MW01005382

THE LOEB CLASSICAL LIBRARY

FOUNDED BY JAMES LOEB 1911

EDITED BY

JEFFREY HENDERSON

PLATO

IV

LCL 167

PLATO

CRATYLUS · PARMENIDES
GREATER HIPPIAS
LESSER HIPPIAS

WITH AN ENGLISH TRANSLATION BY

H. N. FOWLER

HARVARD UNIVERSITY PRESS
CAMBRIDGE, MASSACHUSETTS
LONDON, ENGLAND

First published 1926
Revised and reprinted 1939

LOEB CLASSICAL LIBRARY® is a registered trademark
of the President and Fellows of Harvard College

ISBN 978-0-674-99185-9

Printed on acid-free paper and bound by
Edwards Brothers, Ann Arbor, Michigan

CONTENTS

PREFACE

IN this volume the Greek text of the *Parmenides* and *Cratylus* is based upon the Codex Bodleianus or Clarkianus (B) and the Codex Venetus Append. Class. 4, cod. 1 (T). Readings not supported by either of these, and occasionally disagreements between these two manuscripts themselves, are noted in the margin. Later hands of these manuscripts are designated by the letters *b* and *t*. Other manuscripts occasionally mentioned are Codex Venetus Append. Class. 4, cod. 54 (G), and Codex Vindobonensis 54, Suppl. Phil. Gr. 7 (W).

Codex B does not contain the two Hippias dialogues; the text of these is, therefore, based chiefly upon Codex T, with readings from W and Codex Vindobonensis 55, Suppl. Phil. Gr. 39 (F) and occasional use of Codex Vaticanus Palatinus 173 (P) and Codex Venetus Marcianus 189 (S). All readings not supported by T are noted in the margin.

The introductions to the dialogues may, in spite of their extreme brevity, be of some slight service, especially to those who read these dialogues for the first time.

HAROLD N. FOWLER.

LIST OF PLATO'S WORKS showing their division into volumes in this edition and their place in the edition of H. Stephanus (vols. I-III, Paris, 1578).

LIST OF PLATO'S WORKS

CRATYLUS

INTRODUCTION TO THE *CRATYLUS*

In the beginning of the *Cratylus* Hermogenes appeals to Socrates to explain what Cratylus means; for Cratylus has just declared to Hermogenes that "Hermogenes" (Born-of-Hermes) is not really his name, even though he be universally called by it. Socrates is further requested to set forth his own opinion concerning the correctness of names or, in other words, the origin of language and linguistic forms. In the dialogue which ensues, Hermogenes maintains the theory that language is purely a matter of convention. Against this Socrates argues that name-giving, like other arts and sciences, demands technical knowledge, and that names, if they are correct, must have been given by law-givers who possess such knowledge. Most names, or words, are formed by derivation or composition from other words, and Socrates gives many examples of such formation. As the discussion progresses, he develops the theory that the original name-givers believed, like Heracleitus, that all things are in perpetual flux, and embodied that belief in the primary words. By comparison with pictures the conclusion is reached that names are imitations of the realities named. Further examination shows that the results heretofore attained are unsatisfactory. At this point Cratylus takes the place of Hermogenes

as interlocutor and is forced to admit that custom, or convention, plays a part in the formation of words.

The dialogue cannot be satisfactorily translated, because the numerous etymologies cannot be appreciated without some knowledge of Greek ; nevertheless it is interesting, even though the etymologies be not thoroughly understood. Some of them are manifestly absurd, and in some cases the absurdity is obviously intentional. Evidently some current theories of language are satirized in these instances ; in fact, the dialogue appears to contain many references, the meaning of which can only be guessed, because we do not know the persons to whom reference is made. Even so, however, the wit and humour of the dialogue are apparent.

The *Cratylus* cannot be said to be of great importance in the development of the Platonic system, as it treats of a special subject somewhat apart from general philosophic theory ; its interest lies rather in its technical perfection and in the fact that it is the earliest extant attempt to discuss the origin of language. Linguistic science was in Plato's day little more than *a priori* speculation, not a real science based upon wide knowledge of facts ; but this dialogue exhibits such speculation conducted with great brilliancy and remarkable common sense.

The position of the *Cratylus* in the sequence of Plato's works is uncertain. Possibly the rejection (404 B) of the derivation of Ἅιδης from ἀειδής (invisible), which is accepted in the *Phaedo* (80 D), may indicate that the *Cratylus* is the later of the two dialogues.

Hermogenes was the son of Hipponicus and

brother of the wealthy Callias. He was a follower
of Parmenides, as Cratylus was of Heracleitus. Both
are said by Diogenes Laertius (iii. 8) to have been
Plato's teachers. Euthyphro, from whom Socrates
claimed in jest to derive his inspiration, is the same
from whom the dialogue entitled *Euthyphro* derives
its name.

ΚΡΑΤΥΛΟΣ

[Η ΠΕΡΙ ΟΝΟΜΑΤΩΝ ΟΡΘΟΤΗΤΟΣ· ΛΟΓΙΚΟΣ]

ΤΑ ΤΟΥ ΔΙΑΛΟΓΟΥ ΠΡΟΣΩΠΑ

ΕΡΜΟΓΕΝΗΣ, ΚΡΑΤΥΛΟΣ, ΣΩΚΡΑΤΗΣ

1. ΕΡΜ. Βούλει οὖν καὶ Σωκράτει τῷδε ἀνακοινωσώμεθα τὸν λόγον;

ΚΡΑ. Εἴ σοι δοκεῖ.

ΕΡΜ. Κρατύλος φησὶν ὅδε, ὦ Σώκρατες, ὀνόματος ὀρθότητα εἶναι ἑκάστῳ τῶν ὄντων φύσει πεφυκυῖαν, καὶ οὐ τοῦτο εἶναι ὄνομα ὃ ἄν τινες ξυνθέμενοι καλεῖν καλῶσι, τῆς αὑτῶν φωνῆς μόριον ἐπιφθεγγόμενοι, ἀλλὰ ὀρθότητά τινα τῶν B ὀνομάτων πεφυκέναι καὶ Ἕλλησι καὶ βαρβάροις τὴν αὐτὴν ἅπασιν. ἐρωτῶ οὖν αὐτὸν ἐγώ, εἰ αὐτῷ Κρατύλος τῇ ἀληθείᾳ ὄνομα[1]· ὁ δὲ ὁμολογεῖ. "τί δὲ Σωκράτει;" ἔφην. "Σωκράτης," ἦ δ' ὅς. "οὐκοῦν καὶ τοῖς ἄλλοις ἀνθρώποις πᾶσιν, ὅπερ καλοῦμεν ὄνομα ἕκαστον, τοῦτό ἐστιν ἑκάστῳ ὄνομα;" ὁ δέ· "οὔκουν σοί γε," ἦ δ' ὅς, "ὄνομα Ἑρμογένης, οὐδὲ ἂν πάντες καλῶσιν ἄνθρωποι." καὶ ἐμοῦ ἐρωτῶντος καὶ 384 προθυμουμένου εἰδέναι ὅ τι ποτὲ λέγει, οὔτε ἀπο-

[1] ὄνομα Τ: ὄνομα ἐστὶν ἢ οὔ Β.

6

CRATYLUS

[or ON THE CORRECTNESS OF NAMES: logical]

CHARACTERS

Hermogenes, Cratylus, Socrates

HER. Here is Socrates ; shall we take him as a partner in our discussion ?

CRA. If you like.

HER. Cratylus, whom you see here, Socrates, says that everything has a right name of its own, which comes by nature, and that a name is not whatever people call a thing by agreement, just a piece of their own voice applied to the thing, but that there is a kind of inherent correctness in names, which is the same for all men, both Greeks and barbarians. So I ask him whether his name is in truth Cratylus, and he agrees that it is. " And what is Socrates' name ? " I said. " Socrates," said he. " Then that applies to all men, and the particular name by which we call each person is his name?" And he said, "Well, your name is not Hermogenes,[1] even if all mankind call you so." Now, though I am asking him and am exerting myself to find out what in the world he

---

[1] *i.e.* you are no son of Hermes. Hermes was the patron deity of traders, bankers, and the like, and Hermogenes, as is suggested below, was not successful as a money-maker.

7

σαφεῖ οὐδὲν εἰρωνεύεταί τε πρός με, προσποιούμενός τι αὐτὸς ἐν ἑαυτῷ διανοεῖσθαι ὡς εἰδὼς
περὶ αὐτοῦ, ὃ εἰ βούλοιτο σαφῶς εἰπεῖν, ποιήσειεν
ἂν καὶ ἐμὲ ὁμολογεῖν καὶ λέγειν ἅπερ αὐτὸς λέγει.
εἰ οὖν πῃ ἔχεις συμβαλεῖν τὴν Κρατύλου μαντείαν,
ἡδέως ἂν ἀκούσαιμι· μᾶλλον δὲ αὐτῷ σοι ὅπῃ
δοκεῖ περὶ ὀνομάτων ὀρθότητος, ἔτι ἂν ἥδιον
πυθοίμην, εἴ σοι βουλομένῳ ἐστίν.

ΣΩ. Ὦ παῖ Ἱππονίκου Ἑρμόγενες, παλαιὰ
B παροιμία, ὅτι χαλεπὰ τὰ καλά ἐστιν ὅπη ἔχει
μαθεῖν· καὶ δὴ καὶ τὸ περὶ τῶν ὀνομάτων οὐ
σμικρὸν τυγχάνει ὂν μάθημα. εἰ μὲν οὖν ἐγὼ ἤδη
ἠκηκόη παρὰ Προδίκου τὴν πεντηκοντάδραχμον
ἐπίδειξιν, ἣν ἀκούσαντι ὑπάρχει περὶ τοῦτο πεπαι-
δεῦσθαι, ὥς φησιν ἐκεῖνος, οὐδὲν ἂν ἐκώλυέν σε
αὐτίκα μάλα εἰδέναι τὴν ἀλήθειαν περὶ ὀνομάτων
ὀρθότητος· νῦν δὲ οὐκ ἀκήκοα, ἀλλὰ τὴν δραχ-
C μιαίαν· οὔκουν οἶδα πῇ ποτε τὸ ἀληθὲς ἔχει περὶ
τῶν τοιούτων. συζητεῖν μέντοι ἕτοιμός εἰμι καὶ
σοὶ καὶ Κρατύλῳ κοινῇ. ὅτι δὲ οὔ φησί σοι
Ἑρμογένη ὄνομα εἶναι τῇ ἀληθείᾳ, ὥσπερ ὑποπτεύω αὐτὸν σκώπτειν· οἴεται γὰρ ἴσως σε χρημάτων ἐφιέμενον κτήσεως ἀποτυγχάνειν ἑκάστοτε.[1]
ἀλλ', ὃ νῦν δὴ ἔλεγον, εἰδέναι μὲν τὰ τοιαῦτα
χαλεπόν, εἰς τὸ κοινὸν δὲ καταθέντας χρὴ σκοπεῖν,
εἴτε ὡς σὺ λέγεις ἔχει εἴτε ὡς Κρατύλος.

2. ΕΡΜ. Καὶ μὴν ἔγωγε, ὦ Σώκρατες, πολλάκις
δὴ καὶ τούτῳ διαλεχθεὶς καὶ ἄλλοις πολλοῖς, οὐ
D δύναμαι πεισθῆναι ὡς ἄλλη τις ὀρθότης ὀνόματος
ἢ ξυνθήκη καὶ ὁμολογία. ἐμοὶ γὰρ δοκεῖ, ὅ τι ἂν
τίς τῳ θῆται ὄνομα, τοῦτο εἶναι τὸ ὀρθόν· καὶ ἂν

[1] ἑκάστοτε om. T.

means, he does not explain himself at all ; he meets me with dissimulation, claiming to have some special knowledge of his own about it which would, if he chose to speak it out clearly, make me agree entirely with him. Now if you could interpret Cratylus's oracular speech, I should like to hear you ; or rather, I should like still better to hear, if you please, what you yourself think about the correctness of names.

soc. Hermogenes, son of Hipponicus, there is an ancient saying that knowledge of high things is hard to gain ; and surely knowledge of names is no small matter. Now if I had attended Prodicus's fifty-drachma course of lectures, after which, as he himself says, a man has a complete education on this subject, there would be nothing to hinder your learning the truth about the correctness of names at once ; but I have heard only the one-drachma course, and so I do not know what the truth is about such matters. However, I am ready to join you and Cratylus in looking for it. But as for his saying that Hermogenes is not truly your name, I suspect he is making fun of you ; for perhaps he thinks that you want to make money and fail every time. But, as I said, it is difficult to know such things. We must join forces and try to find out whether you are right, or Cratylus.

her. For my part, Socrates, I have often talked with Cratylus and many others, and cannot come to the conclusion that there is any correctness of names other than convention and agreement. For it seems to me that whatever name you give to a thing is its right name ; and if you give up that

PLATO

αὖθίς γε ἕτερον μεταθῆται, ἐκεῖνο δὲ μηκέτι καλῇ,
οὐδὲν ἧττον τὸ ὕστερον ὀρθῶς ἔχειν τοῦ προτέρου,
ὥσπερ τοῖς οἰκέταις ἡμεῖς μετατιθέμεθα[1]· οὐ γὰρ
φύσει ἑκάστῳ πεφυκέναι ὄνομα οὐδὲν οὐδενί, ἀλλὰ
νόμῳ καὶ ἔθει τῶν ἐθισάντων τε καὶ καλούντων.
Ε εἰ δέ πῃ ἄλλῃ ἔχει, ἕτοιμος ἔγωγε καὶ μανθάνειν
καὶ ἀκούειν οὐ μόνον παρὰ Κρατύλου, ἀλλὰ καὶ
παρ' ἄλλου ὁτουοῦν.
385 ΣΩ. Ἴσως μέντοι τὶ λέγεις, ὦ Ἑρμόγενες·
σκεψώμεθα δέ. ὃ ἂν θῇ καλεῖν[2] τις ἕκαστον,
τοῦθ' ἑκάστῳ ὄνομα,

ΕΡΜ. Ἔμοιγε δοκεῖ.

ΣΩ. Καὶ ἐὰν ἰδιώτης καλῇ καὶ ἐὰν πόλις;

ΕΡΜ. Φημί.

ΣΩ. Τί οὖν; ἐὰν ἐγὼ καλῶ ὁτιοῦν τῶν ὄντων,
οἷον ὃ νῦν καλοῦμεν ἄνθρωπον, ἐὰν ἐγὼ τοῦτο
ἵππον προσαγορεύω, ὃ δὲ νῦν ἵππον, ἄνθρωπον,
ἔσται δημοσίᾳ μὲν ὄνομα ἄνθρωπος τῷ αὐτῷ,
ἰδίᾳ δὲ ἵππος; καὶ ἰδίᾳ μὲν αὖ ἄνθρωπος, δημοσίᾳ δὲ ἵππος; οὕτω λέγεις;

Β ΕΡΜ. Ἔμοιγε δοκεῖ.

3. ΣΩ. Φέρε δή μοι τόδε εἰπέ. καλεῖς τι ἀληθῆ
λέγειν καὶ ψευδῆ;

ΕΡΜ. Ἔγωγε.

ΣΩ. Οὐκοῦν εἴη ἂν λόγος ἀληθής, ὁ δὲ ψευδής;

ΕΡΜ. Πάνυ γε.

ΣΩ. Ἆρ' οὖν οὗτος ὃς ἂν τὰ ὄντα λέγῃ ὡς
ἔστιν, ἀληθής· ὃς δ' ἂν ὡς οὐκ ἔστιν, ψευδής;

---

[1] After μετατιθέμεθα Β reads οὐδὲν ἧττον τοῦτ' εἶναι ὀρθὸν τὸ
μετατεθὲν τοῦ πρότερον κειμένου.
[2] θῇ καλεῖν Β: φῇς καλεῖ Τ: φῇς καλῇ Hirschig.

10

name and change it for another, the later name is
no less correct than the earlier, just as we change
the names of our servants ; for I think no name
belongs to any particular thing by nature, but only
by the habit and custom of those who employ it
and who established the usage. But if this is not
the case, I am ready to hear and to learn from
Cratylus or anyone else.

soc. It may be that you are right, Hermogenes ;
but let us see. Whatever name we decide to give
each particular thing is its name ?

her. Yes.

soc. Whether the giver be a private person or a
state ?

her. Yes.

soc. Well, then, suppose I give a name to something or other, designating, for instance, that which
we now call " man " as " horse " and that which we
now call " horse " as " man," will the real name of
the same thing be " man " for the public and "horse"
for me individually, and in the other case " horse "
for the public and " man " for me individually ? Is
that your meaning ?

her. Yes, that is my opinion.

soc. Now answer this question. Is there anything which you call speaking the truth and speaking
falsehood ?

her. Yes.

soc. Then there would be true speech and false
speech ?

her. Certainly.

soc. Then that speech which says things as they
are is true, and that which says them as they are
not is false ?

PLATO

ΕΡΜ. Ναί.

ΣΩ. Ἔστιν ἄρα τοῦτο, λόγῳ λέγειν τὰ ὄντα τε καὶ μή;

ΕΡΜ. Πάνυ γε.

ΣΩ. Ὁ λόγος· δ᾽ ἐστὶν ὁ ἀληθὴς πότερον ὅλος C μὲν ἀληθής, τὰ μόρια δ᾽ αὐτοῦ οὐκ ἀληθῆ;

ΕΡΜ. Οὔκ, ἀλλὰ καὶ τὰ μόρια.

ΣΩ. Πότερον δὲ τὰ μὲν μεγάλα μόρια ἀληθῆ, τὰ δὲ σμικρὰ οὔ· ἢ πάντα;

ΕΡΜ. Πάντα, οἶμαι ἔγωγε.

ΣΩ. Ἔστιν οὖν ὅ τι λέγεις λόγου σμικρότερον μόριον ἄλλο ἢ ὄνομα;

ΕΡΜ. Οὔκ, ἀλλὰ τοῦτο σμικρότατον.

ΣΩ. Καὶ τὸ ὄνομα ἄρα τὸ τοῦ ἀληθοῦς λόγου λέγεται;

ΕΡΜ. Ναί.

ΣΩ. Ἀληθές γε, ὡς φής.

ΕΡΜ. Ναί.

ΣΩ. Τὸ δὲ τοῦ ψευδοῦς μόριον οὐ ψεῦδος;

ΕΡΜ. Φημί.

ΣΩ. Ἔστιν ἄρα ὄνομα ψεῦδος καὶ ἀληθὲς λέγειν, εἴπερ καὶ λόγον;

D ΕΡΜ. Πῶς γὰρ οὔ;

ΣΩ. Ὃ ἂν ἄρα ἕκαστος φῇ τῳ ὄνομα εἶναι, τοῦτό ἐστιν ἑκάστῳ ὄνομα;

ΕΡΜ. Ναί.

ΣΩ. Ἦ καὶ ὁπόσα ἂν φῇ τις ἑκάστῳ ὀνόματα εἶναι, τοσαῦτα ἔσται καὶ τότε ὁπόταν φῇ;

ΕΡΜ. Οὐ γὰρ ἔχω ἔγωγε, ὦ Σώκρατες, ὀνόματος ἄλλην ὀρθότητα ἢ ταύτην, ἐμοὶ μὲν ἕτερον εἶναι καλεῖν ἑκάστῳ ὄνομα, ὃ ἐγὼ ἐθέμην, σοὶ δὲ

12

HER. Yes.

soc. It is possible, then, to say in speech that which is and that which is not?

HER. Certainly.

soc. But is true speech true only as a whole, and are its parts untrue?

HER. No, its parts also are true.

soc. Are the large parts true, but not the small ones, or are all true?

HER. All, in my opinion.

soc. Is there, then, anything which you say is a smaller part of speech than a name?

HER. No, that is the smallest.

soc. And the name is spoken as a part of the true speech?

HER. Yes.

soc. Then it is, according to you, true.

HER. Yes.

soc. And a part of false speech is false, is it not?

HER. It is.

soc. Then it is possible to utter either a false or a true name, since one may utter speech that is either true or false?

HER. Yes, of course.

soc. Then whatever each particular person says is the name of anything, that is its name for that person?

HER. Yes.

soc. And whatever the number of names anyone says a thing has, it will really have that number at the time when he says it?

HER. Yes, Socrates, for I cannot conceive of any other kind of correctness in names than this; I may call a thing by one name, which I gave, and

ἕτερον, ὃ αὖ σύ. οὕτω δὲ καὶ ταῖς πόλεσιν ὁρῶ
E ἰδίᾳ ἐπὶ τοῖς αὐτοῖς κείμενα ὀνόματα, καὶ Ἕλλησι
παρὰ τοὺς ἄλλους Ἕλληνας, καὶ Ἕλλησι παρὰ
βαρβάρους.

4. ΣΩ. Φέρε δὴ ἴδωμεν, ὦ Ἑρμόγενες, πότερον
καὶ τὰ ὄντα οὕτως ἔχειν σοι φαίνεται, ἰδίᾳ αὐτῶν
ἡ οὐσία εἶναι ἑκάστῳ, ὥσπερ Πρωταγόρας ἔλεγεν
386 λέγων πάντων χρημάτων μέτρον εἶναι ἄνθρωπον—
ὡς ἄρα οἷα μὲν ἂν ἐμοὶ φαίνηται τὰ πράγματα,
τοιαῦτα μέν ἐστιν ἐμοί, οἷα δ' ἂν σοί, τοιαῦτα δὲ
σοί—ἢ ἔχειν δοκεῖ σοι αὐτὰ αὑτῶν τινα βεβαιό-
τητα τῆς οὐσίας;

ΕΡΜ. Ἤδη ποτὲ ἔγωγε, ὦ Σώκρατες, ἀπορῶν
καὶ ἐνταῦθα ἐξηνέχθην εἰς ἅπερ Πρωταγόρας
λέγει· οὐ πάνυ τι μέντοι μοι δοκεῖ οὕτως ἔχειν.

ΣΩ. Τί δέ; ἐς τόδε ἤδη ἐξηνέχθης, ὥστε μὴ
B πάνυ σοι δοκεῖν εἶναί τινα ἄνθρωπον πονηρόν;

ΕΡΜ. Οὐ μὰ τόν Δία, ἀλλὰ πολλάκις δὴ αὐτὸ
πέπονθα, ὥστε μοι δοκεῖν πάνυ πονηροὺς εἶναί
τινας ἀνθρώπους, καὶ μάλα συχνούς.

ΣΩ. Τί δέ; πάνυ χρηστοὶ οὔπω σοι ἔδοξαν εἶναι;

ΕΡΜ. Καὶ μάλα ὀλίγοι.

ΣΩ. Ἔδοξαν δ' οὖν;

ΕΡΜ. Ἔμοιγε.

ΣΩ. Πῶς οὖν τοῦτο τίθεσαι; ἆρ' ὧδε· τοὺς μὲν
πάνυ χρηστοὺς πάνυ φρονίμους, τοὺς δὲ πάνυ
πονηροὺς πάνυ ἄφρονας;

C ΕΡΜ. Ἔμοιγε δοκεῖ οὕτως.

ΣΩ. Οἷόν τε οὖν, εἰ Πρωταγόρας ἀληθῆ ἔλεγεν
καὶ ἔστιν αὕτη ἡ ἀλήθεια, τὸ οἷα ἂν δοκῇ ἑκάστῳ
τοιαῦτα καὶ εἶναι, τοὺς μὲν ἡμῶν φρονίμους εἶναι,
τοὺς δὲ ἄφρονας;

14

CRATYLUS

you by another, which you gave. And in the same way, I see that states have their own different names for the same things, and Greeks differ from other Greeks and from barbarians in their use of names.

soc. Now, Hermogenes, let us see. Do you think this is true of the real things, that their reality is a separate one for each person, as Protagoras said with his doctrine that man is the measure of all things—that things are to me such as they seem to me, and to you such as they seem to you—or do you think things have some fixed reality of their own?

her. It has sometimes happened to me, Socrates, to be so perplexed that I have been carried away even into this doctrine of Protagoras; but I do not at all believe he is right.

soc. Well, have you ever been carried away so far as not to believe at all that any man is bad?

her. Lord, no; but I have often been carried away into the belief that certain men, and a good many of them, are very bad.

soc. Well, did you never think any were very good?

her. Very few.

soc. But you did think them so?

her. Yes.

soc. And what is your idea about that? Are the very good very wise and the very bad very foolish?

her. Yes, that is my opinion.

soc. Now if Protagoras is right and the truth is as he says, that all things are to each person as they seem to him, is it possible for some of us to be wise and some foolish?

PLATO

ΕΡΜ. Οὐ δῆτα.

ΣΩ. Καὶ ταῦτά γε, ὡς ἐγῷμαι, σοὶ πάνυ δοκεῖ, φρονήσεως οὔσης καὶ ἀφροσύνης μὴ πάνυ δυνατὸν εἶναι Πρωταγόραν ἀληθῆ λέγειν. οὐδὲν γὰρ ἂν που τῇ ἀληθείᾳ ὁ ἕτερος τοῦ ἑτέρου φρονιμώ-
D τερος εἴη, εἴπερ ἃ ἂν ἑκάστῳ δοκῇ ἑκάστῳ ἀληθῆ ἔσται.

ΕΡΜ. Ἔστι ταῦτα.

5. ΣΩ. Ἀλλὰ μὴν οὐδὲ κατ᾽ Εὐθύδημόν γε, οἶμαι, σοὶ δοκεῖ πᾶσι πάντα ὁμοίως εἶναι ἅμα καὶ ἀεί. οὐδὲ γὰρ ἂν οὕτως εἶεν οἱ μὲν χρηστοί, οἱ δὲ πονηροί, εἰ ὁμοίως ἅπασι καὶ ἀεὶ ἀρετή τε καὶ κακία εἴη.

ΕΡΜ. Ἀληθῆ λέγεις.

ΣΩ. Οὐκοῦν εἰ μήτε πᾶσι πάντα ἐστὶν ὁμοίως ἅμα καὶ ἀεί, μήτε ἑκάστῳ ἰδίᾳ ἕκαστον, δῆλον δὴ ὅτι αὐτὰ αὑτῶν οὐσίαν ἔχοντά τινα βέβαιόν ἐστι
E τὰ πράγματα, οὐ πρὸς ἡμᾶς οὐδὲ ὑφ᾽ ἡμῶν, ἑλκό-μενα ἄνω καὶ κάτω τῷ ἡμετέρῳ φαντάσματι, ἀλλὰ καθ᾽ αὑτὰ πρὸς τὴν αὑτῶν οὐσίαν ἔχοντα ᾗπερ πέφυκεν.

ΕΡΜ. Δοκεῖ μοι, ὦ Σώκρατες, οὕτω.

ΣΩ. Πότερον οὖν αὐτὰ μὲν ἂν εἴη οὕτω πεφυ-κότα, αἱ δὲ πράξεις αὐτῶν οὐ κατὰ τὸν αὐτὸν τρόπον; ἢ οὐ καὶ αὗται[1] ἕν τι εἶδος τῶν ὄντων εἰσίν, αἱ πράξεις;

ΕΡΜ. Πάνυ γε καὶ αὗται.[1]

387 ΣΩ. Κατὰ τὴν αὑτῶν ἄρα φύσιν καὶ αἱ πράξεις πράττονται, οὐ κατὰ τὴν ἡμετέραν δόξαν. οἷον ἐάν τι ἐπιχειρήσωμεν ἡμεῖς τῶν ὄντων τέμνειν, πότερον ἡμῖν τμητέον ἕκαστον ὡς ἂν ἡμεῖς βουλώ-

[1] αὗται Heindorf: αὐταὶ BT.

16

HER. No, it is not.

soc. And you are, I imagine, strongly of the opinion that if wisdom and folly exist, it is quite impossible that Protagoras is right, for one man would not in reality be at all wiser than another if whatever seems to each person is really true to him.

HER. Quite right.

soc. But neither do you believe with Euthydemus that all things belong equally to all men at the same time and perpetually,[1] for on this assumption also some could not be good and others bad, if virtue and its opposite were always equally possessed by all.

HER. True.

soc. Then if neither all things belong equally to all men at the same time and perpetually nor each thing to each man individually, it is clear that things have some fixed reality of their own, not in relation to us nor caused by us ; they do not vary, swaying one way and another in accordance with our fancy, but exist of themselves in relation to their own reality imposed by nature.

HER. I think, Socrates, that is the case.

soc. Can things themselves, then, possess such a nature as this, and that of their actions be different ? Or are not actions also a class of realities ?

HER. Certainly they are.

soc. Then actions also are performed according to their own nature, not according to our opinion. For instance, if we undertake to cut anything, ought we to cut it as we wish, and with whatever

[1] The doctrine here attributed to Euthydemus is not expressly enunciated by him in the dialogue which bears his name, but it is little more than a comprehensive statement of the several doctrines there proclaimed by him and his brother Dionysodorus.

μεθα καὶ ᾧ ἂν βουληθῶμεν, ἢ ἐὰν μὲν κατὰ τὴν
φύσιν βουληθῶμεν ἕκαστον τέμνειν τοῦ τέμνειν
τε καὶ τέμνεσθαι καὶ ᾧ πέφυκε, τεμοῦμέν τε
καὶ πλέον τι ἡμῖν ἔσται καὶ ὀρθῶς πράξομεν
τοῦτο, ἐὰν δὲ παρὰ φύσιν, ἐξαμαρτησόμεθά τε
καὶ οὐδὲν πράξομεν;

B   ΕΡΜ. Ἔμοιγε δοκεῖ οὕτω.

ΣΩ. Οὐκοῦν καὶ ἐὰν κάειν τι ἐπιχειρήσωμεν,
οὐ κατὰ πᾶσαν δόξαν δεῖ κάειν, ἀλλὰ κατὰ τὴν
ὀρθήν· αὕτη δ' ἐστὶν ἧ πέφυκεν[1] ἕκαστον κάεσθαί
τε καὶ κάειν καὶ ᾧ πέφυκεν[1];

ΕΡΜ. Ἔστι ταῦτα.

ΣΩ. Οὐκοῦν καὶ τἆλλα οὕτω;

ΕΡΜ. Πάνυ γε.

6. ΣΩ. Ἆρ' οὖν οὐ καὶ τὸ λέγειν μία τις τῶν
πράξεών ἐστιν;

ΕΡΜ. Ναί.

ΣΩ. Πότερον οὖν ἧ ἄν τῳ δοκῇ λεκτέον εἶναι,
C   ταύτῃ λέγων ὀρθῶς λέξει, ἢ ἐὰν μὲν ἧ πέφυκε
τὰ πράγματα λέγειν τε καὶ λέγεσθαι καὶ ᾧ, ταύτῃ
καὶ τούτῳ λέγῃ, πλέον τέ τι ποιήσει καὶ ἐρεῖ,
ἂν δὲ μή, ἐξαμαρτήσεταί τε καὶ οὐδὲν ποιήσει;

ΕΡΜ. Οὕτω μοι δοκεῖ, ὡς λέγεις.

ΣΩ. Οὐκοῦν τοῦ λέγειν μόριον τὸ ὀνομάζειν·
ὀνομάζοντες γάρ που λέγουσι τοὺς λόγους.

ΕΡΜ. Πάνυ γε.

ΣΩ. Οὐκοῦν καὶ τὸ ὀνομάζειν πρᾶξίς τίς ἐστιν,
εἴπερ καὶ τὸ λέγειν πρᾶξίς τις ἦν περὶ τὰ πράγματα;

ΕΡΜ. Ναί.

---

[1] πέφυκεν Hermann : ἐπεφύκει BT.

instrument we wish, or shall we, if we are willing to cut each thing in accordance with the nature of cutting and being cut, and with the natural instrument, succeed in cutting it, and do it rightly, whereas if we try to do it contrary to nature we shall fail and accomplish nothing ?

HER. I think the way is as you suggest.

soc. Then, too, if we undertake to burn anything, we must burn not according to every opinion, but according to the right one ? And that is as each thing naturally burns or is burned and with the natural instrument ?

HER. True.

soc. And all other actions are to be performed in like manner ?

HER. Certainly.

soc. And speaking is an action, is it not ?

HER. Yes.

soc. Then if a man speaks as he fancies he ought to speak, will he speak rightly, or will he succeed in speaking if he speaks in the way and with the instrument in which and with which it is natural for us to speak and for things to be spoken, whereas otherwise he will fail and accomplish nothing ?

HER. I think the way you suggest is the right one.

soc. Now naming is a part of speaking, for in naming I suppose people utter speech.

HER. Certainly.

soc. Then is not naming also a kind of action, if speaking is a kind of action concerned with things ?

HER. Yes.

D ΣΩ. Αἱ δὲ πράξεις ἐφάνησαν ἡμῖν οὐ πρὸς ἡμᾶς
οὖσαι, ἀλλ' αὐτῶν τινα ἰδίαν φύσιν ἔχουσαι;

ΕΡΜ. Ἔστι ταῦτα.

ΣΩ. Οὐκοῦν καὶ ὀνομαστέον ᾗ πέφυκε τὰ πράγματα ὀνομάζειν τε καὶ ὀνομάζεσθαι καὶ ᾧ, ἀλλ'
οὐχ ᾗ ἂν ἡμεῖς βουληθῶμεν, εἴπερ τι τοῖς ἔμπροσθεν μέλλει ὁμολογούμενον εἶναι; καὶ οὕτω μὲν
ἂν πλέον τι ποιοῖμεν καὶ ὀνομάζοιμεν, ἄλλως δὲ
οὔ;

ΕΡΜ. Φαίνεταί μοι.

7. ΣΩ. Φέρε δή, ὃ ἔδει τέμνειν, ἔδει τῳ, φαμέν,
τέμνειν;

ΕΡΜ. Ναί.

E ΣΩ. Καὶ ὃ ἔδει κερκίζειν, ἔδει τῳ κερκίζειν,
καὶ ὃ ἔδει τρυπᾶν, ἔδει τῳ τρυπᾶν;

ΕΡΜ. Πάνυ γε.

ΣΩ. Καὶ ὃ ἔδει δὴ ὀνομάζειν, ἔδει τῳ ὀνομάζειν;

388 ΕΡΜ. Ἔστι ταῦτα.

ΣΩ. Τί δὲ ἦν ἐκεῖνο ᾧ ἔδει τρυπᾶν;

ΕΡΜ. Τρύπανον.

ΣΩ. Τί δὲ ᾧ κερκίζειν;

ΕΡΜ. Κερκίς.

ΣΩ. Τί δὲ ᾧ ὀνομάζειν;

ΕΡΜ. Ὄνομα.

ΣΩ. Εὖ λέγεις. ὄργανον ἄρα τί ἐστι καὶ τὸ
ὄνομα.

ΕΡΜ. Πάνυ γε.

ΣΩ. Εἰ οὖν ἐγὼ ἐροίμην· τί ἦν ὄργανον ἡ κερκίς; οὐχ ᾧ κερκίζομεν;

20

soc. But we saw that actions are not merely relative to us, but possess a separate nature of their own ?

her. True.

soc. Then in naming also, if we are to be consistent with our previous conclusions, we cannot follow our own will, but the way and the instrument which the nature of things prescribes must be employed, must they not ? And if we pursue this course we shall be successful in our naming, but otherwise we shall fail.

her. I think you are right.

soc. And again, what has to be cut, we said, has to be cut with something.

her. Certainly.

soc. And what has to be woven, has to be woven with something, and what has to be bored, has to be bored with something ?

her. Certainly.

soc. And then what has to be named, has to be named with something ?

her. True.

soc. And what is that with which we have to bore ?

her. A borer.

soc. And that with which we weave ?

her. A shuttle.

soc. And that with which we must name ?

her. A name.

soc. Right. A name also, then, is a kind of instrument.

her. Certainly.

soc. Then if I were to ask " What instrument is the shuttle ? " Is it not that with which we weave ?

ΕΡΜ. Ναί.

Β ΣΩ. Κερκίζοντες δὲ τί δρῶμεν; οὐ τὴν κρόκην καὶ τοὺς στήμονας συγκεχυμένους διακρίνομεν;

ΕΡΜ. Ναί.

ΣΩ. Οὐκοῦν καὶ περὶ τρυπάνου ἕξεις οὕτως εἰπεῖν καὶ περὶ τῶν ἄλλων;

ΕΡΜ. Πάνυ γε.

ΣΩ. Ἔχεις δὴ καὶ περὶ ὀνόματος οὕτως εἰπεῖν; ὀργάνῳ ὄντι τῷ ὀνόματι ὀνομάζοντες τί ποιοῦμεν;

ΕΡΜ. Οὐκ ἔχω λέγειν.

ΣΩ. Ἆρ' οὐ[1] διδάσκομέν τι ἀλλήλους καὶ τὰ πράγματα διακρίνομεν ἧ ἔχει;

ΕΡΜ. Πάνυ γε.

8. ΣΩ. Ὄνομα ἄρα διδασκαλικόν τί ἐστιν ὄρ-
C γανον καὶ διακριτικὸν τῆς οὐσίας, ὥσπερ κερκὶς ὑφάσματος.

ΕΡΜ. Ναί.

ΣΩ. Ὑφαντικὸν δέ γε ἡ κερκίς;

ΕΡΜ. Πῶς δ' οὔ;

ΣΩ. Ὑφαντικὸς μὲν ἄρα κερκίδι καλῶς χρήσεται· καλῶς δ' ἐστὶν ὑφαντικῶς· διδασκαλικὸς δὲ ὀνό-ματι, καλῶς δ' ἐστὶ διδασκαλικῶς.

ΕΡΜ. Ναί.

ΣΩ. Τῷ τίνος οὖν ἔργῳ ὁ ὑφάντης καλῶς χρή-σεται, ὅταν τῇ κερκίδι χρῆται;

ΕΡΜ. Τῷ τοῦ τέκτονος.

ΣΩ. Πᾶς δὲ τέκτων ἢ ὁ τὴν τέχνην ἔχων;

ΕΡΜ. Ὁ τὴν τέχνην.

D ΣΩ. Τῷ τίνος δὲ ἔργῳ ὁ τρυπητὴς καλῶς χρή-σεται ὅταν τῷ τρυπάνῳ χρῆται;

ΕΡΜ. Τῷ τοῦ χαλκέως.

---

[1] οὐ Stephanus : οὖν ΒΤ.

22

HER. Yes.

soc. And what do we do when we weave? Do we not separate the mingled threads of warp and woof?

HER. Yes.

soc. And you could give a similar answer about the borer and the rest, could you not?

HER. Certainly.

soc. And can you say something of the same kind about a name? The name being an instrument, what do we do with it when we name?

HER. I cannot tell.

soc. Do we not teach one another something, and separate things according to their natures?

HER. Certainly.

soc. A name is, then, an instrument of teaching and of separating reality, as a shuttle is an instrument of separating the web?

HER. Yes.

soc. But the shuttle is an instrument of weaving?

HER. Of course.

soc. The weaver, then, will use the shuttle well, and well means like a weaver; and a teacher will use a name well, and well means like a teacher.

HER. Yes.

soc. Whose work will the weaver use well when he uses the shuttle?

HER. The carpenter's.

soc. Is every one a carpenter, or he who has the skill?

HER. He who has the skill.

soc. And whose work will the hole-maker use when he uses the borer?

HER. The smith's.

ΣΩ. Ἆρ' οὖν πᾶς χαλκεὺς ἢ ὁ τὴν τέχνην ἔχων;

ΕΡΜ. Ὁ τὴν τέχνην.

ΣΩ. Εἶεν. τῷ δὲ τίνος ἔργῳ ὁ διδασκαλικὸς χρήσεται, ὅταν τῷ ὀνόματι χρῆται;

ΕΡΜ. Οὐδὲ τοῦτ' ἔχω.

ΣΩ. Οὐδὲ τοῦτό γ' ἔχεις εἰπεῖν, τίς παραδίδωσιν ἡμῖν τὰ ὀνόματα οἷς χρώμεθα;

ΕΡΜ. Οὐ δῆτα.

ΣΩ. Ἆρ' οὐχὶ ὁ νόμος δοκεῖ σοι ὁ παραδιδοὺς αὐτά;

ΕΡΜ. Ἔοικεν.

Ε ΣΩ. Νομοθέτου ἄρα ἔργῳ χρήσεται ὁ διδασκαλικός, ὅταν ὀνόματι χρῆται;

ΕΡΜ. Δοκεῖ μοι.

ΣΩ. Νομοθέτης δέ σοι δοκεῖ πᾶς εἶναι ἀνὴρ ἢ ὁ τὴν τέχνην ἔχων;

ΕΡΜ. Ὁ τὴν τέχνην.

ΣΩ. Οὐκ ἄρα παντὸς ἀνδρός, ὦ Ἑρμόγενες, 389 ὄνομα θέσθαι, ἀλλά τινος ὀνοματουργοῦ· οὗτος δ' ἐστίν, ὡς ἔοικεν, ὁ νομοθέτης, ὃς δὴ τῶν δημιουργῶν σπανιώτατος ἐν¹ ἀνθρώποις γίγνεται.

ΕΡΜ. Ἔοικεν.

9. ΣΩ. Ἴθι δή, ἐπίσκεψαι ποῖ βλέπων ὁ νομοθέτης τὰ ὀνόματα τίθεται· ἐκ τῶν ἔμπροσθεν δὲ ἀνάσκεψαι. ποῖ βλέπων ὁ τέκτων τὴν κερκίδα ποιεῖ; ἆρ' οὐ πρὸς τοιοῦτόν τι ὃ ἐπεφύκει κερκίζειν;

ΕΡΜ. Πάνυ γε.

ΣΩ. Τί δέ; ἂν καταγῇ αὐτῷ ἡ κερκὶς ποιοῦντι, Β πότερον πάλιν ποιήσει ἄλλην πρὸς τὴν κατεαγυῖαν βλέπων, ἢ πρὸς ἐκεῖνο τὸ εἶδος, πρὸς ὅπερ καὶ ἦν κατέαξεν ἐποίει;

¹ ἐν om. T.

24

soc. And is every one a smith, or he who has the skill ?

her. He who has the skill.

soc. And whose work will the teacher use when he uses the name ?

her. I cannot tell that, either.

soc. And can you not tell this, either, who gives us the names we use ?

her. No.

soc. Do you not think it is the law that gives them to us ?

her. Very likely.

soc. Then the teacher, when he uses a name, will be using the work of a lawgiver ?

her. I think so.

soc. Do you think every man is a lawgiver, or only he who has the skill ?

her. He who has the skill.

soc. Then it is not for every man, Hermogenes, to give names, but for him who may be called the name-maker ; and he, it appears, is the lawgiver, who is of all the artisans among men the rarest.

her. So it appears.

soc. See now what the lawgiver has in view in giving names. Look at it in the light of what has gone before. What has the carpenter in view when he makes a shuttle ? Is it not something the nature of which is to weave ?

her. Certainly.

soc. Well, then, if the shuttle breaks while he is making it, will he make another with his mind fixed on that which is broken, or on that form with reference to which he was making the one which he broke ?

ΕΡΜ. Πρὸς ἐκεῖνο, ἔμοιγε δοκεῖ.

ΣΩ. Οὐκοῦν ἐκεῖνο δικαιότατ' ἂν αὐτὸ ὃ ἔστιν κερκὶς καλέσαιμεν;

ΕΡΜ. Ἔμοιγε δοκεῖ.

ΣΩ. Οὐκοῦν ἐπειδὰν δέῃ λεπτῷ ἱματίῳ ἢ παχεῖ ἢ λινῷ ἢ ἐρεῷ ἢ ὁποιῳοῦν τινι κερκίδα ποιεῖν, πάσας μὲν δεῖ τὸ τῆς κερκίδος ἔχειν εἶδος, οἷα δ'
C ἑκάστῳ καλλίστη πέφυκε, ταύτην ἀποδιδόναι τὴν φύσιν εἰς τὸ ἔργον ἕκαστον;

ΕΡΜ. Ναί.

ΣΩ. Καὶ περὶ τῶν ἄλλων δὴ ὀργάνων ὁ αὐτὸς τρόπος· τὸ φύσει ἑκάστῳ πεφυκὸς ὄργανον ἐξευρόντα δεῖ ἀποδοῦναι εἰς ἐκεῖνο ἐξ οὗ ἂν ποιῇ[1], οὐχ οἷον ἂν αὐτὸς βουληθῇ, ἀλλ' οἷον ἐπεφύκει. τὸ φύσει γὰρ ἑκάστῳ, ὡς ἔοικε, τρύπανον πεφυκὸς εἰς τὸν σίδηρον δεῖ ἐπίστασθαι τιθέναι.

ΕΡΜ. Πάνυ γε.

ΣΩ. Καὶ τὴν φύσει κερκίδα ἑκάστῳ πεφυκυῖαν εἰς ξύλον.

ΕΡΜ. Ἔστι ταῦτα.

D ΣΩ. Φύσει γὰρ ἦν ἑκάστῳ εἴδει ὑφάσματος, ὡς ἔοικεν, ἑκάστη κερκίς, καὶ τἆλλα οὕτως.

ΕΡΜ. Ναί.

ΣΩ. Ἆρ' οὖν, ὦ βέλτιστε, καὶ τὸ ἑκάστῳ φύσει πεφυκὸς ὄνομα τὸν νομοθέτην ἐκεῖνον εἰς τοὺς φθόγγους καὶ τὰς συλλαβὰς δεῖ ἐπίστασθαι τιθέναι, καὶ βλέποντα πρὸς αὐτὸ ἐκεῖνο ὃ ἔστιν ὄνομα, πάντα τὰ ὀνόματα ποιεῖν τε καὶ τίθεσθαι, εἰ μέλλει κύριος εἶναι ὀνομάτων θέτης; εἰ δὲ μὴ εἰς τὰς αὐτὰς συλλαβὰς ἕκαστος ὁ νομοθέτης τίθησιν,

---

[1] ποιῇ Τ : ποιῇ τὸ ἔργον Β.

HER. On that form, in my opinion.

soc. Then we should very properly call that the absolute or real shuttle?

HER. Yes, I think so.

soc. Then whenever he has to make a shuttle for a light or a thick garment, or for one of linen or of wool or of any kind whatsoever, all of them must contain the form or ideal of shuttle, and in each of his products he must embody the nature which is naturally best for each?

HER. Yes.

soc. And the same applies to all other instruments. The artisan must discover the instrument naturally fitted for each purpose and must embody that in the material of which he makes the instrument, not in accordance with his own will, but in accordance with its nature. He must, it appears, know how to embody in the iron the borer fitted by nature for each special use.

HER. Certainly.

soc. And he must embody in the wood the shuttle fitted by nature for each kind of weaving.

HER. True.

soc. For each kind of shuttle is, it appears, fitted by nature for its particular kind of weaving, and the like is true of other instruments.

HER. Yes.

soc. Then, my dear friend, must not the lawgiver also know how to embody in the sounds and syllables that name which is fitted by nature for each object? Must he not make and give all his names with his eye fixed upon the absolute or ideal name, if he is to be an authoritative giver of names? And if different lawgivers do not embody it in the

27

οὐδὲν δεῖ τοῦτο ἀγνοεῖν· οὐδὲ γὰρ εἰς τὸν αὐτὸν
E σίδηρον ἅπας χαλκεὺς τίθησιν, τοῦ αὐτοῦ ἕνεκα
ποιῶν τὸ αὐτὸ ὄργανον· ἀλλ' ὅμως, ἕως ἂν τὴν
390 αὐτὴν ἰδέαν ἀποδιδῷ, ἐάντε ἐν ἄλλῳ σιδήρῳ,
ὅμως ὀρθῶς ἔχει τὸ ὄργανον, ἐάντε ἐνθάδε ἐάντε
ἐν βαρβάροις τις ποιῇ. ἦ γάρ;

ΕΡΜ. Πάνυ γε.

ΣΩ. Οὐκοῦν οὕτως ἀξιώσεις καὶ τὸν νομοθέτην
τόν τε ἐνθάδε καὶ τὸν ἐν τοῖς βαρβάροις, ἕως ἂν
τὸ τοῦ ὀνόματος εἶδος ἀποδιδῷ τὸ προσῆκον
ἑκάστῳ ἐν ὁποιαισοῦν συλλαβαῖς, οὐδὲν χείρω
νομοθέτην εἶναι τὸν ἐνθάδε ἢ τὸν ὁπουοῦν ἄλλοθι;

ΕΡΜ. Πάνυ γε.

Β 10. ΣΩ. Τίς οὖν ὁ γνωσόμενος εἰ τὸ προσῆκον
εἶδος κερκίδος ἐν ὁποιῳοῦν ξύλῳ κεῖται; ὁ
ποιήσας, ὁ τέκτων, ἢ ὁ χρησόμενος, ὁ ὑφάντης;

ΕΡΜ. Εἰκὸς μὲν μᾶλλον, ὦ Σώκρατες, τὸν χρη-
σόμενον.

ΣΩ. Τίς οὖν ὁ τῷ τοῦ λυροποιοῦ ἔργῳ χρησόμενος; ἆρ' οὐχ οὗτος, ὃς ἐπίσταιτο ἂν ἐργαζο-
μένῳ κάλλιστα ἐπιστατεῖν καὶ εἰργασμένον γνοίη
εἴτ' εὖ εἴργασται εἴτε μή;

ΕΡΜ. Πάνυ γε.

ΣΩ. Τίς;

ΕΡΜ. Ὁ κιθαριστής.

ΣΩ. Τίς δὲ ὁ τῷ τοῦ ναυπηγοῦ;

C ΕΡΜ. Κυβερνήτης.

ΣΩ. Τίς δὲ τῷ τοῦ νομοθέτου ἔργῳ ἐπιστατήσειέ
τ' ἂν κάλλιστα καὶ εἰργασμένον κρίνειε καὶ ἐνθάδε
καὶ ἐν τοῖς βαρβάροις; ἆρ' οὐχ ὅσπερ χρήσεται;

same syllables, we must not forget this ideal name on that account; for different smiths do not embody the form in the same iron, though making the same instrument for the same purpose, but so long as they reproduce the same ideal, though it be in different iron, still the instrument is as it should be, whether it be made here or in foreign lands, is it not?

HER. Certainly.

soc. On this basis, then, you will judge the law-giver, whether he be here or in a foreign land, so long as he gives to each thing the proper form of the name, in whatsoever syllables, to be no worse lawgiver, whether here or anywhere else, will you not?

HER. Certainly.

soc. Now who is likely to know whether the proper form of shuttle is embodied in any piece of wood? The carpenter who made it, or the weaver who is to use it?

HER. Probably the one who is to use it, Socrates.

soc. Then who is to use the work of the lyre-maker? Is not he the man who would know best how to superintend the making of the lyre and would also know whether it is well made or not when it is finished?

HER. Certainly.

soc. Who is he?

HER. The lyre-player.

soc. And who would know best about the work of the ship-builder?

HER. The navigator.

soc. And who can best superintend the work of the lawgiver and judge of it when it is finished, both here and in foreign countries? The user, is it not?

29

ΕΡΜ. Ναί.

ΣΩ. Ἆρ' οὖν οὐχ ὁ ἐρωτᾶν ἐπιστάμενος οὗτός ἐστιν;

ΕΡΜ. Πάνυ γε.

ΣΩ. Ὁ δὲ αὐτὸς καὶ ἀποκρίνεσθαι;

ΕΡΜ. Ναί.

ΣΩ. Τὸν δὲ ἐρωτᾶν καὶ ἀποκρίνεσθαι ἐπιστάμενον ἄλλο τι σὺ καλεῖς ἢ διαλεκτικόν;

ΕΡΜ. Οὔκ, ἀλλὰ τοῦτο.

D ΣΩ. Τέκτονος μὲν ἄρα ἔργον ἐστὶν ποιῆσαι πηδάλιον ἐπιστατοῦντος κυβερνήτου, εἰ μέλλει καλὸν εἶναι τὸ πηδάλιον.

ΕΡΜ. Φαίνεται.

ΣΩ. Νομοθέτου δέ γε, ὡς ἔοικεν, ὄνομα, ἐπιστάτην ἔχοντος διαλεκτικὸν ἄνδρα, εἰ μέλλει καλῶς ὀνόματα θήσεσθαι.

ΕΡΜ. Ἔστι ταῦτα.

ΣΩ. Κινδυνεύει ἄρα, ὦ Ἑρμόγενες, εἶναι οὐ φαῦλον, ὡς σὺ οἴει, ἡ τοῦ ὀνόματος θέσις, οὐδὲ φαύλων ἀνδρῶν οὐδὲ τῶν ἐπιτυχόντων. καὶ Κρατύλος ἀληθῆ λέγει λέγων φύσει τὰ ὀνόματα εἶναι
E τοῖς πράγμασι, καὶ οὐ πάντα δημιουργὸν ὀνομάτων εἶναι, ἀλλὰ μόνον ἐκεῖνον τὸν ἀποβλέποντα εἰς τὸ τῇ φύσει ὄνομα ὂν ἑκάστῳ καὶ δυνάμενον αὐτοῦ τὸ εἶδος τιθέναι εἴς τε τὰ γράμματα καὶ τὰς συλλαβάς.

ΕΡΜ. Οὐκ ἔχω, ὦ Σώκρατες, ὅπως χρὴ πρὸς ἃ λέγεις ἐναντιοῦσθαι. ἴσως μέντοι οὐ ῥᾴδιόν
391 ἐστιν οὕτως ἐξαίφνης πεισθῆναι, ἀλλὰ δοκῶ μοι ὧδε ἂν μᾶλλον πιθέσθαί σοι,[1] εἴ μοι δείξειας ἥντινα φῂς εἶναι τὴν φύσει ὀρθότητα ὀνόματος.

ΣΩ. Ἐγὼ μέν, ὦ μακάριε Ἑρμόγενες, οὐδε-

HER. Yes.

soc. And is not this he who knows how to ask questions ?

HER. Certainly.

soc. And the same one knows also how to make replies ?

HER. Yes.

soc. And the man who knows how to ask and answer questions you call a dialectician ?

HER. Yes, that is what I call him.

soc. The work of the carpenter, then, is to make a rudder under the supervision of the steersman, if the rudder is to be a good one.

HER. Evidently.

soc. And the work of the lawgiver, as it seems, is to make a name, with the dialectician as his supervisor, if names are to be well given.

HER. True.

soc. Then, Hermogenes, the giving of names can hardly be, as you imagine, a trifling matter, or a task for trifling or casual persons : and Cratylus is right in saying that names belong to things by nature and that not every one is an artisan of names, but only he who keeps in view the name which belongs by nature to each particular thing and is able to embody its form in the letters and syllables.

HER. I do not know how to answer you, Socrates ; nevertheless it is not easy to change my conviction so suddenly. I think you would be more likely to convince me, if you were to show me just what it is that you say is the natural correctness of names.

soc. I, my dear Hermogenes, do not say that there

---

[1] ἀλλὰ . . . πιθέσθαι TG : om. B, Schanz : σοι Burnet after Schanz : τίθεσθαί σε pr. T : πείθεσθαί σε pr. G.

μίαν λέγω, ἀλλ' ἐπελάθου γε ὧν ὀλίγον πρότερον
ἔλεγον, ὅτι οὐκ εἰδείην, ἀλλὰ σκεψοίμην μετὰ σοῦ.
νῦν δὲ σκοπουμένοις ἡμῖν, ἐμοί τε καὶ σοί, τοσοῦτον
μὲν ἤδη φαίνεται παρὰ τὰ πρότερα, φύσει τέ τινα
ὀρθότητα ἔχον εἶναι τὸ ὄνομα καὶ οὐ παντὸς
B ἀνδρὸς ἐπίστασθαι καλῶς[1] αὐτὸ πράγματι ὁτῳοῦν
θέσθαι· ἢ οὔ;

ΕΡΜ. Πάνυ γε.

11. ΣΩ. Οὐκοῦν τὸ μετὰ τοῦτο χρὴ ζητεῖν,
εἴπερ ἐπιθυμεῖς εἰδέναι, ἥτις ποτ' αὖ ἐστιν αὐτοῦ
ἡ ὀρθότης.

ΕΡΜ. Ἀλλὰ μὴν ἐπιθυμῶ γε εἰδέναι.

ΣΩ. Σκόπει τοίνυν.

ΕΡΜ. Πῶς οὖν χρὴ σκοπεῖν;

ΣΩ. Ὀρθοτάτη μὲν τῆς σκέψεως, ὦ ἑταῖρε, μετὰ
τῶν ἐπισταμένων, χρήματα ἐκείνοις τελοῦντα καὶ
χάριτας κατατιθέμενον. εἰσὶ δὲ οὗτοι οἱ σοφισταί,
C οἷσπερ καὶ ὁ ἀδελφός σου Καλλίας πολλὰ τελέσας
χρήματα σοφὸς δοκεῖ εἶναι. ἐπειδὴ δὲ οὐκ ἐγκρατὴς εἶ τῶν πατρῴων, λιπαρεῖν χρὴ τὸν ἀδελφὸν
καὶ δεῖσθαι αὐτοῦ διδάξαι σε τὴν ὀρθότητα περὶ
τῶν τοιούτων, ἣν ἔμαθεν παρὰ Πρωταγόρου.

ΕΡΜ. Ἄτοπος μέντ' ἂν εἴη μου, ὦ Σώκρατες,
ἡ δέησις, εἰ τὴν μὲν ἀλήθειαν τὴν Πρωταγόρου
ὅλως οὐκ ἀποδέχομαι, τὰ δὲ τῇ τοιαύτῃ ἀληθείᾳ
ῥηθέντα ἀγαπῴην ὥς του ἄξια.

ΣΩ. Ἀλλ' εἰ μὴ αὖ σε ταῦτα ἀρέσκει, παρ'
D Ὁμήρου χρὴ μανθάνειν καὶ παρὰ τῶν ἄλλων
ποιητῶν.

ΕΡΜ. Καὶ τί λέγει, ὦ Σώκρατες, Ὅμηρος περὶ
ὀνομάτων, καὶ ποῦ;

[1] καλῶς om. T.

is any. You forget what I said a while ago, that I did not know, but would join you in looking for the truth. And now, as we are looking, you and I, we already see one thing we did not know before, that names do possess a certain natural correctness, and that not every man knows how to give a name well to anything whatsoever. Is not that true ?

HER. Certainly.

SOC. Then our next task is to try to find out, if you care to know about it, what kind of correctness that is which belongs to names.

HER. To be sure I care to know.

SOC. Then investigate.

HER. How shall I investigate ?

SOC. The best way to investigate, my friend, is with the help of those who know ; and you make sure of their favour by paying them money. They are the sophists, from whom your brother Callias got his reputation for wisdom by paying them a good deal of money. But since you have not the control of your inheritance, you ought to beg and beseech your brother to teach you the correctness which he learned of Protagoras about such matters.

HER. It would be an absurd request for me, Socrates, if I, who reject the *Truth* [1] of Protagoras altogether, should desire what is said in such a *Truth*, as if it were of any value.

SOC. Then if you do not like that, you ought to learn from Homer and the other poets.

HER. Why, Socrates, what does Homer say about names, and where ?

---

[1] *Truth* was the title of a book by Protagoras.

PLATO

ΣΩ. Πολλαχοῦ· μέγιστα δὲ καὶ κάλλιστα ἐν οἷς
διορίζει ἐπὶ τοῖς αὐτοῖς ἅ τε οἱ ἄνθρωποι ὀνόματα
καλοῦσι καὶ οἱ θεοί. ἢ οὐκ οἴει αὐτὸν μέγα τι
καὶ θαυμάσιον λέγειν ἐν τούτοις περὶ ὀνομάτων
ὀρθότητος; δῆλον γὰρ δὴ ὅτι οἵ γε θεοὶ αὐτὰ
E καλοῦσιν πρὸς ὀρθότητα ἅπερ ἐστὶ φύσει ὀνό-
ματα· ἢ σὺ οὐκ οἴει;
ΕΡΜ. Εὖ οἶδα μὲν οὖν ἔγωγε, εἴπερ καλοῦσιν,
ὅτι ὀρθῶς καλοῦσιν. ἀλλὰ ποῖα ταῦτα λέγεις;
ΣΩ. Οὐκ οἶσθα ὅτι περὶ τοῦ ποταμοῦ τοῦ ἐν
τῇ Τροίᾳ, ὃς ἐμονομάχει τῷ Ἡφαίστῳ, ὃν Ξάνθον,
φησί, καλέουσι θεοί, ἄνδρες δὲ Σκάμανδρον;
ΕΡΜ. Ἔγωγε.
392 ΣΩ. Τί οὖν δή; οὐκ οἴει τοῦτο σεμνόν τι εἶναι
γνῶναι, ὅπῃ ποτὲ ὀρθῶς ἔχει ἐκεῖνον τὸν ποταμὸν
Ξάνθον καλεῖν μᾶλλον ἢ Σκάμανδρον; εἰ δὲ
βούλει, περὶ τῆς ὄρνιθος, ἣν λέγει ὅτι

χαλκίδα κικλήσκουσι θεοί, ἄνδρες δὲ κύμινδιν,

φαῦλον ἡγεῖ τὸ μάθημα, ὅσῳ ὀρθότερόν ἐστι
καλεῖσθαι χαλκὶς κυμίνδιδος τῷ αὐτῷ ὀρνέῳ; ἢ
τὴν Βατίειάν τε καὶ Μυρίνην, καὶ ἄλλα πολλὰ
B καὶ τούτου τοῦ ποιητοῦ καὶ ἄλλων; ἀλλὰ ταῦτα
μὲν ἴσως μείζω ἐστὶν ἢ κατ' ἐμὲ καὶ σὲ ἐξευρεῖν·
ὁ δὲ Σκαμάνδριός[1] τε καὶ ὁ Ἀστυάναξ ἀνθρω-
πινώτερον διασκέψασθαι, ὡς ἐμοὶ δοκεῖ, καὶ ῥᾷον,
ἅ φησιν ὀνόματα εἶναι τῷ τοῦ Ἕκτορος υἱεῖ,
τίνα ποτὲ λέγει τὴν ὀρθότητα αὐτῶν. οἶσθα
γὰρ δήπου ταῦτα τὰ ἔπη, ἐν οἷς ἔνεστιν ἃ ἐγὼ
λέγω.

[1] Σκαμάνδριός] Σκάμανδρός BT.

[1] Homer, Iliad, xxi. 342-380.   [2] Ibid. xx. 74.

soc. In many passages; but chiefly and most admirably in those in which he distinguishes between the names by which gods and men call the same things. Do you not think he gives in those passages great and wonderful information about the correctness of names? For clearly the gods call things by the names that are naturally right. Do you not think so?

her. Of course I know that if they call things, they call them rightly. But what are these instances to which you refer?

soc. Do you not know that he says about the river in Troyland which had the single combat with Hephaestus,[1] " whom the gods call Xanthus, but men call Scamander " ? [2]

her. Oh yes.

soc. Well, do you not think this is a grand thing to know, that the name of that river is rightly Xanthus, rather than Scamander? Or, if you like, do you think it is a slight thing to learn about the bird which he says " gods call chalcis, but men call cymindis," [3] that it is much more correct for the same bird to be called chalcis than cymindis? Or to learn that the hill men call Batieia is called by the gods Myrina's tomb,[4] and many other such statements by Homer and other poets? But perhaps these matters are too high for us to understand; it is, I think, more within human power to investigate the names Scamandrius and Astyanax, and understand what kind of correctness he ascribes to these, which he says are the names of Hector's son You recall, of course, the lines which contain the words to which I refer.

[3] *Ibid.* xiv. 291. [4] *Ibid.* ii. 813 f.

ΕΡΜ. Πάνυ γε.

ΣΩ. Πότερον οὖν οἴει Ὅμηρον ὀρθότερον ἡγεῖσθαι τῶν ὀνομάτων κεῖσθαι τῷ παιδί, τὸν Ἀστυάνακτα ἢ τὸν Σκαμάνδριον;

C ΕΡΜ. Οὐκ ἔχω λέγειν.

12. ΣΩ. Ὧδε δὴ σκόπει. εἴ τις ἔροιτό σε, πότερον οἴει ὀρθότερον καλεῖν τὰ ὀνόματα τοὺς φρονιμωτέρους ἢ τοὺς ἀφρονεστέρους;

ΕΡΜ. Δῆλον δὴ ὅτι τοὺς φρονιμωτέρους, φαίην ἄν.

ΣΩ. Πότερον οὖν αἱ γυναῖκες ἐν ταῖς πόλεσιν φρονιμώτεραί σοι δοκοῦσιν εἶναι ἢ οἱ ἄνδρες, ὡς τὸ ὅλον εἰπεῖν γένος;

ΕΡΜ. Οἱ ἄνδρες.

ΣΩ. Οὐκοῦν οἶσθα ὅτι Ὅμηρος τὸ παιδίον τὸ τοῦ Ἕκτορος ὑπὸ τῶν Τρώων φησὶν καλεῖσθαι

D Ἀστυάνακτα, Σκαμάνδριον δὲ δῆλον ὅτι ὑπὸ τῶν γυναικῶν, ἐπειδὴ οἵ γε ἄνδρες αὐτὸν Ἀστυάνακτα ἐκάλουν;

ΕΡΜ. Ἔοικέ γε.

ΣΩ. Οὐκοῦν καὶ Ὅμηρος τοὺς Τρῶας σοφωτέρους ἡγεῖτο ἢ τὰς γυναῖκας αὐτῶν;

ΕΡΜ. Οἶμαι ἔγωγε.

ΣΩ. Τὸν Ἀστυάνακτα ἄρα ὀρθότερον ᾤετο κεῖσθαι τῷ παιδὶ ἢ τὸν Σκαμάνδριον;

ΕΡΜ. Φαίνεται.

ΣΩ. Σκοπῶμεν δὴ διὰ τί ποτε. ἢ αὐτὸς ἡμῖν κάλλιστα ὑφηγεῖται τὸ διότι; φησὶν γάρ·

E οἶος γάρ σφιν ἔρυτο πόλιν καὶ τείχεα μακρά.

διὰ ταῦτα δή, ὡς ἔοικεν, ὀρθῶς ἔχει καλεῖν τὸν τοῦ σωτῆρος υἱὸν Ἀστυάνακτα τούτου ὃ ἔσῳζεν ὁ πατὴρ αὐτοῦ, ὥς φησιν Ὅμηρος.

CRATYLUS

HER. Certainly.

SOC. Which of the names of the boy do you imagine Homer thought was more correct, Astyanax or Scamandrius?

HER. I cannot say.

SOC. Look at it in this way: suppose you were asked, "Do the wise or the unwise give names more correctly?"

HER. "The wise, obviously," I should say.

SOC. And do you think the women or the men of a city, regarded as a class in general, are the wiser?

HER. The men.

SOC. And do you not know that Homer says the child of Hector was called Astyanax by the men of Troy;[1] so he must have been called Scamandrius by the women, since the men called him Astyanax?

HER. Yes, probably.

SOC. And Homer too thought the Trojan men were wiser than the women?

HER. I suppose he did.

SOC. Then he thought Astyanax was more rightly the boy's name than Scamandrius?

HER. So it appears.

SOC. Let us, then, consider the reason for this. Does he not himself indicate the reason most admirably? For he says—

He alone defended their city and long walls.[2]

Therefore, as it seems, it is right to call the son of the defender Astyanax (Lord of the city), ruler of that which his father, as Homer says, defended.

[1] Homer, *Iliad*, xxii. 506.
[2] *Ibid.* xxii. 507; but the verb is in the second person, addressed by Hecuba to Hector after his death.

ΕΡΜ. Φαίνεταί μοι.

ΣΩ. Τί δή ποτε; οὐ γάρ πω οὐδ᾽ αὐτὸς ἔγωγε μανθάνω, ὦ Ἑρμόγενες· σὺ δὲ μανθάνεις;

ΕΡΜ. Μὰ Δί᾽ οὐκ ἔγωγε.

393 ΣΩ. Ἀλλ᾽ ἆρα, ὠγαθέ, καὶ τῷ Ἕκτορι αὐτὸς ἔθετο τὸ ὄνομα Ὅμηρος;

ΕΡΜ. Τί δή;

ΣΩ. Ὅτι μοι δοκεῖ καὶ τοῦτο παραπλήσιόν τι εἶναι τῷ Ἀστυάνακτι, καὶ ἔοικεν Ἑλληνικοῖς ταῦτα τὰ ὀνόματα. ὁ γὰρ ἄναξ καὶ ὁ ἕκτωρ σχεδόν τι ταὐτὸν σημαίνει, βασιλικὰ ἀμφότερα εἶναι τὰ ὀνόματα· οὗ γὰρ ἄν τις ἄναξ ᾖ, καὶ ἕκτωρ δήπου ἐστὶν τούτου· δῆλον γὰρ ὅτι κρατεῖ B τε αὐτοῦ καὶ κέκτηται καὶ ἔχει αὐτό. ἢ οὐδέν σοι δοκῶ λέγειν, ἀλλὰ λανθάνω καὶ ἐμαυτὸν οἰόμενός τινος ὥσπερ ἴχνους ἐφάπτεσθαι τῆς Ὁμήρου δόξης περὶ ὀνομάτων ὀρθότητος;

ΕΡΜ. Μὰ Δί᾽ οὐ σύ γε, ὡς ἐμοὶ δοκεῖς, ἀλλὰ ἴσως του ἐφάπτει.

13. ΣΩ. Δίκαιόν γέ τοί ἐστιν, ὡς ἐμοὶ φαίνεται, τὸν λέοντος ἔκγονον λέοντα καλεῖν καὶ τὸν ἵππου ἔκγονον ἵππον. οὔ τι λέγω ἐὰν ὥσπερ τέρας γένηται ἐξ ἵππου ἄλλο τι ἢ ἵππος, ἀλλ᾽ C οὗ ἂν ᾖ τοῦ γένους ἔκγονον τὴν φύσιν, τοῦτο λέγω· ἐὰν βοὸς ἔκγονον φύσει ἵππος παρὰ φύσιν τέκῃ μόσχον, οὐ πῶλον κλητέον ἀλλὰ μόσχον· οὐδ᾽ ἂν ἐξ ἀνθρώπου, οἶμαι, μὴ τὸ ἀνθρώπου ἔκγονον γένηται, ἄλλο ἂν[1] τὸ ἔκγονον ἄνθρωπος κλητέος· καὶ τὰ δένδρα ὡσαύτως καὶ τἆλλα ἅπαντα· ἢ οὐ ξυνδοκεῖ;

---

[1] ἄλλο ἂν] ἀλλ᾽ οὗ ἂν BT : secl. Peipers.

HER. That is clear to me.

soc. Indeed ? I do not yet understand about it myself, Hermogenes. Do you ?

HER. No, by Zeus, I do not.

soc. But, my good friend, did not Homer himself also give Hector his name ?

HER. Why do you ask that ?

soc. Because that name seems to me similar to Astyanax, and both names seem to be Greek. For lord ($ἄναξ$) and holder ($ἕκτωρ$) mean nearly the same thing, indicating that they are names of a king ; for surely a man is holder of that of which he is lord ; for it is clear that he rules it and possesses it and holds it. Or does it seem to you that there is nothing in what I am saying, and am I wrong in imagining that I have found a clue to Homer's opinion about the correctness of names ?

HER. No, by Zeus, you are not wrong, in my opinion ; I think perhaps you have found a clue.

soc. It is right, I think, to call a lion's offspring a lion and a horse's offspring a horse. I am not speaking of prodigies, such as the birth of some other kind of creature from a horse, but of the natural offspring of each species after its kind. If a horse, contrary to nature, should bring forth a calf, the natural offspring of a cow, it should be called a calf, not a colt, nor if any offspring that is not human should be born from a human being, should that other offspring be called a human being ; and the same applies to trees and all the rest. Do you not agree ?

PLATO

ΕΡΜ. Ξυνδοκεῖ.

ΣΩ. Καλῶς λέγεις· φύλαττε γάρ με, μή πη
παρακρούσωμαί σε. κατὰ γὰρ τὸν αὐτὸν λόγον
κἂν ἐκ βασιλέως γίγνηταί τι ἔκγονον, βασιλεὺς
D κλητέος· εἰ δὲ ἐν ἑτέραις συλλαβαῖς ἢ ἐν ἑτέραις
τὸ αὐτὸ σημαίνει, οὐδὲν πρᾶγμα· οὐδ' εἰ πρόσ-
κειταί τι γράμμα ἢ¹ ἀφήρηται, οὐδὲν οὐδὲ τοῦτο,
ἕως ἂν ἐγκρατὴς ᾖ ἡ οὐσία τοῦ πράγματος δηλου-
μένη ἐν τῷ ὀνόματι.

ΕΡΜ. Πῶς τοῦτο λέγεις;

ΣΩ. Οὐδὲν ποικίλον, ἀλλ' ὥσπερ τῶν στοιχείων
οἶσθα ὅτι ὀνόματα λέγομεν, ἀλλ' οὐκ αὐτὰ τὰ
στοιχεῖα, πλὴν τεττάρων, τοῦ ε καὶ τοῦ υ καὶ
τοῦ ο καὶ τοῦ ω· τοῖς δ' ἄλλοις φωνήεσί τε καὶ
E ἀφώνοις οἶσθα ὅτι περιτιθέντες ἄλλα γράμματα
λέγομεν, ὀνόματα ποιοῦντες· ἀλλ' ἕως ἂν αὐτοῦ
δηλουμένην τὴν δύναμιν ἐντιθῶμεν, ὀρθῶς ἔχει
ἐκεῖνο τὸ ὄνομα καλεῖν ὃ αὐτὸ ἡμῖν δηλώσει.
οἷον τὸ βῆτα· ὁρᾷς ὅτι τοῦ η καὶ τοῦ τ καὶ τοῦ
α προστεθέντων οὐδὲν ἐλύπησεν, ὥστε μὴ οὐχὶ
τὴν ἐκείνου τοῦ στοιχείου φύσιν δηλῶσαι ὅλῳ
τῷ ὀνόματι οὗ ἐβούλετο ὁ νομοθέτης· οὕτως
ἠπιστήθη καλῶς θέσθαι τοῖς γράμμασι τὰ ὀνόματα.

ΕΡΜ. Ἀληθῆ μοι δοκεῖς λέγειν.

ΣΩ. Οὐκοῦν καὶ περὶ βασιλέως ὁ αὐτὸς λόγος;
394 ἔσται γάρ ποτε ἐκ βασιλέως βασιλεύς, καὶ ἐξ
ἀγαθοῦ ἀγαθός, καὶ ἐκ καλοῦ καλός, καὶ τἆλλα
πάντα οὕτως, ἐξ ἑκάστου γένους ἕτερον τοιοῦτον
ἔκγονον, ἐὰν μὴ τέρας γίγνηται· κλητέον δὴ

---

¹ ἢ T: οὐδ' B: οὐδ' εἰ al.

HER. Yes.

soc. Good; but keep watch of me, and do not let me trick you; for by the same argument any offspring of a king should be called a king; and whether the same meaning is expressed in one set of syllables or another makes no difference; and if a letter is added or subtracted, that does not matter either, so long as the essence of the thing named remains in force and is made plain in the name.

HER. What do you mean?

soc. Something quite simple. For instance, when we speak of the letters of the alphabet, you know, we speak their names, not merely the letters themselves, except in the case of four, e, v, o, and ω.[1] We make names for all the other vowels and consonants by adding other letters to them; and so long as we include the letter in question and make its force plain, we may properly call it by that name, and that will designate it for us. Take beta, for instance, The addition of e (η), t (τ), and a (a) does no harm and does not prevent the whole name from making clear the nature of that letter which the lawgiver wished to designate; he knew so well how to give names to letters.

HER. I think you are right.

soc. Does not the same reasoning apply to a king? A king's son will probably be a king, a good man's good, a handsome man's handsome, and so forth; the offspring of each class will be of the same class, unless some unnatural birth takes

[1] In Plato's time the names epsilon, ypsilon, omicron, and omega were not yet in vogue. The names used were εἶ, ὖ, οὖ, and ὦ.

ταὐτὰ ὀνόματα. ποικίλλειν δὲ ἔξεστι ταῖς συλλαβαῖς, ὥστε δόξαι ἂν τῷ ἰδιωτικῶς ἔχοντι ἕτερα
εἶναι ἀλλήλων τὰ αὐτὰ ὄντα· ὥσπερ ἡμῖν τὰ
τῶν ἰατρῶν φάρμακα χρώμασιν ἢ ὀσμαῖς πεποικιλ-
μένα ἄλλα φαίνεται τὰ αὐτὰ ὄντα, τῷ δέ γε ἰατρῷ,
B ἅτε τὴν δύναμιν τῶν φαρμάκων σκοπουμένῳ, τὰ
αὐτὰ φαίνεται, καὶ οὐκ ἐκπλήττεται ὑπὸ τῶν προσ-
όντων. οὕτω δὲ ἴσως καὶ ὁ ἐπιστάμενος περὶ
ὀνομάτων τὴν δύναμιν αὐτῶν σκοπεῖ, καὶ οὐκ
ἐκπλήττεται εἴ τι πρόσκειται γράμμα ἢ μετά-
κειται ἢ ἀφῄρηται, ἢ καὶ ἐν ἄλλοις παντάπασιν
γράμμασίν ἐστιν ἡ τοῦ ὀνόματος δύναμις. ὥσπερ
ὃ νῦν δὴ ἐλέγομεν, Ἀστυάναξ τε καὶ Ἕκτωρ
οὐδὲν τῶν αὐτῶν γραμμάτων ἔχει πλὴν τοῦ τ,
C ἀλλ᾽ ὅμως ταὐτὸν σημαίνει. καὶ Ἀρχέπολίς γε
τῶν μὲν γραμμάτων τί ἐπικοινωνεῖ; δηλοῖ δὲ
ὅμως τὸ αὐτό· καὶ ἄλλα πολλά ἐστιν, ἃ οὐδὲν
ἀλλ᾽ ἢ βασιλέα σημαίνει· καὶ ἄλλα γε αὖ στρα-
τηγόν, οἷον Ἆγις καὶ Πολέμαρχος καὶ Εὐ-
πόλεμος· καὶ ἰατρικά γε ἕτερα, Ἰατροκλῆς καὶ
Ἀκεσίμβροτος· καὶ ἕτερα ἂν ἴσως συχνὰ εὕροιμεν
ταῖς μὲν συλλαβαῖς καὶ τοῖς γράμμασι διαφω-
νοῦντα, τῇ δὲ δυνάμει ταὐτὸν φθεγγόμενα. φαίνεται οὕτως ἢ οὔ;

D ΕΡΜ. Πάνυ μὲν οὖν.

ΣΩ. Τοῖς μὲν δὴ κατὰ φύσιν γιγνομένοις τὰ
αὐτὰ ἀποδοτέον ὀνόματα.

ΕΡΜ. Πάνυ γε.

14. ΣΩ. Τί δὲ τοῖς παρὰ φύσιν, οἳ ἂν ἐν τέ-
ρατος εἴδει γένωνται; οἷον ὅταν ἐξ ἀνδρὸς ἀγαθοῦ καὶ θεοσεβοῦς ἀσεβὴς γένηται, ἆρ᾽ οὐχ ὥσπερ

place; so they should be called by the same names. But variety in the syllables is admissible, so that names which are the same appear different to the uninitiated, just as the physicians' drugs, when prepared with various colours and perfumes, seem different to us, though they are the same, but to the physician, who considers only their medicinal value, they seem the same, and he is not confused by the additions. So perhaps the man who knows about names considers their value and is not confused if some letter is added, transposed, or subtracted, or even if the force of the name is expressed in entirely different letters. So, for instance, in the names we were just discussing, Astyanax and Hector, none of the letters is the same, except *t*, but nevertheless they have the same meaning. And what letters has Archepolis (ruler of the city) in common with them? Yet it means the same thing; and there are many other names which mean simply "king." Others again mean "general," such as Agis (leader), Polemarchus (war-lord), and Eupolemus (good warrior); and others indicate physicians, as Iatrocles (famous physician) and Acesimbrotus (healer of mortals); and we might perhaps find many others which differ in syllables and letters, but express the same meaning. Do you think that is true, or not?

HER. Certainly.

SOC. To those, then, who are born in accordance with nature the same names should be given.

HER. Yes.

SOC. And how about those who are born contrary to nature as prodigies? For instance, when an impious son is born to a good and pious man, ought

PLATO

ἐν τοῖς ἔμπροσθεν, κἂν ἵππος βοὸς ἔκγονον τέκῃ, οὐ τοῦ τεκόντος δήπου ἔδει τὴν ἐπωνυμίαν ἔχειν, ἀλλὰ τοῦ γένους οὗ εἴη;

ΕΡΜ. Πάνυ γε.

Ε ΣΩ. Καὶ τῷ ἐκ τοῦ εὐσεβοῦς ἄρα γενομένῳ ἀσεβεῖ τὸ τοῦ γένους ὄνομα ἀποδοτέον.

ΕΡΜ. Ἔστι ταῦτα.

ΣΩ. Οὐ Θεόφιλον, ὡς ἔοικεν, οὐδὲ Μνησίθεον οὐδὲ τῶν τοιούτων οὐδέν· ἀλλ' ὅ τι τἀναντία τούτοις σημαίνει, ἐάνπερ τῆς ὀρθότητος τυγχάνῃ τὰ ὀνόματα.

ΕΡΜ. Παντός γε μᾶλλον, ὦ Σώκρατες.

ΣΩ. Ὥσπερ γε καὶ ὁ Ὀρέστης, ὦ Ἑρμόγενες, κινδυνεύει ὀρθῶς ἔχειν, εἴτε τις τύχη ἔθετο αὐτῷ τὸ ὄνομα εἴτε καὶ ποιητής τις, τὸ θηριῶδες τῆς φύσεως καὶ τὸ ἄγριον αὐτοῦ καὶ τὸ ὀρεινὸν ἐνδεικνύμενος τῷ ὀνόματι.

395 ΕΡΜ. Φαίνεται οὕτως, ὦ Σώκρατες.

ΣΩ. Ἔοικεν δέ γε καὶ τῷ πατρὶ αὐτοῦ κατὰ φύσιν τὸ ὄνομα εἶναι.

ΕΡΜ. Φαίνεται.

ΣΩ. Κινδυνεύει γὰρ τοιοῦτός τις εἶναι ὁ Ἀγαμέμνων, οἷος ἂν δόξειεν αὐτῷ διαπονεῖσθαι καὶ καρτερεῖν, τέλος ἐπιτιθεὶς τοῖς δόξασι δι' ἀρετήν. σημεῖον δὲ αὐτοῦ ἡ ἐν Τροίᾳ μονὴ τοῦ πλήθους τε καὶ καρτερία.[1] ὅτι οὖν ἀγαστὸς κατὰ τὴν ἐπιμονὴν οὗτος ὁ ἀνήρ, ἐνσημαίνει τὸ ὄνομα ὁ Β Ἀγαμέμνων. ἴσως δὲ καὶ ὁ Ἀτρεὺς ὀρθῶς ἔχει. ὅ τε γὰρ τοῦ Χρυσίππου αὐτῷ φόνος καὶ ἃ πρὸς τὸν Θυέστην ὡς ὠμὰ διεπράττετο, πάντα ταῦτα ζημιώδη καὶ ἀτηρὰ πρὸς ἀρετήν· ἡ οὖν τοῦ ὀνόματος ἐπωνυμία σμικρὸν παρακλίνει καὶ ἐπι-

[1] καρτερία E Hermann al.: καρτερίας BT.

44

he not, as in our former example when a mare brought forth a calf, **to** have the designation of the class to which he belongs, instead of that of his parent ?

HER. Certainly.

SOC. Then the impious son of a pious father ought to receive the name of his class.

HER. True.

SOC. Not Theophilus (beloved of God) or Mnesitheus (mindful of God) or anything of that sort ; but something of opposite meaning, if names are correct.

HER. Most assuredly, Socrates.

SOC. As the name of Orestes (mountain man) is undoubtedly correct, Hermogenes, whether it was given him by chance or by some poet who indicated by the name the fierceness, rudeness, and mountain-wildness of his nature.

HER. So it seems, Socrates.

SOC. And his father's name also appears to be in accordance with nature.

HER. It seems so.

SOC. Yes, for Agamemnon (admirable for remaining) is one who would resolve to toil to the end and to endure, putting the finish upon his resolution by virtue. And a proof of this is his long retention of the host at Troy and his endurance. So the name Agamemnon denotes that this man is admirable for remaining. And so, too, the name of Atreus is likely to be correct ; for his murder of Chrysippus and the cruelty of his acts to Thyestes are all damaging and ruinous ($\dot{\alpha}\tau\eta\rho\dot{\alpha}$) to his virtue. Now the form of his name is slightly deflected and hidden,

κεκάλυπται, ὥστε μὴ πᾶσι δηλοῦν τὴν φύσιν τοῦ
ἀνδρός· τοῖς δ' ἐπαΐουσι περὶ ὀνομάτων ἱκανῶς
δηλοῖ ὃ βούλεται ὁ Ἀτρεύς. καὶ γὰρ κατὰ τὸ
C ἀτειρὲς καὶ κατὰ τὸ ἄτρεστον καὶ κατὰ τὸ ἀτηρὸν
πανταχῇ ὀρθῶς αὐτῷ τὸ ὄνομα κεῖται. δοκεῖ δέ
μοι καὶ τῷ Πέλοπι τὸ ὄνομα ἐμμέτρως κεῖσθαι·
σημαίνει γὰρ τοῦτο τὸ ὄνομα τὸν τὰ ἐγγὺς ὁρῶντα
ἄξιον εἶναι ταύτης τῆς ἐπωνυμίας.[1]

ΕΡΜ. Πῶς δή;

ΣΩ. Οἷόν που καὶ κατ' ἐκείνου λέγεται τοῦ
ἀνδρὸς ἐν τῷ τοῦ Μυρτίλου φόνῳ οὐδὲν οἷον[2] τε
γενέσθαι προνοηθῆναι οὐδὲ προϊδεῖν τῶν πόρρω τῶν
εἰς τὸ πᾶν γένος, ὅσης αὐτὸ[3] δυστυχίας ἐνεπίμπλα,
D τὸ ἐγγὺς μόνον ὁρῶν καὶ τὸ παραχρῆμα—τοῦτο
δ' ἐστὶ πέλας—ἡνίκα προεθυμεῖτο λαβεῖν παντὶ
τρόπῳ τὸν τῆς Ἱπποδαμείας γάμον. τῷ δὲ Ταντάλῳ καὶ πᾶς ἂν ἡγήσαιτο τοὔνομα ὀρθῶς καὶ κατὰ
φύσιν τεθῆναι, εἰ ἀληθῆ τὰ περὶ αὐτὸν λεγόμενα.

ΕΡΜ. Τὰ ποῖα ταῦτα;

ΣΩ. Ἅ τέ που ἔτι ζῶντι δυστυχήματα ἐγένετο
πολλὰ καὶ δεινά, ὧν καὶ τέλος ἡ πατρὶς αὐτοῦ
ὅλη ἀνετράπετο, καὶ τελευτήσαντι ἐν Ἅιδου ἡ
E ὑπὲρ τῆς κεφαλῆς τοῦ λίθου ταλαντεία[4] θαυμαστῶς ὡς σύμφωνος τῷ ὀνόματι· καὶ ἀτεχνῶς ἔοικεν,
ὥσπερ ἂν εἴ τις βουλόμενος ταλάντατον ὀνομάσαι
ἀποκρυπτόμενος ὀνομάσειε καὶ εἴποι ἀντ' ἐκείνου
Τάνταλον, τοιοῦτόν τι καὶ τούτῳ τὸ ὄνομα ἔοικεν
ἐκπορίσαι ἡ τύχη τῆς φήμης. φαίνεται δὲ καὶ
τῷ πατρὶ αὐτοῦ λεγομένῳ τῷ Διὶ παγκάλως τὸ

---

[1] ἄξιον . . . ἐπωνυμίας om. by nearly all editors.
[2] οἷον b : οἵῳ BT.   [3] αὐτὸ b : αὐτῷ BT.
[4] ταλαντεία Spalding : τανταλεία BT.

CRATYLUS

so that it does not make the man's nature plain to every one ; but to those who understand about names it makes the meaning of Atreus plain enough : for indeed in view of his stubbornness (ἀτειρές) and fearlessness (ἄτρεστον) and ruinous acts (ἀτηρόν) the name is correctly given to him on every ground. And I think Pelops also has a fitting name ; for this name means that he who sees only what is near deserves this designation.

HER. How is that ?

soc. Why it is said of him that in murdering Myrtilus he was quite unable to forecast or foresee the ultimate effects upon his whole race, and all the misery with which it was overwhelmed, because he saw only the near at hand and the immediate—that is to say, πέλας (near)—in his eagerness to win by all means the hand of Hippodameia. And anyone would think the name of Tantalus was given rightly and in accordance with nature, if the stories about him are true.

HER. What are the stories ?

soc. The many terrible misfortunes that happened to him both in his life, the last of which was the utter overthrow of his country, and in Hades, after his death, the balancing (ταλαντεία) of the stone above his head, in wonderful agreement with his name ; and it seems exactly as if someone who wished to call him most wretched (ταλάντατον) disguised the name and said Tantalus instead ; in some such way as that chance seems to have affected his name in the legend. And his father also, who is said to be Zeus, appears to have a very excellent

ὄνομα κεῖσθαι· ἔστι δὲ οὐ ῥᾴδιον κατανοῆσαι.
396 ἀτεχνῶς γάρ ἐστιν οἷον λόγος τὸ τοῦ Διὸς ὄνομα·
διελόντες δὲ αὐτὸ διχῇ οἱ μὲν τῷ ἑτέρῳ μέρει,
οἱ δὲ τῷ ἑτέρῳ χρώμεθα· οἱ μὲν γὰρ Ζῆνα, οἱ
δὲ Δία καλοῦσιν· συντιθέμενα δ' εἰς ἓν δηλοῖ τὴν
φύσιν τοῦ θεοῦ, ὃ δὴ προσήκειν φαμὲν ὀνόματι
οἵῳ τε εἶναι ἀπεργάζεσθαι. οὐ γὰρ ἔστιν ἡμῖν
καὶ τοῖς ἄλλοις πᾶσιν ὅστις ἐστὶν αἴτιος μᾶλλον
τοῦ ζῆν ἢ ὁ ἄρχων τε καὶ βασιλεὺς τῶν πάντων.
B συμβαίνει οὖν ὀρθῶς ὀνομάζεσθαι οὗτος ὁ θεὸς
εἶναι, δι' ὃν ζῆν ἀεὶ πᾶσι τοῖς ζῶσιν ὑπάρχει.
διείληπται δὲ δίχα, ὥσπερ λέγω, ἓν ὂν τὸ ὄνομα,
τῷ Διὶ καὶ τῷ Ζηνί. τοῦτον δὲ Κρόνου υἱὸν
εἶναι ὑβριστικὸν μὲν ἄν τις δόξειεν εἶναι ἀκούσαντι ἐξαίφνης, εὔλογον δὲ μεγάλης τινὸς διανοίας
ἔκγονον εἶναι τὸν Δία· κόρον γὰρ σημαίνει οὐ
παῖδα, ἀλλὰ τὸ καθαρὸν αὐτοῦ καὶ ἀκήρατον τοῦ
νοῦ. ἔστι δὲ οὗτος Οὐρανοῦ υἱός, ὡς λόγος· ἡ
δὲ αὖ ἐς τὸ ἄνω ὄψις καλῶς ἔχει τοῦτο τὸ ὄνομα
C καλεῖσθαι, οὐρανία, ὁρῶσα τὰ ἄνω, ὅθεν δὴ καὶ
φασιν, ὦ Ἑρμόγενες, τὸν καθαρὸν νοῦν παρα-
γίγνεσθαι οἱ μετεωρολόγοι, καὶ τῷ οὐρανῷ ὀρθῶς τὸ ὄνομα κεῖσθαι· εἰ δ' ἐμεμνήμην τὴν Ἡσιόδου γενεαλογίαν, τίνας ἔτι τοὺς ἀνωτέρω προγόνους λέγει τούτων, οὐκ ἂν ἐπαυόμην διεξιὼν ὡς
ὀρθῶς αὐτοῖς τὰ ὀνόματα κεῖται, ἕως ἀπεπειράθην
τῆς σοφίας ταυτησὶ τί ποιήσει, εἰ ἄρα ἀπερεῖ ἢ
οὔ, ἣ ἐμοὶ ἐξαίφνης νῦν οὑτωσὶ προσπέπτωκεν
D ἄρτι οὐκ οἶδ' ὁπόθεν.

ΕΡΜ. Καὶ μὲν δή, ὦ Σώκρατες, ἀτεχνῶς γέ
μοι δοκεῖς ὥσπερ οἱ ἐνθουσιῶντες ἐξαίφνης χρησμῳδεῖν.

name, but it is not easy to understand; for the
name of Zeus is exactly like a sentence; we divide
it into two parts, and some of us use one part,
others the other; for some call him Zena (Ζῆνα),
and others Dia (Δία); but the two in combination
express the nature of the god, which is just what we
said a name should be able to do. For certainly
no one is so much the author of life (ζῆν) for us and
all others as the ruler and king of all. Thus this
god is correctly named, through whom (δι᾽ ὅν) all
living beings have the gift of life (ζῆν). But, as I
say, the name is divided, though it is one name,
into the two parts, Dia and Zena. And it might
seem, at first hearing, highly irreverent to call him
the son of Cronus and reasonable to say that Zeus
is the offspring of some great intellect; and so
he is, for κόρος (for Κρόνος) signifies not child, but
the purity (καθαρόν) and unblemished nature of his
mind. And Cronus, according to tradition, is the
son of Uranus; but the upward gaze is rightly
called by the name urania (οὐρανία), looking at the
things above (ὁρῶ τὰ ἄνω), and the astronomers say,
Hermogenes, that from this looking people acquire
a pure mind, and Uranus is correctly named. If I
remembered the genealogy of Hesiod and the still
earlier ancestors of the gods he mentions, I would
have gone on examining the correctness of their
names until I had made a complete trial whether
this wisdom which has suddenly come to me, I know
not whence, will fail or not.

HER. Indeed, Socrates, you do seem to me to be
uttering oracles, exactly like an inspired prophet.

PLATO

15. ΣΩ. Καὶ αἰτιῶμαί γε, ὦ Ἑρμόγενες, μάλιστα αὐτὴν ἀπὸ Εὐθύφρονος τοῦ Προσπαλτίου προσπεπτωκέναι μοι. ἕωθεν γὰρ πολλὰ αὐτῷ συνῆ καὶ παρεῖχον τὰ ὦτα. κινδυνεύει οὖν ἐνθουσιῶν οὐ μόνον τὰ ὦτά μου ἐμπλῆσαι τῆς δαιμονίας σοφίας, ἀλλὰ καὶ τῆς ψυχῆς ἐπειλῆφθαι. δοκεῖ οὖν μοι χρῆναι οὑτωσὶ ἡμᾶς ποιῆσαι· τὸ μὲν
E τήμερον εἶναι χρήσασθαι αὐτῇ καὶ τὰ λοιπὰ περὶ τῶν ὀνομάτων ἐπισκέψασθαι, αὔριον δέ, ἂν καὶ ὑμῖν ξυνδοκῇ, ἀποδιοπομπησόμεθά τε αὐτὴν καὶ καθαρούμεθα ἐξευρόντες ὅστις τὰ τοιαῦτα δεινὸς
397 καθαίρειν, εἴτε τῶν ἱερέων τις εἴτε τῶν σοφιστῶν.
ΕΡΜ. Ἀλλ' ἐγὼ μὲν ξυγχωρῶ· πάνυ γὰρ ἂν ἡδέως τὰ ἐπίλοιπα περὶ τῶν ὀνομάτων ἀκούσαιμι.
ΣΩ. Ἀλλὰ χρὴ οὕτω ποιεῖν. πόθεν οὖν βούλει ἀρξώμεθα διασκοποῦντες, ἐπειδήπερ εἰς τύπον τινὰ ἐμβεβήκαμεν, ἵνα εἰδῶμεν εἰ ἄρα ἡμῖν ἐπιμαρτυρήσει αὐτὰ τὰ ὀνόματα μὴ πάνυ ἀπὸ τοῦ αὐτομάτου οὕτως ἕκαστα κεῖσθαι, ἀλλ' ἔχειν τινὰ
B ὀρθότητα; τὰ μὲν οὖν τῶν ἡρώων καὶ ἀνθρώπων λεγόμενα ὀνόματα ἴσως ἂν ἡμᾶς ἐξαπατήσειεν. πολλὰ μὲν γὰρ αὐτῶν κεῖται κατὰ προγόνων ἐπωνυμίας, οὐδὲν προσῆκον ἐνίοις, ὥσπερ κατ' ἀρχὰς ἐλέγομεν, πολλὰ δὲ ὥσπερ εὐχόμενοι τίθενται, οἷον Εὐτυχίδην καὶ Σωσίαν καὶ Θεόφιλον καὶ ἄλλα πολλά. τὰ μὲν οὖν τοιαῦτα δοκεῖ μοι χρῆναι ἐᾶν· εἰκὸς δὲ μάλιστα ἡμᾶς εὑρεῖν τὰ ὀρθῶς κείμενα περὶ τὰ ἀεὶ ὄντα καὶ πεφυκότα. ἐσπουδάσθαι γὰρ ἐνταῦθα μάλιστα πρέπει τὴν
C θέσιν τῶν ὀνομάτων· ἴσως δ' ἔνια αὐτῶν καὶ ὑπὸ θειοτέρας δυνάμεως ἢ τῆς τῶν ἀνθρώπων ἐτέθη.
50

CRATYLUS

soc. Yes, Hermogenes, and I am convinced that the inspiration came to me from Euthyphro the Prospaltian. For I was with him and listening to him a long time early this morning. So he must have been inspired, and he not only filled my ears but took possession of my soul with his superhuman wisdom. So I think this is our duty : we ought to-day to make use of this wisdom and finish the investigation of names, but to-morrow, if the rest of you agree, we will conjure it away and purify ourselves, when we have found some one, whether priest or sophist, who is skilled in that kind of purifying.

her. I agree, for I should be very glad to hear the rest of the talk about names.

soc. Very well. Then since we have outlined a general plan of investigation, where shall we begin, that we may discover whether the names themselves will bear witness that they are not at all distributed at haphazard, but have a certain correctness ? Now the names of heroes and men might perhaps prove deceptive ; for they are often given because they were names of ancestors, and in some cases, as we said in the beginning, they are quite inappropriate ; many, too, are given as the expression of a prayer, such as Eutychides (fortunate), Sosias (saviour), Theophilus (beloved of God), and many others. I think we had better disregard such as these ; but we are most likely to find the correct names in the nature of the eternal and absolute ; for there the names ought to have been given with the greatest care, and perhaps some of them were given by a power more divine than is that of men.

ΕΡΜ. Δοκεῖς μοι καλῶς λέγειν, ὦ Σώκρατες.

16. ΣΩ. Ἆρ' οὖν οὐ δίκαιον ἀπὸ τῶν θεῶν ἄρχεσθαι σκοπουμένους, πῇ ποτε αὐτὸ τοῦτο τὸ ὄνομα οἱ θεοὶ ὀρθῶς ἐκλήθησαν;

ΕΡΜ. Εἰκός γε.

ΣΩ. Τοιόνδε τοίνυν ἔγωγε ὑποπτεύω· φαίνονταί μοι οἱ πρῶτοι τῶν ἀνθρώπων τῶν περὶ τὴν Ἑλλάδα τούτους μόνους τοὺς θεοὺς ἡγεῖσθαι, οὕσπερ D νῦν πολλοὶ τῶν βαρβάρων, ἥλιον καὶ σελήνην καὶ γῆν καὶ ἄστρα καὶ οὐρανόν· ἅτε οὖν αὐτὰ ὁρῶντες πάντα ἀεὶ ἰόντα δρόμῳ καὶ θέοντα, ἀπὸ ταύτης τῆς φύσεως τῆς τοῦ θεῖν θεοὺς αὐτοὺς ἐπονομάσαι· ὕστερον δὲ κατανοοῦντες τοὺς ἄλλους, πάντας ἤδη τούτῳ τῷ ὀνόματι προσαγορεύειν. ἔοικέ τι ὃ λέγω τῇ ἀληθείᾳ ἢ οὐδέν;

ΕΡΜ. Πάνυ μὲν οὖν ἔοικεν.

ΣΩ. Τί οὖν ἂν μετὰ τοῦτο σκοποῖμεν;

E ΕΡΜ. Δῆλον δὴ ὅτι δαίμονας.[1]

ΣΩ. Καὶ ὡς ἀληθῶς, ὦ Ἑρμόγενες, τί ἄν ποτε νοοῖ τὸ ὄνομα οἱ δαίμονες; σκέψαι, ἄν τί σοι δόξω εἰπεῖν.

ΕΡΜ. Λέγε μόνον.

ΣΩ. Οἶσθα οὖν τίνας φησὶν Ἡσίοδος εἶναι τοὺς δαίμονας;

ΕΡΜ. Οὐκ ἐννοῶ.

ΣΩ. Οὐδὲ ὅτι χρυσοῦν γένος τὸ πρῶτόν φησιν γενέσθαι τῶν ἀνθρώπων;

ΕΡΜ. Οἶδα τοῦτό γε.

---

[1] Δῆλον δὴ ὅτι δαίμονας Burnet: δῆλον δὴ ὅτι δαίμονάς τε καὶ ἥρωας καὶ ἀνθρώπους δαίμονας BT (the last word is usually attributed to Socrates).

CRATYLUS

HER. I think you are right, Socrates.

SOC. Then is it not proper to begin with the gods and see how the gods are rightly called by that name ?

HER. That is reasonable.

SOC. Something of this sort, then, is what I suspect : I think the earliest men in Greece believed only in those gods in whom many foreigners believe to-day—sun, moon, earth, stars, and sky. They saw that all these were always moving in their courses and running, and so they called them gods (θεούς) from this running (θεῖν) nature ; then afterwards, when they gained knowledge of the other gods, they called them all by the same name. Is that likely to be true, or not ?

HER. Yes, very likely.

SOC. What shall we consider next ?

HER. Spirits, obviously.

SOC. Hermogenes, what does the name " spirits " really mean ? See if you think there is anything in what I am going to say.

HER. Go on and say it.

SOC. Do you remember who Hesiod says the spirits are ?

HER. I do not recall it.

SOC. Nor that he says a golden race was the first race of men to be born ?

HER. Yes, I do know that.

53

PLATO

ΣΩ. Λέγει τοίνυν περὶ αὐτοῦ·

αὐτὰρ ἐπειδὴ τοῦτο γένος κατὰ μοῖρ' ἐκάλυψεν,
398 οἱ μὲν δαίμονες ἁγνοὶ ὑποχθόνιοι[1] καλέονται,
ἐσθλοί, ἀλεξίκακοι, φύλακες θνητῶν ἀνθρώπων.

ΕΡΜ. Τί οὖν δή;
ΣΩ. Ὅτι οἶμαι ἐγὼ λέγειν αὐτὸν τὸ χρυσοῦν
γένος οὐκ ἐκ χρυσοῦ πεφυκός, ἀλλ' ἀγαθόν τε
καὶ καλόν. τεκμήριον δέ μοί ἐστιν ὅτι καὶ ἡμᾶς
φησιν σιδηροῦν εἶναι γένος.
ΕΡΜ. Ἀληθῆ λέγεις.
ΣΩ. Οὐκοῦν καὶ τῶν νῦν οἴει ἂν φάναι αὐτὸν
B εἴ τις ἀγαθός ἐστιν, ἐκείνου τοῦ χρυσοῦ γένους
εἶναι;
ΕΡΜ. Εἰκός γε.
ΣΩ. Οἱ δ' ἀγαθοὶ ἄλλο τι ἢ φρόνιμοι;
ΕΡΜ. Φρόνιμοι.
ΣΩ. Τοῦτο τοίνυν παντὸς μᾶλλον λέγει, ὡς ἐμοὶ
δοκεῖ, τοὺς δαίμονας· ὅτι φρόνιμοι καὶ δαήμονες
ἦσαν, δαίμονας αὐτοὺς ὠνόμασεν· καὶ ἔν γε τῇ
ἀρχαίᾳ τῇ ἡμετέρᾳ φωνῇ αὐτὸ συμβαίνει τὸ
ὄνομα. λέγει οὖν καλῶς καὶ οὗτος καὶ ἄλλοι ποιη-
ταὶ πολλοὶ ὅσοι λέγουσιν ὡς, ἐπειδάν τις ἀγαθὸς
C ὢν τελευτήσῃ, μεγάλην μοῖραν καὶ τιμὴν ἔχει
καὶ γίγνεται δαίμων κατὰ τὴν τῆς φρονήσεως
ἐπωνυμίαν. ταύτῃ οὖν τίθεμαι καὶ ἐγὼ[2] πάντ'
ἄνδρα, ὃς ἂν ἀγαθὸς ᾖ, δαιμόνιον εἶναι καὶ ζῶντα
καὶ τελευτήσαντα, καὶ ὀρθῶς δαίμονα καλεῖσθαι.
ΕΡΜ. Καὶ ἐγώ μοι δοκῶ, ὦ Σώκρατες, τούτου
πάνυ σοι σύμψηφος εἶναι. ὁ δὲ δὴ ἥρως τί ἂν εἴη;

---

[1] ὑποχθόνιοι ΒΤ : ἐπιχθόνιοι vulg.

soc. Well, he says of it :

> But since Fate has covered up this race,
> They are called holy spirits under the earth,
> Noble, averters of evil, guardians of mortal men.[1]

her. What of that ?

soc. Why, I think he means that the golden race was not made of gold, but was good and beautiful. And I regard it as a proof of this that he further says we are the iron race.

her. True.

soc. Don't you suppose that if anyone of our day is good, Hesiod would say he was of that golden race ?

her. Quite likely.

soc. But the good are the wise, are they not ?

her. Yes, they are the wise.

soc. This, then, I think, is what he certainly means to say of the spirits : because they were wise and knowing (δαήμονες) he called them spirits (δαίμονες) ; and in the old form of our language the two words are the same. Now he and all the other poets are right, who say that when a good man dies he has a great portion and honour among the dead, and becomes a spirit, a name which is in accordance with the other name of wisdom. And so I assert that every good man, whether living or dead, is of spiritual nature, and is rightly called a spirit.

her. And I, Socrates, believe I quite agree with you in that. But what is the word " hero " ?

---

[1] Hesiod, *Works and Days*, 121 ff.

---

[2] ἐγὼ Hermann : ἐγὼ τὸν δαήμονα BT.

PLATO

ΣΩ. Τοῦτο δὲ οὐ πάνυ χαλεπὸν ἐννοῆσαι. σμικρὸν γὰρ παρῆκται αὐτῶν τὸ ὄνομα, δηλοῦν τὴν
ἐκ τοῦ ἔρωτος γένεσιν.

ΕΡΜ. Πῶς λέγεις;

ΣΩ. Οὐκ οἶσθα ὅτι ἡμίθεοι οἱ ἥρωες;

ΕΡΜ. Τί οὖν;

D   ΣΩ. Πάντες δήπου γεγόνασιν ἐρασθέντος ἢ θεοῦ
θνητῆς ἢ θνητοῦ θεᾶς.[1] ἐὰν οὖν σκοπῇς καὶ τοῦτο
κατὰ τὴν Ἀττικὴν τὴν παλαιὰν φωνήν, μᾶλλον
εἴσει· δηλώσει γάρ σοι ὅτι παρὰ τὸ τοῦ ἔρωτος
ὄνομα, ὅθεν γεγόνασιν οἱ ἥρωες, σμικρὸν παρηγμένον ἐστὶν ὀνόματος χάριν.[2] καὶ ἤτοι τοῦτο λέγει
τοὺς ἥρωας, ἢ ὅτι σοφοὶ ἦσαν καὶ ῥήτορες δεινοὶ[3]
καὶ διαλεκτικοί, ἐρωτᾶν ἱκανοὶ ὄντες· τὸ γὰρ
εἴρειν λέγειν ἐστίν· ὅπερ οὖν ἄρτι λέγομεν, ἐν τῇ
Ἀττικῇ φωνῇ λεγόμενοι οἱ ἥρωες ῥήτορές τινες
E καὶ ἐρωτητικοὶ συμβαίνουσιν, ὥστε ῥητόρων καὶ
σοφιστῶν γένος γίγνεται τὸ ἡρωϊκὸν φῦλον. ἀλλὰ
οὐ τοῦτο χαλεπόν ἐστιν ἐννοῆσαι, ἀλλὰ μᾶλλον τὸ
τῶν ἀνθρώπων, διὰ τί ποτε ἄνθρωποι καλοῦνται·
ἢ[4] σὺ ἔχεις εἰπεῖν;

17. ΕΡΜ. Πόθεν, ὠγαθέ, ἔχω; οὐδ᾽ εἴ τι οἷός
τ᾽ ἂν εἴην εὑρεῖν, οὐ συντείνω διὰ τὸ ἡγεῖσθαι σὲ
μᾶλλον εὑρήσειν ἢ ἐμαυτόν.

399 ΣΩ. Τῇ τοῦ Εὐθύφρονος ἐπιπνοίᾳ πιστεύεις,
ὡς ἔοικας.

---

[1] ἐρασθέντος ἢ θεοῦ θνητῆς ἢ θνητοῦ θεᾶς] ἐρασθέντες ἢ θεοὶ
θνητῆς ἢ θνητοὶ θεᾶς BTG.

[2] ὀνόματος BT, but probably corrupt.

[3] δεινοὶ T (but an erasure precedes): καὶ δεινοὶ B.

[4] ἢ add. Heindorf: om. BT.

---

[1] The old Attic alphabet was officially given up in
favour of the Ionic alphabet in 404 or 403 B.C. The Attic

56

CRATYLUS

soc. That is easy to understand; for the name has been but slightly changed, and indicates their origin from love (ἔρως).

her. What do you mean?

soc. Why, they were all born because a god fell in love with a mortal woman, or a mortal man with a goddess. Now if you consider the word " hero " also in the old Attic pronunciation,¹ you will understand better; for that will show you that it has been only slightly altered from the name of love (Eros), the source from which the heroes spring, to make a name for them. And either this is the reason why they are called heroes, or it is because they were wise and clever orators and dialecticians, able to ask questions (ἐρωτᾶν), for εἴρειν is the same as λέγειν (speak). Therefore, when their name is spoken in the Attic dialect, which I was mentioning just now, the heroes turn out to be orators and askers of questions, so that the heroic race proves to be a race of orators and sophists. That is easy to understand, but the case of men, and the reason why they are called men (ἄνθρωποι), is more difficult. Can you tell me what it is?

her. No, my friend, I cannot; and even if I might perhaps find out, I shall not try, because I think you are more likely to find out than I am.

soc. You have faith in the inspiration of Euthyphro, it seems.

form of the word " hero " is **ΗΕΡΟΣ**, that of " Eros " **ΕΡΟΣ**. The Ionic forms are **ΗΡΩΣ** and **ΕΡΩΣ** respectively. Plato seems to think there was a change in pronunciation, as well as in spelling, and indeed that is quite possible. Or Plato may simply be confusing pronunciation with spelling, as he seems to do in several passages of this dialogue (*cf.* especially 410).

PLATO

ΕΡΜ. Δῆλα δή.

ΣΩ. Ὀρθῶς γε σὺ πιστεύων· ὡς καὶ νῦν γέ μοι φαίνομαι κομψῶς ἐννενοηκέναι, καὶ κινδυνεύσω, ἐὰν μὴ εὐλαβῶμαι, ἔτι τήμερον σοφώτερος τοῦ δέοντος γενέσθαι. σκόπει δὴ ὃ λέγω. πρῶτον μὲν γὰρ τὸ τοιόνδε δεῖ ἐννοῆσαι περὶ ὀνομάτων, ὅτι πολλάκις ἐπεμβάλλομεν γράμματα, τὰ δ᾽ ἐξαιροῦμεν, παρ᾽ ὃ βουλόμεθα ὀνομάζοντες, καὶ τὰς ὀξύτητας μετα-
B βάλλομεν. οἷον Διὶ φίλος· τοῦτο ἵνα ἀντὶ ῥήματος ὄνομα ἡμῖν γένηται, τό τε ἕτερον αὐτόθεν ἰῶτα ἐξείλομεν καὶ ἀντὶ ὀξείας τῆς μέσης συλλαβῆς βαρεῖαν ἐφθεγξάμεθα. ἄλλων δὲ τοὐναντίον ἐμβάλ-λομεν γράμματα, τὰ δὲ βαρύτερα ὀξύτερα[1] φθεγ-γόμεθα.

ΕΡΜ. Ἀληθῆ λέγεις.

ΣΩ. Τούτων τοίνυν ἓν καὶ τὸ τῶν ἀνθρώπων ὄνομα πέπονθεν, ὡς ἐμοὶ δοκεῖ. ἐκ γὰρ ῥήματος ὄνομα γέγονεν, ἑνὸς γράμματος τοῦ ἄλφα ἐξαιρε-θέντος καὶ βαρυτέρας τῆς τελευτῆς γενομένης.

ΕΡΜ. Πῶς λέγεις;

C ΣΩ. Ὧδε. σημαίνει τοῦτο τὸ ὄνομα ὁ ἄνθρω-πος, ὅτι τὰ μὲν ἄλλα θηρία ὧν ὁρᾷ οὐδὲν ἐπισκοπεῖ οὐδὲ ἀναλογίζεται οὐδὲ ἀναθρεῖ, ὁ δὲ ἄνθρωπος ἅμα ἑώρακεν—τοῦτο δ᾽ ἐστὶ[2] ὄπωπε—καὶ ἀναθρεῖ καὶ λογίζεται τοῦτο ὃ ὄπωπεν. ἐντεῦθεν δὴ μόνον τῶν θηρίων ὀρθῶς ὁ ἄνθρωπος ἄνθρωπος ὠνομάσθη, ἀναθρῶν ἃ ὄπωπε.

ΕΡΜ. Τί οὖν; τὸ μετὰ τοῦτο ἔρωμαί σε, ὃ ἡδέως ἂν πυθοίμην;

ΣΩ. Πάνυ γε.

---

[1] ὀξύτερα add. Buttmann: om. BT.
[2] ἐστὶ Eusebius al.: ἐστὶ τὸ BT.

58

CRATYLUS

HER. Evidently.

SOC. And you are right in having it; for just at this very moment I think I have had a clever thought, and if I am not careful, before the day is over I am likely to be wiser than I ought to be. So pay attention. First we must remember in regard to names that we often put in or take out letters, making the names different from the meaning we intend, and we change the accent. Take, for instance, Διὶ φίλος; to change this from a phrase to a name, we took out the second iota and pronounced the middle syllable with the grave instead of the acute accent (Diphilus). In other instances, on the contrary, we insert letters and pronounce grave accents as acute.

HER. True.

SOC. Now it appears to me that the name of men (ἄνθρωπος) underwent a change of that sort. It was a phrase, but became a noun when one letter, alpha, was removed and the accent of the last syllable was dropped.

HER. What do you mean?

SOC. I will tell you. The name " man " (ἄνθρωπος) indicates that the other animals do not examine, or consider, or look up at (ἀναθρεῖ) any of the things that they see, but man has no sooner seen—that is, ὄπωπε—than he looks up at and considers that which he has seen. Therefore of all the animals man alone is rightly called man (ἄνθρωπος), because he looks up at (ἀναθρεῖ) what he has seen (ὄπωπε).

HER. Of course. May I ask you about the next word I should like to have explained?

SOC. Certainly.

D ΕΡΜ. Ὥσπερ τοίνυν μοι δοκεῖ τούτοις ἑξῆς
εἶναί τι χρῆμα. ψυχὴν γάρ που καὶ σῶμά τι καλοῦμεν τοῦ ἀνθρώπου.

ΣΩ. Πῶς γὰρ οὔ;

ΕΡΜ. Πειρώμεθα δὴ καὶ ταῦτα διελεῖν, ὥσπερ τὰ
ἔμπροσθεν.

ΣΩ. Ψυχὴν λέγεις ἐπισκέψασθαι, ὡς εἰκότως τούτου τοῦ ὀνόματος τυγχάνει, ἔπειτ᾽ αὖ τὸ σῶμα;

ΕΡΜ. Ναί.

ΣΩ. Ὡς μὲν τοίνυν ἐκ τοῦ παραχρῆμα λέγειν,
οἶμαί τι τοιοῦτον νοεῖν τοὺς τὴν ψυχὴν ὀνομάσαν-
τας, ὡς τοῦτο ἄρα, ὅταν παρῇ τῷ σώματι, αἴτιόν
E ἐστι τοῦ ζῆν αὐτῷ, τὴν τοῦ ἀναπνεῖν δύναμιν
παρέχον καὶ ἀναψῦχον. ἅμα δὲ ἐκλείποντος τοῦ
ἀναψύχοντος τὸ σῶμα ἀπόλλυταί τε καὶ τελευτᾷ·
ὅθεν δή μοι δοκοῦσιν αὐτὸ ψυχὴν καλέσαι. εἰ δὲ
βούλει, ἔχε ἠρέμα· δοκῶ γάρ μοί τι καθορᾶν
400 πιθανώτερον τούτου τοῖς ἀμφὶ Εὐθύφρονα. τούτου
μὲν γάρ, ὡς ἐμοὶ δοκεῖ, καταφρονήσαιεν ἂν καὶ
ἡγήσαιντο φορτικὸν εἶναι· τόδε δὲ σκόπει, ἐὰν ἄρα
καὶ σοὶ ἀρέσῃ.

ΕΡΜ. Λέγε μόνον.

ΣΩ. Τὴν φύσιν παντὸς τοῦ σώματος, ὥστε καὶ
ζῆν καὶ περιιέναι, τί σοι δοκεῖ ἔχειν τε καὶ ὀχεῖν
ἄλλο ἢ ψυχή;

ΕΡΜ. Οὐδὲν ἄλλο.

ΣΩ. Τί δέ; καὶ τὴν τῶν ἄλλων ἁπάντων φύσιν
οὐ πιστεύεις Ἀναξαγόρᾳ νοῦν καὶ ψυχὴν εἶναι τὴν
διακοσμοῦσαν καὶ ἔχουσαν;

ΕΡΜ. Ἔγωγε.

B ΣΩ. Καλῶς ἄρα ἂν τὸ ὄνομα τοῦτο ἔχοι τῇ
δυνάμει ταύτῃ ἢ φύσιν ὀχεῖ καὶ ἔχει, φυσέχην

60

CRATYLUS

HER. It seems to me to come naturally next after those you have discussed. We speak of man's soul and body.

SOC. Yes, of course.

HER. Let us try to analyse these, as we did the previous words.

SOC. You mean consider " soul " (ψυχή) and see why it is properly called by that name, and likewise " body " (σῶμα) ?

HER. Yes.

SOC. To speak on the spur of the moment, I think those who gave the soul its name had something of this sort in mind : they thought when it was present in the body it was the cause of its living, giving it the power to breathe and reviving it (ἀναψῦχον), and when this revivifying force fails, the body perishes and comes to an end ; therefore, I think, they called it ψυχή. But—please keep still a moment. I fancy I see something which will carry more conviction to Euthyphro and his followers ; for I think they would despise this attempt and would consider it cheap talk. Now see if you like the new one.

HER. I am listening.

SOC. Do you think there is anything which holds and carries the whole nature of the body, so that it lives and moves, except the soul ?

HER. No ; nothing.

SOC. Well, and do you not believe the doctrine of Anaxagoras, that it is mind or soul which orders and holds the nature of all things ?

HER. I do.

SOC. Then there would be an admirable fitness in calling that power which carries and holds (ἔχει)

61

PLATO

ἐπονομάζειν. ἔξεστι δὲ καὶ ψυχὴν κομψευόμενον
λέγειν.

ΕΡΜ. Πάνυ μὲν οὖν, καὶ δοκεῖ γέ μοι τοῦτο
ἐκείνου τεχνικώτερον εἶναι.

ΣΩ. Καὶ γὰρ ἔστιν· γελοῖον μέντοι φαίνεται ὡς
ἀληθῶς ὀνομαζόμενον ὡς ἐτέθη.

ΕΡΜ. Ἀλλὰ δὴ τὸ μετὰ τοῦτο πῶς φῶμεν ἔχειν;

ΣΩ. Τὸ σῶμα λέγεις;

ΕΡΜ. Ναί.

ΣΩ. Πολλαχῇ μοι δοκεῖ τοῦτό γε· ἂν μὲν καὶ
σμικρόν τις παρακλίνῃ, καὶ πάνυ. καὶ γὰρ σῆμά
C τινές φασιν αὐτὸ εἶναι τῆς ψυχῆς, ὡς τεθαμμένης ἐν
τῷ νῦν παρόντι· καὶ διότι αὖ τούτῳ σημαίνει ἃ ἂν
σημαίνῃ ἡ ψυχή, καὶ ταύτῃ σῆμα ὀρθῶς καλεῖσθαι.
δοκοῦσι μέντοι μοι μάλιστα θέσθαι οἱ ἀμφὶ Ὀρφέα
τοῦτο τὸ ὄνομα, ὡς δίκην διδούσης τῆς ψυχῆς ὧν δὴ
ἕνεκα δίδωσιν· τοῦτον δὲ περίβολον ἔχειν, ἵνα σῴ-
ζηται, δεσμωτηρίου εἰκόνα· εἶναι οὖν τῆς ψυχῆς
τοῦτο, ὥσπερ αὐτὸ ὀνομάζεται, ἕως ἂν ἐκτείσῃ τὰ
ὀφειλόμενα, τὸ σῶμα, καὶ οὐδὲν δεῖν παράγειν
οὐδὲ[1] γράμμα.

D 18. ΕΡΜ. Ταῦτα μέν μοι δοκεῖ ἱκανῶς, ὦ Σώκρατες, εἰρῆσθαι· περὶ δὲ τῶν θεῶν. τῶν ὀνομάτων, οἷον καὶ περὶ τοῦ Διὸς νῦν δὴ ἔλεγες, ἔχοιμεν
ἄν που κατὰ τὸν αὐτὸν τρόπον ἐπισκέψασθαι, κατὰ
τίνα ποτὲ ὀρθότητα αὐτῶν τὰ ὀνόματα κεῖται;

ΣΩ. Ναὶ μὰ Δία ἡμεῖς γε, ὦ Ἑρμόγενες, εἴπερ
γε νοῦν ἔχοιμεν, ἕνα μὲν τὸν κάλλιστον τρόπον, ὅτι
περὶ θεῶν οὐδὲν ἴσμεν, οὔτε περὶ αὐτῶν οὔτε περὶ
τῶν ὀνομάτων, ἅττα ποτὲ ἑαυτοὺς καλοῦσιν· δῆλον

---

[1] οὐδὲ Τ: οὐδὲν Β: οὐδ' ἐν Burnet.

CRATYLUS

nature (φύσιν) φυσέχη : and this may be refined and pronounced ψυχή.

HER. Certainly ; and I think this is a more scientific explanation than the other.

SOC. Yes, it is. But it seems actually absurd that the name was given with such truth.

HER. Now what shall we say about the next word ?

SOC. You mean " body " (σῶμα) ?

HER. Yes.

SOC. I think this admits of many explanations, if a little, even very little, change is made ; for some say it is the tomb (σῆμα) of the soul, their notion being that the soul is buried in the present life ; and again, because by its means the soul gives any signs which it gives, it is for this reason also properly called " sign " (σῆμα). But I think it most likely that the Orphic poets gave this name, with the idea that the soul is undergoing punishment for something ; they think it has the body as an enclosure to keep it safe, like a prison, and this is, as the name itself denotes, the safe (σῶμα) for the soul, until the penalty is paid, and not even a letter needs to be changed.

HER. I think, Socrates, enough has been said about these words ; but might we not consider the names of the gods in the same way in which you were speaking about that of Zeus a few minutes ago, and see what kind of correctness there is in them ?

SOC. By Zeus, Hermogenes, we, if we are sensible, must recognize that there is one most excellent kind, since of the gods we know nothing, neither of them nor of their names, whatever they may be,

γὰρ ὅτι ἐκεῖνοί γε τἀληθῆ καλοῦσι. δεύτερος δ' αὖ
Ε τρόπος ὀρθότητος, ὥσπερ ἐν ταῖς εὐχαῖς νόμος
ἐστὶν ἡμῖν εὔχεσθαι, οἵτινές τε καὶ ὁπόθεν χαίρουσιν
ὀνομαζόμενοι, ταῦτα καὶ ἡμᾶς αὐτοὺς καλεῖν, ὡς
401 ἄλλο μηδὲν εἰδότας· καλῶς γὰρ δὴ ἔμοιγε δοκεῖ
νενομίσθαι. εἰ οὖν βούλει, σκοπῶμεν ὥσπερ προειπόντες τοῖς θεοῖς ὅτι περὶ αὐτῶν οὐδὲν ἡμεῖς
σκεψόμεθα—οὐ γὰρ ἀξιοῦμεν οἷοί τ' ἂν εἶναι
σκοπεῖν—ἀλλὰ περὶ τῶν ἀνθρώπων, ἥν ποτέ
τινα[1] δόξαν ἔχοντες ἐτίθεντο αὐτοῖς τὰ ὀνόματα·
τοῦτο γὰρ ἀνεμέσητον.

ΕΡΜ. Ἀλλά μοι δοκεῖς, ὦ Σώκρατες, μετρίως λέγειν, καὶ οὕτω ποιῶμεν.

Β ΣΩ. Ἄλλο τι οὖν ἀφ' Ἑστίας ἀρχώμεθα κατὰ
τὸν νόμον;

ΕΡΜ. Δίκαιον γοῦν.

ΣΩ. Τί οὖν ἄν τις φαίη διανοούμενον τὸν ὀνομά-
σαντα Ἑστίαν ὀνομάσαι;

ΕΡΜ. Οὐ μὰ τὸν Δία οὐδὲ τοῦτο οἶμαι ῥᾴδιον
εἶναι.

ΣΩ. Κινδυνεύουσι γοῦν, ὠγαθὲ Ἑρμόγενες, οἱ
πρῶτοι τὰ ὀνόματα τιθέμενοι οὐ φαῦλοι εἶναι, ἀλλὰ
μετεωρολόγοι καὶ ἀδολέσχαι τινές.

ΕΡΜ. Τί δή;

ΣΩ. Καταφαίνεταί μοι ἡ θέσις τῶν ὀνομάτων
τοιούτων τινῶν ἀνθρώπων· καὶ ἐάν τις τὰ ξενικὰ
C ὀνόματα ἀνασκοπῇ, οὐχ ἧττον ἀνευρίσκεται ὃ
ἕκαστον βούλεται. οἷον καὶ ἐν τούτῳ ὃ ἡμεῖς
" οὐσίαν " καλοῦμεν, εἰσὶν οἳ " ἐσσίαν " καλοῦσιν,
οἳ δ' αὖ " ὠσίαν." πρῶτον μὲν οὖν κατὰ τὸ
ἕτερον ὄνομα τούτων ἡ τῶν πραγμάτων οὐσία

---

[1] ἥν ποτέ τινα ΒΤ: ἥντινά ποτε vulg.

64

by which they call themselves, for it is clear that they use the true names. But there is a second kind of correctness, that we call them, as is customary in prayers, by whatever names and patronymics are pleasing to them, since we know no other. Now I think that is an excellent custom. So, if you like, let us first make a kind of announcement to the gods, saying that we are not going to investigate about them—for we do not claim to be able to do that—but about men, and let us inquire what thought men had in giving them their names ; for in that there is no impiety.

HER. I think, Socrates, you are right ; let us do as you say.

soc. Shall we, then, begin with Hestia, according to custom ?

HER. That is the proper thing.

soc. Then what would you say the man had in mind who gave Hestia her name ?

HER. By Zeus, I think that is no more easy question than the other.

soc. At any rate, my dear Hermogenes, the first men who gave names were no ordinary persons, but high thinkers and great talkers.

HER. What then ?

soc. I am sure the names were given by men of that kind ; and if foreign names are examined, the meaning of each of them is equally evident. Take, for instance, that which we call οὐσία (reality, essence) ; some people call it ἐσσία, and still others ὠσία. First, then, in connexion with the second of these forms, it is reasonable that the essence of

" Ἑστία " καλεῖσθαι ἔχει λόγον· καὶ ὅτι γε αὖ
ἡμεῖς τὸ τῆς οὐσίας μετέχον " ἔστιν "[1] φαμέν, καὶ
κατὰ τοῦτο ὀρθῶς ἂν καλοῖτο Ἑστία· ἐοίκαμεν
γὰρ καὶ ἡμεῖς τὸ παλαιὸν " ἐσσίαν " καλεῖν τὴν
οὐσίαν. ἔτι δὲ καὶ κατὰ τὰς θυσίας ἄν τις ἐννοήσας
D ἡγήσαιτο οὕτω νοεῖν ταῦτα τοὺς τιθεμένους· τὸ
γὰρ πρὸ πάντων θεῶν τῇ Ἑστίᾳ πρώτῃ προθύειν
εἰκὸς ἐκείνους οἵτινες τὴν πάντων οὐσίαν " ἐσσίαν "[2]
ἐπωνόμασαν. ὅσοι δ᾽ αὖ " ὠσίαν," σχεδόν τι αὖ
οὗτοι καθ᾽ Ἡράκλειτον ἂν ἡγοῖντο τὰ ὄντα ἰέναι τε
πάντα καὶ μένειν οὐδέν· τὸ οὖν αἴτιον καὶ τὸ ἀρχη-
γὸν αὐτῶν εἶναι τὸ ὠθοῦν, ὅθεν δὴ καλῶς ἔχειν
αὐτὸ " ὠσίαν " ὠνομάσθαι. καὶ ταῦτα μὲν δὴ
E ταύτῃ ὡς παρὰ μηδὲν εἰδότων εἰρήσθω· μετὰ δ᾽
Ἑστίαν δίκαιον Ῥέαν καὶ Κρόνον ἐπισκέψασθαι.
καίτοι τό γε τοῦ Κρόνου ὄνομα ἤδη διήλθομεν. ἴσως
μέντοι οὐδὲν λέγω.

19. ΕΡΜ. Τί δή, ὦ Σώκρατες;

ΣΩ. Ὠγαθέ, ἐννενόηκά τι σμῆνος σοφίας.

ΕΡΜ. Ποῖον δὴ τοῦτο;

402 ΣΩ. Γελοῖον μὲν πάνυ εἰπεῖν, οἶμαι μέντοι τινὰ
πιθανότητα ἔχον.

ΕΡΜ. Τίνα ταύτην;

ΣΩ. Τὸν Ἡράκλειτόν μοι δοκῶ καθορᾶν παλαί᾽
ἄττα σοφὰ λέγοντα, ἀτεχνῶς τὰ ἐπὶ Κρόνου καὶ
Ῥέας, ἃ καὶ Ὅμηρος ἔλεγεν.

ΕΡΜ. Πῶς τοῦτο λέγεις;

ΣΩ. Λέγει που Ἡράκλειτος ὅτι πάντα χωρεῖ καὶ
οὐδὲν μένει, καὶ ποταμοῦ ῥοῇ ἀπεικάζων τὰ ὄντα
λέγει ὡς δὶς ἐς τὸν αὐτὸν ποταμὸν οὐκ ἂν ἐμβαίης.

---

[1] ἔστιν Burnet: ἔστι Badham: ἑστίαν Β: ἑστίαν Τ.
[2] ἐσσίαν Burnet: ἑστίαν Τ: ἑστίαν Β.

things be called Hestia ; and moreover, because we ourselves say of that which partakes of reality " it is " (ἔστιν), the name Hestia would be correct in this connexion also ; for apparently we also called οὐσία (reality) ἐσσία in ancient times. And besides, if you consider it in connexion with sacrifices, you would come to the conclusion that those who established them understood the name in that way ; for those who called the essence of things ἐσσία would naturally sacrifice to Hestia first of all the gods. Those on the other hand, who say ὠσία would agree well enough with Heracleitus that all things move and nothing remains still. So they would say the cause and ruler of things was the pushing power (ὠθοῦν), wherefore it had been rightly named ὠσία. But enough of this, considering that we know nothing. After Hestia it is right to consider Rhea and Cronus. The name of Cronus, however, has already been discussed. But perhaps I am talking nonsense.

HER. Why, Socrates ?

SOC. My friend, I have thought of a swarm of wisdom.

HER. What is it ?

SOC. It sounds absurd, but I think there is some probability in it.

HER. What is this probability ?

SOC. I seem to have a vision of Heracleitus saying some ancient words of wisdom as old as the reign of Cronus and Rhea, which Homer said too.

HER. What do you mean by that ?

SOC. Heracleitus says, you know, that all things move and nothing remains still, and he likens the universe to the current of a river, saying that you cannot step twice into the same stream.

PLATO

ΕΡΜ. Ἔστι ταῦτα.

B ΣΩ. Τί οὖν; δοκεῖ σοι ἀλλοιότερον Ἡρακλείτου νοεῖν ὁ τιθέμενος τοῖς τῶν ἄλλων θεῶν προγόνοις " Ῥέαν" τε καὶ " Κρόνον"; ἆρα οἴει ἀπὸ τοῦ αὐτομάτου αὐτὸν ἀμφοτέροις ῥευμάτων ὀνόματα θέσθαι; ὥσπερ αὖ Ὅμηρος " Ὠκεανόν τε θεῶν γένεσίν" φησι " καὶ μητέρα Τηθύν"· οἶμαι δὲ καὶ Ἡσίοδος. λέγει δέ που καὶ Ὀρφεὺς ὅτι

Ὠκεανὸς πρῶτος καλλίρροος[1] ἦρξε γάμοιο,
C ὅς ῥα κασιγνήτην ὁμομήτορα Τηθὺν ὄπυιεν.

ταῦτ᾽ οὖν σκόπει ὅτι καὶ ἀλλήλοις συμφωνεῖ καὶ πρὸς τὰ τοῦ Ἡρακλείτου πάντα τείνει.

ΕΡΜ. Φαίνει τί μοι λέγειν, ὦ Σώκρατες· τὸ μέντοι τῆς Τηθύος οὐκ ἐννοῶ ὄνομα τί βούλεται.

ΣΩ. Ἀλλὰ μὴν τοῦτό γε ὀλίγου αὐτὸ λέγει ὅτι πηγῆς ὄνομα ἐπικεκρυμμένον ἐστίν. τὸ γὰρ διατ-
D τώμενον καὶ τὸ ἠθούμενον πηγῆς ἀπείκασμά ἐστιν· ἐκ δὲ τούτων ἀμφοτέρων τῶν ὀνομάτων ἡ Τηθὺς τὸ ὄνομα ξύγκειται.

ΕΡΜ. Τοῦτο μέν, ὦ Σώκρατες, κομψόν.

ΣΩ. Τί δ᾽ οὐ μέλλει[2]; ἀλλὰ τί τὸ μετὰ τοῦτο; τὸν μὲν Δία εἴπομεν.

ΕΡΜ. Ναί.

ΣΩ. Τοὺς ἀδελφοὺς δὴ αὐτοῦ λέγωμεν, τόν τε Ποσειδῶ καὶ τὸν Πλούτωνα καὶ τὸ ἕτερον ὄνομα ὃ ὀνομάζουσιν αὐτόν.

ΕΡΜ. Πάνυ γε.

ΣΩ. Τὸ μὲν τοίνυν τοῦ Ποσειδῶνός μοι φαίνεται ὠνομάσθαι ὑπὸ[3] τοῦ πρώτου ὀνομάσαντος, ὅτι

[1] καλλίρροος] καλλιρόους B: καλλιρρόους T.
[2] μέλλει] μέλλω BT.   [3] ὑπὸ cod. Gudianus: om. BT

68

HER. True.

soc. Well, don't you think he who gave to the ancestors of the other gods the names " Rhea " and " Cronus " had the same thought as Heracleitus ? Do you think he gave both of them the names of streams merely by chance ? Just so Homer, too, says—

Ocean the origin of the gods, and their mother Tethys ; [1]

and I believe Hesiod says that also. Orpheus, too, says—

Fair-flowing Ocean was the first to marry, and he wedded his sister Tethys, daughter of his mother.

See how they agree with each other and all tend towards the doctrine of Heracleitus.

HER. I think there is something in what you say, Socrates ; but I do not know what the name of Tethys means.

soc. Why, the name itself almost tells that it is the name of a spring somewhat disguised ; for that which is strained ($\delta\iota\alpha\tau\tau\acute{\omega}\mu\epsilon\nu o\nu$) and filtered ($\mathring{\eta}\theta o\acute{\nu}\mu\epsilon\nu o\nu$) represents a spring, and the name Tethys is compounded of those two words.

HER. That is very neat, Socrates.

soc. Of course it is. But what comes next ? Zeus we discussed before.

HER. Yes.

soc. Let us, then, speak of his brothers, Poseidon and Pluto, including also the other name of the latter.

HER. By all means.

soc. I think Poseidon's name was given by him who first applied it, because the power of the sea

[1] Homer, *Iliad*, xiv. 201, 302.

PLATO

Ε αὐτὸν βαδίζοντα ἐπέσχεν ἡ τῆς θαλάττης φύσις
καὶ οὐκέτι εἴασεν προελθεῖν, ἀλλ' ὥσπερ δεσμὸς
τῶν ποδῶν αὐτῷ ἐγένετο. τὸν οὖν ἄρχοντα τῆς
δυνάμεως ταύτης θεὸν ὠνόμασεν Ποσειδῶνα, ὡς
ποσίδεσμον ὄντα· τὸ δὲ ε ἔγκειται ἴσως εὐπρε-
πείας ἕνεκα. τάχα δὲ οὐκ ἂν τοῦτο λέγοι, ἀλλ'
ἀντὶ τοῦ σίγμα δύο λάβδα τὸ πρῶτον ἐλέγετο,
403 ὡς πολλὰ εἰδότος τοῦ θεοῦ. ἴσως δὲ ἀπὸ τοῦ
σείειν ὁ σείων ὠνόμασται· πρόσκειται δὲ τὸ πῖ
καὶ τὸ δέλτα. τὸ δὲ Πλούτωνος, τοῦτο μὲν κατὰ
τὴν τοῦ πλούτου δόσιν, ὅτι ἐκ τῆς γῆς κάτωθεν
ἀνίεται ὁ πλοῦτος, ἐπωνομάσθη· ὁ δὲ Ἅιδης, οἱ
πολλοὶ μέν μοι δοκοῦσιν ὑπολαμβάνειν τὸ ἀειδὲς
προσειρῆσθαι τῷ ὀνόματι τούτῳ, καὶ φοβούμενοι
τὸ ὄνομα Πλούτωνα καλοῦσιν αὐτόν.

Β   ΕΡΜ. Σοὶ δὲ πῶς φαίνεται, ὦ Σώκρατες;
    20. ΣΩ. Πολλαχῇ ἔμοιγε δοκοῦσιν ἄνθρωποι δι-
ημαρτηκέναι περὶ τούτου τοῦ θεοῦ τῆς δυνάμεως
καὶ φοβεῖσθαι αὐτὸν οὐκ ἄξιον ὄν.[1] ὅτι τε γάρ,
ἐπειδὰν ἅπαξ τις ἡμῶν ἀποθάνῃ, ἀεὶ ἐκεῖ ἐστιν,
φοβοῦνται, καὶ ὅτι ἡ ψυχὴ γυμνὴ τοῦ σώματος
παρ' ἐκεῖνον ἀπέρχεται, καὶ τοῦτο πεφόβηνται· τὰ
δ' ἐμοὶ δοκεῖ πάντα ἐς ταὐτόν τι συντείνειν, καὶ
ἡ ἀρχὴ τοῦ θεοῦ καὶ τὸ ὄνομα.
    ΕΡΜ. Πῶς δή;
C   ΣΩ. Ἐγώ σοι ἐρῶ ἅ γέ μοι φαίνεται. εἰπὲ γάρ
μοι, δεσμὸς ζῴω ὁτῳοῦν ὥστε μένειν ὁπουοῦν,
πότερος ἰσχυρότερός ἐστιν, ἀνάγκη ἢ ἐπιθυμία;
    ΕΡΜ. Πολὺ διαφέρει, ὦ Σώκρατες, ἡ ἐπιθυμία.
    ΣΩ. Οἴει οὖν τὸν Ἅιδην οὐκ ἂν πολλοὺς ἐκ-
φεύγειν, εἰ μὴ τῷ ἰσχυροτάτῳ δεσμῷ ἔδει τοὺς
ἐκεῖσε ἰόντας;

70

restrained him as he was walking and hindered his
advance ; it acted as a bond (δεσμός) of his feet
(ποδῶν). So he called the lord of this power
Poseidon, regarding him as a foot-bond (ποσί-δεσμον).
The e is inserted perhaps for euphony. But possibly
that may not be right ; possibly two lambdas were
originally pronounced instead of the sigma, because
the god knew (εἰδότος) many (πολλά) things. Or it
may be that from his shaking he was called the
Shaker (ὁ σείων), and the pi and delta are additions.
As for Pluto, he was so named as the giver of wealth
(πλοῦτος), because wealth comes up from below out
of the earth. And Hades—I fancy most people
think that this is a name of the Invisible (ἀειδής),
so they are afraid and call him Pluto.

HER. And what do you think yourself, Socrates ?

SOC. I think people have many false notions
about the power of this god, and are unduly afraid
of him. They are afraid because when we are once
dead we remain in his realm for ever, and they are
also terrified because the soul goes to him without
the covering of the body. But I think all these
facts, and the office and the name of the god, point
in the same direction.

HER. How so ?

SOC. I will tell you my own view. Please answer
this question : Which is the stronger bond upon
any living being to keep him in any one place,
desire, or compulsion ?

HER. Desire, Socrates, is much stronger.

SOC. Then do you not believe there would be
many fugitives from Hades, if he did not bind with
the strongest bond those who go to him there ?

---

[1] ὃν add. Baiter: om. BT.

PLATO

ΕΡΜ. Δῆλα δή.

ΣΩ. Ἐπιθυμίᾳ ἄρα τινί αὐτούς, ὡς ἔοικε, δεῖ, εἴπερ τῷ μεγίστῳ δεσμῷ δεῖ, καὶ οὐκ ἀνάγκῃ.

ΕΡΜ. Φαίνεται.

ΣΩ. Οὐκοῦν ἐπιθυμίαι αὖ πολλαί εἰσιν;

ΕΡΜ. Ναί.

D ΣΩ. Τῇ μεγίστῃ ἄρα ἐπιθυμίᾳ τῶν ἐπιθυμιῶν δεῖ αὐτούς, εἴπερ μέλλει τῷ μεγίστῳ δεσμῷ κατέχειν.

ΕΡΜ. Ναί.

ΣΩ. Ἔστιν οὖν τις μείζων ἐπιθυμία ἢ ὅταν τίς τῳ συνὼν οἴηται δι᾽ ἐκεῖνον ἔσεσθαι ἀμείνων ἀνήρ;

ΕΡΜ. Μὰ Δί᾽ οὐδ᾽ ὁπωστιοῦν, ὦ Σώκρατες.

ΣΩ. Διὰ ταῦτα ἄρα φῶμεν, ὦ Ἑρμόγενες, οὐδένα δεῦρο ἐθελῆσαι ἀπελθεῖν τῶν ἐκεῖθεν, οὐδὲ αὐτὰς τὰς Σειρῆνας, ἀλλὰ κατακεκηλῆσθαι ἐκείνας
E τε καὶ τοὺς ἄλλους πάντας· οὕτω καλούς τινας, ὡς ἔοικεν, ἐπίσταται λόγους λέγειν ὁ Ἅιδης, καὶ ἔστιν, ὥς γ᾽ ἐκ τοῦ λόγου τούτου, ὁ θεὸς οὗτος τέλεος σοφιστής τε καὶ μέγας εὐεργέτης τῶν παρ᾽ αὑτῷ, ὅς γε καὶ τοῖς ἐνθάδε τοσαῦτα ἀγαθὰ ἀνίησιν· οὕτω πολλὰ αὐτῷ τὰ περιόντα ἐκεῖ ἐστιν, καὶ τὸν Πλούτωνα ἀπὸ τούτου ἔσχε τὸ ὄνομα. καὶ τὸ αὖ μὴ ἐθέλειν συνεῖναι τοῖς ἀνθρώποις ἔχουσι τὰ σώματα, ἀλλὰ τότε συγγίγνεσθαι,
404 ἐπειδὰν ἡ ψυχὴ καθαρὰ ᾖ πάντων τῶν περὶ τὸ σῶμα κακῶν καὶ ἐπιθυμιῶν, οὐ φιλοσόφου δοκεῖ σοι εἶναι καὶ εὖ ἐντεθυμημένου[1] ὅτι οὕτω μὲν ἂν κατέχοι αὐτοὺς δήσας τῇ περὶ ἀρετὴν ἐπιθυμίᾳ,

---

[1] φιλοσόφου . . . ἐντεθυμημένου Heusde: φιλόσοφον . . . ἐντεθυμημένον ΒΤ.

CRATYLUS

HER. Of course there would.

SOC. Apparently, then, if he binds them with the strongest bond, he binds them by some kind of desire, not by compulsion.

HER. Yes, that is plain.

SOC. There are many desires, are there not?

HER. Yes.

SOC. Then he binds with the desire which is the strongest of all, if he is to restrain them with the strongest bond.

HER. Yes.

SOC. And is there any desire stronger than the thought of being made a better man by association with some one?

HER. No, by Zeus, Socrates, there certainly is not.

SOC. Then, Hermogenes, we must believe that this is the reason why no one has been willing to come away from that other world, not even the Sirens, but they and all others have been overcome by his enchantments, so beautiful, as it appears, are the words which Hades has the power to speak; and from this point of view this god is a perfect sophist and a great benefactor of those in his realm, he who also bestows such great blessings upon us who are on earth; such abundance surrounds him there below, and for this reason he is called Pluto. Then, too, he refuses to consort with men while they have bodies, but only accepts their society when the soul is pure of all the evils and desires of the body. Do you not think this shows him to be a philosopher and to understand perfectly that under these conditions he could restrain them by binding them with the desire of virtue, but that so long as they

ἔχοντας δὲ τὴν τοῦ σώματος πτοίησιν καὶ μανίαν
οὐδ' ἂν ὁ Κρόνος δύναιτο ὁ πατὴρ συγκατέχειν
αὐτῷ ἐν τοῖς δεσμοῖς δήσας τοῖς αὑτοῦ λεγο-
μένοις;

ΕΡΜ. Κινδυνεύεις τὶ λέγειν, ὦ Σώκρατες.

B ΣΩ. Καὶ τό γε ὄνομα ὁ Ἅιδης, ὦ Ἑρμόγενες,
πολλοῦ δεῖ ἀπὸ τοῦ ἀειδοῦς[1] ἐπωνομάσθαι, ἀλλὰ
πολὺ μᾶλλον ἀπὸ τοῦ πάντα τὰ καλὰ εἰδέναι, ἀπὸ
τούτου ὑπὸ τοῦ νομοθέτου Ἅιδης ἐκλήθη.

21. ΕΡΜ. Εἶεν· τί δὲ Δήμητρά τε καὶ Ἥραν
καὶ Ἀπόλλω καὶ Ἀθηνᾶν καὶ Ἥφαιστον καὶ
Ἄρη καὶ τοὺς ἄλλους θεούς, πῶς λέγομεν;

ΣΩ. Δημήτηρ μὲν φαίνεται κατὰ τὴν δόσιν τῆς
ἐδωδῆς διδοῦσα ὡς μήτηρ Δημήτηρ κεκλῆσθαι,

C Ἥρα δὲ ἐρατή τις, ὥσπερ οὖν καὶ λέγεται ὁ
Ζεὺς αὐτῆς ἐρασθεὶς ἔχειν.[2] ἴσως δὲ μετεωρο-
λογῶν ὁ νομοθέτης τὸν ἀέρα Ἥραν ὠνόμασεν
ἐπικρυπτόμενος, θεὶς τὴν ἀρχὴν ἐπὶ τελευτήν·
γνοίης δ' ἄν, εἰ πολλάκις λέγοις τὸ τῆς Ἥρας
ὄνομα. Φερρέφαττα δέ, πολλοὶ μὲν καὶ τοῦτο
φοβοῦνται τὸ ὄνομα καὶ τὸν Ἀπόλλω, ὑπὸ ἀπει-
ρίας, ὡς ἔοικεν, ὀνομάτων ὀρθότητος. καὶ γὰρ
μεταβάλλοντες σκοποῦνται τὴν Φερσεφόνην, καὶ
δεινὸν αὐτοῖς φαίνεται· τὸ δὲ μηνύει σοφὴν εἶναι

D τὴν θεόν· ἅτε γὰρ φερομένων τῶν πραγμάτων τὸ
ἐφαπτόμενον καὶ ἐπαφῶν καὶ δυνάμενον ἐπακο-
λουθεῖν σοφία ἂν εἴη. Φερέπαφα οὖν διὰ τὴν
σοφίαν καὶ τὴν ἐπαφὴν τοῦ φερομένου ἡ θεὸς ἂν
ὀρθῶς καλοῖτο, ἢ τοιοῦτόν τι—δι' ὅπερ καὶ σύν-

---

[1] ἀειδοῦς P : ἀιδοῦς BT.
[2] ἐρασθεὶς ἔχειν liber Bessarionis : ὁ ἐρασθεὶς ἔχει BT.

CRATYLUS

are infected with the unrest and madness of the body, not even his father Cronus could hold them to himself, though he bound them with his famous chains ?

HER. There seems to be something in that, Socrates.

SOC. And the name "Hades" is not in the least derived from the invisible (ἀειδές), but far more probably from knowing (εἰδέναι) all noble things, and for that reason he was called Hades by the lawgiver.

HER. Very well; what shall we say of Demeter, Hera, Apollo, Athena, Hephaestus, Ares, and the other gods ?

SOC. Demeter appears to have been called Demeter, because like a mother (μήτηρ) she gives the gift of food, and Hera is a lovely one (ἐρατή), as indeed, Zeus is said to have married her for love. But perhaps the lawgiver had natural phenomena in mind, and called her Hera (Ἥρα) as a disguise for ἀήρ (air), putting the beginning at the end. You would understand, if you were to repeat the name Hera over and over. And Pherephatta!—How many people fear this name, and also Apollo ! I imagine it is because they do not know about correctness of names. You see they change the name to Phersephone and its aspect frightens them. But really the name indicates that the goddess is wise ; for since things are in motion (φερόμενα), that which grasps (ἐφαπτόμενον) and touches (ἐπαφῶν) and is able to follow them is wisdom. Pherepapha, or something of that sort, would therefore be the correct name of the goddess, because she is wise and touches that which is in motion (ἐπαφὴ τοῦ φερομένου)

εστιν αὐτῇ ὁ Ἅιδης σοφὸς ὤν, διότι τοιαύτη ἐστίν—
νῦν δὲ αὐτῆς ἐκκλίνουσι τὸ ὄνομα εὐστομίαν περὶ
πλείονος ποιούμενοι τῆς ἀληθείας, ὥστε Φερρέ-
φατταν αὐτὴν καλεῖν. ταὐτὸν δὲ καὶ περὶ τὸν
E Ἀπόλλω, ὅπερ λέγω, πολλοὶ πεφόβηνται περὶ τὸ
ὄνομα τοῦ θεοῦ, ὥς τι δεινὸν μηνύοντος· ἢ οὐκ
ᾔσθησαι;

ΕΡΜ. Πάνυ μὲν οὖν, καὶ ἀληθῆ λέγεις.

ΣΩ. Τὸ δέ γ᾽ ἐστίν, ὡς ἐμοὶ δοκεῖ, κάλλιστα
κείμενον πρὸς τὴν δύναμιν τοῦ θεοῦ.

ΕΡΜ. Πῶς δή;

ΣΩ. Ἐγὼ πειράσομαι φράσαι ὅ γέ μοι φαίνεται·
405 οὐ γὰρ ἔστιν ὅ τι ἂν μᾶλλον ὄνομα ἥρμοσεν ἓν
ὂν τέτταρσι δυνάμεσι ταῖς τοῦ θεοῦ, ὥστε πασῶν
ἐφάπτεσθαι καὶ δηλοῦν τρόπον τινὰ μουσικήν τε
καὶ μαντικὴν καὶ ἰατρικὴν καὶ τοξικήν.

ΕΡΜ. Λέγε δή· ἄτοπον γάρ τί μοι λέγεις τὸ
ὄνομα εἶναι.

22. ΣΩ. Εὐάρμοστον μὲν οὖν, ἅτε μουσικοῦ
ὄντος τοῦ θεοῦ· πρῶτον μὲν γὰρ ἡ κάθαρσις καὶ
οἱ καθαρμοὶ καὶ κατὰ τὴν ἰατρικὴν καὶ κατὰ τὴν
μαντικὴν καὶ αἱ τοῖς ἰατρικοῖς φαρμάκοις καὶ
B αἱ τοῖς μαντικοῖς περιθειώσεις τε καὶ τὰ λουτρὰ
τὰ ἐν τοῖς τοιούτοις καὶ αἱ περιρράνσεις, πάντα
ἕν τι ταῦτα δύναιτ᾽ ἄν, καθαρὸν παρέχειν τὸν
ἄνθρωπον καὶ κατὰ τὸ σῶμα καὶ κατὰ τὴν ψυχήν·
ἢ οὔ;

ΕΡΜ. Πάνυ μὲν οὖν.

ΣΩ. Οὐκοῦν ὁ καθαίρων θεὸς καὶ ὁ ἀπολούων
τε καὶ ἀπολύων τῶν τοιούτων κακῶν οὗτος ἂν
εἴη;

ΕΡΜ. Πάνυ μὲν οὖν.

—and this is the reason why Hades, who is wise, consorts with her, because she is wise—but people have altered her name, attaching more importance to euphony than to truth, and they call her Phere-phatta. Likewise in the case of Apollo, as I say, many people are afraid because of the name of the god, thinking that it has some terrible meaning. Have you not noticed that?

HER. Certainly; what you say is true.

SOC. But really the name is admirably appropriate to the power of the god.

HER. How is that?

SOC. I will try to tell you what I think about it; for no single name could more aptly indicate the four functions of the god, touching upon them all and in a manner declaring his power in music, prophecy, medicine, and archery.

HER. Go on; you seem to imply that it is a remarkable name.

SOC. His name and nature are in harmony; you see he is a musical god. For in the first place, purification and purgations used in medicine and in soothsaying, and fumigations with medicinal and magic drugs, and the baths and sprinklings connected with that sort of thing all have the single function of making a man pure in body and soul, do they not?

HER. Certainly.

SOC. But this is the god who purifies and washes away (ἀπολούων) and delivers (ἀπολύων) from such evils, is he not?

HER. Certainly.

77

ΣΩ. Κατὰ μὲν τοίνυν τὰς ἀπολύσεις τε καὶ
C ἀπολούσεις, ὡς ἰατρὸς ὢν τῶν τοιούτων, Ἀπολούων ἂν ὀρθῶς καλοῖτο· κατὰ δὲ τὴν μαντικὴν
καὶ τὸ ἀληθές τε καὶ τὸ ἁπλοῦν—ταὐτὸν γάρ
ἐστιν—, ὥσπερ οὖν οἱ Θετταλοὶ καλοῦσιν αὐτόν,
ὀρθότατ' ἂν καλοῖτο· Ἅπλουν[1] γάρ φασι πάντες
Θετταλοὶ τοῦτον τὸν θεόν. διὰ δὲ τὸ ἀεὶ βολῶν
ἐγκρατὴς εἶναι τοξικῇ Ἀειβάλλων ἐστίν. κατὰ
δὲ τὴν μουσικὴν δεῖ ὑπολαβεῖν[2] ὅτι τὸ ἄλφα σημαίνει πολλαχοῦ τὸ ὁμοῦ, καὶ ἐνταῦθα τὴν ὁμοῦ
πόλησιν καὶ περὶ τὸν οὐρανόν, οὓς δὴ πόλους
καλοῦσιν, καὶ[3] περὶ τὴν ἐν τῇ ᾠδῇ ἁρμονίαν, ἣ
D δὴ συμφωνία καλεῖται, ὅτι ταῦτα πάντα, ὥς φασιν
οἱ κομψοὶ περὶ μουσικὴν καὶ ἀστρονομίαν, ἁρμονίᾳ
τινὶ πολεῖ ἅμα πάντα· ἐπιστατεῖ δὲ οὗτος ὁ
θεὸς τῇ ἁρμονίᾳ ὁμοπολῶν αὐτὰ πάντα καὶ κατὰ
θεοὺς καὶ κατ' ἀνθρώπους· ὥσπερ οὖν τὸν ὁμοκέλευθον καὶ ὁμόκοιτιν ἀκόλουθον καὶ ἄκοιτιν
ἐκαλέσαμεν, μεταβαλόντες ἀντὶ τοῦ ὁμο ἄλφα,[4]
οὕτω καὶ Ἀπόλλωνα ἐκαλέσαμεν, ὃς ἦν Ὁμοπο-
E λῶν, ἕτερον λάβδα ἐμβαλόντες,[5] ὅτι ὁμώνυμον
ἐγίγνετο τῷ χαλεπῷ ὀνόματι. ὅπερ καὶ νῦν
ὑποπτεύοντές τινες διὰ τὸ μὴ ὀρθῶς σκοπεῖσθαι
τὴν δύναμιν τοῦ ὀνόματος φοβοῦνται αὐτὸ ὡς
σημαῖνον φθοράν τινα· τὸ δέ,[6] ὥσπερ ἄρτι ἐλέγετο,
406 πασῶν ἐφαπτόμενον κεῖται τῶν τοῦ θεοῦ δυνάμεων,
ἁπλοῦ, ἀεὶ βάλλοντος, ἀπολούοντος, ὁμοπολοῦν-
τος. τὰς δὲ Μούσας τε καὶ ὅλως τὴν μουσικὴν

---

[1] Ἅπλουν Boeckh : ἁπλῶν B : ἁπλόν T.
[2] After ὑπολαβεῖν, the words ὥσπερ τὸν ἀκόλουθόν τε καὶ τὴν
ἄκοιτιν of the mss. were bracketed by Ast.
[3] καὶ t : καὶ τὴν BT.

CRATYLUS

soc. With reference, then, to his acts of delivering and his washings, as being the physician of such diseases, he might properly be called Apoluon (ἀπολούων, the washer), and with reference to soothsaying and truth and simplicity—for the two are identical—he might most properly be called by the name the Thessalians use ; for all Thessalians call the god Aplun. And because he is always by his archery controller of darts (βολῶν) he is ever darting (ἀεὶ βάλλων). And with reference to music we have to understand that *alpha* often signifies " together," and here it denotes moving together in the heavens about the poles, as we call them, and harmony in song, which is called concord ; for, as the ingenious musicians and astronomers tell us, all these things move together by a kind of harmony. And this god directs the harmony, making them all move together, among both gods and men ; and so, just as we call the ὁμοκέλευθον (him who accompanies), and ὁμόκοιτιν (bedfellow), by changing the ὁμο to *alpha*, ἀκόλουθον and ἄκοιτιν, so also we called him Apollo who was Homopolo, and the second lambda was inserted, because without it the name sounded of disaster (ἀπολῶ, ἀπόλωλα, etc.). Even as it is, some have a suspicion of this, because they do not properly regard the force of the name, and therefore they fear it, thinking that it denotes some kind of ruin. But in fact, as was said, the name touches upon all the qualities of the god, as simple, ever-darting, purifying, and accompanying. The Muses and music in general are named, ap-

---

4 ἀντὶ τοῦ ὁμο ἄλφα Hermann: ἀντὶ τοῦ ἄλφα B : ἀντὶ τοῦ ὦ ᾱ T.   5 ἐμβαλόντες G : ἐμβάλλοντες BT.
6 τὸ δέ codex Gudianus : τὸ δὲ πολύ BT.

79

PLATO

ἀπὸ τοῦ μῶσθαι, ὡς ἔοικεν, καὶ τῆς ζητήσεώς
τε καὶ φιλοσοφίας τὸ ὄνομα τοῦτο ἐπωνόμασεν.
Λητὼ δὲ ἀπὸ τῆς πρᾳότητος τῆς θεοῦ, κατὰ τὸ
ἐθελήμονα εἶναι ὧν ἄν τις δέηται. ἴσως δὲ ὡς
οἱ ξένοι καλοῦσιν—πολλοὶ γὰρ Ληθὼ καλοῦσιν—
ἔοικεν οὖν πρὸς τὸ μὴ τραχὺ τοῦ ἤθους ἀλλ'
B ἥμερόν τε καὶ λεῖον Ληθὼ κεκλῆσθαι ὑπὸ τῶν
τοῦτο καλούντων. Ἄρτεμις δὲ διὰ τὸ[1] ἀρτεμὲς
φαίνεται καὶ τὸ κόσμιον, διὰ τὴν τῆς παρθενίας
ἐπιθυμίαν· ἴσως δὲ ἀρετῆς ἵστορα τὴν θεὸν ἐκάλεσεν ὁ καλέσας, τάχα δ' ἂν καὶ ὡς τὸν ἄροτον
μισησάσης τὸν ἀνδρὸς ἐν γυναικί· ἢ διὰ τούτων
τι ἢ διὰ πάντα ταῦτα τὸ ὄνομα τοῦτο ὁ τιθέμενος
ἔθετο τῇ θεῷ.

23. ΕΡΜ. Τί δὲ ὁ Διόνυσός τε καὶ ἡ Ἀφροδίτη;
ΣΩ. Μεγάλα, ὦ παῖ Ἱππονίκου, ἐρωτᾷς. ἀλλὰ
ἔστι γὰρ καὶ σπουδαίως εἰρημένος ὁ τρόπος τῶν
C ὀνομάτων τούτοις τοῖς θεοῖς καὶ παιδικῶς. τὸν
μὲν οὖν σπουδαῖον ἄλλους τινὰς ἐρώτα, τὸν δὲ
παιδικὸν οὐδὲν κωλύει διελθεῖν· φιλοπαίσμονες
γὰρ καὶ οἱ θεοί. ὅ τε γὰρ Διόνυσος εἴη ἂν ὁ
διδοὺς τὸν οἶνον Διδοίνυσος ἐν παιδιᾷ καλούμενος,
οἶνος δ', ὅτι οἴεσθαι νοῦν ἔχειν ποιεῖ τῶν πινόν-
των τοὺς πολλοὺς οὐκ ἔχοντας, οἰόνους δικαιότατ'
ἂν καλούμενος. περὶ δὲ Ἀφροδίτης οὐκ ἄξιον
Ἡσιόδῳ ἀντιλέγειν, ἀλλὰ ξυγχωρεῖν ὅτι διὰ τὴν
D ἐκ[2] τοῦ ἀφροῦ γένεσιν Ἀφροδίτη ἐκλήθη.

ΕΡΜ. Ἀλλὰ μὴν οὐδ' Ἀθηνᾶς Ἀθηναῖός γ' ὤν,
ὦ Σώκρατες, ἐπιλήσει, οὐδ' Ἡφαίστου τε καὶ
Ἄρεως.

ΣΩ. Οὐδὲ εἰκός γε.

[1] δὲ διὰ τὸ Stephanus: δὲ τὸ BT.   [2] ἐκ add. Hermann.

80

CRATYLUS

parently, from μῶσθαι, searching, and philosophy ;
and Leto from her gentleness, because whatever is
asked of her, she is willing (ἐθελήμων). But perhaps
her name is Letho, as she is called by many foreigners ;
and those who call her by that name seem to do so
on account of the mild and gentle (λεῖον, Ληθώ)
kindness of her character. Artemis appears to get
her name from her healthy (ἀρτεμές) and well-
ordered nature, and her love of virginity ; or perhaps
he who named her meant that she is learned in
virtue (ἀρετή), or possibly, too, that she hates sexual
intercourse (ἄροτον μισεῖ) of man and woman ; or he
who gave the goddess her name may have given it
for any or all of these reasons.

HER. What of Dionysus and Aphrodite ?

SOC. You ask great things of me, son of Hipponicus. You see there is both a serious and a facetious
account of the form of the name of these deities.
You will have to ask others for the serious one ;
but there is nothing to hinder my giving you the
facetious account, for the gods also have a sense of
humour. Dionysus, the giver (διδούς) of wine (οἶνος),
might be called in jest Didoinysus, and wine, because
it makes most drinkers think (οἴεσθαι) they have
wit (νοῦς) when they have not, might very justly
be called Oeonus (οἰόνους). As for Aphrodite,
we need not oppose Hesiod ; we can accept his
derivation of the name from her birth out of the
foam (ἀφροῦ).

HER. But surely you, as an Athenian, will not
forget Athena, nor Hephaestus and Ares.

SOC. That is not likely.

PLATO

ΕΡΜ. Οὐ γάρ.

ΣΩ. Οὐκοῦν τὸ μὲν ἕτερον ὄνομα αὐτῆς οὐ χαλεπὸν εἰπεῖν δι' ὃ κεῖται.

ΕΡΜ. Τὸ ποῖον;

ΣΩ. Παλλάδα που αὐτὴν καλοῦμεν.

ΕΡΜ. Πῶς γὰρ οὔ;

ΣΩ. Τοῦτο μὲν τοίνυν ἀπὸ τῆς ἐν τοῖς ὅπλοις
E ὀρχήσεως ἡγούμενοι τεθῆναι ὀρθῶς ἄν, ὡς ἐγῷμαι,
ἡγοίμεθα· τὸ γάρ που ἢ αὐτὸν ἤ τι ἄλλο μετεω-
407 ρίζειν ἢ ἀπὸ τῆς γῆς ἢ ἐν ταῖς χερσὶν πάλλειν τε καὶ
πάλλεσθαι καὶ ὀρχεῖν καὶ ὀρχεῖσθαι καλοῦμεν.

ΕΡΜ. Πάνυ μὲν οὖν.

ΣΩ. Παλλάδα μὲν τοίνυν ταύτῃ.

ΕΡΜ. Καὶ ὀρθῶς γε. ἀλλὰ δὴ τὸ ἕτερον πῶς
λέγεις;

ΣΩ. Τὸ τῆς Ἀθηνᾶς;

ΕΡΜ. Ναί.

ΣΩ. Τοῦτο ἐμβριθέστερον, ὦ φίλε. ἐοίκασι δὴ
καὶ οἱ παλαιοὶ τὴν Ἀθηνᾶν νομίζειν ὥσπερ οἱ νῦν
B περὶ Ὅμηρον δεινοί. καὶ γὰρ τούτων οἱ πολλοὶ
ἐξηγούμενοι τὸν ποιητήν φασι τὴν Ἀθηνᾶν αὐτὸν
νοῦν τε καὶ διάνοιαν πεποιηκέναι, καὶ ὁ τὰ ὀνόματα
ποιῶν ἔοικε τοιοῦτόν τι περὶ αὐτῆς διανοεῖσθαι,
ἔτι δὲ μειζόνως λέγων θεοῦ νόησιν ὡσπερεὶ λέγει
ὅτι ἁ θεονόα[1] ἐστὶν αὕτη, τῷ ἄλφα ξενικῶς ἀντὶ τοῦ
ἦτα χρησάμενος καὶ τὸ ἰῶτα καὶ τὸ σῖγμα ἀφελών.
ἴσως δὲ οὐδὲ ταύτῃ, ἀλλ' ὡς τὰ θεῖα νοούσης
αὐτῆς διαφερόντως τῶν ἄλλων Θεονόην ἐκάλεσεν.
οὐδὲν δὲ ἀπέχει καὶ τὴν ἐν τῷ ἤθει νόησιν ὡς οὖσαν
C τὴν θεὸν ταύτην Ἠθονόην μὲν βούλεσθαι προσ-

---

[1] ἁ θεονόα Buttmann : ἡ θεονόη B : ἡ θονόη T.

CRATYLUS

HER. No.

SOC. It is easy to tell the reason of one of her two names.

HER. What name?

SOC. We call her Pallas, you know.

HER. Yes, of course.

SOC. Those of us are right, I fancy, who think this name is derived from armed dances, for lifting oneself or anything else from the ground or in the hands is called shaking (πάλλειν) and being shaken, or dancing and being danced.

HER. Yes, certainly.

SOC. So that is the reason she is called Pallas.

HER. And rightly called so. But what can you say of her other name?

SOC. You mean Athena?

HER. Yes.

SOC. That is a weightier matter, my friend. The ancients seem to have had the same belief about Athena as the interpreters of Homer have now; for most of these, in commenting on the poet, say that he represents Athena as mind (νοῦς) and intellect (διάνοια); and the maker of her name seems to have had a similar conception of her, but he gives her the still grander title of " mind of God " (ἡ θεοῦ νόησις), seeming to say that she is ἁ θεονόα; here he used the alpha in foreign fashion instead of eta, and dropped out the iota and sigma. But perhaps that was not his reason; he may have called her Theonoë because she has unequalled knowledge of divine things (τὰ θεῖα νοοῦσα). Perhaps, too, he may have wished to identify the goddess with wisdom of character (ἐν ἤθει νόησις) by calling her Ethonoë; and then he himself or others after-

83

ειπεῖν· παραγαγὼν δὲ ἢ αὐτὸς ἤ τινες ὕστερον ἐπὶ
τὸ κάλλιον, ὡς ᾤοντο, Ἀθηνάαν ἐκάλεσαν.

ΕΡΜ. Τί δὲ δὴ τὸν Ἥφαιστον, πῇ λέγεις;

ΣΩ. Ἦ τὸν γενναῖον τὸν φάεος ἵστορα ἐρωτᾷς;

ΕΡΜ. Ἔοικα.

ΣΩ. Οὐκοῦν οὗτος μὲν παντὶ δῆλος Φαῖστος ὤν,
τὸ ἦτα προσελκυσάμενος;

ΕΡΜ. Κινδυνεύει, ἐὰν μή πῇ σοι, ὡς ἔοικεν, ἔτι
ἄλλῃ δόξῃ.

ΣΩ. Ἀλλ᾽ ἵνα μὴ δόξῃ, τὸν Ἄρη ἐρώτα.

ΕΡΜ. Ἐρωτῶ.

D ΣΩ. Οὐκοῦν, εἰ μὲν βούλει, κατὰ τὸ ἄρρεν τε
καὶ κατὰ τὸ ἀνδρεῖον Ἄρης ἂν εἴη· εἰ δ᾽ αὖ κατὰ
τὸ σκληρόν τε καὶ ἀμετάστροφον, ὃ δὴ ἄρρατον
καλεῖται, καὶ ταύτῃ ἂν πανταχῇ πολεμικῷ θεῷ
πρέποι Ἄρη καλεῖσθαι.

ΕΡΜ. Πάνυ μὲν οὖν.

ΣΩ. Ἐκ μὲν οὖν τῶν θεῶν πρὸς θεῶν ἀπαλλαγῶμεν, ὡς ἐγὼ δέδοικα περὶ αὐτῶν διαλέγεσθαι·
περὶ δὲ ἄλλων ὧντινων[1] βούλει πρόβαλλέ μοι,
ὄφρα ἴδηαι οἷοι Εὐθύφρονος ἵπποι.

E ΕΡΜ. Ἀλλὰ ποιήσω ταῦτα, ἔτι γε ἓν ἐρόμενός
σε περὶ Ἑρμοῦ, ἐπειδή με καὶ οὔ φησιν Κρατύλος
Ἑρμογένη εἶναι. πειρώμεθα οὖν τὸν Ἑρμῆν σκέ-
ψασθαι τί καὶ νοεῖ τὸ ὄνομα, ἵνα καὶ εἰδῶμεν εἰ τὶ
ὅδε λέγει.

ΣΩ. Ἀλλὰ μὴν τοῦτό γε ἔοικε περὶ λόγον τι
εἶναι ὁ Ἑρμῆς, καὶ τὸ ἑρμηνέα εἶναι καὶ τὸ ἄγγελον
408 καὶ τὸ κλοπικόν τε καὶ τὸ ἀπατηλὸν ἐν λόγοις καὶ
τὸ ἀγοραστικόν, περὶ λόγου δύναμίν ἐστιν πᾶσα

---

[1] ἄλλων ὧντινων codex Parisinus 1813: ἄλλων τινῶν B:
ἄλλων εἴ τινων T.

wards improved the name, as they thought, and called her Athenaa.

HER. And how do you explain Hephaestus?

SOC. You ask about "the noble master of light"?

HER. To be sure.

SOC. Hephaestus is Phaestus, with the eta added by attraction; anyone could see that, I should think.

HER. Very likely, unless some other explanation occurs to you, as it probably will.

SOC. To prevent that, ask about Ares.

HER. I do ask.

SOC. Ares, then, if you like, would be named for his virility and courage, or for his hard and unbending nature, which is called ἄρρατον; so Ares would be in every way a fitting name for the god of war.

HER. Certainly.

SOC. For God's sake, let us leave the gods, as I am afraid to talk about them; but ask me about any others you please, "that you may see what" Euthyphro's "horses are."[1]

HER. I will do so, but first one more god. I want to ask you about Hermes, since Cratylus says I am not Hermogenes (son of Hermes). Let us investigate the name of Hermes, to find out whether there is anything in what he says.

SOC. Well then, this name "Hermes" seems to me to have to do with speech; he is an interpreter (ἑρμηνεύς) and a messenger, is wily and deceptive in speech, and is oratorical. All this activity is

---

[1] *Cf.* Homer, *Iliad*, v. 221, viii. 105.

αὕτη ἡ πραγματεία· ὅπερ οὖν καὶ ἐν τοῖς πρόσθεν
ἐλέγομεν, τὸ εὕρειν λόγου χρεία ἐστί, τὸ δέ, οἷον
καὶ Ὅμηρος πολλαχοῦ λέγει, ἐμήσατό φησιν, τοῦτο
δὲ μηχανήσασθαί ἐστιν. ἐξ ἀμφοτέρων οὖν τούτων
τὸν τὸ λέγειν τε καὶ τὸν λόγον μησάμενον—τὸ δὲ
λέγειν δή ἐστιν εὕρειν—τοῦτον τὸν θεὸν ὡσπερεὶ
B ἐπιτάττει ἡμῖν ὁ νομοθέτης· ὦ ἄνθρωποι, ὃς τὸ
εὕρειν ἐμήσατο, δικαίως ἂν καλοῖτο ὑπὸ ὑμῶν
Εἰρέμης· νῦν δὲ ἡμεῖς, ὡς οἰόμεθα, καλλωπίζοντες
τὸ ὄνομα Ἑρμῆν καλοῦμεν· καὶ ἥ γε Ἶρις ἀπὸ
τοῦ εὕρειν ἔοικεν κεκλημένη, ὅτι ἄγγελος ἦν.[1]

ΕΡΜ. Νὴ τὸν Δία, εὖ ἄρα μοι δοκεῖ Κρατύλος
λέγειν τὸ ἐμὲ μὴ εἶναι Ἑρμογένη· οὔκουν εὐμή-
χανός γέ εἰμι λόγου.

24. ΣΩ. Καὶ τό γε τὸν Πᾶνα τοῦ Ἑρμοῦ εἶναι
υἱὸν διφυῆ ἔχει τὸ εἰκός, ὦ ἑταῖρε.

C ΕΡΜ. Πῶς δή;

ΣΩ. Οἶσθα ὅτι ὁ λόγος τὸ πᾶν σημαίνει καὶ
κυκλεῖ καὶ πολεῖ ἀεί, καὶ ἔστι διπλοῦς, ἀληθής τε
καὶ ψευδής.

ΕΡΜ. Πάνυ γε.

ΣΩ. Οὐκοῦν τὸ μὲν ἀληθὲς αὐτοῦ λεῖον καὶ θεῖον
καὶ ἄνω οἰκοῦν ἐν τοῖς θεοῖς, τὸ δὲ ψεῦδος κάτω
ἐν τοῖς πολλοῖς τῶν ἀνθρώπων καὶ τραχὺ καὶ
τραγικόν· ἐνταῦθα γὰρ πλεῖστοι οἱ μῦθοί τε καὶ τὰ
ψεύδη ἐστίν, περὶ τὸν τραγικὸν βίον.

ΕΡΜ. Πάνυ γε.

ΣΩ. Ὀρθῶς ἄρ' ἂν[2] ὁ πᾶν μηνύων καὶ ἀεὶ πολῶν

---

[1] καὶ ἥ γε Ἶρις . . . ἄγγελος ἦν bracketed by Heindorf and others.
[2] ἂν add. Stallbaum.

concerned with the power of speech. Now, as I said before, εἴρειν denotes the use of speech; moreover, Homer often uses the word ἐμήσατο, which means " contrive." From these two words, then, the lawgiver imposes upon us the name of this god who contrived speech and the use of speech —εἴρειν means " speak "—and tells us : " Ye human beings, he who contrived speech (εἴρειν ἐμήσατο) ought to be called Eiremes by you." We, however, have beautified the name, as we imagine, and call him Hermes. Iris also seems to have got her name from εἴρειν, because she is a messenger.

HER. By Zeus, I believe Cratylus was right in saying I was not Hermogenes ; I certainly am no good contriver of speech.

SOC. And it is reasonable, my friend, that Pan is the double-natured son of Hermes.

HER. How is that ?

SOC. You know that speech makes all things (πᾶν) known and always makes them circulate and move about, and is twofold, true and false.

HER. Certainly.

SOC. Well, the true part is smooth and divine and dwells aloft among the gods, but falsehood dwells below among common men, is rough and like the tragic goat[1] ; for tales and falsehoods are most at home there, in the tragic life.

HER. Certainly.

SOC. Then Pan, who declares and always moves (ἀεὶ πολῶν) all, is rightly called goat-herd (αἰπόλος),

[1] The chorus of the primitive performances from which tragedy developed appeared as satyrs, clad in goat-skins. Hence the name τραγῳδία (goat-song). The adjective τραγικός may mean either " goat-like " or " tragic." In this passage it has both meanings.

D Πὰν αἰπόλος εἴη, διφυὴς Ἑρμοῦ υἱός, τὰ μὲν
ἄνωθεν λεῖος, τὰ δὲ κάτωθεν τραχὺς καὶ τραγο-
ειδής. καὶ ἔστιν ἤτοι λόγος ἢ λόγου ἀδελφὸς ὁ
Πάν, εἴπερ Ἑρμοῦ υἱός ἐστιν· ἀδελφῷ δὲ ἐοικέναι
ἀδελφὸν οὐδὲν θαυμαστόν. ἀλλ' ὅπερ ἐγὼ ἔλεγον,
ὦ μακάριε, ἀπαλλαγῶμεν ἐκ τῶν θεῶν.

ΕΡΜ. Τῶν γε τοιούτων, ὦ Σώκρατες, εἰ βούλει.
περὶ δὲ τῶν τοιῶνδε[1] τί σε κωλύει διελθεῖν, οἷον
ἡλίου τε καὶ σελήνης καὶ ἄστρων καὶ γῆς καὶ
E αἰθέρος καὶ ἀέρος καὶ πυρὸς καὶ ὕδατος καὶ ὡρῶν
καὶ ἐνιαυτοῦ;

ΣΩ. Συχνὰ μέν μοι προστάττεις, ὅμως δέ, εἴπερ
σοι κεχαρισμένον ἔσται, ἐθέλω.

ΕΡΜ. Καὶ μὴν χαριεῖ.

ΣΩ. Τί δὴ οὖν πρῶτον βούλει; ἢ ὥσπερ εἶπες,
τὸν ἥλιον διέλθωμεν;

ΕΡΜ. Πάνυ γε.

ΣΩ. Ἔοικε τοίνυν κατάδηλον γενόμενον ἂν μᾶλ-
409 λον, εἰ τῷ Δωρικῷ τις ὀνόματι χρῷτο· ἅλιον γὰρ
καλοῦσιν οἱ Δωριῆς· ἅλιος οὖν εἴη μὲν ἂν κατὰ τὸ
ἁλίζειν εἰς ταὐτὸ τοὺς ἀνθρώπους, ἐπειδὰν ἀνατείλῃ,
εἴη δ' ἂν καὶ τῷ περὶ τὴν γῆν ἀεὶ εἰλεῖν ἰών, ἐοίκοι
δ' ἂν καὶ ὅτι ποικίλλει ἰὼν τὰ γιγνόμενα ἐκ τῆς γῆς·
τὸ δὲ ποικίλλειν καὶ αἰολεῖν ταὐτόν.

ΕΡΜ. Τί δὲ ἡ σελήνη;

ΣΩ. Τοῦτο δὲ τὸ ὄνομα φαίνεται τὸν Ἀναξ-
αγόραν πιέζειν.

ΕΡΜ. Τί δή;

ΣΩ. Ἔοικε δηλοῦντι[2] παλαιότερον ὃ ἐκεῖνος

---

[1] περὶ δὲ τῶν τοιῶνδε b : περὶ τῶν τοιῶνδε Β : περὶ τῶν
τοιούτων δὲ Τ : περὶ δὲ τῶν τοιούτων G.
[2] δηλοῦντι Heusde : δηλοῦν τι ΒΤ.

being the double-natured son of Hermes, smooth in his upper parts, rough and goat-like in his lower parts. And Pan, if he is the son of Hermes, is either speech or the brother of speech, and that brother resembles brother is not at all surprising. But, as I said, my friend, let us get away from the gods.

HER. From such gods as those, if you like, Socrates ; but why should you not tell of another kind of gods, such as sun, moon, stars, earth, ether, air, fire, water, the seasons, and the year ?

SOC. You are imposing a good many tasks upon me ; however, if it will give you pleasure, I am willing.

HER. It will give me pleasure.

SOC. What, then, do you wish first ? Shall we discuss the sun ("Ηλιος), as you mentioned it first ?

HER. By all means.

SOC. I think it would be clearer if we were to use the Doric form of the name. The Dorians call it "Αλιος. Now ἅλιος might be derived from collecting (ἁλίζειν) men when he rises, or because he always turns (ἀεὶ εἰλεῖν) about the earth in his course, or because he variegates the products of the earth, for variegate is identical with αἰολεῖν.

HER. And what of the moon, Selene ?

SOC. That name appears to put Anaxagoras in an uncomfortable position.

HER. How so ?

SOC. Why, it seems to have anticipated by many

Β νεωστὶ ἔλεγεν, ὅτι ἡ σελήνη ἀπὸ τοῦ ἡλίου ἔχει
τὸ φῶς.

ΕΡΜ. Πῶς δή;

ΣΩ. Τὸ μέν που σέλας καὶ τὸ φῶς ταὐτόν.

ΕΡΜ. Ναί.

ΣΩ. Νέον δέ που καὶ ἕνον ἀεί ἐστι περὶ τὴν
σελήνην τοῦτο τὸ φῶς, εἴπερ ἀληθῆ οἱ Ἀναξαγό-
ρειοι λέγουσιν· κύκλῳ γάρ που ἀεὶ αὐτὴν περιιὼν
νέον ἀεὶ ἐπιβάλλει, ἔνον δὲ ὑπάρχει τὸ τοῦ προτέρου
μηνός.

ΕΡΜ. Πάνυ γε.

ΣΩ. Σελαναίαν δέ γε καλοῦσιν αὐτὴν πολλοί.

ΕΡΜ. Πάνυ γε.

ΣΩ. Ὅτι δὲ σέλας νέον τε καὶ ἔνον ἔχει ἀεί,
C Σελαενονεοάεια[1] μὲν δικαιότατ' ἂν τῶν ὀνομάτων
καλοῖτο, συγκεκροτημένον δὲ σελαναία κέκληται.

ΕΡΜ. Διθυραμβῶδές γε τοῦτο τοὔνομα, ὦ Σώκρατες. ἀλλὰ τὸν μῆνα καὶ τὰ ἄστρα πῶς λέγεις;

ΣΩ. Ὁ μὲν μεὶς ἀπὸ τοῦ μειοῦσθαι εἴη ἂν
μείης ὀρθῶς κεκλημένος, τὰ δ' ἄστρα ἔοικε τῆς
ἀστραπῆς ἐπωνυμίαν ἔχειν. ἡ δὲ ἀστραπή, ὅτι
τὰ ὦπα ἀναστρέφει, ἀναστρωπὴ ἂν εἴη, νῦν δὲ
ἀστραπὴ καλλωπισθεῖσα κέκληται.

ΕΡΜ. Τί δὲ τὸ πῦρ καὶ τὸ ὕδωρ;

D ΣΩ. Τὸ πῦρ ἀπορῶ· καὶ κινδυνεύει ἤτοι ἡ τοῦ
Εὐθύφρονός με μοῦσα ἐπιλελοιπέναι, ἢ τοῦτό τι
παγχάλεπον εἶναι· σκέψαι οὖν ἣν εἰσάγω μηχανὴν
ἐπὶ πάντα τὰ τοιαῦτα ἃ ἂν ἀπορῶ.

---

[1] Σελαενονεοάεια Heindorf: σελαεννεοάεια Β: σέλλαεν-
νεοάεια Τ.

90

years the recent doctrine of Anaxagoras, that the moon receives its light from the sun.

HER. How is that ?

SOC. Σέλας (gleam) and φῶς (light) are the same thing.

HER. Yes.

SOC. Now the light is always new and old about the moon, if the Anaxagoreans are right ; for they say the sun, in its continuous course about the moon, always sheds new light upon it, and the light of the previous month persists.

HER. Certainly.

SOC. The moon is often called Σελαναία.

HER. Certainly.

SOC. Because it has always a new and old gleam (σέλας νέον τε καὶ ἕνον) the very most fitting name for it would be Σελαενονεοάεια, which has been compressed into Σελαναία.

HER. That is a regular *opéra bouffe* name, Socrates. But what have you to say of the month (μήν) and the stars ?

SOC. The word " month " (μείς) would be properly pronounced μείης, from μειοῦσθαι, " to grow less," and I think the stars (ἄστρα) get their name from ἀστραπή (lightning). But ἀστραπή, because it turns our eyes upwards (τὰ ὦπα ἀναστρέφει), would be called ἀναστρωπή, which is now pronounced more prettily ἀστραπή.

HER. And what of πῦρ (fire) and ὕδωρ (water) ?

SOC. Πῦρ is too much for me. It must be that either the muse of Euthyphro has deserted me or this is a very difficult word. Now just note the contrivance I introduce in all cases like this which are too much for me.

ΕΡΜ. Τίνα δή;

ΣΩ. Ἐγώ σοι ἐρῶ. ἀπόκριναι γάρ μοι· ἔχοις ἂν
εἰπεῖν πῦρ κατὰ τίνα τρόπον καλεῖται;

ΕΡΜ. Μὰ Δί᾽ οὐκ ἔγωγε.

25. ΣΩ. Σκέψαι δὴ ὃ ἐγὼ ὑποπτεύω περὶ
αὐτοῦ. ἐννοῶ γὰρ ὅτι πολλὰ οἱ Ἕλληνες ὀνόματα
Ε ἄλλως τε καὶ οἱ ὑπὸ τοῖς βαρβάροις οἰκοῦντες παρὰ
τῶν βαρβάρων εἰλήφασιν.

ΕΡΜ. Τί οὖν δή;

ΣΩ. Εἴ τις ζητοῖ ταῦτα κατὰ τὴν Ἑλληνικὴν
φωνὴν ὡς εἰκότως κεῖται, ἀλλὰ μὴ κατ᾽ ἐκείνην ἐξ
ἧς τὸ ὄνομα τυγχάνει ὄν, οἶσθα ὅτι ἀποροῖ ἄν.

ΕΡΜ. Εἰκότως γε.

410 ΣΩ. Ὅρα τοίνυν καὶ τοῦτο τὸ ὄνομα τὸ πῦρ μή
τι βαρβαρικὸν ᾖ. τοῦτο γὰρ οὔτε ῥᾴδιον προσάψαι
ἐστὶν Ἑλληνικῇ φωνῇ, φανεροί τ᾽ εἰσὶν οὕτως αὐτὸ
καλοῦντες Φρύγες, σμικρόν τι παρακλίνοντες· καὶ
τό γε ὕδωρ καὶ τὰς κύνας καὶ ἄλλα πολλά.

ΕΡΜ. Ἔστι ταῦτα.

ΣΩ. Οὐ τοίνυν δεῖ ταῦτα προσβιάζεσθαι, ἐπεὶ
ἔχοι γ᾽ ἄν τις εἰπεῖν περὶ αὐτῶν. τὸ μὲν οὖν πῦρ
Β καὶ τὸ ὕδωρ ταύτῃ ἀπωθοῦμαι· ὁ δὲ δὴ[1] ἀὴρ
ἆρά γε, ὦ Ἑρμόγενες, ὅτι αἴρει τὰ ἀπὸ τῆς γῆς, ἀὴρ
κέκληται; ἢ ὅτι ἀεὶ ῥεῖ; ἢ ὅτι πνεῦμα ἐξ αὐτοῦ
γίγνεται ῥέοντος; οἱ γὰρ ποιηταί που τὰ πνεύματα
ἀήτας καλοῦσιν· ἴσως οὖν λέγει, ὥσπερ ἂν εἰ
εἴποι πνευματόρρουν, ἀητόρρουν.[2] τὸν δὲ αἰθέρα
τῇδέ πῃ ὑπολαμβάνω, ὅτι ἀεὶ θεῖ περὶ τὸν ἀέρα
ῥέων ἀειθεὴρ δικαίως ἂν καλοῖτο. γῆ δὲ μᾶλλον

---

[1] δὴ G : om. BT.
[2] After ἀητόρρουν the MSS. read ὅθεν δὴ βούλεται αὐτὸν οὕτως
εἰπεῖν, ὅτι ἐστὶν ἀήρ, "whence he means that he says it is
air." Bracketed by Heindorf.

CRATYLUS

HER. What contrivance ?

SOC. I will tell you. Answer me ; can you tell the reason of the word πῦρ ?

HER. Not I, by Zeus.

SOC. See what I suspect about it. I know that many Greeks, especially those who are subject to the barbarians, have adopted many foreign words.

HER. What of that ?

SOC. If we should try to demonstrate the fitness of those words in accordance with the Greek language, and not in accordance with the language from which they are derived, you know we should get into trouble.

HER. Naturally.

SOC. Well, this word πῦρ is probably foreign ; for it is difficult to connect it with the Greek language, and besides, the Phrygians have the same word, only slightly altered. The same is the case with ὕδωρ (water), κύων (dog), and many other words.

HER. Yes, that is true.

SOC. So we must not propose forced explanations of these words, though something might be said about them. I therefore set aside πῦρ and ὕδωρ in this way. But is air called ἀήρ because it raises (αἴρει) things from the earth, or because it is always flowing (ἀεὶ ῥεῖ), or because wind arises from its flow ? The poets call the winds ἀήτας, " blasts." Perhaps the poet means to say " air-flow " (ἀητόρρουν), as he might say " wind-flow " (πνευματόρρουν). The word αἰθήρ (ether) I understand in this way : because it always runs and flows about the air (ἀεὶ θεῖ περὶ τὸν ἀέρα ῥέων), it may properly be called ἀειθεήρ. The word γῆ (earth) shows the meaning

93

PLATO

C σημαίνει ὃ βούλεται ἐάν τις γαῖαν ὀνομάσῃ· γαῖα
γὰρ γεννήτειρα ἂν εἴη ὀρθῶς κεκλημένη, ὥς φησιν
Ὅμηρος· τὸ γὰρ γεγάασιν γεγενῆσθαι λέγει. εἶεν·
τί οὖν ἡμῖν ἦν τὸ μετὰ τοῦτο;

ΕΡΜ. Ὧραι, ὦ Σώκρατες, καὶ ἐνιαυτὸς καὶ
ἔτος.

ΣΩ. Αἱ μὲν δὴ ὧραι Ἀττικιστὶ ὡς τὸ παλαιὸν
ῥητέον, εἴπερ βούλει τὸ εἰκὸς εἰδέναι· ὧραι γάρ
εἰσι διὰ τὸ ὁρίζειν χειμῶνάς τε καὶ θέρη καὶ
πνεύματα καὶ τοὺς καρποὺς τοὺς ἐκ τῆς γῆς·
ὁρίζουσαι δὲ δικαίως ἂν ὧραι καλοῖντο. ἐνιαυ-
D τὸς δὲ καὶ ἔτος κινδυνεύει ἕν τι εἶναι. τὸ γὰρ τὰ
φυόμενα καὶ τὰ γιγνόμενα ἐν μέρει ἕκαστον
προάγον εἰς φῶς καὶ αὐτὸ ἐν αὑτῷ ἐξετάζον,
τοῦτο, ὥσπερ ἐν τοῖς πρόσθεν τὸ τοῦ Διὸς ὄνομα
δίχα διῃρημένον οἱ μὲν Ζῆνα, οἱ δὲ Δία ἐκάλουν,
οὕτω καὶ ἐνταῦθα οἱ μὲν ἐνιαυτόν, ὅτι ἐν ἑαυτῷ,
οἱ δὲ ἔτος, ὅτι ἐτάζει· ὁ δὲ ὅλος λόγος ἐστὶν τὸ
ἐν αὑτῷ ἐτάζον τοῦτο προσαγορεύεσθαι ἓν ὂν
δίχα, ὥστε δύο ὀνόματα γεγονέναι, ἐνιαυτόν τε
E καὶ ἔτος, ἐξ ἑνὸς λόγου.

ΕΡΜ. Ἀλλὰ δῆτα, ὦ Σώκρατες, πολὺ ἐπιδίδως.
ΣΩ. Πόρρω ἤδη, οἶμαι, φαίνομαι σοφίας ἐλαύνειν.
ΕΡΜ. Πάνυ μὲν οὖν.
ΣΩ. Τάχα μᾶλλον φήσεις.

411 26. ΕΡΜ. Ἀλλὰ μετὰ τοῦτο τὸ εἶδος ἔγωγε
ἡδέως ἂν θεασαίμην ταῦτα τὰ καλὰ ὀνόματα τίνι
ποτὲ ὀρθότητι κεῖται, τὰ περὶ τὴν ἀρετήν, οἷον
φρόνησίς τε καὶ σύνεσις καὶ δικαιοσύνη καὶ τἆλλα
τὰ τοιαῦτα πάντα.

better in the form γαῖα; for γαῖα is a correct word for "mother," as Homer says, for he uses γεγάασιν to mean γεγενῆσθαι (be born). Well, now what came next?

HER. The seasons, Socrates, and the two words for year.

SOC. The word ὧραι (seasons) should be pronounced in the old Attic fashion, ὅραι, if you wish to know the probable meaning; ὅραι exist to divide winters and summers and winds and the fruits of the earth; and since they divide (ὁρίζουσι), they would rightly be called ὅραι. The two words for year, ἐνιαυτός and ἔτος, are really one. For that which brings to light within itself the plants and animals, each in its turn, and examines them, is called by some ἐνιαυτός, because of its activity within itself (ἐν ἑαυτῷ), and by others ἔτος, because it examines (ἐτάζει), just as we saw before that the name of Zeus was divided and some said Δία and others Ζῆνα. The whole phrase is "that which examines within itself (τὸ ἐν αὑτῷ ἐτάζον), and this one phrase is divided in speech so that the two words ἐνιαυτός and ἔτος are formed from one phrase.

HER. Truly, Socrates, you are going ahead at a great rate.

SOC. Yes, I fancy I am already far along on the road of wisdom.

HER. I am sure you are.

SOC. You will be surer presently.

HER. Now after the class of words you have explained, I should like to examine the correctness of the noble words that relate to virtue, such as wisdom, intelligence, justice, and all the others of that sort.

PLATO

ΣΩ. Ἐγείρεις μέν, ὦ ἑταῖρε, οὐ φαῦλον γένος
ὀνομάτων· ὅμως δὲ ἐπειδήπερ τὴν λεοντῆν ἐνδέ-
δυκα, οὐκ ἀποδειλιατέον, ἀλλ' ἐπισκεπτέον, ὡς
ἔοικε, φρόνησιν καὶ σύνεσιν καὶ γνώμην καὶ ἐπιστήμην καὶ τἆλλα δὴ ἃ φῇς πάντα ταῦτα τὰ καλὰ
B ὀνόματα.

ΕΡΜ. Πάνυ μὲν οὖν οὐ δεῖ ἡμᾶς προαποστῆναι.

ΣΩ. Καὶ μήν, νὴ τὸν κύνα, δοκῶ γέ μοι οὐ
κακῶς μαντεύεσθαι, ὃ καὶ νῦν δὴ ἐνενόησα, ὅτι
οἱ πάνυ παλαιοὶ ἄνθρωποι οἱ τιθέμενοι τὰ ὀνόματα
παντὸς μᾶλλον, ὥσπερ καὶ τῶν νῦν οἱ πολλοὶ τῶν
σοφῶν, ὑπὸ τοῦ πυκνὰ περιστρέφεσθαι ζητοῦντες
ὅπῃ ἔχει τὰ ὄντα ἀεὶ[1] εἰλιγγιῶσιν, κἄπειτα αὐτοῖς
φαίνεται περιφέρεσθαι τὰ πράγματα καὶ πάντως
C φέρεσθαι. αἰτιῶνται δὴ οὐ τὸ ἔνδον τὸ παρὰ
σφίσιν πάθος αἴτιον εἶναι ταύτης τῆς δόξης, ἀλλὰ
αὐτὰ τὰ πράγματα οὕτω πεφυκέναι, οὐδὲν αὐτῶν
μόνιμον εἶναι οὐδὲ βέβαιον, ἀλλὰ ῥεῖν καὶ φέρεσθαι
καὶ μεστὰ εἶναι πάσης φορᾶς καὶ γενέσεως ἀεί.
λέγω δὲ ἐννοήσας πρὸς πάντα τὰ νῦν δὴ ὀνόματα.

ΕΡΜ. Πῶς δὴ τοῦτο, ὦ Σώκρατες;

ΣΩ. Οὐ κατενόησας ἴσως τὰ ἄρτι λεγόμενα,
ὅτι παντάπασιν ὡς φερομένοις τε καὶ ῥέουσι καὶ
γιγνομένοις τοῖς πράγμασι τὰ ὀνόματα ἐπίκειται.

ΕΡΜ. Οὐ πάνυ ἐνεθυμήθην.

D ΣΩ. Καὶ μὴν πρῶτον μὲν τοῦτο ὃ πρῶτον εἴπομεν παντάπασιν ὡς ἐπὶ τοιούτων ἐστίν.

ΕΡΜ. Τὸ ποῖον;

ΣΩ. Ἡ φρόνησις· φορᾶς γάρ ἐστι καὶ ῥοῦ
νόησις. εἴη δ' ἂν καὶ ὄνησιν ὑπολαβεῖν φορᾶς

---

[1] ἀεὶ T : om. B.

soc. You are stirring up a mighty tribe of words, my friend ; however, since I have put on the lion helmet, I must not play the coward, but must, it seems, examine wisdom, intelligence, thought, knowledge, and all the other noble words of which you speak.

her. Certainly we must not stop until that is done.

soc. By the dog, I believe I have a fine intuition which has just come to me, that the very ancient men who invented names were quite like most of the present philosophers who always get dizzy as they turn round and round in their search for the nature of things, and then the things seem to them to turn round and round and be in motion. They think the cause of this belief is not an affection within themselves, but that the nature of things really is such that nothing is at rest or stable, but everything is flowing and moving and always full of constant motion and generation. I say this because I thought of it with reference to all these words we are now considering.

her. How is that, Socrates ?

soc. Perhaps you did not observe that the names we just mentioned are given under the assumption that the things named are moving and flowing and being generated.

her. No, I did not notice that at all.

soc. Surely the first one we mentioned is subject to such assumptions.

her. What is the word ?

soc. Wisdom (φρόνησις) ; for it is perception (νόησις) of motion (φορᾶς) and flowing (ῥοῦ) ; or it might be understood as benefit (ὄνησις) of motion

97

ἀλλ᾽ οὖν περί γε τὸ φέρεσθαί ἐστιν. εἰ δὲ βούλει,
ἡ γνώμη παντάπασιν δηλοῖ γονῆς σκέψιν καὶ
νώμησιν· τὸ γὰρ νωμᾶν καὶ τὸ σκοπεῖν ταὐτόν.
εἰ δὲ βούλει, αὐτὸ ἡ νόησις τοῦ νέου ἐστὶν ἕσις·
τὸ δὲ νέα εἶναι τὰ ὄντα σημαίνει γιγνόμενα ἀεὶ
E εἶναι· τούτου οὖν ἐφίεσθαι τὴν ψυχὴν μηνύει τὸ
ὄνομα ὁ θέμενος τὴν νεόεσιν. οὐ γὰρ νόησις τὸ
ἀρχαῖον ἐκαλεῖτο, ἀλλ᾽ ἀντὶ τοῦ ἦτα εἶ ἔδει λέγειν
δύο, νεόεσιν. σωφροσύνη δὲ σωτηρία οὗ νῦν δὴ
412 ἐσκέμμεθα, φρονήσεως. καὶ μὴν ἥ γε ἐπιστήμη
μηνύει ὡς φερομένοις τοῖς πράγμασιν ἑπομένης
τῆς ψυχῆς τῆς ἀξίας λόγου, καὶ οὔτε ἀπολειπο-
μένης οὔτε προθεούσης· διὸ δὴ ἐμβάλλοντας δεῖ
τὸ εἶ ἐπεΐστήμην[1] αὐτὴν ὀνομάζειν. σύνεσις δ᾽
αὖ οὕτω μὲν δόξειεν ἂν ὥσπερ συλλογισμὸς εἶναι·
ὅταν δὲ συνιέναι λέγῃ, ταὐτὸν παντάπασιν τῷ
ἐπίστασθαι συμβαίνει λεγόμενον· συμπορεύεσθαι
B γὰρ λέγει τὴν ψυχὴν τοῖς πράγμασι τὸ συνιέναι.
ἀλλὰ μὴν ἥ γε σοφία φορᾶς ἐφάπτεσθαι σημαίνει.
σκοτωδέστερον δὲ τοῦτο καὶ ξενικώτερον· ἀλλὰ
δεῖ ἐκ τῶν ποιητῶν ἀναμιμνήσκεσθαι ὅτι πολλαχοῦ λέγουσιν περὶ ὅτου ἂν τύχωσιν τῶν ἀρ-
χομένων ταχὺ προϊέναι ἐσύθη φασίν. Λακωνικῷ
δὲ ἀνδρὶ τῶν εὐδοκίμων καὶ ὄνομα ἦν Σοῦς· τὴν
γὰρ ταχεῖαν ὁρμὴν οἱ Λακεδαιμόνιοι τοῦτο καλοῦσιν. ταύτης οὖν τῆς φορᾶς ἐπαφὴν σημαίνει
ἡ σοφία, ὡς φερομένων τῶν ὄντων. καὶ μὴν τό
C γε ἀγαθόν, τοῦτο τῆς φύσεως πάσης τῷ ἀγαστῷ
βούλεται τὸ ὄνομα ἐπικεῖσθαι. ἐπειδὴ γὰρ πορεύεται τὰ ὄντα, ἔνι μὲν ἄρ᾽ αὐτοῖς τάχος, ἔνι δὲ

---

[1] ἐπεΐστήμην Heindorf : ἐπιστήμην BT.

CRATYLUS

(φορᾶς); in either case it has to do with motion. And γνώμη (thought), if you please, certainly denotes contemplation and consideration of generation (γονῆς νώμησις); for to consider is the same as to contemplate. Or, if you please, νόησις (intelligence) is merely ἕσις (desire) τοῦ νεοῦ (of the new); but that things are new shows that they are always being generated; therefore the soul's desire for generation is declared by the giver of the name νεόεσις; for in antiquity the name was not νόησις, but two epsilons had to be spoken instead of the eta. Σωφροσύνη (self-restraint) is σωτηρία (salvation) of φρόνησις (wisdom), which we have just been discussing. And ἐπιστήμη (knowledge) indicates that the soul which is of any account accompanies (ἕπεται) things in their motion, neither falling behind them nor running in front of them; therefore we ought to insert an epsilon and call it ἐπεϊστήμη. Σύνεσις (intelligence) in its turn is a kind of reckoning together; when one says συνιέναι (understand), the same thing as ἐπίστασθαι is said; for συνιέναι means that the soul goes with things. Certainly σοφία (wisdom) denotes the touching of motion. This word is very obscure and of foreign origin; but we must remember that the poets often say of something which begins to advance rapidly ἐσύθη (it rushed). There was a famous Laconian whose name was Σοῦς (Rush), for this is the Laconian word for rapid motion. Now σοφία signifies the touching (ἐπαφή) of this rapid motion, the assumption being that things are in motion. And the word ἀγαθόν (good) is intended to denote the admirable (ἀγαστόν) in all nature. For since all things are in motion, they possess quickness and slowness; now

βραδυτής. ἔστιν οὖν οὐ πᾶν τὸ ταχύ, ἀλλὰ τὶ
αὐτοῦ ἀγαστόν. τοῦ θοοῦ[1] δὴ τῷ ἀγαστῷ αὕτη
ἡ ἐπωνυμία ἐστίν, τἀγαθόν.

27. Δικαιοσύνη δέ, ὅτι μὲν ἐπὶ τῇ τοῦ δικαίου
συνέσει τοῦτο κεῖται τὸ ὄνομα, ῥάδιον συμβαλεῖν·
αὐτὸ δὲ τὸ δίκαιον χαλεπόν. καὶ γὰρ δὴ καὶ ἔοικε
μέχρι μέν του ὁμολογεῖσθαι παρὰ πολλῶν, ἔπειτα
D δὲ ἀμφισβητεῖσθαι. ὅσοι γὰρ ἡγοῦνται τὸ πᾶν
εἶναι ἐν πορείᾳ,[2] τὸ μὲν πολὺ αὐτοῦ ὑπολαμ-
βάνουσιν τοιοῦτόν τι εἶναι οἷον οὐδὲν ἄλλο ἢ
χωρεῖν, διὰ δὲ τούτου παντὸς εἶναί τι διεξιόν,
δι' οὗ πάντα τὰ γιγνόμενα γίγνεσθαι· εἶναι δὲ
τάχιστον τοῦτο καὶ λεπτότατον. οὐ γὰρ ἂν
δύνασθαι ἄλλως διὰ τοῦ ὄντος ἰέναι παντός, εἰ
μὴ λεπτότατόν τε ἦν ὥστε αὐτὸ μηδὲν στέγειν,
καὶ τάχιστον ὥστε χρῆσθαι ὥσπερ ἑστῶσι τοῖς
ἄλλοις. ἐπεὶ δ' οὖν ἐπιτροπεύει τὰ ἄλλα πάντα
E διαϊόν, τοῦτο τὸ ὄνομα ἐκλήθη ὀρθῶς δίκαιον, εὐστομίας ἕνεκα τὴν τοῦ κάππα δύναμιν προσλα-
βόν. μέχρι μὲν οὖν ἐνταῦθα, ὃ νῦν δὴ ἐλέγομεν,
παρὰ πολλῶν ὁμολογεῖται τοῦτο εἶναι τὸ δίκαιον·
413 ἐγὼ δέ, ὦ Ἑρμόγενες, ἅτε λιπαρὴς ὢν περὶ αὐτοῦ,
ταῦτα μὲν πάντα διαπέπυσμαι ἐν ἀπορρήτοις, ὅτι
τοῦτ' ἔστι τὸ δίκαιον καὶ τὸ αἴτιον—δι' ὃ γὰρ
γίγνεται, τοῦτ' ἔστι τὸ αἴτιον—καὶ Δία[3] καλεῖν ἔφη
τις τοῦτο ὀρθῶς ἔχειν διὰ ταῦτα· ἐπειδὰν δ'
ἠρέμα αὐτοὺς ἐπανερωτῶ ἀκούσας ταῦτα μηδὲν
ἧττον, " Τί οὖν ποτ' ἔστιν, ὦ ἄριστε, δίκαιον, εἰ
τοῦτο οὕτως ἔχει; " δοκῶ τε ἤδη μακρότερα τοῦ

---

[1] τοῦ θοοῦ Baiter : τοῦτο οὗ ΒΤ.
[2] ἐν πορείᾳ liber Bessarionis : εὐπορίᾳ Β : εὐπορίᾳ Τ.
[3] Δία Hermann : ἰδίᾳ ΒΤ.

CRATYLUS

not all that is swift, but only part of it, is admirable ;
this name ἀγαθόν is therefore given to the admirable
(ἀγαστόν) part of the swift (θοοῦ). It is easy to
conjecture that the word δικαιοσύνη applies to the
understanding (σύνεσις) of the just (τοῦ δικαίου) ;
but the word δίκαιον (just) is itself difficult. Up to
a certain point, you see, many men seem to agree
about it, but beyond that they differ. For those
who think the universe is in motion believe that the
greater part of it is of such a nature as to be a mere
receptacle, and that there is some element which
passes through all this, by means of which all created
things are generated. And this element must be
very rapid and very subtle ; for it could not pass
through all the universe unless it were very subtle,
so that nothing could keep it out, and it must be
very swift, so that all other things are relatively at
rest. Since, then, it superintends and passes through
(διαϊόν) all other things, this is rightly called by
the name δίκαιον, the sound of the kappa being
added merely for the sake of euphony. Up to this
point, as I said just now, many men agree about
justice (δίκαιον) ; and I, Hermogenes, being very
much in earnest about it, have persistently asked
questions and have been told in secret teachings
that this is justice, or the cause—for that through
which creation takes place is a cause—and some one
told me that it was for this reason rightly called
Zeus (Δία). But when, after hearing this, I nevertheless ask them quietly, " What then, my most
excellent friend, if this is true, is justice ? " they
101

προσήκοντος ἐρωτᾶν καὶ ὑπὲρ τὰ ἐσκαμμένα ἅλ-
B λεσθαι. ἱκανῶς γάρ μέ φασι πεπύσθαι[1] καὶ ἐπι-
χειροῦσιν βουλόμενοι ἀποπιμπλάναι με ἄλλος ἄλλα
ἤδη λέγειν, καὶ οὐκέτι συμφωνοῦσιν. ὁ μὲν γὰρ
τίς φησιν τοῦτο εἶναι δίκαιον, τὸν ἥλιον· τοῦτον
γὰρ μόνον διαϊόντα καὶ κάοντα ἐπιτροπεύειν τὰ
ὄντα. ἐπειδὰν οὖν τῳ λέγω αὐτὸ ἄσμενος ὡς
καλόν τι ἀκηκοώς, καταγελᾷ μου οὗτος ἀκούσας
καὶ ἐρωτᾷ εἰ οὐδὲν δίκαιον οἶμαι εἶναι ἐν τοῖς
ἀνθρώποις ἐπειδὰν ὁ ἥλιος δύῃ. λιπαροῦντος οὖν
C ἐμοῦ ὅτι αὖ ἐκεῖνος λέγει αὐτό, τὸ πῦρ φησιν·
τοῦτο δὲ οὐ ῥᾴδιόν ἐστιν εἰδέναι· ὁ δὲ οὐκ αὐτὸ
τὸ πῦρ φησιν, ἀλλ' αὐτὸ τὸ θερμὸν τὸ ἐν τῷ πυρὶ
ἐνόν. ὁ δὲ τούτων μὲν πάντων καταγελᾶν φησιν.
εἶναι δὲ τὸ δίκαιον ὃ λέγει Ἀναξαγόρας, νοῦν
εἶναι τοῦτο· αὐτοκράτορα γὰρ αὐτὸν ὄντα καὶ
οὐδενὶ μεμιγμένον πάντα φησὶν αὐτὸν κοσμεῖν τὰ
πράγματα διὰ πάντων ἰόντα. ἐνταῦθα δὴ ἐγώ,
ὦ φίλε, πολὺ ἐν πλείονι ἀπορίᾳ εἰμὶ ἢ πρὶν ἐπι-
χειρῆσαι μανθάνειν περὶ τοῦ δικαίου ὅ τι ποτ'
D ἔστιν. ἀλλ' οὖν οὗπερ ἕνεκα ἐσκοποῦμεν, τό γε
ὄνομα τοῦτο φαίνεται αὐτῷ διὰ ταῦτα κεῖσθαι.

ΕΡΜ. Φαίνει μοι, ὦ Σώκρατες, ταῦτα μὲν ἀκηκοέναι του καὶ οὐκ αὐτοσχεδιάζειν.

ΣΩ. Τί δὲ τἆλλα;

ΕΡΜ. Οὐ πάνυ.

28. ΣΩ. Ἄκουε δή· ἴσως γὰρ ἄν σε καὶ τὰ
ἐπίλοιπα ἐξαπατήσαιμι ὡς οὐκ ἀκηκοὼς λέγω.
μετὰ γὰρ δικαιοσύνην τί ἡμῖν λείπεται; ἀνδρείαν,
E οἶμαι, οὔπω διήλθομεν. ἀδικία μὲν γὰρ δῆλον
ὅτι ἐστὶν ὄντως ἐμπόδισμα τοῦ διαϊόντος, ἀνδρεία

---

[1] πεπύσθαι Schanz : πεπύσθαι ἀκηκοέναι BT.

think I am asking too many questions and am leaping over the trenches.[1] They say I have been told enough ; they try to satisfy me by saying all sorts of different things, and they no longer agree. For one says the sun is justice, for the sun alone superintends all things, passing through and burning (διαϊόντα καὶ καίοντα) them. Then when I am pleased and tell this to some one, thinking it is a fine answer, he laughs at me and asks if I think there is no justice among men when the sun has set. So I beg him to tell me what he thinks it is, and he says " Fire." But this is not easy to understand. He says it is not actual fire, but heat in the abstract that is in the fire. Another man says he laughs at all these notions, and that justice is what Anaxagoras says it is, mind ; for mind, he says, is ruled only by itself, is mixed with nothing, orders all things, and passes through them. Then, my friend, I am far more perplexed than before I undertook to learn about the nature of justice. But I think the name—and that was the subject of our investigation —was given for the reasons I have mentioned.

HER. I think, Socrates, you must have heard this from some one and are not inventing it yourself.

SOC. And how about the rest of my talk ?

HER. I do not at all think you had heard that.

SOC. Listen then ; perhaps I may deceive you into thinking that all I am going to say is my own. What remains to consider after justice ? I think we have not yet discussed courage. It is plain enough that injustice (ἀδικία) is really a mere hindrance of that which passes through (τοῦ διαϊόντος),

---

[1] A trench was the limit of the leap for the pentathletes.

δὲ σημαίνει ὡς ἐν μάχῃ ἐπονομαζομένης τῆς
ἀνδρείας· μάχην δ' εἶναι ἐν τῷ ὄντι, εἴπερ ῥεῖ,
οὐκ ἄλλο τι ἢ τὴν ἐναντίαν ῥοήν· ἐὰν οὖν τις
ἐξέλῃ τὸ δέλτα τοῦ ὀνόματος τῆς ἀνδρείας, αὐτὸ
μηνύει τὸ ἔργον τὸ ὄνομα ἡ ἀνρεία. δῆλον οὖν
ὅτι οὐ πάσῃ ῥοῇ ἡ ἐναντία ῥοὴ ἀνδρεία ἐστίν, ἀλλὰ
414 τῇ παρὰ τὸ δίκαιον ῥεούσῃ· οὐ γὰρ ἂν ἐπῃνεῖτο
ἡ ἀνδρεία. καὶ τὸ ἄρρεν καὶ ὁ ἀνὴρ ἐπὶ παρα-
πλησίῳ τινὶ τούτῳ ἐστί, τῇ ἄνω ῥοῇ. γυνὴ δὲ
γονή μοι φαίνεται βούλεσθαι εἶναι. τὸ δὲ θῆλυ
ἀπὸ τῆς θηλῆς τι φαίνεται ἐπωνομάσθαι· ἡ δὲ
θηλὴ ἆρά γε, ὦ Ἑρμόγενες, ὅτι τεθηλέναι ποιεῖ
ὥσπερ τὰ ἀρδόμενα;

ΕΡΜ. Ἔοικέν γε, ὦ Σώκρατες.

ΣΩ. Καὶ μὴν αὐτό γε τὸ θάλλειν τὴν αὔξην μοι
δοκεῖ ἀπεικάζειν τὴν τῶν νέων, ὅτι ταχεῖα καὶ
B ἐξαιφνιδία γίγνεται. οἱόνπερ οὖν μεμίμηται τῷ
ὀνόματι, συναρμόσας ἀπὸ τοῦ θεῖν καὶ ἅλλεσθαι
τὸ ὄνομα. ἀλλ' οὐ γὰρ ἐπισκοπεῖς με ὥσπερ
ἐκτὸς δρόμου φερόμενον, ἐπειδὰν λείου ἐπιλά-
βωμαι· ἐπίλοιπα δὲ ἡμῖν ἔτι συχνὰ[1] τῶν δοκούν-
των σπουδαίων εἶναι.

ΕΡΜ. Ἀληθῆ λέγεις.

ΣΩ. Ὧν γ' ἔστιν ἓν καὶ τέχνην ἰδεῖν ὅ τι ποτὲ
βούλεται εἶναι. .

ΕΡΜ. Πάνυ μὲν οὖν.

ΣΩ. Οὐκοῦν τοῦτό γε ἕξιν νοῦ σημαίνει, τὸ μὲν
ταῦ ἀφελόντι, ἐμβαλόντι δὲ τὸ οὗ μεταξὺ τοῦ χῖ
C καὶ τοῦ νῦ καὶ τοῦ νῦ καὶ[2] τοῦ ἦτα;

---

[1] ἐπίλοιπα . . . συχνὰ Burnet : λοιπὰ . . . συχνὰ ἐπὶ BT
(ἐστι vulg.).
[2] τοῦ νῦ καὶ add. Stephanus.

CRATYLUS

but the word ἀνδρεία (courage) implies that courage got its name in battle, and if the universe is flowing, a battle in the universe can be nothing else than an opposite current or flow (ῥοή). Now if we remove the *delta* from the word ἀνδρεία, the word ἀνρεία signifies exactly that activity. Of course it is clear that not the current opposed to every current is courage, but only that opposed to the current which is contrary to justice ; for otherwise courage would not be praised. The words ἄρρεν (male) and ἀνήρ (man) refer, like ἀνδρεία, to the upward (ἄνω) current or flow. The word γυνή (woman) seems to me to be much the same as γονή (birth). I think θῆλυ (female) is derived from θηλή (teat) ; and is not θηλή, Hermogenes, so called because it makes things flourish (τεθηλέναι), like plants wet with showers ?

HER. Very likely, Socrates.

soc. And again, the word θάλλειν (flourish) seems to me to figure the rapid and sudden growth of the young. Something of that sort the name-giver has reproduced in the name, which he compounded of θεῖν (run) and ἄλλεσθαι (jump). You do not seem to notice how I rush along outside of the race-course, when I get on smooth ground. But we still have plenty of subjects left which seem to be serious.

HER. True.

soc. One of which is to see what the word τέχνη (art, science) means.

HER. Certainly.

soc. Does not this denote possession of mind, if you remove the tau and insert omicron between the chi and the nu and the nu and the eta (making ἐχονόη) ?

PLATO

ΕΡΜ. Καὶ μάλα γε γλίσχρως, ὦ Σώκρατες.

ΣΩ. Ὦ μακάριε, οὐκ οἶσθ' ὅτι τὰ πρῶτα ὀνόματα τεθέντα κατακέχωσται ἤδη ὑπὸ τῶν βου-
λομένων τραγῳδεῖν αὐτά, περιτιθέντων γράμματα καὶ ἐξαιρούντων εὐστομίας ἕνεκα καὶ πανταχῇ στρεφόντων καὶ ὑπὸ καλλωπισμοῦ καὶ ὑπὸ
χρόνου. ἐπεὶ ἐν τῷ κατόπτρῳ οὐ δοκεῖ σοι
ἄτοπον εἶναι τὸ ἐμβεβλῆσθαι τὸ ῥῶ; ἀλλὰ τοιαῦ-
D τα, οἶμαι, ποιοῦσιν οἱ τῆς μὲν ἀληθείας οὐδὲν
φροντίζοντες, τὸ δὲ στόμα πλάττοντες, ὥστ'
ἐπεμβάλλοντες πολλὰ ἐπὶ τὰ πρῶτα ὀνόματα
τελευτῶντες ποιοῦσιν μηδ' ἂν ἕνα ἀνθρώπων
συνεῖναι ὅ τι ποτὲ βούλεται τὸ ὄνομα· ὥσπερ καὶ
τὴν σφίγγα ἀντὶ φικός[1] σφίγγα καλοῦσιν, καὶ
ἄλλα πολλά.

ΕΡΜ. Ταῦτα μὲν ἔστιν οὕτως, ὦ Σώκρατες.

ΣΩ. Εἰ δ' αὖ τις ἐάσει καὶ ἐντιθέναι καὶ ἐξαιρεῖν
ἅττ' ἂν βούληταί τις εἰς τὰ ὀνόματα, πολλὴ εὐ-
πορία ἔσται καὶ πᾶν ἂν παντί τις ὄνομα πράγματι
προσαρμόσειεν.

E   ΕΡΜ. Ἀληθῆ λέγεις.

ΣΩ. Ἀληθῆ μέντοι. ἀλλὰ τὸ μέτριον, οἶμαι,
δεῖ φυλάττειν καὶ τὸ εἰκὸς σὲ τὸν σοφὸν ἐπιστάτην.

ΕΡΜ. Βουλοίμην ἄν.

29. ΣΩ. Καὶ ἐγώ σοι συμβούλομαι, ὦ Ἑρμό-
415 γενες. ἀλλὰ μὴ λίαν, ὦ δαιμόνιε, ἀκριβολογοῦ,
μή με ἀπογυιώσῃς μένεος. ἔρχομαι γὰρ ἐπὶ τὴν
κορυφὴν ὧν εἴρηκα, ἐπειδὰν μετὰ τέχνην μηχανὴν ἐπισκεψώμεθα. μηχανὴ γάρ μοι δοκεῖ τοῦ
ἄνειν ἐπὶ πολὺ σημεῖον εἶναι· τὸ γὰρ μῆκός πως
τὸ πολὺ σημαίνει· ἐξ ἀμφοῖν οὖν τούτοιν σύγ-

[1] φικὸς after Hesiod, Theog. 326 : σφιγγὸς B : φιγὸς T.

106

HER. It does it very poorly, Socrates.

soc. My friend, you do not bear in mind that the original words have before now been completely buried by those who wished to dress them up, for they have added and subtracted letters for the sake of euphony and have distorted the words in every way for ornamentation or merely in the lapse of time. Do you not, for instance, think it absurd that the letter rho is inserted in the word κάτοπτρον (mirror)? I think that sort of thing is the work of people who care nothing for truth, but only for the shape of their mouths; so they keep adding to the original words until finally no human being can understand what in the world the word means. So the sphinx, for instance, is called sphinx, instead of phix, and there are many other examples.

HER. Yes, that is true, Socrates.

soc. And if we are permitted to insert and remove any letters we please in words, it will be perfectly easy to fit any name to anything.

HER. True.

soc. Yes, quite true. But I think you, as a wise director, must observe the rule of moderation and probability.

HER. I should like to do so.

soc. And I, too, Hermogenes. But do not, my friend, demand too much precision, lest you " enfeeble me of my might."[1] For now that τέχνη (art) is disposed of, I am nearing the loftiest height of my subject, when once we have investigated μηχανή (contrivance). For I think μηχανή signifies ἄνειν ἐπὶ πολύ (much accomplishment); for μῆκος (length) has about the same meaning as τὸ πολύ (much),

---

[1] Homer, *Iliad*, vi. 265.

κεῖται, μήκους τε καὶ τοῦ ἄνειν, τὸ ὄνομα ἡ μηχανή. ἀλλ᾽, ὅπερ νῦν δὴ[1] εἶπον, ἐπὶ τὴν κορυφὴν
δεῖ τῶν εἰρημένων ἐλθεῖν· ἀρετὴ γὰρ καὶ κακία
ὅ τι βούλεται τὰ ὀνόματα ζητητέα. τὸ μὲν οὖν
B ἕτερον οὔπω καθορῶ, τὸ δ᾽ ἕτερον δοκεῖ μοι κατάδηλον εἶναι. συμφωνεῖ γὰρ τοῖς ἔμπροσθεν πᾶσιν.
ἅτε γὰρ ἰόντων τῶν πραγμάτων, πᾶν τὸ κακῶς
ἰὸν κακία ἂν εἴη· τοῦτο δὲ ὅταν ἐν ψυχῇ ᾖ τὸ
κακῶς ἰέναι ἐπὶ τὰ πράγματα, μάλιστα τὴν τοῦ
ὅλου ἐπωνυμίαν ἔχει τῆς κακίας. τὸ δὲ κακῶς
ἰέναι ὅ τι ποτ᾽ ἔστιν, δοκεῖ μοι δηλοῦν καὶ ἐν τῇ
δειλίᾳ, ὃ οὔπω διήλθομεν ἀλλ᾽ ὑπερέβημεν, δέον
C αὐτὸ μετὰ τὴν ἀνδρείαν σκέψασθαι· δοκοῦμεν δέ
μοι καὶ ἄλλα πολλὰ ὑπερβεβηκέναι. ἡ δ᾽ οὖν
δειλία τῆς ψυχῆς σημαίνει δεσμὸν εἶναι ἰσχυρόν·
τὸ γὰρ λίαν ἰσχύς τίς ἐστιν· δεσμὸς οὖν ὁ λίαν
καὶ ὁ μέγιστος τῆς ψυχῆς ἡ δειλία ἂν εἴη· ὥσπερ
γε καὶ ἡ ἀπορία κακόν, καὶ πᾶν, ὡς ἔοικεν, ὅ τι
ἂν ἐμποδὼν ᾖ τῷ ἰέναι[2] καὶ πορεύεσθαι. τοῦτ᾽
οὖν φαίνεται τὸ κακῶς ἰέναι δηλοῦν, τὸ ἰσχομένως
τε καὶ ἐμποδιζομένως πορεύεσθαι, ὃ δὴ ψυχὴ
ὅταν ἔχῃ, κακία μεστὴ γίγνεται. εἰ δ᾽ ἐπὶ τοιούτοις ἡ κακία ἐστὶν τοὔνομα, τοὐναντίον τούτου
ἡ ἀρετὴ ἂν εἴη, σημαῖνον πρῶτον μὲν εὐπορίαν,
D ἔπειτα δὲ λελυμένην τὴν ῥοὴν τῆς ἀγαθῆς ψυχῆς
εἶναι ἀεί, ὥστε τὸ ἀσχέτως καὶ τὸ ἀκωλύτως
ἀεὶ ῥέον ἐπωνυμίαν εἴληφεν, ὡς ἔοικε, τοῦτο

[1] νῦν δή] δὴ νῦν BT.   [2] ἰέναι b: εἶναι BT.

CRATYLUS

and the name μηχανή is composed of these two,
μῆκος and ἄνειν. But, as I was just saying, we
must go on to the loftiest height of our subject;
we must search for the meaning of the words ἀρετή
(virtue) and κακία (wickedness). Now one of them
I cannot yet see; but the other seems to be quite
clear, since it agrees with everything we have said
before. For inasmuch as all things are in motion,
everything that moves badly (κακῶς ἰόν) would be
evil (κακία); and when this evil motion in relation
to its environment exists in the soul, it receives the
general name κακία (evil) in the special sense of
wickedness. But the nature of evil motion (κακῶς
ἰέναι) is made clear, I think, also in the word δειλία
(cowardice), which we have not yet discussed. We
passed it by, when we ought to have examined it
after ἀνδρεία (courage); and I fancy we passed over
a good many other words. Now the meaning of
δειλία is " a strong bond of the soul "; for λίαν
(excessively) is, in a way, expressive of strength ;
so δειλία would be the excessive or greatest bond
(δεσμός, δεῖν) of the soul; and so, too, ἀπορία
(perplexity) is an evil, as is everything, apparently,
which hinders motion and progress (πορεύεσθαι).
This, then, seems to be the meaning of evil motion
(κακῶς ἰέναι), that advance is halting and impeded ;
and the soul that is infected by it becomes filled
with wickedness (κακία). If these are the reasons
for the name of wickedness, virtue (ἀρετή) would
be the opposite of this ; it would signify first ease
of motion, and secondly that the flow of the good
soul is always unimpeded, and therefore it has
received this name, which designates that which
always flows (ἀεὶ ῥέον) without let or hindrance.

109

τοὔνομα. ὀρθῶς μὲν ἔχει ἀειρείτην καλεῖν, ἴσως
δὲ αἱρετὴν λέγει, ὡς οὔσης ταύτης τῆς ἔξεως
αἱρετωτάτης· συγκεκρότηται δὲ καὶ καλεῖται ἀρετή.
καὶ ἴσως με αὖ φήσεις πλάττειν· ἐγὼ δέ φημι,
εἴπερ ὃ ἔμπροσθεν εἶπον ὀρθῶς ἔχει, ἡ κακία,
Ε καὶ τοῦτο τὸ ὄνομα τὴν ἀρετὴν ὀρθῶς ἔχειν.

416 ΕΡΜ. Τὸ δὲ δὴ κακόν, δι' οὗ πολλὰ τῶν ἔμπροσθεν
εἴρηκας, τί ἂν νοοῖ τοὔνομα;

ΣΩ. Ἄτοπόν τι νὴ Δία ἔμοιγε δοκεῖ καὶ χαλεπὸν συμβαλεῖν. ἐπάγω οὖν καὶ τούτῳ ἐκείνην τὴν
μηχανήν.

ΕΡΜ. Ποίαν ταύτην;

ΣΩ. Τὴν τοῦ βαρβαρικόν τι καὶ τοῦτο φάναι εἶναι.

ΕΡΜ. Καὶ ἔοικάς γε ὀρθῶς λέγοντι. ἀλλ' εἰ
δοκεῖ, ταῦτα μὲν ἐῶμεν, τὸ δὲ καλὸν καὶ τὸ αἰσχρὸν πειρώμεθα ἰδεῖν πῇ εὐλόγως ἔχει.

ΣΩ. Τὸ μὲν τοίνυν αἰσχρὸν καὶ δὴ κατάδηλόν
Β μοι φαίνεται ὃ νοεῖ· καὶ τοῦτο γὰρ τοῖς ἔμπροσθεν ὁμολογεῖται. τὸ γὰρ ἐμποδίζον καὶ ἴσχον
τῆς ῥοῆς τὰ ὄντα λοιδορεῖν μοι φαίνεται διὰ
παντὸς ὁ τὰ ὀνόματα τιθείς, καὶ νῦν τῷ ἀεὶ ἴσχοντι
τὸν ῥοῦν τοῦτο τὸ ὄνομα ἔθετο ἀεισχοροῦν· νῦν
δὲ συγκροτήσαντες αἰσχρὸν καλοῦσιν.

ΕΡΜ. Τί δὲ τὸ καλόν;

ΣΩ. Τοῦτο χαλεπώτερον κατανοῆσαι· καίτοι λέγει[1] γε αὐτό· ἁρμονίᾳ μόνον καὶ μήκει τοῦ οὗ
παρῆκται.

C ΕΡΜ. Πῶς δή;

ΣΩ. Τῆς διανοίας τις ἔοικεν ἐπωνυμία εἶναι
τοῦτο τὸ ὄνομα.

ΕΡΜ. Πῶς λέγεις;

[1] λέγει ΒΤ : λέγουσι G.

110

It is properly called ἀειρειτή, or perhaps also αἱρετή, indicating that this condition is especially to be chosen ; but it has been compressed and is pronounced ἀρετή. Perhaps you will say this is another invention of mine ; but I say if what I said just now about κακία is right, this about the name of ἀρετή is right too.

HER. But what is the meaning of the word κακόν which you used in many of your derivations ?

SOC. By Zeus, I think it is a strange word and hard to understand ; so I apply to it that contrivance of mine.

HER. What contrivance ?

SOC. The claim of foreign origin, which I advance in this case as in those others.

HER. Well, probably you are right. But, if you please, let us drop these words and try to discover the reasons for the words καλόν (beautiful, noble) and αἰσχρόν (base).

SOC. I think the meaning of αἰσχρόν is clear, and this also agrees with what has been said before. For the giver of names appears to me throughout to denounce that which hinders and restrains things from flowing, and in this instance he gave to that which always restrains the flow (ἀεὶ ἴσχει τὸν ῥοῦν) this name ἀεισχοροῦν, which is now compressed and pronounced αἰσχρόν.

HER. What about καλόν ?

SOC. That is harder to understand, and yet it expresses its meaning : it has been altered merely in accent and in the length of the o.

HER. How is that ?

SOC. I think this word denotes intellect.

HER. What do you mean ?

ΣΩ. Φέρε, τί οἴει σὺ εἶναι τὸ αἴτιον κληθῆναι ἑκάστῳ τῶν ὄντων; ἆρ' οὐκ ἐκεῖνο τὸ τὰ ὀνόματα θέμενον;

ΕΡΜ. Πάντως που.

ΣΩ. Οὐκοῦν διάνοια ἂν εἴη τοῦτο ἤτοι θεῶν ἢ ἀνθρώπων ἢ ἀμφότερα;

ΕΡΜ. Ναί.

ΣΩ. Οὐκοῦν τὸ καλέσαν τὰ πράγματα καὶ τὸ καλοῦν[1] ταὐτόν ἐστιν τοῦτο, διάνοια;

ΕΡΜ. Φαίνεται.

ΣΩ. Οὐκοῦν καὶ ὅσα μὲν ἂν νοῦς τε καὶ διάνοια ἐργάσηται, ταῦτά ἐστι τὰ ἐπαινετά, ἃ[2] δὲ μή, ψεκτά;

ΕΡΜ. Πάνυ γε.

D ΣΩ. Τὸ οὖν ἰατρικὸν ἰατρικὰ ἐργάζεται καὶ τὸ τεκτονικὸν τεκτονικά; ἢ πῶς λέγεις;

ΕΡΜ. Οὕτως ἔγωγε.

ΣΩ. Καὶ τὸ καλὸν ἄρα καλά;

ΕΡΜ. Δεῖ γέ τοι.

ΣΩ. Ἔστι δέ γε τοῦτο, ὥς φαμεν, διάνοια;

ΕΡΜ. Πάνυ γε.

ΣΩ. Ὀρθῶς ἄρα φρονήσεως αὕτη ἡ ἐπωνυμία ἐστὶν τὸ καλὸν τῆς τὰ τοιαῦτα ἀπεργαζομένης, ἃ δὴ καλὰ φάσκοντες εἶναι ἀσπαζόμεθα.

ΕΡΜ. Φαίνεται.

E 30. ΣΩ. Τί οὖν ἔτι ἡμῖν λοιπὸν τῶν τοιούτων;

ΕΡΜ. Ταῦτα τὰ περὶ τὸ ἀγαθόν τε καὶ καλόν, 417 συμφέροντά τε καὶ λυσιτελοῦντα καὶ ὠφέλιμα καὶ κερδαλέα καὶ τἀναντία τούτων.

ΣΩ. Οὐκοῦν τὸ μὲν συμφέρον ἤδη που κἂν σὺ

---

[1] καλοῦν Badham: καλὸν BT.   [2] ἃ Heindorf: τὰ BT.

112

soc. Why, what do you think is the cause why anything is called by a name? Is it not the power which gave the name?

her. Why, certainly.

soc. And is not that power the intellect either of gods or of men or both?

her. Yes.

soc. Are not that which called things by name and that which calls them by name (τὸ καλοῦν) the same thing, namely intellect?

her. Yes, clearly.

soc. And are not all works which are done by mind and intelligence worthy of praise, and those that are not done by them worthy of blame?

her. Certainly.

soc. Does not the medical power perform medical works and the power of carpentry works of carpentry? Do you agree to that?

her. I agree.

soc. And the beautiful performs beautiful works?

her. It must do so.

soc. And the beautiful is, we say, intellect?

her. Certainly.

soc. Then this name, the beautiful, is rightly given to mind, since it accomplishes the works which we call beautiful and in which we delight.

her. Evidently.

soc. What further words of this sort are left for us?

her. Those that are related to the good and the beautiful, such as συμφέροντα (advantageous), λυσιτελοῦντα (profitable), ὠφέλιμα (useful), κερδαλέα (gainful), and their opposites.

soc. You might by this time be able to find the

113

εὕροις ἐκ τῶν πρότερον ἐπισκοπῶν· τῆς γὰρ
ἐπιστήμης ἀδελφόν τι φαίνεται. οὐδὲν γὰρ ἄλλο
δηλοῖ ἢ τὴν ἅμα φορὰν τῆς ψυχῆς μετὰ τῶν
πραγμάτων, καὶ τὰ ὑπὸ τοῦ τοιούτου πραττόμενα
συμφέροντά τε καὶ σύμφορα κεκλῆσθαι ἀπὸ τοῦ
συμπεριφέρεσθαι ἔοικε. τὸ δέ γε κερδαλέον ἀπὸ
B τοῦ κέρδους. κέρδος δὲ νῦ ἀντὶ τοῦ δέλτα ἀπο-
διδόντι ἐς τὸ ὄνομα δηλοῖ ὃ βούλεται· τὸ γὰρ
ἀγαθὸν κατ' ἄλλον τρόπον ὀνομάζει. ὅτι γὰρ
κεράννυται ἐς πάντα διεξιόν, ταύτην αὐτοῦ τὴν
δύναμιν ἐπονομάζων ἔθετο τοὔνομα· δέλτα δ'[1]
ἐνθεὶς ἀντὶ τοῦ νῦ κέρδος ἐφθέγξατο.

ΕΡΜ. Λυσιτελοῦν δὲ τί δή;

ΣΩ. Ἔοικεν, ὦ Ἑρμόγενες, οὐχὶ καθάπερ οἱ
κάπηλοι αὐτῷ χρῶνται, ἐὰν τὸ ἀνάλωμα ἀπολύῃ
C οὐ ταύτῃ λέγειν μοι δοκεῖ τὸ λυσιτελοῦν, ἀλλ' ὅτι
τάχιστον ὂν τοῦ ὄντος ἵστασθαι οὐκ ἐᾷ τὰ πράγματα, οὐδὲ τέλος λαβοῦσαν τὴν φορὰν τοῦ φέρεσθαι
στῆναί τε καὶ παύσασθαι, ἀλλ' ἀεὶ λύει αὐτῆς,
ἄν τι ἐπιχειρῇ τέλος ἐγγίγνεσθαι, καὶ παρέχει
ἄπαυστον καὶ ἀθάνατον αὐτήν· ταύτῃ μοι δοκεῖ
ἐπιφημίσαι τὸ ἀγαθὸν λυσιτελοῦν· τὸ γὰρ τῆς
φορᾶς λύον τὸ τέλος λυσιτελοῦν καλέσαι. ὠφέλιμον δὲ ξενικὸν τοὔνομα, ᾧ καὶ Ὅμηρος πολλαχοῦ κέχρηται, τῷ ὀφέλλειν· ἔστι δὲ τοῦτο τοῦ
αὔξειν καὶ ποιεῖν ἐπωνυμία.

D 31. ΕΡΜ. Τὰ δὲ δὴ τούτων ἐναντία πῶς ἔχει
ἡμῖν;

ΣΩ. Ὅσα μὲν ἀπόφησιν αὐτῶν, ὥς γέ μοι
δοκεῖ, οὐδὲν δεῖ ταῦτα διεξιέναι.

---

[1] δ' add. Becker: om. BT.

CRATYLUS

meaning of συμφέρον by yourself in the light of the
previous explanations, for it appears to be own
brother to ἐπιστήμη. It means nothing else but
the motion (φορά) of the soul in company with the
world, and naturally things which are done by such
a power are called συμφέροντα and σύμφορα because
they are carried round with (συμπεριφέρεσθαι) the
world. But κερδαλέον is from κέρδος (gain). If
you restore nu in the word κέρδος in place of the
delta, the meaning is plain ; it signifies good, but in
another way. Because it passes through and is
mingled (κεράννυται) with all things, he who named
it gave it this name which indicates that function ;
but he inserted a delta instead of nu and said κέρδος.

HER. And what is λυσιτελοῦν ?

SOC. I do not think, Hermogenes, the name-giver
gives the meaning to λυσιτελοῦν which it has in
the language of tradesfolk, when profit sets free
(ἀπολύει) the sum invested, but he means that
because it is the swiftest thing in the world it does
not allow things to remain at rest and does not allow
the motion to come to any end (τέλος) of movement
or to stop or pause, but always, if any end of the
motion is attempted, it sets it free, making it
unceasing and immortal. It is in this sense, I think,
that the good is dubbed λυσιτελοῦν, for it frees
(λύει) the end (τέλος) of the motion. But the
word ὠφέλιμον is a foreign one, which Homer often
uses in the verbal form ὀφέλλειν. This is a synonym
of " increase " and " create."

HER. What shall be our explanations of the
opposites of these ?

SOC. Those of them that are mere negatives,
need, I think, no discussion.

ΕΡΜ. Ποῖα ταῦτα;

ΣΩ. Ἀσύμφορον καὶ ἀνωφελὲς καὶ ἀλυσιτελὲς καὶ ἀκερδές.

ΕΡΜ. Ἀληθῆ λέγεις.

ΣΩ. Ἀλλὰ βλαβερόν γε καὶ ζημιῶδες.

ΕΡΜ. Ναί.

ΣΩ. Καὶ τὸ μέν γε βλαβερὸν τὸ βλάπτον τὸν E ῥοῦν εἶναι λέγει· τὸ δὲ βλάπτον αὖ σημαίνει βουλό-μενον ἅπτειν· τὸ δὲ ἅπτειν καὶ δεῖν ταὐτόν ἐστι, τοῦτο δὲ πανταχοῦ ψέγει. τὸ βουλόμενον οὖν ἅπτειν ῥοῦν ὀρθότατα μὲν ἂν εἴη βουλαπτεροῦν, καλλωπισθὲν δὲ καλεῖσθαί μοι φαίνεται βλαβερόν.

ΕΡΜ. Ποικίλα γέ σοι, ὦ Σώκρατες, ἐκβαίνει τὰ ὀνόματα. καὶ γὰρ νῦν μοι ἔδοξας ὥσπερ τοῦ τῆς Ἀθηνάας νόμου προαύλιον στομαυλῆσαι, τοῦτο 418 τὸ ὄνομα προειπὼν τὸ βουλαπτεροῦν.

ΣΩ. Οὐκ ἔγωγε, ὦ Ἑρμόγενες, αἴτιος, ἀλλ᾽ οἱ θέμενοι τὸ ὄνομα.

ΕΡΜ. Ἀληθῆ λέγεις· ἀλλὰ δὴ τὸ ζημιῶδες τί ἂν εἴη;

ΣΩ. Τί δ᾽ ἂν εἴη ποτὲ ζημιῶδες; θέασαι, ὦ Ἑρμόγενες, ὡς ἐγὼ ἀληθῆ λέγω λέγων ὅτι προσ-τιθέντες γράμματα καὶ ἐξαιροῦντες σφόδρα ἀλ-λοιοῦσι τὰς τῶν ὀνομάτων διανοίας, οὕτως ὥστε σμικρὰ πάνυ παραστρέφοντες ἐνίοτε τἀναντία B ποιεῖν σημαίνειν· οἷον καὶ ἐν τῷ δέοντι· ἐνενόησα γὰρ αὐτὸ καὶ ἀνεμνήσθην ἄρτι ἀπὸ τοῦδε, ὃ ἔμελλόν σοι ἐρεῖν, ὅτι ἡ μὲν νέα φωνὴ ἡμῖν ἡ καλὴ αὕτη καὶ τοὐναντίον περιέτρεψε μηνύειν τὸ

116

CRATYLUS

HER. Which are those?

soc. Disadvantageous, useless, unprofitable, and ungainful.

HER. True.

soc. But βλαβερόν (harmful) and ζημιῶδες (hurtful) do need it.

HER. Yes.

soc. And βλαβερόν means that which harms (βλάπτον) the flow (ῥοῦν); but βλάπτον means "wishing to fasten" (ἅπτειν), and ἅπτειν is the same thing as δεῖν (bind), which the name-giver constantly finds fault with. Now τὸ βουλόμενον ἅπτειν ῥοῦν (that which wishes to fasten the flow) would most correctly be called βουλαπτεροῦν, but is called βλαβερόν merely, as I think, to make it prettier.

HER. Elaborate names these are, Socrates, that result from your method. Just now, when you pronounced βουλαπτεροῦν, you looked as if you had made up your mouth to whistle the flute-prelude of the hymn to Athena.

soc. Not I, Hermogenes, am responsible, but those who gave the name.

HER. True. Well, what is the origin of ζημιῶδες?

soc. What can the origin of ζημιῶδες be? See, Hermogenes, how true my words are when I say that by adding and taking away letters people alter the sense of words so that even by very slight changes they sometimes make them mean the opposite of what they meant before; as, for instance, in the case of the word δέον (obligation, right), for that just occurred to me and I was reminded of it by what I was going to say to you, that this fine modern language of ours has turned δέον and also ζημιῶδες round, so that each has the

117

δέον καὶ τὸ ζημιῶδες, ἀφανίζουσα ὅ τι νοεῖ, ἡ
δὲ παλαιὰ ἀμφότερον δηλοῖ ὃ βούλεται τοὔνομα.

ΕΡΜ. Πῶς λέγεις;

ΣΩ. Ἐγώ σοι ἐρῶ. οἶσθα ὅτι οἱ παλαιοὶ οἱ
ἡμέτεροι τῷ ἰῶτα καὶ τῷ δέλτα εὖ μάλα ἐχρῶντο,
C καὶ οὐχ ἥκιστα αἱ γυναῖκες, αἵπερ μάλιστα τὴν
ἀρχαίαν φωνὴν σῴζουσι. νῦν δὲ ἀντὶ μὲν τοῦ ἰῶτα
ἢ εἶ ἢ ἦτα μεταστρέφουσιν, ἀντὶ δὲ τοῦ δέλτα
ζῆτα, ὡς δὴ μεγαλοπρεπέστερα ὄντα.

ΕΡΜ. Πῶς δή;

ΣΩ. Οἷον οἱ μὲν ἀρχαιότατοι ἱμέραν τὴν ἡμέραν
ἐκάλουν, οἱ δὲ ἐμέραν, οἱ δὲ νῦν ἡμέραν.

ΕΡΜ. Ἔστι ταῦτα.

ΣΩ. Οἶσθα οὖν ὅτι μόνον τοῦτο δηλοῖ τὸ ἀρχαῖον ὄνομα τὴν διάνοιαν τοῦ θεμένου; ὅτι γὰρ
ἀσμένοις τοῖς ἀνθρώποις καὶ ἱμείρουσιν ἐκ τοῦ
D σκότους τὸ φῶς ἐγίγνετο, ταύτῃ ὠνόμασαν ἱμέραν.[1]

ΕΡΜ. Φαίνεται.

ΣΩ. Νῦν δέ γε τετραγῳδημένον οὐδ' ἂν κατα-
νοήσαις ὅ τι βούλεται ἡ ἡμέρα. καίτοι τινὲς
οἴονται, ὡς δὴ ἡ ἡμέρα ἥμερα ποιεῖ, διὰ ταῦτα
ὠνομάσθαι αὐτὴν οὕτως.

ΕΡΜ. Δοκεῖ μοι.

ΣΩ. Καὶ τό γε ζυγὸν οἶσθα ὅτι δυογὸν οἱ παλαιοὶ
ἐκάλουν.

ΕΡΜ. Πάνυ γε.

ΣΩ. Καὶ τὸ μέν γε ζυγὸν οὐδὲν δηλοῖ, τὸ δὲ τοῖν
E δυοῖν ἕνεκα τῆς δέσεως ἐς τὴν ἀγωγὴν ἐπωνόμασται δυογὸν δικαίως· νῦν δὲ ζυγόν. καὶ ἄλλα
πάμπολλα οὕτως ἔχει.

---

[1] ἱμέραν dt : ἡμέραν BT.

CRATYLUS

opposite of its original meaning, whereas the ancient language shows clearly the real sense of both words.

HER. What do you mean?

SOC. I will tell you. You know that our ancestors made good use of the sounds of iota and delta, and that is especially true of the women, who are most addicted to preserving old forms of speech. But nowadays people change iota to eta or epsilon, and delta to zeta, thinking they have a grander sound.

HER. How is that?

SOC. For instance, in the earliest times they called day ἱμέρα, others said ἑμέρα, and now they say ἡμέρα.

HER. That is true.

SOC. Only the ancient word discloses the intention of the name-giver, don't you know? For day comes out of darkness to men; they welcome it and long (ἱμείρουσι) for it, and so they called it ἱμέρα.

HER. That is clear.

SOC. But now ἡμέρα is masquerading so that you could not guess its meaning. Why, some people think day is called ἡμέρα because it makes things gentle (ἥμερα).

HER. I believe they do.

SOC. And you know the ancients called ζυγόν (yoke) δυογόν.

HER. Certainly.

SOC. And ζυγόν conveys no clear meaning, but the name δυογόν is quite properly given to that which binds two together for the purpose of draught; now, however, we say ζυγόν. There are a great many other such instances.

PLATO

ΕΡΜ. Φαίνεται.

ΣΩ. Κατὰ ταῦτα τοίνυν πρῶτον μὲν τὸ δέον οὕτω λεγόμενον τοὐναντίον σημαίνει πᾶσι τοῖς περὶ τὸ ἀγαθὸν ὀνόμασιν· ἀγαθοῦ γὰρ ἰδέα οὖσα τὸ δέον φαίνεται δεσμὸς εἶναι καὶ κώλυμα φορᾶς, ὥσπερ ἀδελφὸν ὂν τοῦ βλαβεροῦ.

ΕΡΜ. Καὶ μάλα, ὦ Σώκρατες, οὕτω φαίνεται.

ΣΩ. Ἀλλ' οὐκ ἐὰν τῷ ἀρχαίῳ ὀνόματι χρῇ, ὃ 419 πολὺ μᾶλλον εἰκός ἐστιν ὀρθῶς κεῖσθαι ἢ τὸ νῦν, ἀλλ' ὁμολογήσει τοῖς πρόσθεν ἀγαθοῖς, ἐὰν ἀντὶ τοῦ εἶ τὸ ἰῶτα ἀποδιδῷς, ὥσπερ τὸ παλαιόν· διὸν γὰρ αὖ σημαίνει, ἀλλ' οὐ δέον, τἀγαθόν, ὅπερ δὴ ἐπαινεῖ. καὶ οὕτω οὐκ ἐναντιοῦται αὐτὸς αὑτῷ ὁ τὰ ὀνόματα τιθέμενος, ἀλλὰ δέον καὶ ὠφέλιμον καὶ λυσιτελοῦν καὶ κερδαλέον καὶ ἀγαθὸν καὶ ξυμφέρον καὶ εὔπορον τὸ αὐτὸ φαίνεται, ἑτέροις ὀνόμασι σημαῖνον τὸ διακοσμοῦν καὶ ἰὸν[1] πανταχοῦ ἐγκεκω-
B μιασμένον, τὸ δὲ ἴσχον καὶ δοῦν ψεγόμενον. καὶ δὴ καὶ τὸ ζημιῶδες, ἐὰν κατὰ τὴν ἀρχαίαν φωνὴν ἀποδῷς ἀντὶ τοῦ ζῆτα δέλτα, φανεῖταί σοι κεῖσθαι τὸ ὄνομα ἐπὶ τῷ δοῦντι τὸ ἰόν, ἐπονομασθὲν δημι-ῶδες.

32. ΕΡΜ. Τί δὲ δὴ ἡδονὴ καὶ λύπη καὶ ἐπιθυμία καὶ τὰ τοιαῦτα, ὦ Σώκρατες;

ΣΩ. Οὐ πάνυ χαλεπά μοι φαίνεται, ὦ Ἑρμόγενες. ἥ τε γὰρ ἡδονή, ἡ πρὸς τὴν ὄνησιν ἔοικε τείνουσα πρᾶξις τοῦτο ἔχειν τὸ ὄνομα—τὸ δέλτα δὲ ἔγκειται, ὥστε ἡδονὴ ἀντὶ ἡονῆς καλεῖται—ἥ τε λύπη ἀπὸ

_____
[1] ἰὸν Bekker: ὂν ΒΤ.

120

HER. Yes, that is plain.

soc. Similarly the word δέον (obligation) at first, when spoken in this way, denotes the opposite of all words connected with the good ; for although it is a form of good, δέον seems to be a bond (δεσμός) and hindrance of motion, own brother, as it were, to βλαβερόν.

HER. Yes, Socrates, it certainly does seem so.

soc. But it does not, if you employ the ancient word, which is more likely to be right than the present one. You will find that it agrees with the previous words for " good," if instead of the epsilon you restore the iota, as it was in old times ; for διόν (going through), not δέον, signifies good, which the name-giver praises. And so the giver of names does not contradict himself, but δέον (obligation, right), ὠφέλιμον (useful), λυσιτελοῦν (profitable), κερδαλέον (gainful), ἀγαθόν (good), ξυμφέρον (advantageous), and εὔπορον (prosperous), are plainly identical, signifying under different names the principle of arrangement and motion which has constantly been praised, whereas the principle of constraint and bondage is found fault with. And likewise in the case of ζημιῶδες, if you restore the ancient delta in place of the zeta, you will see that the name, pronounced δημιῶδες, was given to that which binds motion (δοῦντι τὸ ἰόν).

HER. What of ἡδονή (pleasure) and λύπη (pain) and ἐπιθυμία (desire), and the like, Socrates ?

soc. I do not think they are at all difficult, Hermogenes, for ἡδονή appears to have this name because it is the action that tends towards advantage (ἡ πρὸς τὴν ὄνησιν τείνουσα) ; the delta is inserted, so that we say ἡδονή instead of ἡονή. Λύπη appears to

PLATO

C τῆς διαλύσεως τοῦ σώματος ἔοικεν ἐπωνομάσθαι, ἣν ἐν τούτῳ τῷ πάθει ἴσχει τὸ σῶμα. καὶ ἥ γε ἀνία τὸ ἐμποδίζον τοῦ ἰέναι. ἡ δὲ ἀλγηδὼν ξενικόν τι φαίνεταί μοι, ἀπὸ τοῦ ἀλγεινοῦ ὠνομασμένον. ὀδύνη δὲ ἀπὸ τῆς ἐνδύσεως τῆς λύπης κεκλημένη[1] ἔοικεν. ἀχθηδὼν δέ, καὶ παντὶ δῆλον ἀπεικασμένον τὸ ὄνομα τῷ τῆς φορᾶς βάρει. χαρὰ δὲ τῇ διαχύσει καὶ εὐπορίᾳ τῆς ῥοῆς τῆς ψυχῆς ἔοικε κεκλημένη.[1]

D τέρψις δὲ ἀπὸ τοῦ τερπνοῦ· τὸ δὲ τερπνὸν ἀπὸ τῆς διὰ τῆς ψυχῆς ἕρψεως πνοῇ ἀπεικασθὲν κέκληται, ἐν δίκῃ μὲν ἂν ἕρπνουν καλούμενον, ὑπὸ χρόνου δὲ τερπνὸν παρηγμένον. εὐφροσύνη δὲ οὐδὲν προσδεῖται τοῦ διότι ῥηθῆναι· παντὶ γὰρ δῆλον ὅτι ἀπὸ τοῦ εὖ τοῖς πράγμασι τὴν ψυχὴν ξυμφέρεσθαι τοῦτο ἔλαβε τὸ ὄνομα, εὐφεροσύνην,[2] τό γε δίκαιον· ὅμως δὲ αὐτὸ καλοῦμεν εὐφροσύνην. οὐδ᾽ ἐπιθυμία

E χαλεπόν· τῇ γὰρ ἐπὶ τὸν θυμὸν ἰούσῃ δυνάμει δῆλον ὅτι τοῦτο ἐκλήθη τὸ ὄνομα· θυμὸς δὲ ἀπὸ τῆς θύσεως καὶ ζέσεως τῆς ψυχῆς ἔχοι ἂν τοῦτο τὸ ὄνομα. ἀλλὰ μὴν ἵμερός γε τῷ μάλιστα ἕλκοντι τὴν ψυχὴν ῥῷ ἐπωνομάσθη· ὅτι γὰρ ἰέμενος ῥεῖ

420 καὶ ἐφιέμενος τῶν πραγμάτων, καὶ οὕτω δὴ ἐπισπᾷ σφόδρα τὴν ψυχὴν διὰ τὴν ἕσιν τῆς ῥοῆς, ἀπὸ ταύτης οὖν πάσης τῆς δυνάμεως ἵμερος ἐκλήθη. καὶ μὴν πόθος αὖ καλεῖται σημαίνων οὐ τοῦ παρόντος εἶναι,[3] ἀλλὰ τοῦ ἄλλοθί που ὄντος καὶ ἀπόντος, ὅθεν πόθος ἐπωνόμασται, ὃς τότε, ὅταν

---

[1] κεκλημένῃ Stallbaum : κεκλημένη BT.
[2] εὐφεροσύνην Bekker : εὐφροσύνην B : ἐφερωσυνην T.
[3] After εἶναι the words ἱμέρου καὶ ῥεύματος (longing and stream) of the mss. are bracketed by Ast and others.

CRATYLUS

have received its name from the dissolution (διάλυσις) of the body which takes place through pain. Ἀνία (sorrow) is that which hinders motion (ἰέναι). Ἀλγηδών (distress) is, I think, a foreign word, derived from ἀλγεινός (distressing). Ὀδύνη (grief) appears to be so called from the putting on of pain (τῆς ἐνδύσεως τῆς λύπης). Ἀχθηδών (vexation) has a name, as anyone can see, made in the likeness of the weight (ἄχθος, burden) which vexation imposes upon motion. Χαρά (joy) seems to have its name from the plenteous diffusion (διάχυσις) of the flow of the soul. Τέρψις (delight) is from τερπνόν (delightful); and τερπνόν is called from the creeping (ἕρψις) of the soul, which is likened to a breath (πνοή), and would properly be called ἕρπνουν, but the name has been changed in course of time to τερπνόν. Εὐφροσύνη (mirth) needs no explanation, for it is clear to anyone that from the motion of the soul in harmony (εὖ) with the universe, it received the name εὐφεροσύνη, as it rightfully is ; but we call it εὐφροσύνη. Nor is there any difficulty about ἐπιθυμία (desire), for this name was evidently given to the power that goes (ἰοῦσα) into the soul (θυμός). And θυμός has its name from the raging (θύσις) and boiling of the soul. The name ἵμερος (longing) was given to the stream (ῥοῦς) which most draws the soul ; for because it flows with a rush (ἰέμενος) and with a desire for things and thus draws the soul on through the impulse of its flowing, all this power gives it the name of ἵμερος. And the word πόθος (yearning) signifies that it pertains not to that which is present, but to that which is elsewhere (ἄλλοθί που) or absent, and therefore the same feeling which is called ἵμερος when its

123

PLATO

παρῇ οὗ τις ἐφίετο, ἵμερος ἐκαλεῖτο· ἀπογενο-
μένου δὲ ὁ αὐτὸς οὗτος πόθος ἐκλήθη. ἔρως δέ,
ὅτι ἐσρεῖ ἔξωθεν καὶ οὐκ οἰκεία ἐστὶν ἡ ῥοὴ αὕτη
B τῷ ἔχοντι, ἀλλ᾽ ἐπείσακτος διὰ τῶν ὀμμάτων,
διὰ ταῦτα ἀπὸ τοῦ ἐσρεῖν ἔσρος τό γε παλαιὸν
ἐκαλεῖτο—τῷ γὰρ οὗ ἀντὶ τοῦ ὦ ἐχρώμεθα—, νῦν
δ᾽ ἔρως κέκληται διὰ τὴν τοῦ ὦ ἀντὶ τοῦ οὗ μεταλ-
λαγήν. ἀλλὰ τί ἔτι σὺ¹ λέγεις ὅτι σκοπῶμεν;
ΕΡΜ. Δόξα καὶ τὰ τοιαῦτα πῇ σοι φαίνεται;
ΣΩ. Δόξα δὴ ἤτοι² τῇ διώξει ἐπωνόμασται, ἣν ἡ
ψυχὴ διώκουσα τὸ εἰδέναι ὅπῃ ἔχει τὰ πράγματα
πορεύεται, ἢ τῇ ἀπὸ τοῦ τόξου βολῇ. ἔοικε δὲ
τούτῳ μᾶλλον. ἡ γοῦν οἴησις τούτῳ ξυμφωνεῖ.
C οἴσιν γὰρ³ τῆς ψυχῆς ἐπὶ πᾶν⁴ πρᾶγμα, οἷόν ἐστιν
ἕκαστον τῶν ὄντων, δηλούσῃ προσέοικεν, ὥσπερ
γε καὶ ἡ βουλή πως⁵ τὴν βολήν, καὶ τὸ βούλεσθαι
τὸ ἐφίεσθαι σημαίνει καὶ τὸ⁶ βουλεύεσθαι· πάντα
ταῦτα δόξῃ ἑπόμεν᾽ ἄττα φαίνεται τῆς βολῆς
ἀπεικάσματα, ὥσπερ αὖ καὶ τοὐναντίον ἡ ἀβουλία
ἀτυχία δοκεῖ εἶναι, ὡς οὐ βαλόντος οὐδὲ τυχόντος
οὗ τ᾽⁷ ἔβαλλε⁸ καὶ ὃ ἐβούλετο καὶ περὶ οὗ ἐβου-
λεύετο καὶ οὗ ἐφίετο.
D ΕΡΜ. Ταῦτα ἤδη μοι δοκεῖς, ὦ Σώκρατες,
πυκνότερα ἐπάγειν.
ΣΩ. Τέλος γὰρ ἤδη θέω.⁹ ἀνάγκην δ᾽ οὖν ἔτι
βούλομαι διαπερᾶναι, ὅτι τούτοις ἑξῆς ἐστι, καὶ τὸ
ἑκούσιον. τὸ μὲν οὖν ἑκούσιον, τὸ εἶκον καὶ μὴ

¹ σὺ Heindorf : οὐ BT.
² δὴ ἤτοι cod. Laurentinus 85. 17 : δὲ ἤτοι BT : δή τοι Schanz.
³ οἴσιν γὰρ t in marg. : οἴσειν· ἴσως γὰρ B : εἰσὶν γὰρ T : οἴσιν· ἴσως γὰρ W. ⁴ πᾶν T : τὸ B.
⁵ πως Hermann : πρὸς BT. ⁶ τὸ add. Heindorf.
⁷ οὗ τ᾽ Burnet : οὔτ᾽ B : οὔτ᾽ b : οὗ T.

124

CRATYLUS

object is present, is called πόθος when it is absent.
And ἔρως (love) is so called because it flows in
(ἐσρεῖ) from without, and this flowing is not inherent
in him who has it, but is introduced through the eyes ;
for this reason it was in ancient times called ἔσρος,
from ἐσρεῖν—for we used to employ omicron instead
of omega—but now it is called ἔρως through the
change of omicron to omega. Well, what more
is there that you want to examine ?

HER. What is your view about δόξα (opinion) and
the like ?

SOC. Δόξα is derived either from the pursuit
(δίωξις) which the soul carries on as it pursues the
knowledge of the nature of things, or from the
shooting of the bow (τόξον) ; the latter is more
likely ; at any rate οἴησις (belief) supports this view,
for it appears to mean the motion (οἶσις) of the soul
towards the essential nature of every individual
thing, just as βουλή (intention) denotes shooting
(βολή) and βούλεσθαι (wish), as well as βουλεύεσθαι
(plan), denotes aiming at something. All these
words seem to follow δόξα and to express the idea
of shooting, just as ἀβουλία (ill-advisedness), on the
other hand, appears to be a failure to hit, as if a
person did not shoot or hit that which he shot at or
wished or planned or desired.

HER. I think you are hurrying things a bit,
Socrates.

SOC. Yes, for I am running the last lap now.
But I think I must still explain ἀνάγκη (compulsion)
and ἑκούσιον (voluntary) because they naturally
come next. Now by the word ἑκούσιον is expressed

8 ἔβαλλε Heindorf: ἐβάλλετο BT.
9 θέω Adam: θεῶ T: θεω B: θεῷ vulg.

ἀντιτυποῦν, ἀλλ᾿, ὥσπερ λέγω, εἶκον τῷ ἰόντι
δεδηλωμένον ἂν εἴη τούτῳ τῷ ὀνόματι, τῷ κατὰ
τὴν βούλησιν γιγνομένῳ· τὸ δὲ ἀναγκαῖον καὶ
ἀντίτυπον, παρὰ τὴν βούλησιν ὄν, τὸ περὶ τὴν
ἁμαρτίαν ἂν εἴη καὶ ἀμαθίαν, ἀπείκασται δὲ τῇ
E κατὰ τὰ ἄγκη[1] πορείᾳ, ὅτι δύσπορα καὶ τραχέα καὶ
λάσια ὄντα ἴσχει τοῦ ἰέναι. ἐντεῦθεν οὖν ἴσως
ἐκλήθη ἀναγκαῖον, τῇ διὰ τοῦ ἄγκους ἀπεικασθὲν πορείᾳ. ἕως δὲ πάρεστιν ἡ ῥώμη, μὴ
ἀνιῶμεν αὐτήν· ἀλλὰ καὶ σὺ μὴ ἀνίει, ἀλλὰ ἐρώτα.

33. ερμ. Ἐρωτῶ δὴ τὰ μέγιστα καὶ τὰ κάλ-
421 λιστα, τήν τε ἀλήθειαν καὶ τὸ ψεῦδος καὶ τὸ ὂν καὶ
αὐτὸ τοῦτο περὶ ὧν νῦν ὁ λόγος ἡμῖν ἐστιν,
ὄνομα, δι᾿ ὅ τι τὸ ὄνομα ἔχει.

σω. Μαίεσθαι οὖν καλεῖς τι;

ερμ. Ἔγωγε, τό γε ζητεῖν.

σω. Ἔοικε τοίνυν ἐκ λόγου ὀνόματι συγκεκροτη-
μένῳ, λέγοντος ὅτι τοῦτ᾿ ἔστιν ὄν, οὗ τυγχάνει
ζήτημα ὄν,[2] τὸ ὄνομα. μᾶλλον δὲ ἂν αὐτὸ γνοίης
ἐν ᾧ λέγομεν τὸ ὀνομαστόν· ἐνταῦθα γὰρ σαφῶς
B λέγει τοῦτο εἶναι ὂν οὗ μάσμα ἐστίν.[3] ἡ δ᾿ ἀλήθεια, καὶ τοῦτο τοῖς ἄλλοις ἔοικε.[4] ἡ γὰρ θεία τοῦ
ὄντος φορὰ ἔοικε προσειρῆσθαι τούτῳ τῷ ῥήματι,
τῇ ἀληθείᾳ, ὡς θεία οὖσα ἄλη. τὸ δὲ[5] ψεῦδος
τοὐναντίον τῇ φορᾷ· πάλιν γὰρ αὖ λοιδορούμενον
ἥκει τὸ ἰσχόμενον καὶ τὸ ἀναγκαζόμενον ἡσυχάζειν,
ἀπείκασται δὲ τοῖς καθεύδουσι· τὸ ψῖ δὲ προσγενό-
μενον ἐπικρύπτει τὴν βούλησιν τοῦ ὀνόματος· τὸ

---

[1] τὰ ἄγκη b: ἀνάγκην BT.   [2] ὄν add. Burnet.
[3] ὂν οὗ μαῖσμα ἐστίν Heusde (μάσμα Buttmann): ὀνόμασμά
ἐστιν BT.
[4] ἔοικε Hermann: ἔοικε συγκεκροτῆσθαι BT.
[5] δὲ om. BT.

the yielding (εἶκον) and not opposing, but, as I say, yielding to the motion which is in accordance with the will; but the compulsory (τὸ ἀναγκαῖον) and resistant, being contrary to the will, is associated with error and ignorance; so it is likened to walking through ravines (ἄγκη), because they are hard to traverse, rough, and rugged, and retard motion; the word ἀναγκαῖον may, then, originate in a comparison with progress through a ravine. But let us not cease to use my strength, so long as it lasts; and do not you cease from asking questions.

HER. I ask, then, about the greatest and noblest words, truth (ἀλήθεια), falsehood (ψεῦδος), being (τὸ ὄν), and why name, the subject of our whole discourse, has the name ὄνομα.

SOC. Does the word μαίεσθαι (search) mean anything to you?

HER. Yes, it means " seek."

SOC. The word ὄνομα seems to be a word composed from a sentence signifying " this is a being about which our search is." You can recognize that more readily in the adjective ὀνομαστόν, for that says clearly that this is ὂν οὗ μάσμα ἐστίν (being of which the search is). And ἀλήθεια (truth) is like the others; for the divine motion of the universe is, I think, called by this name, ἀλήθεια, because it is a divine wandering (θεία ἄλη). But ψεῦδος (false-hood) is the opposite of motion; for once more that which is held back and forced to be quiet is found fault with, and it is compared to slumberers (εὕδουσι); but the addition of the psi conceals the meaning of the word. The words τὸ ὄν (being) and

127

PLATO

δὲ ὂν καὶ ἡ οὐσία ὁμολογεῖ τῷ ἀληθεῖ, τὸ ἰῶτα
ἀπολαβόν· ἰὸν γὰρ σημαίνει· καὶ τὸ οὐκ ὂν αὖ,
C ὥς τινες καὶ ὀνομάζουσιν αὐτὸ οὐκ ἰόν.

ΕΡΜ. Ταῦτα μέν μοι δοκεῖς, ὦ Σώκρατες,
ἀνδρείως πάνυ διακεκροτηκέναι· εἰ δέ τίς σε
ἔροιτο τοῦτο τὸ ἰὸν καὶ τὸ ῥέον καὶ τὸ δοῦν, τίνα
ἔχει ὀρθότητα ταῦτα τὰ ὀνόματα—

ΣΩ. Τί ἂν αὐτῷ ἀποκρινaίμεθα, λέγεις; ἦ γάρ;

ΕΡΜ. Πάνυ μὲν οὖν.

ΣΩ. Ἓν μὲν τοίνυν ἄρτι που ἐπορισάμεθα ὥστε
δοκεῖν τὶ λέγειν ἀποκρινόμενοι.

ΕΡΜ. Τὸ ποῖον τοῦτο;

ΣΩ. Φάναι, ὃ ἂν μὴ γιγνώσκωμεν, βαρβαρικόν
D τι τοῦτ' εἶναι. εἴη μὲν οὖν ἴσως ἄν τι τῇ ἀληθείᾳ
καὶ τοιοῦτον αὐτῶν, εἴη δὲ κἂν ὑπὸ παλαιότητος τὰ
πρῶτα τῶν ὀνομάτων ἀνεύρετα εἶναι· διὰ γὰρ τὸ
πανταχῇ στρέφεσθαι τὰ ὀνόματα οὐδὲν θαυμαστὸν
ἂν εἴη, εἰ ἡ¹ παλαιὰ φωνὴ πρὸς τὴν νυνὶ βαρβαρικῆς
μηδὲν διαφέρει.²

ΕΡΜ. Καὶ οὐδέν γε ἀπὸ τρόπου λέγεις.

ΣΩ. Λέγω γὰρ οὖν εἰκότα. οὐ μέντοι μοι δοκεῖ
προφάσεις ἀγὼν δέχεσθαι, ἀλλὰ προθυμητέον
ταῦτα διασκέψασθαι. ἐνθυμηθῶμεν δέ, εἴ τις ἀεί,
E δι' ὧν ἂν λέγηται τὸ ὄνομα, ἐκεῖνα ἀνερήσεται³ τὰ
ῥήματα, καὶ αὖθις αὖ, δι' ὧν ἂν τὰ ῥήματα λεχθῇ,
ἐκεῖνα πεύσεται, καὶ τοῦτο μὴ παύσεται ποιῶν,
ἆρ' οὐκ ἀνάγκη τελευτῶντα ἀπειπεῖν τὸν ἀποκρινόμενον;

ΕΡΜ. Ἔμοιγε δοκεῖ.

---

¹ εἴη εἰ ἡ bt: εἴη BT.
² διαφέρει bt: διαφέρειν BT.
³ ἀνερήσεται Bekker: ἐρήσεται B: ἂν ἐρήσεται T.

128

CRATYLUS

οὐσία (existence) agree with ἀληθής, with the loss of iota, for they mean "going" (ἰόν). And οὐκ ὄν (not being) means οὐκ ἰόν (not going), and indeed some people pronounce it so.

HER. I think you have knocked these words to pieces manfully, Socrates; but if anyone should ask you what propriety or correctness there was in these words that you have employed—ἰόν and ῥέον and δοῦν——

SOC. What answer should I make? Is that your meaning?

HER. Yes, exactly.

SOC. We acquired just now one way of making an answer with a semblance of sense in it.

HER. What way was that?

SOC. Saying, if there is a word we do not know about, that it is of foreign origin. Now this may be true of some of them, and also on account of the lapse of time it may be impossible to find out about the earliest words; for since words get twisted in all sorts of ways, it would not be in the least wonderful if the ancient Greek word should be identical with the modern foreign one.

HER. That is not unlikely.

SOC. It is indeed quite probable. However, we must play the game[1] and investigate these questions vigorously. But let us bear in mind that if a person asks about the words by means of which names are formed, and again about those by means of which those words were formed, and keeps on doing this indefinitely, he who answers his questions will at last give up; will he not?

HER. Yes, I think so.

[1] A proverbial expression.

422 ΣΩ. Πότε οὖν ἀπειπὼν ὁ ἀπαγορεύων δικαίως
παύοιτ᾿ ἄν; ἆρ᾿ οὐκ ἐπειδὰν ἐπ᾿ ἐκείνοις γένηται
τοῖς ὀνόμασιν, ἃ ὡσπερεὶ στοιχεῖα τῶν ἄλλων
ἐστὶ καὶ λόγων καὶ ὀνομάτων; ταῦτα γάρ που
οὐκέτι δίκαιον φανῆναι ἐξ ἄλλων ὀνομάτων ξυγκείμενα, ἂν οὕτως ἔχῃ. οἷον νῦν δὴ τὸ ἀγαθὸν
ἔφαμεν ἐκ τοῦ ἀγαστοῦ καὶ ἐκ τοῦ θοοῦ ξυγκεῖ-
σθαι· τὸ δὲ θοὸν ἴσως φαῖμεν ἂν ἐξ ἑτέρων, ἐκεῖνα
B δὲ ἐξ ἄλλων· ἀλλ᾿ ἐάν ποτέ γε λάβωμεν ὃ οὐκέτι
ἔκ τινων ἑτέρων ξύγκειται ὀνομάτων, δικαίως ἂν
φαῖμεν ἐπὶ στοιχείῳ τε ἤδη εἶναι καὶ οὐκέτι τοῦτο
ἡμᾶς δεῖν εἰς ἄλλα ὀνόματα ἀναφέρειν.

ΕΡΜ. Ἔμοιγε δοκεῖς ὀρθῶς λέγειν.

ΣΩ. Ἆρ᾿ οὖν καὶ νῦν ἃ ἐρωτᾷς τὰ ὀνόματα
στοιχεῖα ὄντα τυγχάνει, καὶ δεῖ αὐτῶν ἄλλῳ τινὶ
τρόπῳ ἤδη τὴν ὀρθότητα ἐπισκέψασθαι, ἥτις ἐστίν;

ΕΡΜ. Εἰκός γε.

ΣΩ. Εἰκὸς δῆτα, ὦ Ἑρμόγενες· πάντα γοῦν
φαίνεται τὰ ἔμπροσθεν εἰς ταῦτα ἀνεληλυθέναι.
C εἰ δὲ τοῦτο οὕτως ἔχει, ὥς μοι δοκεῖ ἔχειν, δεῦρο
αὖ συνεπίσκεψαι μετ᾿ ἐμοῦ, μή τι παραληρήσω
λέγων οἵαν δεῖ τὴν τῶν πρώτων ὀνομάτων ὀρθότητα εἶναι.

ΕΡΜ. Λέγε μόνον, ὡς ὅσον γε δυνάμεως παρ᾿
ἐμοί ἐστιν συνεπισκέψομαι.

34. ΣΩ. Ὅτι μὲν τοίνυν μία γέ τις ἡ ὀρθότης
παντὸς ὀνόματος καὶ πρώτου καὶ ὑστάτου, καὶ
οὐδὲν διαφέρει τῷ ὄνομα εἶναι οὐδὲν αὐτῶν, οἶμαι
καὶ σοὶ ξυνδοκεῖ.

ΕΡΜ. Πάνυ γε.

D ΣΩ. Ἀλλὰ μὴν ὧν γε νῦν δὴ[1] διεληλύθαμεν

[1] δὴ add. Heindorf.

soc. Now at what point will he be right in giving up and stopping? Will it not be when he reaches the names which are the elements of the other names and words? For these, if they are the elements, can no longer rightly appear to be composed of other names. For instance, we said just now that ἀγαθόν was composed of ἀγαστόν and θοόν; and perhaps we might say that θοόν was composed of other words, and those of still others; but if we ever get hold of a word which is no longer composed of other words, we should be right in saying that we had at last reached an element, and that we must no longer refer to other words for its derivation.

her. I think you are right.

soc. Are, then, these words about which you are now asking elements, and must we henceforth investigate their correctness by some other method?

her. Probably.

soc. Yes, probably, Hermogenes; at any rate, all the previous words were traced back to these. But if this be true, as I think it is, come to my aid again and help me in the investigation, that I may not say anything foolish in declaring what principle must underlie the correctness of the earliest names.

her. Go on, and I will help you to the best of my ability.

soc. I think you agree with me that there is but one principle of correctness in all names, the earliest as well as the latest, and that none of them is any more a name than the rest.

her. Certainly.

soc. Now the correctness of all the names we

τῶν ὀνομάτων ἡ ὀρθότης τοιαύτη τις ἐβούλετο
εἶναι, οἷα δηλοῦν οἷον ἕκαστόν ἐστι τῶν ὄντων.

ΕΡΜ. Πῶς γὰρ οὔ;

ΣΩ. Τοῦτο μὲν ἄρα οὐδὲν ἧττον καὶ τὰ πρῶτα
δεῖ ἔχειν καὶ τὰ ὕστερα, εἴπερ ὀνόματα ἔσται.

ΕΡΜ. Πάνυ γε.

ΣΩ. Ἀλλὰ τὰ μὲν ὕστερα, ὡς ἔοικε, διὰ τῶν προτέρων οἷά τε ἦν τοῦτο ἀπεργάζεσθαι.

ΕΡΜ. Φαίνεται.

ΣΩ. Εἶεν· τὰ δὲ δὴ πρῶτα, οἷς οὔπω ἕτερα ὑπόκειται, τίνι τρόπῳ κατὰ τὸ δυνατὸν ὅτι μάλιστα
E φανερὰ ἡμῖν ποιήσει τὰ ὄντα, εἴπερ μέλλει ὀνόματα
εἶναι; ἀπόκριναι δέ μοι τόδε· εἰ φωνὴν μὴ εἴχομεν
μηδὲ γλῶτταν, ἐβουλόμεθα δὲ δηλοῦν ἀλλήλοις
τὰ πράγματα, ἆρ’ οὐκ ἄν, ὥσπερ νῦν οἱ ἐνεοί,
ἐπεχειροῦμεν ἂν σημαίνειν ταῖς χερσὶ καὶ τῇ
κεφαλῇ καὶ τῷ ἄλλῳ σώματι;

ΕΡΜ. Πῶς γὰρ ἂν ἄλλως, ὦ Σώκρατες;

423 ΣΩ. Εἰ μέν γ’, οἶμαι, τὸ ἄνω καὶ τὸ κοῦφον
ἐβουλόμεθα δηλοῦν, ᾔρομεν ἂν πρὸς τὸν οὐρανὸν
τὴν χεῖρα, μιμούμενοι αὐτὴν τὴν φύσιν τοῦ πράγ-
ματος· εἰ δὲ τὰ¹ κάτω καὶ τὰ βαρέα, πρὸς τὴν
γῆν· καὶ εἰ ἵππον θέοντα ἤ τι ἄλλο τῶν ζῴων
ἐβουλόμεθα δηλοῦν, οἶσθα ὅτι ὡς ὁμοιότατ’ ἂν
τὰ ἡμέτερα αὐτῶν σώματα καὶ σχήματα ἐποιοῦμεν
ἐκείνοις.

ΕΡΜ. Ἀνάγκη μοι δοκεῖ ὡς λέγεις ἔχειν.

ΣΩ. Οὕτω γὰρ ἄν, οἶμαι, δήλωμά του² ἐγίγνετο,
B μιμησαμένου, ὡς ἔοικε, τοῦ σώματος ἐκεῖνο ὃ
ἐβούλετο δηλῶσαι.

---

¹ τὰ G: om. BT.
² δήλωμα τοῦ σώματος BT : σώματος bracketed by Schanz.

have discussed was based upon the intention of showing the nature of the things named.

HER. Yes, of course.

soc. And this principle of correctness must be present in all names, the earliest as well as the later ones, if they are really to be names.

HER. Certainly.

soc. But the later ones, apparently, were able to accomplish this by means of the earlier ones.

HER. Evidently.

soc. Well, then, how can the earliest names, which are not as yet based upon any others, make clear to us the nature of things, so far as that is possible, which they must do if they are to be names at all ? Answer me this question : If we had no voice or tongue, and wished to make things clear to one another, should we not try, as dumb people actually do, to make signs with our hands and head and person generally ?

HER. Yes. What other method is there, Socrates ?

soc. If we wished to designate that which is above and is light, we should, I fancy, raise our hand towards heaven in imitation of the nature of the thing in question ; but if the things to be designated were below or heavy, we should extend our hands towards the ground ; and if we wished to mention a galloping horse or any other animal, we should, of course, make our bodily attitudes as much like theirs as possible.

HER. I think you are quite right ; there is no other way.

soc. For the expression of anything, I fancy, would be accomplished by bodily imitation of that which was to be expressed.

133

PLATO

ΕΡΜ. Ναί.

ΣΩ. Ἐπειδὴ δὲ φωνῇ τε καὶ γλώττῃ καὶ στόματι βουλόμεθα δηλοῦν, ἆρ' οὐ τότε ἑκάστου δήλωμα ἡμῖν ἔσται τὸ ἀπὸ τούτων γιγνόμενον, ὅταν μίμημα γένηται διὰ τούτων περὶ ὁτιοῦν;

ΕΡΜ. Ἀνάγκη μοι δοκεῖ.

ΣΩ. Ὄνομ' ἄρ' ἐστίν, ὡς ἔοικε, μίμημα φωνῇ ἐκείνου ὃ μιμεῖται, καὶ ὀνομάζει ὁ μιμούμενος τῇ φωνῇ ὃ ἂν μιμῆται.

ΕΡΜ. Δοκεῖ μοι.

C ΣΩ. Μὰ Δί' ἀλλ' οὐκ¹ ἐμοί πω δοκεῖ καλῶς λέγεσθαι, ὦ ἑταῖρε.

ΕΡΜ. Τί δή;

ΣΩ. Τοὺς τὰ πρόβατα μιμουμένους τούτους καὶ τοὺς ἀλεκτρυόνας καὶ τὰ ἄλλα ζῷα ἀναγκαζοίμεθ' ἂν ὁμολογεῖν ὀνομάζειν ταῦτα ἅπερ μιμοῦνται.

ΕΡΜ. Ἀληθῆ λέγεις.

ΣΩ. Καλῶς οὖν ἔχειν δοκεῖ σοι;

ΕΡΜ. Οὐκ ἔμοιγε. ἀλλὰ τίς ἄν, ὦ Σώκρατες, μίμησις εἴη τὸ ὄνομα;

ΣΩ. Πρῶτον μέν, ὡς ἐμοὶ δοκεῖ, οὐκ ἐὰν καθάπερ τῇ μουσικῇ μιμούμεθα τὰ πράγματα οὕτω D μιμώμεθα, καίτοι φωνῇ γε καὶ τότε μιμούμεθα· ἔπειτα οὐκ ἐὰν ἅπερ ἡ μουσικὴ μιμεῖται² καὶ ἡμεῖς μιμώμεθα, οὔ μοι δοκοῦμεν ὀνομάσειν. λέγω δέ τοι τοῦτο·³ ἔστι τοῖς πράγμασι φωνὴ καὶ σχῆμα ἑκάστῳ, καὶ χρῶμά γε πολλοῖς;

ΕΡΜ. Πάνυ γε.

ΣΩ. Ἔοικε τοίνυν οὐκ ἐάν τις ταῦτα μιμῆται,

¹ ἀλλ' οὐκ Hermann (γρ. Τ): οὐκ ἀλλ' Β: οὔκ ἀλλ' Τ.
² μιμεῖται g: μιμῆται BGT.
³ δέ τοι τοῦτο G: δέ τι τοῦτο ΒΤ.

134

CRATYLUS

HER. Yes.

soc. And when we wish to express anything by voice or tongue or mouth, will not our expression by these means be accomplished in any given instance when an imitation of something is accomplished by them ?

HER. I think that is inevitable.

soc. A name, then, it appears, is a vocal imitation of that which is imitated, and he who imitates with his voice names that which he imitates.

HER. I think that is correct.

soc. By Zeus, I do not think it is quite correct, yet, my friend.

HER. Why not ?

soc. We should be obliged to agree that people who imitate sheep and cocks and other animals were naming those which they imitate.

HER. Yes, so we should.

soc. And do you think that is correct ?

HER. No, I do not ; but, Socrates, what sort of an imitation is a name ?

soc. In the first place we shall not, in my opinion, be making names, if we imitate things as we do in music, although musical imitation also is vocal ; and secondly we shall make no names by imitating that which music imitates. What I mean is this : all objects have sound and shape, and many have colour, have they not ?

HER. Certainly.

soc. Well then, the art of naming is not employed

PLATO

οὐδὲ περὶ ταύτας τὰς μιμήσεις ἡ τέχνη ἡ ὀνο-
μαστικὴ εἶναι. αὗται μὲν γάρ εἰσιν ἡ μὲν μου-
σική, ἡ δὲ γραφική· ἢ γάρ;

ΕΡΜ. Ναί.

Ε ΣΩ. Τί δὲ δὴ τόδε; οὐ καὶ οὐσία δοκεῖ σοι
εἶναι ἑκάστῳ, ὥσπερ καὶ χρῶμα καὶ ἃ νῦν δὴ
ἐλέγομεν; πρῶτον αὐτῷ τῷ χρώματι καὶ τῇ
φωνῇ οὐκ ἔστιν οὐσία τις ἑκατέρῳ αὐτῶν καὶ
τοῖς ἄλλοις πᾶσιν ὅσα ἠξίωται ταύτης τῆς προσ-
ρήσεως, τοῦ εἶναι;

ΕΡΜ. Ἔμοιγε δοκεῖ.

ΣΩ. Τί οὖν; εἴ τις αὐτὸ τοῦτο μιμεῖσθαι δύναιτο ἑκάστου, τὴν οὐσίαν, γράμμασί τε καὶ συλλαβαῖς, ἆρ' οὐκ ἂν δηλοῖ ἕκαστον ὃ ἔστιν; ἢ οὔ;

424 ΕΡΜ. Πάνυ μὲν οὖν.

ΣΩ. Καὶ τί ἂν φαίης τὸν τοῦτο δυνάμενον,
ὥσπερ τοὺς προτέρους τὸν μὲν μουσικὸν ἔφησθα,
τὸν δὲ γραφικόν. τοῦτον δὲ τίνα;

ΕΡΜ. Τοῦτο ἔμοιγε δοκεῖ, ὦ Σώκρατες, ὅπερ
πάλαι ζητοῦμεν,[1] οὗτος ἂν εἶναι ὁ ὀνομαστικός.

35. ΣΩ. Εἰ ἄρα τοῦτο ἀληθές, ἤδη ἔοικεν ἐπισκεπτέον περὶ ἐκείνων τῶν ὀνομάτων ὧν σὺ
ἤρου, περὶ ῥοῆς τε καὶ τοῦ ἰέναι καὶ σχέσεως, εἰ
τοῖς γράμμασι καὶ ταῖς συλλαβαῖς τοῦ ὄντος
Β ἐπιλαμβάνεται αὐτῶν ὥστε ἀπομιμεῖσθαι τὴν
οὐσίαν, εἴτε καὶ οὔ;

ΕΡΜ. Πάνυ μὲν οὖν.

ΣΩ. Φέρε δή, ἴδωμεν, πότερον ἄρα ταῦτα μόνα
ἐστὶ τῶν πρώτων ὀνομάτων ἢ καὶ ἄλλα πολλά.

ΕΡΜ. Οἶμαι ἔγωγε καὶ ἄλλα.

ΣΩ. Εἰκὸς γάρ. ἀλλὰ τίς ἂν εἴη ὁ τρόπος τῆς

---

[1] ζητοῦμεν cod. Vindobonensis 31 : ἐξητοῦμεν ΒΤ.

in the imitation of those qualities, and has nothing to do with them. The arts which are concerned with them are music and design, are they not?

HER. Yes.

soc. Here is another point. Has not each thing an essential nature, just as it has a colour and the other qualities we just mentioned? Indeed, in the first place, have not colour and sound and all other things which may properly be said to exist, each and all an essential nature?

HER. I think so.

soc. Well, then, if anyone could imitate this essential nature of each thing by means of letters and syllables, he would show what each thing really is, would he not?

HER. Certainly.

soc. And what will you call him who can do this, as you called the others musician and painter? What will you call this man?

HER. I think, Socrates, he is what we have been looking for all along, the name-maker.

soc. If that is the case, is it our next duty to consider whether in these names about which you were asking—flow, motion, and restraint—the name-maker grasps with his letters and syllables the reality of the things named and imitates their essential nature, or not?

HER. Certainly.

soc. Well now, let us see whether those are the only primary names, or there are others.

HER. I think there are others.

soc. Yes, most likely there are. Now what is

διαιρέσεως ὅθεν ἄρχεται μιμεῖσθαι ὁ μιμούμενος;
ἆρα οὐκ ἐπείπερ συλλαβαῖς τε καὶ γράμμασιν ἡ
μίμησις τυγχάνει οὖσα τῆς οὐσίας, ὀρθότατόν ἐστι
διελέσθαι τὰ στοιχεῖα πρῶτον, ὥσπερ οἱ ἐπιχει-
C ροῦντες τοῖς ῥυθμοῖς τῶν στοιχείων πρῶτον τὰς
δυνάμεις διείλοντο, ἔπειτα τῶν συλλαβῶν καὶ
οὕτως ἤδη ἔρχονται ἐπὶ τοὺς ῥυθμοὺς σκεψόμενοι,
πρότερον δ' οὔ;

ΕΡΜ. Ναί.

ΣΩ. Ἆρ' οὖν καὶ ἡμᾶς οὕτω δεῖ πρῶτον μὲν
τὰ φωνήεντα διελέσθαι, ἔπειτα τῶν ἑτέρων κατὰ
εἴδη τά τε ἄφωνα καὶ ἄφθογγα—οὑτωσὶ γάρ που
λέγουσιν οἱ δεινοὶ περὶ τούτων—καὶ τὰ αὖ φωνήεντα μὲν οὔ, οὐ μέντοι γε ἄφθογγα; καὶ αὐτῶν
τῶν φωνηέντων ὅσα διάφορα εἴδη ἔχει ἀλλήλων;
D καὶ ἐπειδὰν ταῦτα διελώμεθα εὖ πάντα[1] αὖ οἷς[2]
δεῖ ὀνόματα ἐπιθεῖναι, εἰ ἔστιν εἰς ἃ ἀναφέρεται
πάντα ὥσπερ τὰ στοιχεῖα, ἐξ ὧν ἔστιν ἰδεῖν αὐτά
τε καὶ εἰ ἐν αὐτοῖς ἔνεστιν εἴδη κατὰ τὸν αὐτὸν
τρόπον ὥσπερ ἐν τοῖς στοιχείοις· ταῦτα πάντα
καλῶς διαθεασαμένους ἐπίστασθαι ἐπιφέρειν ἕκαστον κατὰ τὴν ὁμοιότητα, ἐάντε ἓν ἑνὶ δέῃ ἐπιφέρειν,
ἐάντε συγκεραννύντα πολλά,[3] ὥσπερ οἱ ζωγράφοι
βουλόμενοι ἀφομοιοῦν ἐνίοτε μὲν ὄστρεον μόνον
E ἐπήνεγκαν, ἐνίοτε δὲ ὁτιοῦν ἄλλο τῶν φαρμάκων,
ἔστι δὲ ὅτε πολλὰ συγκεράσαντες, οἷον ὅταν
ἀνδρείκελον σκευάζωσιν ἢ ἄλλο τι τῶν τοιούτων,
ὡς ἄν, οἶμαι, δοκῇ ἑκάστη ἡ εἰκὼν δεῖσθαι ἑκάστου φαρμάκου· οὕτω δὴ καὶ ἡμεῖς τὰ στοιχεῖα
ἐπὶ τὰ πράγματα ἐποίσομεν, καὶ ἓν ἐπὶ ἕν, οὗ

---

[1] εὖ πάντα Beck : τὰ ὄντα εὖ πάντα ΒΤ.
[2] αὖ οἷς Badham : αὖθις ΒΤ.　　[3] πολλά Τ : πολλὰ ἑνί Β.

the method of division with which the imitator
begins his imitation ? Since the imitation of the
essential nature is made with letters and syllables,
would not the most correct way be for us to separate
the letters first, just as those who undertake the
practice of rhythms separate first the qualities of
the letters, then those of the syllables, and then,
but not till then, come to the study of rhythms ?

HER. Yes.

SOC. Must not we, too, separate first the vowels,
then in their several classes the consonants or mutes,
as they are called by those who specialize in phonetics,
and also the letters which are neither vowels nor
mutes, as well as the various classes that exist
among the vowels themselves ? And when we have
made all these divisions properly, we must in turn
give names to the things which ought to have them,
if there are any names to which they can all, like
the letters, be referred, from which it is possible
to see what their nature is and whether there are
any classes among them, as there are among letters.
When we have properly examined all these points,
we must know how to apply each letter with reference
to its fitness, whether one letter is to be applied to
one thing or many are to be combined ; just as
painters, when they wish to produce an imitation,
sometimes use only red, sometimes some other colour,
and sometimes mix many colours, as when they are
making a picture of a man or something of that
sort, employing each colour, I suppose, as they think
the particular picture demands it. In just this way
we, too, shall apply letters to things, using one

PLATO

ἂν δοκῇ δεῖν, καὶ σύμπολλα, ποιοῦντες ὃ δὴ
συλλαβὰς καλοῦσιν, καὶ συλλαβὰς αὖ συντιθέντες,
425 ἐξ ὧν τά τε ὀνόματα καὶ τὰ ῥήματα συντίθενται·
καὶ πάλιν ἐκ τῶν ὀνομάτων καὶ ῥημάτων μέγα
ἤδη τι καὶ καλὸν καὶ ὅλον συστήσομεν, ὥσπερ
ἐκεῖ τὸ ζῷον τῇ γραφικῇ, ἐνταῦθα τὸν λόγον τῇ
ὀνομαστικῇ ἢ ῥητορικῇ ἢ ἥτις ἐστὶν ἡ τέχνη.
μᾶλλον δὲ οὐχ ἡμεῖς, ἀλλὰ λέγων ἐξηνέχθην. συν-
έθεσαν μὲν γὰρ οὕτως ᾗπερ[1] σύγκειται οἱ παλαιοί·
ἡμᾶς δὲ δεῖ, εἴπερ τεχνικῶς ἐπιστησόμεθα σκο-
B πεῖσθαι αὐτὰ πάντα, οὕτω διελομένους, εἴτε κατὰ
τρόπον τά τε πρῶτα ὀνόματα κεῖται καὶ τὰ ὕστερα,
εἴτε μή, οὕτω θεᾶσθαι· ἄλλως δὲ συνείρειν μὴ
φαῦλον ᾖ καὶ οὐ καθ᾽ ὁδόν, ὦ φίλε Ἑρμόγενες.

ΕΡΜ. Ἴσως νὴ Δί᾽, ὦ Σώκρατες.

36. ΣΩ. Τί οὖν; σὺ πιστεύεις σαυτῷ οἷός τ᾽
ἂν εἶναι ταῦτα οὕτω διελέσθαι; ἐγὼ μὲν γὰρ
οὔ.

ΕΡΜ. Πολλοῦ ἄρα δέω ἔγωγε.

ΣΩ. Ἐάσομεν οὖν, ἢ βούλει οὕτως ὅπως ἂν
δυνώμεθα, καὶ ἂν σμικρόν τι αὐτῶν οἷοί τ᾽ ὦμεν
C κατιδεῖν, ἐπιχειρῶμεν, προειπόντες, ὥσπερ ὀλίγον
πρότερον τοῖς θεοῖς, ὅτι οὐδὲν εἰδότες τῆς ἀληθείας τὰ τῶν ἀνθρώπων δόγματα περὶ αὐτῶν
εἰκάζομεν, οὕτω δὲ καὶ νῦν αὖ εἰπόντες ἡμῖν
αὐτοῖς ἴωμεν, ὅτι εἰ μέν τι χρῆν[2] αὐτὰ διελέσθαι
εἴτε ἄλλον ὁντινοῦν εἴτε ἡμᾶς, οὕτως ἔδει αὐτὰ
διαιρεῖσθαι, νῦν δὲ τὸ λεγόμενον κατὰ δύναμιν
δεήσει ἡμᾶς περὶ αὐτῶν πραγματεύεσθαι; δοκεῖ
ταῦτα, ἢ πῶς λέγεις;

---

[1] ᾗπερ] εἴπερ BT.
[2] χρῆν Ast : χρηστὸν ἔδει BT.

letter for one thing, when that seems to be required, or many letters together, forming syllables, as they are called, and in turn combining syllables, and by their combination forming nouns and verbs. And from nouns and verbs again we shall finally construct something great and fair and complete. Just as in our comparison we made the picture by the art of painting, so now we shall make language by the art of naming, or of rhetoric, or whatever it be. No, not we ; I said that too hastily. For the ancients gave language its existing composite character ; and we, if we are to examine all these matters with scientific ability, must take it to pieces as they put it together and see whether the words, both the earliest and the later, are given systematically or not ; for if they are strung together at haphazard, it is a poor, unmethodical performance, my dear Hermogenes.

HER. By Zeus, Socrates, may be it is.

SOC. Well, do you believe you could take them to pieces in that way ? I do not believe I could.

HER. Then I am sure I could not.

SOC. Shall we give up then ? Or shall we do the best we can and try to see if we are able to understand even a little about them, and, just as we said to the gods a while ago that we knew nothing about the truth but were guessing at human opinion about them, so now, before we proceed, shall we say to ourselves that if anyone, whether we or some one else, is to make any analysis of names, he will have to analyse them in the way we have described, and we shall have to study them, as the saying is, with all our might ? Do you agree, or not ?

PLATO

ΕΡΜ. Πάνυ μὲν οὖν σφόδρα ἔμοιγε δοκεῖ.

D ΣΩ. Γελοῖα μὲν οἶμαι φανεῖσθαι, ὦ Ἑρμόγενες, γράμμασι καὶ συλλαβαῖς τὰ πράγματα μεμιμημένα κατάδηλα γιγνόμενα· ὅμως δὲ ἀνάγκη. οὐ γὰρ ἔχομεν τούτου βέλτιον, εἰς ὅ τι ἐπανενέγκωμεν περὶ ἀληθείας τῶν πρώτων ὀνομάτων, εἰ μὴ ἄρα βούλει,[1] ὥσπερ οἱ τραγῳδιοποιοὶ ἐπειδάν τι ἀπορῶσιν ἐπὶ τὰς μηχανὰς καταφεύγουσι θεοὺς αἴροντες, καὶ ἡμεῖς οὕτως εἰπόντες ἀπαλλαγῶμεν, ὅτι τὰ πρῶτα ὀνόματα οἱ θεοὶ ἔθεσαν
E καὶ διὰ ταῦτα ὀρθῶς ἔχει. ἆρα καὶ ἡμῖν κράτιστος οὗτος τῶν λόγων; ἢ ἐκεῖνος, ὅτι παρὰ βαρβάρων τινῶν αὐτὰ παρειλήφαμεν, εἰσὶ δὲ ἡμῶν
426 ἀρχαιότεροι βάρβαροι; ἢ ὅτι ὑπὸ παλαιότητος ἀδύνατον αὐτὰ ἐπισκέψασθαι, ὥσπερ καὶ τὰ βαρβαρικά; αὗται γὰρ ἂν πᾶσαι ἐκδύσεις εἶεν καὶ μάλα κομψαὶ τῷ μὴ ἐθέλοντι λόγον διδόναι περὶ τῶν πρώτων ὀνομάτων ὡς ὀρθῶς κεῖται. καίτοι ὅτῳ τις τρόπῳ τῶν πρώτων ὀνομάτων τὴν ὀρθότητα μὴ οἶδεν, ἀδύνατόν που τῶν γε ὑστέρων εἰδέναι, ἃ ἐξ ἐκείνων ἀνάγκη δηλοῦσθαι ὧν τις πέρι μηδὲν οἶδεν· ἀλλὰ δῆλον ὅτι τὸν φάσκοντα περὶ αὐτῶν τεχνικὸν εἶναι περὶ τῶν πρώτων ὀνομάτων μάλιστά τε
B καὶ καθαρώτατα δεῖ ἔχειν ἀποδεῖξαι, ἢ εὖ εἰδέναι ὅτι τά γε ὕστερα ἤδη φλυαρήσει. ἢ σοὶ ἄλλως δοκεῖ;

ΕΡΜ. Οὐδ' ὁπωστιοῦν, ὦ Σώκρατες, ἄλλως.

ΣΩ. Ἃ μὲν τοίνυν ἐγὼ ᾔσθημαι περὶ τῶν πρώτων ὀνομάτων πάνυ μοι δοκεῖ ὑβριστικὰ εἶναι καὶ γελοῖα. τούτων οὖν σοι μεταδώσω, ἂν βούλῃ· σὺ δ' ἄν τι ἔχῃς βέλτιόν ποθεν λαβεῖν, πειρᾶσθαι καὶ ἐμοὶ μεταδιδόναι.

[1] βούλει Hermann : δεῖ ΒΤ.

142

HER. Yes, I agree most heartily.

SOC. It will, I imagine, seem ridiculous that things are made manifest through imitation in letters and syllables; nevertheless it cannot be otherwise. For there is no better theory upon which we can base the truth of the earliest names, unless you think we had better follow the example of the tragic poets, who, when they are in a dilemma, have recourse to the introduction of gods on machines. So we may get out of trouble by saying that the gods gave the earliest names, and therefore they are right. Is that the best theory for us? Or perhaps this one, that we got the earliest names from some foreign folk and the foreigners are more ancient than we are? Or that it is impossible to investigate them because of their antiquity, as is also the case with the foreign words? All these are merely very clever evasions on the part of those who refuse to offer any rational theory of the correctness of the earliest names. And yet if anyone is, no matter why, ignorant of the correctness of the earliest names, he cannot know about that of the later, since they can be explained only by means of the earliest, about which he is ignorant. No, it is clear that anyone who claims to have scientific knowledge of names must be able first of all to explain the earliest names perfectly, or he can be sure that what he says about the later will be nonsense. Or do you disagree?

HER. No, Socrates, not in the least.

SOC. Now I think my notions about the earliest names are quite outrageous and ridiculous. I will impart them to you, if you like; if you can find anything better, please try to impart it to me.

PLATO

ΕΡΜ. Ποιήσω ταῦτα. ἀλλὰ θαρρῶν λέγε.

C 37. ΣΩ. Πρῶτον μὲν τοίνυν τὸ ῥῶ ἔμοιγε
φαίνεται ὥσπερ ὄργανον εἶναι πάσης τῆς κινήσεως, ἣν οὐδ᾽ εἴπομεν δι᾽ ὅ τι ἔχει τοῦτο τοὔνομα·
ἀλλὰ γὰρ δῆλον ὅτι ἴεσις βούλεται εἶναι· οὐ γὰρ
ἦτα ἐχρώμεθα ἀλλὰ εἶ τὸ παλαιόν. ἡ δὲ ἀρχὴ
ἀπὸ τοῦ κίειν—ξενικὸν δὲ τοὔνομα—τοῦτο δ᾽
ἐστὶν ἰέναι. εἰ οὖν τις τὸ παλαιὸν αὐτῆς εὕροι
ὄνομα εἰς τὴν ἡμετέραν φωνὴν συμβαῖνον, ἴεσις
ἂν ὀρθῶς καλοῖτο· νῦν δὲ ἀπό τε τοῦ ξενικοῦ
τοῦ κίειν καὶ ἀπὸ τῆς τοῦ ἦτα μεταβολῆς καὶ τῆς
τοῦ νῦ ἐνθέσεως κίνησις κέκληται, ἔδει δὲ κιείνησιν
D καλεῖσθαι ἢ εἶσιν. ἡ δὲ στάσις ἀπόφασις τοῦ
ἰέναι βούλεται εἶναι, διὰ δὲ τὸν καλλωπισμὸν
στάσις ὠνόμασται. τὸ δὲ οὖν ῥῶ τὸ στοιχεῖον,
ὥσπερ λέγω, καλὸν ἔδοξεν ὄργανον εἶναι τῆς
κινήσεως τῷ τὰ ὀνόματα τιθεμένῳ πρὸς τὸ ἀφομοιοῦν τῇ φορᾷ· πολλαχοῦ γοῦν χρῆται αὐτῷ εἰς
αὐτήν· πρῶτον μὲν ἐν αὐτῷ τῷ ῥεῖν καὶ ῥοῇ
διὰ τούτου τοῦ γράμματος τὴν φορὰν μιμεῖται,
E εἶτα ἐν τῷ τρόμῳ, εἶτα ἐν τῷ τρέχειν,[1] ἔτι δὲ ἐν
τοῖς τοιοῖσδε ῥήμασιν, οἷον κρούειν, θραύειν,
ἐρείκειν, θρύπτειν, κερματίζειν, ῥυμβεῖν· πάντα
ταῦτα τὸ πολὺ ἀπεικάζει διὰ τοῦ ῥῶ· ἑώρα[2] γάρ,
οἶμαι, τὴν γλῶτταν ἐν τούτῳ ἥκιστα μένουσαν,
μάλιστα δὲ σειομένην· διὸ φαίνεταί μοι τούτῳ
πρὸς ταῦτα κατακεχρῆσθαι. τῷ δὲ αὖ ἰῶτα πρὸς
τὰ λεπτὰ πάντα, ἃ δὴ μάλιστα διὰ πάντων ἴοι ἄν.
427 διὰ ταῦτα τὸ ἰέναι καὶ τὸ ἵεσθαι[3] διὰ τοῦ ἰῶτα

---

[1] τρέχειν codex Parisinus 1813: τραχεῖ ΒΤ.
[2] ἑώρα Heindorf: ἑῶ ΒΤ.
[3] ἵεσθαι Schanz: ἱενέσθαι Β: ἵεσθαι Τ.

HER. I will do so. Go on, and do not be afraid.

SOC. First, then, the letter rho seems to me to be an instrument expressing all motion. We have not as yet said why motion has the name κίνησις; but it evidently should be ἵεσις, for in old times we did not employ eta, but epsilon. And the beginning of κίνησις is from κίειν, a foreign word equivalent to ἰέναι (go). So we should find that the ancient word corresponding to our modern form would be ἵεσις; but now by the employment of the foreign word κίειν, change of epsilon to eta, and the insertion of nu it has become κίνησις, though it ought to be κιείνεσις or εἶσις. And στάσις (rest) signifies the negation of motion, but is called στάσις for euphony. Well, the letter rho, as I was saying, appeared to be a fine instrument expressive of motion to the name-giver who wished to imitate rapidity, and he often applies it to motion. In the first place, in the words ῥεῖν (flow) and ῥοή (current) he imitates their rapidity by this letter, then in τρόμος (trembling) and in τρέχειν (run), and also in such words as κρούειν (strike), θραύειν (break), ἐρείκειν (rend), θρύπτειν (crush), κερματίζειν (crumble), ῥυμβεῖν (whirl), he expresses the action of them all chiefly by means of the letter rho; for he observed, I suppose, that the tongue is least at rest and most agitated in pronouncing this letter, and that is probably the reason why he employed it for these words. Iota again, he employs for everything subtle, which can most readily pass through all things. Therefore he imitates the nature of ἰέναι (go) and ἵεσθαι (hasten) by means of iota, just as he has imitated

ἀπομιμεῖται, ὥσπερ γε διὰ τοῦ φῖ καὶ τοῦ ψῖ καὶ
τοῦ σῖγμα καὶ τοῦ ζῆτα, ὅτι πνευματώδη τὰ
γράμματα, πάντα τὰ τοιαῦτα μεμίμηται αὐτοῖς
ὀνομάζων, οἷον τὸ ψυχρὸν καὶ τὸ ζέον καὶ τὸ
σείεσθαι καὶ ὅλως σεισμόν. καὶ ὅταν που τὸ
φυσῶδες μιμῆται, πανταχοῦ ἐνταῦθα ὡς τὸ πολὺ
τὰ τοιαῦτα γράμματα ἐπιφέρειν φαίνεται ὁ τὰ
ὀνόματα τιθέμενος. τῆς δ' αὖ τοῦ δέλτα συμ-
πιέσεως καὶ τοῦ ταῦ καὶ ἀπερείσεως τῆς γλώττης
B τὴν δύναμιν χρήσιμον φαίνεται ἡγήσασθαι πρὸς
τὴν μίμησιν τοῦ δεσμοῦ καὶ τῆς στάσεως. ὅτι
δὲ ὀλισθάνει μάλιστα ἐν τῷ λάβδα ἡ γλῶττα κατ-
ιδών, ἀφομοιῶν ὠνόμασε τά τε λεῖα καὶ αὐτὸ τὸ
ὀλισθάνειν καὶ τὸ λιπαρὸν καὶ τὸ κολλῶδες καὶ
τἆλλα πάντα τὰ τοιαῦτα. ᾗ δὲ ὀλισθανούσης τῆς
γλώττης ἀντιλαμβάνεται ἡ τοῦ γάμμα δύναμις,
τὸ γλίσχρον ἀπεμιμήσατο καὶ γλυκὺ καὶ γλοιῶδες.
C τοῦ δ' αὖ νῦ τὸ εἴσω αἰσθόμενος τῆς φωνῆς, τὸ
ἔνδον καὶ τὰ ἐντὸς ὠνόμασεν, ὡς ἀφομοιῶν τοῖς
γράμμασι τὰ ἔργα. τὸ δ' αὖ ἄλφα τῷ μεγάλῳ
ἀπέδωκε, καὶ τῷ μήκει τὸ ἦτα, ὅτι μεγάλα τὰ
γράμματα. εἰς δὲ τὸ γογγύλον τοῦ οὖ δεόμενος
σημείου, τοῦτο πλεῖστον αὐτῷ εἰς τὸ ὄνομα ἐν-
εκέρασεν. καὶ τἆλλα οὕτω φαίνεται προσβιβάζειν
καὶ κατὰ γράμματα καὶ κατὰ συλλαβὰς ἑκάστῳ
τῶν ὄντων σημεῖόν τε καὶ ὄνομα ποιῶν ὁ νομοθέτης, ἐκ δὲ τούτων τὰ λοιπὰ ἤδη[1] αὐτοῖς τούτοις
συντιθέναι ἀπομιμούμενος. αὕτη μοι φαίνεται, ὦ
D Ἑρμόγενες, βούλεσθαι εἶναι ἡ τῶν ὀνομάτων
ὀρθότης, εἰ μή τι ἄλλο Κρατύλος ὅδε λέγει.

38. ΕΡΜ. Καὶ μήν, ὦ Σώκρατες, πολλά γέ μοι

---

[1] ἤδη cod. Parisinus 1813: ᾔδει BT.

all such notions as ψυχρόν (cold, shivering), ζέον
(seething), σείεσθαι (shake), and σεισμός (shock) by
means of phi, psi, sigma, and zeta, because those
letters are pronounced with much breath. Whenever he imitates that which resembles blowing, the
giver of names always appears to use for the most
part such letters. And again he appears to have
thought that the compression and pressure of the
tongue in the pronunciation of delta and tau was
naturally fitted to imitate the notion of binding
and rest. And perceiving that the tongue has a
gliding movement most in the pronunciation of
lambda, he made the words λεῖα (level), ὀλισθάνειν
(glide) itself, λιπαρόν (sleek), κολλῶδες (glutinous),
and the like to conform to it. Where the gliding of
the tongue is stopped by the sound of gamma he
reproduced the nature of γλισχρόν (glutinous),
γλυκύ (sweet), and γλοιῶδες (gluey). And again,
perceiving that nu is an internal sound, he made
the words ἔνδον (inside) and ἐντός (within), assimilat-
ing the meanings to the letters, and alpha again he
assigned to greatness, and eta to length, because
the letters are large. He needed the sign O for
the expression of γόγγυλον (round), and made it
the chief element of the word. And in this way
the lawgiver appears to apply the other letters,
making by letters and syllables a name for each
and every thing, and from these names he com-
pounds all the rest by imitation. This, Hermogenes,
appears to me to be the theory of the correctness
of names, unless, indeed, Cratylus has some other
view.

HER. Truly, Socrates, as I said in the beginning,

πολλάκις πράγματα παρέχει Κρατύλος, ὥσπερ
κατ' ἀρχὰς ἔλεγον, φάσκων μὲν εἶναι ὀρθότητα ὀνομάτων, ἥτις δ' ἐστὶν οὐδὲν σαφὲς λέγων, ὥστε με
μὴ δύνασθαι εἰδέναι πότερον ἑκὼν ἢ ἄκων οὕτως
ἀσαφῶς ἑκάστοτε περὶ αὐτῶν λέγει. νῦν οὖν μοι,
E ὦ Κρατύλε, ἐναντίον Σωκράτους εἰπὲ πότερον
ἀρέσκει σοι ᾗ λέγει Σωκράτης περὶ ὀνομάτων, ἢ
ἔχεις πῃ ἄλλῃ κάλλιον λέγειν; καὶ εἰ ἔχεις, λέγε,
ἵνα ἤτοι μάθῃς παρὰ Σωκράτους ἢ διδάξῃς ἡμᾶς
ἀμφοτέρους.

ΚΡΑ. Τί δέ, ὦ Ἑρμόγενες; δοκεῖ σοι ῥᾴδιον
εἶναι οὕτω ταχὺ μαθεῖν τε καὶ διδάξαι ὁτιοῦν
πρᾶγμα, μὴ ὅτι τοσοῦτον, ὃ δὴ δοκεῖ ἐν τοῖς
μέγιστον[1] εἶναι;

428 ΕΡΜ. Μὰ Δί', οὐκ ἔμοιγε. ἀλλὰ τὸ τοῦ Ἡσιόδου
καλῶς μοι φαίνεται ἔχειν, τὸ εἰ καί τις σμικρὸν ἐπὶ
σμικρῷ καταθείη, προὔργου εἶναι. εἰ οὖν καὶ
σμικρόν τι οἷός τ' εἶ πλέον ποιῆσαι, μὴ ἀπόκαμνε,
ἀλλ' εὐεργέτει καὶ Σωκράτη τόνδε—δίκαιος δ' εἶ—
καὶ ἐμέ.

ΣΩ. Καὶ μὲν δὴ ἔγωγε καὶ αὐτός, ὦ Κρατύλε,
οὐδὲν ἂν ἰσχυρισαίμην ὧν εἴρηκα, ᾗ δέ μοι ἐφαίνετο
μεθ' Ἑρμογένους ἐπεσκεψάμην, ὥστε τούτου γε
B ἕνεκα θαρρῶν λέγε, εἴ τι ἔχεις βέλτιον, ὡς ἐμοῦ
ἐνδεξομένου. εἰ μέντοι ἔχεις τι σὺ κάλλιον τούτων
λέγειν, οὐκ ἂν θαυμάζοιμι· δοκεῖς γάρ μοι αὐτός
τε ἐσκέφθαι τὰ τοιαῦτα καὶ παρ' ἄλλων μεμαθη-
κέναι. ἐὰν οὖν λέγῃς τι κάλλιον, ἕνα τῶν μαθητῶν
περὶ ὀρθότητος ὀνομάτων καὶ ἐμὲ γράφου.

ΚΡΑ. Ἀλλὰ μὲν δή, ὦ Σώκρατες, ὥσπερ σὺ

[1] ἐν τοῖς μέγιστον liber Bessarionis: ἐν τοῖς μεγίστοις
μέγιστον ΒΤ.

148

CRATYLUS

Cratylus often troubles me a good deal ; he declares that there is such a thing as correctness of names, but does not say clearly what it is ; and so I cannot tell whether he speaks so obscurely about it on any given occasion intentionally or unintentionally. So now, Cratylus, tell me, in the presence of Socrates, do you like what Socrates says about names, or have you a better theory to propose ? And if you have, tell us about it ; then you will either learn from Socrates or instruct both him and me.

CRA. But, Hermogenes, do you think it is an easy matter to learn or teach any subject so quickly, especially so important an one as this, which appears to me to be one of the most important ?

HER. No, by Zeus, I do not. But I think Hesiod is right in saying :

If you can only add little to little, it is worth while.[1]

So now if you can make even a little progress, do not shirk the trouble, but oblige Socrates—you owe it to him—and me.

soc. For that matter, Cratylus, I would not positively affirm any of the things I have said. I merely expressed the opinions which I reached with the help of Hermogenes. So far as I am concerned, you need not hesitate, and if your view is better than mine, I will accept it. And I should not be at all surprised if it were better ; for I think you have not only investigated such matters yourself but have been taught about them by others. So if you have any better theory to propound, put me down as one of your pupils in the course on the correctness of names.

CRA. Yes, Socrates, I have, as you say, paid

[1] Hesiod, *Works and Days*, 359.

PLATO

λέγεις, μεμέληκέν τέ μοι περὶ αὐτῶν καὶ ἴσως ἂν
σε ποιησαίμην μαθητήν. φοβοῦμαι μέντοι μὴ
C τούτου πᾶν τοὐναντίον ᾖ, ὅτι μοί πως ἐπέρχεται
λέγειν πρὸς σὲ τὸ τοῦ Ἀχιλλέως, ὃ ἐκεῖνος ἐν
Λιταῖς πρὸς τὸν Αἴαντα λέγει. φησὶ δὲ

> Αἶαν Διογενὲς Τελαμώνιε, κοίρανε λαῶν,
> πάντα τί μοι κατὰ θυμὸν ἐείσω μυθήσασθαι.

καὶ ἐμοὶ σύ, ὦ Σώκρατες, ἐπιεικῶς φαίνει κατὰ
νοῦν χρησμῳδεῖν, εἴτε παρ' Εὐθύφρονος ἐπίπνους
γενόμενος, εἴτε καὶ ἄλλη τις Μοῦσα πάλαι σε
ἐνοῦσα ἐλελήθει.
D ΣΩ. Ὠγαθὲ Κρατύλε, θαυμάζω καὶ αὐτὸς πάλαι
τὴν ἐμαυτοῦ σοφίαν καὶ ἀπιστῶ. δοκεῖ οὖν μοι
χρῆναι ἐπανασκέψασθαι τί καὶ λέγω. τὸ γὰρ
ἐξαπατᾶσθαι αὐτὸν ὑφ' αὑτοῦ πάντων χαλεπώ-
τατον· ὅταν γὰρ μηδὲ σμικρὸν ἀποστατῇ, ἀλλ'
ἀεὶ παρῇ ὁ ἐξαπατήσων, πῶς οὐ δεινόν; δεῖ δή,
ὡς ἔοικε, θαμὰ μεταστρέφεσθαι ἐπὶ τὰ προειρημένα, καὶ πειρᾶσθαι, τὸ ἐκείνου τοῦ ποιητοῦ,
βλέπειν ἅμα πρόσσω καὶ ὀπίσσω. καὶ δὴ καὶ
E νυνὶ ἡμεῖς ἴδωμεν τί ἡμῖν εἴρηται. ὀνόματος,
φαμέν, ὀρθότης ἐστὶν αὕτη, ἥτις ἐνδείξεται οἷόν ἐστι
τὸ πρᾶγμα· καὶ τοῦτο φῶμεν ἱκανῶς εἰρῆσθαι;
ΚΡΑ. Ἐμοὶ μὲν δοκεῖ πάνυ σφόδρα, ὦ Σώκρατες.
ΣΩ. Διδασκαλίας ἄρα ἕνεκα τὰ ὀνόματα λέγεται;
ΚΡΑ. Πάνυ γε.
ΣΩ. Οὐκοῦν φῶμεν καὶ ταύτην τέχνην εἶναι καὶ
δημιουργοὺς αὐτῆς;
ΚΡΑ. Πάνυ γε.

---

[1] Homer, *Iliad*, ix. 644 f.   [2] *Ibid.* i. 343, iii. 109.

CRATYLUS

attention to these matters, and perhaps I might
make you my pupil. However, I am afraid the
opposite is the case, and I am impelled to say to
you what Achilles says in the " Prayers " to Ajax.
He says : [1]

Ajax, descendant of Zeus, son of Telamon, chief of thy
 people,
All thou hast uttered is good in my sight and pleases my
 spirit.

And so, Socrates, your oracular utterances seem to
me to be much to my mind, whether you are inspired
by Euthyphro or some other Muse has dwelt within
you all along without our knowing it.

soc. My excellent Cratylus, I myself have been
marvelling at my own wisdom all along, and I
cannot believe in it. So I think we ought to re-
examine my utterances. For the worst of all
deceptions is self-deception. How can it help being
terrible, when the deceiver is always present and
never stirs from the spot ? So I think we must
turn back repeatedly to what we have said and must
try, as the poet says, to look " both forwards and
backwards." [2] Then let us now see what we have
said. Correctness of a name, we say, is the quality
of showing the nature of the thing named. Shall
we call that a satisfactory statement ?

cra. I am perfectly satisfied with it, Socrates.

soc. Names, then, are given with a view to
instruction ?

cra. Certainly.

soc. Shall we, then, say that this instruction is
an art and has its artisans ?

cra. Certainly.

PLATO

ΣΩ. Τίνας;

429 ΚΡΑ. Οὗσπερ σὺ κατ᾽ ἀρχὰς ἔλεγες, τοὺς νομοθέτας.

ΣΩ. Πότερον οὖν καὶ ταύτην φῶμεν τὴν τέχνην ἐν τοῖς ἀνθρώποις ἐγγίγνεσθαι ὥσπερ καὶ τὰς ἄλλας, ἢ μή; βούλομαι δὲ λέγειν τὸ τοιόνδε. ζωγράφοι εἰσίν που οἱ μὲν χείρους, οἱ δὲ ἀμείνους;

ΚΡΑ. Πάνυ γε.

ΣΩ. Οὐκοῦν οἱ μὲν ἀμείνους τὰ αὑτῶν ἔργα καλλίω παρέχονται, τὰ ζῷα, οἱ δὲ φαυλότερα; καὶ οἰκοδόμοι ὡσαύτως οἱ μὲν καλλίους τὰς οἰκίας ἐργάζονται, οἱ δὲ αἰσχίους;

ΚΡΑ. Ναί.

B ΣΩ. Ἆρ᾽ οὖν καὶ νομοθέται οἱ μὲν καλλίω τὰ ἔργα τὰ αὑτῶν παρέχονται, οἱ δὲ αἰσχίω;

ΚΡΑ. Οὔ μοι δοκεῖ τοῦτο ἔτι.

ΣΩ. Οὐκ ἄρα δοκοῦσί σοι νόμοι οἱ μὲν βελτίους, οἱ δὲ φαυλότεροι εἶναι;

ΚΡΑ. Οὐ δῆτα.

ΣΩ. Οὐδὲ δὴ ὄνομα, ὡς ἔοικε, δοκεῖ σοι κεῖσθαι τὸ μὲν χεῖρον, τὸ δὲ ἄμεινον;

ΚΡΑ. Οὐ δῆτα.

ΣΩ. Πάντα ἄρα τὰ ὀνόματα ὀρθῶς κεῖται;

ΚΡΑ. Ὅσα γε ὀνόματά ἐστιν.

ΣΩ. Τί οὖν; ὃ καὶ ἄρτι ἐλέγετο, Ἑρμογένει
C τῷδε πότερον μηδὲ ὄνομα τοῦτο κεῖσθαι φῶμεν, εἰ μή τι αὐτῷ Ἑρμοῦ γενέσεως προσήκει, ἢ κεῖσθαι μέν, οὐ μέντοι ὀρθῶς γε;

ΚΡΑ. Οὐδὲ κεῖσθαι ἔμοιγε δοκεῖ, ὦ Σώκρατες, ἀλλὰ δοκεῖν κεῖσθαι, εἶναι δὲ ἑτέρου τοῦτο τοὔνομα, οὗπερ καὶ ἡ φύσις ἡ τὸ ὄνομα δηλοῦσα.

ΣΩ. Πότερον οὐδὲ ψεύδεται, ὅταν τις φῇ Ἑρμο-

soc. Who are they ?

cra. The lawgivers, as you said in the beginning.

soc. Shall we declare that this art arises in men like the other arts, or not ? What I mean is this : Some painters are better, and others worse, are they not ?

cra. Certainly.

soc. And the better produce better works—that is, their paintings—and the others worse works ? And likewise some builders build better houses and others worse ?

cra. Yes.

soc. Then do some lawgivers produce better, and others worse works ?

cra. No ; at that point I cease to agree.

soc. Then you do not think that some laws are better, and some worse ?

cra. No, I do not.

soc. And you do not, it appears, think that one name is better, and another worse ?

cra. No, I do not.

soc. Then all names are correct ?

cra. All that are really names.

soc. How about the name of our friend Hermogenes, which was mentioned a while ago ? Shall we say that it is not his name at all, unless he belongs to the race of Hermes, or that it is his name, but is incorrect ?

cra. I think, Socrates, that it is not his name at all ; it appears to be his, but is really the name of some one else who possesses the nature that makes the name clear.

soc. And when anyone says that our friend is Hermogenes, is he not even speaking falsely ? For

153

γένη αὐτὸν εἶναι; μὴ γὰρ οὐδὲ τοῦτο αὖ ᾖ, τὸ
τοῦτον φάναι Ἑρμογένη εἶναι, εἰ μὴ ἔστιν;

ΚΡΑ. Πῶς λέγεις;

ΣΩ. ᾎρα ὅτι ψευδῆ λέγειν τὸ παράπαν οὐκ ἔστιν,
D ἆρα τοῦτό σοι δύναται ὁ λόγος; συχνοὶ γάρ τινες
οἱ λέγοντες, ὦ φίλε Κρατύλε, καὶ νῦν καὶ πάλαι.

ΚΡΑ. Πῶς γὰρ ἄν, ὦ Σώκρατες, λέγων γέ τις
τοῦτο ὃ λέγει, μὴ τὸ ὂν λέγοι; ἢ οὐ τοῦτό ἐστιν
τὸ ψευδῆ λέγειν, τὸ μὴ τὰ ὄντα λέγειν;

ΣΩ. Κομψότερος μὲν ὁ λόγος ἢ κατ᾽ ἐμὲ καὶ
κατὰ τὴν ἐμὴν ἡλικίαν, ὦ ἑταῖρε· ὅμως μέντοι
εἰπέ μοι τοσόνδε· πότερον λέγειν μὲν οὐ δοκεῖ
E σοι εἶναι ψευδῆ, φάναι δέ;

ΚΡΑ. Οὔ μοι δοκεῖ οὐδὲ φάναι.

ΣΩ. Οὐδὲ εἰπεῖν οὐδὲ προσειπεῖν; οἷον εἴ τις
ἀπαντήσας σοι ἐπὶ ξενίας, λαβόμενος τῆς χειρὸς
εἴποι· χαῖρε, ὦ ξένε Ἀθηναῖε, υἱὲ Σμικρίωνος
Ἑρμόγενες, οὗτος λέξειεν ἂν ταῦτα ἢ φαίη ἂν
ταῦτα ἢ εἴποι ἂν ταῦτα ἢ προσείποι ἂν οὕτω σὲ
μὲν οὔ, Ἑρμογένη δὲ τόνδε; ἢ οὐδένα;

ΚΡΑ. Ἐμοὶ μὲν δοκεῖ, ὦ Σώκρατες, ἄλλως ἂν
οὗτος ταῦτα φθέγξασθαι.

ΣΩ. Ἀλλ᾽ ἀγαπητὸν καὶ τοῦτο. πότερον γὰρ
430 ἀληθῆ ἂν φθέγξαιτο ταῦτα ὁ φθεγξάμενος ἢ ψευδῆ;
ἢ τὸ μέν τι αὐτῶν ἀληθές, τὸ δὲ ψεῦδος; καὶ γὰρ
ἂν καὶ τοῦτο ἐξαρκοῖ.

ΚΡΑ. Ψοφεῖν ἔγωγ᾽ ἂν φαίην τὸν τοιοῦτον,
μάτην αὐτὸν ἑαυτὸν κινοῦντα, ὥσπερ ἂν εἴ τι
χαλκεῖον κινήσειε κρούσας.

39. ΣΩ. Φέρε δή, ἐάν πῃ διαλλαχθῶμεν, ὦ
Κρατύλε· ἆρ᾽ οὐκ ἄλλο μὲν ἂν φαίης τὸ ὄνομα
εἶναι, ἄλλο δὲ ἐκεῖνο οὗ τὸ ὄνομά ἐστιν;

CRATYLUS

perhaps it is not even possible to say that he is
Hermogenes, if he is not.

CRA. What do you mean ?

SOC. Do you mean to say that it is impossible
to speak falsehood at all ? For there are, my dear
Cratylus, many who do so, and who have done so
in the past.

CRA. Why, Socrates, how could anyone who says
that which he says, say that which is not ? Is not
falsehood saying that which is not ?

SOC. Your reasoning is too clever for me at my
age, my friend. However, tell me this : Do you think
it is possible to speak falsehood, but not to say it ?

CRA. Neither to speak nor to say it.

SOC. Nor utter it or use it as a form of address ?
For instance, if some one should meet you in
hospitable fashion, should grasp your hand and say,
" Well met, my friend from Athens, son of Smicrion,
Hermogenes," would he be saying or speaking or
uttering or addressing these words not to you, but
to Hermogenes—or to nobody ?

CRA. I think, Socrates, the man would be pro-
ducing sounds without sense.

SOC. Even that reply is welcome ; for I can ask
whether the words he produced would be true, or
false, or partly true and partly false. Even that
would suffice.

CRA. I should say that the man in such a case
was merely making a noise, going through purpose-
less motions, as if he were beating a bronze pot.

SOC. Let us see, Cratylus, if we cannot come to
terms somehow. You would agree, would you not,
that the name is one thing and the thing of which
it is the name is another ?

ΚΡΑ. Ἔγωγε.

ΣΩ. Οὐκοῦν καὶ τὸ ὄνομα ὁμολογεῖς μίμημά τι
B εἶναι τοῦ πράγματος;

ΚΡΑ. Πάντων μάλιστα.

ΣΩ. Οὐκοῦν καὶ τὰ ζωγραφήματα τρόπον τινὰ
ἄλλον λέγεις μιμήματα εἶναι πραγμάτων τινῶν;

ΚΡΑ. Ναί.

ΣΩ. Φέρε δή—ἴσως γὰρ ἐγὼ οὐ μανθάνω ἅττα
ποτ᾽ ἔστιν ἃ λέγεις, σὺ δὲ τάχ᾽ ἂν ὀρθῶς λέγοις
—ἔστι διανεῖμαι καὶ προσενεγκεῖν ταῦτα ἀμφότερα
τὰ μιμήματα, τά τε ζωγραφήματα κἀκεῖνα τὰ
ὀνόματα, τοῖς πράγμασιν ὧν μιμήματά ἐστιν, ἢ οὔ;
C ΚΡΑ. Ἔστιν.

ΣΩ. Πρῶτον μὲν δὴ σκόπει τόδε. ἆρ᾽ ἄν τις
τὴν μὲν τοῦ ἀνδρὸς εἰκόνα τῷ ἀνδρὶ ἀποδοίη, τὴν δὲ
τῆς γυναικὸς τῇ γυναικί, καὶ τἆλλα οὕτως;

ΚΡΑ. Πάνυ μὲν οὖν.

ΣΩ. Οὐκοῦν καὶ τοὐναντίον τὴν μὲν τοῦ ἀνδρὸς
τῇ γυναικί, τὴν δὲ τῆς γυναικὸς τῷ ἀνδρί;

ΚΡΑ. Ἔστι καὶ ταῦτα.

ΣΩ. Ἆρ᾽ οὖν αὗται αἱ διανομαὶ ἀμφότεραι
ὀρθαί, ἢ ἡ ἑτέρα;

ΚΡΑ. Ἡ ἑτέρα.

ΣΩ. Ἡ ἂν ἑκάστῳ, οἶμαι, τὸ προσῆκόν τε καὶ
τὸ ὅμοιον ἀποδιδῷ.

ΚΡΑ. Ἔμοιγε δοκεῖ.

ΣΩ. Ἵνα τοίνυν μὴ μαχώμεθα ἐν τοῖς λόγοις
D ἐγώ τε καὶ σύ, φίλοι ὄντες, ἀπόδεξαί μου ὃ λέγω.
τὴν τοιαύτην γάρ, ὦ ἑταῖρε, καλῶ ἔγωγε διανομὴν
ἐπ᾽ ἀμφοτέροις μὲν τοῖς μιμήμασιν, τοῖς τε ζῴοις
καὶ τοῖς ὀνόμασιν, ὀρθήν, ἐπὶ δὲ τοῖς ὀνόμασι
πρὸς τῷ ὀρθὴν καὶ ἀληθῆ· τὴν δ᾽ ἑτέραν, τὴν τοῦ

CRATYLUS

CRA. Yes, I should.

soc. And you agree that the name is an imitation of the thing named ?

CRA. Most assuredly.

soc. And you agree that paintings also are imitations, though in a different way, of things ?

CRA. Yes.

soc. Well then—for perhaps I do not understand, and you may be right—can both of these imitations, the paintings and the names, be assigned and applied to the things which they imitate, or not ?

CRA. They can.

soc. First, then, consider this question : Can we assign the likeness of the man to the man and that of the woman to the woman, and so forth ?

CRA. Certainly.

soc. And can we conversely attribute that of the man to the woman, and the woman's to the man ?

CRA. That is also possible.

soc. And are these assignments both correct, or only the former ?

CRA. The former.

soc. The assignment, in short, which attributes to each that which belongs to it and is like it.

CRA. That is my view.

soc. To put an end to contentious argument between you and me, since we are friends, let me state my position. I call that kind of assignment in the case of both imitations—paintings and names —correct, and in the case of names not only correct, but true ; and the other kind, which gives and

ἀνομοίου δόσιν τε καὶ ἐπιφοράν, οὐκ ὀρθήν, καὶ ψευδῆ ὅταν ἐπ᾽ ὀνόμασιν ᾖ.

ΚΡΑ. Ἀλλ᾽ ὅπως μή, ὦ Σώκρατες, ἐν μὲν τοῖς ζωγραφήμασιν ᾖ τοῦτο, τὸ μὴ ὀρθῶς διανέμειν, E ἐπὶ δὲ τοῖς ὀνόμασιν οὔ, ἀλλ᾽ ἀναγκαῖον ᾖ ἀεὶ ὀρθῶς.

ΣΩ. Πῶς λέγεις; τί τοῦτο ἐκείνου διαφέρει; ἆρ᾽ οὐκ ἔστι προσελθόντα ἀνδρί τῳ εἰπεῖν, ὅτι "τουτί ἐστι σὸν γράμμα," καὶ δεῖξαι αὐτῷ, ἂν μὲν τύχῃ, ἐκείνου εἰκόνα, ἂν δὲ τύχῃ, γυναικός; τὸ δὲ δεῖξαι λέγω εἰς τὴν τῶν ὀφθαλμῶν αἴσθησιν καταστῆσαι.

ΚΡΑ. Πάνυ γε.

ΣΩ. Τί δέ; πάλιν αὐτῷ τούτῳ προσελθόντα εἰπεῖν, ὅτι "τουτί ἐστιν σὸν ὄνομα"; ἔστι δέ που καὶ τὸ ὄνομα μίμημα, ὥσπερ τὸ ζωγράφημα. 431 τοῦτο δὴ λέγω· ἆρ᾽ οὐκ ἂν εἴη αὐτῷ εἰπεῖν, ὅτι "τουτί ἐστι σὸν ὄνομα," καὶ μετὰ τοῦτο εἰς τὴν τῆς ἀκοῆς αὖ αἴσθησιν καταστῆσαι, ἂν μὲν τύχῃ, τὸ ἐκείνου μίμημα, εἰπόντα ὅτι ἀνήρ, ἂν δὲ τύχῃ, τὸ τοῦ θήλεος τοῦ ἀνθρωπίνου γένους, εἰπόντα ὅτι γυνή; οὐ δοκεῖ σοι τοῦτο οἷόν τ᾽ εἶναι καὶ γίγνεσθαι ἐνίοτε;

ΚΡΑ. Ἐθέλω σοι, ὦ Σώκρατες, ξυγχωρῆσαι, καὶ ἔστω οὕτως.

ΣΩ. Καλῶς γε σὺ ποιῶν, ὦ φίλε, εἰ ἔστι τοῦτο οὕτως· οὐδὲν γὰρ δεῖ νῦν πάνυ διαμάχεσθαι περὶ B αὐτοῦ. εἰ δ᾽ οὖν ἔστι τοιαύτη τις διανομὴ καὶ ἐνταῦθα, τὸ μὲν ἕτερον τούτων ἀληθεύειν βουλόμεθα καλεῖν, τὸ δ᾽ ἕτερον ψεύδεσθαι. εἰ δὲ τοῦτο οὕτως ἔχει, καὶ ἔστι μὴ ὀρθῶς διανέμειν τὰ ὀνόματα μηδὲ ἀποδιδόναι τὰ προσήκοντα ἑκάστῳ, ἀλλ᾽ ἐνίοτε τὰ μὴ προσήκοντα, εἴη ἂν καὶ ῥήματα

applies the unlike imitation, I call incorrect and, in the case of names, false.

CRA. But it may be, Socrates, that this incorrect assignment is possible in the case of paintings, and not in the case of names, which must be always correctly assigned.

SOC. What do you mean ? What difference is there between the two ? Can I not step up to a man and say, " This is your portrait," and show him perhaps his own likeness or, perhaps, that of a woman ? And by " show " I mean bring before the sense of sight.

CRA. Certainly.

SOC. Well, then, can I not step up to the same man again and say, " This is your name " ? A name is an imitation, just as a picture is. Very well ; can I not say to him, " This is your name," and then bring before his sense of hearing perhaps the imitation of himself, saying that it is a man, or perhaps the imitation of the female of the human species, saying that it is a woman ? Do you not believe that this is possible and sometimes happens ?

CRA. I am willing to concede it, Socrates, and grant that you are right.

SOC. That is a good thing for you to do, my friend, if I am right ; for now we need no longer argue about the matter. If, then, some such assignment of names takes place, we will call one kind speaking truth, and the other speaking falsehood. But if this is accepted, and if it is possible to assign names incorrectly and to give to objects not the names that befit them, but sometimes those that are unfitting, it would be possible to treat verbs in the same way.

159

ταὐτὸν τοῦτο ποιεῖν. εἰ δὲ ῥήματα καὶ ὀνόματα
ἔστιν οὕτω τιθέναι, ἀνάγκη καὶ λόγους· λόγοι
γάρ που, ὡς ἐγῷμαι, ἡ τούτων ξύνθεσίς ἐστιν·
C ἢ πῶς λέγεις, ὦ Κρατύλε;

ΚΡΑ. Οὕτω· καλῶς γάρ μοι δοκεῖς λέγειν.

ΣΩ. Οὐκοῦν εἰ γράμμασιν αὖ τὰ πρῶτα ὀνόματα
ἀπεικάζομεν, ἔστιν ὥσπερ ἐν τοῖς ζωγραφήμασιν
καὶ πάντα τὰ προσήκοντα χρώματά τε καὶ σχήματα ἀποδοῦναι, καὶ μὴ πάντα αὖ, ἀλλ' ἔνια ἐλ-
λείπειν, ἔνια δὲ καὶ προστιθέναι, καὶ πλείω καὶ
μείζω· ἢ οὐκ ἔστιν;

ΚΡΑ. Ἔστιν.

ΣΩ. Οὐκοῦν ὁ μὲν ἀποδιδοὺς πάντα καλὰ τὰ
γράμματά τε καὶ τὰς εἰκόνας ἀποδίδωσιν, ὁ δὲ ἢ
προστιθεὶς ἢ ἀφαιρῶν γράμματα μὲν καὶ εἰκόνας
ἐργάζεται καὶ οὗτος, ἀλλὰ πονηράς;

D ΚΡΑ. Ναί.

ΣΩ. Τί δὲ ὁ διὰ τῶν συλλαβῶν τε καὶ γραμμάτων τὴν οὐσίαν τῶν πραγμάτων ἀπομιμούμενος;
ἆρα οὐ κατὰ τὸν αὐτὸν λόγον, ἂν μὲν πάντα ἀποδῷ
τὰ προσήκοντα, καλὴ ἡ εἰκὼν ἔσται—τοῦτο δ'
ἐστὶν ὄνομα—ἐὰν δὲ σμικρὰ ἐλλείπῃ ἢ προστιθῇ
ἐνίοτε, εἰκὼν μὲν γενήσεται, καλὴ δὲ οὔ; ὥστε
τὰ μὲν καλῶς εἰργασμένα ἔσται τῶν ὀνομάτων, τὰ
δὲ κακῶς;

ΚΡΑ. Ἴσως.

E ΣΩ. Ἴσως ἄρα ἔσται ὁ μὲν ἀγαθὸς δημιουργὸς
ὀνομάτων, ὁ δὲ κακός;

ΚΡΑ. Ναί.

ΣΩ. Οὐκοῦν τούτῳ ὁ νομοθέτης ἦν ὄνομα.

ΚΡΑ. Ναί.

ΣΩ. Ἴσως ἄρα νὴ Δί' ἔσται, ὥσπερ ἐν ταῖς ἄλλαις

160

And if verbs and nouns can be assigned in this way, the same must be true of sentences ; for sentences are, I conceive, a combination of verbs and nouns. What do you say to that, Cratylus ?

CRA. I agree ; I think you are right.

SOC. If, then, we compare the earliest words to sketches, it is possible in them, as in pictures, to reproduce all the appropriate colours and shapes, or not all ; some may be wanting, and some may be added, and they may be too many or too large. Is not that true ?

CRA. Yes, it is.

SOC. Then he who reproduces all, produces good sketches and pictures, and he who adds or takes away produces also sketches and pictures, but bad ones ?

CRA. Yes.

SOC. And how about him who imitates the nature of things by means of letters and syllables ? By the same principle, if he gives all that is appropriate, the image—that is to say, the name—will be good, and if he sometimes omits or adds a little, it will be an image, but not a good one ; and therefore some names are well and others badly made. Is that not true ?

CRA. Perhaps.

SOC. Perhaps, then, one artisan of names will be good, and another bad ?

CRA. Yes.

SOC. The name of such an artisan was lawgiver ?

CRA. Yes.

SOC. Perhaps, then, by Zeus, as is the case in

161

τέχναις, καὶ νομοθέτης ὁ μὲν ἀγαθός, ὁ δὲ κακός, ἐάνπερ τὰ ἔμπροσθεν ἐκεῖνα ὁμολογηθῇ ἡμῖν.

ΚΡΑ. Ἔστι ταῦτα. ἀλλ᾽ ὁρᾷς, ὦ Σώκρατες, ὅταν ταῦτα τὰ γράμματα, τό τε ἄλφα καὶ τὸ βῆτα καὶ ἕκαστον τῶν στοιχείων, τοῖς ὀνόμασιν ἀπο-
432 διδῶμεν τῇ γραμματικῇ τέχνῃ, ἐάν τι ἀφέλωμεν ἢ προσθῶμεν ἢ μεταθῶμέν τι, οὐ[1] γέγραπται μὲν ἡμῖν τὸ ὄνομα, οὐ μέντοι ὀρθῶς, ἀλλὰ τὸ παράπαν οὐδὲ γέγραπται, ἀλλ᾽ εὐθὺς ἕτερόν ἐστιν, ἐάν τι τούτων πάθῃ.

ΣΩ. Μὴ γὰρ οὐ καλῶς σκοπῶμεν οὕτω σκοποῦν-τες, ὦ Κρατύλε.

ΚΡΑ. Πῶς δή;

ΣΩ. Ἴσως ὅσα ἔκ τινος ἀριθμοῦ ἀναγκαῖον εἶναι ἢ μὴ εἶναι, πάσχοι ἂν τοῦτο ὃ σὺ λέγεις, ὥσπερ καὶ αὐτὰ τὰ δέκα ἢ ὅστις βούλει ἄλλος ἀριθμός,
Β ἐὰν ἀφέλῃς τι ἢ προσθῇς, ἕτερος εὐθὺς γέγονε· τοῦ δὲ ποιοῦ τινος καὶ ξυμπάσης εἰκόνος μὴ οὐχ αὕτη ᾖ[2] ἡ ὀρθότης, ἀλλὰ τὸ ἐναντίον οὐδὲ τὸ παράπαν δέῃ πάντα ἀποδοῦναι, οἷόν ἐστιν ᾧ[3] εἰκάζει, εἰ μέλλει εἰκὼν εἶναι. σκόπει δέ, εἰ τὶ λέγω. ἆρ᾽ ἂν δύο πράγματα εἴη τοιάδε, οἷον Κρατύλος καὶ Κρατύλου εἰκών, εἴ τις θεῶν μὴ μόνον τὸ σὸν χρῶμα καὶ σχῆμα ἀπεικάσειεν ὥσπερ οἱ ζωγράφοι, ἀλλὰ καὶ τὰ ἐντὸς πάντα τοιαῦτα ποιήσειεν οἷάπερ τὰ σά, καὶ μαλακότητας
C καὶ θερμότητας τὰς αὐτὰς ἀποδοίη, καὶ κίνησιν καὶ ψυχὴν καὶ φρόνησιν οἷαπερ ἡ παρὰ σοὶ ἐνθείη αὐτοῖς, καὶ ἑνὶ λόγῳ πάντα ἅπερ σὺ ἔχεις, τοιαῦτα ἕτερα καταστήσειεν πλησίον σου; πότερον Κρατύ-

---

[1] οὐ add. Bekker.   [2] ᾖ add. Heindorf
[3] ᾧ Burnet: ὃ BT.

the other arts, one lawgiver may be good and another bad, if we accept our previous conclusions.

CRA. That is true. But you see, Socrates, when by the science of grammar we assign these letters—alpha, beta, and the rest—to names, if we take away or add or transpose any letter, it is not true that the name is written, but written incorrectly ; it is not written at all, but immediately becomes a different word, if any such thing happens to it.

SOC. Perhaps we are not considering the matter in the right way.

CRA. Why not ?

SOC. It may be that what you say would be true of those things which must necessarily consist of a certain number or cease to exist at all, as ten, for instance, or any number you like, if you add or subtract anything is immediately another number ; but this is not the kind of correctness which applies to quality or to images in general ; on the contrary, the image must not by any means reproduce all the qualities of that which it imitates, if it is to be an image. See if I am not right. Would there be two things, Cratylus and the image of Cratylus, if some god should not merely imitate your colour and form, as painters do, but should also make all the inner parts like yours, should reproduce the same flexibility and warmth, should put into them motion, life, and intellect, such as exist in you, and in short, should place beside you a duplicate of all your qualities ? Would there be in such an

PLATO

λος ἂν καὶ εἰκὼν Κρατύλου τότ' εἴη τὸ τοιοῦτον, ἢ δύο Κρατύλοι;

ΚΡΑ. Δύο ἔμοιγε δοκοῦσιν, ὦ Σώκρατες, Κρατύλοι.

40. ΣΩ. Ὁρᾷς οὖν, ὦ φίλε, ὅτι ἄλλην χρὴ εἰκόνος ὀρθότητα ζητεῖν καὶ ὧν νῦν δὴ ἐλέγομεν, D καὶ οὐκ ἀναγκάζειν, ἐάν τι ἀπῇ ἢ προσῇ, μηκέτι αὐτὴν εἰκόνα εἶναι; ἢ οὐκ αἰσθάνει ὅσου ἐνδέουσιν αἱ εἰκόνες τὰ αὐτὰ ἔχειν ἐκείνοις ὧν εἰκόνες εἰσίν;

ΚΡΑ. Ἔγωγε.

ΣΩ. Γελοῖα γοῦν, ὦ Κρατύλε, ὑπὸ τῶν ὀνομάτων πάθοι ἂν ἐκεῖνα ὧν ὀνόματά ἐστι τὰ ὀνόματα, εἰ πάντα πανταχῇ αὐτοῖς ὁμοιωθείη. διττὰ γὰρ ἄν που πάντα γένοιτο, καὶ οὐκ ἂν ἔχοι αὐτῶν εἰπεῖν οὐδεὶς¹ οὐδέτερον ὁπότερόν ἐστι τὸ μὲν αὐτό, τὸ δὲ ὄνομα.

ΚΡΑ. Ἀληθῆ λέγεις.

ΣΩ. Θαρρῶν τοίνυν, ὦ γενναῖε, ἔα καὶ ὄνομα τὸ E μὲν εὖ κεῖσθαι, τὸ δὲ μή, καὶ μὴ ἀνάγκαζε πάντ' ἔχειν τὰ γράμματα, ἵνα κομιδῇ ᾖ τοιοῦτον οἷόνπερ οὗ ὄνομά ἐστιν, ἀλλ' ἔα καὶ τὸ μὴ προσῆκον γράμμα ἐπιφέρειν. εἰ δὲ γράμμα, καὶ ὄνομα ἐν λόγῳ· εἰ δὲ ὄνομα, καὶ λόγον ἐν λόγῳ μὴ προσήκοντα τοῖς πράγμασιν ἐπιφέρεσθαι, καὶ μηδὲν ἧττον ὀνομάζεσθαι τὸ πρᾶγμα καὶ λέγεσθαι, ἕως ἂν ὁ τύπος ἐνῇ τοῦ πράγματος περὶ οὗ ἂν ὁ λόγος 433 ᾖ, ὥσπερ ἐν τοῖς τῶν στοιχείων ὀνόμασιν, εἰ μέμνησαι ἃ νῦν δὴ ἐγὼ καὶ Ἑρμογένης ἐλέγομεν.

ΚΡΑ. Ἀλλὰ μέμνημαι.

ΣΩ. Καλῶς τοίνυν. ὅταν γὰρ τοῦτο ἐνῇ, κἂν

¹ οὐδεὶς add. Burnet.

164

event Cratylus and an image of Cratylus, or two Cratyluses ?

CRA. I should say, Socrates, two Cratyluses.

SOC. Then don't you see, my friend, that we must look for some other principle of correctness in images and in names, of which we were speaking, and must not insist that they are no longer images if anything be wanting or be added ? Do you not perceive how far images are from possessing the same qualities as the originals which they imitate ?

CRA. Yes, I do.

SOC. Surely, Cratylus, the effect produced by the names upon the things of which they are the names would be ridiculous, if they were to be entirely like them in every respect. For everything would be duplicated, and no one could tell in any case which was the real thing and which the name.

CRA. Quite true.

SOC. Then do not be faint-hearted, but have the courage to admit that one name may be correctly and another incorrectly given ; do not insist that it must have all the letters and be exactly the same as the thing named, but grant that an inappropriate letter may be employed. But if a letter, then grant that also a noun in a clause, and if a noun, then also a clause in a sentence may be employed which is not appropriate to the things in question, and the thing may none the less be named and described, so long as the intrinsic quality of the thing named is retained, as is the case in the names of the letters of the alphabet, if you remember what Hermogenes and I were saying a while ago.

CRA. Yes, I remember.

SOC. Very well, then. So long as this intrinsic

μὴ πάντα τὰ προσήκοντα ἔχῃ, λέξεταί γε τὸ
πρᾶγμα, καλῶς, ὅταν πάντα, κακῶς δέ, ὅταν
ὀλίγα· λέγεσθαι δ' οὖν, ὦ μακάριε, ἐῶμεν, ἵνα
μὴ ὄφλωμεν ὥσπερ οἱ ἐν Αἰγίνῃ νύκτωρ περιιόντες
ὀψὲ ὁδοῦ, καὶ ἡμεῖς ἐπὶ τὰ πράγματα δόξωμεν
αὐτῇ τῇ ἀληθείᾳ οὕτω πως ἐληλυθέναι ὀψιαίτερον
B τοῦ δέοντος, ἢ ζήτει τινὰ ἄλλην ὀνόματος ὀρθότητα,
καὶ μὴ ὁμολόγει δήλωμα συλλαβαῖς καὶ γράμμασι
πράγματος ὄνομα εἶναι. εἰ γὰρ ταῦτα ἀμφότερα
ἐρεῖς, οὐχ οἷός τ' ἔσει συμφωνεῖν σαυτῷ.

ΚΡΑ. Ἀλλά μοι δοκεῖς γε, ὦ Σώκρατες, μετρίως
λέγειν, καὶ οὕτω τίθεμαι.

ΣΩ. Ἐπειδὴ τοίνυν ταῦτα ἡμῖν ξυνδοκεῖ, μετὰ
ταῦτα τάδε σκοπῶμεν· εἰ μέλλει, φαμέν, καλῶς
κεῖσθαι τὸ ὄνομα, τὰ προσήκοντα δεῖ αὐτὸ γράμματα ἔχειν;

ΚΡΑ. Ναί.

C ΣΩ. Προσήκει δὲ τὰ ὅμοια τοῖς πράγμασιν;

ΚΡΑ. Πάνυ γε.

ΣΩ. Τὰ μὲν ἄρα καλῶς κείμενα οὕτω κεῖται·
εἰ δὲ μή τι καλῶς ἐτέθη, τὸ μὲν ἂν πολὺ ἴσως ἐκ
προσηκόντων εἴη γραμμάτων καὶ ὁμοίων, εἴπερ
ἔσται εἰκών, ἔχοι δ' ἄν τι καὶ οὐ προσῆκον, δι'
ὃ οὐκ ἂν καλὸν εἴη οὐδὲ καλῶς εἰργασμένον τὸ
ὄνομα. οὕτω φαμὲν ἢ ἄλλως;

ΚΡΑ. Οὐδὲν δεῖ, οἶμαι, διαμάχεσθαι, ὦ Σώ-
κρατες· ἐπεὶ οὐκ ἀρέσκει γέ με τὸ φάναι ὄνομα
μὲν εἶναι, μὴ μέντοι καλῶς γε κεῖσθαι.

ΣΩ. Πότερον τοῦτο οὐκ ἀρέσκει σε, τὸ εἶναι τὸ
D ὄνομα δήλωμα τοῦ πράγματος;

166

quality is present, even though the name have not all the proper letters, the thing will still be named; well, when it has all the proper letters; badly, when it has only a few of them. Let us, then, grant this, my friend, or we shall get into trouble, like the belated night wanderers in the road at Aegina,[1] and in very truth we shall be found to have arrived too late; otherwise you must look for some other principle of correctness in names, and must not admit that a name is the representation of a thing in syllables and letters. For if you maintain both positions, you cannot help contradicting yourself.

CRA. Well, Socrates, I think what you say is reasonable, and I accept it.

SOC. Then since we are agreed about this, let us consider the next point. If a name, we say, is to be a good one, it must have the proper letters?

CRA. Yes.

SOC. And the proper letters are those which are like the things named?

CRA. Yes, certainly.

SOC. That is, then, the method by which well-given names are given. But if any name is not well given, the greater part of it may perhaps, if it is to be an image at all, be made up of proper and like letters, but it may contain some inappropriate element, and is on that account not good or well made. Is that our view?

CRA. I suppose, Socrates, there is no use in keeping up my contention; but I am not satisfied that it can be a name and not be well given.

SOC. Are you not satisfied that the name is the representation of a thing?

---

[1] This seems to refer to some story unknown to us.

ΚΡΑ. Ἐμέ γε.¹

ΣΩ. Ἀλλὰ τὸ εἶναι τῶν ὀνομάτων τὰ μὲν ἐκ
προτέρων ξυγκείμενα, τὰ δὲ πρῶτα, οὐ καλῶς²
σοι δοκεῖ λέγεσθαι;

ΚΡΑ. Ἔμοιγε.

ΣΩ. Ἀλλὰ τὰ πρῶτα εἰ μέλλει δηλώματά τινων
γίγνεσθαι, ἔχεις τινὰ καλλίω τρόπον τοῦ δηλώματα
αὐτὰ γενέσθαι ἄλλον ἢ αὐτὰ ποιῆσαι ὅτι μάλιστα
E τοιαῦτα οἷα ἐκεῖνα ἃ δεῖ δηλοῦν αὐτά; ἢ³ ὅδε
μᾶλλόν σε ἀρέσκει ὁ τρόπος ὃν Ἑρμογένης λέγει
καὶ ἄλλοι πολλοί, τὸ ξυνθήματα εἶναι τὰ ὀνόματα
καὶ δηλοῦν τοῖς ξυνθεμένοις, προειδόσι δὲ τὰ
πράγματα, καὶ εἶναι ταύτην ὀρθότητα ὀνόματος,
ξυνθήκην, διαφέρειν δὲ οὐδέν, ἐάντε τις ξυνθῆται
ὥσπερ νῦν ξύγκειται, ἐάντε καὶ τοὐναντίον ἐπὶ
μὲν ᾧ⁴ νῦν σμικρόν, μέγα καλεῖν, ἐπὶ δὲ ᾧ μέγα,
σμικρόν; πότερός σε ὁ τρόπος ἀρέσκει;

434 ΚΡΑ. Ὅλῳ καὶ παντὶ διαφέρει, ὦ Σώκρατες, τὸ
ὁμοιώματι δηλοῦν ὅ τι ἄν τις δηλοῖ, ἀλλὰ μὴ τῷ
ἐπιτυχόντι.

ΣΩ. Καλῶς λέγεις. οὐκοῦν εἴπερ ἔσται τὸ ὄνομα
ὅμοιον τῷ πράγματι, ἀναγκαῖον πεφυκέναι τὰ
στοιχεῖα ὅμοια τοῖς πράγμασιν, ἐξ ὧν τὰ πρῶτα
ὀνόματά τις ξυνθήσει; ὧδε δὲ λέγω· ἆρά ποτ'
ἄν⁵ τις ξυνέθηκεν ὃ νῦν δὴ ἐλέγομεν ζωγράφημα
ὅμοιόν τῳ τῶν ὄντων, εἰ μὴ φύσει ὑπῆρχε φάρμα-
B κεῖα ὅμοια ὄντα, ἐξ ὧν ξυντίθεται τὰ ζωγραφού-
μενα, ἐκείνοις ἃ μιμεῖται ἡ γραφική· ἢ ἀδύνατον;

ΚΡΑ. Ἀδύνατον.

---

¹ ἐμέ γε Bekker: ἔμοιγε B: ἔμοι T.
² οὐ καλῶς t: οὐκ ἄλλως B (om. T γε ἀλλὰ . . . ἔμοι).
³ ἢ] ἤ T: καὶ ἢ B: καὶ ἢ b.

CRATYLUS

CRA. Yes.

soc. And do you not think it is true that some names are composed of earlier ones and others are primary ?

CRA. Yes.

soc. But if the primary names are to be representations of any things, can you suggest any better way of making them representations than by making them as much as possible like the things which they are to represent ? Or do you prefer the theory advanced by Hermogenes and many others, who claim that names are conventional and represent things to those who established the convention and knew the things beforehand, and that convention is the sole principle of correctness in names, and it makes no difference whether we accept the existing convention or adopt an opposite one according to which small would be called great and great small ? Which of these two theories do you prefer ?

CRA. Representing by likeness the thing represented is absolutely and entirely superior to representation by chance signs.

soc. You are right. Then if the name is like the thing, the letters of which the primary names are to be formed must be by their very nature like the things, must they not ? Let me explain. Could a painting, to revert to our previous comparison, ever be made like any real thing, if there were no pigments out of which the painting is composed, which were by their nature like the objects which the painter's art imitates ? Is not that impossible ?

CRA. Yes, it is impossible.

---

⁴ ᾧ V : ὅ BT (but by emendation in B).
⁵ ἆρά ποτ' ἄν vulg.: ἆρα ὁπότ' ἄν BT.

ΣΩ. Οὐκοῦν ὡσαύτως καὶ ὀνόματα οὐκ ἄν ποτε ὅμοια γένοιτο οὐδενί, εἰ μὴ ὑπάρξει ἐκεῖνα πρῶτον ὁμοιότητά τινα ἔχοντα, ἐξ ὧν ξυντίθεται τὰ ὀνόματα, ἐκείνοις ὧν ἐστι τὰ ὀνόματα μιμήματα; ἔστι δέ, ἐξ ὧν συνθετέον, στοιχεῖα;

ΚΡΑ. Ναί.

41. ΣΩ. Ἤδη τοίνυν καὶ σὺ κοινώνει τοῦ λόγου C οὗπερ ἄρτι Ἑρμογένης. φέρε, καλῶς σοι δοκοῦμεν λέγειν ὅτι τὸ ῥῶ τῇ φορᾷ καὶ κινήσει καὶ σκληρότητι προσέοικεν, ἢ οὐ καλῶς;

ΚΡΑ. Καλῶς ἔμοιγε.

ΣΩ. Τὸ δὲ λάβδα τῷ λείῳ καὶ μαλακῷ καὶ οἷς νῦν δὴ ἐλέγομεν,

ΚΡΑ. Ναί.

ΣΩ. Οἶσθα οὖν, ὅτι ἐπὶ τῷ αὐτῷ ἡμεῖς μέν φαμεν σκληρότης, Ἐρετριῆς δὲ σκληρότηρ;

ΚΡΑ. Πάνυ γε.

ΣΩ. Πότερον οὖν τό τε ῥῶ καὶ τὸ σῖγμα ἔοικεν ἀμφότερα τῷ αὐτῷ, καὶ δηλοῖ ἐκείνοις τε τὸ αὐτὸ τελευτῶντος τοῦ ῥῶ καὶ ἡμῖν τοῦ σῖγμα, ἢ τοῖς ἑτέροις ἡμῶν οὐ δηλοῖ;

D ΚΡΑ. Δηλοῖ μὲν οὖν ἀμφοτέροις.

ΣΩ. Πότερον ᾗ ὅμοια τυγχάνει ὄντα τὸ ῥῶ καὶ τὸ σῖγμα, ἢ ᾗ μή;

ΚΡΑ. Ἧι ὅμοια.

ΣΩ. Ἦ οὖν ὅμοιά ἐστι πανταχῇ;

ΚΡΑ. Πρός γε τὸ ἴσως φορὰν δηλοῦν.

ΣΩ. Ἦ καὶ τὸ λάβδα ἐγκείμενον; οὐ τὰ ἐναντίον δηλοῖ σκληρότητος;

ΚΡΑ. Ἴσως γὰρ οὐκ ὀρθῶς ἔγκειται, ὦ Σώκρατες·

soc. In the same way, names can never be like anything unless those elements of which the names are composed exist in the first place and possess some kind of likeness to the things which the names imitate ; and the elements of which they are composed are the letters, are they not ?

cra. Yes.

soc. Then I must now ask you to consider with me the subject which Hermogenes and I discussed a while ago. Do you think I am right in saying that rho is expressive of speed, motion, and hardness, or not ?

cra. You are right.

soc. And lambda is like smoothness, softness, and the other qualities we mentioned ?

cra. Yes.

soc. You know, of course, that we call the same thing σκληρότης (hardness) which the Eretrians call σκληρότηρ ?

cra. Certainly.

soc. Have rho and sigma both a likeness to the same thing, and does the final rho mean to them just what the sigma means to us, or is there to one of us no meaning ?

cra. They mean the same to both.

soc. In so far as rho and sigma are alike, or in so far as they are not ?

cra. In so far as they are alike.

soc. And are they alike in all respects ?

cra. Yes ; at least for the purpose of expressing motion equally.

soc. But how about the lambda in σκληρότης ? Does it not express the opposite of hardness ?

cra. Well, perhaps it has no right to be there,

171

ὥσπερ καὶ ἃ νῦν δὴ σὺ πρὸς Ἑρμογένη ἔλεγες ἐξαιρῶν τε καὶ ἐντιθεὶς γράμματα οὗ δέοι, καὶ ὀρθῶς ἐδόκεις ἔμοιγε. καὶ νῦν ἴσως ἀντὶ τοῦ λάβδα ῥῶ δεῖ λέγειν.

E ΣΩ. Εὖ λέγεις. τί οὖν; νῦν ὡς λέγομεν, οὐδὲν μανθάνομεν ἀλλήλων, ἐπειδάν τις φῇ σκληρόν, οὐδὲ οἶσθα σὺ νῦν ὅ τι ἐγὼ λέγω;

ΚΡΑ. Ἔγωγε, διά γε τὸ ἔθος, ὦ φίλτατε.

ΣΩ. Ἔθος δὲ λέγων οἴει τι διάφορον λέγειν ξυνθήκης; ἢ ἄλλο τι λέγεις τὸ ἔθος ἢ ὅτι ἐγώ, ὅταν τοῦτο φθέγγωμαι, διανοοῦμαι ἐκεῖνο, σὺ δὲ γιγνώσκεις ὅτι ἐκεῖνο διανοοῦμαι; οὐ τοῦτο λέγεις;

435 ΚΡΑ. Ναί.

ΣΩ. Οὐκοῦν εἰ γιγνώσκεις ἐμοῦ φθεγγομένου, δήλωμά σοι γίγνεται παρ' ἐμοῦ;

ΚΡΑ. Ναί.

ΣΩ. Ἀπὸ τοῦ ἀνομοίου γε ἢ ὃ διανοούμενος φθέγγομαι, εἴπερ τὸ λάβδα ἀνόμοιόν ἐστι τῇ ᾗ φῂς σὺ σκληρότητι· εἰ δὲ τοῦτο οὕτως ἔχει, τί ἄλλο ἢ αὐτὸς σαυτῷ ξυνέθου καί σοι γίγνεται ἡ ὀρθότης τοῦ ὀνόματος ξυνθήκη, ἐπειδή γε δηλοῖ καὶ τὰ ὅμοια καὶ τὰ ἀνόμοια γράμματα, ἔθους τε καὶ ξυνθήκης τυχόντα; εἰ δ' ὅτι μάλιστα μή ἐστι

B τὸ ἔθος ξυνθήκη, οὐκ ἂν καλῶς ἔτι ἔχοι λέγειν τὴν ὁμοιότητα δήλωμα εἶναι, ἀλλὰ τὸ ἔθος· ἐκεῖνο γάρ, ὡς ἔοικε, καὶ ὁμοίῳ καὶ ἀνομοίῳ δηλοῖ. ἐπειδὴ δὲ ταῦτα ξυγχωροῦμεν, ὦ Κρατύλε—τὴν γὰρ σιγήν σου ξυγχώρησιν θήσω—ἀναγκαῖόν που καὶ ξυνθήκην τι καὶ ἔθος ξυμβάλλεσθαι πρὸς δήλωσιν ὧν διανοούμενοι λέγομεν· ἐπεί, ὦ βέλ-

Socrates; it may be like the cases that came up in your talk with Hermogenes, when you removed or inserted letters where that was necessary. I think you did right; and in this case perhaps we ought to put a rho in place of the lambda.

soc. Excellent. However, do we not understand one another when anyone says σκληρόν, using the present pronunciation, and do you not now know what I mean?

cra. Yes, but that is by custom, my friend.

soc. In saying " custom " do you think you are saying anything different from convention? Do you not mean by " convention " that when I speak I have a definite meaning and you recognize that I have that meaning? Is not that what you mean?

cra. Yes.

soc. Then if you recognize my meaning when I speak, that is an indication given to you by me.

cra. Yes.

soc. The indication comes from something which is unlike my meaning when I speak, if in your example σκληρότης the lambda is unlike hardness; and if this is true, did you not make a convention with yourself, since both like and unlike letters, by the influence of custom and convention, produce indication? And even if custom is entirely distinct from convention, we should henceforth be obliged to say that custom, not likeness, is the principle of indication, since custom, it appears, indicates both by the like and by the unlike. And since we grant this, Cratylus—for I take it that your silence gives consent—both convention and custom must contribute something towards the indication of our meaning when we speak. For, my friend, if you

τιστε, εἰ θέλεις ἐπὶ τὸν ἀριθμὸν ἐλθεῖν, πόθεν οἴει
ἕξειν ὀνόματα ὅμοια ἑνὶ ἑκάστῳ τῶν ἀριθμῶν
C ἐπενεγκεῖν, ἐὰν μὴ ἐᾷς τι τὴν σὴν ὁμολογίαν καὶ
ξυνθήκην κῦρος ἔχειν τῶν ὀνομάτων ὀρθότητος
πέρι; ἐμοὶ μὲν οὖν καὶ αὐτῷ ἀρέσκει μὲν κατὰ
τὸ δυνατὸν ὅμοια εἶναι τὰ ὀνόματα τοῖς πράγμασιν·
ἀλλὰ μὴ ὡς ἀληθῶς, τὸ τοῦ Ἑρμογένους, γλίσχρα
ᾖ ἡ ὁλκὴ αὕτη τῆς ὁμοιότητος, ἀναγκαῖον δὲ ᾖ
καὶ τῷ φορτικῷ τούτῳ προσχρῆσθαι, τῇ ξυνθήκῃ,
εἰς ὀνομάτων ὀρθότητα. ἐπεὶ ἴσως κατά γε τὸ
δυνατὸν κάλλιστ᾽ ἂν λέγοιτο ὅταν ἢ πᾶσιν ἢ ὡς
πλείστοις ὁμοίοις[1] λέγηται, τοῦτο δ᾽ ἐστὶ προσ-
D ήκουσιν, αἴσχιστα δὲ τοὐναντίον. τόδε δέ μοι
ἔτι εἰπὲ μετὰ ταῦτα, τίνα ἡμῖν δύναμιν ἔχει τὰ
ὀνόματα καὶ τί φῶμεν αὐτὰ καλὸν ἀπεργάζεσθαι;

42. ΚΡΑ. Διδάσκειν ἔμοιγε δοκεῖ, ὦ Σώκρατες,
καὶ τοῦτο πάνυ ἁπλοῦν εἶναι, ὃς ἂν τὰ ὀνόματα
ἐπίστηται, ἐπίστασθαι καὶ τὰ πράγματα.

ΣΩ. Ἴσως γάρ, ὦ Κρατύλε, τὸ τοιόνδε λέγεις,
ὡς ἐπειδάν τις εἰδῇ τὸ ὄνομα οἷόν ἐστιν — ἔστι δὲ
οἷόνπερ τὸ πρᾶγμα—εἴσεται δὴ καὶ τὸ πρᾶγμα,
E ἐπείπερ ὅμοιον τυγχάνει ὂν τῷ ὀνόματι, τέχνη δὲ
μία ἄρ᾽ ἐστὶν ἡ αὐτὴ πάντων τῶν ἀλλήλοις ὁμοίων.
κατὰ τοῦτο δή μοι δοκεῖς λέγειν ὡς ὃς ἂν τὰ
ὀνόματα εἰδῇ εἴσεται καὶ τὰ πράγματα.

ΚΡΑ. Ἀληθέστατα λέγεις.

ΣΩ. Ἔχε δή, ἴδωμεν τίς ποτ᾽ ἂν εἴη ὁ τρόπος
οὗτος τῆς διδασκαλίας τῶν ὄντων ὃν σὺ λέγεις νῦν,
καὶ πότερον ἔστι μὲν καὶ ἄλλος, οὗτος μέντοι
βελτίων, ἢ οὐδ᾽ ἔστιν ἄλλος ἢ οὗτος. ποτέρως
οἴει;

---

[1] ὁμοίοις Heindorf: ὁμοίως ΒΤ.

will just turn your attention to numbers, where do you think you can possibly get names to apply to each individual number on the principle of likeness, unless you allow agreement and convention on your part to control the correctness of names ? I myself prefer the theory that names are, so far as is possible, like the things named ; but really this attractive force of likeness is, as Hermogenes says, a poor thing, and we are compelled to employ in addition this commonplace expedient, convention, to establish the correctness of names. Probably language would be, within the bounds of possibility, most excellent when all its terms, or as many as possible, were based on likeness, that is to say, were appropriate, and most deficient under opposite conditions. But now answer the next question. What is the function of names, and what good do they accomplish ?

CRA. I think, Socrates, their function is to instruct, and this is the simple truth, that he who knows the names knows also the things named.

SOC. I suppose, Cratylus, you mean that when anyone knows the nature of the name—and its nature is that of the thing—he will know the thing also, since it is like the name, and the science of all things which are like each other is one and the same. It is, I fancy, on this ground that you say whoever knows names will know things also.

CRA. You are perfectly right.

SOC. Now let us see what this manner of giving instruction is, to which you refer, and whether there is another method, but inferior to this, or there is no other at all. What do you think ?

175

PLATO

436 ΚΡΑ. Οὕτως ἔγωγε, οὐ πάνυ τι εἶναι ἄλλον, τοῦτον δὲ καὶ μόνον καὶ βέλτιστον.

ΣΩ. Πότερον δὲ καὶ εὕρεσιν τῶν ὄντων τὴν αὐτὴν ταύτην εἶναι, τὸν τὰ ὀνόματα εὑρόντα καὶ ἐκεῖνα ηὑρηκέναι ὧν ἐστὶ τὰ ὀνόματα· ἢ ζητεῖν μὲν καὶ εὑρίσκειν ἕτερον δεῖν τρόπον, μανθάνειν δὲ τοῦτον;

ΚΡΑ. Πάντων μάλιστα καὶ ζητεῖν καὶ εὑρίσκειν τὸν αὐτὸν τρόπον τοῦτον κατὰ ταῦτά.

ΣΩ. Φέρε δή, ἐννοήσωμεν, ὦ Κρατύλε, εἴ τις ζητῶν τὰ πράγματα ἀκολουθοῖ τοῖς ὀνόμασι, B σκοπῶν οἷον ἕκαστον βούλεται εἶναι, ἆρ' ἐννοεῖς ὅτι οὐ σμικρὸς κίνδυνός ἐστιν ἐξαπατηθῆναι;

ΚΡΑ. Πῶς;

ΣΩ. Δῆλον ὅτι ὁ θέμενος πρῶτος τὰ ὀνόματα, οἷα ἡγεῖτο εἶναι τὰ πράγματα, τοιαῦτα ἐτίθετο καὶ τὰ ὀνόματα, ὥς φαμεν. ἦ γάρ;

ΚΡΑ. Ναί.

ΣΩ. Εἰ οὖν ἐκεῖνος μὴ ὀρθῶς ἡγεῖτο, ἔθετο δὲ οἷα ἡγεῖτο, τί οἴει ἡμᾶς τοὺς ἀκολουθοῦντας αὐτῷ πείσεσθαι; ἄλλο τι ἢ ἐξαπατηθήσεσθαι;

ΚΡΑ. Ἀλλὰ μὴ οὐχ οὕτως ἔχῃ,[1] ὦ Σώκρατες, C ἀλλ' ἀναγκαῖον ἦ εἰδότα τίθεσθαι τὸν τιθέμενον τὰ ὀνόματα· εἰ δὲ μή, ὅπερ πάλαι ἐγὼ ἔλεγον, οὐδ' ἂν ὀνόματα εἴη. μέγιστον δέ σοι ἔστω τεκμήριον ὅτι οὐκ ἔσφαλται τῆς ἀληθείας ὁ τιθέμενος· οὐ γὰρ ἄν ποτε οὕτω ξύμφωνα ἦν αὐτῷ ἅπαντα· ἢ οὐκ ἐνενόεις αὐτὸς λέγων ὡς πάντα κατὰ ταὐτὸν[2] καὶ ἐπὶ ταὐτὸν ἐγίγνετο τὰ ὀνόματα;

ΣΩ. Ἀλλὰ τοῦτο μέν, ὠγαθὲ Κρατύλε, οὐδέν

[1] ἔχῃ B: ἔχει T.
[2] κατὰ ταὐτὸν cod. Gudianus: κατ' αὐτὸ B: om. T.

176

CRATYLUS

CRA. I think there is no other at all ; this is both the best and the only method.

SOC. Do you think this is also the method of discovering realities, and that he who has discovered the names has discovered also the things named ; or do you think inquiry and discovery demand another method, and this belongs to instruction ?

CRA. I most certainly think inquiry and discovery follow this same method and in the same way.

SOC. Let us consider the matter, Cratylus. Do you not see that he who in his inquiry after things follows names and examines into the meaning of each one runs great risks of being deceived ?

CRA. How so ?

SOC. Clearly he who first gave names, gave such names as agreed with his conception of the nature of things. That is our view, is it not ?

CRA. Yes.

SOC. Then if his conception was incorrect, and he gave the names according to his conception, what do you suppose will happen to us who follow him ? Can we help being deceived ?

CRA. But, Socrates, surely that is not the case. He who gave the names must necessarily have known ; otherwise, as I have been saying all along, they would not be names at all. And there is a decisive proof that the name-giver did not miss the truth, one which you must accept ; for otherwise his names would not be so universally consistent. Have you not yourself noticed in speaking that all names were formed by the same method and with the same end in view ?

SOC. But that, Cratylus, is no counter argument.

PLATO

ἐστιν ἀπολόγημα. εἰ γὰρ τὸ πρῶτον σφαλεὶς ὁ
D τιθέμενος τἆλλα ἤδη πρὸς τοῦτ' ἐβιάζετο καὶ αὑτῷ
ξυμφωνεῖν ἠνάγκαζεν, οὐδὲν ἄτοπον, ὥσπερ τῶν
διαγραμμάτων ἐνίοτε τοῦ πρώτου σμικροῦ καὶ
ἀδήλου ψεύδους γενομένου, τὰ λοιπὰ πάμπολλα
ἤδη ὄντα ἑπόμενα ὁμολογεῖν ἀλλήλοις. δεῖ δὴ
περὶ τῆς ἀρχῆς παντὸς πράγματος παντὶ ἀνδρὶ
τὸν πολὺν λόγον εἶναι καὶ τὴν πολλὴν σκέψιν εἴτε
ὀρθῶς εἴτε μὴ ὑπόκειται· ἐκείνης δὲ ἐξετασθείσης
ἱκανῶς, τὰ λοιπὰ φαίνεσθαι ἐκείνῃ ἑπόμενα. οὐ
E μέντοι ἀλλὰ θαυμάζοιμ' ἄν, εἰ καὶ τὰ ὀνόματα ξυμφωνεῖ αὐτὰ αὑτοῖς. πάλιν γὰρ ἐπισκεψώμεθα ἃ τὸ
πρότερον διήλθομεν. ὡς τοῦ παντὸς ἰόντος τε καὶ
φερομένου καὶ ῥέοντός φαμεν σημαίνειν ἡμῖν τὴν
οὐσίαν τὰ ὀνόματα. ἄλλο τι οὕτω σοι δοκεῖ δηλοῦν;
437 ΚΡΑ. Πάνυ σφόδρα, καὶ ὀρθῶς γε σημαίνει.

ΣΩ. Σκοπῶμεν δὴ ἐξ αὐτῶν ἀναλαβόντες πρῶτον μὲν τοῦτο τὸ ὄνομα, τὴν ἐπιστήμην, ὡς ἀμφί-
βολόν ἐστι καὶ μᾶλλον ἔοικε σημαίνοντι ὅτι ἵστησιν
ἡμῶν ἐπὶ τοῖς πράγμασι τὴν ψυχὴν ἢ ὅτι ξυμ-
περιφέρεται, καὶ ὀρθότερόν ἐστιν ὥσπερ νῦν αὐτοῦ
τὴν ἀρχὴν λέγειν μᾶλλον ἢ ἐμβάλλοντας[1] τὸ εἶ
ἐπεϊστήμην,[2] ἀλλὰ τὴν ἐμβολὴν ποιήσασθαι ἀντὶ
τῆς ἐν τῷ εἶ ἐν τῷ ἰῶτα. ἔπειτα τὸ βέβαιον, ὅτι
βάσεώς τινός ἐστιν καὶ στάσεως μίμημα, ἀλλ' οὐ
B φορᾶς. ἔπειτα ἡ ἱστορία αὐτό που σημαίνει, ὅτι
ἵστησι τὸν ῥοῦν. καὶ τὸ πιστὸν ἱστὰν παντάπασι
σημαίνει. ἔπειτα δὲ ἡ μνήμη παντί που μηνύει,
ὅτι μονή ἐστιν ἐν τῇ ψυχῇ, ἀλλ' οὐ φορά. εἰ δὲ
βούλει, ἡ ἁμαρτία καὶ ἡ ξυμφορά, εἰ κατὰ τὸ

---

[1] ἐμβάλλοντας T: ἐκβάλλοντας B.
[2] ἐπεϊστήμην Heindorf: ἐπιστήμην BT: πιστήμην al.

CRATYLUS

For if the giver of names erred in the beginning and thenceforth forced all other names into agreement with his own initial error, there is nothing strange about that. It is just so sometimes in geometrical diagrams ; the initial error is small and unnoticed, but all the numerous deductions are wrong, though consistent. Every one must therefore give great care and great attention to the beginning of any undertaking, to see whether his foundation is right or not. If that has been considered with proper care, everything else will follow. However, I should be surprised if names are really consistent. Let us review our previous discussion. Names, we said, indicate nature to us, assuming that all things are in motion and flux. Do you not think they do so ?

CRA. Yes, and they indicate it correctly.

SOC. Let us first take up again the word ἐπιστήμη (knowledge) and see how ambiguous it is, seeming to indicate that it makes our soul stand still (ἵστησιν) at things, rather than that it is carried round with them, so it is better to speak the beginning of it as we now do than to insert the epsilon and say ἐπεϊστήμη ; we should insert an iota rather than an epsilon. Then take βέβαιον (firm), which expresses position and rest, not motion. And ἱστορία (inquiry) means much the same, that it stops (ἵστησι) the flow. And πιστόν (faithful) most certainly means that which stops (ἱστάν) motion. Then again, anyone can see that μνήμη (memory) expresses rest (μονή) in the soul, not motion. On the other hand, ἁμαρτία (error) and ξυμφορά (misfortune), if you consider

179

PLATO

ὄνομά τις ἀκολουθήσει, φανεῖται ταὐτὸν τῇ ξυνέσει ταύτῃ καὶ ἐπιστήμῃ καὶ τοῖς ἄλλοις πᾶσι τοῖς περὶ τὰ σπουδαῖα ὀνόμασιν. ἔτι τοίνυν ἡ ἀμαθία καὶ ἡ ἀκολασία παραπλησία τούτοις φαίνεται· ἡ C μὲν γὰρ τοῦ ἅμα θεῷ ἰόντος πορεία φαίνεται, ἡ ἀμαθία, ἡ δ' ἀκολασία παντάπασιν ἀκολουθία τοῖς πράγμασι φαίνεται. καὶ οὕτως, ἃ νομίζομεν ἐπὶ τοῖς κακίστοις ὀνόματα εἶναι, ὁμοιότατ' ἂν φαίνοιτο τοῖς ἐπὶ τοῖς καλλίστοις. οἶμαι δὲ καὶ ἄλλα πόλλ' ἄν τις εὕροι εἰ πραγματεύοιτο, ἐξ ὧν οἰηθείη ἂν αὖ πάλιν τὸν τὰ ὀνόματα τιθέμενον οὐχὶ ἰόντα οὐδὲ φερόμενα ἀλλὰ μένοντα τὰ πράγματα σημαίνειν.

ΚΡΑ. Ἀλλ', ὦ Σώκρατες, ὁρᾷς ὅτι τὰ πολλὰ D ἐκείνως ἐσήμαινεν.

ΣΩ. Τί οὖν τοῦτο, ὦ Κρατύλε; ὥσπερ ψήφους διαριθμησόμεθα τὰ ὀνόματα, καὶ ἐν τούτῳ ἔσται ἡ ὀρθότης; ὁπότερα ἂν πλείω φαίνηται τὰ ὀνόματα σημαίνοντα, ταῦτα δὴ ἔσται τἀληθῆ;

ΚΡΑ. Οὔκουν εἰκός γε.

43. ΣΩ. Οὐδ' ὁπωστιοῦν, ὦ φίλε. καὶ ταῦτα 438 μέν γε αὐτοῦ ἐάσωμεν,[1] ἐπανέλθωμεν δὲ πάλιν

---

[1] After ἐάσωμεν d adds in the margin τάδε δὲ ἐπισκεψώμεθα, εἰ ἡμῖν καὶ τῇδε ὁμολογεῖς εἴτε καὶ οὔ. φέρε, τοὺς τὰ ὀνόματα ἐν ταῖς πόλεσι τιθεμένους ἑκάστοτε, ἔν τε ταῖς Ἑλληνικαῖς καὶ βαρβαρικαῖς, οὐκ ἀρτίως ὁμολογοῦμεν νομοθέτας εἶναι καὶ τὴν τέχνην τὴν τοῦτο δυναμένην νομοθετικήν ; ΚΡΑ. Πάνυ γε.   ΣΩ. Λέγε δή, οἱ πρῶτοι νομοθέται τὰ πρῶτα ὀνόματα πότερον γιγνώσκοντες τὰ πράγματα, οἷς ἐτίθεντο, ἐτίθεντο ἢ ἀγνοοῦντες ; ΚΡΑ. Οἶμαι μὲν ἔγώ, ὦ Σώκρατες, γιγνώσκοντες.   ΣΩ. Οὐ γάρ πω (l. που), ὦ ἑταῖρε Κρατύλε, ἀγνοοῦντές γε.   ΚΡΑ. Οὔ μοι δοκεῖ.   " And let us consider whether you agree with me in this also. Have we not just now been agreeing that those who make the names in the various cities, whether Greek or barbarian, are lawgivers and possess the science of lawgiving which

180

CRATYLUS

merely the form of the names, will appear to be the same as σύνεσις (intellect) and ἐπιστήμη and all the other names of good significance. Moreover, ἀμαθία (ignorance) and ἀκολασία (unrestraint) also appear to be like them; for the former, ἀμαθία, seems to be τοῦ ἅμα θεῷ ἰόντος πορεία (the progress of one who goes with God), and ἀκολασία seems to be exactly ἀκολουθία τοῖς πράγμασιν (movement in company with things). And so names which we believe have the very worst meanings appear to be very like those which have the best. And I think we could, if we took pains, find many other words which would lead us to reverse our judgement and believe that the giver of names meant that things were not in progress or in motion, but were at rest.

CRA. But, Socrates, you see that most of the names indicate motion.

SOC. What of that, Cratylus? Are we to count names like votes, and shall correctness rest with the majority? Are those to be the true names which are found to have that one of the two meanings which is expressed by the greater number?

CRA. That is not reasonable.

SOC. No, not in the least, my friend. Now let us drop this and return to the point at which we

---

has the power of giving names? CRA. Certainly. SOC. Well then, did the first lawgivers give the first names with knowledge of the things to which they gave them, or in ignorance? CRA. With knowledge of them, I think, Socrates. SOC. Yes, for they certainly did not give them in ignorance. CRA. No, I do not think they did."

The same late hand adds ἐκ ποίων δὲ, indicating that ἐπανέλθωμεν . . . KPA. εἰδότα (below) are to be omitted.

181

ὅθεν δεῦρο μετέβημεν. ἄρτι γὰρ ἐν τοῖς πρόσθεν, εἰ μέμνησαι, τὸν τιθέμενον τὰ ὀνόματα ἀναγκαῖον ἔφησθα εἶναι εἰδότα τίθεσθαι οἷς ἐτίθετο. πότερον οὖν ἔτι σοι δοκεῖ οὕτως ἢ οὔ;

ΚΡΑ. Ἔτι.

ΣΩ. Ἦ καὶ τὸν τὰ πρῶτα τιθέμενον εἰδότα φῂς τίθεσθαι;

ΚΡΑ. Εἰδότα.

ΣΩ. Ἐκ ποίων οὖν ὀνομάτων ἢ μεμαθηκὼς ἢ
B εὑρηκὼς ἦν τὰ πράγματα, εἴπερ τά γε πρῶτα μή πω ἔκειτο, μαθεῖν δ᾽ αὖ φαμεν τὰ πράγματα καὶ εὑρεῖν ἀδύνατον εἶναι ἄλλως ἢ τὰ ὀνόματα μαθόντας ἢ αὐτοὺς ἐξευρόντας οἷά ἐστι;

ΚΡΑ. Δοκεῖς τί μοι λέγειν, ὦ Σώκρατες.

ΣΩ. Τίνα οὖν τρόπον φῶμεν αὐτοὺς εἰδότας θέσθαι ἢ νομοθέτας εἶναι, πρὶν καὶ ὁτιοῦν ὄνομα κεῖσθαί τε καὶ ἐκείνους εἰδέναι, εἴπερ μὴ ἔστι τὰ πράγματα μαθεῖν ἀλλ᾽ ἢ ἐκ τῶν ὀνομάτων;
C ΚΡΑ. Οἶμαι μὲν ἐγὼ τὸν ἀληθέστατον λόγον περὶ τούτων εἶναι, ὦ Σώκρατες, μείζω τινὰ δύναμιν εἶναι ἢ ἀνθρωπείαν τὴν θεμένην τὰ πρῶτα ὀνόματα τοῖς πράγμασιν, ὥστε ἀναγκαῖον εἶναι αὐτὰ ὀρθῶς ἔχειν.

ΣΩ. Εἶτα, οἴει, ἐναντία ἂν ἐτίθετο αὐτὸς αὑτῷ ὁ θείς, ὢν[1] δαίμων τις ἢ θεός; ἢ οὐδέν σοι ἐδοκοῦμεν ἄρτι λέγειν;

ΚΡΑ. Ἀλλὰ μὴ οὐκ ᾖ[2] τούτων τὰ ἕτερα ὀνόματα.

ΣΩ. Πότερα, ὦ ἄριστε, τὰ ἐπὶ τὴν στάσιν

---

[1] ὁ θεὶς ὢν t: ὁ θήσων BT.
[2] ᾖ vulg.: ἦν BT.

digressed. A little while ago, you may remember, you said he who gave names must have known the things to which he gave them. Do you still hold that opinion, or not ? "

CRA. I do.

SOC. And you say that he who gave the first names also knew the things which he named ?

CRA. Yes, he knew them.

SOC. But from what names had he learned or discovered the things, if the first names had not yet been given, and if we declare that it is impossible to learn or discover things except by learning or ourselves discovering the names ?

CRA. I think there is something in what you say, Socrates.

SOC. How can we assert that they gave names or were lawgivers with knowledge, before any name whatsoever had been given, and before they knew any names, if things cannot be learned except through their names ?

CRA. I think the truest theory of the matter, Socrates, is that the power which gave the first names to things is more than human, and therefore the names must necessarily be correct.

SOC. Then, in your opinion, he who gave the names, though he was a spirit or a god, would have given names which made him contradict himself ? Or do you think there is no sense in what we were saying just now ?

CRA. But, Socrates, those that make up one of the two classes are not really names.

SOC. Which of the two, my excellent friend ; the class of those which point towards rest or of those

ἄγοντα ἢ τὰ ἐπὶ τὴν φοράν; οὐ γάρ που κατὰ
τὸ ἄρτι λεχθὲν πλήθει κριθήσεται.

D ΚΡΑ. Οὗτοι[1] δὴ δίκαιόν γε, ὦ Σώκρατες.

ΣΩ. Ὀνομάτων οὖν στασιασάντων, καὶ τῶν μὲν
φασκόντων ἑαυτὰ εἶναι τὰ ὅμοια τῇ ἀληθείᾳ, τῶν
δ' ἑαυτά, τίνι ἔτι διακρινοῦμεν, ἢ ἐπὶ τί ἐλθόντες;
οὐ γάρ που ἐπὶ ὀνόματά γε ἕτερα ἄλλα τούτων·
οὐ γὰρ ἔστιν, ἀλλὰ δῆλον ὅτι ἄλλ' ἄττα ζητητέα
πλὴν ὀνομάτων, ἃ ἡμῖν ἐμφανιεῖ ἄνευ ὀνομάτων
ὁπότερα τούτων ἐστὶ τἀληθῆ, δείξαντα δῆλον ὅτι
E τὴν ἀλήθειαν τῶν ὄντων.

ΚΡΑ. Δοκεῖ μοι οὕτω.

ΣΩ. Ἔστιν ἄρα, ὡς ἔοικεν, ὦ Κρατύλε, δυνατὸν
μαθεῖν ἄνευ ὀνομάτων τὰ ὄντα, εἴπερ ταῦτα οὕτως
ἔχει.

ΚΡΑ. Φαίνεται.

ΣΩ. Διὰ τίνος ἄλλου οὖν ἔτι προσδοκᾷς ἂν αὐτὰ
μαθεῖν; ἆρα δι' ἄλλου του ἢ οὗπερ εἰκός τε καὶ
δικαιότατον, δι' ἀλλήλων γε, εἴ πῃ ξυγγενῆ ἐστιν,
καὶ αὐτὰ δι' αὑτῶν; τὸ γάρ που ἕτερον ἐκείνων
καὶ ἀλλοῖον ἕτερον ἄν τι καὶ ἀλλοῖον[2] σημαίνοι,
ἀλλ' οὐκ ἐκεῖνα.

ΚΡΑ. Ἀληθῆ μοι φαίνει λέγειν.

439 ΣΩ. Ἔχε δὴ πρὸς Διός· τὰ δὲ ὀνόματα οὐ
πολλάκις μέντοι ὡμολογήσαμεν τὰ καλῶς κείμενα
ἐοικότα εἶναι ἐκείνοις ὧν ὀνόματα κεῖται, καὶ
εἶναι εἰκόνας τῶν πραγμάτων;

ΚΡΑ. Ναί.

ΣΩ. Εἰ οὖν ἔστι μὲν ὅτι μάλιστα δι' ὀνομάτων
τὰ πράγματα μανθάνειν, ἔστι δὲ καὶ δι' αὐτῶν,

---

[1] οὗτοι Heindorf: οὕτω BT.
[2] ἀλλοῖον Heusde: ἄλλο ὂν BT.

184

that point towards motion? We agreed just now that the matter is not to be determined by mere numbers.

CRA. No; that would not be right, Socrates.

SOC. Then since the names are in conflict, and some of them claim that *they* are like the truth, and others that *they* are, how can we decide, and upon what shall we base our decision? Certainly not upon other names differing from these, for there are none. No, it is plain that we must look for something else, not names, which shall show us which of these two kinds are the true names, which of them, that is to say, show the truth of things.

CRA. That is my opinion.

SOC. Then if that is true, Cratylus, it seems that things may be learned without names.

CRA. So it appears.

SOC. What other way is left by which you could expect to know them? What other than the natural and the straightest way, through each other, if they are akin, and through themselves? For that which is other and different from them would signify not them, but something other and different.

CRA. I think that is true.

SOC. Stop for Heaven's sake! Did we not more than once agree that names which are rightly given are like the things named and are images of them?

CRA. Yes.

SOC. Then if it be really true that things can be learned either through names or through themselves

ποτέρα ἂν εἴη καλλίων καὶ σαφεστέρα ἡ μάθησις;
ἐκ τῆς εἰκόνος μανθάνειν αὐτήν τε αὐτήν, εἰ
καλῶς εἴκασται, καὶ τὴν ἀλήθειαν ἧς ἦν εἰκών,
B ἢ ἐκ τῆς ἀληθείας αὐτήν τε αὐτὴν καὶ τὴν εἰκόνα
αὐτῆς, εἰ πρεπόντως εἴργασται;

ΚΡΑ. Ἐκ τῆς ἀληθείας μοι δοκεῖ ἀνάγκη εἶναι.

ΣΩ. Ὅντινα μὲν τοίνυν τρόπον δεῖ μανθάνειν
ἢ εὑρίσκειν τὰ ὄντα, μεῖζον ἴσως ἐστὶν ἐγνωκέναι
ἢ κατ' ἐμὲ καὶ σέ· ἀγαπητὸν δὲ καὶ τοῦτο ὁμο-
λογήσασθαι, ὅτι οὐκ ἐξ ὀνομάτων, ἀλλὰ πολὺ
μᾶλλον αὐτὰ ἐξ αὑτῶν καὶ μαθητέον καὶ ζητητέον
ἢ ἐκ τῶν ὀνομάτων.

ΚΡΑ. Φαίνεται, ὦ Σώκρατες.

44. ΣΩ. Ἔτι τοίνυν τόδε σκεψώμεθα, ὅπως μὴ
ἡμᾶς τὰ πολλὰ ταῦτα ὀνόματα ἐς ταὐτὸν τείνοντα
C ἐξαπατᾷ,[1] εἴ τῷ¹ ὄντι μὲν οἱ θέμενοι αὐτὰ δια-
νοηθέντες γε² ἔθεντο ὡς ἰόντων ἁπάντων ἀεὶ καὶ
ῥεόντων—φαίνονται γὰρ ἔμοιγε καὶ αὐτῷ³ οὕτω
διανοηθῆναι—, τὸ δ', εἰ ἔτυχεν, οὐχ οὕτως ἔχει,
ἀλλ' οὗτοι αὐτοί τε ὥσπερ εἴς τινα δίνην ἐμ-
πεσόντες κυκῶνται καὶ ἡμᾶς ἐφελκόμενοι προσεμ-
βάλλουσιν. σκέψαι γάρ, ὦ θαυμάσιε Κρατύλε, ὃ
ἔγωγε πολλάκις ὀνειρώττω. πότερον φῶμέν τι
εἶναι αὐτὸ καλὸν καὶ ἀγαθὸν καὶ ἓν ἕκαστον τῶν
D ὄντων οὕτω, ἢ μή;

ΚΡΑ. Ἔμοιγε δοκεῖ, ὦ Σώκρατες.

ΣΩ. Αὐτὸ τοίνυν ἐκεῖνο σκεψώμεθα, μὴ εἰ
πρόσωπόν τί ἐστι καλὸν ἤ τι τῶν τοιούτων, καὶ
δοκεῖ ταῦτα πάντα ῥεῖν· ἀλλ' αὐτό, φῶμεν, τὸ καλὸν
οὐ τοιοῦτον ἀεί ἐστιν οἷόν ἐστιν;

---

¹ ἐξαπατᾷ, εἰ Wyttenbach: ἐξαπατᾶται καὶ Β: ἐξαπατᾷ
καί Τ. ² γε Ast: τε ΒΤ. ³ αὐτῷ Heindorf: αὐτοὶ ΒΤ.

which would be the better and surer way of learning ? To learn from the image whether it is itself a good imitation and also to learn the truth which it imitates, or to learn from the truth both the truth itself and whether the image is properly made ?

CRA. I think it is certainly better to learn from the truth.

SOC. How realities are to be learned or discovered is perhaps too great a question for you or me to determine ; but it is worth while to have reached even this conclusion, that they are to be learned and sought for, not from names but much better through themselves than through names.

CRA. That is clear, Socrates.

SOC. Then let us examine one further point to avoid being deceived by the fact that most of these names tend in the same direction. Suppose it should prove that although those who gave the names gave them in the belief that all things are in motion and flux—I myself think they did have that belief— still in reality that is not the case, and the name-givers themselves, having fallen into a kind of vortex, are whirled about, dragging us along with them. Consider, my worthy Cratylus, a question about which I often dream. Shall we assert that there is any absolute beauty, or good, or any other absolute existence, or not ?

CRA. I think there is, Socrates.

SOC. Then let us consider the absolute, not whether a particular face, or something of that sort, is beautiful, or whether all these things are in flux. Is not, in our opinion, absolute beauty always such as it is ?

ΚΡΑ. Ἀνάγκη.

ΣΩ. Ἆρ᾽ οὖν οἷόν τε προσειπεῖν αὐτὸ ὀρθῶς, εἰ ἀεὶ ὑπεξέρχεται, πρῶτον μὲν ὅτι ἐκεῖνό ἐστιν, ἔπειτα ὅτι τοιοῦτον, ἢ ἀνάγκη ἅμα ἡμῶν λεγόντων ἄλλο αὐτὸ εὐθὺς γίγνεσθαι καὶ ὑπεξιέναι καὶ μηκέτι οὕτως ἔχειν;

ΚΡΑ. Ἀνάγκη.

Ε   ΣΩ. Πῶς οὖν ἂν εἴη τὶ ἐκεῖνο ὃ μηδέποτε ὡσαύτως ἔχει; εἰ γάρ ποτε ὡσαύτως ἴσχει, ἔν γ᾽ ἐκείνῳ τῷ χρόνῳ δῆλον ὅτι οὐδὲν μεταβαίνει· εἰ δὲ ἀεὶ ὡσαύτως ἔχει καὶ τὸ αὐτό ἐστι, πῶς ἂν τοῦτό γε μεταβάλλοι ἢ κινοῖτο, μηδὲν ἐξιστάμενον τῆς αὑτοῦ ἰδέας;

ΚΡΑ. Οὐδαμῶς.

ΣΩ. Ἀλλὰ μὴν οὐδ᾽ ἂν γνωσθείη γε ὑπ᾽ οὐδε-
440 νός. ἅμα γὰρ ἂν ἐπιόντος τοῦ γνωσομένου ἄλλο καὶ ἀλλοῖον γίγνοιτο, ὥστε οὐκ ἂν γνωσθείη ἔτι ὁποῖόν γέ τί ἐστιν ἢ πῶς ἔχον· γνῶσις δὲ δήπου οὐδεμία γιγνώσκει ὃ γιγνώσκει μηδαμῶς ἔχον.

ΚΡΑ. Ἔστιν ὡς λέγεις.

ΣΩ. Ἀλλ᾽ οὐδὲ γνῶσιν εἶναι φάναι εἰκός, ὦ Κρατύλε, εἰ μεταπίπτει πάντα χρήματα καὶ μηδὲν μένει. εἰ μὲν γὰρ αὐτὸ τοῦτο, ἡ γνῶσις, τοῦ γνῶσις εἶναι μὴ μεταπίπτει,[1] μένοι τε ἂν ἀεὶ ἡ γνῶσις καὶ εἴη γνῶσις· εἰ δὲ καὶ αὐτὸ τὸ εἶδος
Β μεταπίπτει τῆς γνώσεως, ἅμα τ᾽ ἂν μεταπίπτοι εἰς ἄλλο εἶδος γνώσεως καὶ οὐκ ἂν εἴη γνῶσις· εἰ δὲ ἀεὶ μεταπίπτει, ἀεὶ οὐκ ἂν εἴη γνῶσις, καὶ ἐκ τούτου τοῦ λόγου οὔτε τὸ γνωσόμενον οὔτε τὸ

---

[1] μεταπίπτει PD: μεταπίπτοι Β (by correction): μετα-πίπτ$^{εἰ}_{ῃ}$ T.

CRA. That is inevitable.

SOC. Can we, then, if it is always passing away, correctly say that it is this, then that it is that, or must it inevitably, in the very instant while we are speaking, become something else and pass away and no longer be what it is ?

CRA. That is inevitable.

SOC. How, then, can that which is never in the same state be anything ? For if it is ever in the same state, then obviously at that time it is not changing ; and if it is always in the same state and is always the same, how can it ever change or move without relinquishing its own form ?

CRA. It cannot do so at all.

SOC. No, nor can it be known by anyone. For at the moment when he who seeks to know it approaches, it becomes something else and different, so that its nature and state can no longer be known ; and surely there is no knowledge which knows that which is in no state.

CRA. It is as you say.

SOC. But we cannot even say that there is any knowledge, if all things are changing and nothing remains fixed ; for if knowledge itself does not change and cease to be knowledge, then knowledge would remain, and there would be knowledge ; but if the very essence of knowledge changes, at the moment of the change to another essence of knowledge there would be no knowledge, and if it is always changing, there will always be no knowledge, and by this reasoning there will be neither any-

189

γνωσθησόμενον ἂν εἴη· εἰ δὲ ἔστι μὲν ἀεὶ τὸ
γιγνῶσκον, ἔστι δὲ τὸ γιγνωσκόμενον, ἔστι δὲ τὸ
καλόν, ἔστι δὲ τὸ ἀγαθόν, ἔστι δὲ ἓν ἕκαστον τῶν
ὄντων, οὔ μοι φαίνεται ταῦτα ὅμοια ὄντα, ἃ νῦν
C ἡμεῖς λέγομεν, ῥοῇ οὐδὲν οὐδὲ φορᾷ. ταῦτ᾽ οὖν
πότερόν ποτε οὕτως ἔχει ἢ ἐκείνως ὡς οἱ περὶ
Ἡράκλειτόν τε λέγουσι καὶ ἄλλοι πολλοί, μὴ οὐ
ῥᾴδιον ᾖ ἐπισκέψασθαι, οὐδὲ πάνυ νοῦν ἔχοντος
ἀνθρώπου ἐπιτρέψαντα ὀνόμασιν αὐτὸν καὶ τὴν
αὑτοῦ ψυχὴν θεραπεύειν, πεπιστευκότα ἐκείνοις
καὶ τοῖς θεμένοις αὐτά, διισχυρίζεσθαι ὥς τι
εἰδότα, καὶ αὑτοῦ τε καὶ τῶν ὄντων καταγιγνώ-
σκειν ὡς οὐδὲν ὑγιὲς οὐδενός, ἀλλὰ πάντα ὥσπερ
κεράμια ῥεῖ, καὶ ἀτεχνῶς ὥσπερ οἱ κατάρρῳ
D νοσοῦντες ἄνθρωποι οὕτως οἴεσθαι καὶ τὰ πράγματα διακεῖσθαι, ὑπὸ ῥεύματός τε καὶ κατάρρου
πάντα τὰ χρήματα ἔχεσθαι. ἴσως μὲν οὖν δή, ὦ
Κρατύλε, οὕτως ἔχει, ἴσως δὲ καὶ οὔ. σκοπεῖσθαι
οὖν χρὴ ἀνδρείως τε καὶ εὖ, καὶ μὴ ῥᾳδίως ἀποδέχεσθαι—ἔτι γὰρ νέος εἶ καὶ ἡλικίαν ἔχεις—,
σκεψάμενον δέ, ἐὰν εὕρῃς, μεταδιδόναι καὶ ἐμοί.

ΚΡΑ. Ἀλλὰ ποιήσω ταῦτα. εὖ μέντοι ἴσθι, ὦ
Σώκρατες, ὅτι οὐδὲ νυνὶ ἀσκέπτως ἔχω, ἀλλά μοι
σκοπουμένῳ καὶ πράγματα ἔχοντι πολὺ μᾶλλον
E ἐκείνως φαίνεται ἔχειν ὡς Ἡράκλειτος λέγει.

ΣΩ. Εἰς αὖθις τοίνυν με, ὦ ἑταῖρε, διδάξεις, ἐπειδὰν ἥκῃς· νῦν δέ, ὥσπερ παρεσκεύασαι, πορεύου
εἰς ἀγρόν· προπέμψει δέ σε καὶ Ἑρμογένης ὅδε.

ΚΡΑ. Ταῦτ᾽ ἔσται, ὦ Σώκρατες, ἀλλὰ καὶ σὺ
πειρῶ ἔτι ἐννοεῖν ταῦτα ἤδη.

one to know nor anything to be known. But if
there is always that which knows and that which
is known—if the beautiful, the good, and all the
other verities exist—I do not see how there is any
likeness between these conditions of which I am
now speaking and flux or motion. Now whether
this is the nature of things, or the doctrine of
Heracleitus and many others is true, is another
question ; but surely no man of sense can put
himself and his soul under the control of names,
and trust in names and their makers to the point of
affirming that he knows anything ; nor will he
condemn himself and all things and say that there
is no health in them, but that all things are flowing
like leaky pots, or believe that all things are just
like people afflicted with catarrh, flowing and running
all the time. Perhaps, Cratylus, this theory is true,
but perhaps it is not. Therefore you must consider
courageously and thoroughly and not accept anything carelessly—for you are still young and in
your prime ; then, if after investigation you find
the truth, impart it to me.

CRA. I will do so. However, I assure you,
Socrates, that I have already considered the matter,
and after toilsome consideration I think the doctrine
of Heracleitus is much more likely to be true.

SOC. Some other time, then, my friend, you will
teach me, when you come back ; but now go into
the country as you have made ready to do ; and
Hermogenes here will go with you a bit.

CRA. Very well, Socrates, and I hope you also
will continue to think of these matters.

PARMENIDES

INTRODUCTION TO THE *PARMENIDES*

This dialogue is narrated by Cephalus of Clazomenae, who tells how it was repeated to him by Antiphon. The latter had himself heard it from Pythodorus, who was present as a listener when Parmenides conversed with Socrates and others.

Parmenides, the great Eleatic philosopher, is described as a man of about sixty-five years of age, and Socrates is said to have been at the time a young man. If we assume twenty years as the age of Socrates, the imaginary date of the dialogue would be about 449 B.C., from which it results that Parmenides was born not far from 514 B.C., some twenty-five years later than the date frequently given on the authority of Diogenes Laertius (ix. 23). Zeno of Elea is described as a man of about forty years, and probably he really was not far from twenty-five years younger than Parmenides. The other persons of the dialogue are Adeimantus and Glaucon, Plato's brothers, both of whom appear also in the *Republic* and the *Symposium*, Antiphon, their half-brother, Aristoteles, who was one of the Thirty Tyrants, and Pythodorus, son of Isolochus. This Pythodorus was a general in the Peloponnesian War.

The introduction (126 A to 137 B) gives the dramatic setting, introduces the speakers, and

195

exhibits the futility of some of Zeno's paradoxes, which the youthful Socrates shows to be no paradoxes at all (to 130 A). Then (to 137 B), in a brief discussion carried on by Parmenides and Socrates, some of the chief difficulties of the doctrine of ideas, at least in its extreme form, are set forth. The objections to this doctrine are not answered, and the dialogue proceeds in the form of a lecture by Parmenides, interrupted only by brief questions or expressions of assent on the part of Aristoteles who, being the youngest man present, serves as interlocutor.

To show his method, Parmenides chooses to discuss first the hypothesis that one is or exists, and then the hypothesis that one is not or does not exist. As the principle of dichotomy is elaborately illustrated by the Eleatic Stranger in the *Sophist*, so here the method of division by contradictories or opposites is illustrated by Parmenides. The conclusion reached is : Whether the one is or is not, the one and the others, in relation to themselves and to each other, all in every way are and are not, and appear and do not appear. This seems to be a *reductio ad absurdum* of the Eleatic doctrines and methods, put into the mouth of the chief of the Eleatic school. Yet this is the school of thought for which Plato appears to have had the greatest respect, and he always speaks of Parmenides as a thinker to be reverenced.

It is hardly to be supposed that the whole purpose of this dialogue is to show the difficulties inherent in the doctrine of ideas and in the Eleatic doctrine of being, since these are the doctrines which Plato elsewhere advocates or, at least, treats with most

profound respect. Yet this negative result is all that appears with any clearness. There can be no doubt that Plato's contemporaries, living in the atmosphere of philosophical discussion which pervaded the Athens of those days, understood many allusions which are lost to us, and were able to appreciate Plato's point of view more fully than any modern scholar can hope to do, but even for them the result of this dialogue must have been chiefly, if not entirely, negative. In greater or less degree the same is true of several other dialogues which appear to belong to nearly the same date as the *Parmenides*. Such are the *Theaetetus*, the *Cratylus*, the *Sophist*, the *Statesman*, and the *Philebus*. These all seem to be more or less polemical, and in most of them the interest in method is evident. It may be that more positive results were reached by Plato in his oral teaching, or that these dialogues were to be followed by a series of more positively constructive treatises which were never actually written. The *Parmenides*, like other dialogues of nearly the same date, may be regarded rather as a preparatory exercise than as a definitive presentation of Platonic doctrine.

There are special annotated editions of the *Parmenides* by Thomas Maguire (Dublin, 1882) and W. W. Waddell (Glasgow, 1894).

ΠΑΡΜΕΝΙΔΗΣ

[Η ΠΕΡΙ ΙΔΕΩΝ· ΛΟΓΙΚΟΣ]

ΤΑ ΤΟΥ ΔΙΑΛΟΓΟΥ ΠΡΟΣΩΠΑ

ΚΕΦΑΛΟΣ, ΑΔΕΙΜΑΝΤΟΣ, ΑΝΤΙΦΩΝ, ΓΛΑΥΚΩΝ, ΠΥΘΟΔΩΡΟΣ, ΣΩΚΡΑΤΗΣ, ΖΗΝΩΝ, ΠΑΡΜΕΝΙΔΗΣ, ΑΡΙΣΤΟΤΕΛΗΣ

1. ΚΕΦ. Ἐπειδὴ Ἀθήναζε οἴκοθεν ἐκ Κλαζομενῶν ἀφικόμεθα, κατ᾽ ἀγορὰν ἐνετύχομεν Ἀδειμάντῳ τε καὶ Γλαύκωνι· καί μου λαβόμενος τῆς χειρὸς ὁ Ἀδείμαντος· "χαῖρ᾽," ἔφη, " ὦ Κέφαλε, καὶ εἴ του δέει τῶν τῇδε ὧν ἡμεῖς δυνατοί, φράζε."

" Ἀλλὰ μὲν δή," εἶπον ἐγώ, "πάρειμί γε ἐπ᾽ αὐτὸ τοῦτο, δεησόμενος ὑμῶν."

" Λέγοις ἄν," ἔφη, "τὴν δέησιν."

B   Καὶ ἐγὼ εἶπον· "τῷ ἀδελφῷ ὑμῶν τῷ ὁμομητρίῳ τί ἦν ὄνομα; οὐ γὰρ μέμνημαι. παῖς δέ που ἦν, ὅτε τὸ πρότερον ἐπεδήμησα δεῦρο ἐκ Κλαζομενῶν· πολὺς δὲ ἤδη χρόνος ἐξ ἐκείνου. τῷ μὲν γὰρ πατρί, δοκῶ, Πυριλάμπης ὄνομα."

" Πάνυ γε," ἔφη.

" Αὐτῷ δέ γε;"

" Ἀντιφῶν.[1]   ἀλλὰ τί μάλιστα πυνθάνει;"

[1] αὐτῷ δέ γε; ἀντιφῶν B: αὐτῷ δέ γε ἀντιφῶν (spoken by Adeimantus) T.

198

PARMENIDES

[or ON IDEAS: LOGICAL]

CHARACTERS

CEPHALUS, ADEIMANTUS, ANTIPHON, GLAUCON,
PYTHODORUS, SOCRATES, ZENO, PARMENIDES,
ARISTOTELES

CEPH. When we came from our home at Clazomenae to Athens, we met Adeimantus and Glaucon in the market-place. Adeimantus took me by the hand and said, " Welcome, Cephalus ; if there is anything we can do for you here, let us know."

" Why," said I, " that is just why I am here, to ask a favour of you."

" Tell us," said he, " what it is."

And I said, " What was your half-brother's name ? I don't remember. He was only a boy when I came here from Clazomenae before ; and that is now a long time ago. His father's name, I believe, was Pyrilampes."

" Yes," said he.

" And what is his own name ? "

" Antiphon. But why do you ask ? "

" Οἶδ'," εἶπον ἐγώ, " πολῖταί τ' ἐμοί[1] εἰσι, μάλα
φιλόσοφοι, ἀκηκόασί τε ὅτι οὗτος ὁ Ἀντιφῶν
Πυθοδώρῳ τινὶ Ζήνωνος ἑταίρῳ πολλὰ ἐντετύχηκε,
C καὶ τοὺς λόγους, οὓς ποτε Σωκράτης καὶ Ζήνων
καὶ Παρμενίδης διελέχθησαν, πολλάκις ἀκούσας
τοῦ Πυθοδώρου ἀπομνημονεύει."

" Ἀληθῆ," ἔφη, " λέγεις."

" Τούτων τοίνυν," εἶπον, " δεόμεθα διακοῦσαι."

" Ἀλλ' οὐ χαλεπόν," ἔφη· " μειράκιον γὰρ ὢν
αὐτοὺς εὖ μάλα διεμελέτησεν, ἐπεὶ νῦν γε κατὰ τὸν
πάππον τε καὶ ὁμώνυμον πρὸς ἱππικῇ τὰ πολλὰ
διατρίβει. ἀλλ' εἰ δεῖ, ἴωμεν παρ' αὐτόν· ἄρτι γὰρ
ἐνθένδε οἴκαδε οἴχεται, οἰκεῖ δὲ ἐγγὺς ἐν Μελίτῃ."

127 Ταῦτα εἰπόντες ἐβαδίζομεν, καὶ κατελάβομεν τὸν
Ἀντιφῶντα οἴκοι χαλινόν τινα χαλκεῖ ἐκδιδόντα
σκευάσαι· ἐπειδὴ δὲ ἐκείνου ἀπηλλάγη οἵ τε
ἀδελφοὶ ἔλεγον αὐτῷ ὧν ἕνεκα παρεῖμεν, ἀνεγνώ-
ρισέ τέ με ἐκ τῆς προτέρας ἐπιδημίας καὶ ἠσπά-
ζετο, καὶ δεομένων ἡμῶν διελθεῖν τοὺς λόγους,
τὸ μὲν πρῶτον ὤκνει—πολὺ γὰρ ἔφη ἔργον εἶναι—
ἔπειτα μέντοι διηγεῖτο. ἔφη δὲ δὴ ὁ Ἀντιφῶν
λέγειν τὸν Πυθόδωρον ὅτι ἀφίκοιντό ποτε εἰς
B Παναθήναια τὰ μεγάλα Ζήνων τε καὶ Παρμενίδης.
τὸν μὲν οὖν Παρμενίδην εὖ μάλα ἤδη πρεσβύτην
εἶναι, σφόδρα πολιόν, καλὸν δὲ κἀγαθὸν τὴν ὄψιν,
περὶ ἔτη μάλιστα πέντε καὶ ἑξήκοντα· Ζήνωνα
δὲ ἐγγὺς ἐτῶν τετταράκοντα τότε εἶναι, εὐμήκη
δὲ καὶ χαρίεντα ἰδεῖν· καὶ λέγεσθαι αὐτὸν παιδικὰ
τοῦ Παρμενίδου γεγονέναι. καταλύειν δὲ αὐτοὺς
C ἔφη παρὰ τῷ Πυθοδώρῳ ἐκτὸς τείχους ἐν Κερα-

---

[1] τ' ἐμοί Stephanus : τέ μοι T : μοί B.

"These gentlemen," I said, "are fellow-citizens of mine, who are very fond of philosophy. They have heard that this Antiphon had a good deal to do with a friend of Zeno's named Pythodorus, that Pythodorus often repeated to him the conversation which Socrates, Zeno, and Parmenides once had together, and that he remembers it."

"That is true," said he.

"Well," I said, "we should like to hear it."

"There is no difficulty about that," said he; "for when he was a youth he studied it with great care; though now he devotes most of his time to horses, like his grandfather Antiphon. If that is what you want, let us go to him. He has just gone home from here, and he lives close by in Melite."

Thereupon we started, and we found Antiphon at home, giving a smith an order to make a bridle. When he had got rid of the smith and his brothers told him what we were there for, he remembered me from my former visit and greeted me cordially, and when we asked him to repeat the conversation, he was at first unwilling—for he said it was a good deal of trouble—but afterwards he did so. Antiphon, then, said that Pythodorus told him that Zeno and Parmenides once came to the Great Panathenaea; that Parmenides was already quite elderly, about sixty-five years old, very white-haired, and of handsome and noble countenance; Zeno was at that time about forty years of age; he was tall and good-looking, and there was a story that Parmenides had been in love with him. He said that they lodged with Pythodorus outside of the wall, in Cerameicus,

μεικῷ· οἳ δὴ καὶ ἀφικέσθαι τόν τε Σωκράτη καὶ
ἄλλους τινὰς μετ᾽ αὐτοῦ πολλούς, ἐπιθυμοῦντας
ἀκοῦσαι τῶν τοῦ Ζήνωνος γραμμάτων· τότε γὰρ
αὐτὰ πρῶτον ὑπ᾽ ἐκείνων κομισθῆναι· Σωκράτη
δὲ εἶναι τότε σφόδρα νέον. ἀναγιγνώσκειν οὖν
αὐτοῖς τὸν Ζήνωνα αὐτόν, τὸν δὲ Παρμενίδην
τυχεῖν ἔξω ὄντα· καὶ εἶναι πάνυ βραχὺ ἔτι λοιπὸν
τῶν λόγων ἀναγιγνωσκομένων, ἡνίκα αὐτός τε
D ἐπεισελθεῖν ἔφη ὁ Πυθόδωρος ἔξωθεν καὶ τὸν
Παρμενίδην μετ᾽ αὐτοῦ καὶ Ἀριστοτέλη τὸν τῶν
τριάκοντα γενόμενον, καὶ σμίκρ᾽ ἄττα ἔτι ἐπ-
ακοῦσαι τῶν γραμμάτων· οὐ μὴν αὐτός γε, ἀλλὰ
καὶ πρότερον ἀκηκοέναι τοῦ Ζήνωνος.

2. Τὸν οὖν Σωκράτη ἀκούσαντα πάλιν τε κε-
λεῦσαι τὴν πρώτην ὑπόθεσιν τοῦ πρώτου λόγου
ἀναγνῶναι, καὶ ἀναγνωσθείσης·

E "Πῶς," φάναι, "ὦ Ζήνων, τοῦτο λέγεις; εἰ
πολλά ἐστι τὰ ὄντα, ὡς ἄρα δεῖ αὐτὰ ὅμοιά τε
εἶναι καὶ ἀνόμοια, τοῦτο δὲ δὴ ἀδύνατον· οὔτε
γὰρ τὰ ἀνόμοια ὅμοια οὔτε τὰ ὅμοια ἀνόμοια
οἷόν τε εἶναι; οὐχ οὕτω λέγεις;"

"Οὕτω," φάναι τὸν Ζήνωνα.

"Οὐκοῦν εἰ ἀδύνατον τά τε ἀνόμοια ὅμοια
εἶναι καὶ τὰ ὅμοια ἀνόμοια, ἀδύνατον δὴ καὶ
πολλὰ εἶναι· εἰ γὰρ πολλὰ εἴη, πάσχοι ἂν τὰ
ἀδύνατα. ἆρα τοῦτό ἐστιν ὃ βούλονταί σου οἱ
λόγοι, οὐκ ἄλλο τι ἢ διαμάχεσθαι παρὰ πάντα τὰ
λεγόμενα, ὡς οὐ πολλά ἐστι; καὶ τούτου αὐτοῦ
οἴει σοι τεκμήριον εἶναι ἕκαστον τῶν λόγων,
ὥστε καὶ ἡγεῖ τοσαῦτα τεκμήρια παρέχεσθαι,
ὅσουσπερ λόγους γέγραφας, ὡς οὐκ ἔστι πολλά;
128 οὕτω λέγεις, ἢ ἐγὼ οὐκ ὀρθῶς καταμανθάνω;"

and that Socrates and many others with him went there because they wanted to hear Zeno's writings, which had been brought to Athens for the first time by them. Socrates was then very young. So Zeno himself read aloud to them, and Parmenides was not in the house. Pythodorus said the reading of the treatises was nearly finished when he came in himself with Parmenides and Aristoteles (the one who was afterwards one of the thirty), so they heard only a little that remained of the written works. He himself, however, had heard Zeno read them before.

Socrates listened to the end, and then asked that the first thesis of the first treatise be read again. When this had been done, he said :

" Zeno, what do you mean by this ? That if existences are many, they must be both like and unlike, which is impossible ; for the unlike cannot be like, nor the like unlike ? Is not that your meaning ? "

" Yes," said Zeno.

" Then if it is impossible for the unlike to be like and the like unlike, it is impossible for existences to be many ; for if they were to be many, they would experience the impossible. Is that the purpose of your treatises, to maintain against all arguments that existences are not many ? And you think each of your treatises is a proof of this very thing, and therefore you believe that the proofs you offer that existences are not many are as many as the treatises you have written ? Is that your meaning, or have I misunderstood ? "

"Οὔκ, ἀλλά," φάναι τὸν Ζήνωνα, "καλῶς συνῆκας ὅλον τὸ γράμμα ὃ βούλεται."

"Μανθάνω," εἰπεῖν τὸν Σωκράτη, "ὦ Παρμενίδη, ὅτι Ζήνων ὅδε οὐ μόνον τῇ ἄλλῃ σου φιλίᾳ βούλεται ᾠκειῶσθαι,[1] ἀλλὰ καὶ τῷ συγγράμματι. ταὐτὸν γὰρ γέγραφε τρόπον τινὰ ὅπερ[2] σύ, μεταβάλλων δὲ ἡμᾶς πειρᾶται ἐξαπατᾶν ὡς ἕτερόν τι λέγων. σὺ μὲν γὰρ ἐν τοῖς ποιήμασιν ἓν φῂς B εἶναι τὸ πᾶν, καὶ τούτων τεκμήρια παρέχει καλῶς τε καὶ εὖ· ὅδε δὲ αὖ οὐ πολλά φησιν εἶναι, τεκμήρια δὲ καὶ αὐτὸς παμπολλα καὶ παμμεγέθη παρέχεται. τὸ οὖν τὸν μὲν ἓν φάναι, τὸν δὲ μὴ πολλά, καὶ οὕτως ἑκάτερον λέγειν ὥστε μηδὲν τῶν αὐτῶν εἰρηκέναι δοκεῖν σχεδόν τι λέγοντας ταὐτά, ὑπὲρ ἡμᾶς τοὺς ἄλλους φαίνεται ὑμῖν τὰ εἰρημένα εἰρῆσθαι."

"Ναί," φάναι τὸν Ζήνωνα, "ὦ Σώκρατες. σὺ δ' οὖν τὴν ἀλήθειαν τοῦ γράμματος οὐ πανC ταχοῦ ᾔσθησαι· καίτοι ὥσπερ γε αἱ Λάκαιναι σκύλακες εὖ μεταθεῖς τε καὶ ἰχνεύεις τὰ λεχθέντα· ἀλλὰ πρῶτον μέν σε τοῦτο λανθάνει, ὅτι οὐ παντάπασιν οὕτω σεμνύνεται τὸ γράμμα, ὥστε ἅπερ σὺ λέγεις διανοηθὲν γραφῆναι, τοὺς ἀνθρώπους δὲ ἐπικρυπτόμενον ὥς τι μέγα διαπραττόμενον· ἀλλὰ σὺ μὲν εἶπες τῶν συμβεβηκότων τι, ἔστι δὲ τό γε ἀληθὲς βοήθειά τις ταῦτα τὰ γράμματα τῷ Παρμενίδου λόγῳ πρὸς τοὺς ἐπιχειροῦντας D αὐτὸν κωμῳδεῖν ὡς εἰ ἓν ἔστι, πολλὰ καὶ γελοῖα συμβαίνει πάσχειν τῷ λόγῳ καὶ ἐναντία αὐτῷ. ἀντιλέγει δὴ οὖν τοῦτο τὸ γράμμα πρὸς τοὺς τὰ

---

[1] οἰκειῶσθαι BT: corr. B²t.
[2] ὅπερ Proclus: ὅνπερ B: ὅ*περ T.

"No," said Zeno, "you have grasped perfectly the general intent of the work."

"I see, Parmenides," said Socrates, "that Zeno here wishes to be very close to you not only in his friendship, but also in his writing. For he has written much the same thing as you, but by reversing the process he tries to cheat us into the belief that he is saying something new. For you, in your poems, say that the all is one, and you furnish proofs of this in fine and excellent fashion ; and he, on the other hand, says it is not many, and he also furnishes very numerous and weighty proofs. That one of you says it is one, and the other that it is not many, and that each of you expresses himself so that although you say much the same you seem not to have said the same things at all, appears to the rest of us a feat of expression quite beyond our power."

"Yes, Socrates," said Zeno, "but you have not perceived all aspects of the truth about my writings. You follow the arguments with a scent as keen as a Laconian hound's, but you do not observe that my treatise is not by any means so pretentious that it could have been written with the intention you ascribe to it, of disguising itself as a great performance in the eyes of men. What you mentioned is a mere accident, but in truth these writings are meant to support the argument of Parmenides against those who attempt to jeer at him and assert that if the all is one many absurd results follow which contradict his theory. Now this treatise opposes

πολλὰ λέγοντας, καὶ ἀνταποδίδωσι ταὐτὰ[1] καὶ
πλείω τοῦτο βουλόμενον δηλοῦν, ὡς ἔτι γε-
λοιότερα πάσχοι ἂν αὐτῶν ἡ ὑπόθεσις, εἰ πολλά
ἐστιν, ἢ ἡ τοῦ ἓν εἶναι, εἴ τις ἱκανῶς ἐπεξίοι. διὰ
τοιαύτην δὴ φιλονεικίαν ὑπὸ νέου ὄντος ἐμοῦ
Ε ἐγράφη, καί τις αὐτὸ ἔκλεψε γραφέν, ὥστε οὐδὲ
βουλεύσασθαι ἐξεγένετο εἴτ᾽ ἐξοιστέον αὐτὸ εἰς
τὸ φῶς εἴτε μή.   ταύτῃ οὖν σε λανθάνει, ὦ Σώκρατες, ὅτι οὐχ ὑπὸ νέου φιλονεικίας οἴει αὐτὸ
γεγράφθαι, ἀλλ᾽ ὑπὸ πρεσβυτέρου φιλοτιμίας·
ἐπεί, ὅπερ γ᾽ εἶπον, οὐ κακῶς ἀπείκασας."
    3. " Ἀλλ᾽ ἀποδέχομαι," φάναι τὸν Σωκράτη,
" καὶ ἡγοῦμαι ὡς λέγεις ἔχειν. τόδε δέ μοι εἰπέ·
οὐ νομίζεις εἶναι αὐτὸ καθ᾽ αὑτὸ εἶδός τι ὁμοιότη-
129 τος, καὶ τῷ τοιούτῳ αὖ ἄλλο τι ἐναντίον, ὃ ἔστιν
ἀνόμοιον· τούτοιν δὲ δυοῖν ὄντοιν καὶ ἐμὲ καὶ
σὲ καὶ τἆλλα ἃ δὴ πολλὰ καλοῦμεν μεταλαμβάνειν; καὶ τὰ μὲν τῆς ὁμοιότητος μεταλαμβάνοντα ὅμοια γίγνεσθαι ταύτῃ τε καὶ κατὰ
τοσοῦτον ὅσον ἂν μεταλαμβάνῃ, τὰ δὲ τῆς ἀν-
ομοιότητος ἀνόμοια, τὰ δὲ ἀμφοτέρων ἀμφότερα;
εἰ δὲ καὶ πάντα ἐναντίων ὄντων ἀμφοτέρων μεταλαμβάνει, καὶ ἔστι τῷ μετέχειν ἀμφοῖν ὅμοιά
Β τε καὶ ἀνόμοια αὐτὰ αὑτοῖς, τί θαυμαστόν; εἰ
μὲν γὰρ αὐτὰ τὰ ὅμοιά τις ἀπέφαινεν ἀνόμοια
γιγνόμενα ἢ τὰ ἀνόμοια ὅμοια, τέρας ἄν, οἶμαι,
ἦν· εἰ δὲ τὰ τούτων μετέχοντα ἀμφοτέρων ἀμφότερα ἀποφαίνει πεπονθότα, οὐδὲν ἔμοιγε, ὦ Ζήνων,
ἄτοπον δοκεῖ εἶναι, οὐδέ γε εἰ ἓν ἅπαντα ἀποφαίνει τις τῷ μετέχειν τοῦ ἑνὸς καὶ ταὐτὰ ταῦτα

---

[1] ταὐτὰ Schleiermacher : ταῦτα Β : om. T.

the advocates of the many and gives them back their ridicule with interest, for its purpose is to show that their hypothesis that existences are many, if properly followed up, leads to still more absurd results than the hypothesis that they are one. It was in such a spirit of controversy that I wrote it when I was young, and when it was written some one stole it, so that I could not even consider whether it should be published or not. So, Socrates, you are not aware of this and you think that the cause of its composition was not the controversial spirit of a young man, but the ambition of an old one. In other respects, as I said, you guessed its meaning pretty well."

" I see," said Socrates, " and I accept your explanation. But tell me, do you not believe there is an idea of likeness in the abstract, and another idea of unlikeness, the opposite of the first, and that you and I and all things which we call many partake of these two ? And that those which partake of likeness become like, and those which partake of unlikeness become unlike, and those which partake of both become both like and unlike, all in the manner and degree of their participation ? And even if all things partake of both opposites, and are enabled by their participation to be both like and unlike themselves, what is there wonderful about that ? For if anyone showed that the absolute like becomes unlike, or the unlike like, that would, in my opinion, be a wonder ; but if he shows that things which partake of both become both like and unlike, that seems to me, Zeno, not at all strange, not even if he shows that all things are one by participation in unity and that the same are also

πολλὰ τῷ πλήθους αὖ μετέχειν· ἀλλ' εἰ ὃ ἔστιν
ἕν, αὐτὸ τοῦτο πολλὰ ἀποδείξει καὶ αὖ τὰ πολλὰ
C δὴ ἕν, τοῦτο ἤδη θαυμάσομαι. καὶ περὶ τῶν
ἄλλων ἁπάντων ὡσαύτως· εἰ μὲν αὐτὰ τὰ γένη
τε καὶ εἴδη ἐν αὑτοῖς ἀποφαίνοι τἀναντία ταῦτα
πάθη πάσχοντα, ἄξιον θαυμάζειν· εἰ δ' ἐμὲ ἕν
τις ἀποδείξει ὄντα καὶ πολλά, τί θαυμαστόν,
λέγων, ὅταν μὲν βούληται πολλὰ ἀποφαίνειν, ὡς
ἕτερα μὲν τὰ ἐπὶ δεξιά μού ἐστιν, ἕτερα δὲ τὰ
ἐπ' ἀριστερά, καὶ ἕτερα μὲν τὰ πρόσθεν, ἕτερα
δὲ τὰ ὄπισθεν, καὶ ἄνω καὶ κάτω ὡσαύτως· πλή-
D θους γάρ, οἶμαι, μετέχω· ὅταν δὲ ἕν, ἐρεῖ ὡς
ἑπτὰ ἡμῶν ὄντων εἷς ἐγώ εἰμι ἄνθρωπος μετέχων
καὶ τοῦ ἑνός· ὥστε ἀληθῆ ἀποφαίνει ἀμφότερα.
ἐὰν οὖν τις τοιαῦτα ἐπιχειρῇ πολλὰ καὶ ἓν ταὐτὰ
ἀποφαίνειν, λίθους καὶ ξύλα καὶ τὰ τοιαῦτα,
φήσομεν αὐτὸν πολλὰ καὶ ἓν ἀποδεικνύναι, οὐ τὸ
ἓν πολλὰ οὐδὲ τὰ πολλὰ ἕν, οὐδέ τι θαυμαστὸν
λέγειν, ἀλλ' ἅπερ ἂν πάντες ὁμολογοῖμεν· ἐὰν δέ
τις, ὃ νῦν δὴ ἐγὼ ἔλεγον, πρῶτον μὲν διαιρῆται
χωρὶς αὐτὰ καθ' αὑτὰ τὰ εἴδη, οἷον ὁμοιότητά
E τε καὶ ἀνομοιότητα καὶ πλῆθος καὶ τὸ ἓν καὶ
στάσιν καὶ κίνησιν καὶ πάντα τὰ τοιαῦτα, εἶτα
ἐν ἑαυτοῖς ταῦτα δυνάμενα συγκεράννυσθαι καὶ
διακρίνεσθαι ἀποφαίνῃ, ἀγαίμην ἂν ἔγωγ'," ἔφη,
"θαυμαστῶς, ὦ Ζήνων. ταῦτα δὲ ἀνδρείως μὲν
πάνυ ἡγοῦμαι πεπραγματεῦσθαι· πολὺ μέντ' ἂν
ὧδε μᾶλλον, ὡς λέγω, ἀγασθείην, εἴ τις ἔχοι τὴν
αὐτὴν ταύτην ἀπορίαν ἐν αὐτοῖς τοῖς εἴδεσι
130 παντοδαπῶς πλεκομένην, ὥσπερ ἐν τοῖς ὁρωμένοις διήλθετε, οὕτως καὶ ἐν τοῖς λογισμῷ λαμ-
βανομένοις ἐπιδεῖξαι."

many by participation in multitude; but if he shows that absolute unity is also many and the absolute many again are one, then I shall be amazed. The same applies to all other things. If he shows that the kinds and ideas in and by themselves possess these opposite qualities, it is marvellous; but if he shows that I am both one and many, what marvel is there in that? He will say, when he wishes to show that I am many, that there are my right parts and my left parts, my front parts and my back parts, likewise upper and lower, all different; for I do, I suppose, partake of multitude; and when he wishes to show that I am one, he will say that we here are seven persons, of whom I am one, a man, partaking also of unity; and so he shows that both assertions are true. If anyone then undertakes to show that the same things are both many and one—I mean such things as stones, sticks, and the like—we shall say that he shows that they are many and one, but not that the one is many or the many one; he says nothing wonderful, but only what we should all accept. If, however, as I was saying just now, he first distinguishes the abstract ideas, such as likeness and unlikeness, multitude and unity, rest and motion, and the like, and then shows that they can be mingled and separated, I should," said he, " be filled with amazement, Zeno. Now I think this has been very manfully discussed by you; but I should, as I say, be more amazed if anyone could show in the abstract ideas, which are intellectual conceptions, this same multifarious and perplexing entanglement which you described in visible objects."

4. Λέγοντος δή, ἔφη ὁ Πυθόδωρος, τοῦ Σωκράτους ταῦτα αὐτὸς μὲν ἂν[1] οἴεσθαι ἐφ᾽ ἑκάστου
ἄχθεσθαι τόν τε Παρμενίδην καὶ τὸν Ζήνωνα,
τοὺς δὲ πάνυ τε αὐτῷ προσέχειν τὸν νοῦν καὶ
θαμὰ εἰς ἀλλήλους βλέποντας μειδιᾶν ὡς ἀγα-
μένους τὸν Σωκράτη. ὅπερ οὖν καὶ παυσαμένου
αὐτοῦ εἰπεῖν τὸν Παρμενίδην· "ὦ Σώκρατες,"
B φάναι, "ὡς ἄξιος εἶ ἄγασθαι τῆς ὁρμῆς τῆς ἐπὶ
τοὺς λόγους. καί μοι εἰπέ, αὐτὸς σὺ οὕτω διῄρη-
σαι ὡς λέγεις, χωρὶς μὲν εἴδη αὐτὰ ἄττα, χωρὶς
δὲ τὰ τούτων αὖ μετέχοντα; καί τί σοι δοκεῖ
εἶναι αὐτὴ ὁμοιότης χωρὶς ἧς ἡμεῖς ὁμοιότητος
ἔχομεν, καὶ ἓν δὴ καὶ πολλὰ καὶ πάντα ὅσα νῦν
δὴ Ζήνωνος ἤκουες;"

"Ἔμοιγε," φάναι τὸν Σωκράτη.

"Ἦ καὶ τὰ τοιάδε," εἰπεῖν τὸν Παρμενίδην,
"οἷον δικαίου τι εἶδος αὐτὸ καθ᾽ αὑτὸ καὶ καλοῦ
καὶ ἀγαθοῦ καὶ πάντων αὖ τῶν τοιούτων;"

"Ναί," φάναι.

C "Τί δ᾽, ἀνθρώπου εἶδος χωρὶς ἡμῶν καὶ τῶν
οἷοι ἡμεῖς ἐσμὲν πάντων, αὐτό τι εἶδος ἀνθρώπου
ἢ πυρὸς ἢ καὶ ὕδατος;"

"Ἐν ἀπορίᾳ," φάναι, "πολλάκις δή, ὦ Παρμενίδη, περὶ αὐτῶν γέγονα, πότερα χρὴ φάναι
ὥσπερ περὶ ἐκείνων ἢ ἄλλως."

"Ἦ καὶ περὶ τῶνδε, ὦ Σώκρατες, ἃ καὶ γελοῖα
δόξειεν ἂν εἶναι, οἷον θρὶξ καὶ πηλὸς καὶ ῥύπος ἢ
ἄλλο τι ἀτιμότατόν τε καὶ φαυλότατον, ἀπορεῖς
εἴτε χρὴ φάναι καὶ τούτων ἑκάστου εἶδος εἶναι
D χωρίς, ὃν ἄλλο αὖ τῶν ὧν[2] ἡμεῖς μεταχειριζό-
μεθα, εἴτε καὶ μή;"

---

[1] ἂν add. Burnet.   [2] αὖ τῶν ὧν Heindorf: αὐτῶν ἢ ὧν BT.

PARMENIDES

Pythodorus said that he thought at every word, while Socrates was saying this, Parmenides and Zeno would be angry, but they paid close attention to him and frequently looked at each other and smiled, as if in admiration of Socrates, and when he stopped speaking Parmenides expressed their approval. " Socrates," he said, " what an admirable talent for argument you have ! Tell me, did you invent this distinction yourself, which separates abstract ideas from the things which partake of them ? And do you think there is such a thing as abstract likeness apart from the likeness which we possess, and abstract one and many, and the other abstractions of which you heard Zeno speaking just now ? "

" Yes, I do," said Socrates.

" And also," said Parmenides, " abstract ideas of the just, the beautiful, the good, and all such conceptions ? "

" Yes," he replied.

" And is there an abstract idea of man, apart from us and all others such as we are, or of fire or water ? "

" I have often," he replied, " been very much troubled, Parmenides, to decide whether there are ideas of such things, or not."

" And are you undecided about certain other things, which you might think rather ridiculous, such as hair, mud, dirt, or anything else particularly vile and worthless ? Would you say that there is an idea of each of these distinct and different from the things with which we have to do, or not ? "

211

" Οὐδαμῶς," φάναι τὸν Σωκράτη, " ἀλλὰ ταῦτα
μέν γε ἅπερ ὁρῶμεν, ταῦτα καὶ εἶναι· εἶδος δέ
τι αὐτῶν οἰηθῆναι εἶναι μὴ λίαν ᾖ ἄτοπον. ἤδη
μέντοι ποτέ με καὶ ἔθραξε μή τι ᾖ περὶ πάντων
ταὐτόν· ἔπειτα ὅταν ταύτῃ στῶ, φεύγων οἴχομαι,
δείσας μή ποτε εἴς τινα βυθὸν φλυαρίας[1] ἐμπεσὼν
διαφθαρῶ· ἐκεῖσε δ' οὖν ἀφικόμενος, εἰς ἃ νῦν δὴ
ἐλέγομεν εἴδη ἔχειν, περὶ ἐκεῖνα πραγματευόμενος
διατρίβω."

E " Νέος γὰρ εἶ ἔτι," φάναι τὸν Παρμενίδην,
" ὦ Σώκρατες, καὶ οὔπω σου ἀντείληπται φιλο-
σοφία ὡς ἔτι ἀντιλήψεται κατ' ἐμὴν δόξαν, ὅτε
οὐδὲν αὐτῶν ἀτιμάσεις· νῦν δὲ ἔτι πρὸς ἀνθρώπων
ἀποβλέπεις δόξας διὰ τὴν ἡλικίαν.

5. Τόδε οὖν μοι εἰπέ. δοκεῖ σοι, ὡς φής, εἶναι
εἴδη ἄττα, ὧν τάδε τὰ ἄλλα μεταλαμβάνοντα τὰς
131 ἐπωνυμίας αὐτῶν ἴσχειν, οἷον ὁμοιότητος μὲν
μεταλαβόντα ὅμοια, μεγέθους δὲ μεγάλα, κάλλους
δὲ καὶ δικαιοσύνης δίκαιά τε καὶ καλὰ γίγνεσθαι;"

" Πάνυ γε," φάναι τὸν Σωκράτη.

" Οὐκοῦν ἤτοι ὅλου τοῦ εἴδους ἢ μέρους ἕκαστον
τὸ μεταλαμβάνον μεταλαμβάνει; ἢ ἄλλη τις ἂν
μετάληψις χωρὶς τούτων γένοιτο;"

" Καὶ πῶς ἄν;" εἶπεν.

" Πότερον οὖν δοκεῖ σοι ὅλον τὸ εἶδος ἐν ἑκάστῳ
εἶναι τῶν πολλῶν ἓν ὄν, ἢ πῶς;"

" Τί γὰρ κωλύει," φάναι τὸν Σωκράτη, " ὦ
Παρμενίδη, ἐνεῖναι[2];"

B " Ἕν ἄρα ὂν καὶ ταὐτὸν ἐν πολλοῖς χωρὶς οὖσιν

---

[1] φλυαρίας Par. 1836, Proclus (CD), Syenesius, *Origines*:
φλυαρίαν BT.
[2] ἐνεῖναι Schleiermacher: ἐν εἶναι BT: secl. Burnet.

" By no means," said Socrates. " No, I think these things are such as they appear to us, and it would be quite absurd to believe that there is an idea of them; and yet I am sometimes disturbed by the thought that perhaps what is true of one thing is true of all. Then when I have taken up this position, I run away for fear of falling into some abyss of nonsense and perishing; so when I come to those things which we were just saying do have ideas, I stay and busy myself with them."

" Yes, for you are still young," said Parmenides, " and philosophy has not yet taken hold upon you, Socrates, as I think it will later. Then you will not despise them; but now you still consider people's opinions, on account of your youth. Well, tell me; do you think that, as you say, there are ideas, and that these other things which partake of them are named from them, as, for instance, those that partake of likeness become like, those that partake of greatness great, those that partake of beauty and justice just and beautiful? "

" Certainly," said Socrates.

" Well then, does each participant object partake of the whole idea, or of a part of it? Or could there be some other third kind of participation?

" How could there be? " said he.

" Do you think the whole idea, being one, is in each of the many participants, or what? "

" Yes, for what prevents it from being in them, Parmenides? " said Socrates.

" Then while it is one and the same, the whole

ὅλον ἅμα ἐνέσται, καὶ οὕτως αὐτὸ αὑτοῦ χωρὶς
ἂν εἴη.”

“ Οὐκ ἄν, εἴ γε,” φάναι, “ οἷον[1] ἡμέρα[2] μία καὶ
ἡ αὐτὴ οὖσα πολλαχοῦ ἅμα ἐστὶ καὶ οὐδέν τι
μᾶλλον αὐτὴ αὑτῆς χωρίς ἐστιν, εἰ οὕτω καὶ
ἕκαστον τῶν εἰδῶν ἓν ἐν πᾶσιν ἅμα ταὐτὸν εἴη.”

“ Ἡδέως γε,” φάναι, “ ὦ Σώκρατες, ἓν ταὐτὸν
ἅμα πολλαχοῦ ποιεῖς, οἷον εἰ ἱστίῳ καταπετάσας
πολλοὺς ἀνθρώπους φαίης ἓν ἐπὶ πολλοῖς εἶναι
C ὅλον. ἢ οὐ τὸ τοιοῦτον ἡγεῖ λέγειν;”

“ Ἴσως,” φάναι.

“ Ἦ οὖν ὅλον ἐφ’ ἑκάστῳ τὸ ἱστίον εἴη ἄν, ἢ
μέρος αὐτοῦ ἄλλο ἐπ’ ἄλλῳ;”

“ Μέρος.”

“ Μεριστὰ ἄρα,” φάναι, “ ὦ Σώκρατες, ἔστιν
αὐτὰ τὰ εἴδη, καὶ τὰ μετέχοντα αὐτῶν μέρους ἂν
μετέχοι, καὶ οὐκέτι ἐν ἑκάστῳ ὅλον, ἀλλὰ μέρος
ἑκάστου ἂν εἴη.”

“ Φαίνεται οὕτω γε.”

“ Ἦ οὖν ἐθελήσεις, ὦ Σώκρατες, φάναι τὸ ἓν
εἶδος ἡμῖν τῇ ἀληθείᾳ μερίζεσθαι, καὶ ἔτι ἓν
ἔσται;”

“ Οὐδαμῶς,” εἰπεῖν.

“ Ὅρα γάρ,” φάναι· “ εἰ αὐτὸ τὸ μέγεθος
D μεριεῖς καὶ ἕκαστον τῶν πολλῶν μεγάλων μεγέθους μέρει σμικροτέρῳ αὐτοῦ τοῦ μεγέθους μέγα
ἔσται, ἆρα οὐκ ἄλογον φανεῖται;”

“ Πάνυ γ’,” ἔφη.

“ Τί δέ; τοῦ ἴσου μέρος[3] ἕκαστον σμικρὸν

---

[1] οἷον εἰ BT : οἷον Proclus.
[2] ἡμέρα εἴη BT : εἴη secl. Heindorf.
[3] μέρος Proclus : μέρους BT (corr. t).

of it would be in many separate individuals at once, and thus it would itself be separate from itself."

"No," he replied, "for it might be like day, which is one and the same, is in many places at once, and yet is not separated from itself; so each idea, though one and the same, might be in all its participants at once."

"That," said he, "is very neat, Socrates; you make one to be in many places at once, just as if you should spread a sail over many persons and then should say it was one and all of it was over many. Is not that about what you mean?"

"Perhaps it is," said Socrates.

"Would the whole sail be over each person, or a particular part over each?"

"A part over each."

"Then," said he, "the ideas themselves, Socrates, are divisible into parts, and the objects which partake of them would partake of a part, and in each of them there would be not the whole, but only a part of each idea."

"So it appears."

"Are you, then, Socrates, willing to assert that the one idea is really divided and will still be one?"

"By no means," he replied.

"No," said Parmenides, "for if you divide absolute greatness, and each of the many great things is great by a part of greatness smaller than absolute greatness, is not that unreasonable?"

"Certainly," he said.

"Or again, will anything by taking away a

ἀπολαβόν τι ἕξει ᾧ ἐλάττονι ὄντι αὐτοῦ τοῦ ἴσου
τὸ ἔχον ἴσον τῳ ἔσται;"

" Ἀδύνατον."

" Ἀλλὰ τοῦ σμικροῦ μέρος τις ἡμῶν ἕξει, τούτου
δὲ αὐτοῦ τὸ σμικρὸν μεῖζον ἔσται ἅτε μέρους
ἑαυτοῦ ὄντος, καὶ οὕτω δὴ αὐτὸ τὸ σμικρὸν μεῖζον
ἔσται· ᾧ δ' ἂν προστεθῇ τὸ ἀφαιρεθέν, τοῦτο
Ε σμικρότερον ἔσται ἀλλ' οὐ μεῖζον ἢ πρίν."

" Οὐκ ἂν γένοιτο," φάναι, " τοῦτό γε."

" Τίνα οὖν τρόπον," εἰπεῖν, " ὦ Σώκρατες, τῶν
εἰδῶν σοι τὰ ἄλλα μεταλήψεται, μήτε κατὰ μέρη
μήτε κατὰ ὅλα μεταλαμβάνειν δυνάμενα;"

" Οὐ μὰ τὸν Δία," φάναι, " οὔ μοι δοκεῖ εὔκολον
εἶναι τὸ τοιοῦτον οὐδαμῶς διορίσασθαι."

" Τί δὲ δή; πρὸς τόδε πῶς ἔχεις;"

" Τὸ ποῖον;"

132   " Οἶμαί σε ἐκ τοῦ τοιοῦδε ἓν ἕκαστον εἶδος
οἴεσθαι εἶναι· ὅταν πόλλ' ἄττα μεγάλα σοι δόξῃ
εἶναι, μία τις ἴσως δοκεῖ ἰδέα ἡ αὐτὴ εἶναι ἐπὶ
πάντα ἰδόντι, ὅθεν ἓν τὸ μέγα ἡγεῖ εἶναι."

" Ἀληθῆ λέγεις," φάναι.

" Τί δ' αὐτὸ τὸ μέγα καὶ τἆλλα τὰ μεγάλα, ἐὰν
ὡσαύτως τῇ ψυχῇ ἐπὶ πάντα ἴδῃς, οὐχὶ ἕν τι αὖ
μέγα φανεῖται, ᾧ ταῦτα πάντα ἀνάγκη[1] μεγάλα
φαίνεσθαι;"

" Ἔοικεν."

" Ἄλλο ἄρα εἶδος μεγέθους ἀναφανήσεται, παρ'
αὐτό τε τὸ μέγεθος γεγονὸς καὶ τὰ μετέχοντα
Β αὐτοῦ· καὶ ἐπὶ τούτοις αὖ πᾶσιν ἕτερον, ᾧ ταῦτα

---

[1] ἀνάγκη om. B.

particular small part of equality possess something by means of which, when it is less than absolute equality, its possessor will be equal to anything else ? "

" That is impossible."

" Or let one of us have a part of the small ; the small will be greater than this, since this is a part of it, and therefore the absolute small will be greater ; but that to which the part of the small is added will be smaller, not greater, than before."

" That," said he, " is impossible."

" How, then, Socrates, will other things partake of those ideas of yours, if they cannot partake of them either as parts or as wholes ? "

" By Zeus," he replied, " I think that is a very hard question to determine."

" Well, what do you think of this ? "

" Of what ? "

" I fancy your reason for believing that each idea is one is something like this ; when there is a number of things which seem to you to be great, you may think, as you look at them all, that there is one and the same idea in them, and hence you think the great is one."

" That is true," he said.

" But if with your mind's eye you regard the absolute great and these many great things in the same way, will not another great appear beyond, by which all these must appear to be great ? "

" So it seems."

" That is, another idea of greatness will appear, in addition to absolute greatness and the objects which partake of it ; and another again in addition to these, by reason of which they are all great ;

PLATO

πάντα μεγάλα ἔσται· καὶ οὐκέτι δὴ ἓν ἕκαστόν
σοι τῶν εἰδῶν ἔσται, ἀλλ' ἄπειρα τὸ πλῆθος.''

6. "'Ἀλλά,'' φάναι, "ὦ Παρμενίδη,'' τὸν Σωκράτη, "μὴ τῶν εἰδῶν ἕκαστον ᾖ τούτων νόημα,
καὶ οὐδαμοῦ αὐτῷ προσήκῃ[1] ἐγγίγνεσθαι ἄλλοθι
ἢ ἐν ψυχαῖς· οὕτω γὰρ ἂν ἕν γε ἕκαστον εἴη καὶ
οὐκ ἂν ἔτι πάσχοι ἃ νῦν δὴ ἐλέγετο.''

"Τί οὖν;'' φάναι, "ἓν ἕκαστόν ἐστι τῶν νο-η-
μάτων, νόημα δὲ οὐδενός;''

"'Ἀλλ' ἀδύνατον,'' εἰπεῖν.

"'Ἀλλὰ τινός;''

"Ναί.''

C   "Ὄντος ἢ οὐκ ὄντος;''

"Ὄντος.''

"Οὐχ ἑνός τινος, ὃ ἐπὶ πᾶσιν ἐκεῖνο τὸ νόημα
ἐπὸν νοεῖ,[2] μίαν τινὰ οὖσαν ἰδέαν;''

"Ναί.''

"Εἶτα οὐκ εἶδος ἔσται τοῦτο τὸ νοούμενον ἓν
εἶναι, ἀεὶ ὂν τὸ αὐτὸ ἐπὶ πᾶσιν;''

"'Ἀνάγκη αὖ φαίνεται.''

"Τί δὲ δή;'' εἰπεῖν τὸν Παρμενίδην, "οὐκ
ἀνάγκη ᾗ[3] τἆλλα φὴς τῶν εἰδῶν μετέχειν, ἢ δοκεῖ
σοι ἐκ νοημάτων ἕκαστον εἶναι καὶ πάντα νοεῖν, ἢ
νοήματα ὄντα ἀνόητα εἶναι;''

"'Ἀλλ' οὐδὲ τοῦτο,'' φάναι, "ἔχει λόγον, ἀλλ',
D ὦ Παρμενίδη, μάλιστα ἔμοιγε καταφαίνεται ὧδε
ἔχειν· τὰ μὲν εἴδη ταῦτα ὥσπερ παραδείγματα
ἑστάναι ἐν τῇ φύσει, τὰ δὲ ἄλλα τούτοις ἐοικέναι
καὶ εἶναι ὁμοιώματα· καὶ ἡ μέθεξις αὕτη τοῖς

---

[1] προσήκῃ Proclus : προσήκει BT.
[2] ἐπὸν νοεῖ Proclus (cod. B) : ἐπὸν νοεῖν T : εἶπον νοεῖν B.

and each of your ideas will no longer be one, but their number will be infinite."

" But, Parmenides," said Socrates, " each of these ideas may be only a thought, which can exist only in our minds ; then each might be one, without being exposed to the consequences you have just mentioned."

" But," he said, " is each thought one, but a thought of nothing ? "

" That is impossible," he replied.

" But of something ? "

" Yes."

" Of something that is, or that is not ? "

" Of something that is."

" A thought of some single element which that thought thinks of as appertaining to all and as being one idea ? "

" Yes."

" Then will not this single element, which is thought of as one and as always the same in all, be an idea ? "

" That, again, seems inevitable."

" Well then," said Parmenides, " does not the necessity which compels you to say that all other things partake of ideas, oblige you also to believe either that everything is made of thoughts, and all things think, or that, being thoughts, they are without thought ? "

" That is quite unreasonable, too," he said, " but Parmenides, I think the most likely view is, that these ideas exist in nature as patterns, and the other things resemble them and are imitations of them ;

---

[3] ἀνάγκῃ ᾖ Waddell : ἀνάγκῃ ᾔ B : ἀναγκη ᾖ T : ἀνάγκη εἰ Proclus.

PLATO

ἄλλοις γίγνεσθαι τῶν εἰδῶν οὐκ ἄλλη τις ἢ εἰκα-
σθῆναι αὐτοῖς."

"Εἰ οὖν τι," ἔφη, "ἔοικε τῷ εἴδει, οἷόν τε
ἐκεῖνο τὸ εἶδος μὴ ὅμοιον εἶναι τῷ εἰκασθέντι,
καθ' ὅσον αὐτῷ ἀφωμοιώθη; ἢ ἔστι τις μηχανὴ
τὸ ὅμοιον μὴ ὁμοίῳ ὅμοιον εἶναι;"

"Οὐκ ἔστι."

"Τὸ δὲ ὅμοιον τῷ ὁμοίῳ ἆρ' οὐ μεγάλη ἀνάγκη
E ἑνὸς τοῦ αὐτοῦ εἴδους μετέχειν;"

"Ἀνάγκη."

"Οὗ δ' ἂν τὰ ὅμοια μετέχοντα ὅμοια ᾖ, οὐκ
ἐκεῖνο ἔσται αὐτὸ τὸ εἶδος;"

"Παντάπασι μὲν οὖν."

"Οὐκ ἄρα οἷόν τέ τι τῷ εἴδει ὅμοιον εἶναι,
οὐδὲ τὸ εἶδος ἄλλῳ· εἰ δὲ μή, παρὰ τὸ εἶδος ἀεὶ
ἄλλο ἀναφανήσεται εἶδος, καὶ ἂν ἐκεῖνό τῳ ὅμοιον
133 ᾖ,[1] ἕτερον αὖ, καὶ οὐδέποτε παύσεται ἀεὶ καινὸν
εἶδος γιγνόμενον, ἐὰν τὸ εἶδος τῷ ἑαυτοῦ μετέχοντι
ὅμοιον γίγνηται."

"Ἀληθέστατα λέγεις."

"Οὐκ ἄρα ὁμοιότητι τἆλλα τῶν εἰδῶν μεταλαμβάνει, ἀλλά τι ἄλλο δεῖ ζητεῖν ᾧ μεταλαμβάνει."

"Ἔοικεν."

"Ὁρᾷς οὖν," φάναι, "ὦ Σώκρατες, ὅση ἡ
ἀπορία, ἐάν τις ὡς εἴδη ὄντα αὐτὰ καθ' αὐτὰ διορί-
ζηται;"

"Καὶ μάλα."

"Εὖ τοίνυν ἴσθι," φάναι, "ὅτι ὡς ἔπος εἰπεῖν
B οὐδέπω ἅπτει αὐτῆς ὅση ἐστὶν ἡ ἀπορία, εἰ ἓν
εἶδος ἕκαστον τῶν ὄντων ἀεί τι ἀφοριζόμενος
θήσεις."

[1] ᾖ] ἢ BT.

220

PARMENIDES

their participation in ideas is assimilation to them,
that and nothing else."

" Then if anything," he said, " resembles the
idea, can that idea avoid being like the thing which
resembles it, in so far as the thing has been made to
resemble it ; or is there any possibility that the
like be unlike its like ? "

" No, there is none."

" And must not necessarily the like partake of
the same idea as its like ? "

" It must."

" That by participation in which like things
are made like, will be the absolute idea, will it not ? "

" Certainly."

" Then it is impossible that anything be like the
idea, or the idea like anything ; for if they are alike,
some further idea, in addition to the first, will
always appear, and if that is like anything, still
another, and a new idea will always be arising, if
the idea is like that which partakes of it."

" Very true."

" Then it is not by likeness that other things
partake of ideas ; we must seek some other method
of participation."

" So it seems."

" Do you see, then, Socrates, how great the
difficulty is, if we maintain that ideas are separate,
independent entities ? "

" Yes, certainly."

" You may be sure," he said, " that you do not
yet, if I may say so, grasp the greatness of the
difficulty involved in your assumption that each
idea is one and is something distinct from concrete
things."

" Πῶς δή; " εἰπεῖν.

" Πολλὰ μὲν καὶ ἄλλα," φάναι, " μέγιστον δὲ τόδε. εἴ τις φαίη μηδὲ προσήκειν αὐτὰ γιγνώσκεσθαι ὄντα τοιαῦτα οἷά φαμεν δεῖν εἶναι τὰ εἴδη, τῷ ταῦτα λέγοντι οὐκ ἂν ἔχοι τις ἐνδείξασθαι ὅτι ψεύδεται, εἰ μὴ πολλῶν μὲν τύχοι ἔμπειρος ὢν ὁ ἀμφισβητῶν καὶ μὴ ἀφυής, ἐθέλοι δὲ πάνυ πολλὰ καὶ πόρρωθεν πραγματευομένου C τοῦ ἐνδεικνυμένου ἕπεσθαι, ἀλλ' ἀπίθανος εἴη ὁ ἄγνωστα ἀναγκάζων αὐτὰ εἶναι."

" Πῇ δή, ὦ Παρμενίδη; " φάναι τὸν Σωκράτη.

" Ὅτι, ὦ Σώκρατες, οἶμαι ἂν καὶ σὲ καὶ ἄλλον, ὅστις αὐτήν τινα καθ' αὑτὴν ἑκάστου οὐσίαν τίθεται εἶναι, ὁμολογῆσαι ἂν πρῶτον μὲν μηδεμίαν αὐτῶν εἶναι ἐν ἡμῖν."

" Πῶς γὰρ ἂν αὐτὴ καθ' αὑτὴν ἔτι εἴη; " φάναι τὸν Σωκράτη.

" Καλῶς λέγεις," εἰπεῖν. " οὐκοῦν καὶ ὅσαι τῶν ἰδεῶν πρὸς ἀλλήλας εἰσὶν αἵ εἰσιν, αὐταὶ πρὸς αὑτὰς τὴν οὐσίαν ἔχουσιν, ἀλλ' οὐ πρὸς τὰ παρ' D ἡμῖν εἴτε ὁμοιώματα εἴτε ὅπῃ δή τις αὐτὰ τίθεται, ὧν ἡμεῖς μετέχοντες εἶναι ἕκαστα ἐπονομαζόμεθα· τὰ δὲ παρ' ἡμῖν ταῦτα ὁμώνυμα ὄντα ἐκείνοις αὐτὰ αὖ πρὸς αὑτά ἐστιν ἀλλ' οὐ πρὸς τὰ εἴδη, καὶ ἑαυτῶν ἀλλ' οὐκ ἐκείνων ὅσα αὖ ὀνομάζεται οὕτως."

" Πῶς λέγεις; " φάναι τὸν Σωκράτη.

" Οἷον," φάναι τὸν Παρμενίδην, " εἴ τις ἡμῶν του δεσπότης ἢ δοῦλός ἐστιν, οὐκ αὐτοῦ δεσπότου E δή που, ὃ ἔστι δεσπότης, ἐκείνου δοῦλός ἐστιν, οὐδὲ αὐτοῦ δούλου, ὃ ἔστι δοῦλος, δεσπότης ὁ δεσπότης, ἀλλ' ἄνθρωπος ὢν ἀνθρώπου ἀμφότερα

" How is that ? " said he.

" There are many reasons," he said, " but the greatest is this : if anyone should say that the ideas cannot even be known if they are such as we say they must be, no one could prove to him that he was wrong, unless he who argued that they could be known were a man of wide education and ability and were willing to follow the proof through many long and elaborate details ; he who maintains that they cannot be known would be unconvinced."

" Why is that, Parmenides ? " said Socrates.

" Because, Socrates, I think that you or anyone else who claims that there is an absolute idea of each thing would agree in the first place that none of them exists in us."

" No, for if it did, it would no longer be absolute," said Socrates.

" You are right," he said. " Then those absolute ideas which are relative to one another have their own nature in relation to themselves, and not in relation to the likenesses, or whatever we choose to call them, which are amongst us, and from which we receive certain names as we participate in them. And these concrete things, which have the same names with the ideas, are likewise relative only to themselves, not to the ideas, and belong to themselves, not to the like-named ideas."

" What do you mean ? " said Socrates.

" For instance," said Parmenides, " if one of us is master or slave of anyone, he is not the slave of master in the abstract, nor is the master the master of slave in the abstract ; each is a man and is master

ταῦτά ἐστιν· αὕτη δὲ δεσποτεία αὐτῆς δουλείας
ἐστὶν ὅ ἐστι, καὶ δουλεία ὡσαύτως αὕτη δουλεία
αὐτῆς δεσποτείας, ἀλλ' οὐ τὰ ἐν ἡμῖν πρὸς ἐκεῖνα
τὴν δύναμιν ἔχει οὐδὲ ἐκεῖνα πρὸς ἡμᾶς, ἀλλ',
134 ὃ λέγω, αὐτὰ αὑτῶν καὶ πρὸς αὐτὰ ἐκεῖνά τέ ἐστι,
καὶ τὰ παρ' ἡμῖν ὡσαύτως πρὸς ἑαυτά. ἢ οὐ
μανθάνεις ὃ λέγω;"

"Πάνυ γ'," εἰπεῖν τὸν Σωκράτη, "μανθάνω."

7. "Οὐκοῦν καὶ ἐπιστήμη," φάναι, "αὐτὴ
μὲν ὃ ἐστιν ἐπιστήμη τῆς ὃ ἐστιν ἀλήθεια αὐτῆς
ἂν ἐκείνης εἴη ἐπιστήμη;"

"Πάνυ γε."

"Ἑκάστη δὲ αὖ τῶν ἐπιστημῶν, ἣ ἔστιν,
ἑκάστου τῶν ὄντων, ὃ ἔστιν, εἴη ἂν ἐπιστήμη· ἢ
οὔ;"

"Ναί."

"Ἡ δὲ παρ' ἡμῖν ἐπιστήμη οὐ τῆς παρ' ἡμῖν
ἂν ἀληθείας εἴη, καὶ αὖ ἑκάστη ἡ παρ' ἡμῖν ἐπι-
B στήμη τῶν παρ' ἡμῖν ὄντων ἑκάστου ἂν ἐπιστήμη
συμβαίνοι εἶναι;"

"Ἀνάγκη."

"Ἀλλὰ μὴν αὐτά γε τὰ εἴδη, ὡς ὁμολογεῖς,
οὔτε ἔχομεν οὔτε παρ' ἡμῖν οἷόν τε εἶναι."

"Οὐ γὰρ οὖν."

"Γιγνώσκεται δέ γέ που ὑπ' αὐτοῦ τοῦ εἴδους
τοῦ τῆς ἐπιστήμης αὐτὰ τὰ γένη ἃ ἔστιν ἕκαστα;"

"Ναί."

"Ὅ γε ἡμεῖς οὐκ ἔχομεν."

"Οὐ γάρ."

"Οὐκ ἄρα ὑπό γε ἡμῶν γιγνώσκεται τῶν εἰδῶν
οὐδέν, ἐπειδὴ αὐτῆς ἐπιστήμης οὐ μετέχομεν."

"Οὐκ ἔοικεν."

or slave of a man ; but mastership in the abstract is mastership of slavery in the abstract, and likewise slavery in the abstract is slavery to mastership in the abstract, but our slaves and masters are not relative to them, nor they to us ; they, as I say, belong to themselves and are relative to themselves and likewise our slaves and masters are relative to themselves. You understand what I mean, do you not ? "

" Certainly," said Socrates, " I understand."

" Then knowledge also, if abstract or absolute, would be knowledge of abstract or absolute truth ? "

" Certainly."

" And likewise each kind of absolute knowledge would be knowledge of each kind of absolute being, would it not ? "

" Yes."

" And would not the knowledge that exists among us be the knowledge of the truth that exists among us, and each kind of our knowledge be the knowledge of each kind of truth that exists among us ? "

" Yes, that is inevitable."

" But the ideas themselves, as you agree, we have not, neither can they be among us "

" No, they cannot."

" And the various classes of ideas are known by the absolute idea of knowledge ? "

" Yes."

" Which we do not possess."

" No, we do not."

" Then none of the ideas is known by us, since we do not partake of absolute knowledge."

" Apparently not."

PLATO

" Ἄγνωστον ἄρα ἡμῖν ἐστὶ καὶ αὐτὸ τὸ καλὸν ὃ
C ἔστι καὶ τὸ ἀγαθὸν καὶ πάντα ἃ δὴ ὡς ἰδέας αὐτὰς
οὔσας ὑπολαμβάνομεν."

" Κινδυνεύει."

" Ὅρα δὴ ἔτι τούτου δεινότερον τόδε."

" Τὸ ποῖον;"

" Φαίης ἄν που,[1] εἴπερ ἔστιν αὐτό τι γένος
ἐπιστήμης, πολὺ αὐτὸ ἀκριβέστερον εἶναι ἢ τὴν
παρ᾽ ἡμῖν ἐπιστήμην, καὶ κάλλος καὶ τἆλλα πάντα
οὕτως."

" Ναί."

" Οὐκοῦν εἴπερ τι ἄλλο αὐτῆς ἐπιστήμης μετέχει, οὐκ ἄν τινα μᾶλλον ἢ θεὸν φαίης ἔχειν τὴν
ἀκριβεστάτην ἐπιστήμην;"

" Ἀνάγκη."

D " Ἆρ᾽ οὖν οἷός τε αὖ ἔσται ὁ θεὸς τὰ παρ᾽ ἡμῖν
γιγνώσκειν αὐτὴν ἐπιστήμην ἔχων;"

" Τί γὰρ οὔ;"

" Ὅτι," ἔφη ὁ Παρμενίδης, " ὡμολόγηται ἡμῖν,
ὦ Σώκρατες, μήτ᾽ ἐκεῖνα τὰ εἴδη πρὸς τὰ παρ᾽
ἡμῖν τὴν δύναμιν ἔχειν ἣν ἔχει, μήτε τὰ παρ᾽ ἡμῖν
πρὸς ἐκεῖνα, ἀλλ᾽ αὐτὰ πρὸς αὑτὰ ἑκάτερα."

" Ὡμολόγηται γάρ."

" Οὐκοῦν εἰ παρὰ τῷ θεῷ αὕτη ἐστὶν ἡ ἀκριβεστάτη δεσποτεία καὶ αὕτη ἡ ἀκριβεστάτη ἐπιστήμη,
οὔτ᾽ ἂν ἡ δεσποτεία ἡ ἐκείνων ἡμῶν ποτε ἂν δε-
E σπόσειεν, οὔτ᾽ ἂν ἡ ἐπιστήμη ἡμᾶς γνοίη οὐδέ τι
ἄλλο τῶν παρ᾽ ἡμῖν, ἀλλὰ ὁμοίως ἡμεῖς τ᾽ ἐκείνων
οὐκ ἄρχομεν τῇ παρ᾽ ἡμῖν ἀρχῇ οὐδὲ γιγνώσκομεν
τοῦ θείου οὐδὲν τῇ ἡμετέρᾳ ἐπιστήμῃ, ἐκεῖνοί τε
αὖ κατὰ τὸν αὐτὸν λόγον οὔτε δεσπόται ἡμῶν

[1] που T: ἢ οὔ B.

" Then the absolute good and the beautiful and all which we conceive to be absolute ideas are unknown to us."

" I am afraid they are."

" Now we come to a still more fearful consequence."

" What is it ? "

" You would say, no doubt, that if there is an absolute kind of knowledge, it is far more accurate than our knowledge, and the same of beauty and all the rest ? "

" Yes."

" And if anything partakes of absolute knowledge, you would say that there is no one more likely than God to possess this most accurate knowledge ? "

" Of course."

" Then will it be possible for God to know human things, if he has absolute knowledge ? "

" Why not ? "

" Because," said Parmenides, " we have agreed that those ideas are not relative to our world, nor our world to them, but each only to themselves."

" Yes, we have agreed to that."

" Then if this most perfect mastership and this most accurate knowledge are with God, his mastership can never rule us, nor his knowledge know us or anything of our world ; we do not rule the gods with our authority, nor do we know anything of the divine with our knowledge, and by the same reasoning, they likewise, being gods, are not

εἰσὶν οὔτε γιγνώσκουσι τὰ ἀνθρώπεια πράγματα
θεοὶ ὄντες."

" Ἀλλὰ μὴ λίαν," ἔφη, " θαυμαστὸς ὁ λόγος ᾖ,[1]
εἴ τις τὸν θεὸν ἀποστερήσει[2] τοῦ εἰδέναι."

" Ταῦτα μέντοι, ὦ Σώκρατες," ἔφη ὁ Παρμε-
135 νίδης, " καὶ ἔτι ἄλλα πρὸς τούτοις πάνυ πολλὰ
ἀναγκαῖον ἔχειν τὰ εἴδη, εἰ εἰσὶν αὗται αἱ ἰδέαι
τῶν ὄντων καὶ ὁριεῖταί τις αὐτό τι ἕκαστον εἶδος·
ὥστε ἀπορεῖν τε τὸν ἀκούοντα καὶ ἀμφισβητεῖν ὡς
οὔτε ἔστι ταῦτα, εἴ τε ὅτι μάλιστα εἴη, πολλὴ
ἀνάγκη αὐτὰ εἶναι τῇ ἀνθρωπίνῃ φύσει ἄγνωστα·
καὶ ταῦτα λέγοντα δοκεῖν τε τὶ λέγειν, καί, ὃ
ἄρτι ἐλέγομεν, θαυμαστῶς ὡς δυσανάπειστον εἶναι.
καὶ ἀνδρὸς πάνυ μὲν εὐφυοῦς τοῦ δυνησομένου
μαθεῖν ὡς ἔστι γένος τι ἑκάστου καὶ οὐσία αὐτὴ
Β καθ᾽ αὑτήν, ἔτι δὲ θαυμαστοτέρου τοῦ εὑρήσοντος
καὶ ἄλλον δυνησομένου διδάξαι ταῦτα πάντα ἱκανῶς
διευκρινησάμενον."

" Συγχωρῶ σοι," ἔφη, " ὦ Παρμενίδη," ὁ
Σωκράτης· " πάνυ γάρ μοι κατὰ νοῦν λέγεις."

" Ἀλλὰ μέντοι," εἶπεν ὁ Παρμενίδης, " εἴ γέ
τις δή, ὦ Σώκρατες, αὖ μὴ ἐάσει[3] εἴδη τῶν ὄντων
εἶναι, εἰς πάντα τὰ νῦν δὴ καὶ ἄλλα τοιαῦτα ἀπο-
βλέψας, μηδέ τι[4] ὁριεῖται εἶδος ἑνὸς ἑκάστου,
οὐδὲ ὅπῃ τρέψει τὴν διάνοιαν ἕξει, μὴ ἐῶν ἰδέαν
C τῶν ὄντων ἑκάστου τὴν αὐτὴν ἀεὶ εἶναι, καὶ οὕτως
τὴν τοῦ διαλέγεσθαι δύναμιν παντάπασι διαφθερεῖ.
τοῦ τοιούτου μὲν οὖν μοι δοκεῖς καὶ μᾶλλον ᾐσθῆ-
σθαι."

" Ἀληθῆ λέγεις," φάναι.

---

[1] ᾖ add. Heindorf.
[2] ἀποστερήσει Stephanus : ἀποστερήσειε BT.

PARMENIDES

our masters and have no knowledge of human affairs."

" But surely this," said he, " is a most amazing argument, if it makes us deprive God of knowledge."

" And yet, Socrates," said Parmenides, " these difficulties and many more besides are inseparable from the ideas, if these ideas of things exist and we declare that each of them is an absolute idea. Therefore he who hears such assertions is confused in his mind and argues that the ideas do not exist, and even if they do exist cannot by any possibility be known by man ; and he thinks that what he says is reasonable, and, as I was saying just now, he is amazingly hard to convince. Only a man of very great natural gifts will be able to understand that everything has a class and absolute essence, and only a still more wonderful man can find out all these facts and teach anyone else to analyse them properly and understand them."

" I agree with you, Parmenides," said Socrates, " for what you say is very much to my mind."

" But on the other hand," said Parmenides, " if anyone, with his mind fixed on all these objections and others like them, denies the existence of ideas of things, and does not assume an idea under which each individual thing is classed, he will be quite at a loss, since he denies that the idea of each thing is always the same, and in this way he will utterly destroy the power of carrying on discussion. You seem to have been well aware of this."

" Quite true," he said.

---

³ ἐάσῃ BT.   ⁴ μὴ δέτι B : μηδ' ὅτι T.

229

8. " Τί οὖν ποιήσεις φιλοσοφίας πέρι; πῇ τρέψει ἀγνοουμένων τούτων;"

" Οὐ πάνυ μοι δοκῶ καθορᾶν ἔν γε τῷ παρόντι."

" Πρῲ γάρ," εἰπεῖν, " πρὶν γυμνασθῆναι, ὦ Σώκρατες, ὁρίζεσθαι ἐπιχειρεῖς καλόν τέ τι καὶ δίκαιον καὶ ἀγαθὸν καὶ ἓν ἕκαστον τῶν εἰδῶν. D ἐνενόησα γὰρ καὶ πρῴην σου ἀκούων διαλεγομένου ἐνθάδε Ἀριστοτέλει τῷδε. καλὴ μὲν οὖν καὶ θεία, εὖ ἴσθι, ἡ ὁρμή, ἣν ὁρμᾷς ἐπὶ τοὺς λόγους· ἕλκυσον δὲ σαυτὸν καὶ γύμνασαι μᾶλλον διὰ τῆς δοκούσης ἀχρήστου εἶναι καὶ καλουμένης ὑπὸ τῶν πολλῶν ἀδολεσχίας, ἕως ἔτι νέος εἶ· εἰ δὲ μή, σὲ διαφεύξεται ἡ ἀλήθεια."

" Τίς οὖν ὁ τρόπος," φάναι, " ὦ Παρμενίδη, τῆς γυμνασίας;"

" Οὗτος," εἰπεῖν, " ὅνπερ ἤκουσας Ζήνωνος. E πλὴν τοῦτό γέ σου καὶ πρὸς τοῦτον ἠγάσθην εἰπόντος ὅτι οὐκ εἴας ἐν τοῖς ὁρωμένοις οὐδὲ περὶ ταῦτα τὴν πλάνην ἐπισκοπεῖν, ἀλλὰ περὶ ἐκεῖνα ἃ μάλιστά τις ἂν λόγῳ λάβοι καὶ εἴδη ἂν ἡγήσαιτο εἶναι."

" Δοκεῖ γάρ μοι," ἔφη, " ταύτῃ γε οὐδὲν χαλεπὸν εἶναι καὶ ὅμοια καὶ ἀνόμοια καὶ ἄλλο ὁτιοῦν τὰ ὄντα πάσχοντα ἀποφαίνειν."

" Καὶ καλῶς γ'," ἔφη. " χρὴ δὲ καὶ τόδε ἔτι πρὸς τούτῳ ποιεῖν, μὴ μόνον εἰ ἔστιν ἕκαστον 136 ὑποτιθέμενον σκοπεῖν τὰ ξυμβαίνοντα ἐκ τῆς ὑποθέσεως, ἀλλὰ καὶ εἰ μὴ ἔστι τὸ αὐτὸ τοῦτο ὑποτίθεσθαι, εἰ βούλει μᾶλλον γυμνασθῆναι."

" Πῶς λέγεις;" φάναι.

" Οἷον," ἔφη, " εἰ βούλει περὶ ταύτης τῆς ὑποθέσεως, ἣν Ζήνων ὑπέθετο, εἰ πολλά ἐστι, τί χρὴ

" Then what will become of philosophy ? To what can you turn, if these things are unknown ? "

" I do not see at all, at least not at present."

" No, Socrates," he said, " for you try too soon, before you are properly trained, to define the beautiful, the just, the good, and all the other ideas. You see I noticed it when I heard you talking yesterday with Aristoteles here. Your impulse towards dialectic is noble and divine, you may be assured of that ; but exercise and train yourself while you are still young in an art which seems to be useless and is called by most people mere loquacity ; otherwise the truth will escape you."

" What, then, Parmenides," he said, " is the method of training ? "

" That which you heard Zeno practising," said he. " However, even when you were speaking to him I was pleased with you, because you would not discuss the doubtful question in terms of visible objects or in relation to them, but only with reference to what we conceive most entirely by the intellect and may call ideas."

" Yes," he said, " that is because I think that in that way it is quite easy to show that things experience likeness or unlikeness or anything else."

" Quite right," said he, " but if you wish to get better training, you must do something more than that ; you must consider not only what happens if a particular hypothesis is true, but also what happens if it is not true."

" What do you mean ? " he said.

" Take, for instance," he replied, " that hypothesis of Zeno's ; if the many exist, you should inquire what

ξυμβαίνειν καὶ αὐτοῖς τοῖς πολλοῖς πρὸς αὐτὰ καὶ
πρὸς τὸ ἓν καὶ τῷ ἑνὶ πρός τε αὐτὸ καὶ πρὸς τὰ
πολλά· καὶ αὖ εἰ μή ἐστι πολλά, πάλιν σκοπεῖν,
τί ξυμβήσεται καὶ τῷ ἑνὶ καὶ τοῖς πολλοῖς καὶ
B πρὸς αὐτὰ καὶ πρὸς ἄλληλα· καὶ αὖθις αὖ ἐὰν
ὑποθῇ, εἰ ἔστιν ὁμοιότης ἢ εἰ μὴ ἔστι, τί ἐφ' ἑκατέ-
ρας τῆς ὑποθέσεως ξυμβήσεται καὶ αὐτοῖς τοῖς
ὑποτεθεῖσι καὶ τοῖς ἄλλοις καὶ πρὸς αὐτὰ καὶ πρὸς
ἄλληλα. καὶ περὶ ἀνομοίου ὁ αὐτὸς λόγος καὶ
περὶ κινήσεως καὶ στάσεως καὶ περὶ γενέσεως καὶ
φθορᾶς καὶ περὶ αὐτοῦ τοῦ εἶναι καὶ τοῦ μὴ εἶναι·
καὶ ἑνὶ λόγῳ, περὶ ὅτου ἂν ἀεὶ ὑποθῇ ὡς ὄντος καὶ
ὡς οὐκ ὄντος καὶ ὁτιοῦν ἄλλο πάθος πάσχοντος,
C δεῖ σκοπεῖν τὰ ξυμβαίνοντα πρὸς αὐτὸ καὶ πρὸς
ἓν ἕκαστον τῶν ἄλλων, ὅ τι ἂν προέλῃ, καὶ πρὸς
πλείω καὶ πρὸς ξύμπαντα ὡσαύτως· καὶ τἆλλα αὖ
πρὸς αὐτά τε καὶ πρὸς ἄλλο ὅ τι ἂν προαιρῇ ἀεί,
ἐάντε ὡς ὂν ὑποθῇ ὃ ὑπετίθεσο, ἐάντε ὡς μὴ ὄν,
εἰ μέλλεις τελέως γυμνασάμενος κυρίως διόψεσθαι
τὸ ἀληθές."

"'Αμήχανον," ἔφη, "λέγεις, ὦ Παρμενίδη,
πραγματείαν, καὶ οὐ σφόδρα μανθάνω. ἀλλά μοι
τί οὐ διῆλθες αὐτὸς ὑποθέμενός τι, ἵνα μᾶλλον
καταμάθω;"

D "Πολὺ ἔργον," φάναι, "ὦ Σώκρατες, προστάττεις ὡς τηλικῷδε."

"'Αλλὰ σύ," εἰπεῖν τὸν Σωκράτη, "Ζήνων,
τί οὐ διῆλθες ἡμῖν;"

Καὶ τὸν Ζήνωνα ἔφη γελάσαντα φάναι· "αὐτοῦ,
ὦ Σώκρατες, δεώμεθα Παρμενίδου. μὴ γὰρ οὐ
φαῦλον ᾖ ὃ λέγει. ἢ οὐχ ὁρᾷς ὅσον ἔργον προσ-

will happen to the many themselves in relation to themselves and to the one, and to the one in relation to itself and to the many, and also what will happen to the one and the many in relation to themselves and to each other, if the many do not exist. And likewise if you suppose the existence or non-existence of likeness, what will happen to the things supposed and to other things in relation to themselves and to each other under each of the two hypotheses. The same applies to unlikeness and to motion and rest, creation and destruction, and even to being and not being. In brief, whatever the subject of your hypothesis, if you suppose that it is or is not, or that it experiences any other affection, you must consider what happens to it and to any other particular things you may choose, and to a greater number and to all in the same way ; and you must consider other things in relation to themselves and to anything else you may choose in any instance, whether you suppose that the subject of your hypothesis exists or does not exist, if you are to train yourself completely to see the truth perfectly."

"Parmenides," he said, " it is a stupendous amount of study which you propose, and I do not understand very well. Why do you not yourself frame an hypothesis and discuss it, to make me understand better ? "

"That is a great task, Socrates," he said, " to impose upon a man of my age."

"But you, Zeno," said Socrates, " why do not you do it for us ? "

Pythodorus said that Zeno answered with a smile : " Let us ask it of Parmenides himself, Socrates ; for there is a great deal in what he says,

τάττεις· εἰ μὲν οὖν πλείους ἦμεν, οὐκ ἂν ἄξιον ἦν
δεῖσθαι· ἀπρεπῆ γὰρ τὰ τοιαῦτα πολλῶν ἐναντίον
λέγειν ἄλλως τε καὶ τηλικούτῳ· ἀγνοοῦσιν γὰρ
E οἱ πολλοὶ ὅτι ἄνευ ταύτης τῆς διὰ πάντων διεξ-
όδου τε καὶ πλάνης ἀδύνατον ἐντυχόντα τῷ ἀληθεῖ
νοῦν σχεῖν. ἐγὼ μὲν οὖν, ὦ Παρμενίδη, Σωκράτει
συνδέομαι, ἵνα καὶ αὐτὸς διακούσω διὰ χρόνου."

9. Ταῦτα δὴ εἰπόντος τοῦ Ζήνωνος, ἔφη ὁ Ἀντιφῶν φάναι τὸν Πυθόδωρον, αὐτόν τε δεῖσθαι τοῦ
Παρμενίδου καὶ τὸν Ἀριστοτέλη καὶ τοὺς ἄλλους,
ἐνδείξασθαι ὃ λέγοι καὶ μὴ ἄλλως ποιεῖν. τὸν
οὖν Παρμενίδην· "ἀνάγκη," φάναι, "πείθεσθαι.
137 καί τοι δοκῶ μοι τὸ τοῦ Ἰβυκείου ἵππου πεπονθέναι, ᾧ ἐκεῖνος ἀθλητῇ ὄντι καὶ πρεσβυτέρῳ, ὑφ᾽
ἅρματι μέλλοντι ἀγωνιεῖσθαι καὶ δι᾽ ἐμπειρίαν
τρέμοντι τὸ μέλλον, ἑαυτὸν ἀπεικάζων ἄκων ἔφη
καὶ αὐτὸς οὕτω πρεσβύτης ὢν εἰς τὸν ἔρωτα ἀναγκά-
ζεσθαι ἰέναι· κἀγώ μοι δοκῶ μεμνημένος μάλα
φοβεῖσθαι πῶς χρὴ τηλικόνδε ὄντα διανεῦσαι
τοιοῦτόν τε καὶ τοσοῦτον πέλαγος[1] λόγων· ὅμως
δὲ δεῖ γὰρ χαρίζεσθαι, ἐπειδὴ καί, ὃ[2] Ζήνων
B λέγει, αὐτοί ἐσμεν. πόθεν οὖν δὴ ἀρξόμεθα καὶ
τί πρῶτον ὑποθησόμεθα; ἢ βούλεσθε, ἐπειδήπερ
δοκεῖ πραγματειώδη παιδιὰν παίζειν, ἀπ᾽ ἐμαυτοῦ
ἄρξωμαι καὶ τῆς ἐμαυτοῦ ὑποθέσεως, περὶ τοῦ
ἑνὸς αὐτοῦ ὑποθέμενος, εἴτε ἓν ἔστιν εἴτε μὴ ἕν,
τί χρὴ ξυμβαίνειν;"

"Πάνυ μὲν οὖν," φάναι τὸν Ζήνωνα.

"Τίς οὖν;" εἰπεῖν, "μοι ἀποκρινεῖται; ἢ ὁ

___

[1] πέλαγος Stephanus (fr. Ficinus), and Proclus seems to
have had this reading: πλῆθος BT.
[2] ὃ Bekker: ὁ BT.

and perhaps you do not see how heavy a task you are imposing upon him. If there were more of us, it would not be fair to ask it of him; for it is not suitable for him to speak on such subjects before many, especially at his age; for the many do not know that except by this devious passage through all things the mind cannot attain to the truth. So I, Parmenides, join Socrates in his request, that I myself may hear the method, which I have not heard for a long time."

Antiphon said that Pythodorus told him that when Zeno said this he himself and Antisthenes and the rest begged Parmenides to show his meaning by an example and not to refuse. And Parmenides said : " I must perforce do as you ask. And yet I feel very much like the horse in the poem of Ibycus [1] —an old race-horse who was entered for a chariot race and was trembling with fear of what was before him, because he knew it by experience. Ibycus says he is compelled to fall in love against his will in his old age, and compares himself to the horse. So I am filled with terror when I remember through what a fearful ocean of words I must swim, old man that I am. However, I will do it, for I must be obliging, especially since we are, as Zeno says, alone. Well, how shall we begin? What shall be our first hypothesis? Or, since you are determined that I must engage in a laborious pastime, shall I begin with myself, taking my own hypothesis and discussing the consequences of the supposition that the one exists or that it does not exist ? "

" By all means," said Zeno.

" Who then," said he, " is to answer my questions ?

[1] Ibycus, fragm. 2 Bergk.

νεώτατος; ἥκιστα γὰρ ἂν πολυπραγμονοῖ, καὶ
ἃ οἴεται μάλιστ' ἂν ἀποκρίνοιτο· καὶ ἅμα ἐμοὶ
ἀνάπαυλα ἂν εἴη ἡ ἐκείνου ἀπόκρισις."

C   " Ἕτοιμός σοι, ὦ Παρμενίδη," φάναι, " τοῦτο,"
τὸν Ἀριστοτέλη· ' ἐμὲ γὰρ λέγεις τὸν νεώτατον
λέγων· ἀλλ' ἐρώτα ὡς ἀποκρινουμένου."

10. " Εἶεν δή," φάναι· " εἰ ἕν ἐστιν, ἄλλο τι
οὐκ ἂν εἴη πολλὰ τὸ ἕν;" " πῶς γὰρ ἄν;" " οὔτε
ἄρα μέρος αὐτοῦ οὔτε ὅλον αὐτὸ δεῖ εἶναι." " τί
δή;" " τὸ μέρος που ὅλου μέρος¹ ἐστίν." " Ναί."
" Τί δὲ τὸ ὅλον; οὐχὶ οὗ ἂν μέρος μηδὲν ἀπῇ,
ὅλον ἂν εἴη;" " πάνυ γε." " ἀμφοτέρως ἄρα
τὸ ἓν ἐκ μερῶν ἂν εἴη, ὅλον τε ὂν καὶ μέρη ἔχον."
D " ἀνάγκη." " ἀμφοτέρως ἂν ἄρα οὕτως τὸ ἓν
πολλὰ εἴη, ἀλλ' οὐχ ἕν." " ἀληθῆ." " δεῖ δέ
γε μὴ πολλὰ ἀλλ' ἓν αὐτὸ εἶναι." " δεῖ." " οὔτ'
ἄρα ὅλον ἔσται οὔτε μέρη ἕξει, εἰ ἓν ἔσται τὸ ἕν."
" οὐ γάρ."

" Οὐκοῦν εἰ μηδὲν ἔχει μέρος, οὔτ' ἂν ἀρχὴν οὔτε
τελευτὴν οὔτε μέσον ἔχοι· μέρη γὰρ ἂν ἤδη αὐτοῦ
τὰ τοιαῦτα εἴη." " ὀρθῶς." " καὶ μὴν τελευτή
γε καὶ ἀρχὴ πέρας ἑκάστου." " πῶς δ' οὔ;"
" ἄπειρον ἄρα τὸ ἕν, εἰ μήτε ἀρχὴν μήτε τελευτὴν
ἔχει." " ἄπειρον." " καὶ ἄνευ σχήματος ἄρα·
E οὔτε γὰρ² ἂν στρογγύλου οὔτε εὐθέος μετέχει.³"
" πῶς;" " στρογγύλου γέ πού ἐστι τοῦτο, οὗ
ἂν τὰ ἔσχατα πανταχῇ ἀπὸ τοῦ μέσου ἴσον
ἀπέχῃ." " ναί." " καὶ μὴν εὐθύ γε, οὗ ἂν τὸ
μέσον ἀμφοῖν τοῖν ἐσχάτοιν ἐπίπροσθεν ᾖ." " οὕτως." " οὐκοῦν μέρη ἂν ἔχοι τὸ ἓν καὶ πόλλ' ἂν

---

¹ ὅλου μέρους B: μέρος ὅλου T.   ² γὰρ BT: γὰρ ἂν vulg.
³ μετέχει Proclus: μετέχοι BT.

Shall we say the youngest? He would be least likely to be over-curious and most likely to say what he thinks ; and moreover his replies would give me a chance to rest."

" I am ready, Parmenides, to do that," said Aristoteles, " for I am the youngest, so you mean me. Ask your questions and I will answer."

" Well then," said he, " if the one exists, the one cannot be many, can it ? " " No, of course not." " Then there can be no parts of it, nor can it be a whole." " How is that ? " " The part surely is part of a whole." " Yes." " And what is the whole ? Is not a whole that of which no part is wanting ? " " Certainly." " Then in both cases the one would consist of parts, being a whole and having parts." " Inevitably." " Then in both cases the one would be many, not one." " True." " Yet it must be not many, but one." " Yes." " Then the one, if it is to be one, will not be a whole and will not have parts." " No."

" And if it has no parts, it can have no beginning, or middle, or end, for those would be parts of it ? " " Quite right." " Beginning and end are, however, the limits of everything." " Of course." " Then the one, if it has neither beginning nor end, is unlimited." " Yes, it is unlimited." " And it is without form, for it partakes neither of the round nor of the straight." " How so ? " " The round, of course, is that of which the extremes are every-where equally distant from the centre." " Yes." " And the straight, again, is that of which the middle is in the nearest line between the two extremes." " It is." " Then the one would have parts and would

εἴη, εἴτε εὐθέος σχήματος εἴτε περιφεροῦς μετέχοι."
" πάνυ μὲν οὖν." " οὔτε ἄρα εὐθὺ οὔτε περιφερές
138 ἐστιν, ἐπείπερ οὐδὲ μέρη ἔχει." " ὀρθῶς."

" Καὶ μὴν τοιοῦτόν γε ὂν οὐδαμοῦ ἂν εἴη· οὔτε
γὰρ ἐν ἄλλῳ οὔτε ἐν ἑαυτῷ εἴη." " πῶς δή;"
" ἐν ἄλλῳ μὲν ὂν κύκλῳ που ἂν περιέχοιτο ὑπ᾽
ἐκείνου ἐν ᾧ ἐνείη,¹ καὶ πολλαχοῦ ἂν αὐτοῦ
ἅπτοιτο πολλοῖς· τοῦ δὲ ἑνός τε καὶ ἀμεροῦς καὶ
κύκλου μὴ μετέχοντος ἀδύνατον πολλαχῇ κύκλῳ
ἅπτεσθαι." " ἀδύνατον." " ἀλλὰ μὴν αὐτό γε
ἐν ἑαυτῷ ὂν κἂν ἑαυτῷ² εἴη περιέχον οὐκ ἄλλο
B ἢ αὐτό,³ εἴπερ καὶ ἐν ἑαυτῷ εἴη· ἔν τῳ γὰρ τι
εἶναι μὴ περιέχοντι ἀδύνατον." " ἀδύνατον γάρ."
" οὐκοῦν ἕτερον μὲν ἄν τι εἴη αὐτὸ τὸ περιέχον,
ἕτερον δὲ τὸ περιεχόμενον· οὐ γὰρ ὅλον γε ἄμφω
ταὐτὸν ἅμα πείσεται καὶ ποιήσει· καὶ οὕτω τὸ
ἓν οὐκ ἂν εἴη ἔτι ἓν ἀλλὰ δύο." " οὐ γὰρ οὖν."
" οὐκ ἄρα ἐστίν που τὸ ἕν, μήτε ἐν ἑαυτῷ μήτε ἐν
ἄλλῳ ἐνόν." " οὐκ ἔστιν."

11. " Ὅρα δή, οὕτως ἔχον εἰ οἷόν τέ ἐστιν
ἑστάναι ἢ κινεῖσθαι." " τί δὴ γὰρ οὔ;" " ὅτι
C κινούμενόν γε⁴ ἢ φέροιτο ἢ ἀλλοιοῖτο ἄν· αὗται
γὰρ μόναι κινήσεις." " ναί." " ἀλλοιούμενον δὲ
τὸ ἓν ἑαυτοῦ ἀδύνατόν που ἓν ἔτι εἶναι." " ἀδύνατον." " οὐκ ἄρα κατ᾽ ἀλλοίωσίν γε κινεῖται."
" οὐ φαίνεται." " ἀλλ᾽ ἆρα τῷ φέρεσθαι;"
" ἴσως." " καὶ μὴν εἰ φέροιτο τὸ ἕν, ἤτοι ἐν τῷ
αὐτῷ ἂν περιφέροιτο κύκλῳ ἢ μεταλλάττοι χώραν
ἑτέραν ἐξ ἑτέρας." " ἀνάγκη." " οὐκοῦν κύκλῳ

¹ ἐνείη Heindorf: ἂν ἐν εἴη B: ἂν εἴη T.
² ἑαυτῷ B: ἑαυτὸ T, Proclus.
³ αὐτὸ Diels: αὐτὸ BT, Proclus.
⁴ γε b, Proclus al.: τε BT, Stobaeus.

be many, whether it partook of straight or of round form." "Certainly." "Then it is neither straight nor round, since it has no parts." "Right."

"Moreover, being of such a nature, it cannot be anywhere, for it could not be either in anything else or in itself." "How is that?" "If it were in something else, it would be encircled by that in which it would be and would be touched in many places by many parts of it; but that which is one and without parts and does not partake of the circular nature cannot be touched by a circle in many places." "No, it cannot." "But, furthermore, being in itself it would also be surrounding with itself naught other than itself, if it were in itself; for nothing can be in anything which does not surround it." "No, it cannot." "Then that which surrounds would be other than that which is surrounded; for a whole cannot be both active and passive in the same action; and thus one would be no longer one, but two." "True." "Then the one is not anywhere, neither in itself nor in something else." "No, it is not."

"This being the case, see whether it can be either at rest or in motion." "Why not?" "Because if in motion it would be either moving in place or changing; for those are the only kinds of motion." "Yes." "But the one, if changing to something other than itself, cannot any longer be one." "It cannot." "Then it is not in motion by the method of change." "Apparently not." "But by moving in place?" "Perhaps." "But if the one moved in place, it would either revolve in the same spot or pass from one place to another." "Yes, it must do so." "And that which revolves

239

μὲν περιφερόμενον ἐπὶ μέσου βεβηκέναι ἀνάγκη,
καὶ τὰ περὶ τὸ μέσον φερόμενα ἄλλα μέρη ἔχειν
D ἑαυτοῦ. ᾧ δὲ μήτε μέσου μήτε μερῶν προσήκει,
τίς μηχανὴ τοῦτο κύκλῳ ποτ᾽ ἐπὶ τοῦ μέσου
ἐνεχθῆναι;" "οὐδεμία." "ἀλλὰ δὴ χώραν ἀμεί-
βον ἄλλοτ᾽ ἄλλοθι γίγνεται καὶ οὕτω κινεῖται;"
"εἴπερ γε δή." "οὐκοῦν εἶναι μέν που ἔν τινι
αὐτὸ[1] ἀδύνατον ἐφάνη;" "ναί." "ἆρ᾽ οὖν γίγνεσθαι ἔτι ἀδυνατώτερον;" "οὐκ ἐννοῶ ὅπη."
"εἰ ἔν τῳ τι γίγνεται, οὐκ ἀνάγκη μήτε πω ἐν
ἐκείνῳ εἶναι ἔτι ἐγγιγνόμενον, μήτ᾽ ἔτι ἔξω ἐκείνου
παντάπασιν, εἴπερ ἤδη ἐγγίγνεται;" "ἀνάγκη."
E "εἰ ἄρα τι ἄλλο πείσεται τοῦτο, ἐκεῖνο ἂν μόνον
πάσχοι οὗ μέρη εἴη· τὸ μὲν γὰρ ἄν τι αὐτοῦ ἤδη
ἐν ἐκείνῳ, τὸ δὲ ἔξω εἴη ἅμα· τὸ δὲ μὴ ἔχον μέρη
οὐχ οἷόν τέ που ἔσται τρόπῳ οὐδενὶ ὅλον ἅμα μήτε
ἐντὸς εἶναι τινὸς μήτε ἔξω." "ἀληθῆ." "οὗ
δὲ μήτε μέρη εἰσὶ μήθ᾽ ὅλον τυγχάνει ὄν, οὐ πολὺ
ἔτι ἀδυνατώτερον ἐγγίγνεσθαί που, μήτε κατὰ
μέρη μήτε κατὰ ὅλον ἐγγιγνόμενον;" "φαίνε-
139 ται." "οὔτ᾽ ἄρα ποι ἰὸν καὶ ἔν τῳ γιγνόμενον
χώραν ἀλλάττει, οὔτ᾽ ἐν τῷ αὐτῷ περιφερόμενον
οὔτε ἀλλοιούμενον." "οὐκ ἔοικεν." "κατὰ
πᾶσαν ἄρα κίνησιν τὸ ἓν ἀκίνητον." "ἀκίνητον."
"ἀλλὰ μὴν καὶ εἶναί γέ φαμεν ἔν τινι αὐτὸ ἀδύνατον." "φαμὲν γάρ." "οὐδ᾽ ἄρα ποτὲ ἐν τῷ
αὐτῷ ἐστιν." "τί δή;" "ὅτι ἤδη ἂν ἐν ἐκείνῳ
εἴη, ἐν ᾧ τῷ αὐτῷ ἐστίν." "πάνυ μὲν οὖν."
"ἀλλ᾽ οὔτε ἐν ἑαυτῷ οὔτε ἐν ἄλλῳ οἷόν τε ἦν
αὐτῷ ἐνεῖναι.[2]" "οὐ γὰρ οὖν." "οὐδέποτε ἄρα
B ἐστὶ τὸ ἓν ἐν τῷ αὐτῷ." "οὐκ ἔοικεν." "ἀλλὰ

---

[1] αὐτῷ BT: αὐτὸ vulg.   [2] ἐνεῖναι b: ἐν εἶναι BT.

must rest upon a centre and have other parts which turn about the centre ; but what possible way is there for that which has no centre and no parts to revolve upon a centre ? " " There is none." " But does it change its place by coming into one place at one time and another at another, and move in that way ? " " Yes, if it moves at all." " Did we not find that it could not be in anything ? " " Yes." " And is it not still more impossible for it to come into anything ? " " I do not understand why." " If anything comes into anything, it must be not yet in it, while it is still coming in, nor still entirely outside of it, if it is already coming in, must it not ? " " It must." " Now if anything goes through this process, it can be only that which has parts ; for a part of it could be already in the other, and the rest outside ; but that which has no parts cannot by any possibility be entirely neither inside nor outside of anything at the same time." " True." " But is it not still more impossible for that which has no parts and is not a whole to come into anything, since it comes in neither in parts nor as a whole ? " " Clearly." " Then it does not change its place by going anywhere or into anything, nor does it revolve in a circle, nor change." " Apparently not." " Then the one is without any kind of motion." " It is motionless." " Furthermore, we say that it cannot be in anything." " We do." " Then it is never in the same." " Why is that ? " " Because it would then be in that with which the same is identical." " Certainly." " But we saw that it cannot be either in itself or in anything else." " No, it cannot." " Then the one is never in the same." " Apparently not." " But that which is

PLATO

μὴν τό γε μηδέποτε ἐν τῷ αὐτῷ ὂν οὔθ᾽ ἡσυχίαν
ἄγει οὔθ᾽ ἕστηκεν." "οὐ γὰρ οἷόν τε." "τὸ
ἓν ἄρα, ὡς ἔοικεν, οὔθ᾽ ἕστηκεν οὔτε κινεῖται."
"οὔκουν δὴ φαίνεταί γε."

"Οὐδὲ μὴν ταὐτόν γε οὔθ᾽ ἑτέρῳ οὔτε ἑαυτῷ
ἔσται, οὐδ᾽ αὖ ἕτερον οὔτε αὐτοῦ οὔτε ἑτέρου
ἂν εἴη." "πῇ δή;" "ἕτερον μέν που ἑαυτοῦ ὂν
ἑνὸς ἕτερον ἂν εἴη καὶ οὐκ ἂν εἴη ἕν." "ἀληθῆ."
"καὶ μὴν ταὐτόν γε ἑτέρῳ ὂν ἐκεῖνο ἂν εἴη, αὐτὸ
C δ᾽ οὐκ ἂν εἴη· ὥστε οὐδ᾽ ἂν οὕτως εἴη ὅπερ ἔστιν,
ἕν, ἀλλ᾽ ἕτερον ἑνός." "οὐ γὰρ οὖν." "ταὐτὸν
μὲν ἄρα ἑτέρῳ ἢ ἕτερον ἑαυτοῦ οὐκ ἔσται." "οὐ
γάρ." "ἕτερον δέ γε ἑτέρου οὐκ ἔσται, ἕως ἂν
ᾖ ἕν. οὐ γὰρ ἑνὶ προσήκει ἑτέρῳ τινὸς εἶναι,
ἀλλὰ μόνῳ ἑτέρῳ ἑτέρου, ἄλλῳ δὲ οὐδενί." "ὀρθῶς." "τῷ μὲν ἄρα ἓν εἶναι οὐκ ἔσται ἕτερον·
ἢ οἴει;" "οὐ δῆτα." "ἀλλὰ μὴν εἰ μὴ τούτῳ,
οὐχ ἑαυτῷ ἔσται· εἰ δὲ μὴ αὑτῷ, οὐδὲ αὐτό· αὐτὸ
D δὲ μηδαμῇ ὂν ἕτερον οὐδενὸς ἔσται ἕτερον."
"ὀρθῶς." "οὐδὲ μὴν ταὐτὸν ἑαυτῷ ἔσται."
"πῶς δ᾽ οὔ; "οὐχ ἥπερ τοῦ ἑνὸς φύσις, αὐτὴ[1]
δήπου καὶ τοῦ ταὐτοῦ." "τί δή;" "ὅτι οὐκ,
ἐπειδὰν ταὐτὸν γένηταί τῳ τι, ἓν γίγνεται." "ἀλλὰ
τί μήν;" "τοῖς πολλοῖς ταὐτὸν γενόμενον πολλὰ
ἀνάγκη γίγνεσθαι, ἀλλ᾽ οὐχ ἕν." "ἀληθῆ." "ἀλλ᾽
εἰ τὸ ἓν καὶ τὸ ταὐτὸν μηδαμῇ διαφέρει, ὁπότε
τι ταὐτὸν ἐγίγνετο, ἀεὶ ἂν ἓν ἐγίγνετο, καὶ
ὁπότε ἕν, ταὐτόν." "πάνυ γε." "εἰ ἄρα τὸ
E ἓν ἑαυτῷ ταὐτὸν ἔσται, οὐχ ἓν ἑαυτῷ ἔσται.

---

[1] αὐτὴ Proclus : αὕτη B : αὐτὴ T.

never in the same is neither motionless nor at rest."
" No, it cannot be so." " The one, then, it appears,
is neither in motion nor at rest." " No, apparently
not."

" Neither, surely, can it be the same with another
or with itself; nor again other than itself or
another." " Why not ? " " If it were other than
itself, it would be other than one and would not be
one." " True." " And, surely, if it were the same
with another, it would be that other, and would
not be itself; therefore in this case also it would
not be that which it is, namely one, but other than
one." " Quite so." " Then it will not be the same
as another, nor other than itself." " No." " But
it will not be other than another, so long as it is
one. For one cannot be other than anything;
only other, and nothing else, can be other than
another." " Right." " Then it will not be other
by reason of being one, will it ? " " Certainly not."
" And if not for this reason, not by reason of itself;
and if not by reason of itself, not itself; but since
itself is not other at all, it will not be other than
anything." " Right." " And yet one will not be
the same with itself." " Why not ? " " The nature
of one is surely not the same as that of the same."
" Why ? " " Because when a thing becomes the
same as anything, it does not thereby become one."
" But why not ? " " That which becomes the same
as many, becomes necessarily many, not one."
" True." " But if the one and the same were
identical, whenever anything became the same it
would always become one, and when it became one,
the same." " Certainly." " Then if the one is the
same with itself, it will not be one with itself; and

καὶ οὕτω ἓν ὂν οὐχ ἓν ἔσται· ἀλλὰ μὴν τοῦτό γε
ἀδύνατον· ἀδύνατον ἄρα καὶ τῷ ἑνὶ ἢ ἑτέρου
ἕτερον εἶναι ἢ ἑαυτῷ ταὐτόν." "ἀδύνατον."
"οὕτω δὴ ἕτερόν γε ἢ ταὐτὸν τὸ ἓν οὔτ' ἂν
αὑτῷ οὔτ' ἂν ἑτέρῳ εἴη." "οὐ γὰρ οὖν."

"Οὐδὲ μὴν ὅμοιόν τινι ἔσται οὐδ' ἀνόμοιον
οὔθ' ἑαυτῷ οὔθ' ἑτέρῳ." "τί δή;" "ὅτι τὸ
ταὐτόν που πεπονθὸς ὅμοιον." "ναί." "τοῦ δέ
γε ἑνὸς χωρὶς ἐφάνη τὴν φύσιν τὸ ταὐτόν." "ἐφάνη
140 γάρ." "ἀλλὰ μὴν εἴ τι πέπονθε χωρὶς τοῦ ἓν
εἶναι τὸ ἕν, πλείω ἂν εἶναι πεπόνθοι ἢ ἕν, τοῦτο
δὲ ἀδύνατον." "ναί." "οὐδαμῶς ἔστιν ἄρα ταὐτὸν πεπονθὸς εἶναι τὸ ἓν οὔτε ἄλλῳ οὔθ' ἑαυτῷ."
"οὐ φαίνεται." "οὐδὲ ὅμοιον ἄρα δυνατὸν αὐτὸ
εἶναι οὔτε ἄλλῳ οὔθ' ἑαυτῷ." "οὐκ ἔοικεν."
"οὐδὲ μὴν ἕτερόν γε πέπονθεν εἶναι τὸ ἕν· καὶ
γὰρ οὕτω πλείω ἂν πεπόνθοι εἶναι ἢ ἕν." "πλείω
γάρ." "τό γε μὴν ἕτερον πεπονθὸς ἢ ἑαυτοῦ ἢ
B ἄλλου ἀνόμοιον ἂν εἴη ἢ ἑαυτῷ ἢ ἄλλῳ, εἴπερ τὸ
ταὐτὸν πεπονθὸς ὅμοιον." "ὀρθῶς." "τὸ δέ γε
ἕν, ὡς ἔοικεν, οὐδαμῶς ἕτερον πεπονθὸς οὐδαμῶς
ἀνόμοιόν ἐστιν οὔθ' ἑαυτῷ οὔθ' ἑτέρῳ." "οὐ
γὰρ οὖν." "οὔτε ἄρα ὅμοιον οὔτε ἀνόμοιον οὔθ'
ἑτέρῳ οὔτε ἑαυτῷ ἂν εἴη τὸ ἕν." "οὐ φαίνεται."

"Καὶ μὴν τοιοῦτόν γε ὂν οὔτε ἴσον οὔτε ἄνισον
ἔσται οὔτε ἑαυτῷ οὔτε ἄλλῳ." "πῇ;" "ἴσον
μὲν ὂν τῶν αὐτῶν μέτρων ἔσται ἐκείνῳ ᾧ ἂν
ἴσον ᾖ." "ναί." "μεῖζον δέ που ἢ ἔλαττον ὄν,
C οἷς μὲν ἂν ξύμμετρον ᾖ, τῶν μὲν ἐλαττόνων πλείω

thus, being one, it will not be one; this, however, is impossible; it is therefore impossible for one to be either the other of other or the same with itself." "Impossible." "Thus the one cannot be either other or the same to itself or another." "No, it cannot." "And again it will not be like or unlike anything, either itself or another." "Why not?" "Because the like is that which is affected in the same way." "Yes." "But we saw that the same was of a nature distinct from that of the one." "Yes, so we did." "But if the one were affected in any way apart from being one, it would be so affected as to be more than one, and that is impossible." "Yes." "Then the one cannot possibly be affected in the same way as another or as itself." "Evidently not." "Then it cannot be like another or itself." "No, so it appears." "Nor can the one be so affected as to be other; for in that case it would be so affected as to be more than one." "Yes, it would be more." "But that which is affected in a way other than itself or other, would be unlike itself or other, if that which is affected in the same way is like." "Right." "But the one, as it appears, being never affected in a way other than itself or other, is never unlike either itself or other." "Evidently not." "Then the one will be neither like nor unlike either other or itself." "So it seems."

"Since, then, it is of such a nature, it can be neither equal nor unequal to itself or other." "Why not?" "If it is equal, it is of the same measures as that to which it is equal." "Yes." "And if it is greater or less than things with which it is commensurate, it will have more measures than the

μέτρα ἕξει, τῶν δὲ μειζόνων ἐλάττω." "ναί."
"οἷς δ' ἂν μὴ σύμμετρον, τῶν μὲν σμικροτέρων,
τῶν δὲ μειζόνων μέτρων ἔσται." "πῶς γὰρ οὔ;"
"οὐκοῦν ἀδύνατον τὸ μὴ μετέχον τοῦ αὐτοῦ ἢ
μέτρων τῶν αὐτῶν εἶναι ἢ ἄλλων ὡντινωνοῦν
τῶν αὐτῶν;" "ἀδύνατον." "ἴσον μὲν ἄρα
οὔτ' ἂν ἑαυτῷ οὔτε ἄλλῳ εἴη μὴ τῶν αὐτῶν μέτρων
ὄν." "οὔκουν φαίνεταί γε." "ἀλλὰ μὴν πλειόνων γε μέτρων ὂν ἢ ἐλαττόνων, ὁσωνπερ μέτρων,
D τοσούτων καὶ μερῶν ἂν εἴη· καὶ οὕτως αὖ οὐκέτι
ἓν ἔσται, ἀλλὰ τοσαῦτα ὁσαπερ καὶ τὰ μέτρα."
"ὀρθῶς." "εἰ δέ γε ἑνὸς μέτρου εἴη, ἴσον ἂν
γίγνοιτο τῷ μέτρῳ· τοῦτο δὲ ἀδύνατον ἐφάνη,
ἴσον τῳ[1] αὐτὸ εἶναι." "ἐφάνη γάρ." "οὔτε
ἄρα ἑνὸς μέτρου μετέχον οὔτε πολλῶν οὔτε ὀλίγων,
οὔτε τὸ παράπαν τοῦ αὐτοῦ μετέχον, οὔτε ἑαυτῷ
ποτε, ὡς ἔοικεν, ἔσται ἴσον οὔτε ἄλλῳ· οὐδ' αὖ
μεῖζον οὐδὲ ἔλαττον οὔτε ἑαυτοῦ οὔτε ἑτέρου."
"παντάπασι μὲν οὖν οὕτω."

E 12. "Τί δέ; πρεσβύτερον ἢ νεώτερον ἢ τὴν
αὐτὴν ἡλικίαν ἔχειν τὸ ἓν δοκεῖ τῳ[2] δυνατὸν
εἶναι;" "τί δὴ γὰρ οὔ;" "ὅτι που ἡλικίαν
μὲν τὴν αὐτὴν ἔχον ἢ αὐτῷ ἢ ἄλλῳ ἰσότητος
χρόνου καὶ ὁμοιότητος μεθέξει, ὧν ἐλέγομεν οὐ
μετεῖναι τῷ ἑνί, οὔθ' ὁμοιότητος οὔτε ἰσότητος."
"ἐλέγομεν γὰρ οὖν." "καὶ μὴν καὶ ὅτι ἀν-
ομοιότητός τε καὶ ἀνισότητος οὐ μετέχει, καὶ
τοῦτο ἐλέγομεν." "πάνυ μὲν οὖν." "πῶς οὖν οἷόν
141 τε ἔσται τινὸς ἢ πρεσβύτερον ἢ νεώτερον εἶναι ἢ
τὴν αὐτὴν ἡλικίαν ἔχειν τῳ[2] τοιοῦτον ὄν;" "οὐδαμῶς." "οὐκ ἄρ' ἂν εἴη νεώτερόν γε οὐδὲ

---

[1] τῳ] αὐτῷ B : τῷ T.　　　　　　　　[2] τῳ] τῷ BT.

things which are less and less measures than the
things which are greater." "Yes." "And in the
case of things with which it is not commensurate,
it will have smaller measures than some and greater
measures than others." "Of course." "Is it not
impossible for that which does not participate in
sameness to have either the same measures or
anything else the same?" "Impossible." "Then
not having the same measures, it cannot be equal
either to itself or to anything else." "No, apparently
not." "But whether it have more measures or
less, it will have as many parts as measures; and
thus one will be no longer one, but will be as many
as are its measures." "Right." "But if it were
of one measure, it would be equal to the measure;
but we have seen that it cannot be equal to anything."
"Yes, so we have." "Then it will partake neither
of one measure, nor of many, nor of few; nor will
it partake at all of the same, nor will it ever, apparently, be equal to itself or to anything else;
nor will it be greater or less than itself or another."
"Perfectly true."

"Well, does anyone believe that the one can
be older or younger or of the same age? " "Why
not?" "Because if it has the same age as itself
or as anything else, it will partake of equality and
likeness of time, and we said the one had no part
in likeness or equality." "Yes, we said that."
"And we said also that it does not partake of unlikeness or inequality." "Certainly." "How, then,
being of such a nature, can it be either younger
or older or of the same age as anything?" "In
no way." "Then the one cannot be younger or

PLATO

πρεσβύτερον οὐδὲ τὴν αὐτὴν ἡλικίαν ἔχον τὸ ἓν
οὔτε αὑτῷ οὔτε ἄλλῳ.'' ''οὐ φαίνεται.'' '' ἆρ'
οὖν οὐδὲ ἐν χρόνῳ τὸ παράπαν δύναιτ' ἂν εἶναι
τὸ ἕν, εἰ τοιοῦτον εἴη; ἢ οὐκ ἀνάγκη, ἐάν τι ᾖ
ἐν χρόνῳ, ἀεὶ αὐτὸ αὑτοῦ πρεσβύτερον γίγνεσθαι;'' ''ἀνάγκη.'' ''οὐκοῦν τό γε πρεσβύτερον
ἀεὶ νεωτέρου πρεσβύτερον;'' ''τί μήν;'' ''τὸ
B πρεσβύτερον ἄρα ἑαυτοῦ γιγνόμενον καὶ νεώτερον
ἑαυτοῦ ἅμα γίγνεται, εἴπερ μέλλει ἔχειν ὅτου
πρεσβύτερον γίγνεται.'' ''πῶς λέγεις;'' ''ὧδε·
διάφορον ἕτερον ἑτέρου οὐδὲν δεῖ γίγνεσθαι ἤδη
ὄντος διαφόρου, ἀλλὰ τοῦ μὲν ἤδη ὄντος ἤδη εἶναι,
τοῦ δὲ γεγονότος γεγονέναι, τοῦ δὲ μέλλοντος
μέλλειν, τοῦ δὲ γιγνομένου οὔτε γεγονέναι οὔτε
μέλλειν οὔτε εἶναί πω διάφορον, ἀλλὰ γίγνεσθαι
καὶ ἄλλως οὐκ εἶναι.'' ''ἀνάγκη γάρ.'' ''ἀλλὰ
C μὴν τό γε πρεσβύτερον διαφορότης νεωτέρου ἐστὶ
καὶ οὐδενὸς ἄλλου.'' ''ἔστι γάρ.'' ''τὸ ἄρα
πρεσβύτερον ἑαυτοῦ γιγνόμενον ἀνάγκη καὶ νεώτερον ἅμα ἑαυτοῦ γίγνεσθαι.'' ''ἔοικεν.'' ''ἀλλὰ
μὴν καὶ μήτε πλείω ἑαυτοῦ γίγνεσθαι χρόνον
μήτ' ἐλάττω, ἀλλὰ τὸν ἴσον χρόνον καὶ γίγνεσθαι
ἑαυτῷ καὶ εἶναι καὶ γεγονέναι καὶ μέλλειν ἔσεσθαι.'' ''ἀνάγκη γὰρ οὖν καὶ ταῦτα.'' ''ἀνάγκη
ἄρα ἐστίν, ὡς ἔοικεν, ὅσα γε ἐν χρόνῳ ἐστὶ καὶ
D μετέχει τοῦ τοιούτου, ἕκαστον αὐτῶν τὴν αὐτήν
τε αὐτὸ αὑτῷ ἡλικίαν ἔχειν καὶ πρεσβύτερόν τε
αὑτοῦ ἅμα καὶ νεώτερον γίγνεσθαι.'' ''κινδυνεύει.'' ''ἀλλὰ μὴν τῷ γε ἑνὶ τῶν τοιούτων
παθημάτων οὐδὲν μετῆν.'' ''οὐ γὰρ μετῆν.''

248

older or of the same age as anything." "No, evidently not." "And can the one exist in time at all, if it is of such a nature? Must it not, if it exists in time, always be growing older than itself?" "It must." "And the older is always older than something younger?" "Certainly." "Then that which grows older than itself grows at the same time younger than itself, if it is to have something than which it grows older." "What do you mean?" "This is what I mean: A thing which is different from another does not have to become different from that which is already different, but it must be different from that which is already different, it must have become different from that which has become so, it will have to be different from that which will be so, but from that which is becoming different it cannot have become, nor can it be going to be, nor can it already be different; it must become different, and that is all." "There is no denying that." "But surely the notion 'older' is a difference with respect to the younger and to nothing else." "Yes, so it is." "But that which is becoming older than itself must at the same time be becoming younger than itself." "So it appears." "But surely it cannot become either for a longer or for a shorter time than itself; it must become and be and be about to be for an equal time with itself." "That also is inevitable." "Apparently, then, it is inevitable that everything which exists in time and partakes of time is of the same age as itself and is also at the same time becoming older and younger than itself." "I see no escape from that." "But the one had nothing to do with such affections." "No, it had not." "It has nothing

" οὐδὲ ἄρα χρόνου αὐτῷ μέτεστιν, οὐδ' ἔστιν ἔν τινι χρόνῳ." " οὔκουν δή, ὥς γε ὁ λόγος αἱρεῖ."

" Τί οὖν; τὸ ἦν καὶ τὸ γέγονε καὶ τὸ ἐγίγνετο οὐ χρόνου μέθεξιν δοκεῖ σημαίνειν τοῦ ποτὲ γεγο-
E νότος;" " καὶ μάλα." " τί δέ; τὸ ἔσται καὶ τὸ γενήσεται καὶ τὸ γενηθήσεται οὐ τοῦ ἔπειτά που[1] μέλλοντος;" " ναί." " τὸ δὲ δὴ ἔστι καὶ τὸ γίγνεται οὐ τοῦ νῦν παρόντος;" " πάνυ μὲν οὖν." " εἰ ἄρα τὸ ἓν μηδαμῇ μηδενὸς μετέχει χρόνου, οὔτε ποτὲ γέγονεν οὔτ' ἐγίγνετο οὔτ' ἦν ποτέ, οὔτε νῦν γέγονεν οὔτε γίγνεται οὔτ' ἔστιν, οὔτ' ἔπειτα γενήσεται οὔτε γενηθήσεται οὔτ' ἔσται." " ἀληθέστατα." " ἔστιν οὖν οὐσίας ὅπως ἄν τι μετάσχοι ἄλλως ἢ κατὰ τούτων τι;" " οὐκ ἔστιν." " οὐδαμῶς ἄρα τὸ ἓν οὐσίας μετέχει." " οὐκ ἔοικεν." " οὐδαμῶς ἄρα ἔστι τὸ ἕν." " οὐ φαίνεται." " οὐδ' ἄρα οὕτως ἔστιν ὥστε ἓν εἶναι· εἴη γὰρ ἂν ἤδη ὂν καὶ οὐσίας μετέχον· ἀλλ' ὡς ἔοικε, τὸ ἓν οὔτε ἕν ἐστιν οὔτε ἔστιν, εἰ δεῖ τῷ
142 τοιῷδε λόγῳ πιστεύειν." " κινδυνεύει." " ὃ δὲ μὴ ἔστι, τούτῳ τῷ μὴ ὄντι εἴη ἄν τι αὐτῷ ἢ αὐτοῦ;" " καὶ πῶς;" " οὐδ' ἄρα ὄνομά ἐστιν αὐτῷ οὐδὲ λόγος οὐδέ τις ἐπιστήμη οὐδὲ αἴσθησις οὐδὲ δόξα." " οὐ φαίνεται." " οὐδ' ὀνομάζεται ἄρα οὐδὲ λέγεται οὐδὲ δοξάζεται οὐδὲ γιγνώσκεται, οὐδέ τι τῶν ὄντων αὐτοῦ αἰσθάνεται." " οὐκ ἔοικεν." " ἦ δυνατὸν οὖν περὶ τὸ ἓν ταῦθ' οὕτως ἔχειν;" " οὔκουν ἔμοιγε δοκεῖ."

13. " Βούλει οὖν ἐπὶ τὴν ὑπόθεσιν πάλιν ἐξ
B ἀρχῆς ἐπανέλθωμεν, ἐάν τι ἡμῖν ἐπανιοῦσιν ἀλ-λοῖον φανῇ;" " πάνυ μὲν οὖν βούλομαι." " οὐκ-

―――――――
[1] ἔπειτά που G. Hermann : ἔπειτα τοῦ BT.

PARMENIDES

to do with time, and does not exist in time." " No, that is the result of the argument."

" Well, and do not the words ' was,' ' has become,' and ' was becoming ' appear to denote participation in past time ? " " Certainly." " And ' will be,' ' will become,' and ' will be made to become,' in future time ? " " Yes." " And ' is ' and ' is becoming ' in the present ? " " Certainly." " Then if the one has no participation in time whatsoever, it neither has become nor became nor was in the past, it has neither become nor is it becoming nor is it in the present, and it will neither become nor be made to become nor will it be in the future." " Very true." " Can it then partake of being in any other way than in the past, present, or future ? " " It cannot." " Then the one has no share in being at all." " Apparently not." " Then the one is not at all." " Evidently not." " Then it has no being even so as to be one, for if it were one, it would be and would partake of being ; but apparently one neither is nor is one, if this argument is to be trusted." " That seems to be true." " But can that which does not exist have anything pertaining or belonging to it ? " " Of course not." " Then the one has no name, nor is there any description or knowledge or perception or opinion of it." " Evidently not." " And it is neither named nor described nor thought of nor known, nor does any existing thing perceive it." " Apparently not." " Is it possible that all this is true about the one ? " " I do not think so."

" Shall we then return to our hypothesis and see if a review of our argument discloses any new point of view ? " " By all means." " We say, then,

251

PLATO

οὖν ἓν εἰ ἔστιν, φαμέν, τὰ συμβαίνοντα περὶ
αὐτοῦ, ποῖά ποτε τυγχάνει ὄντα, διομολογητέα
ταῦτα· οὐχ οὕτω;" "ναί." "ὅρα δὴ ἐξ ἀρχῆς.
ἓν εἰ ἔστιν, ἆρα οἷόν τε αὐτὸ εἶναι μέν, οὐσίας δὲ
μὴ μετέχειν;" "οὐχ οἷόν τε." "οὐκοῦν καὶ ἡ
οὐσία τοῦ ἑνὸς εἴη ἂν οὐ ταὐτὸν οὖσα τῷ ἑνί·
οὐ γὰρ ἂν ἐκείνη ἦν ἐκείνου οὐσία, οὐδ' ἂν ἐκεῖνο
C τὸ ἓν ἐκείνης μετεῖχεν, ἀλλ' ὅμοιον ἂν ἦν λέγειν
ἕν τε εἶναι καὶ ἓν ἕν. νῦν δὲ οὐχ αὕτη ἐστὶν ἡ
ὑπόθεσις, εἰ ἓν ἕν, τί¹ χρὴ ξυμβαίνειν, ἀλλ' εἰ ἓν
ἔστιν· οὐχ οὕτω;" "πάνυ μὲν οὖν." "οὐκοῦν
ὡς ἄλλο τι σημαῖνον τὸ ἔστι τοῦ ἕν;" "ἀνάγκη."
"ἆρα οὖν ἄλλο ἢ ὅτι οὐσίας μετέχει τὸ ἕν, τοῦτ'
ἂν εἴη τὸ λεγόμενον, ἐπειδάν τις συλλήβδην εἴπῃ
ὅτι ἓν ἔστιν;" "πάνυ γε." "πάλιν δὴ λέγωμεν,
ἓν εἰ ἔστι, τί συμβήσεται. σκόπει οὖν, εἰ οὐκ
ἀνάγκη ταύτην τὴν ὑπόθεσιν τοιοῦτον ὂν τὸ ἓν
σημαίνειν, οἷον μέρη ἔχειν;" "πῶς;" "ὧδε·
D εἰ τὸ ἔστι τοῦ ἑνὸς ὄντος λέγεται καὶ τὸ ἓν τοῦ
ὄντος ἑνός, ἔστι δὲ οὐ τὸ αὐτὸ ἥ τε οὐσία καὶ τὸ
ἕν, τοῦ αὐτοῦ δὲ ἐκείνου οὗ ὑπεθέμεθα, τοῦ ἑνὸς
ὄντος, ἆρα οὐκ ἀνάγκη τὸ μὲν ὅλον ἓν ὂν εἶναι
αὐτό, τούτου δὲ γίγνεσθαι μόρια τό τε ἓν καὶ τὸ
εἶναι;" "ἀνάγκη." "πότερον οὖν ἑκάτερον τῶν
μορίων τούτων μόριον μόνον προσεροῦμεν, ἢ
τοῦ ὅλου μόριον τό γε μόριον προσρητέον;"
"τοῦ ὅλου." "καὶ ὅλον ἄρα ἐστίν, ὃ ἂν ἓν ᾖ,
καὶ μόριον ἔχει." "πάνυ γε." "τί οὖν; τῶν
μορίων ἑκάτερον τούτων τοῦ ἑνὸς ὄντος, τό τε
E ἓν καὶ τὸ ὄν, ἆρα ἀπολείπεσθον ἢ τὸ ἓν τοῦ εἶναι
μορίου ἢ τὸ ὂν τοῦ ἑνὸς μορίου;" "οὐκ ἂν εἴη."

¹ ἓν ἕν, τί] ἓν ἐντι B: ἓν τι T.

252

that if the one exists, we must come to an agreement about the consequences, whatever they may be, do we not?" "Yes." "Now consider the first point. If one is, can it be and not partake of being?" "No, it cannot." "Then the being of one will exist, but will not be identical with one; for if it were identical with one, it would not be the being of one, nor would one partake of it, but the statement that one is would be equivalent to the statement that one is one; but our hypothesis is not if one is one, what will follow, but if one is. Do you agree?" "Certainly." "In the belief that 'one' and 'being' differ in meaning?" "Most assuredly." "Then if we say concisely 'one is,' it is equivalent to saying that one partakes of being?" "Certainly." "Let us again say what will follow if one is; and consider whether this hypothesis must not necessarily show that one is of such a nature as to have parts." "How does that come about?" "In this way: If being is predicated of the one which exists and unity is predicated of being which is one, and being and the one are not the same, but belong to the existent one of our hypothesis, must not the existent one be a whole of which the one and being are parts?" "Inevitably." "And shall we call each of these parts merely a part, or must it, in so far as it is a part, be called a part of the whole?" "A part of the whole." "Whatever one, then, exists is a whole and has a part." "Certainly." "Well then, can either of these two parts of existent one —unity and being—abandon the other? Can unity cease to be a part of being or being to be a part of unity?" "No." "And again each of the parts

"πάλιν ἄρα καὶ τῶν μορίων ἑκάτερον τό τε ἓν
ἴσχει καὶ τὸ ὄν, καὶ γίγνεται τὸ ἐλάχιστον ἐκ
δυοῖν αὖ μορίοιν τὸ μόριον, καὶ κατὰ τὸν αὐτὸν
λόγον οὕτως ἀεί, ὅτιπερ ἂν μόριον γένηται, τούτω
τὼ μορίω[1] ἀεὶ ἴσχει· τό τε γὰρ ἓν τὸ ὂν ἀεὶ ἴσχει
143 καὶ τὸ ὂν τὸ ἕν· ὥστε ἀνάγκη δύ' ἀεὶ γιγνόμενον
μηδέποτε ἓν εἶναι." "παντάπασι μὲν οὖν."
"οὐκοῦν ἄπειρον ἂν τὸ πλῆθος οὕτω τὸ ἓν ὂν
εἴη;" "ἔοικεν."

"Ἴθι δὴ καὶ τῇδε ἔτι." "πῇ;" "οὐσίας
φαμὲν μετέχειν τὸ ἕν, διὸ ἔστιν;" "ναί." "καὶ
διὰ ταῦτα δὴ τὸ ἓν ὂν πολλὰ ἐφάνη." "οὕτως."
"τί δέ; αὐτὸ τὸ ἕν, ὃ δή φαμεν οὐσίας μετέχειν,
ἐὰν αὐτὸ τῇ διανοίᾳ μόνον καθ' αὑτὸ λάβωμεν
ἄνευ τούτου οὗ φαμεν μετέχειν, ἆρά γε ἓν μόνον
φανήσεται ἢ καὶ πολλὰ τὸ αὐτὸ τοῦτο;" "ἕν,
B οἶμαι ἔγωγε." "ἴδωμεν[2] δή· ἄλλο τι ἕτερον μὲν
ἀνάγκη τὴν οὐσίαν αὐτοῦ εἶναι, ἕτερον δὲ αὐτό,
εἴπερ μὴ οὐσία τὸ ἕν, ἀλλ' ὡς ἓν οὐσίας μετέσχεν;"
"ἀνάγκη." "οὐκοῦν εἰ ἕτερον μὲν ἡ οὐσία,
ἕτερον δὲ τὸ ἕν, οὔτε τῷ ἓν τὸ ἓν τῆς οὐσίας ἕτερον
οὔτε τῷ οὐσία εἶναι ἡ οὐσία τοῦ ἑνὸς ἄλλο, ἀλλὰ
τῷ ἑτέρῳ τε καὶ ἄλλῳ ἕτερα ἀλλήλων." "πάνυ
μὲν οὖν." "ὥστε οὐ ταὐτόν ἐστιν οὔτε τῷ ἑνὶ
οὔτε τῇ οὐσίᾳ τὸ ἕτερον." "πῶς γάρ;"

"Τί οὖν; ἐὰν προελώμεθα αὐτῶν εἴτε βούλει
C τὴν οὐσίαν καὶ τὸ ἕτερον εἴτε τὴν οὐσίαν καὶ
τὸ ἓν εἴτε τὸ ἓν καὶ τὸ ἕτερον, ἆρ' οὐκ ἐν ἑκάστῃ
τῇ προαιρέσει προαιρούμεθά τινε ὣ ὀρθῶς ἔχει
καλεῖσθαι ἀμφοτέρω;" "πῶς;" "ὧδε· ἔστιν
οὐσίαν εἰπεῖν;" "ἔστιν." "καὶ αὖθις εἰπεῖν

---

[1] τούτῳ τῷ μορίῳ B pr. T.   [2] ἴδωμεν] εἰδῶμεν ΒΤ.

possesses unity and being, and the smallest of parts is composed of these two parts, and thus by the same argument any part whatsoever has always these two parts ; for always unity has being and being has unity ; and, therefore, since it is always becoming two, it can never be one." " Certainly." " Then it results that the existent one would be infinite in number ? " " Apparently."

" Let us make another fresh start." " In what direction ? " " We say that the one partakes of being, because it is ? " " Yes." " And for that reason the one, because it is, was found to be many." " Yes." " Well then, will the one, which we say partakes of being, if we form a mental conception of it alone by itself, without that of which we say it partakes, be found to be only one, or many ? " " One, I should say." " Just let us see ; must not the being of one be one thing and one itself another, if the one is not being, but, considered as one, partakes of being ? " " Yes, that must be so." " Then if being is one thing and one is another, one is not other than being because it is one, nor is being other than one because it is being, but they differ from each other by virtue of being other and different." " Certainly." " Therefore the other is neither the same as one nor as being." " Certainly not." " Well, then, if we make a selection among them, whether we select being and the other, or being and one, or one and the other, in each instance we select two things which may properly be called both ? " " What do you mean ? " " I will explain. We can speak of being ? " " Yes." " And we can

ἕν;" "καὶ τοῦτο." "ἆρ' οὖν οὐχ ἑκάτερον
αὐτοῖν εἴρηται;" "ναί." "τί δ' ὅταν εἴπω
οὐσία τε καὶ ἕν, ἆρα οὐκ ἀμφοτέρω;" "πάνυ
γε." "οὐκοῦν καὶ ἐὰν οὐσία τε καὶ ἕτερον ἢ
ἕτερόν τε καὶ ἕν, καὶ οὕτω πανταχῶς ἐφ' ἑκάστου
D ἄμφω λέγω;" "ναί." "ᾧ δ' ἂν ἄμφω ὀρθῶς
προσαγορεύησθον, ἆρα οἷόν τε ἄμφω μὲν αὐτὼ
εἶναι, δύο δὲ μή;" "οὐχ οἷόν τε." "ᾧ¹ δ' ἂν
δύο ἦτον, ἔστι τις μηχανὴ μὴ οὐχ ἑκάτερον αὐτοῖν
ἓν εἶναι;" "οὐδεμία." "τούτων ἄρα ἐπείπερ
σύνδυο² ἕκαστα ξυμβαίνει εἶναι, καὶ ἓν ἂν εἴη
ἕκαστον." "φαίνεται." "εἰ δὲ ἓν ἕκαστον αὐτῶν ἐστί, συντεθέντος ἑνὸς ὁποιουοῦν ἡτινιοῦν
συζυγίᾳ οὐ τρία γίγνεται τὰ πάντα;" "ναί."
"τρία δὲ οὐ περιττὰ καὶ τὰ δύο ἄρτια;" "πῶς
E δ' οὔ;" "τί δέ; δυοῖν ὄντοιν οὐκ ἀνάγκη εἶναι
καὶ δίς, καὶ τριῶν ὄντων τρίς, εἴπερ ὑπάρχει
τῷ τε δύο τὸ δὶς ἓν καὶ τῷ τρία τὸ τρὶς ἕν;"
"ἀνάγκη." "δυοῖν δὲ ὄντοιν καὶ δὶς οὐκ ἀνάγκη
δύο δὶς εἶναι; καὶ τριῶν καὶ τρὶς οὐκ ἀνάγκη
αὖ τρία τρὶς εἶναι;" "πῶς δ' οὔ;" "τί δέ;
τριῶν ὄντων καὶ δὶς ὄντων καὶ δυοῖν ὄντοιν καὶ
τρὶς ὄντοιν οὐκ ἀνάγκη τε τρία δὶς εἶναι καὶ δύο
τρίς³;" "πολλή γε." "ἄρτιά τε ἄρα ἀρτιάκις
144 ἂν εἴη καὶ περιττὰ περιττάκις καὶ ἄρτια περιττάκις καὶ περιττὰ ἀρτιάκις." "ἔστιν οὕτω."
"εἰ οὖν ταῦτα οὕτως ἔχει, οἴει τινὰ ἀριθμὸν
ὑπολείπεσθαι, ὃν οὐκ ἀνάγκη εἶναι;" "οὐδαμῶς
γε." "εἰ ἄρα ἔστιν ἕν, ἀνάγκη καὶ ἀριθμὸν εἶναι."
"ἀνάγκη." "ἀλλὰ μὴν ἀριθμοῦ γε ὄντος πόλλ'
ἂν εἴη καὶ πλῆθος ἄπειρον τῶν ὄντων· ἢ οὐκ
ἄπειρος ἀριθμὸς πλήθει καὶ μετέχων οὐσίας γί-
256

also speak of one ? " " Yes, that too." " Then
have we not spoken of each of them ? " " Yes."
" And when I speak of being and one, do I not
speak of both ? " " Certainly." " And also when
I speak of being and other, or other and one, in
every case I speak of each pair as both ? " " Yes."
" If things are correctly called both, can they be
both without being two ? " " They cannot." " And
if things are two, must not each of them be one ? "
" Certainly." " Then since the units of these pairs
are together two, each must be individually one."
" That is clear." " But if each of them is one, by
the addition of any sort of one to any pair whatsoever
the total becomes three ? " " Yes." " And three
is an odd number, and two is even ? " " Of course."
" Well, when there are two units, must there not
also be twice, and when there are three, thrice,
that is, if two is twice one and three is thrice one ? "
" There must." " But if there are two and twice,
must there not also be twice two ? And again, if
there are three and thrice, must there not be thrice
three ? " " Of course." " Well then, if there are
three and twice and two and thrice, must there not
also be twice three and thrice two ? " " Inevitably."
" Then there would be even times even, odd times
odd, odd times even, and even times odd." " Yes."
" Then if that is true, do you believe any number
is left out, which does not necessarily exist ? " " By
no means." " Then if one exists, number must
also exist." " It must." " But if number exists,
there must be many, indeed an infinite multitude,
of existences ; or is not number infinite in multitude

---

¹ ὧ] ὧ̣ B : ὧ T.   ² σύνδυο Stephanus : οὖν δύο B : σὺν δύο T.
³ δύο τρίς in marg. b, Proclus suppl.: τρία δὶς B : δὶς τρία T.

γνεται;" "καὶ πάνυ γε." "οὐκοῦν εἰ πᾶς ἀριθμὸς οὐσίας μετέχει, καὶ τὸ μόριον ἕκαστον τοῦ
ἀριθμοῦ μετέχοι ἂν αὐτῆς;" "ναί."

B 14. "Ἐπὶ πάντα ἄρα πολλὰ ὄντα ἡ οὐσία νενέμηται καὶ οὐδενὸς ἀποστατεῖ τῶν ὄντων, οὔτε
τοῦ σμικροτάτου οὔτε τοῦ μεγίστου; ἢ τοῦτο
μὲν καὶ ἄλογον ἐρέσθαι; πῶς γὰρ ἂν δὴ οὐσία
γε τῶν ὄντων του ἀποστατοῖ[1];" "οὐδαμῶς."
"κατακεκερμάτισται ἄρα ὡς οἷόν τε σμικρότατα
καὶ μέγιστα καὶ πανταχῶς ὄντα, καὶ μεμέρισται
C πάντων μάλιστα, καὶ ἔστι μέρη ἀπέραντα τῆς οὐσίας."
"ἔχει οὕτω." "πλεῖστα ἄρα ἐστὶ τὰ μέρη
αὐτῆς." "πλεῖστα μέντοι." "τί οὖν; ἔστι τι
αὐτῶν ὃ ἔστι μὲν μέρος τῆς οὐσίας, οὐδὲν μέντοι
μέρος;" "καὶ πῶς ἂν τοῦτο[2] γένοιτο;" "ἀλλ'
εἴπερ γε, οἶμαι, ἔστιν, ἀνάγκη αὐτὸ ἀεί, ἕωσ-
περ ἂν ᾖ, ἕν γέ τι εἶναι, μηδὲν δὲ ἀδύνατον."
"ἀνάγκη." "πρὸς ἅπαντι ἄρα ἑκάστῳ τῷ τῆς
οὐσίας μέρει πρόσεστι τὸ ἕν, οὐκ ἀπολειπόμενον
οὔτε σμικροτέρου οὔτε μείζονος μέρους οὔτε ἄλλου
D οὐδενός." "οὕτω." "ἆρα οὖν ἓν ὂν πολλαχοῦ
ἅμα ὅλον ἐστί; τοῦτο ἄθρει." "ἀλλ' ἀθρῶ καὶ
ὁρῶ ὅτι ἀδύνατον." "μεμερισμένον ἄρα, εἴπερ μὴ
ὅλον· ἄλλως γάρ που οὐδαμῶς ἅμα ἅπασι τοῖς
τῆς οὐσίας μέρεσιν παρέσται ἢ μεμερισμένον."
"ναί." "καὶ μὴν τό γε μεριστὸν πολλὴ ἀνάγκη
εἶναι τοσαῦτα ὅσαπερ μέρη." "ἀνάγκη." "οὐκ
ἄρα ἀληθῆ ἄρτι ἐλέγομεν λέγοντες ὡς πλεῖστα
μέρη ἡ οὐσία νενεμημένη εἴη. οὐδὲ γὰρ πλείω
E τοῦ ἑνὸς νενέμηται, ἀλλ' ἴσα, ὡς ἔοικε, τῷ ἑνί.

---

[1] ἀποστατοῖ corr. T: ἀποστατοίη Stobaeus: ἀποστατεῖ B
pr. T.   [2] τοῦτο] τοι τοῦτο BT.

and participant of existence ? " " Certainly it is."
" Then if all number partakes of existence, every
part of number will partake of it ? " " Yes."

" Existence, then, is distributed over all things,
which are many, and is not wanting in any existing
thing from the greatest to the smallest ? Indeed,
is it not absurd even to ask that question ? For
how can existence be wanting in any existing thing ? "
" It cannot by any means." " Then it is split up
into the smallest and greatest and all kinds of
existences ; nothing else is so much divided, and
in short the parts of existence are infinite." " That
is true." " Its parts are the most numerous of all."
" Yes, they are the most numerous." " Well, is
there any one of them which is a part of existence,
but is no part ? " " How could that be ? " " But
if there is, it must, I imagine, so long as it is, be
some one thing ; it cannot be nothing." " That
is inevitable." " Then unity is an attribute of
every part of existence and is not wanting to a
smaller or larger or any other part." " True."
" Can the one be in many places at once and still
be a whole ? Consider that question." " I am
considering and I see that it is impossible." " Then
it is divided into parts, if it is not a whole ; for it
cannot be attached to all the parts of existence at
once unless it is divided." " I agree." " And
that which is divided into parts must certainly be
as numerous as its parts." " It must." " Then
what we said just now—that existence was divided
into the greatest number of parts—was not true ;
for it is not divided, you see, into any more parts
than one, but, as it seems, into the same number

259

οὔτε γὰρ τὸ ὂν τοῦ ἑνὸς ἀπολείπεται οὔτε τὸ ἓν
τοῦ ὄντος, ἀλλ' ἐξισοῦσθον δύο ὄντε ἀεὶ παρὰ
πάντα." "παντάπασιν οὕτω φαίνεται." "τὸ ἓν
ἄρα αὐτὸ κεκερματισμένον ὑπὸ τῆς οὐσίας πολλά
τε καὶ ἄπειρα τὸ πλῆθός ἐστιν." "φαίνεται."
"οὐ μόνον ἄρα τὸ ὂν ἓν πολλά ἐστιν, ἀλλὰ καὶ
αὐτὸ τὸ ἓν ὑπὸ τοῦ ὄντος διανενεμημένον πολλὰ
ἀνάγκη εἶναι." "παντάπασι μὲν οὖν."

15. "Καὶ μὴν ὅτι γε ὅλου τὰ μόρια μόρια,
πεπερασμένον ἂν εἴη κατὰ τὸ ὅλον τὸ ἕν· ἢ οὐ
περιέχεται ὑπὸ τοῦ ὅλου τὰ μόρια;" "ἀνάγκη."
"ἀλλὰ μὴν τό γε περιέχον πέρας ἂν εἴη." "πῶς
δ' οὔ;" "τὸ ἓν ἄρα ὂν ἕν τέ ἐστί που καὶ πολλά,
καὶ ὅλον καὶ μόρια, καὶ πεπερασμένον καὶ ἄπειρον
πλήθει." "φαίνεται." "ἆρ' οὖν οὐκ, ἐπείπερ
πεπερασμένον, καὶ ἔσχατα ἔχον;" "ἀνάγκη."
"τί δ'; εἰ ὅλον, οὐ καὶ ἀρχὴν ἂν ἔχοι καὶ μέσον
καὶ τελευτήν; ἢ οἷόν τέ τι ὅλον εἶναι ἄνευ τριῶν
τούτων; κἂν του¹ ἓν ὁτιοῦν αὐτῶν ἀποστατῇ,
ἐθελήσει ἔτι ὅλον εἶναι;" "οὐκ ἐθελήσει." "καὶ
ἀρχὴν δή, ὡς ἔοικεν, καὶ τελευτὴν καὶ μέσον ἔχοι
ἂν τὸ ἕν." "ἔχοι." "ἀλλὰ μὴν τό γε μέσον
ἴσον τῶν ἐσχάτων ἀπέχει· οὐ γὰρ ἂν ἄλλως μέσον
εἴη." "οὐ γάρ." "καὶ σχήματος δή τινος,
ὡς ἔοικε, τοιοῦτον ὂν μετέχοι ἂν τὸ ἕν, ἤτοι εὐθέος ἢ στρογγύλου ἤ τινος μικτοῦ ἐξ ἀμφοῖν."
"μετέχοι γὰρ ἄν."

"Ἆρ' οὖν οὕτως ἔχον οὐκ αὐτό τε ἐν ἑαυτῷ
ἔσται καὶ ἐν ἄλλῳ;" "πῶς;" "τῶν μερῶν
που ἕκαστον ἐν τῷ ὅλῳ ἐστὶ καὶ οὐδὲν ἐκτὸς τοῦ
ὅλου." "οὕτως." "πάντα δὲ τὰ μέρη ὑπὸ τοῦ
ὅλου περιέχεται;" "ναί." "καὶ μὴν τά γε

PARMENIDES

as one; for existence is not wanting to the one,
nor the one to existence, but being two they are
equal throughout." "That is perfectly clear."
"The one, then, split up by existence, is many
and infinite in number." "Clearly." "Then not
only the existent one is many, but the absolute one
divided by existence, must be many." "Certainly."

"And because the parts are parts of a whole,
the one would be limited by the whole; or are not
the parts included by the whole?" "They must
be so." "But surely that which includes is a
limit." "Of course." "Then the existent one is,
apparently, both one and many, a whole and parts,
limited and of infinite number." "So it appears."
"Then if limited it has also extremes?" "Certainly." "Yes, and if it is a whole, will it not
have a beginning, a middle, and an end? Or can
there be any whole without these three? And if
any one of these is wanting, will it still be a whole?"
"It will not." "Then the one, it appears, will
have a beginning, a middle, and an end." "It
will." "But surely the middle is equally distant
from the extremes; for otherwise it would not be
a middle." "No." "And the one, apparently,
being of such a nature, will partake of some shape,
whether straight or round or a mixture of the two."
"Yes, it will."

"This being the case, will not the one be in
itself and in other?" "How is that?" "Each
of the parts doubtless is in the whole and none is
outside of the whole." "True." "And all the
parts are included in the whole?" "Yes." "And

---

¹ τον Schleiermacher : τοῦ BT.

261

πάντα μέρη τὰ αὑτοῦ τὸ ἕν ἐστι, καὶ οὔτε τι
πλέον οὔτε ἔλαττον ἢ πάντα.” “οὐ γάρ.” “οὐκοῦν καὶ τὸ ὅλον τὸ ἕν ἐστιν;” “πῶς δ’ οὔ;”
“εἰ ἄρα πάντα τὰ μέρη ἐν ὅλῳ τυγχάνει ὄντα,
ἔστι δὲ τά τε πάντα τὸ ἓν καὶ αὐτὸ τὸ ὅλον, περιέχεται δὲ ὑπὸ τοῦ ὅλου τὰ πάντα, ὑπὸ τοῦ ἑνὸς
ἂν περιέχοιτο τὸ ἕν, καὶ οὕτως ἂν ἤδη τὸ ἓν αὐτὸ
ἐν ἑαυτῷ εἴη.” “φαίνεται.” “ἀλλὰ μέντοι τό
γε ὅλον αὖ οὐκ ἐν τοῖς μέρεσίν ἐστιν, οὔτε ἐν
D πᾶσιν οὔτε ἔν τινι. εἰ γὰρ ἐν πᾶσιν, ἀνάγκη καὶ
ἐν ἑνί· ἔν τινι γὰρ ἑνὶ μὴ ὂν οὐκ ἂν ἔτι που δύναιτο
ἔν γε ἅπασιν εἶναι· εἰ δὲ τοῦτο μὲν τὸ ἓν τῶν
ἁπάντων ἐστί, τὸ δὲ ὅλον ἐν τούτῳ μὴ ἔνι,¹ πῶς
ἔτι ἔν γε τοῖς πᾶσιν ἐνέσται²;” “οὐδαμῶς.”
“οὐδὲ μὴν ἔν τισι τῶν μερῶν. εἰ γὰρ ἔν τισι
τὸ ὅλον εἴη, τὸ πλέον ἂν ἐν τῷ ἐλάττονι εἴη, ὅ
ἐστιν ἀδύνατον.” “ἀδύνατον γάρ.” “μὴ ὂν δ’
ἐν πλέοσι μηδ’ ἐν ἑνὶ μηδ’ ἐν ἅπασι τοῖς μέρεσι
τὸ ὅλον οὐκ ἀνάγκη ἐν ἑτέρῳ τινὶ εἶναι ἢ μηδαμοῦ
E ἔτι εἶναι;” “ἀνάγκη.” “οὐκοῦν μηδαμοῦ μὲν
ὂν οὐδὲν ἂν εἴη, ὅλον δὲ ὄν, ἐπειδὴ οὐκ ἐν αὑτῷ
ἐστίν, ἀνάγκη ἐν ἄλλῳ εἶναι;” “πάνυ γε.”
“ᾗ μὲν ἄρα τὸ ἓν ὅλον, ἐν ἄλλῳ ἐστίν· ᾗ δὲ τὰ
πάντα μέρη ὄντα τυγχάνει, αὐτὸ ἐν ἑαυτῷ· καὶ
οὕτω τὸ ἓν ἀνάγκη αὐτό τε ἐν ἑαυτῷ εἶναι καὶ
ἐν ἑτέρῳ.” “ἀνάγκη.”
“Οὕτω δὴ πεφυκὸς τὸ ἓν ἆρ’ οὐκ ἀνάγκη καὶ
κινεῖσθαι καὶ ἑστάναι;” “πῇ;” “ἕστηκε μέν
που, εἴπερ αὐτὸ ἐν ἑαυτῷ ἐστίν. ἐν γὰρ ἑνὶ ὂν
146 καὶ ἐκ τούτου μὴ μεταβαῖνον ἐν τῷ αὐτῷ ἂν εἴη,
ἐν ἑαυτῷ.” “ἔστι γάρ.” “τὸ δέ γε ἐν τῷ αὐτῷ
ἀεὶ ὂν ἑστὸς δήπου ἀνάγκη ἀεὶ εἶναι.” “πάνυ

surely the one is all its parts, neither more nor
less than all." "Certainly." "But the whole is
the one, is it not?" "Of course." "Then if all
the parts are in the whole and all the parts are the
one and the one is also the whole, and all the parts
are included in the whole, the one will be included
in the one, and thus the one will be in itself."
"Evidently." "But the whole is not in the parts,
neither in all of them nor in any. For if it is in
all, it must be in one, for if it were wanting in any
one it could no longer be in all; for if this one is
one of all, and the whole is not in this one, how can
it still be in all?" "It cannot in any way." "Nor
can it be in some of the parts; for if the whole were
in some parts, the greater would be in the less, which
is impossible." "Yes, it is impossible." "But
not being in one or several or all of the parts, it
must be in something else or cease to be anywhere
at all?" "It must." "And if it were nowhere,
it would be nothing, but being a whole, since it is
not in itself, it must be in something else, must it
not?" "Certainly." "Then the one, inasmuch
as it is a whole, is in other; and inasmuch as it is
all its parts, it is in itself; and thus one must be
both in itself and in other." "It must."

"This being its nature, must not the one be
both in motion and at rest?" "How is that?"
"It is at rest, no doubt, if it is in itself; for being
in one, and not passing out from this, it is in the
same, namely in itself." "It is." "But that
which is always in the same, must always be at
rest." "Certainly." "Well, then, must not, on

---

¹ ἔνι corr. Ven. 189: ἐνὶ B: ἐνὶ T.
² ἐνέσται Par. 1836: ἐν ἔσται BT.

γε." "τί δέ; τὸ ἐν ἑτέρῳ ἀεὶ ὂν οὐ τὸ ἐναντίον
ἀνάγκη μηδέποτ' ἐν τῷ αὐτῷ εἶναι, μηδέποτε
δὲ ὂν ἐν τῷ αὐτῷ μηδὲ ἑστάναι, μὴ ἑστὸς δὲ
κινεῖσθαι;" "οὕτως." "ἀνάγκη ἄρα τὸ ἕν,
αὐτό τε ἐν ἑαυτῷ ἀεὶ ὂν καὶ ἐν ἑτέρῳ, ἀεὶ κινεῖ-
σθαί τε καὶ ἑστάναι." "φαίνεται."

"Καὶ μὴν ταὐτόν γε δεῖ εἶναι αὐτὸ ἑαυτῷ καὶ
B ἕτερον ἑαυτοῦ, καὶ τοῖς ἄλλοις ὡσαύτως ταὐτόν
τε καὶ ἕτερον εἶναι, εἴπερ καὶ τὰ πρόσθεν πέπονθεν." "πῶς;" "πᾶν που πρὸς ἅπαν ὧδε ἔχει.
ἢ ταὐτόν ἐστιν ἢ ἕτερον· ἢ ἐὰν μὴ ταὐτὸν ἦ μηδ'
ἕτερον, μέρος ἂν εἴη τούτου πρὸς ὃ οὕτως ἔχει,
ἢ ὡς πρὸς μέρος ὅλον ἂν εἴη." "φαίνεται."
"ἆρ' οὖν τὸ ἓν αὐτὸ αὑτοῦ μέρος ἐστίν;" "οὐδαμῶς." "οὐδ' ἄρα ὡς πρὸς μέρος αὐτὸ αὑτοῦ
ὅλον ἂν εἴη, πρὸς ἑαυτὸ μέρος ὄν." "οὐ γὰρ
οἷόν τε." "ἀλλ' ἄρα ἕτερόν ἐστιν ἑνὸς τὸ ἕν;"
C "οὐ δῆτα." "οὐδ' ἄρα ἑαυτοῦ γε ἕτερον ἂν εἴη."
"οὐ μέντοι." "εἰ οὖν μήτε ἕτερον μήθ' ὅλον
μήτε μέρος αὐτὸ πρὸς ἑαυτό ἐστιν, οὐκ ἀνάγκη
ἤδη ταὐτὸν εἶναι αὐτὸ ἑαυτῷ;" "ἀνάγκη."
"τί δέ; τὸ ἑτέρωθι ὂν αὐτὸ ἑαυτοῦ ἐν τῷ αὐτῷ
ὄντος ἑαυτῷ οὐκ ἀνάγκη αὐτὸ ἑαυτοῦ ἕτερον
εἶναι, εἴπερ καὶ ἑτέρωθι ἔσται;" "ἔμοιγε δοκεῖ."
"οὕτω μὴν ἐφάνη ἔχον τὸ ἕν, αὐτό τε ἐν ἑαυτῷ
ὂν ἅμα καὶ ἐν ἑτέρῳ." "ἐφάνη γάρ." "ἕτερον
ἄρα, ὡς ἔοικεν, εἴη ταύτῃ ἂν ἑαυτοῦ τὸ ἕν."
D "ἔοικεν." "τί οὖν; εἰ τού τι[1] ἕτερόν ἐστιν,
οὐχ ἑτέρου ὄντος ἕτερον ἔσται;" "ἀνάγκη."

16. "Οὐκοῦν ὅσα μὴ ἕν ἐστιν, ἅπανθ' ἕτερα
τοῦ ἑνός, καὶ τὸ ἓν τῶν μὴ ἕν;" "πῶς δ' οὔ;"

---

[1] εἴ τού τι G : εἰ του τι BT.

the contrary, that which is always in other be never in the same, and being never in the same be not at rest, and being not at rest be in motion?" "True." "Then the one, being always in itself and in other, must always be in motion and at rest." "That is clear."

"And again, it must be the same with itself and other than itself, and likewise the same with all other things and other than they, if what we have said is true." "How is that?" "Everything stands to everything in one of the following relations : it is either the same or other ; or if neither the same or other, its relation is that of a part to a whole or of a whole to a part." "Obviously." "Now is the one a part of itself?" "By no means." "Then it cannot, by being a part in relation to itself, be a whole in relation to itself, as a part of itself." "No, that is impossible." "Nor can it be other than itself." "Certainly not." "Then if it is neither other nor a part nor a whole in relation to itself, must it not therefore be the same with itself?" "It must." "Well, must not that which is in another place than itself—the self being in the same place with itself—be other than itself, if it is to be in another place?" "I think so." "Now we saw that this was the case with one, for it was in itself and in other at the same time." "Yes, we saw that it was so." "Then by this reasoning the one appears to be other than itself." "So it appears." "Well then, if a thing is other than something, will it not be other than that which is other than it?" "Certainly." "Are not all things which are not one, other than one, and the one other than the not one?" "Of course."

PLATO

" ἕτερον ἄρα ἂν εἴη τὸ ἓν τῶν ἄλλων." " ἕτερον."
" ὅρα δή· αὐτό τε ταὐτὸν καὶ τὸ ἕτερον ἆρ' οὐκ
ἐναντία ἀλλήλοις;" " πῶς δ' οὔ;" " ἢ οὖν
ἐθελήσει ταὐτὸν ἐν τῷ ἑτέρῳ ἢ τὸ ἕτερον ἐν ταὐτῷ
ποτὲ εἶναι;" " οὐκ ἐθελήσει." " εἰ ἄρα τὸ
ἕτερον ἐν ταὐτῷ μηδέποτε ἔσται, οὐδὲν ἔστι τῶν
E ὄντων ἐν ᾧ ἐστιν τὸ ἕτερον χρόνον οὐδένα. εἰ
γὰρ ὁντινοῦν εἴη ἔν τῳ, ἐκεῖνον ἂν τὸν χρόνον ἐν
ταὐτῷ εἴη τὸ ἕτερον. οὐχ οὕτως;" " οὕτως."
" ἐπειδὴ δ' οὐδέποτε ἐν τῷ αὐτῷ ἐστιν, οὐδέποτε
ἔν τινι τῶν ὄντων ἂν εἴη τὸ ἕτερον." " ἀληθῆ."
" οὔτ' ἄρα ἐν τοῖς μὴ ἓν οὔτε ἐν τῷ ἑνὶ ἐνείη[1] ἂν
τὸ ἕτερον." " οὐ γὰρ οὖν." " οὐκ ἄρα τῷ
ἑτέρῳ γ' ἂν εἴη τὸ ἓν τῶν μὴ ἓν οὐδὲ τὰ μὴ ἓν
τοῦ ἑνὸς ἕτερα." " οὐ γάρ." " οὐδὲ μὴν ἑαυτοῖς γε ἕτερ' ἂν εἴη ἀλλήλων, μὴ μετέχοντα τοῦ
147 ἑτέρου." " πῶς γάρ;" " εἰ δὲ μήτε αὑτοῖς
ἕτερά ἐστι μήτε τῷ ἑτέρῳ, οὐ πάντη ἤδη ἂν ἐκ-
φεύγοι τὸ μὴ ἕτερα εἶναι ἀλλήλων;" " ἐκ-
φεύγοι." " ἀλλὰ μὴν οὐδὲ τοῦ ἑνός γε μετέχει
τὰ μὴ ἕν· οὐ γὰρ ἂν μὴ ἓν ἦν, ἀλλά πη ἂν ἓν ἦν."
" ἀληθῆ." " οὐδ' ἂν ἀριθμὸς ε η ἄρα τὰ μὴ
ἕν· οὐδὲ γὰρ ἂν οὕτω μὴ ἓν ἦν παντάπασιν, ἀριθμόν γε ἔχοντα." " οὐ γὰρ οὖν." " τί δέ; τὰ
μὴ ἓν τοῦ ἑνὸς ἄρα μόριά ἐστιν; ἢ κἂν οὕτω
μετεῖχε τοῦ ἑνὸς τὰ μὴ ἕν;" " μετεῖχεν." " εἰ
B ἄρα πάντη τὸ μὲν ἕν ἐστι, τὰ δὲ μὴ ἕν, οὔτ' ἂν
μόριον τῶν μὴ ἓν τὸ ἓν εἴη οὔτε ὅλον ὡς μορίων·[2]

---

[1] ἐνείη] ἐν εἴη B : εἴη T.
[2] μορίων corr. Ven. 189 : μορίου BT.

" Then the one would be other than the others."
" Yes, it is other." " Consider ; are not the
absolute same and the absolute other opposites of
one another ? " " Of course." " Then will the
same ever be in the other, or the other in the same ? "
" No." " Then if the other can never be in the
same, there is no existing thing in which the other
is during any time ; for if it were in anything during
any time whatsoever, the other would be in the same,
would it not ? " " Yes, it would." " But since
the other is never in the same, it can never be in
any existing thing." " True." " Then the other
cannot be either in the not one or in the one." " No,
it cannot." " Then not by reason of the other will
the one be other than the not one or the not one
other than the one." " No." " And surely they
cannot by reason of themselves be other than one
another, if they do not partake of the other." " Of
course not." " But if they are not other than one
another either by reason of themselves or by reason
of the other, will it not be quite impossible for
them to be other than one another at all ? " " Quite
impossible." " But neither can the not one partake
of the one ; for in that case they would not be not
one, but would be one." " True." " Nor can the
not one be a number ; for in that case, too, since
they would possess number, they would not be
not one at all." " No, they would not." " Well,
then, are the not one parts of the one ? Or would
the not one in that case also partake of the one ? "
" Yes, they would partake of it." " If, then, in
every way the one is one and the not one are not
one, the one cannot be a part of the not one, nor a
whole of which the not one are parts, nor are the

οὔτε αὖ τὰ μὴ ἓν τοῦ ἑνὸς μόρια, οὔτε ὅλα ὡς μορίῳ τῷ ἑνί." "οὐ γάρ." "ἀλλὰ μὴν ἔφαμεν τὰ μήτε μόρια μήτε ὅλα μήτε ἕτερα ἀλλήλων ταὐτὰ ἔσεσθαι ἀλλήλοις." "ἔφαμεν γάρ." "φῶμεν ἄρα καὶ τὸ ἓν πρὸς τὰ μὴ ἓν οὕτως ἔχον τὸ αὐτὸ εἶναι αὐτοῖς;" "φῶμεν." "τὸ ἓν ἄρα, ὡς ἔοικεν, ἕτερόν τε τῶν ἄλλων ἐστὶν καὶ ἑαυτοῦ καὶ ταὐτὸν ἐκείνοις τε καὶ ἑαυτῷ." "κινδυνεύει
C φαίνεσθαι ἔκ γε τοῦ λόγου."

"Ἆρ' οὖν καὶ ὅμοιόν τε καὶ ἀνόμοιον ἑαυτῷ τε καὶ τοῖς ἄλλοις;" "ἴσως." "ἐπειδὴ γοῦν ἕτερον τῶν ἄλλων ἐφάνη, καὶ τἆλλά που ἕτερ' ἂν ἐκείνου εἴη." "τί μήν;" "οὐκοῦν οὕτως ἕτερον τῶν ἄλλων, ὥσπερ καὶ τἆλλα ἐκείνου, καὶ οὔτε μᾶλλον οὔτε ἧττον;" "τί γὰρ ἄν;" "εἰ ἄρα μήτε μᾶλλον μήτε ἧττον, ὁμοίως." "ναί." "οὐκοῦν ᾗ ἕτερον εἶναι πέπονθεν τῶν ἄλλων καὶ τἆλλα ἐκείνου ὡσαύτως, ταύτῃ ταὐτὸν ἂν πεπον-
D θότα εἶεν τό τε ἓν τοῖς ἄλλοις καὶ τἆλλα τῷ ἑνί." "πῶς λέγεις;" "ὧδε· ἕκαστον τῶν ὀνομάτων οὐκ ἐπί τινι καλεῖς;" "ἔγωγε." "τί οὖν; τὸ αὐτὸ ὄνομα εἴποις ἂν πλεονάκις ἢ ἅπαξ;" "ἔγω-γε." "πότερον οὖν ἐὰν μὲν ἅπαξ εἴπῃς, ἐκεῖνο προσαγορεύεις οὗπέρ ἐστι τοὔνομα, ἐὰν δὲ πολ-λάκις, οὐκ ἐκεῖνο; ἢ ἐάντε ἅπαξ ἐάντε πολλάκις ταὐτὸν ὄνομα φθέγξῃ, πολλὴ ἀνάγκη σε ταὐτὸν καὶ λέγειν ἀεί;" "τί μήν;" "οὐκοῦν καὶ τὸ ἕτε-ρον ὄνομά ἐστιν ἐπί τινι;" "πάνυ γε." "ὅταν

not one parts of the one, nor a whole of which the one is a part." "No." "But we said that things which are neither parts nor wholes of one another, nor other than one another, are the same as one another." "Yes, we did." "Shall we say, then, that since the relations of the one and the not one are such as we have described, the two are the same as one another?" "Yes, let us say that." "The one, then, is, it appears, other than all other things and than itself, and is also the same as other things and as itself." "That appears to be the result of our argument."

"Is it, then, also like and unlike itself and others?" "Perhaps." "At any rate, since it was found to be other than others, the others must also be other than it." "Of course." "Then it is other than the others just as the others are other than it, neither more nor less?" "Certainly." "And if neither more nor less, then in like degree?" "Yes." "In so far as it is so affected as to be other than the others and the others are affected in the same way in relation to the one, to that degree the one will be affected in the same way as the others and the others in the same way as the one." "What do you mean?" "I will explain. You give a particular name to a thing?" "Yes." "Well, you can utter the same name once or more than once?" "Yes." "And do you name that to which the name belongs when you utter it once, but not when you utter it many times? Or must you always mean the same thing when you utter the same name, whether once or repeatedly?" "The same thing, of course." "The word 'other' is the name of something, is it not?" "Certainly."

E ἆρα αὐτὸ φθέγγῃ, ἐάντε ἅπαξ ἐάντε πολλάκις, οὐκ
ἐπ' ἄλλῳ οὐδὲ ἄλλο τι ὀνομάζεις ἢ ἐκεῖνο οὗπερ
ἦν ὄνομα." "ἀνάγκη." "ὅταν δὴ λέγωμεν ὅτι
ἕτερον μὲν τἆλλα τοῦ ἑνός, ἕτερον δὲ τὸ ἓν τῶν
ἄλλων, δὶς τὸ ἕτερον εἰπόντες οὐδέν τι μᾶλλον ἐπ'
ἄλλῃ, ἀλλ' ἐπ' ἐκείνῃ τῇ φύσει αὐτὸ ἀεὶ λέγομεν,
ἧσπερ ἦν τοὔνομα." "πάνυ μὲν οὖν." "ἦ[1]
148 ἆρα ἕτερον τῶν ἄλλων τὸ ἓν καὶ τἆλλα τοῦ ἑνός,
κατ' αὐτὸ τὸ[2] ἕτερον πεπονθέναι οὐκ ἄλλο, ἀλλὰ
τὸ αὐτὸ ἂν πεπονθὸς εἴη τὸ ἓν τοῖς ἄλλοις· τὸ δέ
που ταὐτὸν πεπονθὸς ὅμοιον· οὐχί;" "ναί."
"ᾗ δὴ τὸ ἓν ἕτερον τῶν ἄλλων πέπονθεν εἶναι,
κατ' αὐτὸ τοῦτο ἅπαν ἅπασιν ὅμοιον ἂν εἴη· ἅπαν
γὰρ ἁπάντων ἕτερόν ἐστιν." "ἔοικεν."

17. "Ἀλλὰ μὴν τό γε ὅμοιον τῷ ἀνομοίῳ[3]
ἐναντίον." "ναί." "οὐκοῦν καὶ τὸ ἕτερον τῷ
ταὐτῷ.[4]" "καὶ τοῦτο." "ἀλλὰ μὴν καὶ τοῦτό
γ' ἐφάνη, ὡς ἄρα τὸ ἓν τοῖς ἄλλοις ταὐτόν."
B "ἐφάνη γάρ." "τοὐναντίον δέ γε πάθος ἐστὶ τὸ
εἶναι ταὐτὸν τοῖς ἄλλοις τῷ ἕτερον εἶναι τῶν
ἄλλων." "πάνυ γε." "ᾗ γε μὴν ἕτερον, ὅμοιον
ἐφάνη." "ναί." "ᾗ ἄρα ταὐτόν, ἀνόμοιον ἔσται
κατὰ τοὐναντίον πάθος τῷ ὁμοιοῦντι πάθει.
ὡμοίου δέ που τὸ ἕτερον;" "ναί." "ἀνομοιώ-
σει ἄρα τὸ ταὐτόν, ἢ οὐκ ἐναντίον ἔσται τῷ ἑτέρῳ."
C "ἔοικεν." "ὅμοιον ἄρα καὶ ἀνόμοιον ἔσται τὸ
ἓν τοῖς ἄλλοις, ᾗ μὲν ἕτερον, ὅμοιον, ᾗ δὲ ταὐτόν,
ἀνόμοιον." "ἔχει γὰρ οὖν δή, ὡς ἔοικεν, καὶ
τοιοῦτον λόγον." "καὶ γὰρ τόνδε ἔχει." "τίνα;"

---

[1] ᾗ] ἢ B : ἦ T : εἰ vulg.
[2] κατ' αὐτὸ τὸ Thomson : κατὰ ταυτὸ BT.
[3] τῷ ἀνομοίῳ] τῷ ὁμοίῳ B : τῶν ἀνομοίων T.
[4] ταὐτῷ in marg. T : αὐτῷ BT.

" Then when you utter it, whether once or many times, you apply it to nothing else, and you name nothing else, than that of which it is the name." " Assuredly." " Now when we say that the others are other than the one, and the one is other than the others, though we use the word ' other ' twice, we do not for all that apply it to anything else, but we always apply it to that nature of which it is the name." " Certainly." " In so far as the one is other than the others and the others are other than the one, the one and the others are not in different states, but in the same state ; but whatever is in the same state is like, is it not ? " " Yes." " Then in so far as the one is in the state of being other than the others, just so far everything is like all other things ; for everything is other than all other things." " So it appears." " But the like is opposed to the unlike." " Yes." " And the other to the same." " That is also true." " But this, too, was shown, that the one is the same as the others." " Yes, it was." " And being the same as the others is the opposite of being other than the others." " Certainly." " In so far as it was other it was shown to be like." " Yes." " Then in so far as it is the same it will be unlike, since it has a quality which is the opposite of the quality which makes it like, for the other made it like." " Yes." " Then the same will make it unlike ; otherwise the same will not be the opposite of the other." " So it appears." " Then the one will be both like and unlike the others, like in so far as it is other, unlike in so far as it is the same." " Yes, that sort of conclusion seems to be tenable." " But there is another besides " " What is it ? " " In

PLATO

" ἢ ταὐτὸν πέπονθε, μὴ ἀλλοῖον πεπονθέναι, μὴ
ἀλλοῖον δὲ πεπονθὸς μὴ ἀνόμοιον, μὴ ἀνόμοιον δὲ
ὅμοιον εἶναι· ἢ δ' ἄλλο πέπονθεν, ἀλλοῖον, ἀλλοῖον δὲ ὂν ἀνόμοιον εἶναι." "ἀληθῆ λέγεις."
"ταὐτόν τε ἄρα ὂν τὸ ἓν τοῖς ἄλλοις καὶ ὅτι ἕτερόν ἐστι, κατ' ἀμφότερα καὶ καθ' ἑκάτερον, ὅμοιόν
D τε ἂν εἴη καὶ ἀνόμοιον τοῖς ἄλλοις." "πάνυ γε."
"οὐκοῦν καὶ ἑαυτῷ ὡσαύτως, ἐπείπερ ἕτερόν τε
ἑαυτοῦ καὶ ταὐτὸν ἑαυτῷ ἐφάνη, κατ' ἀμφότερα
καὶ κατὰ ἑκάτερον ὅμοιόν τε καὶ ἀνόμοιον φανήσεται;" "ἀνάγκη."

"Τί δὲ δή; περὶ τοῦ ἅπτεσθαι τὸ ἓν αὑτοῦ
καὶ τῶν ἄλλων καὶ τοῦ μὴ ἅπτεσθαι πέρι πῶς ἔχει,
σκόπει." "σκοπῶ." "αὐτὸ γάρ που ἐν ἑαυτῷ
ὅλῳ τὸ ἓν ἐφάνη ὄν." "ὀρθῶς." "οὐκοῦν καὶ
ἐν τοῖς ἄλλοις τὸ ἕν;" "ναί." "ᾗ μὲν ἄρα ἐν
E τοῖς ἄλλοις, τῶν ἄλλων ἅπτοιτο ἄν· ᾗ δὲ αὐτὸ ἐν
ἑαυτῷ, τῶν μὲν ἄλλων ἀπείργοιτο ἅπτεσθαι,
αὐτὸ δὲ αὐτοῦ ἅπτοιτο ἂν ἐν ἑαυτῷ ὄν." "φαίνεται." "οὕτω μὲν δὴ ἅπτοιτο ἂν τὸ ἓν αὑτοῦ τε
καὶ τῶν ἄλλων." "ἅπτοιτο." "τί δὲ τῇδε;
ἆρ' οὐ πᾶν τὸ μέλλον ἅψεσθαί τινος ἐφεξῆς δεῖ
κεῖσθαι ἐκείνῳ οὗ μέλλει ἅπτεσθαι, ταύτην τὴν
ἕδραν κατέχον ἢ ἂν μετ' ἐκείνην ᾗ[1] ᾗ[2] ἂν κέηται,
ἅπτεται;" "ἀνάγκη." "καὶ τὸ ἓν ἄρα εἰ μέλλει αὐτὸ αὑτοῦ ἅψεσθαι, ἐφεξῆς δεῖ εὐθὺς μεθ'
ἑαυτὸ κεῖσθαι, τὴν ἐχομένην χώραν κατέχον ἐκείνης ἐν[3] ᾗ αὐτό ἐστιν." "δεῖ γὰρ οὖν." "οὐκοῦν
149 δύο μὲν ὂν τὸ ἓν ποιήσειεν ἂν ταῦτα καὶ ἐν δυοῖν
χώραιν ἅμα γένοιτο· ἕως δ' ἂν ᾖ ἕν, οὐκ ἐθε-

---

[1] ᾗ ἕδρα BT: ἕδρα om. Bekker: ἕδραν Heindorf.
[2] ᾗ B: ᾗ T.　　　　　　[3] ἐν T: om. B.

so far as it is in the same state, the one is not in another state, and not being in another state it is not unlike, and not being unlike it is like ; but in so far as it is in another state, it is of another sort, and being of another sort it is unlike." "True." " Then the one, because it is the same as the others and because it is other than the others, for both these reasons or for either of them would be both like and unlike the others." " Certainly." " And likewise, since it has been shown to be other than itself and the same as itself, the one will for both these reasons or for either of them be both like and unlike itself." " That is inevitable."

" Now, then, consider the question whether the one touches or does not touch itself and other things." " I am considering." " The one was shown, I think, to be in the whole of itself." " Right." " And the one is also in other things ? " " Yes." " Then by reason of being in the others it would touch them, and by reason of being in itself it would be prevented from touching the others, but would touch itself, since it is in itself." " That is clear." " Thus the one would touch itself and the other things." " It would." " But how about this ? Must not everything which is to touch anything be next to that which it is to touch, and occupy that position which, being next to that of the other, touches it ? " " It must." " Then the one, if it is to touch itself, must lie next to itself and occupy the position next to that in which it is." " Yes, it must." " The one, then, might do this if it were two, and might be in two places at once ; but so long as it

λήσει;" "οὐ γὰρ οὖν." "ἡ αὐτὴ ἄρα ἀνάγκη
τῷ ἑνὶ μήτε δύο εἶναι μήτε ἅπτεσθαι αὐτῷ αὑτοῦ." "ἡ αὐτή." "ἀλλ' οὐδὲ μὴν τῶν ἄλλων
ἅψεται." "τί δή;" "ὅτι, φαμέν, τὸ μέλλον
ἅψεσθαι χωρὶς ὂν ἐφεξῆς δεῖ ἐκείνῳ εἶναι οὗ μέλλει ἅψεσθαι, τρίτον δὲ αὐτῶν ἐν μέσῳ μηδὲν
εἶναι." "ἀληθῆ." "δύο ἄρα δεῖ τὸ ὀλίγιστον
εἶναι, εἰ μέλλει ἅψις εἶναι." "δεῖ." "ἐὰν δὲ
B τοῖν δυοῖν ὅροιν τρίτον προσγένηται ἑξῆς, αὐτὰ
μὲν τρία ἔσται, αἱ δὲ ἅψεις δύο." "ναί." "καὶ
οὕτω δὴ ἀεὶ ἑνὸς προσγιγνομένου μία καὶ ἅψις
προσγίγνεται, καὶ συμβαίνει τὰς ἅψεις τοῦ πλήθους τῶν ἀριθμῶν μιᾷ ἐλάττους εἶναι. ᾧ γὰρ τὰ
πρῶτα δύο ἐπλεονέκτησε τῶν ἅψεων εἰς τὸ πλείω
εἶναι τὸν ἀριθμὸν ἢ τὰς ἅψεις, τῷ ἴσῳ τούτῳ καὶ
ὁ ἔπειτα ἀριθμὸς πᾶς πασῶν τῶν ἅψεων πλεον-
C εκτεῖ. ἤδη γὰρ τὸ λοιπὸν ἅμα ἕν τε τῷ ἀριθμῷ
προσγίγνεται καὶ μία ἅψις ταῖς ἅψεσιν." "ὀρθῶς." "ὅσα ἄρα ἐστὶ τὰ ὄντα τὸν ἀριθμόν, ἀεὶ
μιᾷ αἱ ἅψεις ἐλάττους εἰσὶν αὐτῶν." "ἀληθῆ."
"εἰ δέ γε ἓν μόνον ἐστί, δυὰς δὲ μὴ ἔστιν, ἅψις
οὐκ ἂν εἴη." "πῶς γάρ;" "οὐκοῦν, φαμέν,
τὰ ἄλλα τοῦ ἑνὸς οὔτε ἕν ἐστιν οὔτε μετέχει αὐτοῦ, εἴπερ ἄλλα ἐστίν." "οὐ γάρ." "οὐκ ἄρα
ἔνεστιν[1] ἀριθμὸς ἐν τοῖς ἄλλοις, ἑνὸς μὴ ἐνόντος[2]
ἐν αὐτοῖς." "πῶς γάρ;" "οὔτ' ἄρα ἕν ἐστι
D τὰ ἄλλα οὔτε δύο οὔτε ἄλλου ἀριθμοῦ ἔχοντα
ὄνομα οὐδέν." "οὔ." "τὸ ἓν ἄρα μόνον ἐστὶν
ἕν, καὶ δυὰς οὐκ ἂν εἴη." "οὐ φαίνεται." "ἅψις
ἄρα οὐκ ἔστι δυοῖν μὴ ὄντοιν." "οὐκ ἔστιν."
"οὔτ' ἄρα τὸ ἓν τῶν ἄλλων ἅπτεται οὔτε τὰ ἄλλα

¹ ἔνεστιν b: ἔν ἐστιν BT.   ² ἐνόντος b: ἐν ὄντος B: ὄντος T.

PARMENIDES

is one, it will not ? "   " No, it will not."   " The one
can no more touch itself than it can be two."   " No."
" Nor, again, will it touch the others."   " Why
not ? "   " Because, as we agreed, that which is to
touch anything must be outside of that which it is
to touch, and next it, and there must be no third
between them."   " True."   " Then there must be
two, at least, if there is to be contact."   " There
must."   " And if to the two a third be added in
immediate succession, there will be three terms
and two contacts."   " Yes."   " And thus whenever
one is added, one contact also is added, and the
number of contacts is always one less than the
number of terms ; for every succeeding number of
terms exceeds the number of all the contacts just
as much as the first two terms exceeded the number
of their contacts. For after the first every addi-
tional term adds one to the number of contacts."
" Right."   " Then whatever the number of terms,
the contacts are always one less."   " True."   " But
if only one exists, and not two, there can be no
contact."   " Of course not."   " We affirm that
those things which are other than one are not one
and do not partake of oneness, since they are other."
" They do not."   " Then there is no number in
others, if one is not in them."   " Of course not."
" Then the others are neither one nor two, nor have
they the name of any other number."   " No."
" The one is, then, only one, and there can be no
two."   " That is clear."   " There is no contact if
there are no two terms."   " No, there is none."
" Then the one does not touch the others, nor the

τοῦ ἑνός, ἐπείπερ ἅψις οὐκ ἔστιν." "οὐ γὰρ
οὖν." "οὕτω δὴ κατὰ πάντα ταῦτα τὸ ἓν τῶν
τε ἄλλων καὶ ἑαυτοῦ ἅπτεταί τε καὶ οὐχ ἅπτεται."
"ἔοικεν."

18. "Ἆρ' οὖν καὶ ἴσον ἐστὶ καὶ ἄνισον αὐτῷ
τε καὶ τοῖς ἄλλοις;" "πῶς;" "εἰ μεῖζον εἴη
E τὸ ἓν ἢ τἆλλα ἢ ἔλαττον, ἢ αὖ τἆλλα τοῦ ἑνὸς
μείζω ἢ ἐλάττω, ἆρα οὐκ ἂν τῷ μὲν ἓν εἶναι τὸ
ἓν καὶ τὰ ἄλλα ἄλλα τοῦ ἑνὸς οὔτε τι μεῖζω οὔτε
τι ἐλάττω ἂν εἴη ἀλλήλων αὐταῖς γε ταύταις ταῖς
οὐσίαις· ἀλλ' εἰ μὲν πρὸς τῷ τοιαῦτα εἶναι ἑκάτερα
ἰσότητα ἔχοιεν, ἴσα ἂν εἴη πρὸς ἄλληλα· εἰ δὲ τὰ
μὲν μέγεθος, τὸ¹ δὲ σμικρότητα, ἢ καὶ μέγεθος
μὲν τὸ ἕν, σμικρότητα δὲ τἆλλα, ὁποτέρῳ μὲν
τῷ εἴδει μέγεθος προσείη, μεῖζον ἂν εἴη, ᾧ δὲ
σμικρότης, ἔλαττον;" "ἀνάγκη." "οὐκοῦν ἐστόν
γέ² τινε τούτω εἴδη, τό τε μέγεθος καὶ ἡ σμικρότης;
οὐ γὰρ ἄν που μὴ ὄντε γε ἐναντίω τε ἀλλήλοιν
εἴτην καὶ ἐν τοῖς οὖσιν ἐγγιγνοίσθην." "πῶς γὰρ
150 ἄν;" "εἰ ἄρα ἐν τῷ ἑνὶ σμικρότης ἐγγίγνεται, ἤτοι
ἐν ὅλῳ ἂν ἢ ἐν μέρει αὐτοῦ ἐνείη." "ἀνάγκη."
"τί δ' εἰ ἐν ὅλῳ ἐγγίγνοιτο; οὐχὶ ἢ ἐξ ἴσου ἂν
τῷ ἑνὶ δι' ὅλου αὐτοῦ τεταμένη εἴη ἢ περιέχουσα
αὐτό;" "δῆλον δή." "ἆρ' οὖν οὐκ ἐξ ἴσου μὲν
οὖσα ἡ σμικρότης τῷ ἑνὶ ἴση ἂν αὐτῷ εἴη, περιέχουσα δὲ μείζων;" "πῶς δ' οὔ;" "δυνατὸν
οὖν σμικρότητα ἴσην τῳ εἶναι ἢ μείζω τινός, καὶ
πράττειν γε τὰ μεγέθους τε καὶ ἰσότητος, ἀλλὰ
B μὴ τὰ ἑαυτῆς;" "ἀδύνατον." "ἐν μὲν ὅλῳ ἄρα τῷ

---

¹ τὸ Par. 1810: τὰ ΒΤ.   ² γέ al.: τέ ΒΤ.

others the one, since there is no contact." " No, certainly not." " Thus on all these grounds the one touches and does not touch itself and the others." " So it appears."

" And is the one both equal and unequal to itself and the others ? " " How is that ? " " If the one were greater or less than the others, or, again, the others greater or less than the one, is it not true that the one, considered merely as one, and the others, considered merely as others, would be neither greater nor less than one another, so far as their own natures are concerned ; but if in addition to their own natures they both possessed equality, they would be equal to one another ; or if the others possessed greatness and the one small-ness, or *vice versa*, that class to which greatness was added would be greater, and that to which smallness was added would be smaller ? " " Certainly." " These two ideas, greatness and smallness, exist, do they not ? For if they did not exist, they could not be opposites of one another and could not come into being in things." " That is obvious." " Then if smallness comes into being in the one, it would be either in a part or in the whole of it." " Neces-sarily." " What if it be in the whole of one ? Will it not either be on an equality with the one, extending throughout the whole of it, or else contain it ? " " Clearly." " And if smallness be on an equality with the one, will it not be equal to the one, and if it contain the one, greater than the one ? " " Of course." " But can smallness be equal to anything or greater than anything, performing the functions of greatness or equality and not its own functions ? " " No, it cannot." " Then smallness

277

ἑνὶ οὐκ ἂν εἴη σμικρότης, ἀλλ' εἴπερ, ἐν μέρει."
" ναί." " οὐδὲ¹ γε ἐν παντὶ αὖ τῷ μέρει· εἰ δὲ
μή, ταὐτὰ ποιήσει ἅπερ πρὸς τὸ ὅλον· ἴση ἔσται
ἢ μείζων τοῦ μέρους ἐν ᾧ ἂν ἀεὶ ἐνῇ." " ἀνάγκη."
" οὐδενί ποτε ἄρα ἐνέσται τῶν ὄντων σμικρότης,
μήτ' ἐν μέρει μήτ' ἐν ὅλῳ ἐγγιγνομένη· οὐδέ τι
ἔσται σμικρὸν πλὴν αὐτῆς σμικρότητος." " οὐκ
ἔοικεν." " οὐδ' ἄρα μέγεθος ἐνέσται ἐν αὐτῷ.
C μεῖζον γὰρ ἄν τι εἴη ἄλλο καὶ πλὴν αὐτοῦ μεγέθους,
ἐκεῖνο ἐν ᾧ τὸ μέγεθος ἐνείη, καὶ ταῦτα σμικροῦ
αὐτῷ οὐκ ὄντος, οὗ ἀνάγκη ὑπερέχειν, ἐάνπερ
ᾖ μέγα· τοῦτο δὲ ἀδύνατον, ἐπειδὴ σμικρότης
οὐδαμοῦ ἔνι." " ἀληθῆ." " ἀλλὰ μὴν αὐτὸ μέγεθος οὐκ ἄλλου μεῖζον ἢ αὐτῆς σμικρότητος, οὐδὲ
σμικρότης ἄλλου ἔλαττον ἢ αὐτοῦ μεγέθους."
" οὐ γάρ." " οὔτε ἄρα τὰ ἄλλα μείζω τοῦ
ἑνὸς οὐδὲ ἐλάττω, μήτε μέγεθος μήτε σμικρότητα
D ἔχοντα, οὔτε αὐτὼ τούτω πρὸς τὸ ἓν ἔχετον τὴν
δύναμιν τὴν τοῦ ὑπερέχειν καὶ ὑπερέχεσθαι, ἀλλὰ
πρὸς ἀλλήλω, οὔτε αὖ τὸ ἓν τούτοιν οὐδὲ τῶν
ἄλλων μεῖζόν τ' ἂν οὐδ' ἔλαττον εἴη, μήτε μέγεθος
μήτε σμικρότητα ἔχον." " οὔκουν φαίνεταί γε."
" ἆρ' οὖν, εἰ μήτε μεῖζον μήτε ἔλαττον τὸ ἓν τῶν
ἄλλων, ἀνάγκη αὐτὸ ἐκείνων μήτε ὑπερέχειν μήτε
ὑπερέχεσθαι;" " ἀνάγκη." " οὐκοῦν τό γε μήτε
ὑπερέχον μήτε ὑπερεχόμενον πολλὴ ἀνάγκη ἐξ
ἴσου εἶναι, ἐξ ἴσου δὲ ὂν ἴσον εἶναι." " πῶς γὰρ
E οὔ;" " καὶ μὴν καὶ αὐτό γε τὸ ἓν πρὸς ἑαυτὸ
οὕτως ἂν ἔχοι· μήτε μέγεθος ἐν ἑαυτῷ μήτε
σμικρότητα ἔχον οὔτ' ἂν ὑπερέχοιτο οὔτ' ἂν

---

¹ οὐδέ Hermann : οὔτε B : οὔτι T.

cannot exist in the whole of the one, but, if at all, only in a part of it." "Yes." "And neither can it exist in a whole part, for then it will behave just as it did in relation to the whole; it will be equal to or greater than the part in which it happens to exist." "Inevitably." "Then smallness will never exist in anything, either in a part or in a whole, nor will anything be small except absolute smallness." "So it appears." "Nor will greatness exist in the one. For in that case, something other than absolute greatness and differing from it, namely that in which greatness exists, would be greater, and that although there is no smallness in it, which greatness must exceed, if it be great. But this is impossible, since smallness exists nowhere." "True." "But absolute greatness is not greater than anything but absolute smallness, and absolute smallness is not smaller than anything but absolute greatness." "No." "Then other things are neither greater nor smaller than the one, if they have neither greatness nor smallness, nor have even these two the power of exceeding or being exceeded in relation to the one, but only in relation to each other, nor can the one be greater or less than these two or than other things, since it has neither greatness nor smallness." "Evidently not." "Then if the one is neither greater nor smaller than the others, it can neither exceed them nor be exceeded by them?" "Certainly not." "Then that which neither exceeds nor is exceeded must be on an equality, and being on an equality, must be equal." "Of course." "And the one will be in the same relation to itself also; if it have in itself neither greatness nor smallness, it cannot be exceeded by itself or exceed

279

PLATO

ὑπερέχοι ἑαυτοῦ, ἀλλ' ἐξ ἴσου ὂν ἴσον ἂν εἴη
ἑαυτῷ." "πάνυ μὲν οὖν." "τὸ ἓν ἄρα ἑαυτῷ
τε καὶ τοῖς ἄλλοις ἴσον ἂν εἴη." "φαίνεται."
"καὶ μὴν αὐτό γε ἐν ἑαυτῷ ὂν καὶ περὶ ἑαυτὸ
ἂν εἴη ἔξωθεν, καὶ περιέχον μὲν μεῖζον ἂν ἑαυτοῦ
151 εἴη, περιεχόμενον δὲ ἔλαττον, καὶ οὕτω μεῖζον ἂν
καὶ ἔλαττον εἴη αὐτὸ ἑαυτοῦ τὸ ἕν." "εἴη γὰρ
ἄν." "οὐκοῦν καὶ τόδε ἀνάγκη, μηδὲν εἶναι
ἐκτὸς τοῦ ἑνός τε καὶ τῶν ἄλλων;" "πῶς γὰρ
οὔ;" "ἀλλὰ μὴν καὶ εἶναί που δεῖ τό γε ὂν ἀεί."
"ναί." "οὐκοῦν τό γε ἔν τῳ ὂν ἐν μείζονι ἔσται
ἔλαττον ὄν; οὐ γὰρ ἂν ἄλλως ἕτερον ἐν ἑτέρῳ εἴη."
"οὐ γάρ." "ἐπειδὴ δὲ οὐδὲν ἕτερον ἔστι χωρὶς
τῶν ἄλλων καὶ τοῦ ἑνός, δεῖ δὲ αὐτὰ ἔν τῳ εἶναι,
οὐκ ἀνάγκη ἤδη ἐν ἀλλήλοις εἶναι, τά τε ἄλλα ἐν
B τῷ ἑνὶ καὶ τὸ ἓν ἐν τοῖς ἄλλοις, ἢ μηδαμοῦ εἶναι;"
"φαίνεται." "ὅτι μὲν ἄρα τὸ ἓν ἐν τοῖς ἄλλοις
ἔνεστι, μείζω ἂν εἴη τὰ ἄλλα τοῦ ἑνός, περιέχοντα
αὐτό, τὸ δὲ ἓν ἔλαττον τῶν ἄλλων, περιεχόμενον·
ὅτι δὲ τὰ ἄλλα ἐν τῷ ἑνί, τὸ ἓν τῶν ἄλλων κατὰ
τὸν αὐτὸν λόγον μεῖζον ἂν εἴη, τὰ δὲ ἄλλα τοῦ
ἑνὸς ἐλάττω." "ἔοικεν." "τὸ ἓν ἄρα ἴσον τε
καὶ μεῖζον καὶ ἔλαττόν ἐστιν αὐτό τε αὑτοῦ καὶ
τῶν ἄλλων." "φαίνεται." "καὶ μὴν εἴπερ μεῖζον
καὶ ἔλαττον καὶ ἴσον, ἴσων ἂν εἴη μέτρων καὶ
C πλειόνων καὶ ἐλαττόνων αὑτῷ καὶ τοῖς ἄλλοις,
ἐπειδὴ δὲ μέτρων, καὶ μερῶν." "πῶς δ' οὔ;"
"ἴσων μὲν ἄρα μέτρων ὂν καὶ πλειόνων καὶ
ἐλαττόνων, καὶ ἀριθμῷ ἔλαττον ἂν καὶ πλέον εἴη
αὐτό τε αὑτοῦ καὶ τῶν ἄλλων καὶ ἴσον αὑτῷ τε

PARMENIDES

itself; it would be on an equality with and equal to itself." "Certainly." "The one is, then, equal to itself and to the others." "Evidently." "But the one, being within itself, would also be contained by itself, and since it contains itself it would be greater than itself, and since it is contained by itself it would be less than itself; thus the one would be both greater and less than itself." "Yes, it would." "And is it true, moreover, that nothing can exist outside of the one and the others?" "Of course." "But that which exists must always exist somewhere." "Yes." "And that which exists in anything will be smaller and will exist in the greater? One thing cannot exist in another in any other way, can it?" "No, it cannot." "But since there is nothing else apart from the one and the others, and they must be in something, must they not be in one another, the others in the one and the one in the others, or else be nowhere at all?" "Clearly." "And because the one is in the others, the others will be greater than the one, since they contain it, and the one less than the others, since it is contained; but because the others are in the one, the one will by the same reasoning be greater than the others, and the others less than the one." "So it appears." "Then the one is equal to and greater and less than itself and the others." "Evidently." "And if equal and greater and less, it will be of equal and more and less measures with itself and the others, and since of equal, more, and less measures, of equal, more, and less parts." "Of course." "And being of equal and more and less measures, it will be less and more in number than itself and the others and likewise equal in

281

PLATO

καὶ τοῖς ἄλλοις κατὰ ταὐτά." "πῶς;" "ὧν-
περ μεῖζόν ἐστι, πλειόνων που καὶ μέτρων ἂν εἴη
αὐτῶν· ὅσων δὲ μέτρων, καὶ μερῶν· καὶ ὧν
ἔλαττον, ὡσαύτως· καὶ οἷς ἴσον, κατὰ ταὐτά."
"οὕτως." "οὐκοῦν ἑαυτοῦ μεῖζον καὶ ἔλαττον
D ὂν καὶ ἴσον ἴσων ἂν εἴη μέτρων καὶ πλειόνων καὶ
ἐλαττόνων αὑτῷ, ἐπειδὴ δὲ μέτρων, καὶ μερῶν;"
"πῶς δ' οὔ;" "ἴσων μὲν ἄρα μερῶν ὂν αὑτῷ
ἴσον ἂν τὸ πλῆθος αὑτῷ εἴη, πλειόνων δὲ πλέον,
ἐλαττόνων δὲ ἔλαττον τὸν ἀριθμὸν αὑτοῦ." "φαίνεται." "οὐκοῦν καὶ πρὸς τἆλλα ὡσαύτως ἕξει
τὸ ἕν; ὅτι μὲν μεῖζον αὐτῶν φαίνεται, ἀνάγκη
πλέον εἶναι καὶ τὸν ἀριθμὸν αὐτῶν· ὅτι δὲ σμικρότερον, ἔλαττον· ὅτι δὲ ἴσον μεγέθει, ἴσον καὶ
τὸ πλῆθος εἶναι τοῖς ἄλλοις;" "ἀνάγκη." "οὕτω
E δὴ αὖ, ὡς ἔοικε, τὸ ἕν καὶ ἴσον καὶ πλέον καὶ
ἔλαττον τὸν ἀριθμὸν αὐτό τε αὑτοῦ ἔσται καὶ
τῶν ἄλλων." "ἔσται."

19. "Ἆρ' οὖν καὶ χρόνου μετέχει τὸ ἕν, καὶ
ἐστί τε καὶ γίγνεται νεώτερόν τε καὶ πρεσβύτερον
αὐτό τε ἑαυτοῦ καὶ τῶν ἄλλων, καὶ οὔτε νεώτερον
οὔτε πρεσβύτερον οὔτε ἑαυτοῦ οὔτε τῶν ἄλλων,
χρόνου μετέχον;" "πῶς;" "εἶναι μέν που
αὐτῷ ὑπάρχει, εἴπερ ἕν ἐστιν." "ναί." "τὸ
δὲ εἶναι ἄλλο τί ἐστιν ἢ μέθεξις οὐσίας μετὰ χρόνου
152 τοῦ παρόντος, ὥσπερ τὸ ἦν μετὰ τοῦ παρεληλυ-
θότος καὶ αὖ τὸ ἔσται μετὰ τοῦ μέλλοντος οὐσίας
ἐστὶ κοινωνία;" "ἔστι γάρ." "μετέχει μὲν
ἄρα χρόνου, εἴπερ καὶ τοῦ εἶναι." "πάνυ γε."
"οὐκοῦν πορευομένου τοῦ χρόνου;" "ναί."

282

number to itself and the others." "How is that?"
"If it is greater than any things, it will be of more
measures than they; and of as many parts as
measures. Similarly if it is less or equal, the number
of parts will be less or equal." "True." "Then
one, being greater and less than itself and equal to
itself, will be of more and less measures than itself
and of equal measures with itself, and if of measures,
of parts also?" "Of course." "And being of
equal parts with itself, it will also be equal in number
to itself, and if of more parts, more in number, and
if of less parts, less in number than itself." "Clearly."
"And will not the one possess the same relation
towards other things? Because it is shown to be
greater than they, must it not also be more in
number than they; and because it is smaller, less
in number? And because it is equal in size, must
it not be also equal in number to the others?"
"Yes, it must." "And so once more, as it appears,
the one will be equal to, greater than, and less than
itself and other things in number." "Yes, it will."

"And does the one partake of time; and if it
partakes of time, is it and does it become younger
and older than itself and other things, and neither
younger nor older than itself and the others?"
"What do you mean?" "If one is, it is thereby shown
to be." "Yes." "But is 'to be' anything else
than participation in existence together with present
time, just as 'was' denotes participation in existence
together with past time, and 'will be' similar
participation together with future time?" "True."
"Then the one partakes of time if it partakes of
being." "Certainly." "And the time in which
it partakes is always moving forward?" "Yes."

" ἀεὶ ἄρα πρεσβύτερον γίγνεται ἑαυτοῦ, εἴπερ προέρχεται κατὰ χρόνον." " ἀνάγκη." " ἆρ' οὖν μεμνήμεθα ὅτι νεωτέρου γιγνομένου τὸ πρεσβύτερον πρεσβύτερον γίγνεται; " " μεμνήμεθα." " οὐκοῦν ἐπειδὴ πρεσβύτερον ἑαυτοῦ γίγνεται τὸ

B ἕν, νεωτέρου ἂν γιγνομένου ἑαυτοῦ πρεσβύτερον γίγνοιτο; " " ἀνάγκη." " γίγνεται μὲν δὴ νεώτερόν τε καὶ πρεσβύτερον αὑτοῦ οὕτως." " ναί."
" ἔστι δὲ πρεσβύτερον ἆρ' οὐχ ὅταν κατὰ τὸν νῦν χρόνον ᾖ γιγνόμενον τὸν μεταξὺ τοῦ ἦν τε καὶ ἔσται; οὐ γάρ που πορευόμενόν γε ἐκ τοῦ ποτὲ εἰς τὸ ἔπειτα ὑπερβήσεται τὸ νῦν." " οὐ γάρ."
" ἆρ' οὖν οὐκ ἐπίσχει τότε τοῦ γίγνεσθαι πρε-

C σβύτερον, ἐπειδὰν τῷ νῦν ἐντύχῃ καὶ οὐ γίγνεται, ἀλλ' ἔστι τότ' ἤδη πρεσβύτερον; προϊὸν γὰρ οὐκ ἄν ποτε ληφθείη ὑπὸ τοῦ νῦν. τὸ γὰρ προϊὸν οὕτως ἔχει ὡς ἀμφοτέρων ἐφάπτεσθαι, τοῦ τε νῦν καὶ τοῦ ἔπειτα, τοῦ μὲν νῦν ἀφιέμενον, τοῦ δ' ἔπειτα ἐπιλαμβανόμενον, μεταξὺ ἀμφοτέρων γιγνόμενον, τοῦ τε ἔπειτα καὶ τοῦ νῦν." " ἀληθῆ."
" εἰ δέ γε ἀνάγκη μὴ παρελθεῖν τὸ νῦν πᾶν τὸ γιγνόμενον, ἐπειδὰν κατὰ τοῦτο ᾖ, ἐπίσχει ἀεὶ

D τοῦ γίγνεσθαι καὶ ἔστι τότε τοῦτο ὅ τι ἂν τύχῃ γιγνόμενον." " φαίνεται." " καὶ τὸ ἓν ἄρα, ὅταν πρεσβύτερον γιγνόμενον ἐντύχῃ τῷ νῦν, ἐπέσχεν τοῦ γίγνεσθαι καὶ ἔστι τότε πρεσβύτερον." " πάνυ μὲν οὖν." " οὐκοῦν οὗπερ ἐγίγνετο πρεσβύτερον, τούτου καὶ ἔστιν· ἐγίγνετο δὲ αὑτοῦ; " " ναί."
" ἔστι δὲ τὸ πρεσβύτερον νεωτέρου πρεσβύτερον; " " ἔστιν." " καὶ νεώτερον ἄρα τότε αὑτοῦ ἐστι τὸ ἕν, ὅταν πρεσβύτερον γιγνόμενον ἐντύχῃ τῷ

E νῦν." " ἀνάγκη." " τό γε μὴν νῦν ἀεὶ πάρεστι
284

PARMENIDES

" Then it is always growing older than itself, if it moves forward with the time." " Certainly." " Now, do we not remember that there is something becoming younger when the older becomes older than it ? " " Yes, we do." " Then the one, since it becomes older than itself, would become older than a self which becomes younger ? " " There is no doubt of it." " Thus the one becomes older and younger than itself." " Yes." " And it is older (is it not ?) when in becoming older it is in the present time, between the past and the future ; for in going from the past to the future it cannot avoid the present." " No, it cannot." " Then is it not the case that it ceases to become older when it arrives at the present, and no longer becomes, but actually is older ? For while it moves forward it can never be arrested by the present, since that which moves forward touches both the present and the future, letting the present go and seizing upon the future, proceeding or becoming between the two, the present and the future." " True." " But if everything that is becoming is unable to avoid and pass by the present, then when it reaches the present it always ceases to become and straightway is that which it happens to be becoming." " Clearly." " The one, then, when in becoming older it reaches the present, ceases to become and straightway is older." " Certainly." " It therefore is older than that than which it was becoming older ; and it was becoming older than itself." " Yes." " And that which is older is older than that which is younger, is it not ? " " It is." " Then the one is younger than itself, when in becoming older it reaches the present." " Undoubtedly." " But the present is

285

τῷ ἑνὶ διὰ παντὸς τοῦ εἶναι· ἔστι γὰρ ἀεὶ νῦν ὅτανπερ ᾖ.” “πῶς γὰρ οὔ;” “ἀεὶ ἄρα ἐστί τε καὶ γίγνεται πρεσβύτερον ἑαυτοῦ καὶ νεώτερον τὸ ἕν.” “ἔοικεν.” “πλείω δὲ χρόνον αὐτὸ ἑαυτοῦ ἔστιν ἢ γίγνεται, ἢ τὸν ἴσον;” “τὸν ἴσον.” “ἀλλὰ μὴν τόν γε ἴσον χρόνον ἢ γιγνόμενον ἢ ὂν τὴν αὐτὴν ἡλικίαν ἔχει.” “πῶς δ' οὔ;” “τὸ δὲ τὴν αὐτὴν ἡλικίαν ἔχον οὔτε πρεσβύτερον οὔτε νεώτερόν ἐστιν.” “οὐ γάρ.” “τὸ ἓν ἄρα τὸν ἴσον χρόνον αὐτὸ ἑαυτῷ καὶ γιγνόμενον καὶ ὂν οὔτε νεώτερον οὔτε πρεσβύτερον ἑαυτοῦ ἐστιν οὐδὲ[1] γίγνεται.” “οὔ μοι δοκεῖ.” “τί δέ; τῶν 153 ἄλλων;” “οὐκ ἔχω λέγειν.” “τόδε γε μὴν ἔχεις λέγειν, ὅτι τὰ ἄλλα τοῦ ἑνός, εἴπερ ἕτερά ἐστιν, ἀλλὰ μὴ ἕτερον, πλείω ἐστὶν ἑνός· ἕτερον μὲν γὰρ ὂν ἓν ἂν ἦν· ἕτερα δὲ ὄντα πλείω ἑνός ἐστι καὶ πλῆθος ἂν ἔχοι.” “ἔχοι γὰρ ἄν.” “πλῆθος δὲ ὂν ἀριθμοῦ πλείονος ἂν μετέχοι ἢ τοῦ ἑνός.” “πῶς δ' οὔ;” “τί οὖν; ἀριθμοῦ φήσομεν τὰ πλείω γίγνεσθαί τε καὶ γεγονέναι πρότερον, ἢ τὰ ἐλάττω;” “τὰ ἐλάττω.” “τὸ ὀλίγιστον ἄρα πρῶτον· τοῦτο δ' ἐστὶ τὸ ἕν. ἦ B γάρ;” “ναί.” “πάντων ἄρα τὸ ἓν πρῶτον γέγονε τῶν ἀριθμὸν ἐχόντων. ἔχει δὲ καὶ τἆλλα πάντα ἀριθμόν, εἴπερ ἄλλα καὶ μὴ ἄλλο ἐστίν.” “ἔχει γάρ.” “πρῶτον δέ γε, οἶμαι, γεγονὸς πρότερον γέγονε, τὰ δὲ ἄλλα ὕστερον· τὰ δ' ὕστερον γεγονότα νεώτερα τοῦ πρότερον γεγονότος· καὶ οὕτως ἂν εἴη τἆλλα νεώτερα τοῦ ἑνός,

---

[1] οὐδὲ Heindorf: οὔτε B.

PARMENIDES

inseparable from the one throughout its whole existence ; for it always is now whenever it is." " Of course." " Always, then, the one is and is becoming younger than itself." " So it appears." " And is it or does it become for a longer time than itself, or for an equal time ? " " For an equal time." " But that which is or becomes for an equal time is of the same age." " Of course." " But that which is of the same age is neither older nor younger." " No." " Then the one, since it is and becomes for an equal time with itself, neither is nor becomes older or younger than itself." " I agree." " Well, then, is it or does it become older or younger than other things ? " " I cannot tell." " But you can at any rate tell that the others, if they are others, not an other—plural, not singular—are more than one ; for if they were an other, they would be one ; but since they are others, they are more than one and have multitude." " Yes, they have." " And being a multitude, they would partake of a number greater than one." " Of course." " Well, which shall we say come and have come into being first, the greater or the smaller numbers ? " " The smaller." Then the smallest comes into being first ; and that is the one, is it not ? " " Yes." " The one, therefore, has come into being first of all things that have number ; but all others also have number, if they are others and not an other." " They have." " And since it came into being first, it came into being, I suppose, before the others, and the others later ; but things which have come into being later are younger than that which came into being before them ; and thus the other things would be younger than the one,

287

τὸ δὲ ἓν πρεσβύτερον τῶν ἄλλων." "εἴη γὰρ
ἄν."

20. "Τί δὲ τόδε; ἆρ' ἂν εἴη τὸ ἓν παρὰ φύσιν
τὴν αὑτοῦ γεγονός, ἢ ἀδύνατον;" "ἀδύνατον."
C "ἀλλὰ μὴν μέρη γε ἔχον ἐφάνη τὸ ἕν, εἰ δὲ μέρη,
καὶ ἀρχὴν καὶ τελευτὴν καὶ μέσον." "ναί."
"οὐκοῦν πάντων πρῶτον ἀρχὴ γίγνεται, καὶ
αὐτοῦ τοῦ ἑνὸς καὶ ἑκάστου τῶν ἄλλων, καὶ μετὰ
τὴν ἀρχὴν καὶ τἆλλα πάντα μέχρι τοῦ τέλους;"
"τί μήν;" "καὶ μὴν μόριά γε φήσομεν ταῦτ'
εἶναι πάντα τἆλλα τοῦ ὅλου τε καὶ ἑνός, αὐτὸ δὲ
ἐκεῖνο ἅμα τῇ τελευτῇ γεγονέναι ἕν τε καὶ ὅλον."
"φήσομεν γάρ." "τελευτὴ δέ γε, οἶμαι, ὕστατον γίγνεται· τούτῳ δ' ἅμα τὸ ἓν πέφυκε γί-
D γνεσθαι· ὥστ' εἴπερ ἀνάγκη αὐτὸ τὸ ἓν μὴ παρὰ
φύσιν γίγνεσθαι, ἅμα τελευτῇ ἂν γεγονὸς ὕστατον
ἂν τῶν ἄλλων πεφυκὸς εἴη γίγνεσθαι." "φαίνεται." "νεώτερον ἄρα τῶν ἄλλων τὸ ἕν ἐστι, τὰ
δ' ἄλλα τοῦ ἑνὸς πρεσβύτερα." "οὕτως αὖ μοι
φαίνεται." "τί δὲ δή; ἀρχὴν ἢ ἄλλο μέρος
ὁτιοῦν τοῦ ἑνὸς ἢ ἄλλου ὁτουοῦν, ἐάνπερ μέρος
ᾖ ἀλλὰ μὴ μέρη, οὐκ ἀναγκαῖον ἓν εἶναι, μέρος
γε ὄν;" "ἀνάγκη." "οὐκοῦν τὸ ἓν ἅμα τε τῷ
E πρώτῳ γιγνομένῳ γίγνοιτ' ἂν καὶ ἅμα τῷ δευ-
τέρῳ, καὶ οὐδενὸς ἀπολείπεται τῶν ἄλλων γιγνο-
μένων, ὅτιπερ ἂν προσγίγνηται ὁτῳοῦν, ἕως ἂν
πρὸς τὸ ἔσχατον διελθὸν ὅλον ἓν γένηται, οὔτε
μέσου οὔτε πρώτου οὔτε ἐσχάτου οὔτε ἄλλου
οὐδενὸς ἀπολειφθὲν ἐν τῇ γενέσει." "ἀληθῆ."
288

and the one older than the other things." "Yes, they would."

"Here is another question : Can the one have come into being contrary to its own nature, or is that impossible ? " " It is impossible." " But surely the one was shown to have parts, a beginning, a middle, and an end." "Yes." " And the beginning of everything—of one and everything else alike—comes into being first, and after the beginning come all the other parts until the end arrives, do they not ? " " Certainly." " And we shall say also that all these others are parts of the whole and the one, and that it has become one and whole at the moment when the end arrives." "Yes, we shall say that." " The end, I imagine, comes into being last ; and at that moment the one naturally comes into being ; so that if the absolute one cannot come into being contrary to its own nature, since it has come into being simultaneously with the end, its nature must be such that it comes into being after all the others." " That is clear." " Then the one is younger than the others and the others are older than the one." " I think that is clear, too." " Well, must not a beginning or any other part whatsoever of one or of anything else whatsoever, if it be a part, not parts, be one, since it is a part ? " " It must." " Then the one would come into being simultaneously with the first part and with the second, and it is not wanting in any part which comes into being in addition to any part whatsoever which may precede it, until it reaches the end and becomes complete one ; it will not be wanting in the middle, nor in the first, nor in the last, nor in any other part in the process of coming into

PLATO

" πᾶσιν ἄρα τοῖς ἄλλοις τὴν αὐτὴν ἡλικίαν ἴσχει
τὸ ἕν. ὥστ' εἰ μὴ παρὰ φύσιν πέφυκεν αὐτὸ τὸ
ἕν, οὔτε πρότερον οὔτε ὕστερον τῶν ἄλλων γεγονὸς
154 ἂν εἴη, ἀλλ' ἅμα. καὶ κατὰ τοῦτον τὸν λόγον τὸ
ἕν τῶν ἄλλων οὔτε πρεσβύτερον οὔτε νεώτερον ἂν
εἴη, οὐδὲ τἆλλα τοῦ ἑνός· κατὰ δὲ τὸν πρόσθεν
πρεσβύτερόν τε καὶ νεώτερον, καὶ τἆλλα ἐκείνου
ὡσαύτως." " πάνυ μὲν οὖν." " ἔστι μὲν δὴ
οὕτως ἔχον τε καὶ γεγονός. ἀλλὰ τί αὖ περὶ τοῦ
γίγνεσθαι αὐτὸ πρεσβύτερόν τε καὶ νεώτερον τῶν
ἄλλων καὶ τἆλλα τοῦ ἑνός, καὶ μήτε νεώτερον
μήτε πρεσβύτερον γίγνεσθαι; ἆρα ὥσπερ περὶ
τοῦ εἶναι, οὕτω καὶ περὶ τοῦ γίγνεσθαι ἔχει, ἢ
B ἑτέρως;" " οὐκ ἔχω λέγειν." " ἀλλ' ἐγὼ τοσόν-
δε γε, ὅτι εἰ καὶ ἔστιν πρεσβύτερον ἕτερον
ἑτέρου, γίγνεσθαί γε αὐτὸ πρεσβύτερον ἔτι ἢ ὡς
τὸ πρῶτον εὐθὺς γενόμενον διήνεγκε τῇ ἡλικίᾳ
οὐκ ἂν ἔτι δύναιτο, οὐδ' αὖ τὸ νεώτερον ὂν ἔτι
νεώτερον γίγνεσθαι· ἀνίσοις γὰρ ἴσα προστι-
θέμενα, χρόνῳ τε καὶ ἄλλῳ ὁτῳοῦν, ἴσῳ ποιεῖ
διαφέρειν ἀεὶ ὅσῳπερ ἂν τὸ πρῶτον διενέγκῃ."
" πῶς γὰρ οὔ;" " οὐκ ἄρα τό γε ὂν τοῦ¹ ὄντος
C γίγνοιτ' ἄν ποτε πρεσβύτερον οὐδὲ νεώτερον,
εἴπερ ἴσῳ διαφέρει ἀεὶ τὴν ἡλικίαν· ἀλλ' ἔστι καὶ
γέγονε πρεσβύτερον, τὸ δὲ νεώτερον, γίγνεται δ'
οὔ." " ἀληθῆ." " καὶ τὸ ἓν ἄρα ὂν τῶν ἄλλων
ὄντων οὔτε πρεσβύτερόν ποτε οὔτε νεώτερον
γίγνεται." " οὐ γὰρ οὖν." " ὅρα δέ, εἰ τῇδε
πρεσβύτερα καὶ νεώτερα γίγνεται." " πῇ δή;"

¹ τοῦ ἑνὸς BT : ἑνὸς secl. Schleiermacher.

being." "True." "Then one has the same age as all the others; so that the absolute one, unless it is naturally contrary to nature, could not have come into being either before or after the others, but only simultaneously with them. And by this reasoning the one would be neither older nor younger than the others nor the others than the one, but of the same age; but by the previous reasoning the one would be both older and younger than the others, and likewise the others than the one." "Certainly." "In this state, then, it is and in this way it has come into being. But what about the one becoming older and younger than the others, and the others than the one, and becoming neither older nor younger? Is it the same with becoming as with being, or otherwise?" "I cannot say." "But I can say as much as this, that even if one thing be older than another, it cannot become older by any greater difference in age than that which existed at first, nor if younger can it become younger by any greater difference; for the addition of equals to unequals, whether in time or anything else whatsoever, makes the difference always equal to that which existed at first." "Yes, of course." "Then that which exists can never become older or younger than that which exists, if the difference in age is always the same; but it is and has become older, and the other is and has become younger, but it does not become so." "True." "And the one, since it exists, never becomes either older or younger than the other things." "No, it does not." "But see whether they become older and younger in this way" "In what way?" "Because the one was

PLATO

" ἢ τό τε ἓν τῶν ἄλλων ἐφάνη πρεσβύτερον καὶ
τἆλλα τοῦ ἑνός." "τί οὖν;" "ὅταν τὸ ἓν τῶν
D ἄλλων πρεσβύτερον ᾖ, πλείω που χρόνον γέγονεν
ἢ τὰ ἄλλα." "ναί." "πάλιν δὴ σκόπει· ἐὰν
πλέονι καὶ ἐλάττονι χρόνῳ προστιθῶμεν τὸν ἴσον
χρόνον, ἆρα τῷ ἴσῳ μορίῳ διοίσει τὸ πλέον τοῦ
ἐλάττονος ἢ σμικροτέρῳ;" "σμικροτέρῳ." "οὐκ
ἄρα ἔσται, ὅτιπερ τὸ πρῶτον ἦν πρὸς τἆλλα
ἡλικίᾳ διαφέρον τὸ ἕν, τοῦτο καὶ εἰς τὸ ἔπειτα,
ἀλλὰ ἴσον λαμβάνον χρόνον τοῖς ἄλλοις ἔλαττον
ἀεὶ τῇ ἡλικίᾳ διοίσει αὐτῶν ἢ πρότερον· ἢ οὔ;"
E "ναί." "οὐκοῦν τό γε ἔλαττον διαφέρον ἡλικίᾳ
πρός τι ἢ πρότερον νεώτερον γίγνοιτ' ἂν ἢ ἐν τῷ
πρόσθεν πρὸς ἐκεῖνα πρὸς ἃ ἦν πρεσβύτερον
πρότερον;" "νεώτερον." "εἰ δὲ ἐκεῖνο νεώτερον, οὐκ ἐκεῖνα αὖ τὰ ἄλλα πρὸς τὸ ἓν πρεσβύτερα
ἢ πρότερον;" "πάνυ γε." "τὸ μὲν νεώτερον
ἄρα γεγονὸς πρεσβύτερον γίγνεται πρὸς τὸ πρότερον γεγονός τε καὶ πρεσβύτερον ὄν, ἔστι δὲ οὐδέποτε πρεσβύτερον, ἀλλὰ γίγνεται ἀεὶ ἐκείνου
πρεσβύτερον· ἐκεῖνο μὲν γὰρ ἐπὶ τὸ νεώτερον
155 ἐπιδίδωσιν, τὸ δ' ἐπὶ τὸ πρεσβύτερον. τὸ δ' αὖ
πρεσβύτερον τοῦ νεωτέρου νεώτερον γίγνεται
ὡσαύτως. ἰόντε γὰρ αὐτοῖν εἰς τὸ ἐναντίον τὸ
ἐναντίον ἀλλήλοιν γίγνεσθον, τὸ μὲν νεώτερον
πρεσβύτερον τοῦ πρεσβυτέρου, τὸ δὲ πρεσβύτερον
νεώτερον τοῦ νεωτέρου· γενέσθαι δὲ οὐκ ἂν οἴω
τε εἴτην. εἰ γὰρ γένοιντο, οὐκ ἂν ἔτι γίγνοιντο,
ἀλλ' εἶεν ἄν. νῦν δὲ γίγνονται μὲν πρεσβύτερα

found to be older than the others, and the others than the one." "What then?" "When the one is older than the others, it has come into being a longer time than the others." "Yes." "Then consider again. If we add an equal to a greater and to a less time, will the greater differ from the less by the same or by a smaller fraction?" "By a smaller fraction." "Then the proportional difference in age which existed originally between the one and the others will not continue afterwards, but if an equal time be added to the one and the others, the difference in their ages will constantly diminish, will it not?" "Yes." "And that which differs less in age from something than before becomes younger than before in relation to those things than which it formerly was older?" "Yes, it becomes younger." "But if the one becomes younger, must not those other things in turn become older than formerly in relation to the one?" "'Certainly." "Then that which came into being later, becomes older in relation to the older, which came into being earlier; yet it never is older, but is always becoming older; for the latter always tends towards being younger, and the former towards being older. And conversely the older becomes in the same way younger than the younger. For as they are moving in opposite directions, they are becoming the opposites of one another, the younger older than the older, and the older younger than the younger; but they cannot finish the process of becoming; for if they finished the process of becoming, they would no longer be becoming, they would be. But as the case is, they become older and younger than one another

ἀλλήλων καὶ νεώτερα· τὸ μὲν ἓν τῶν ἄλλων
νεώτερον γίγνεται, ὅτι πρεσβύτερον ἐφάνη ὂν καὶ
B πρότερον γεγονός, τὰ δὲ ἄλλα τοῦ ἑνὸς πρεσβύτερα, ὅτι ὕστερα γέγονε. κατὰ δὲ τὸν αὐτὸν
λόγον καὶ τἆλλα οὕτω πρὸς τὸ ἓν ἴσχει, ἐπειδήπερ
αὐτοῦ πρεσβύτερα ἐφάνη καὶ πρότερα γεγονότα."
"φαίνεται γὰρ οὖν οὕτως." "οὐκοῦν ᾗ μὲν
οὐδὲν ἕτερον ἑτέρου πρεσβύτερον γίγνεται οὐδὲ
νεώτερον, κατὰ τὸ ἴσῳ ἀριθμῷ ἀλλήλων ἀεὶ
διαφέρειν, οὔτε τὸ ἓν τῶν ἄλλων πρεσβύτερον
γίγνοιτ᾽ ἂν οὐδὲ νεώτερον, οὔτε τἆλλα τοῦ ἑνός·
ᾗ δὲ ἄλλῳ ἀεὶ μορίῳ διαφέρειν ἀνάγκη τὰ πρότερα
C τῶν ὑστέρων γενόμενα καὶ τὰ ὕστερα τῶν προτέρων, ταύτῃ δὴ ἀνάγκη πρεσβύτερά τε καὶ
νεώτερα ἀλλήλων γίγνεσθαι τά τε ἄλλα τοῦ ἑνὸς
καὶ τὸ ἓν τῶν ἄλλων;" "πάνυ μὲν οὖν." "κατὰ
δὴ πάντα ταῦτα τὸ ἓν αὐτό τε αὑτοῦ καὶ τῶν
ἄλλων πρεσβύτερον καὶ νεώτερον ἔστι τε καὶ
γίγνεται, καὶ οὔτε πρεσβύτερον οὔτε νεώτερον
οὔτ᾽ ἔστιν οὔτε γίγνεται οὔτε αὑτοῦ οὔτε τῶν
ἄλλων." "παντελῶς μὲν οὖν." "ἐπειδὴ δὲ
χρόνου μετέχει τὸ ἓν καὶ τοῦ πρεσβύτερόν τε καὶ
D νεώτερον γίγνεσθαι, ἆρ᾽ οὐκ ἀνάγκη καὶ τοῦ ποτὲ
μετέχειν καὶ τοῦ ἔπειτα καὶ τοῦ νῦν, εἴπερ χρόνου
μετέχει;" "ἀνάγκη." "ἦν ἄρα τὸ ἓν καὶ ἔστι
καὶ ἔσται καὶ ἐγίγνετο καὶ γίγνεται καὶ γενήσεται."
"τί μήν;" "καὶ εἴη ἄν τι ἐκείνῳ καὶ ἐκείνου,
καὶ ἦν καὶ ἔστιν καὶ ἔσται." "πάνυ γε." "καὶ
ἐπιστήμη δὴ εἴη ἂν αὐτοῦ καὶ δόξα καὶ αἴσθησις,
εἴπερ καὶ νῦν ἡμεῖς περὶ αὐτοῦ πάντα ταῦτα
πράττομεν." "ὀρθῶς λέγεις." "καὶ ὄνομα δὴ

—the one becomes younger than the others, because, as we saw, it is older and came into being earlier, and the others are becoming older than the one, because they came into being later. By the same reasoning the others stand in the same relation to the one, since they were seen to be older than the one and to have come into being earlier." "Yes, that is clear." "Then from the point of view that no one thing becomes older or younger than another, inasmuch as they always differ by an equal number, the one cannot become older or younger than the others, nor the others than the one ; but in so far as that which comes into being earlier must always differ by a different proportional part from that which comes into being later, and *vice versa*—from this point of view the one and the others must necessarily become both older and younger than one another, must they not ? " "Certainly." "For all these reasons, then, the one both is and becomes both older and younger than both itself and the others, and neither is nor becomes either older or younger than either itself or the others." "Perfectly true." "But since the one partakes of time and can become older and younger, must it not also partake of the past, the future, and the present ? " "It must." "Then the one was and is and will be and was becoming and is becoming and will become." "Certainly." "And there would be and was and is and will be something which is in relation to it and belongs to it ? " "Certainly." "And there would be knowledge and opinion and perception of it ; there must be, if we are now carrying on all this discussion about it." "You are right." "And it has a

καὶ λόγος ἔστιν αὐτῷ, καὶ ὀνομάζεται καὶ λέγεται·
Ε καὶ ὅσαπερ καὶ περὶ τὰ ἄλλα τῶν τοιούτων τυγχάνει ὄντα, καὶ περὶ τὸ ἓν ἔστιν." "παντελῶς
μὲν οὖν ἔχει οὕτως."

21. "Ἔτι δὴ τὸ τρίτον λέγωμεν. τὸ ἓν εἰ
ἔστιν οἷον διεληλύθαμεν, ἆρ᾽ οὐκ ἀνάγκη αὐτό,
ἕν τε ὂν καὶ πολλὰ καὶ μήτε ἓν μήτε πολλὰ καὶ
μετέχον χρόνου, ὅτι μὲν ἔστιν ἕν, οὐσίας μετέχειν
ποτέ, ὅτι δ᾽ οὐκ ἔστι, μὴ μετέχειν αὖ ποτὲ οὐσίας;"
"ἀνάγκη." "ἆρ᾽ οὖν, ὅτε μετέχει, οἷόν τε ἔσται
τότε μὴ μετέχειν, ἢ ὅτε μὴ μετέχει, μετέχειν;"
"οὐχ οἷόν τε." "ἐν ἄλλῳ ἄρα χρόνῳ μετέχει
καὶ ἐν ἄλλῳ οὐ μετέχει· οὕτω γὰρ ἂν μόνως τοῦ
156 αὐτοῦ μετέχοι τε καὶ οὐ μετέχοι." "ὀρθῶς."
"οὐκοῦν ἔστι καὶ οὗτος χρόνος, ὅτε μεταλαμβάνει τοῦ εἶναι καὶ ὅτε ἀπαλλάττεται αὐτοῦ; ἢ
πῶς οἷόν τε ἔσται τοτὲ μὲν ἔχειν τὸ αὐτό, τοτὲ
δὲ μὴ ἔχειν, ἐὰν μή ποτε καὶ λαμβάνῃ αὐτὸ καὶ
ἀφίῃ;" "οὐδαμῶς." "τὸ δὴ οὐσίας μεταλαμβάνειν ἆρά γε οὐ γίγνεσθαι καλεῖς;" "ἔγωγε."
"τὸ δὲ ἀπαλλάττεσθαι οὐσίας ἆρα οὐκ ἀπόλλυσθαι;" "καὶ πάνυ γε." "τὸ ἓν δή, ὡς ἔοικε,
λαμβάνον τε καὶ ἀφιὲν οὐσίαν γίγνεταί τε καὶ
Β ἀπόλλυται." "ἀνάγκη." "ἓν δὲ καὶ πολλὰ ὂν
καὶ γιγνόμενον καὶ ἀπολλύμενον ἆρ᾽ οὐχ, ὅταν
μὲν γίγνηται ἕν, τὸ πολλὰ εἶναι ἀπόλλυται, ὅταν
δὲ πολλά, τὸ ἓν εἶναι ἀπόλλυται;" "πάνυ γε."
"ἓν δὲ γιγνόμενον καὶ πολλὰ ἆρ᾽ οὐκ ἀνάγκη
διακρίνεσθαί τε καὶ συγκρίνεσθαι;" "πολλή γε."
"καὶ μὴν ἀνόμοιόν γε καὶ ὅμοιον ὅταν γίγνηται,
ὁμοιοῦσθαί τε καὶ ἀνομοιοῦσθαι;" "ναί." "καὶ
ὅταν μεῖζον καὶ ἔλαττον καὶ ἴσον, αὐξάνεσθαί τε

name and definition, is named and defined, and all
the similar attributes which pertain to other things
pertain also to the one." " That is perfectly true."
    " Let us discuss the matter once more and for
the third· time. If the one is such as we have
described it, being both one and many and neither
one nor many, and partakes of time, must it not,
because one is, sometimes partake of being, and
again because one is not, sometimes not partake
of being ? " " Yes, it must." " And can one,
when it partakes of being, not partake of it, or partake
of it when it does not partake of it ? " " No, it
cannot." " Then it partakes at one time and does
not partake at another ; for that is the only way
in which it can partake and not partake of the same
thing." " True." " And is there not also a time
when it assumes being and when it gives it up ?
How can it sometimes have and sometimes not have
the same thing, unless it receives it at some time
and again loses it ? " " There is no other way at all."
" But would you not say that receiving existence
is generation or becoming ? " " Yes." " And losing
existence is destruction ? " " Certainly." " The
one, then, as it appears, since it receives and loses
existence, is generated and destroyed." " Inevitably." " And being one and many and being
generated and destroyed, when it becomes one
its existence as many is destroyed, and when it
becomes many its existence as one is destroyed, is
it not ? " " Certainly." " And in becoming one
and many, must it not be separated and combined ? "
" Inevitably." " And when it becomes like and
unlike, it must be assimilated and dissimilated ? "
" Yes." " And when it becomes greater and

PLATO

C καὶ φθίνειν καὶ ἰσοῦσθαι;" "οὕτως." "ὅταν
δὲ κινούμενόν τε ἵστηται καὶ ὅταν ἑστὸς ἐπὶ τὸ
κινεῖσθαι μεταβάλλῃ, δεῖ δή που αὐτό γε μηδ᾽
ἐν ἑνὶ χρόνῳ εἶναι." "πῶς δή;" "ἑστός τε
πρότερον ὕστερον κινεῖσθαι καὶ πρότερον κινούμενον ὕστερον ἑστάναι, ἄνευ μὲν τοῦ μεταβάλλειν
οὐχ οἷόν τε ἔσται ταῦτα πάσχειν." "πῶς γάρ;"
"χρόνος δέ γε οὐδεὶς ἔστιν, ἐν ᾧ τι οἷόν τε ἅμα
μήτε κινεῖσθαι μήτε ἑστάναι." "οὐ γὰρ οὖν."
"ἀλλ᾽ οὐδὲ μὴν μεταβάλλει ἄνευ τοῦ μεταβάλλειν." "οὐκ εἰκός." "πότ᾽ οὖν μεταβάλλει;
οὔτε γὰρ ἑστὸς ὂν[1] οὔτε κινούμενον μεταβάλλει
D οὔτε ἐν χρόνῳ ὄν." "οὐ γὰρ οὖν." "ἆρ᾽ οὖν
ἔστι τὸ ἄτοπον τοῦτο, ἐν ᾧ τότ᾽ ἂν εἴη, ὅτε μεταβάλλει;" "τὸ ποῖον δή;" "τὸ ἐξαίφνης. τὸ
γὰρ ἐξαίφνης τοιόνδε τι ἔοικε σημαίνειν, ὡς ἐξ
ἐκείνου μεταβάλλον εἰς ἑκάτερον. οὐ γὰρ ἔκ γε
τοῦ ἑστάναι ἑστῶτος ἔτι μεταβάλλει, οὐδ᾽ ἐκ τῆς
κινήσεως κινουμένης ἔτι μεταβάλλει· ἀλλὰ ἡ ἐξαίφνης αὕτη φύσις ἄτοπός τις ἐγκάθηται μεταξὺ
E τῆς κινήσεώς τε καὶ στάσεως, ἐν χρόνῳ οὐδενὶ
οὖσα, καὶ εἰς ταύτην δὴ καὶ ἐκ ταύτης τό τε
κινούμενον μεταβάλλει ἐπὶ τὸ ἑστάναι καὶ τὸ
ἑστὸς ἐπὶ τὸ κινεῖσθαι." "κινδυνεύει." "καὶ
τὸ ἓν δή, εἴπερ ἕστηκέ τε καὶ κινεῖται, μεταβάλλοι ἂν ἐφ᾽ ἑκάτερα· μόνως γὰρ ἂν οὕτως
ἀμφότερα ποιοῖ· μεταβάλλον δ᾽ ἐξαίφνης μεταβάλλει, καὶ ὅτε μεταβάλλει, ἐν οὐδενὶ χρόνῳ ἂν
εἴη, οὐδὲ κινοῖτ᾽ ἂν τότε, οὐδ᾽ ἂν σταίη." "οὐ
γάρ." "ἆρ᾽ οὖν οὕτω καὶ πρὸς τὰς ἄλλας μετα-
βολὰς ἔχει, ὅταν ἐκ τοῦ εἶναι εἰς τὸ ἀπόλλυσθαι

[1] ὂν B : ἂν T.

298

smaller and equal, it must be increased and diminished
and equalized ? " " Yes." " And when being in
motion it comes to rest, and when being at rest it
changes to motion, it must itself be in no time at
all." " How is that ? " " It is impossible for it to
be previously at rest and afterwards in motion, or
previously in motion and afterwards at rest, without
changing." " Of course." " And there is no time
in which anything can be at once neither in motion
nor at rest." " No, there is none." " And certainly
it cannot change without changing." " I should
say not." " Then when does it change ? For it
does not change when it is at rest or when
it is in motion or when it is in time." " No, it
does not." " Does this strange thing, then, exist,
in which it would be at the moment when it changes ?'
" What sort of thing is that ? " " The instant.
For the instant seems to indicate a something from
which there is a change in one direction or the
other. For it does not change from rest while it
is still at rest, nor from motion while it is still
moving ; but there is this strange instantaneous
nature, something interposed between motion and
rest, not existing in any time, and into this and out
from this that which is in motion changes into rest
and that which is at rest changes into motion."
" Yes, that must be so." " Then the one, if it is
at rest and in motion, must change in each direction ;
for that is the only way in which it can do both.
But in changing, it changes instantaneously, and when
it changes it can be in no time, and at that instant
it will be neither in motion nor at rest." " No."
" And will the case not be the same in relation
to other changes ? When it changes from being

PLATO

157 μεταβάλλῃ ἢ ἐκ τοῦ μὴ εἶναι εἰς τὸ γίγνεσθαι,
μεταξύ τινων τότε γίγνεται κινήσεών τε καὶ
στάσεων, καὶ οὔτε ἔστι τότε οὔτε οὐκ ἔστι, οὔτε
γίγνεται οὔτε ἀπόλλυται;" "ἔοικε γοῦν."
"κατὰ δὴ τὸν αὐτὸν λόγον καὶ ἐξ ἑνὸς ἐπὶ πολλὰ
ἰὸν καὶ ἐκ πολλῶν ἐφ᾽ ἓν οὔτε ἕν ἐστιν οὔτε πολλά,
οὔτε διακρίνεται οὔτε συγκρίνεται. καὶ ἐξ ὁμοίου
ἐπὶ ἀνόμοιον καὶ ἐξ ἀνομοίου ἐπὶ ὅμοιον ἰὸν οὔτε
ὅμοιον οὔτε ἀνόμοιον, οὔτε ὁμοιούμενον οὔτε
B ἀνομοιούμενον· καὶ ἐκ σμικροῦ ἐπὶ μέγα καὶ ἐπὶ
ἴσον καὶ εἰς τὰ ἐναντία ἰὸν οὔτε σμικρὸν οὔτε
μέγα οὔτε ἴσον, οὔτε αὐξανόμενον οὔτε φθῖνον
οὔτε ἰσούμενον εἴη ἄν." "οὐκ ἔοικε." "ταῦτα
δὴ τὰ παθήματα πάντ᾽ ἂν πάσχοι τὸ ἕν, εἰ ἔστιν."
"πῶς δ᾽ οὔ;"

22. "Τί δὲ τοῖς ἄλλοις προσήκοι ἂν πάσχειν,
ἓν εἰ ἔστιν, ἆρα οὐ σκεπτέον;" "σκεπτέον."
"λέγωμεν δή, ἓν εἰ ἔστι, τἆλλα τοῦ ἑνὸς τί χρὴ
πεπονθέναι;" "λέγωμεν." "οὐκοῦν ἐπείπερ
ἄλλα τοῦ ἑνός ἐστιν, οὔτε τὸ ἕν ἐστι τἆλλα· οὐ
γὰρ ἂν ἄλλα τοῦ ἑνὸς ἦν." "ὀρθῶς." "οὐδὲ
C μὴν στέρεταί γε παντάπασι τοῦ ἑνὸς τἆλλα, ἀλλὰ
μετέχει πῃ." "πῇ δή;" "ὅτι που τὰ ἄλλα τοῦ
ἑνὸς μόρια ἔχοντα ἄλλα ἐστίν· εἰ γὰρ μόρια μὴ
ἔχοι, παντελῶς ἂν ἓν εἴη." "ὀρθῶς." "μόρια
δέ γε, φαμέν, τούτου ἐστίν ὃ ἂν ὅλον ᾖ." "φαμὲν γάρ." "ἀλλὰ μὴν τό γε ὅλον ἓν ἐκ πολλῶν
ἀνάγκη εἶναι, οὗ ἔσται μόρια τὰ μόρια. ἕκαστον
γὰρ τῶν μορίων οὐ πολλῶν μόριον χρὴ εἶναι,
300

to destruction or from not being to becoming, does it not pass into an intermediate stage between certain forms of motion and rest, so that it neither is nor is not, neither comes into being nor is destroyed ? " " Yes, so it appears." " And on the same principle, when it passes from one to many or from many to one, it is neither one nor many, is neither in a process of separation nor in one of combination. And in passing from like to unlike or from unlike to like, it is neither like nor unlike, neither in a process of assimilation nor in one of dissimilation ; and in passing from small to great and to equal and *vice versa*, it is neither small nor great nor equal, neither in a process of increase, nor of diminution, nor of equality " " Apparently not." " All this, then, would happen to the one, if the one exists." " Yes, certainly."

" Must we not consider what is likely to happen to the other things, if the one exists ? " " We must." " Shall we tell, then, what must happen to the things other than one, if one exists ? " " Let us do so." " Well, since they are other than the one, the other things are not the one ; for if they were, they would not be other than the one." " True." " And yet surely the others are not altogether deprived of the one, but they partake of it in a certain way." " In what way ? " " Because the others are other than the one by reason of having parts ; for if they had no parts, they would be altogether one." " True." " But parts, we affirm, belong to that which is a whole." " Yes, we affirm that they do." " But the whole must be one composed of many ; and of this the parts are parts. For each of the parts must be a part, not

ἀλλὰ ὅλου." "πῶς τοῦτο;" "εἴ τι πολλῶν
μόριον εἴη, ἐν οἷς αὐτὸ εἴη, ἑαυτοῦ τε δή που
D μόριον ἔσται, ὃ ἔστιν ἀδύνατον, καὶ τῶν ἄλλων δὴ
ἑνὸς ἑκάστου, εἴπερ καὶ πάντων. ἑνὸς γὰρ μὴ ὂν
μόριον, πλὴν τούτου τῶν ἄλλων ἔσται, καὶ οὕτως
ἑνὸς ἑκάστου οὐκ ἔσται μόριον, μὴ ὂν δὲ μόριον
ἑκάστου οὐδενὸς τῶν πολλῶν ἔσται. μηδενὸς δὲ
ὂν πάντων τούτων τι εἶναι, ὧν οὐδενὸς οὐδέν ἐστι,
καὶ μόριον καὶ ἄλλο ὁτιοῦν ἀδύνατον.[1]" "φαίνεταί γε δή." "οὐκ ἄρα τῶν πολλῶν οὐδὲ πάντων τὸ μόριον μόριον, ἀλλὰ μιᾶς τινὸς ἰδέας καὶ
E ἑνός τινος, ὃ καλοῦμεν ὅλον, ἐξ ἁπάντων ἓν τέλειον
γεγονός, τούτου μόριον ἂν τὸ μόριον εἴη." "παντάπασι μὲν οὖν." "εἰ ἄρα τἆλλα μόρια ἔχει, κἂν
τοῦ ὅλου τε καὶ ἑνὸς μετέχοι." "πάνυ γε." "ἓν
ἄρα ὅλον τέλειον μόρια ἔχον ἀνάγκη εἶναι τἆλλα
τοῦ ἑνός." "ἀνάγκη." "καὶ μὴν καὶ περὶ τοῦ
μορίου γε ἑκάστου ὁ αὐτὸς λόγος. καὶ γὰρ τοῦτο
ἀνάγκη μετέχειν τοῦ ἑνός. εἰ γὰρ ἕκαστον αὐτῶν
158 μόριόν ἐστι, τό γε ἕκαστον εἶναι ἓν δήπου σημαίνει, ἀφωρισμένον μὲν τῶν ἄλλων, καθ' αὑτὸ δὲ
ὄν, εἴπερ ἕκαστον ἔσται." "ὀρθῶς." "μετέχοι
δέ γε ἂν τοῦ ἑνὸς δῆλον ὅτι ἄλλο ὂν ἢ ἕν· οὐ γὰρ
ἂν μετεῖχεν, ἀλλ' ἦν ἂν αὐτὸ ἕν· νῦν δὲ ἑνὶ μὲν
εἶναι πλὴν αὐτῷ τῷ ἑνὶ ἀδύνατόν που." "ἀδύνατον." "μετέχειν δέ γε τοῦ ἑνὸς ἀνάγκη τῷ τε
ὅλῳ καὶ τῷ μορίῳ. τὸ μὲν γὰρ ἓν ὅλον ἔσται, οὗ
μόρια τὰ μόρια· τὸ δ' αὖ ἕκαστον ἓν μόριον τοῦ

---

[1] ἀδύνατον εἶναι BT : εἶναι secl. Heindorf.

PARMENIDES

of many, but of a whole." "How is that?" "If anything is a part of many, and is itself one of the many, it will be a part of itself, which is impossible, and of each one of the others, if it is a part of all. For if it is not a part of some particular one, it will be a part of the rest, with the exception of that one, and thus it will not be a part of each one, and not being a part of each one, it will not be a part of any one of the many. But that which belongs to none cannot belong, whether as a part or as anything else, to all those things to none of which it belongs." "That is clear." "Then the part is a part, not of the many nor of all, but of a single form and a single concept which we call a whole, a perfect unity created out of all; this it is of which the part is a part." "Certainly." "If, then, the others have parts, they will partake of the whole and of the one." "True." "Then the things which are other than one must be a perfect whole which has parts." "Yes, they must." "And the same reasoning applies to each part; for the part must partake of the one. For if each of the parts is a part, the word 'each' implies that it is one, separated from the rest, and existing by itself; otherwise it will not be 'each.'" "True." "But its participation in the one clearly implies that it is other than the one, for if not, it would not partake of the one, but would actually be one; but really it is impossible for anything except one itself to be one." "Yes, it is impossible." "And both the whole and the part must necessarily participate in the one; for the one will be a whole of which the parts are parts, and again each individual one which is a part of a whole will be a part of the

303

PLATO

ὅλου, ὃ ἂν ᾖ μόριον ὅλου." "οὕτως." "οὐκοῦν
B ἕτερα ὄντα τοῦ ἑνὸς μεθέξει τὰ μετέχοντα αὐτοῦ;"
"πῶς δ' οὔ;" "τὰ δ' ἕτερα τοῦ ἑνὸς πολλά που
ἂν εἴη. εἰ γὰρ μήτε ἓν μήτε ἑνὸς πλείω εἴη τἆλλα
τοῦ ἑνός, οὐδὲν ἂν εἴη." "οὐ γὰρ οὖν."

"'Ἐπεὶ δέ γε πλείω ἑνός ἐστι τά τε τοῦ ἑνὸς
μορίου καὶ τὰ τοῦ ἑνὸς ὅλου μετέχοντα, οὐκ
ἀνάγκη ἤδη πλήθει ἄπειρα εἶναι αὐτά γε ἐκεῖνα
τὰ μεταλαμβάνοντα τοῦ ἑνός;" "πῶς;" "ὧδε
ἴδωμεν.[1] ἄλλο τι οὐχ ἓν ὄντα οὐδὲ μετέχοντα τοῦ
ἑνὸς τότε, ὅτε μεταλαμβάνει αὐτοῦ, μεταλαμ-
C βάνει;" "δῆλα δή." "οὐκοῦν πλήθη ὄντα, ἐν
οἷς τὸ ἓν οὐκ ἔνι;" "πλήθη μέντοι." "τί οὖν;
εἰ ἐθέλοιμεν τῇ διανοίᾳ τῶν τοιούτων ἀφελεῖν ὡς
οἷοί τέ ἐσμεν ὅτι ὀλίγιστον, οὐκ ἀνάγκη καὶ τὸ
ἀφαιρεθὲν ἐκεῖνο, εἴπερ τοῦ ἑνὸς μὴ μετέχοι,
πλῆθος εἶναι καὶ οὐχ ἕν;" "ἀνάγκη." "οὐκοῦν
οὕτως ἀεὶ σκοποῦντες αὐτὴν καθ' αὑτὴν τὴν ἑτέραν φύσιν τοῦ εἴδους ὅσον ἂν αὐτῆς ἀεὶ ὁρῶμεν
ἄπειρον ἔσται πλήθει;" "παντάπασι μὲν οὖν."
"καὶ μὴν ἐπειδάν γε ἓν ἕκαστον μόριον μόριον
D γένηται, πέρας ἤδη ἔχει πρὸς ἄλληλα καὶ πρὸς τὸ
ὅλον, καὶ τὸ ὅλον πρὸς τὰ μόρια." "κομιδῇ μὲν
οὖν." "τοῖς ἄλλοις δὴ τοῦ ἑνὸς ξυμβαίνει ἐκ μὲν
τοῦ ἑνὸς καὶ ἐξ ἑαυτῶν κοινωνησάντων, ὡς ἔοικεν,
ἕτερόν τι γίγνεσθαι ἐν ἑαυτοῖς, ὃ δὴ πέρας παρ-
έσχε πρὸς ἄλληλα· ἡ δ' ἑαυτῶν φύσις καθ' ἑαυτὰ
ἀπειρίαν." "φαίνεται." "οὕτω δὴ τὰ ἄλλα τοῦ

[1] ἴδωμεν] εἰδῶμεν BT.

304

whole." " Yes." " And will not the things which participate in the one be other than the one while participating in it ? " " Of course." " But the things which are other than the one will be many ; for if they were neither one nor more than one, they would not be anything." " No."

" But since the things which participate in the one as a part and the one as a whole are more than one, must not those participants in the one be infinite in number ? " " How so ? " " Let us look at the question in this way. Is it not true that at the moment when they begin to participate in the one they are not one and do not participate in one ? " " Clearly." " Then they are multitudes, in which the one is not, are they not ? " " Yes, they are multitudes." " Well, then, if we should subtract from them in thought the smallest possible quantity, must not that which is subtracted, if it has no participation in one, be also a multitude, and not one ? " " It must." " And always when we consider the nature of the class, which makes it other than one, whatever we see of it at any time will be unlimited in number, will it not ? " " Certainly." " And, further, when each part becomes a part, straightway the parts are limited in relation to each other and to the whole, and the whole in relation to the parts." " Undoubtedly." " The result, then, to the things which are other than one is, that from the one and the union of themselves with it there arises, as it appears, something different within themselves which gives them a limitation in relation to one another ; but their own nature, when they are left to themselves, gives them no limits." " So it appears." " Then the things which

ἑνὸς καὶ ὅλα καὶ κατὰ μόρια ἄπειρά τέ ἐστι καὶ
πέρατος μετέχει.'' ''πάνυ γε.''

Ε   '' Οὐκοῦν καὶ ὅμοιά τε καὶ ἀνόμοια ἀλλήλοις τε
καὶ ἑαυτοῖς;'' ''πῇ δή;'' ''ᾗ μέν που ἄπειρά
ἐστι κατὰ τὴν ἑαυτῶν φύσιν πάντα, ταὐτὸν πεπονθότα ἂν εἴη ταύτῃ.'' ''πάνυ γε.'' ''καὶ μὴν ᾗ
γε ἅπαντα πέρατος μετέχει, καὶ ταύτῃ πάντ' ἂν
εἴη ταὐτὸν πεπονθότα.'' ''πῶς δ' οὔ;'' ''ᾗ δέ
γε πεπερασμένα τε εἶναι καὶ ἄπειρα πέπονθεν,
ἐναντία πάθη ἀλλήλοις ὄντα ταῦτα τὰ πάθη πέπον-
159 θεν.'' ''ναί.'' ''τὰ δ' ἐναντία γε ὡς οἷόν τε ἀνομοιότατα.'' ''τί μήν;'' ''κατὰ μὲν ἄρα ἑκάτερον τὸ πάθος ὅμοια ἂν εἴη αὐτά τε αὑτοῖς καὶ
ἀλλήλοις, κατὰ δ' ἀμφότερα ἀμφοτέρως ἐναντιώ-
τατά τε καὶ ἀνομοιότατα.'' ''κινδυνεύει.'' ''οὕτω δὴ τὰ ἄλλα αὐτά τε αὑτοῖς καὶ ἀλλήλοις ὅμοιά
τε καὶ ἀνόμοια ἂν εἴη.'' ''οὕτως.'' ''καὶ ταὐτὰ
δὴ καὶ ἕτερα ἀλλήλων, καὶ κινούμενα καὶ ἑστῶτα,
καὶ πάντα τὰ ἐναντία πάθη οὐκέτι χαλεπῶς εὑρή-
Β σομεν πεπονθότα τἆλλα τοῦ ἑνός, ἐπείπερ καὶ ταῦτα ἐφάνη πεπονθότα.'' ''ὀρθῶς λέγεις.''

23.   '' Οὐκοῦν εἰ ταῦτα μὲν ἤδη ἐῶμεν[1] ὡς φανε-
ρά, ἐπισκοποῖμεν δὲ πάλιν, ἓν εἰ ἔστιν, ἆρα καὶ
οὐχ οὕτως ἔχει τὰ ἄλλα τοῦ ἑνὸς ἢ οὕτω μόνον;''
''πάνυ μὲν οὖν.'' ''λέγωμεν δὴ ἐξ ἀρχῆς, ἓν εἰ
ἔστι, τί χρὴ τὰ ἄλλα τοῦ ἑνὸς πεπονθέναι.'' ''λέγωμεν γάρ.'' ''ἆρ' οὖν οὐ χωρὶς μὲν τὸ ἓν τῶν
ἄλλων, χωρὶς δὲ τἆλλα τοῦ ἑνὸς εἶναι;'' ''τί

---

[1] ἐῶμεν] ἑῶμεν ΒΤ.

are other than one, both as wholes and as parts, are both unlimited and partake of limitation." "Certainly."

"And are they also both like and unlike one another and themselves?" "How is that?" "Inasmuch as they are all by their own nature unlimited, they are all in that respect affected in the same way." "Certainly." "And surely inasmuch as they all partake of limitation, they are all affected in the same way in that respect also." "Obviously." "And inasmuch as they are so affected as to be both limited and limitless, they are affected by affections which are the opposites of one another." "Yes." "But opposites are as unlike as possible." "To be sure." "Then with regard to either one of their two affections they are like themselves and each other, but with regard to both of them together they are utterly opposed and unlike." "Yes, that must be true." "Therefore the others are both like and unlike themselves and one another." "So they are." "And they are the same as one another and also other than one another, they are both in motion and at rest, and since we have proved these cases, we can easily show that the things which are other than one experience all the opposite affections." "You are right."

"Then what if we now drop these matters as evident and again consider whether, if one is, the things other than one are as we have said, and there is no alternative." "Certainly." "Let us then begin at the beginning and ask, if one is, what must happen to the things which are other than one." "By all means." "Must not the one be separate from the others, and the others from

307

PLATO

δή;" " ὅτι που οὐκ ἔστι παρὰ ταῦτα ἕτερον, ὃ
C ἄλλο μέν ἐστι τοῦ ἑνός, ἄλλο δὲ τῶν ἄλλων. πάντα
γὰρ εἴρηται, ὅταν ῥηθῇ τό τε ἓν καὶ τἆλλα."
" πάντα γάρ." " οὐκ ἄρα ἔτ' ἔστιν ἕτερον τούτων, ἐν ᾧ τό τε ἓν ἂν εἴη τῷ αὐτῷ καὶ τἆλλα."
" οὐ γάρ." " οὐδέποτε ἄρα ἐν ταὐτῷ ἐστι τὸ ἓν
καὶ τἆλλα." " οὐκ ἔοικεν." " χωρὶς ἄρα;"
" ναί." " οὐδὲ μὴν μόριά γε ἔχειν φαμὲν τὸ ὡς
ἀληθῶς ἕν." " πῶς γάρ;" " οὔτ' ἄρα ὅλον εἴη
ἂν τὸ ἓν ἐν τοῖς ἄλλοις οὔτε μόρια αὐτοῦ, εἰ χωρίς
τέ ἐστι τῶν ἄλλων καὶ μόρια μὴ ἔχει.[1]" " πῶς
D γάρ;" " οὐδενὶ ἄρα τρόπῳ μετέχοι ἂν τἆλλα τοῦ
ἑνός, μήτε κατὰ μόριόν τι αὐτοῦ μήτε κατὰ ὅλον
μετέχοντα." " οὐκ ἔοικεν." " οὐδαμῇ ἄρα ἓν
τἆλλά ἐστιν, οὐδ' ἔχει ἐν ἑαυτοῖς ἓν οὐδέν." " οὐ
γὰρ οὖν." " οὐδ' ἄρα πολλά ἐστι τἆλλα. ἓν γὰρ
ἂν ἦν ἕκαστον αὐτῶν μόριον τοῦ ὅλου, εἰ πολλὰ ἦν·
νῦν δὲ οὔτε ἓν οὔτε πολλὰ οὔτε ὅλον οὔτε μόριά
ἐστι τἆλλα τοῦ ἑνός, ἐπειδὴ αὐτοῦ οὐδαμῇ μετέχει." " ὀρθῶς." " οὐδ' ἄρα δύο οὐδὲ τρία οὔτε
αὐτά ἐστι τὰ ἄλλα οὔτε ἔνεστιν[2] ἐν αὐτοῖς, εἴπερ
E τοῦ ἑνὸς πανταχῇ στέρεται." " οὕτως."

" Οὐδὲ ὅμοια ἄρα καὶ ἀνόμοια οὔτε αὐτά ἐστι
τῷ ἑνὶ τὰ ἄλλα, οὔτε ἔνεστιν[2] ἐν αὐτοῖς ὁμοιότης
καὶ ἀνομοιότης. εἰ γὰρ ὅμοια καὶ ἀνόμοια αὐτὰ
εἴη ἢ ἔχοι ἐν ἑαυτοῖς ὁμοιότητα καὶ ἀνομοιότητα,
δύο που εἴδη ἐναντία ἀλλήλοις ἔχοι ἂν ἐν ἑαυτοῖς
τὰ ἄλλα τοῦ ἑνός." " φαίνεται." " ἦν δέ γε ἀ-
δύνατον δυοῖν τινοῖν μετέχειν ἃ μηδ' ἑνὸς μετέχοι."

[1] ἔχει] ἔχῃ BT.　　　[2] ἔνεστιν] ἕν ἐστιν BT.

the one ? " " Why is that ? " " Because there is nothing else besides these, which is other than one and other than the others. For when we have said ' one and the others ' we have included all things." " Yes, all things." " Then there is nothing other than these, in which both the one and the others may be." " No." " Then the one and the others can never be in the same." " Apparently not." " Then they are separate ? " " Yes." " And surely we say that what is truly one has no parts." " How can it have parts ? " " Then the one cannot be in the others as a whole, nor can parts of it, if it is separate from the others and has no parts." " Of course not." " Then the others cannot partake of the one in any way ; they can neither partake of any part of it nor of the whole." " No, apparently not." " The others are, then, not one in any sense, nor have they in themselves any unity." " No." " But neither are the others many ; for if they were many, each of them would be one part of the whole ; but actually the things that are other than one are not many nor a whole nor parts, since they do not participate in the one in any way." " Right." " Neither are the others two or three, nor are two or three in them, if they are entirely deprived of unity." " True."

" Nor are the others either themselves like and unlike the one, nor are likeness and unlikeness in them ; for if they were like and unlike or had likeness and unlikeness in them, the things which are other than the one would have in them two elements opposite to one another." " That is clear." " But it is impossible for that to partake of two things which does not even partake of one." " Impossible."

" ἀδύνατον." " οὔτ' ἄρα ὅμοια οὔτ' ἀνόμοιά ἐστιν
160 οὔτ' ἀμφότερα τἆλλα. ὅμοια μὲν γὰρ ἂν ὄντα ἢ
ἀνόμοια ἑνὸς ἂν τοῦ ἑτέρου εἴδους μετέχοι, ἀμφότερα δὲ ὄντα δυοῖν τοῖν ἐναντίοιν· ταῦτα δὲ ἀδύνατα ἐφάνη." " ἀληθῆ."

" Οὐδ' ἄρα τὰ αὐτὰ οὐδ' ἕτερα, οὐδὲ κινούμενα
οὐδὲ ἑστῶτα, οὐδὲ γιγνόμενα οὐδὲ ἀπολλύμενα,
οὐδὲ μείζω οὐδὲ ἐλάττω οὐδὲ ἴσα· οὐδὲ ἄλλο οὐδὲν
πέπονθε τῶν τοιούτων. εἰ γάρ τι τοιοῦτον πεπονθέναι ὑπομένει τὰ ἄλλα, καὶ ἑνὸς καὶ δυοῖν καὶ
τριῶν καὶ περιττοῦ καὶ ἀρτίου μεθέξει, ὧν αὐτοῖς
B ἀδύνατον ἐφάνη μετέχειν τοῦ ἑνός γε πάντη πάντως στερομένοις." " ἀληθέστατα." " οὕτω δὴ ἓν
εἰ ἔστιν, πάντα τέ ἐστι τὸ ἓν καὶ οὐδὲ ἕν¹ ἐστι καὶ
πρὸς ἑαυτὸ καὶ πρὸς τὰ ἄλλα ὡσαύτως." " παντελῶς μὲν οὖν."

24. " Εἶεν· εἰ δὲ δὴ μὴ ἔστι τὸ ἕν, τί χρὴ συμ-
βαίνειν, ἆρ' οὐ σκεπτέον μετὰ τοῦτο²;" " σκεπτέον γάρ." " τίς οὖν ἂν εἴη αὕτη ἡ ὑπόθεσις, εἰ
ἓν μὴ ἔστιν; ἆρά τι διαφέρει τῆσδε, εἰ μὴ ἓν μὴ
ἔστιν;" " διαφέρει μέντοι." " διαφέρει μόνον, ἢ
C καὶ πᾶν τοὐναντίον ἐστὶν εἰπεῖν, εἰ μὴ ἓν μὴ ἔστι
τοῦ εἰ ἓν μὴ ἔστιν;" " πᾶν τοὐναντίον." " τί δ'
εἴ τις λέγοι, εἰ μέγεθος μὴ ἔστιν ἢ σμικρότης μὴ
ἔστιν ἤ τι ἄλλο τῶν τοιούτων, ἆρα ἐφ' ἑκάστου ἂν
δηλοῖ ὅτι ἕτερόν τι λέγοι τὸ μὴ ὄν;" " πάνυ γε."
" οὐκοῦν καὶ νῦν δηλοῖ ὅτι ἕτερον λέγει τῶν ἄλλων τὸ μὴ ὄν, ὅταν εἴπῃ ἓν εἰ μὴ ἔστι, καὶ ἴσμεν ὃ
λέγει;" " ἴσμεν." " πρῶτον μὲν ἄρα γνωστὸν

---

¹ οὐδὲ ἕν T : οὐδέν B.   ² τοῦτο T : ταῦτα B.

"The others are, then, not like nor unlike nor both. For if they were like or unlike, they would partake of one of the two elements, and if they were both, of the two opposites ; and that was shown to be impossible." "True."

"They are, then, neither the same nor other, nor in motion nor at rest, nor becoming nor being destroyed, nor greater nor less nor equal, and they experience no similar affections ; for if the others are subject to such affections, they will participate in one and two and three and odd and even, in which we saw that they cannot participate, if they are in every way utterly deprived of unity." "Very true." "Therefore if one exists, the one is all things and nothing at all in relation both to itself and to all others." "Perfectly true."

"Well, and ought we not next to consider what must happen if one does not exist ?" "Yes, we ought." "What, then, is the sense of this hypothesis—if one does not exist ? Is it different in any way from this—if not one does not exist ?" "Certainly it is different." "Is it merely different, or are the two expressions—if not one does not exist and if one does not exist—complete opposites ?" "They are complete opposites." "Now if a person should say ' if greatness does not exist,' ' if smallness does not exist,' or anything of that sort, would he not make it clear that in each case the thing he speaks of as not existing is different ?" "Certainly." "And in our case does he not make it clear that he means, when he says ' if one is not,' that the thing which is not is different from other things, and do we not know what he means ?" "Yes, we do know." "In the first place, then,

τι λέγει, ἔπειτα ἕτερον τῶν ἄλλων, ὅταν εἴπῃ ἕν,
εἴτε τὸ εἶναι αὐτῷ προσθεὶς εἴτε τὸ μὴ εἶναι·
D οὐδὲν γὰρ[1] ἧττον γιγνώσκεται, τί τὸ λεγόμενον
μὴ εἶναι, καὶ ὅτι διάφορον τῶν ἄλλων. ἢ οὔ;"
"ἀνάγκη." "ὧδε ἄρα λεκτέον ἐξ ἀρχῆς, ἓν εἰ
μὴ ἔστι, τί χρὴ εἶναι. πρῶτον μὲν οὖν αὐτῷ τοῦτο
ὑπάρχειν δεῖ, ὡς ἔοικεν, εἶναι αὐτοῦ ἐπιστήμην, ἢ
μηδὲ ὅ τι λέγεται γιγνώσκεσθαι, ὅταν τις εἴπῃ ἓν
εἰ μὴ ἔστιν." "ἀληθῆ." "οὐκοῦν καὶ τὰ ἄλλα
ἕτερα αὐτοῦ εἶναι, ἢ μηδὲ ἐκεῖνο ἕτερον τῶν ἄλλων
λέγεσθαι;" "πάνυ γε." "καὶ ἑτεροιότης ἄρα
ἐστὶν αὐτῷ πρὸς τῇ ἐπιστήμῃ. οὐ γὰρ τὴν τῶν
E ἄλλων ἑτεροιότητα λέγει, ὅταν τὸ ἓν ἕτερον τῶν
ἄλλων λέγῃ, ἀλλὰ τὴν ἐκείνου." "φαίνεται."
"καὶ μὴν τοῦ γε ἐκείνου καὶ τοῦ τινὸς καὶ τούτου
καὶ τούτῳ καὶ τούτων καὶ πάντων τῶν τοιούτων
μετέχει τὸ μὴ ὂν ἕν. οὐ γὰρ ἂν τὸ ἓν ἐλέγετο οὐδ'
ἂν τοῦ ἑνὸς ἕτερα, οὐδ' ἐκείνῳ ἄν τι ἦν ἢν οὐδ' ἐκείνου, οὐδ' ἄν τι ἐλέγετο, εἰ μήτε τοῦ τινὸς αὐτῷ
μετῆν μήτε τῶν ἄλλων τούτων." "ὀρθῶς."
"εἶναι μὲν δὴ τῷ ἑνὶ οὐχ οἷόν τε, εἴπερ γε μὴ ἔστι,
161 μετέχειν δὲ πολλῶν οὐδὲν κωλύει, ἀλλὰ καὶ ἀνάγκη, εἴπερ τό γε ἓν ἐκεῖνο καὶ μὴ ἄλλο μὴ ἔστιν.
εἰ μέντοι μήτε τὸ ἓν μήτ' ἐκεῖνο μὴ ἔσται, ἀλλὰ
περὶ ἄλλου του ὁ λόγος, οὐδὲ φθέγγεσθαι δεῖ οὐδέν·

---

[1] γὰρ apogr.: om. Tb (οὐδὲν γὰρ . . . μὴ εἶναι om. B:
add. b in marg.)

---

[1] *i.e.* if non-existence cannot be predicated either of the
one (*unitas*) or of that (*illuditas*), but that of which we
predicate non-existence is something else, then we may
as well stop talking. It has just been affirmed that if
that one of which we are speaking, and not something else,
is not, then the one must partake of numerous attributes.

he speaks of something which is known, and secondly of something different from other things, when he says 'one,' whether he adds to it that it is or that it is not ; for that which is said to be non-existent is known none the less, and is known to be different from other things, is it not ? " " Certainly." " Then we should begin at the beginning by asking : if one is not, what must follow ? In the first place this must be true of the one, that there is knowledge of it, or else not even the meaning of the words ' if the one does not exist ' would be known." " True." " And is it not also true that the others differ from the one, or it cannot be said to differ from the others ? " " Certainly." " Then a difference belongs to the one in addition to knowledge ; for when we say that the one differs from the others, we speak of a difference in the one, not in the others." " That is clear." " And the non-existent one partakes of ' that ' and ' some ' and ' this ' and ' relation to this ' and ' these ' and all notions of that sort ; for the one could not be spoken of, nor could the things which are other than one, nor could anything in relation to the one or belonging to it be or be spoken of, if the one did not partake of the notion ' some ' or of those other notions." " True." " It is impossible for the one to be, if it does not exist, but nothing prevents its partaking of many things ; indeed it must do so, if that one of which we are speaking, and not something else, is not. But if neither the one, nor ' that,' is not, but we are speaking of something else, there is no use in saying anything at all ;[1] but if non-existence is

Now it is affirmed that if the converse is true, further discussion is futile.

εἰ δὲ τὸ ἓν ἐκεῖνο καὶ μὴ ἄλλο ὑπόκειται μὴ εἶναι, καὶ τοῦ ἐκείνου καὶ ἄλλων πολλῶν ἀνάγκη αὐτῷ μετεῖναι." "καὶ πάνυ γε."

"Καὶ ἀνομοιότης ἄρα ἐστὶν αὐτῷ πρὸς τὰ ἄλλα. τὰ γὰρ ἄλλα τοῦ ἑνὸς ἕτερα ὄντα ἑτεροῖα καὶ εἴη ἄν." "ναί." "τὰ δ' ἑτεροῖα οὐκ ἀλλοῖα;" "πῶς δ' οὔ;" "τὰ δ' ἀλλοῖα οὐκ ἀνόμοια;" B "ἀνόμοια μὲν οὖν." "οὐκοῦν εἴπερ τῷ ἑνὶ ἀνόμοιά ἐστι, δῆλον ὅτι ἀνομοίῳ τά γε ἀνόμοια ἀνόμοια ἂν εἴη." "δῆλον." "εἴη δὴ ἂν καὶ τῷ ἑνὶ ἀνομοιότης, πρὸς ἣν τὰ ἄλλα ἀνόμοια αὐτῷ ἐστίν." "ἔοικεν." "εἰ δὲ δὴ τῶν ἄλλων ἀνομοιότης ἔστιν αὐτῷ, ἆρ' οὐκ ἀνάγκη ἑαυτοῦ ὁμοιότητα αὐτῷ εἶναι;" "πῶς;" "εἰ ἑνὸς ἀνομοιότης ἔστι τῷ ἑνί, οὐκ ἄν που περὶ τοῦ τοιούτου ὁ λόγος εἴη οἷον τοῦ ἑνός, οὐδ' ἂν ἡ ὑπόθεσις εἴη περὶ ἑνός, ἀλλὰ περὶ ἄλλου ἢ ἑνός." C "πάνυ γε." "οὐ δεῖ δέ γε." "οὐ δῆτα." "δεῖ ἄρα ὁμοιότητα τῷ ἑνὶ αὐτοῦ ἑαυτῷ εἶναι." "δεῖ."

"Καὶ μὴν οὐδ' αὖ ἴσον γ' ἐστὶ τοῖς ἄλλοις. εἰ γὰρ εἴη ἴσον, εἴη τε ἂν ἤδη καὶ ὅμοιον ἂν εἴη αὐτοῖς κατὰ τὴν ἰσότητα· ταῦτα δ' ἀμφότερα ἀδύνατα, εἴπερ μὴ ἔστιν ἕν." "ἀδύνατα." "ἐπειδὴ δὲ οὐκ ἔστι τοῖς ἄλλοις ἴσον, ἆρα οὐκ ἀνάγκη καὶ τἆλλα ἐκείνῳ μὴ ἴσα εἶναι;" "ἀνάγκη." "τὰ δὲ μὴ ἴσα οὐκ ἄνισα;" "ναί." "τὰ δὲ ἄνισα οὐ τῷ ἀνίσῳ ἄνισα;" "πῶς δ' οὔ;" "καὶ ἀνισότητος δὴ μετέχει τὸ ἕν, πρὸς ἣν τἆλλα

the property of that one, and not of something else, then the one must partake of ' that ' and of many other attributes." " Yes, certainly."

" And it will possess unlikeness in relation to other things : for the things which are other than one, being different, will be of a different kind." " Yes." " And are not things which are of a different kind also of another kind ? " " Of course." " And things which are of another kind are unlike, are they not ? " " Yes, they are unlike." " Then if they are unlike the one, the one is evidently unlike the things which are unlike it." " Evidently." " Then the one possesses unlikeness in relation to which the others are unlike." " So it appears." " But if it possesses unlikeness to the others, must it not possess likeness to itself ? " " How is that ? " " If the one possesses unlikeness to the one, our argument will not be concerned with that which is of the nature of the one, and our hypothesis will not relate to the one, but to something other than one." " Certainly." " But that is inadmissible." " It certainly is." " Then the one must possess likeness to itself." " It must."

" And neither is the one equal to the others ; for if it were equal, then it would both be and be like them in respect to equality, both of which are impossible, if one does not exist." " Yes, they are impossible." " And since it is not equal to the others, they cannot be equal to it, can they ? " " Certainly not." " And things which are not equal are unequal, are they not ? " " Yes." " And things which are unequal are unequal to something which is unequal to them ? " " Of course." " Then the one partakes of inequality, in respect to which

PLATO

D αὐτῷ ἐστιν ἄνισα;" "μετέχει." "ἀλλὰ μέντοι
ἀνισότητός γ᾽ ἐστὶ μέγεθός τε καὶ σμικρότης."
"ἔστι γάρ." "ἔστιν ἄρα καὶ μέγεθός τε καὶ
σμικρότης τῷ τοιούτῳ ἑνί;" "κινδυνεύει."
"μέγεθος μὴν καὶ σμικρότης ἀεὶ ἀφέστατον ἀλλήλοιν." "πάνυ γε." "μεταξὺ ἄρα τι αὐτοῖν
ἀεί ἐστιν." "ἔστιν." "ἔχεις οὖν τι ἄλλο εἰπεῖν
μεταξὺ αὐτοῖν ἢ ἰσότητα;" "οὔκ, ἀλλὰ τοῦτο."
"ὅτῳ ἄρα ἔστι μέγεθος καὶ σμικρότης, ἔστι καὶ
ἰσότης αὐτῷ μεταξὺ τούτοιν οὖσα." "φαίνεται."
E "τῷ δὴ[1] ἑνὶ μὴ ὄντι, ὡς ἔοικε, καὶ ἰσότητος ἂν
μετείη καὶ μεγέθους καὶ σμικρότητος." "ἔοικεν."

"Καὶ μὴν καὶ οὐσίας γε δεῖ αὐτὸ μετέχειν πῃ."
"πῶς δή;" "ἔχειν αὐτὸ δεῖ οὕτως ὡς λέγομεν.
εἰ γὰρ μὴ οὕτως ἔχοι,[2] οὐκ ἂν ἀληθῆ λέγοιμεν
ἡμεῖς λέγοντες τὸ ἓν μὴ εἶναι· εἰ δὲ ἀληθῆ, δῆλον
ὅτι ὄντα αὐτὰ λέγομεν. ἢ οὐχ οὕτως;" "οὕτω
μὲν οὖν." "ἐπειδὴ δέ φαμεν ἀληθῆ λέγειν,
162 ἀνάγκη ἡμῖν φάναι καὶ ὄντα λέγειν." "ἀνάγκη."
"ἔστιν ἄρα, ὡς ἔοικε, τὸ ἓν οὐκ ὄν. εἰ γὰρ μὴ
ἔσται μὴ ὄν, ἀλλά τι τοῦ εἶναι ἀνήσει πρὸς τὸ μὴ
εἶναι, εὐθὺς ἔσται ὄν." "παντάπασι μὲν οὖν."
"δεῖ ἄρα αὐτὸ δεσμὸν ἔχειν τοῦ μὴ εἶναι τὸ εἶναι
μὴ ὄν, εἰ μέλλει μὴ εἶναι, ὁμοίως ὥσπερ τὸ ὂν τὸ
μὴ ὂν ἔχειν μὴ εἶναι, ἵνα τελέως αὖ ᾖ.[3] οὕτως
γὰρ ἂν τό τε ὂν μάλιστ᾽ ἂν εἴη καὶ τὸ μὴ ὂν οὐκ
ἂν εἴη, μετέχοντα τὸ μὲν ὂν οὐσίας τοῦ εἶναι ὄν,

---

[1] δὴ Par. 1810, Heindorf from Ficinus : δὲ BT.
[2] ἔχοι Coisl. : ἔχῃ BT.
[3] αὖ εἶναι ἢ BT : αὖ ᾖ (or αὖ ὂν ᾖ) Shorey.

---

[1] i.e. if it ceases to be non-existent, gives up something
of being (as applied to non-existence) to not-being, so that
it no longer is non-existent, but is not non-existent.

the others are unequal to it ? " " Yes, it does."
" But greatness and smallness are constituents of
inequality." " Yes." " Then the one, such as we
are discussing, possesses greatness and smallness ? "
" So it appears." " Now surely greatness and
smallness always keep apart from one another."
" Certainly." " Then there is always something
between them." " There is." " Can you think of
anything between them except equality ? " " No,
only equality." " Then anything which has greatness and smallness has also equality, which is between
the two." " That is clear." " Then the non-
existent one, it appears, partakes of equality and
greatness and smallness." " So it appears."

" And it must also, in a way, partake of existence."
" How is that ? " " It must be in such conditions
as we have been saying ; for if it were not, we should
not be speaking the truth in saying that the one
is not. And if we speak the truth, it is clear that
we say that which is. Am I not right ? " " You
are." " Then inasmuch as we assert that we are
speaking the truth, we necessarily assert that we
say that which is." " Necessarily." " Then, as it
appears, the non-existent one exists. For if it is
not non-existent, but gives up something of being
to not-being,[1] then it will be existent." " Certainly." " Then if it does not exist and is to continue
to be non-existent, it must have the existence of
not-being as a bond, just as being has the non-
existence of not-being, in order to attain its perfect
existence. For in this way the existence of the
existent and the non-existence of the non-existent
would be best assured, when the existent partakes
of the existence of being existent and of the non-

317

B μὴ οὐσίας δὲ τοῦ μὴ[1] εἶναι μὴ ὄν, εἰ μέλλει τελέως εἶναι, τὸ δὲ μὴ ὂν μὴ οὐσίας μὲν τοῦ μὴ εἶναι ὄν,[2] οὐσίας δὲ τοῦ εἶναι μὴ ὄν, εἰ καὶ τὸ μὴ ὂν αὖ τελέως μὴ ἔσται." "ἀληθέστατα." "οὐκοῦν ἐπείπερ τῷ τε ὄντι τοῦ μὴ εἶναι καὶ τῷ μὴ ὄντι τοῦ εἶναι μέτεστι, καὶ τῷ ἑνί, ἐπειδὴ οὐκ ἔστι, τοῦ εἶναι ἀνάγκη μετεῖναι εἰς τὸ μὴ εἶναι." "ἀνάγκη." "καὶ οὐσία δὴ φαίνεται τῷ ἑνί, εἰ μὴ ἔστιν." "φαίνεται." "καὶ μὴ οὐσία ἄρα, εἴπερ μὴ ἔστιν." "πῶς δ' οὔ;"

"Οἷόν τε οὖν τὸ ἔχον πως μὴ ἔχειν οὕτω, μὴ μεταβάλλον ἐκ ταύτης τῆς ἕξεως;" "οὐχ οἷόν τε." "πᾶν ἄρα τὸ τοιοῦτον μεταβολὴν σημαίνει,

C ὃ ἂν οὕτω τε καὶ μὴ οὕτως ἔχῃ." "πῶς δ' οὔ;" "μεταβολὴ δὲ κίνησις· ἢ τί φήσομεν;" "κίνησις." "οὐκοῦν τὸ ἓν ὄν τε καὶ οὐκ ὂν ἐφάνη;" "ναί." "οὕτως ἄρα καὶ οὐχ οὕτως ἔχον φαίνεται." "ἔοικεν." "καὶ κινούμενον ἄρα τὸ οὐκ ὂν ἓν πέφανται, ἐπείπερ καὶ μεταβολὴν ἐκ τοῦ εἶναι ἐπὶ τὸ μὴ εἶναι ἔχον." "κινδυνεύει." "ἀλλὰ μὴν εἰ μηδαμοῦ γέ ἐστι τῶν ὄντων, ὡς οὐκ ἔστιν εἴπερ μὴ ἔστιν, οὐδ' ἂν μεθίσταιτό ποθέν ποι." "πῶς γάρ;" "οὐκ ἄρα τῷ γε μεταβαίνειν κινοῖτ' ἄν." "οὐ γάρ." "οὐδὲ μὴν

D ἐν τῷ αὐτῷ ἂν στρέφοιτο· ταὐτοῦ γὰρ οὐδαμοῦ ἅπτεται. ὂν γὰρ ἐστὶ τὸ ταὐτόν· τὸ δὲ μὴ ὂν ἔν τῳ τῶν ὄντων ἀδύνατον εἶναι." "ἀδύνατον γάρ." "οὐκ ἄρα τὸ ἕν γε μὴ ὂν στρέφεσθαι ἂν δύναιτο ἐν ἐκείνῳ ἐν ᾧ μὴ ἔστιν." "οὐ γὰρ οὖν." "οὐδὲ μὴν ἀλλοιοῦταί που τὸ ἓν ἑαυτοῦ, οὔτε τὸ ὂν οὔτε

---

[1] μὴ add. Shorey.   [2] ὂν Shorey : μὴ ὂν ΒΤ.

existence of not being non-existent, thus assuring
its own perfect existence, and the non-existent
partakes of the non-existence of not being existent
and the existence of being non-existent, and thus
the non-existent also secures its perfect non-
existence." " Very true." " Then since the existent
partakes of non-existence and the non-existent of
existence, the one, since it does not exist, necessarily
partakes of existence to attain non-existence."
" Yes, necessarily." " Clearly, then, the one, if it
does not exist, has existence." " Clearly." " And non-
existence also, if it does not exist." " Of course."

" Well, can anything which is in a certain condition
be not in that condition without changing from it ? "
" No, it cannot." " Then everything of that sort—
if a thing is and is not in a given condition—signifies
a change." " Of course." " But change is motion ;
we agree to that ? " " It is motion." " And did
we not see that the one is and is not ? " " Yes."
" Then we see that it both is and is not in a given
condition." " So it appears." " And we have seen
that the non-existent one has motion, since it
changes from being to not-being." " There is not
much doubt of that." " But if it is nowhere among
existing things—and it is nowhere, if it does not
exist—it cannot move from any place to another."
" Of course not." " Then its motion cannot be
change of place." " No, it cannot." " Nor surely
can it turn in the same spot, for it nowhere touches
the same ; for the same is existent, and the non-
existent cannot be in any existent thing." " No, it
is impossible." " Then the one, being non-existent,
cannot turn in that in which it is not." " No."
" And the one, whether existent or non-existent,

τὸ μὴ ὄν. οὐ γὰρ ἂν ἦν ὁ λόγος ἔτι περὶ τοῦ ἑνός,
εἴπερ ἠλλοιοῦτο αὐτὸ ἑαυτοῦ, ἀλλὰ περὶ ἄλλου
τινός." "ὀρθῶς." "εἰ δὲ μήτ' ἀλλοιοῦται μήτε

E ἐν ταὐτῷ στρέφεται μήτε μεταβαίνει, ἆρ' ἄν πη
ἔτι κινοῖτο;" "πῶς γάρ;" "τό γε μὴν ἀκίνητον ἀνάγκη ἡσυχίαν ἄγειν, τὸ δὲ ἡσυχάζον ἑστάναι." "ἀνάγκη." "τὸ ἓν ἄρα, ὡς ἔοικεν, οὐκ
ὂν ἕστηκέ τε καὶ κινεῖται." "ἔοικεν." "καὶ
μὴν εἴπερ γε κινεῖται, μεγάλη ἀνάγκη αὐτῷ ἀλ-

163 λοιοῦσθαι. ὅπη γὰρ ἄν τι κινηθῇ, κατὰ τοσοῦτον
οὐκέθ' ὡσαύτως ἔχει ὡς εἶχεν, ἀλλ' ἑτέρως."
"οὕτως." "κινούμενον δὴ[1] τὸ ἓν καὶ ἀλλοιοῦται."
"ναί." "καὶ μὴν μηδαμῇ γε κινούμενον οὐδαμῇ
ἂν ἀλλοιοῖτο." "οὐ γάρ." "ᾗ μὲν ἄρα κινεῖται
τὸ οὐκ ὂν ἕν, ἀλλοιοῦται· ᾗ δὲ μὴ κινεῖται, οὐκ
ἀλλοιοῦται." "οὐ γάρ." "τὸ ἓν ἄρα μὴ ὂν
ἀλλοιοῦταί τε καὶ οὐκ ἀλλοιοῦται." "φαίνεται."
"τὸ δ' ἀλλοιούμενον ἆρ' οὐκ ἀνάγκη γίγνεσθαι
μὲν ἕτερον ἢ πρότερον, ἀπόλλυσθαι δὲ ἐκ τῆς

B προτέρας ἕξεως· τὸ δὲ μὴ ἀλλοιούμενον μήτε
γίγνεσθαι μήτε ἀπόλλυσθαι;" "ἀνάγκη." "καὶ
τὸ ἓν ἄρα μὴ ὂν ἀλλοιούμενον μὲν γίγνεταί τε καὶ
ἀπόλλυται, μὴ ἀλλοιούμενον δὲ οὔτε γίγνεται οὔτε
ἀπόλλυται· καὶ οὕτω τὸ ἓν μὴ ὂν γίγνεταί τε καὶ
ἀπόλλυται, καὶ οὔτε γίγνεται οὔτ' ἀπόλλυται."
"οὐ γὰρ οὖν."

25. "Αὖθις δὴ ἐπὶ τὴν ἀρχὴν ἴωμεν πάλιν
ὀψόμενοι εἰ ταὐτὰ ἡμῖν φανεῖται ἅπερ καὶ νῦν, ἢ

---

[1] δὴ Heindorf from Ficinus : δὲ BT.

cannot change into something other than itself;
for if it changed into something other than itself,
our talk would no longer be about the one, but
about something else." "Quite right." "But if
it neither changes into something else, nor turns in
the same spot, nor changes its place, can it still
move in any way ? " " No ; how can it ? " " But
surely that which is without motion must keep still,
and that which keeps still must be at rest." " Yes,
it must." " Then the non-existent one is both at
rest and in motion." "So it appears." "And if it
is in motion, it certainly must change in its nature ;
for if anything is moved in any way, in so far as it
is moved it is no longer in its former condition, but
in a different one." "True." "Then in moving,
the one changes in nature." " Yes." " And yet
when it does not move in any way, it will not change
its nature in any way." "No." "Then in so far
as the non-existent one moves, it changes, and in so
far as it does not move, it does not change." "True."
" Then the non-existent one both changes and does
not change." "So it appears." "And must not
that which changes come into a state of being other
than its previous one, and perish, so far as its previous
state is concerned ; whereas that which does not
change neither comes into being nor perishes ? "
" That is inevitable." " Then the non-existent one,
when it is changed, comes into being and perishes,
and when it is not changed, neither comes into
being nor perishes ; and thus the non-existent one
both comes into being and perishes and neither comes
into being nor perishes." "Quite true."

" Let us now go back again to the beginning and
see whether the conclusions we reach will be the

ἕτερα.” “ἀλλὰ χρή.” “οὐκοῦν ἓν εἰ μὴ ἔστι,
C φαμέν, τί χρὴ περὶ αὐτοῦ ξυμβαίνειν;” “ναί.”
“τὸ δὲ μὴ ἔστιν ὅταν λέγωμεν, ἆρα μή τι ἄλλο
σημαίνει ἢ οὐσίας ἀπουσίαν τούτῳ ᾧ ἂν φῶμεν
μὴ εἶναι;” “οὐδὲν ἄλλο.” “πότερον οὖν, ὅταν
φῶμεν μὴ εἶναί τι, πῶς οὐκ εἶναί φαμεν αὐτό,
πῶς δὲ εἶναι; ἢ τοῦτο τὸ μὴ ἔστι λεγόμενον
ἁπλῶς σημαίνει ὅτι οὐδαμῶς οὐδαμῇ ἔστιν οὐδέ
πῃ μετέχει οὐσίας τό γε μὴ ὄν;” “ἁπλούστατα
μὲν οὖν.” “οὔτε ἄρα εἶναι δύναιτο ἂν τὸ μὴ ὂν
D οὔτε ἄλλως οὐδαμῶς οὐσίας μετέχειν.” “οὐ
γάρ.” “τὸ δὲ γίγνεσθαι καὶ τὸ ἀπόλλυσθαι μή
τι ἄλλο ἦν[1] ἢ τὸ μὲν οὐσίας μεταλαμβάνειν, τὸ δ'
ἀπολλύναι οὐσίαν;” “οὐδὲν ἄλλο.” “ᾧ δέ γε
μηδὲν τούτου μέτεστιν, οὔτ' ἂν λαμβάνοι οὔτ'
ἀπολλύοι αὐτό.” “πῶς γάρ;” “τῷ ἑνὶ ἄρα,
ἐπειδὴ οὐδαμῇ ἔστιν, οὔτε ἐκτέον οὔτε ἀπαλ-
λακτέον οὔτε μεταληπτέον οὐσίας οὐδαμῶς.”
“εἰκός.” “οὔτε ἄρα ἀπόλλυται τὸ μὴ ὂν ἓν
οὔτε γίγνεται, ἐπείπερ οὐδαμῇ μετέχει οὐσίας.”
“οὐ φαίνεται.” “οὐδ' ἄρ' ἀλλοιοῦται οὐδαμῇ·
E ἤδη γὰρ ἂν γίγνοιτό τε καὶ ἀπολλύοιτο τοῦτο
πάσχον.” “ἀληθῆ.” “εἰ δὲ μὴ ἀλλοιοῦται, οὐκ
ἀνάγκη μηδὲ κινεῖσθαι;” “ἀνάγκη.” “οὐδὲ
μὴν ἑστάναι φήσομεν τὸ μηδαμοῦ ὄν. τὸ γὰρ
ἑστὸς ἐν τῷ αὐτῷ τινι δεῖ ἀεὶ εἶναι. “τῷ αὐτῷ·[2]
πῶς γὰρ οὔ;” “οὕτω δὴ αὖ τὸ μὴ ὂν μήτε
ποτὲ ἑστάναι μήτε κινεῖσθαι λέγωμεν.” “μὴ
γὰρ οὖν.” “ἀλλὰ μὴν οὐδ' ἔστι γε αὐτῷ τι τῶν

---

[1] ἦν Heindorf : ἢ BT.
[2] τῷ αὐτῷ BT (B gives it to the other speaker): τὸ αὐτό al.

same as at present, or different." " Yes, we should
do that." " We ask, then, if the one is not, what
will be the consequences in regard to it ? " " Yes."
" Does the expression ' is not ' denote anything else
than the absence of existence in that of which we
say that it is not ? " " No, nothing else." " And
when we say that a thing is not, do we mean that
it is in a way and is not in a way ? Or does the
expression ' is not ' mean without any qualifications
that the non-existent is not in any way, shape, or
manner, and does not participate in being in any
way ? " " Without any qualifications whatsoever."
" Then the non-existent cannot be and cannot in
any other way partake of existence." " No."
" But were coming into being and perishing anything else than receiving and losing existence ? "
" No, nothing else." " But that which has no
participation in it can neither receive it nor lose it."
" Of course not." " Then the one, since it does
not exist in any way, cannot possess or lose or share
in existence at all." " That is reasonable." " Then
the non-existent one neither perishes nor comes
into being, since it participates in no way in existence." " No ; that is clear." " Then it is not
changed in nature at all ; for such change involves
coming into being and perishing." " True." " And
if it is not changed, it cannot move, either, can
it ? " " Certainly not." " And we cannot say that
that which is nowhere is at rest ; for that which is
at rest must always be in some place which is the
same." " Yes, of course, the same place." " Thus
we shall say again that the non-existent one is
neither at rest nor in motion." " No, neither."
" Nor can anything which exists pertain to it ; for

ὄντων. ἤδη γὰρ ἂν του μετέχον ὄντος οὐσίας
164 μετέχοι." "δῆλον." "οὔτε ἄρα μέγεθος οὔτε
σμικρότης οὔτε ἰσότης αὐτῷ ἔστιν." "οὐ γάρ."
"οὐδὲ μὴν ὁμοιότης γε οὐδὲ ἑτεροιότης οὔτε πρὸς
αὐτὸ οὔτε πρὸς τἆλλα εἴη ἂν αὐτῷ." "οὐ φαίνεται." "τί δέ; τἆλλα ἔσθ' ὅπως ἂν εἴη αὐτῷ,
εἰ μηδὲν αὐτῷ δεῖ εἶναι;" "οὐκ ἔστιν." "οὔτε
ἄρα ὅμοια οὔτε ἀνόμοια οὔτε ταὐτὰ οὔθ' ἕτερά
ἐστιν αὐτῷ τὰ ἄλλα." "οὐ γάρ." "τί δέ; τὸ
ἐκείνου ἢ τὸ ἐκείνῳ ἢ τὸ τὶ ἢ τὸ τοῦτο ἢ τὸ τούτου
B ἢ ἄλλου ἢ ἄλλῳ ἢ ποτὲ ἢ ἔπειτα ἢ νῦν ἢ ἐπιστήμη
ἢ δόξα ἢ αἴσθησις ἢ λόγος ἢ ὄνομα ἢ ἄλλο ὁτιοῦν
τῶν ὄντων περὶ τὸ μὴ ὂν ἔσται;" "οὐκ ἔσται."
"οὕτω δὴ ἓν οὐκ ὂν οὐκ ἔχει πως οὐδαμῇ."
"οὔκουν δὴ ἔοικέν γε οὐδαμῇ ἔχειν."

26. "Ἔτι δὴ λέγωμεν, ἓν εἰ μὴ ἔστι, τἆλλα τί
χρὴ πεπονθέναι." "λέγωμεν γάρ." "ἄλλα μέν
που δεῖ αὐτὰ εἶναι· εἰ γὰρ μηδὲ ἄλλα ἐστίν, οὐκ
ἂν περὶ τῶν ἄλλων λέγοιτο." "οὕτω." "εἰ δὲ
περὶ τῶν ἄλλων ὁ λόγος, τά γε ἄλλα ἕτερά ἐστιν.
ἢ οὐκ ἐπὶ τῷ αὐτῷ καλεῖς τό τε ἄλλο καὶ τὸ
C ἕτερον;" "ἔγωγε." "ἕτερον δέ γέ πού φαμεν
τὸ ἕτερον εἶναι ἑτέρου, καὶ τὸ ἄλλο δὴ ἄλλο εἶναι
ἄλλου;" "ναί." "καὶ τοῖς ἄλλοις ἄρα, εἰ μέλλει ἄλλα εἶναι, ἔστι τι οὗ ἄλλα ἔσται." "ἀνάγκη."
"τί δὴ οὖν ἂν εἴη; τοῦ μὲν γὰρ ἑνὸς οὐκ ἔσται
ἄλλα, μὴ ὄντος γε." "οὐ γάρ." "ἀλλήλων ἄρα
ἐστί· τοῦτο γὰρ αὐτοῖς ἔτι λείπεται, ἢ μηδενὸς
εἶναι ἄλλοις." "ὀρθῶς." "κατὰ πλήθη ἄρα
ἕκαστα ἀλλήλων ἄλλα ἐστί. κατὰ ἓν γὰρ οὐκ
ἂν οἷά τε εἴη, μὴ ὄντος ἑνός· ἀλλ' ἕκαστος, ὡς

the moment it partook of anything which exists it would partake of existence." "That is plain." "Then neither greatness nor smallness nor equality pertains to it." "No." "Nor likeness nor difference, either in relation to itself or to other things." "Clearly not." "And can other things pertain to it, if nothing pertains to it?" "Impossible." "Then the other things are neither like it nor unlike it, nor the same nor different." "No." "Well, then, will the notions 'of that' or 'to that' or 'some,' or 'this' or 'of this' or 'of another' or 'to another' or past or future or present or knowledge or opinion or perception or definition or name or anything else which exists pertain to the non-existent?" "No." "Then the non-existent one has no state or condition whatsoever." "It appears to have none whatsoever."

"Let us then discuss further what happens to the other things, if the one does not exist." "Let us do so." "Well, they must exist; for if others do not even exist, there could be no talking about the others." "True." "But if we talk about the others, the others are different. Or do you not regard the words other and different as synonymous?" "Yes, I do." "And we say that the different is different from the different, and the other is other than the other?" "Yes." "Then if the others are to be others, there must be something of which they will be others." "Yes, there must be." "Now what can that be? For they cannot be others of the one, if it does not exist." "No." "Then they are others of each other; for they have no alternative, except to be others of nothing." "True. "They are each, then, others of each other, in groups; for they cannot be so one at a time, if one

PLATO

D ἔοικεν, ὁ ὄγκος αὐτῶν ἄπειρός ἐστι πλήθει, κἂν
τὸ σμικρότατον δοκοῦν εἶναι λάβῃ τις, ὥσπερ
ὄναρ ἐν ὕπνῳ φαίνεται ἐξαίφνης ἀντὶ ἑνὸς δόξαντος
εἶναι πολλὰ καὶ ἀντὶ σμικροτάτου παμμέγεθες
πρὸς τὰ κερματιζόμενα ἐξ αὐτοῦ." "ὀρθότατα."
"τοιούτων δὴ ὄγκων ἄλλα ἀλλήλων ἂν εἴη τἆλλα,
εἰ ἑνὸς μὴ ὄντος ἄλλα ἐστίν." "κομιδῇ μὲν
οὖν." "οὐκοῦν πολλοὶ ὄγκοι ἔσονται, εἷς ἕκαστος
φαινόμενος, ὢν δὲ οὔ, εἴπερ ἓν μὴ ἔσται;" "οὕ-
E τω." "καὶ ἀριθμὸς δὲ εἶναι αὐτῶν δόξει, εἴπερ
καὶ ἓν ἕκαστον, πολλῶν ὄντων." "πάνυ γε."
"καὶ τὰ μὲν δὴ ἄρτια, τὰ δὲ περιττὰ ἐν αὐτοῖς
ὄντα οὐκ ἀληθῶς φαίνεται, εἴπερ ἓν μὴ ἔσται."
"οὐ γὰρ οὖν." "καὶ μὴν καὶ σμικρότατόν γε,
φαμέν, δόξει ἐν¹ αὐτοῖς ἐνεῖναι·² φαίνεται δὲ
τοῦτο πολλὰ καὶ μεγάλα πρὸς ἕκαστον τῶν πολλῶν
165 ὡς σμικρῶν ὄντων." "πῶς δ' οὔ;" "καὶ ἴσος
μὴν τοῖς πολλοῖς καὶ σμικροῖς ἕκαστος ὄγκος
δοξασθήσεται εἶναι. οὐ γὰρ ἂν μετέβαινεν ἐκ
μείζονος εἰς ἔλαττον φαινόμενος, πρὶν εἰς τὸ
μεταξὺ δόξειεν³ ἐλθεῖν· τοῦτο δ' εἴη ἂν φάντασμα
ἰσότητος." "εἰκός." "οὐκοῦν καὶ πρὸς ἄλλον
ὄγκον πέρας ἔχων, αὐτός γε⁴ πρὸς αὑτὸν οὔτε
ἀρχὴν οὔτε πέρας οὔτε μέσον ἔχων;" "πῇ δή;"
"ὅτι ἀεὶ αὐτῶν ὅταν τίς τι λάβῃ τῇ διανοίᾳ ὥς τι
τούτων ὄν, πρό τε τῆς ἀρχῆς ἄλλη ἀεὶ φαίνεται
B ἀρχή, μετά τε τὴν τελευτὴν ἑτέρα ὑπολειπομένη
τελευτή, ἔν τε τῷ μέσῳ ἄλλα μεσαίτερα τοῦ
μέσου, σμικρότερα δέ, διὰ τὸ μὴ δύνασθαι ἑνὸς
αὐτῶν ἑκάστου λαμβάνεσθαι, ἅτε οὐκ ὄντος τοῦ

---

¹ δόξει ἐν Heindorf: δόξειεν ΒΤ.   ² ἐνεῖναι] ἐν εἶναι Β : εἶναι Τ.
³ δόξειεν Τ: δόξειν Β.   ⁴ γε Hermann: τε ΒΤ.

326

does not exist. But each mass of them is unlimited
in number, and even if you take what seems to be
the smallest bit, it suddenly changes, like something
in a dream ; that which seemed to be one is seen
to be many, and instead of very small it is seen to
be very great in comparison with the minute fractions
of it." "Very true." "Such masses of others
would be others of each other, if others exist and
one does not exist." "Certainly." "There will,
then, be many masses, each of which appears to
be one, but is not one, if one does not exist?"
"Yes." "And they will seem to possess number,
if each seems to be one and they are many." "Certainly." "And some will seem to be even and
others odd, but all that will be unreal, if the one
does not exist." "True." "And there will, we
assert, seem to be a smallest among them ; but
this proves to be many and great in comparison
with each of the many minute fractions." "Of
course." "And each mass will be considered equal
to the many minute fractions ; for it could not
appear to pass from greater to smaller, without
seeming to enter that which is between them ;
hence the appearance of equality." "That is
reasonable." "And although it has a limit in
relation to another mass, it has neither beginning
nor limit nor middle in relation to itself?"
"Why is that?" "Because whenever the mind
conceives of any of these as belonging to the masses,
another beginning appears before the beginning,
another end remains after the end, and in the
middle are other more central middles than the
middle, but smaller, because it is impossible to
conceive of each one of them, since the one does

PLATO

ἑνός." "ἀληθέστατα." "θρύπτεσθαι δή,[1] οἶμαι,
κερματιζόμενον ἀνάγκη πᾶν τὸ ὄν, ὃ ἄν τις λάβῃ
τῇ διανοίᾳ. ὄγκος γάρ που ἄνευ ἑνὸς αἰεὶ[2] λαμ-
βάνοιτο ἄν." "πάνυ μὲν οὖν." "οὐκοῦν τό γε
τοιοῦτον πόρρωθεν μὲν ὁρῶντι καὶ ἀμβλὺ ἓν
C φαίνεσθαι[3] ἀνάγκη, ἐγγύθεν δὲ καὶ ὀξὺ νοοῦντι
πλήθει ἄπειρον ἓν ἕκαστον φανῆναι, εἴπερ στέρεται
τοῦ ἑνὸς μὴ ὄντος;" "ἀναγκαιότατον μὲν οὖν."
"οὕτω δὴ ἄπειρά τε καὶ πέρας ἔχοντα καὶ ἓν καὶ
πολλὰ ἕκαστα τἆλλα δεῖ φαίνεσθαι, ἓν εἰ μὴ
ἔστιν, τἆλλα[4] δὲ τοῦ ἑνός." "δεῖ γάρ." "οὐκοῦν
καὶ ὅμοιά τε καὶ ἀνόμοια δόξει εἶναι;" "πῇ
δή;" "οἷον ἐσκιαγραφημένα ἀποστάντι μὲν ἓν
πάντα φαινόμενα ταὐτὸν φαίνεσθαι πεπονθέναι καὶ
D ὅμοια εἶναι." "πάνυ γε." "προσελθόντι δέ γε
πολλὰ καὶ ἕτερα καὶ τῷ τοῦ ἑτέρου φαντάσματι
ἑτεροῖα καὶ ἀνόμοια ἑαυτοῖς." "οὕτω." "καὶ
ὁμοίους δὴ καὶ ἀνομοίους τοὺς ὄγκους αὐτούς τε
ἑαυτοῖς ἀνάγκη φαίνεσθαι καὶ ἀλλήλοις." "πάνυ
μὲν οὖν." "οὐκοῦν καὶ τοὺς αὐτοὺς καὶ ἑτέρους
ἀλλήλων, καὶ ἁπτομένους καὶ χωρὶς ἑαυτῶν, καὶ
κινουμένους πάσας κινήσεις καὶ ἑστῶτας πάντῃ,
καὶ γιγνομένους καὶ ἀπολλυμένους καὶ μηδέτερα,
καὶ πάντα που τὰ τοιαῦτα, ἃ διελθεῖν εὐπετὲς
E ἤδη ἡμῖν, εἰ ἑνὸς μὴ ὄντος πολλὰ ἔστιν." "ἀληθέστατα μὲν οὖν."
27. "Ἔτι δὴ ἅπαξ ἐλθόντες πάλιν ἐπὶ τὴν
ἀρχὴν εἴπωμεν, ἓν εἰ μὴ ἔστι, τἆλλα δὲ τοῦ ἑνός,
τί χρὴ εἶναι." "εἴπωμεν γὰρ οὖν." "οὐκοῦν

---

[1] δή B: δὲ T.   [2] αἰεὶ T: om. B.
[3] ἓν φαίνεσθαι b: ἐμφαίνεσθαι BT.
[4] τἆλλα corr. Ven. 189: ἄλλα B: ἀλλὰ T.

PARMENIDES

not exist." "Very true." "So all being which is
conceived by any mind must, it seems to me, be
broken up into minute fractions; for it would
always be conceived as a mass devoid of one."
"Certainly." "Now anything of that sort, if seen
from a distance and dimly, must appear to be one,
but if seen from close at hand and with keen vision,
each apparent one must prove to be unlimited in
number, if it is really devoid of one, and one does
not exist. Am I right?" "That is perfectly
conclusive." "Therefore the other things must
each and all appear to be unlimited and limited
and one and many, if the things other than one
exist and one does not." "Yes, they must."
"And will they not also appear to be like and unlike?" "Why?" "Just as things in a picture,
when viewed from a distance, appear to be all in
one and the same condition and alike." "Certainly." "But when you come close to them they
appear to be many and different, and, because of
their difference in appearance, different in kind and
unlike each other." "Yes." "And so the groups
of the other things must appear to be like and unlike
themselves and each other." "Certainly." "And
also the same and different, and in contact with one
another and separated, and in all kinds of motion
and in every sort of rest, and coming into being
and perishing, and neither of the two, and all that
sort of thing, which we can easily mention in detail,
if the many exist and the one does not." "Very
true."

"Let us, then, go back once more to the beginning
and tell the consequences, if the others exist and
the one does not." "Let us do so." "Well, the

329

ἓν μὲν οὐκ ἔσται τἆλλα.'' ''πῶς γάρ;'' ''οὐδὲ
μὴν πολλά γε· ἐν γὰρ πολλοῖς οὖσιν ἐνείη[1] ἂν καὶ
ἕν. εἰ γὰρ μηδὲν αὐτῶν ἐστιν ἕν, ἅπαντα οὐδέν
ἐστιν, ὥστε οὐδ' ἂν πολλὰ εἴη.'' ''ἀληθῆ.''
''μὴ ἐνόντος δὲ ἑνὸς ἐν τοῖς ἄλλοις, οὔτε πολλὰ
166 οὔτε ἕν ἐστι τἆλλα.'' ''οὐ γάρ.'' ''οὐδέ γε
φαίνεται ἓν οὐδὲ πολλά.'' ''τί δή;'' ''ὅτι τἆλλα
τῶν μὴ ὄντων οὐδενὶ οὐδαμῆ οὐδαμῶς οὐδεμίαν
κοινωνίαν ἔχει, οὐδέ τι τῶν μὴ ὄντων παρὰ τῶν
ἄλλων τῴ ἐστιν. οὐδὲν γὰρ μέρος ἐστὶ τοῖς μὴ
οὖσιν.'' ''ἀληθῆ.'' ''οὐδ' ἄρα δόξα τοῦ μὴ
ὄντος παρὰ τοῖς ἄλλοις ἐστὶν οὐδέ τι φάντασμα,
οὐδὲ δοξάζεται οὐδαμῆ οὐδαμῶς τὸ μὴ ὂν ἐπὶ[2]
τῶν ἄλλων.'' ''οὐ γὰρ οὖν.'' ''ἓν ἄρα εἰ μὴ
B ἔστιν, οὐδὲ δοξάζεταί τι τῶν ἄλλων ἓν εἶναι οὐδὲ
πολλά· ἄνευ γὰρ ἑνὸς πολλὰ δοξάσαι ἀδύνατον.''
''ἀδύνατον γάρ.'' ''ἓν ἄρα εἰ μὴ ἔστι, τἆλλα
οὔτε ἔστιν οὔτε δοξάζεται ἓν οὐδὲ πολλά.'' ''οὐκ
ἔοικεν.'' ''οὐδ' ἄρα ὅμοια οὐδὲ ἀνόμοια.'' ''οὐ
γάρ.'' ''οὐδὲ μὴν τὰ αὐτά γε οὐδ' ἕτερα, οὐδὲ
ἁπτόμενα οὐδὲ χωρίς, οὐδὲ ἄλλα ὅσα ἐν τοῖς
πρόσθεν διήλθομεν ὡς φαινόμενα αὐτά, τούτων
οὔτε τι ἔστιν οὔτε φαίνεται τἆλλα, ἓν εἰ μὴ ἔστιν.''
C ''ἀληθῆ.'' ''οὐκοῦν καὶ συλλήβδην εἰ εἴποιμεν,
ἓν εἰ μὴ ἔστιν, οὐδέν ἐστιν, ὀρθῶς ἂν εἴποιμεν;''
''παντάπασι μὲν οὖν.'' ''εἰρήσθω τοίνυν τοῦτό
τε καὶ ὅτι, ὡς ἔοικεν, ἓν εἴτ' ἔστιν εἴτε μὴ ἔστιν,
αὐτό τε καὶ τἆλλα καὶ πρὸς αὑτὰ καὶ πρὸς ἄλληλα
πάντα πάντως ἐστί τε καὶ οὐκ ἔστι καὶ φαίνεταί
τε καὶ οὐ φαίνεται.'' ''ἀληθέστατα.''

---

[1] ἐνείη] ἓν εἴη B : εἴη T.   [2] ἐπὶ Schleiermacher : ὑπὸ BT.

others will not be one?" "Of course not." "Nor
will they be many; for if they were many, one
would be contained in them. And if none of
them is one, they are all nothing, so that they
cannot be many." "True." "If one is not
contained in the others, the others are neither
many nor one." "No." "And they do not even
appear to be one or many." "Why is that?"
"Because the others have no communion in any
way whatsoever with anything which is non-existent,
and nothing that is non-existent pertains to any of
the others, for things that are non-existent have
no parts." "True." "Nor is there any opinion
or appearance of the non-existent in connexion
with the others, nor is the non-existent conceived
of in any way whatsoever as related to the others."
"No." "Then if one does not exist, none of the
others will be conceived of as being one or as being
many, either; for it is impossible to conceive of
many without one. "True, it is impossible." "Then
if one does not exist, the others neither are nor are
conceived to be either one or many." "No; so it
seems." "Nor like nor unlike." "No." "Nor
the same nor different, nor in contact nor separate,
nor any of the other things which we were saying
they appeared to be. The others neither are nor
appear to be any of these, if the one does not exist."
"True." "Then if we were to say in a word, 'if the
one is not, nothing is,' should we be right?" "Most
assuredly." "Then let us say that, and we may
add, as it appears, that whether the one is or is
not, the one and the others in relation to themselves
and to each other all in every way are and are not
and appear and do not appear." "Very true."

331

GREATER HIPPIAS

INTRODUCTION TO THE
GREATER HIPPIAS

THE *Greater Hippias* presents the great sophist of Elis as a distinguished representative of his profession, thoroughly imbued with self-confidence and self-importance, and utterly unable to meet the questionings of Socrates. The ostensible subject of the dialogue is The Beautiful, which Socrates asks Hippias to define. Every definition is found to be unsatisfactory, so that the final result is negative. The real purpose of the dialogue seems to be to portray the personality of Hippias and the pertinacity of Socrates in pursuing every question— or rather every answer—until the discomfiture of his interlocutor is complete.

The dialogue is generally (and, in my opinion, rightly) regarded as not the work of Plato. The somewhat frigid humour of Socrates, in pretending that he persists in his interrogations because a " certain man " is sure to find the faults in the definitions proposed, does not necessarily preclude Plato as the author, though nothing closely resembling it is to be found in the dialogues universally accepted. The style resembles that of Plato, though in some particulars it is peculiar. In the *Phaedrus* Plato himself imitates the style of Lysias so closely that the discourse on the lover and the

non-lover has sometimes been regarded as a genuine work of Lysias, and it would not be very difficult for another to write in a style as similar to Plato's as is that of this dialogue. The apparent reference (286 B) to the *Lesser Hippias* proves nothing as to the genuineness of either this dialogue or that. On the whole, there is little probability that this is Plato's work. If it is his, it must be one of his earlier dialogues.

The Greek word καλός has a broader field of application than the English word " beautiful," and it is, therefore, occasionally difficult to render a passage satisfactorily ; for though we may speak of a beautiful act, we can hardly apply the word " beautiful " to laws and constitutions, for example. Then, too, there is no English opposite of " beautiful " which has, even approximately, the widely extended signification of the Greek αἰσχρός. Occasionally, therefore, the direct opposition of καλός and αἰσχρός fails to appear adequately in the English version.

ΙΠΠΙΑΣ ΜΕΙΖΩΝ

[Η ΠΕΡΙ ΤΟΥ ΚΑΛΟΥ· ΑΝΑΤΡΕΠΤΙΚΟΣ]

ΤΑ ΤΟΥ ΔΙΑΛΟΓΟΥ ΠΡΟΣΩΠΑ

ΣΩΚΡΑΤΗΣ, ΙΠΠΙΑΣ

1. ΣΩ. Ἱππίας ὁ καλός τε καὶ σοφός, ὡς διὰ χρόνου ἡμῖν κατῆρας εἰς τὰς Ἀθήνας.

ΙΠ. Οὐ γὰρ σχολή, ὦ Σώκρατες. ἡ γὰρ Ἦλις ὅταν τι δέηται διαπράξασθαι πρός τινα τῶν πόλεων, ἀεὶ ἐπὶ πρῶτον ἐμὲ ἔρχεται τῶν πολιτῶν αἱρουμένη πρεσβευτήν, ἡγουμένη δικαστὴν καὶ ἄγγελον ἱκανώτατον εἶναι τῶν λόγων, οἳ ἂν παρὰ τῶν πόλεων B ἑκάστων λέγωνται. πολλάκις μὲν οὖν καὶ εἰς ἄλλας πόλεις ἐπρέσβευσα, πλεῖστα δὲ καὶ περὶ πλείστων καὶ μεγίστων εἰς Λακεδαίμονα· διὸ δή, ὃ σὺ ἐρωτᾷς, οὐ θαμίζω εἰς τούσδε τοὺς τόπους.

ΣΩ. Τοιοῦτον μέντοι, ὦ Ἱππία, ἔστι τὸ τῇ ἀληθείᾳ σοφόν τε καὶ τέλειον ἄνδρα εἶναι. σὺ γὰρ καὶ ἰδίᾳ ἱκανὸς εἶ παρὰ τῶν νέων πολλὰ χρήματα C λαμβάνων ἔτι πλείω ὠφελεῖν ὧν λαμβάνεις, καὶ αὖ δημοσίᾳ τὴν σαυτοῦ πόλιν ἱκανὸς εὐεργετεῖν, ὥσπερ χρὴ τὸν μέλλοντα μὴ καταφρονήσεσθαι ἀλλ'

336

GREATER HIPPIAS

[or ON THE BEAUTIFUL : refutative]

CHARACTERS

Socrates, Hippias

soc. Hippias, beautiful and wise, what a long time it is since you have put in at the port of Athens !

hipp. I am too busy, Socrates. For whenever Elis needs to have any business transacted with any of the states, she always comes to me first of her citizens and chooses me as envoy, thinking that I am the ablest judge and messenger of the words that are spoken by the several states. So I have often gone as envoy to other states, but most often and concerning the most numerous and important matters to Lacedaemon. For that reason, then, since you ask me, I do not often come to this neighbourhood.

soc. That's what it is, Hippias, to be a truly wise and perfect man ! For you are both in your private capacity able to earn much money from the young and to confer upon them still greater benefits than you receive, and in public affairs you are able to benefit your own state, as a man must who is to be not despised but held in high repute among

PLATO

εὐδοκιμήσειν ἐν τοῖς πολλοῖς. ἀτάρ, ὦ Ἱππία, τί
ποτε τὸ αἴτιον, ὅτι οἱ παλαιοὶ ἐκεῖνοι, ὧν ὀνόματα
μεγάλα λέγεται ἐπὶ σοφίᾳ, Πιττακοῦ τε καὶ
Βίαντος καὶ τῶν ἀμφὶ τὸν Μιλήσιον Θαλῆν καὶ ἔτι
τῶν ὑστέρων μέχρι Ἀναξαγόρου, ὡς ἢ πάντες ἢ οἱ
D πολλοὶ αὐτῶν φαίνονται ἀπεχόμενοι τῶν πολιτικῶν
πράξεων;

ιπ. Τί δ' οἴει, ὦ Σώκρατες, ἄλλο γε ἢ ἀδύνατοι
ἦσαν καὶ οὐχ ἱκανοὶ ἐξικνεῖσθαι φρονήσει ἐπ'
ἀμφότερα, τά τε κοινὰ καὶ τὰ ἴδια;

2. σω. Ἆρ' οὖν πρὸς Διός, ὥσπερ αἱ ἄλλαι
τέχναι ἐπιδεδώκασι καὶ εἰσὶ παρὰ τοὺς νῦν δημιουργοὺς οἱ παλαιοὶ φαῦλοι, οὕτω καὶ τὴν ὑμετέραν
τῶν σοφιστῶν τέχνην ἐπιδεδωκέναι φῶμεν καὶ
εἶναι τῶν ἀρχαίων τοὺς περὶ τὴν σοφίαν φαύλους
πρὸς ὑμᾶς;

ιπ. Πάνυ μὲν οὖν ὀρθῶς λέγεις.

σω. Εἰ ἄρα νῦν ἡμῖν, ὦ Ἱππία, ὁ Βίας ἀναβιώη,
282 γέλωτ' ἂν ὄφλοι πρὸς ὑμᾶς, ὥσπερ καὶ τὸν Δαί-
δαλόν φασιν οἱ ἀνδριαντοποιοί, .νῦν εἰ γενόμενος
τοιαῦτ' ἐργάζοιτο οἷα ἦν ἀφ' ὧν τοὔνομ' ἔσχεν,
καταγέλαστον ἂν εἶναι.

ιπ. Ἔστι μὲν ταῦτα, ὦ Σώκρατες, οὕτως ὡς σὺ
λέγεις· εἴωθα μέντοι ἔγωγε τοὺς παλαιούς τε καὶ
προτέρους ἡμῶν προτέρους τε καὶ μᾶλλον ἐγκωμιά-
ζειν ἢ τοὺς νῦν, εὐλαβούμενος μὲν φθόνον τῶν
ζώντων, φοβούμενος δὲ μῆνιν τῶν τετελευτηκότων.

B σω. Καλῶς γε σύ, ὦ Ἱππία, ὀνομάζων τε καὶ
διανοούμενος, ὡς ἔμοιγε δοκεῖς. συμμαρτυρῆσαι
δέ σοι ἔχω ὅτι ἀληθῆ λέγεις, καὶ τῷ ὄντι ὑμῶν

---

¹ Pittacus of Mitylene, Bias of Priene, and Thales of
Miletus were among the traditional seven wise men.
338

the many. And yet, Hippias, what in the world is the reason why those men of old whose names are called great in respect to wisdom—Pittacus, and Bias, and the Milesian Thales[1] with his followers—and also the later ones, down to Anaxagoras, are all, or most of them, found to refrain from affairs of state ?

HIPP. What else do you suppose, Socrates, than that they were not able to compass by their wisdom both public and private matters ?

SOC. Then for Heaven's sake, just as the other arts have progressed, and the ancients are of no account in comparison with the artisans of to-day, shall we say that your art also has progressed and those of the ancients who were concerned with wisdom are of no account in comparison with you ?

HIPP. Yes, you are quite right.

SOC. Then, Hippias, if Bias were to come to life again now, he would be a laughing-stock in comparison with you, just as the sculptors say that Daedalus,[2] if he were to be born now and were to create such works as those from which he got his reputation, would be ridiculous.

HIPP. That, Socrates, is exactly as you say. I, however, am in the habit of praising the ancients and our predecessors rather than the men of the present day, and more greatly, as a precaution against the envy of the living and through fear of the wrath of those who are dead.

SOC. Yours, Hippias, is a most excellent way, at any rate, of speaking about them and of thinking, it seems to me ; and I can bear you witness that you speak the truth, and that your art really has

[2] Daedalus, the traditional inventor of sculpture.

ἐπιδέδωκεν ἡ τέχνη πρὸς τὸ καὶ τὰ δημόσια
πράττειν δύνασθαι μετὰ τῶν ἰδίων. Γοργίας τε
γὰρ οὗτος ὁ Λεοντῖνος σοφιστὴς δεῦρο ἀφίκετο
δημοσίᾳ οἴκοθεν πρεσβεύων, ὡς ἱκανώτατος ὢν
Λεοντίνων τὰ κοινὰ πράττειν, καὶ ἔν τε τῷ δήμῳ
ἔδοξεν ἄριστα εἰπεῖν, καὶ ἰδίᾳ ἐπιδείξεις ποιούμενος καὶ συνὼν τοῖς νέοις χρήματα πολλὰ εἰργά-
C σατο καὶ ἔλαβεν ἐκ τῆσδε τῆς πόλεως· εἰ δὲ βούλει,
ὁ ἡμέτερος ἑταῖρος Πρόδικος οὗτος πολλάκις μὲν
καὶ ἄλλοτε δημοσίᾳ ἀφίκετο, ἀτὰρ τὰ τελευταῖα
ἔναγχος ἀφικόμενος δημοσίᾳ ἐκ Κέω λέγων τ' ἐν
τῇ βουλῇ πάνυ εὐδοκίμησεν καὶ ἰδίᾳ ἐπιδείξεις
ποιούμενος καὶ τοῖς νέοις συνὼν χρήματα ἔλαβεν
θαυμαστὰ ὅσα. τῶν δὲ παλαιῶν ἐκείνων οὐδεὶς
πώποτε ἠξίωσεν ἀργύριον μισθὸν πράξασθαι οὐδ'
ἐπιδείξεις ποιήσασθαι ἐν παντοδαποῖς ἀνθρώποις
D τῆς ἑαυτοῦ σοφίας· οὕτως ἦσαν εὐήθεις καὶ ἐλελήθει αὐτοὺς ἀργύριον ὡς πολλοῦ ἄξιον εἴη.
τούτων δ' ἑκάτερος πλέον ἀργύριον[1] ἀπὸ σοφίας
εἴργασται ἢ ἄλλος δημιουργὸς ἀφ' ἡστινος τέχνης·
καὶ ἔτι πρότερος τούτων Πρωταγόρας.

3. ιπ. Οὐδὲν γάρ, ὦ Σώκρατες, οἶσθα τῶν καλῶν περὶ τοῦτο. εἰ γὰρ εἰδείης ὅσον ἀργύριον
εἴργασμαι ἐγώ, θαυμάσαις ἄν· καὶ τὰ μὲν ἄλλα ἐῶ,
E ἀφικόμενος δέ ποτε εἰς Σικελίαν, Πρωταγόρου
αὐτόθι ἐπιδημοῦντος καὶ εὐδοκιμοῦντος καὶ πρεσβυτέρου ὄντος πολὺ[2] νεώτερος ὢν ἐν ὀλίγῳ χρόνῳ

---

[1] ἀργύριον F : ἀργυρίου TW.
[2] πολὺ F : καὶ πολὺ TW.

---

[1] The word οὗτος does not indicate that Gorgias was
among those present at the moment, but only that he was
at the time much talked of at Athens. The imaginary, or

progressed in the direction of ability to carry on
public together with private affairs. For this man [1]
Gorgias, the sophist from Leontini, came here from
home in the public capacity of envoy, as being best
able of all the citizens of Leontini to attend to the
interests of the community, and it was the general
opinion that he spoke excellently in the public
assembly, and in his private capacity, by giving
exhibitions and associating with the young, he
earned and received a great deal of money from
this city ; or, if you like, our friend here, Prodicus,
often went to other places in a public capacity, and
the last time, just lately, when he came here in a
public capacity from Ceos, he gained great reputation by his speaking before the Council, and in his
private capacity, by giving exhibitions and associating with the young, he received a marvellous
sum of money ; but none of those ancients ever
thought fit to exact money as payment for his wisdom
or to give exhibitions among people of various places ;
so simple-minded were they, and so unconscious of
the fact that money is of greatest value. But either
of these two has earned more money from his wisdom
than any artisan from his art. And even before these
Protagoras did so.

HIPP. Why, Socrates, you know nothing of the
beauties of this. For if you were to know how
much money I have made, you would be amazed.
I won't mention the rest, but once, when I went
to Sicily, although Protagoras was staying there
and had a great reputation and was the older,
I, who was much younger, made in a very short

dramatic, date of this dialogue, would, then, be shortly
after the time of Gorgias' activity at Athens.

PLATO

πάνυ πλέον ἢ πεντήκοντα καὶ ἑκατὸν μνᾶς εἰρ-
γασάμην, καὶ ἐξ ἑνός γε χωρίου πάνυ σμικροῦ,
Ἰννυκοῦ, πλέον ἢ εἴκοσι μνᾶς· καὶ τοῦτο ἐλθὼν
οἴκαδε φέρων τῷ πατρὶ ἔδωκα, ὥστε ἐκεῖνον καὶ
τοὺς ἄλλους πολίτας θαυμάζειν τε καὶ ἐκπεπλῆχθαι.
καὶ σχεδόν τι οἶμαι ἐμὲ πλείω χρήματα εἰργάσθαι
ἢ ἄλλους σύνδυο οὕστινας βούλει τῶν σοφιστῶν.

ΣΩ. Καλόν γε, ὦ Ἱππία, λέγεις καὶ μέγα τεκμή-
283 ριον σοφίας τῆς τε σεαυτοῦ καὶ τῶν νῦν ἀνθρώπων
πρὸς τοὺς ἀρχαίους ὅσον διαφέρουσι. τῶν γὰρ
προτέρων περὶ Ἀναξαγόρου λέγεται[1] πολλὴ ἀμαθία
κατὰ τὸν σὸν λόγον· τοὐναντίον γὰρ Ἀναξαγόρᾳ
φασὶ συμβῆναι ἢ ὑμῖν· καταλειφθέντων γὰρ αὐτῷ
πολλῶν χρημάτων καταμελῆσαι καὶ ἀπολέσαι
πάντα· οὕτως αὐτὸν ἀνόητα σοφίζεσθαι. λέγουσι
δὲ καὶ περὶ ἄλλων τῶν παλαιῶν ἕτερα τοιαῦτα.
τοῦτο μὲν οὖν μοι δοκεῖς καλὸν τεκμήριον ἀποφαί-
Β νειν περὶ σοφίας τῶν νῦν πρὸς τοὺς προτέρους, καὶ
πολλοῖς συνδοκεῖ ὅτι τὸν σοφὸν αὐτὸν αὑτῷ μάλιστα
δεῖ σοφὸν εἶναι· τούτου δ' ὅρος ἐστὶν ἄρα, ὃς ἂν
πλεῖστον ἀργύριον ἐργάσηται.

4. Καὶ ταῦτα μὲν ἱκανῶς ἐχέτω· τόδε δέ μοι
εἰπέ, σὺ αὐτὸς πόθεν πλεῖστον ἀργύριον εἰργάσω
τῶν πόλεων εἰς ἃς ἀφικνεῖ; ἢ δῆλον ὅτι ἐκ
Λακεδαίμονος, οἷπερ[2] καὶ πλειστάκις ἀφῖξαι;

ΙΠ. Οὐ μὰ τὸν Δία, ὦ Σώκρατες.

ΣΩ. Πῶς φῄς; ἀλλ' ἐλάχιστον;

C ΙΠ. Οὐδὲν μὲν οὖν τὸ παράπαν πώποτε

---

[1] περὶ Ἀναξαγόρου λέγεται bracketed by Stallbaum.
[2] οἷπερ Heindorf: οὗπερ TWF.

time more than one hundred and fifty minas, and in one very small place, Inycus, more than twenty minas ; and when I came home, I took this and gave it to my father, so that he and the other citizens were overwhelmed with amazement. And I pretty well think I have made more money than any other two sophists together.

soc. That's a fine thing you say, Hippias, and strong testimony to your wisdom and that of the men of to-day and to their great superiority to the ancients. For the earlier sophists of the school of Anaxagoras must have been very ignorant to judge from what is said, according to your view ; for they say that what happened to Anaxagoras was the opposite of what happens to you ; for though much money was left him, he neglected it and lost it all ; so senseless was his wisdom. And they tell similar tales about others among the ancients. So this seems to me fine testimony that you adduce for the wisdom of the men of to-day as compared with the earlier men, and many people agree with me that the wise man must be wise for himself especially [1] ; and the test of this is, who makes the most money. Well, so much for that. But tell me this : at which of the cities that you go to did you make the most money ? Or are we to take it that it was at Lacedaemon, where your visits have been most frequent ?

hipp. No, by Zeus, it was not, Socrates.

soc. What's that you say ? But did you make least there ?

hipp. Why, I never made anything at all.

---

[1] Apparently a proverbial expression, like " physician, heal thyself " or " look out for number one."

PLATO

ΣΩ. Τέρας λέγεις καὶ θαυμαστόν, ὦ Ἱππία. καί μοι εἰπέ· ἡ σοφία ἡ σὴ οὐχ οἷα τοὺς συνόντας αὐτῇ καὶ μανθάνοντας εἰς ἀρετὴν βελτίους ποιεῖν;

ΙΠ. Καὶ πολύ γε, ὦ Σώκρατες.

ΣΩ. Ἀλλὰ τοὺς μὲν Ἰνυκίνων¹ υἱεῖς οἷός τε ἦσθα ἀμείνους ποιῆσαι, τοὺς δὲ Σπαρτιατῶν ἠδυνάτεις;

ΙΠ. Πολλοῦ γε δέω.

ΣΩ. Ἀλλὰ δῆτα Σικελιῶται μὲν ἐπιθυμοῦσιν ἀμείνους γίγνεσθαι, Λακεδαιμόνιοι δ᾿ οὔ;

D   ΙΠ. Πάντως γέ² που, ὦ Σώκρατες, καὶ Λακεδαιμόνιοι.

ΣΩ. Ἆρ᾿ οὖν χρημάτων ἐνδείᾳ ἔφευγον τὴν σὴν ὁμιλίαν;

ΙΠ. Οὐ δῆτα, ἐπεὶ ἱκανὰ αὐτοῖς ἐστιν.

ΣΩ. Τί δῆτ᾿ ἂν εἴη ὅτι ἐπιθυμοῦντες καὶ ἔχοντες χρήματα, καὶ σοῦ δυναμένου τὰ μέγιστα αὐτοὺς ὠφελεῖν, οὐ πλήρη σε ἀργυρίου ἀπέπεμψαν; ἀλλ᾿ ἐκεῖνο, μῶν μὴ Λακεδαιμόνιοι σοῦ βέλτιον ἂν παιδεύσειαν τοὺς αὑτῶν παῖδας; ἢ τοῦτο φῶμεν οὕτω, καὶ σὺ συγχωρεῖς;

E   ΙΠ. Οὐδ᾿ ὁπωστιοῦν.

ΣΩ. Πότερον οὖν τοὺς νέους οὐχ οἷός τ᾿ ἦσθα πείθειν ἐν Λακεδαίμονι ὡς σοὶ συνόντες πλέον ἂν εἰς ἀρετὴν ἐπιδιδοῖεν ἢ τοῖς ἑαυτῶν, ἢ τοὺς ἐκείνων πατέρας ἠδυνάτεις πείθειν ὅτι σοὶ χρὴ παραδιδόναι μᾶλλον ἢ αὐτοὺς ἐπιμελεῖσθαι, εἴπερ τι τῶν υἱῶν κήδονται; οὐ γάρ που ἐφθόνουν γε τοῖς ἑαυτῶν παισὶν ὡς βελτίστοις γενέσθαι.

ΙΠ. Οὐκ οἶμαι ἔγωγε φθονεῖν.

¹ Ἰνυκίνων Bekker : ἰνυκινῶν Τ : ἰνυκηνῶν W.
² γέ F : om. TW.

344

soc. That is a prodigious marvel that you tell, Hippias ; and say now : is not your wisdom such as to make those who are in contact with it and learn it, better men in respect to virtue ?

HIPP. Yes, much better, Socrates.

soc. But you were able to make the sons of the Inycenes better, and had no power to improve the sons of the Spartans ?

HIPP. That is far from true.

soc. Well, then, the Siceliotes desire to become better, and the Lacedaemonians do not ?

HIPP. No certainly, Socrates, the Lacedaemonians also desire it.

soc. Then it was for lack of money that they avoided intercourse with you ?

HIPP. Not at all, since they have plenty of money

soc. What, then, could be the reason, that when they desired it and had money, and you had power to confer upon them the greatest benefits, they did not send you away loaded with money ? But I see ; perhaps the Lacedaemonians might educate their own children better than you ? Shall we state it so, and do you agree ?

HIPP. Not in the least.

soc. Then were you not able to persuade the young men at Lacedaemon that they would make more progress towards virtue by associating with you than with their own people, or were you powerless to persuade their fathers that they ought rather to hand them over to you than to care for them themselves, if they are at all concerned for their sons ? For surely they did not begrudge it to their children to beeome as good as possible.

HIPP. I do not think they begrudged it.

ΣΩ. Ἀλλὰ μὴν εὔνομός γ' ἡ Λακεδαίμων.

ΙΠ. Πῶς γὰρ οὔ;

284 ΣΩ. Ἐν δέ γε ταῖς εὐνόμοις πόλεσι τιμιώτατον ἡ ἀρετή.

ΙΠ. Πάνυ γε.

ΣΩ. Σὺ δὲ ταύτην παραδιδόναι ἄλλῳ κάλλιστ' ἀνθρώπων ἐπίστασαι.

ΙΠ. Καὶ πολύ γε, ὦ Σώκρατες.

5. ΣΩ. Ὁ οὖν κάλλιστ' ἐπιστάμενος ἱππικὴν παραδιδόναι ἆρ' οὐκ ἂν ἐν Θετταλίᾳ τῆς Ἑλλάδος μάλιστα τιμῷτο καὶ πλεῖστα χρήματα λαμβάνοι, καὶ ἄλλοθι ὅπου τοῦτο σπουδάζοιτο;

ΙΠ. Εἰκός γε.

ΣΩ. Ὁ δὴ δυνάμενος παραδιδόναι τὰ πλείστου
Β ἄξια μαθήματα εἰς ἀρετὴν οὐκ ἐν Λακεδαίμονι μάλιστα τιμήσεται καὶ πλεῖστα ἐργάσεται χρήματα, ἂν βούληται, καὶ ἐν ἄλλῃ πόλει ἥτις τῶν Ἑλληνίδων εὐνομεῖται; ἀλλ' ἐν Σικελίᾳ, ὦ ἑταῖρε, οἴει μᾶλλον καὶ ἐν Ἰνυκῷ; ταῦτα πειθώμεθα, ὦ Ἱππία; ἐὰν γὰρ σὺ κελεύῃς, πειστέον.

ΙΠ. Οὐ γὰρ πάτριον, ὦ Σώκρατες, Λακεδαιμονίοις κινεῖν τοὺς νόμους, οὐδὲ παρὰ τὰ εἰωθότα παιδεύειν τοὺς υἱεῖς.

ΣΩ. Πῶς λέγεις; Λακεδαιμονίοις οὐ πάτριον
C ὀρθῶς πράττειν ἀλλ' ἐξαμαρτάνειν;

ΙΠ. Οὐκ ἂν φαίην ἔγωγε, ὦ Σώκρατες.

ΣΩ. Οὐκοῦν ὀρθῶς ἂν πράττοιεν βέλτιον ἀλλὰ μὴ χεῖρον παιδεύοντες τοὺς νέους;

346

soc. But certainly Lacedaemon is well governed.

HIPP. Of course it is.

soc. And in well-governed states virtue is most highly honoured.

HIPP. Certainly.

soc. And you know best of all men how to transmit that to another.

HIPP. Much best, Socrates.

soc. Well, he who knows best how to transmit horsemanship would be most honoured in Thessaly of all parts of Greece and would receive most money —and anywhere else where horsemanship is a serious interest, would he not ?

HIPP. Very likely.

soc. Then will not he who is able to transmit the doctrines that are of most value for the acquisition of virtue be most highly honoured in Lacedaemon and make most money, if he so wishes, and in any other of the Greek states that is well governed ? But do you, my friend, think he will fare better in Sicily and at Inycus ? Are we to believe that, Hippias ? For if you tell us to do so, we must believe it.

HIPP. Yes, for it is not the inherited usage of the Lacedaemonians to change their laws or to educate their children differently from what is customary.

soc. What ? For the Lacedaemonians is it the hereditary usage not to act rightly, but to commit errors ?

HIPP. I wouldn't say so, Socrates.

soc. Would they, then, not act rightly in educating the young men better, but not in educating them worse ?

PLATO

ιπ. Ὀρθῶς· ἀλλὰ ξενικὴν παίδευσιν οὐ νόμιμον
αὐτοῖς παιδεύειν, ἐπεὶ εὖ ἴσθι, εἴπερ τις ἄλλος
ἐκεῖθεν χρήματα ἔλαβεν πώποτε ἐπὶ παιδεύσει, καὶ
ἐμὲ ἂν λαβεῖν πολὺ μάλιστα· χαίρουσι γοῦν ἀκούοντες ἐμοῦ καὶ ἐπαινοῦσιν· ἀλλ', ὃ λέγω, οὐ νόμος.

ΣΩ. Νόμον δὲ λέγεις, ὦ Ἱππία, βλάβην πόλεως
D εἶναι ἢ ὠφέλειαν;

ιπ. Τίθεται μέν, οἶμαι, ὠφελείας ἕνεκα, ἐνίοτε
δὲ καὶ βλάπτει, ἐὰν κακῶς τεθῇ ὁ νόμος.

ΣΩ. Τί δέ; οὐχ ὡς ἀγαθὸν μέγιστον πόλει
τίθενται τὸν νόμον οἱ τιθέμενοι; καὶ ἄνευ τούτου
μετὰ εὐνομίας[1] ἀδύνατον οἰκεῖν;

ιπ. Ἀληθῆ λέγεις.

ΣΩ. Ὅταν ἄρα ἀγαθοῦ ἁμάρτωσιν οἱ ἐπιχει-
ροῦντες τοὺς νόμους τιθέναι, νομίμου τε καὶ νόμου
ἡμαρτήκασιν· ἢ πῶς λέγεις;

E ιπ. Τῷ μὲν ἀκριβεῖ λόγῳ, ὦ Σώκρατες, οὕτως
ἔχει· οὐ μέντοι εἰώθασιν ἄνθρωποι ὀνομάζειν
οὕτως.

ΣΩ. Πότερον, ὦ Ἱππία, οἱ εἰδότες ἢ οἱ μὴ
εἰδότες;

ιπ. Οἱ πολλοί.

ΣΩ. Εἰσὶ δ' οὗτοι οἱ εἰδότες τἀληθές, οἱ πολλοί;

ιπ. Οὐ δῆτα.

ΣΩ. Ἀλλὰ μήν που οἵ γ' εἰδότες τὸ ὠφελιμώτερον τοῦ ἀνωφελεστέρου νομιμώτερον ἡγοῦνται
τῇ ἀληθείᾳ πᾶσιν ἀνθρώποις· ἢ οὐ συγχωρεῖς;

ιπ. Ναί, συγχωρῶ, ὅτι γε τῇ ἀληθείᾳ.

[1] εὐνομίας] ἀνομίας T (but εὐ above the line) WF.

348

HIPP. Yes, they would; but it is not lawful for them to give them a foreign education; for you may be sure that if anybody had ever received money there in payment for education, I should have received by far the most; they certainly enjoy hearing me and they applaud me; but, as I say, it is not the law.

SOC. But, Hippias, do you say that law is an injury to the state, or a benefit?

HIPP. It is made, I think, with benefit in view, but sometimes, if the law is badly made, it is injurious.

SOC. Well, then, is it not true that those who make the law make it as the greatest good to the state, and that without this it is impossible to enjoy good government?

HIPP. What you say is true.

SOC. Then, when those who make the laws miss the good, they have missed the lawful and the law; or what do you say?

HIPP. Speaking accurately, Socrates, that is true; however, men are not accustomed to think so.

SOC. The men who know, Hippias, or those who do not know?

HIPP. The many.

SOC. Are these, the many, those who know the truth?

HIPP. Certainly not.

SOC. But surely those who know, think that in truth for all men that which is more beneficial is more lawful than that which is less beneficial; or do you not agree?

HIPP. Yes, I agree that they think it is so in truth.

ΣΩ. Οὐκοῦν ἔστι τε καὶ ἔχει οὕτως, ὡς οἱ εἰδότες ἡγοῦνται;

ιπ. Πάνυ γε.

6. ΣΩ. Ἔστι δέ γε Λακεδαιμονίοις, ὡς σὺ φῄς,
285 ὠφελιμώτερον τὴν ὑπὸ σοῦ παίδευσιν, ξενικὴν οὖσαν, παιδεύεσθαι μᾶλλον ἢ τὴν ἐπιχωρίαν.

ιπ. Καὶ ἀληθῆ γε λέγω.

ΣΩ. Καὶ γὰρ ὅτι τὰ ὠφελιμώτερα νομιμώτερά[1] ἐστι, καὶ τοῦτο λέγεις, ὦ Ἱππία;

ιπ. Εἶπον γάρ.

ΣΩ. Κατὰ τὸν σὸν ἄρα λόγον τοῖς Λακεδαιμονίων υἱέσιν ὑπὸ Ἱππίου παιδεύεσθαι νομιμώτερόν ἐστιν, ὑπὸ δὲ τῶν πατέρων ἀνομώτερον, εἴπερ τῷ ὄντι ὑπὸ σοῦ πλείω ὠφεληθήσονται.

ιπ. Ἀλλὰ μὴν ὠφεληθήσονται, ὦ Σώκρατες.

B ΣΩ. Παρανομοῦσιν ἄρα Λακεδαιμόνιοι οὐ διδόντες σοι χρυσίον καὶ ἐπιτρέποντες τοὺς αὑτῶν υἱεῖς.

ιπ. Συγχωρῶ ταῦτα· δοκεῖς γάρ μοι τὸν λόγοι πρὸς ἐμοῦ λέγειν, καὶ οὐδέν με δεῖ αὐτῷ ἐναντιοῦσθαι.

ΣΩ. Παρανόμους μὲν δή, ὦ ἑταῖρε, τοὺς Λάκωνας εὑρίσκομεν, καὶ ταῦτ' εἰς τὰ μέγιστα, τοὺς νομιμωτάτους δοκοῦντας εἶναι. ἐπαινοῦσι δὲ δή σε πρὸς θεῶν, ὦ Ἱππία, καὶ χαίρουσιν ἀκούοντες
C ποῖα; ἢ δῆλον δὴ ὅτι ἐκεῖνα ἃ σὺ κάλλιστα ἐπίστασαι, τὰ περὶ τὰ ἄστρα τε καὶ τὰ οὐράνια πάθη;

ιπ. Οὐδ' ὁπωστιοῦν· ταῦτά γε οὐδ' ἀνέχονται.

[1] νομιμώτερα F: νομικώτερα TW.

soc. Well, it actually is as those who know think it is, is it not ?

hipp. Certainly.

soc. But for the Lacedaemonians, as you say, it is more beneficial to be educated in your education, which is foreign, than in the local education.

hipp. Yes, and what I say is true.

soc. And do you say this also, Hippias, that beneficial things are more lawful ?

hipp. Yes, I said so.

soc. Then, according to what you say, it is more lawful for the sons of the Lacedaemonians to be educated by Hippias and less lawful for them to be educated by their fathers, if in reality they will be more benefited by you.

hipp. But certainly they will be benefited, Socrates.

soc. Then the Lacedaemonians in not giving you money and entrusting their sons to you, act contrary to law.

hipp. I agree to that ; for you seem to be making your argument in my favour, and there is no need of my opposing it.

soc. Then, my friends, we find that the Lacedaemonians are law-breakers, and that too in the most important affairs—they who are regarded as the most law-abiding of men. But then, for Heaven's sake, Hippias, what sort of discourses are those for which they applaud you and which they enjoy hearing ? Or are they evidently those which you understand most admirably, those about the stars and the phenomena of the heavens ?

hipp. Not in the least ; they won't even endure those.

PLATO

ΣΩ. Ἀλλὰ περὶ γεωμετρίας τι χαίρουσιν ἀκούοντες;

ΙΠ. Οὐδαμῶς, ἐπεὶ οὐδ' ἀριθμεῖν ἐκείνων γε, ὡς ἔπος εἰπεῖν, πολλοὶ ἐπίστανται.

ΣΩ. Πολλοῦ ἄρα δέουσιν περί γε λογισμῶν ἀνέχεσθαί σου ἐπιδεικνυμένου.

ΙΠ. Πολλοῦ μέντοι νὴ Δία.

ΣΩ. Ἀλλὰ δῆτα ἐκεῖνα ἃ σὺ ἀκριβέστατα
D ἐπίστασαι ἀνθρώπων διαιρεῖν, περί τε γραμμάτων δυνάμεως καὶ συλλαβῶν καὶ ῥυθμῶν καὶ ἁρμονιῶν;

ΙΠ. Περὶ ποίων, ὦ 'γαθέ, ἁρμονιῶν καὶ γραμμάτων;

ΣΩ. Ἀλλὰ τίνα μήν ἐστιν ἃ ἡδέως σου ἀκροῶνται καὶ ἐπαινοῦσιν; αὐτός μοι εἰπέ, ἐπειδὴ ἐγὼ οὐχ εὑρίσκω.

ΙΠ. Περὶ τῶν γενῶν, ὦ Σώκρατες, τῶν τε ἡρώων καὶ τῶν ἀνθρώπων, καὶ τῶν κατοικίσεων, ὡς τὸ ἀρχαῖον ἐκτίσθησαν αἱ πόλεις, καὶ συλλήβδην πάσης τῆς ἀρχαιολογίας ἥδιστα ἀκροῶνται, ὥστ' ἔγωγε δι' αὐτοὺς ἠνάγκασμαι ἐκμεμαθηκέναι τε
E καὶ ἐκμεμελετηκέναι πάντα τὰ τοιαῦτα.

ΣΩ. Ναὶ μὰ Δί', ὦ Ἱππία, εὐτύχηκάς γε, ὅτι Λακεδαιμόνιοι οὐ χαίρουσιν ἄν τις αὐτοῖς ἀπὸ Σόλωνος τοὺς ἄρχοντας τοὺς ἡμετέρους καταλέγῃ· εἰ δὲ μή, πράγματ' ἂν εἶχες ἐκμανθάνων.

ΙΠ. Πόθεν, ὦ Σώκρατες; ἅπαξ ἀκούσας πεντήκοντα ὀνόματα ἀπομνημονεύσω.

7. ΣΩ. Ἀληθῆ λέγεις, ἀλλ' ἐγὼ οὐκ ἐνενόησα ὅτι τὸ μνημονικὸν ἔχεις· ὥστ' ἐννοῶ ὅτι εἰκότως σοι χαίρουσιν οἱ Λακεδαιμόνιοι ἅτε πολλὰ εἰδότι,
286 καὶ χρῶνται ὥσπερ ταῖς πρεσβύτισιν οἱ παῖδες πρὸς τὸ ἡδέως μυθολογῆσαι.

352

GREATER HIPPIAS

soc. But they enjoy hearing about geometry?

hipp. Not at all, since one might say that many of them do not even know how to count.

soc. Then they are far from enduring a lecture by you on the processes of thought.

hipp. Far from it indeed, by Zeus.

soc. Well, then, those matters which you of all men know best how to discuss, concerning the value of letters and syllables and rhythms and harmonies?

hipp. Harmonies indeed, my good fellow, and letters!

soc. But then what are the things about which they like to listen to you and which they applaud? Tell me yourself, for I cannot discover them.

hipp. They are very fond of hearing about the genealogies of heroes and men, Socrates, and the foundations of cities in ancient times and, in short, about antiquity in general, so that for their sake I have been obliged to learn all that sort of thing by heart and practise it thoroughly.

soc. By Zeus, Hippias, it is lucky for you that the Lacedaemonians do not enjoy hearing one recite the list of our archons from Solon's time; if they did, you would have trouble in learning it by heart.

hipp. How so, Socrates? After hearing them once, I can remember fifty names.

soc. True, but I did not understand that you possess the science of memory; and so I understand that the Lacedaemonians naturally enjoy you as one who knows many things, and they make use of you as children make use of old women, to tell stories agreeably.

---

¹ ὅτι F : ὅτι γε TW.

353

ιπ. Καὶ ναὶ μὰ Δί', ὦ Σώκρατες, περί γε ἐπιτηδευμάτων καλῶν καὶ ἔναγχος αὐτόθι εὐδοκίμησα
διεξιὼν ἃ χρὴ τὸν νέον ἐπιτηδεύειν. ἔστι γάρ μοι
περὶ αὐτῶν παγκάλως λόγος συγκείμενος, καὶ
ἄλλως εὖ διακείμενος καὶ τοῖς ὀνόμασι· πρόσχημα
δέ μοί ἐστι καὶ ἀρχὴ τοιάδε τις τοῦ λόγου. ἐπειδὴ
ἡ Τροία ἥλω, λέγει ὁ λόγος ὅτι Νεοπτόλεμος
B Νέστορα ἔροιτο, ποῖά ἐστι καλὰ ἐπιτηδεύματα, ἃ
ἄν τις ἐπιτηδεύσας νέος ὢν εὐδοκιμώτατος γένοιτο·
μετὰ ταῦτα δὴ λέγων ἐστὶν ὁ Νέστωρ καὶ ὑπο-
τιθέμενος αὐτῷ πάμπολλα νόμιμα καὶ πάγκαλα.
τοῦτον δὴ καὶ ἐκεῖ ἐπεδειξάμην καὶ ἐνθάδε μέλλω
ἐπιδεικνύναι εἰς τρίτην ἡμέραν, ἐν τῷ Φειδοστράτου
διδασκαλείῳ, καὶ ἄλλα πολλὰ καὶ ἄξια ἀκοῆς·
ἐδεήθη γάρ μου Εὔδικος ὁ Ἀπημάντου. ἀλλ'
ὅπως παρέσει καὶ αὐτὸς καὶ ἄλλους ἄξεις, οἵτινες
C ἱκανοὶ ἀκούσαντες κρῖναι τὰ λεγόμενα.

8. ΣΩ. Ἀλλὰ ταῦτ' ἔσται, ἂν θεὸς ἐθέλῃ, ὦ
Ἱππία. νυνὶ μέντοι βραχύ τί μοι περὶ αὐτοῦ
ἀπόκριναι· καὶ γάρ με εἰς καλὸν ὑπέμνησας.
ἔναγχος γάρ τις, ὦ ἄριστε, εἰς ἀπορίαν με κατ-
έβαλεν ἐν λόγοις τισὶ τὰ μὲν ψέγοντα ὡς αἰσχρά,
τὰ δ' ἐπαινοῦντα ὡς καλά, οὕτω πως ἐρόμενος καὶ
μάλα ὑβριστικῶς· "πόθεν δέ μοι σύ," ἔφη, "ὦ
D Σώκρατες, οἶσθα ὁποῖα καλὰ καὶ αἰσχρά; ἐπεὶ
φέρε, ἔχοις ἂν εἰπεῖν τί ἔστι τὸ καλόν;" καὶ ἐγὼ
διὰ τὴν ἐμὴν φαυλότητα ἠπορούμην τε καὶ οὐκ
εἶχον αὐτῷ κατὰ τρόπον ἀποκρίνασθαι· ἀπιὼν οὖν
ἐκ τῆς συνουσίας ἐμαυτῷ τε ὠργιζόμην καὶ ὠνεί-

HIPP. And by Zeus, Socrates, I have just lately gained reputation there by telling about noble or beautiful pursuits, recounting what those of a young man should be. For I have a very beautiful discourse composed about them, well arranged in its words and also in other respects. And the plan of the discourse, and its beginning, is something like this : After the fall of Troy, the story goes that Neoptolemus asked Nestor what the noble and beautiful pursuits were, by following which a young man would become most famous ; so after that we have Nestor speaking and suggesting to him very many lawful and most beautiful pursuits. That discourse, then, I delivered there and intend to deliver here the day after to-morrow in Pheidostratus's schoolroom, with many other things worth hearing ; for Eudicus, the son of Apemantus, asked me to do so. Now be sure to be there yourself and to bring others who are able to judge of discourses that they hear.

soc. Well, that shall be done, God willing, Hippias. Now, however, give me a brief answer to a question about your discourse, for you reminded me of the beautiful just at the right moment. For recently, my most excellent friend, as I was finding fault with some things in certain speeches as ugly and praising other things as beautiful, a man threw me into confusion by questioning me very insolently somewhat after this fashion : " How, if you please, do you know, Socrates," said he, " what sort of things are beautiful and ugly ? For, come now, could you tell me what the beautiful is ? " And I, being of no account, was at a loss and could not answer him properly ; and so, as I was going away from the company, I was angry with myself and

διζον, καὶ ἠπείλουν, ὁπότε πρῶτον ὑμῶν τῳ τῶν
σοφῶν ἐντύχοιμι, ἀκούσας καὶ μαθὼν καὶ ἐκμε-
λετήσας ἰέναι πάλιν ἐπὶ τὸν ἐρωτήσαντα, ἀναμαχού-
μενος τὸν λόγον. νῦν οὖν, ὃ λέγω, εἰς καλὸν ἥκεις,
E καί με δίδαξον ἱκανῶς αὐτὸ τὸ καλὸν ὅ τι ἔστι, καὶ
πειρῶ μοι ὅτι μάλιστα ἀκριβῶς εἰπεῖν ἀποκρινόμενος, μὴ ἐξελεγχθεὶς τὸ δεύτερον αὖθις γέλωτα
ὄφλω. οἶσθα γὰρ δή που σαφῶς, καὶ σμικρόν
που τοῦτ’ ἂν εἴη μάθημα ὧν σὺ τῶν πολλῶν
ἐπίστασαι.

ιπ. Σμικρὸν μέντοι νὴ Δί’, ὦ Σώκρατες, καὶ
οὐδενὸς ἄξιον, ὡς ἔπος εἰπεῖν.

σω. Ῥᾳδίως ἄρα μαθήσομαι καὶ οὐδείς με
ἐξελέγξει ἔτι.

ιπ. Οὐδεὶς μέντοι· φαῦλον γὰρ ἂν εἴη τὸ ἐμὸν
287 πρᾶγμα καὶ ἰδιωτικόν.

σω. Εὖ γε νὴ τὴν Ἥραν λέγεις, ὦ Ἱππία, εἰ
χειρωσόμεθα τὸν ἄνδρα. ἀτὰρ μή τι κωλύω
μιμούμενος ἐγὼ ἐκεῖνον, ἐὰν σοῦ ἀποκρινομένου
ἀντιλαμβάνωμαι τῶν λόγων, ἵνα ὅτι μάλιστά με
ἐκμελετήσῃς; σχεδὸν γάρ τι ἔμπειρός εἰμι τῶν
ἀντιλήψεων. εἰ οὖν μή τί σοι διαφέρει, βούλομαι
ἀντιλαμβάνεσθαι, ἵν’ ἐρρωμενέστερον μάθω.

ιπ. Ἀλλ’ ἀντιλαμβάνου. καὶ γάρ, ὃ νῦν δὴ εἶπον,
B οὐ μέγα ἐστὶ τὸ ἐρώτημα, ἀλλὰ καὶ πολὺ τούτου
χαλεπώτερα ἂν ἀποκρίνασθαι ἐγώ σε διδάξαιμι,
ὥστε μηδέν’ ἀνθρώπων δύνασθαί σε ἐξελέγχειν.

9. σω. Φεῦ ὡς εὖ λέγεις· ἀλλ’ ἄγ’,[1] ἐπειδὴ καὶ
σὺ κελεύεις, φέρε ὅτι μάλιστ’ ἐκεῖνος γενόμενος
πειρῶμαι σε ἐρωτᾶν. εἰ γὰρ δὴ αὐτῷ τὸν λόγον

---

[1] ἀλλ’ ἄγ’ later hands : ἀλλά γ’ TWF.

reproached myself, and threatened that the first time I met one of you wise men, I would hear and learn and practise and then go back to the man who questioned me to renew the wordy strife. So now, as I say, you have come at the right moment; just teach me satisfactorily what the absolute beautiful is, and try in replying to speak as accurately as possible, that I may not be confuted a second time and be made ridiculous again. For you doubtless know clearly, and this would doubtless be but a small example of your wide learning.

HIPP. Yes, surely, by Zeus, a small one, Socrates, and, I may say, of no value.

SOC. Then I shall learn it easily, and nobody will confute me any more.

HIPP. Nobody, surely; for in that case my profession would be worthless and ordinary.

SOC. That is good, by Hera, Hippias, if we are to worst the fellow. But may I without hindering you imitate him, and when you answer, take exception to what you say, in order that you may give me as much practice as possible? For I am more or less experienced in taking exceptions. So, if it is all the same to you, I wish to take exceptions, that I may learn more vigorously.

HIPP. Oh yes, take exceptions. For, as I said just now, the question is no great matter, but I could teach you to answer much harder ones than this, so that nobody in the world could confute you.

SOC. Oh how good that is! But come, since you tell me to do so, now let me try to play that man's part, so far as possible, and ask you questions. For

τοῦτον ἐπιδείξαιο ὃν φῄς, τὸν περὶ τῶν καλῶν
ἐπιτηδευμάτων, ἀκούσας, ἐπειδὴ παύσαιο λέγων,
ἔροιτ' ἂν οὐ περὶ ἄλλου πρότερον ἢ περὶ τοῦ καλοῦ,
C ἔθος γάρ τι τοῦτ' ἔχει, καὶ εἴποι ἄν· " ὦ ξένε
Ἠλεῖε, ἆρ' οὐ δικαιοσύνῃ δίκαιοί εἰσιν οἱ δίκαιοι;"
ἀπόκριναι δή, ὦ Ἱππία, ὡς ἐκείνου ἐρωτῶντος.

ιπ. Ἀποκρινοῦμαι ὅτι δικαιοσύνῃ.

σω. " Οὐκοῦν ἔστι τι τοῦτο, ἡ δικαιοσύνη;"

ιπ. Πάνυ γε.

σω. " Οὐκοῦν καὶ σοφίᾳ οἱ σοφοί εἰσι σοφοὶ καὶ
τῷ ἀγαθῷ πάντα τἀγαθὰ ἀγαθά;"

ιπ. Πῶς δ' οὔ;

σω. " Οὖσί γέ τισι τούτοις· οὐ γὰρ δή που μὴ
οὖσί γε."

ιπ. Οὖσι μέντοι.

σω. " Ἆρ' οὖν οὐ καὶ τὰ καλὰ πάντα τῷ καλῷ
ἐστι καλά;"

D ιπ. Ναί, τῷ καλῷ.

σω. " Ὄντι γέ τινι τούτῳ;"

ιπ. Ὄντι· ἀλλὰ τί γὰρ μέλλει;

σω. " Εἰπὲ δή, ὦ ξένε," φήσει, " τί ἐστι τοῦτο,
τὸ καλόν;"

ιπ. Ἄλλο τι οὖν, ὦ Σώκρατες, ὁ τοῦτο ἐρωτῶν
δεῖται πυθέσθαι ἢ τί ἐστι καλόν;

σω. Οὔ μοι δοκεῖ, ἀλλ' ὅ τι ἔστι τὸ καλόν, ὦ
Ἱππία.

ιπ. Καὶ τί διαφέρει τοῦτ' ἐκείνου;

σω. Οὐδέν σοι δοκεῖ;

ιπ. Οὐδὲν γὰρ διαφέρει.

if you were to deliver for him this discourse that you mention, the one about beautiful pursuits, when he had heard it, after you had stopped speaking, the very first thing he would ask about would be the beautiful; for he has that sort of habit, and he would say, "Stranger from Elis, is it not by justice that the just are just?" So answer, Hippias, as though he were asking the question.

HIPP. I shall answer that it is by justice.

SOC. "Then this—I mean justice—is something?"

HIPP. Certainly.

SOC. "Then, too, by wisdom the wise are wise and by the good all things are good, are they not?"

HIPP. Of course.

SOC. "And justice, wisdom, and so forth are something; for the just, wise, and so forth would not be such by them, if they were not something."

HIPP. To be sure, they are something.

SOC. "Then are not all beautiful things beautiful by the beautiful?"

HIPP. Yes, by the beautiful.

SOC. "By the beautiful, which is something?"

HIPP. Yes, for what alternative is there?

SOC. "Tell me, then, stranger," he will say, "what is this, the beautiful?"

HIPP. Well, Socrates, does he who asks this question want to find out anything else than what is beautiful?

SOC. I do not think that is what he wants to find out, but what the beautiful is.

HIPP. And what difference is there between the two?

SOC. Do you think there is none?

HIPP. Yes, for there is no difference.

ΣΩ. Ἀλλὰ μέντοι δῆλον ὅτι σὺ κάλλιον οἶσθα. ὅμως δέ, ὦ 'γαθέ, ἄθρει· ἐρωτᾷ γάρ σε οὐ τί ἐστι
E καλόν, ἀλλ' ὅ τί ἐστι τὸ καλόν.

ΙΠ. Μανθάνω, ὦ 'γαθέ, καὶ ἀποκρινοῦμαί γε αὐτῷ ὅ τί ἐστι τὸ καλόν, καὶ οὐ μή ποτε[1] ἐλεγχθῶ. ἔστι γάρ, ὦ Σώκρατες, εὖ ἴσθι, εἰ δεῖ τἀληθὲς λέγειν, παρθένος καλὴ καλόν.

ΣΩ. Καλῶς γε, ὦ Ἱππία, νὴ τὸν κύνα καὶ εὐδόξως ἀπεκρίνω. ἄλλο τι οὖν, ἂν ἐγὼ τοῦτο ἀποκρίνωμαι, τὸ ἐρωτώμενόν τε ἀποκεκριμένος ἔσομαι
288 καὶ ὀρθῶς, καὶ οὐ μή ποτε[1] ἐλεγχθῶ;

ΙΠ. Πῶς γὰρ ἄν, ὦ Σώκρατες, ἐλεγχθείης, ὅ γε πᾶσι δοκεῖ καὶ πάντες σοι μαρτυρήσουσιν οἱ ἀκούοντες ὅτι ὀρθῶς λέγεις;

ΣΩ. Εἶεν· πάνυ μὲν οὖν. φέρε δή, ὦ Ἱππία, πρὸς ἐμαυτὸν ἀναλάβω ὃ λέγεις. ὁ μὲν ἐρήσεταί με οὑτωσί πως· "ἴθι μοι, ὦ Σώκρατες, ἀπόκριναι· ταῦτα πάντα ἃ φῂς καλὰ εἶναι, εἰ τί[2] ἐστιν αὐτὸ τὸ καλόν, ταῦτ' ἂν εἴη καλά;" ἐγὼ δὲ δὴ ἐρῶ ὅτι εἰ παρθένος καλὴ καλόν, ἔστι[3] δι' ὅ[4] ταῦτ' ἂν εἴη καλά.
B ΙΠ. Οἴει οὖν ἔτι αὐτὸν ἐπιχειρήσειν σε ἐλέγχειν ὡς οὐ καλόν ἐστιν ὃ λέγεις, ἢ ἐὰν ἐπιχειρήσῃ, οὐ καταγέλαστον ἔσεσθαι;

ΣΩ. Ὅτι μὲν ἐπιχειρήσει, ὦ θαυμάσιε, εὖ οἶδα· εἰ δ' ἐπιχειρήσας ἔσται καταγέλαστος, αὐτὸ δείξει. ἃ μέντοι ἐρεῖ, ἐθέλω σοι λέγειν.

ΙΠ. Λέγε δή.

10. ΣΩ. "Ὡς γλυκὺς εἶ," φήσει, "ὦ Σώκρατες.

---

[1] ποτε F: om. TW. [2] εἰ τί F: εἴ τι TW.
[3] καλόν, ἔστι Hoeneheek Hissink : καλόν ἔστι TW : καλόν . . . καλά bracketed by Hermann : καλόν, ἔστι τι Schanz.
[4] δι' ὃ] διὸ TW: διότι F.

soc. Well, surely it is plain that you know best; but still, my good friend, consider; for he asked you, not what is beautiful, but what the beautiful is.

HIPP. I understand, my good friend, and I will answer and tell him what the beautiful is, and I shall never be confuted. For be assured, Socrates, if I must speak the truth, a beautiful maiden is beautiful.

soc. Beautifully answered, Hippias, by the dog, and notably! Then if I give this answer, I shall have answered the question that was asked, and shall have answered it correctly, and shall never be confuted?

HIPP. Yes, for how could you, Socrates, be confuted, when you say what everybody thinks, and when all who hear it will bear witness that what you say is correct?

soc. Very well; certainly. Come, then, Hippias, let me rehearse to myself what you say. The man will question me in some such fashion as this: " Come Socrates, answer me. All these things which you say are beautiful, if the absolute beautiful is anything, would be beautiful?" And I shall say that if a beautiful maiden is beautiful, there is something by reason of which these things would be beautiful.

HIPP. Do you think, then, that he will still attempt to refute you and to show that what you say is not beautiful, or, if he does attempt it, that he will not be ridiculous?

soc. That he will attempt it, my admirable friend, I am sure; but whether the attempt will make him ridiculous, the event will show. However, I should like to tell you what he will ask.

HIPP. Do so.

soc. " How charming you are, Socrates! " he will

PLATO

θήλεια δ' ἵππος καλὴ οὐ καλόν, ἣν καὶ ὁ θεὸς ἐν
C τῷ χρησμῷ ἐπήνεσε;" τί φήσομεν, ὦ Ἱππία;
ἄλλο τι ἢ φῶμεν καὶ τὴν ἵππον καλὸν¹ εἶναι, τήν
γε καλήν; πῶς γὰρ ἂν τολμῷμεν² ἔξαρνοι εἶναι τὸ
καλὸν μὴ καλὸν εἶναι;

ΙΠ. Ἀληθῆ λέγεις, ὦ Σώκρατες· ἐπεί τοι καὶ
ὀρθῶς αὐτὸ ὁ θεὸς εἶπεν· πάγκαλαι γὰρ παρ' ἡμῖν
ἵπποι γίγνονται.

ΣΩ. " Εἶεν," φήσει δή· " τί δὲ λύρα καλή; οὐ
καλόν;" φῶμεν, ὦ Ἱππία;

ΙΠ. Ναί.

ΣΩ. Ἐρεῖ τοίνυν μετὰ τοῦτ' ἐκεῖνος, σχεδόν τι εὖ
οἶδα ἐκ τοῦ τρόπου τεκμαιρόμενος· " Ὦ βέλτιστε
σύ, τί δὲ χύτρα καλή; οὐ καλὸν ἄρα;"
D ΙΠ. Ὦ Σώκρατες, τίς δ' ἔστιν ὁ ἄνθρωπος; ὡς
ἀπαίδευτός τις, ὃς οὕτω φαῦλα ὀνόματα ὀνομάζειν
τολμᾷ ἐν σεμνῷ πράγματι.

ΣΩ. Τοιοῦτός τις, ὦ Ἱππία, οὐ κομψὸς ἀλλὰ
συρφετός, οὐδὲν ἄλλο φροντίζων ἢ τὸ ἀληθές.
ἀλλ' ὅμως ἀποκριτέον τῷ ἀνδρί, καὶ ἔγωγε προαπο-
φαίνομαι· εἴπερ ἡ χύτρα κεκεραμευμένη εἴη ὑπ'
ἀγαθοῦ κεραμέως λεία καὶ στρογγύλη καὶ καλῶς
ὠπτημένη, οἷαι τῶν καλῶν χυτρῶν εἰσί τινες
δίωτοι, τῶν ἓξ χόας χωρουσῶν, πάγκαλαι, εἰ

---

¹ καλὸν perhaps F: καλὴν TW.
² τολμῷμεν F: τολμῶμεν TW.

---

¹ Heindorf and other commentators connect this reference
with an oracle quoted by a scholiast on Theocritus, *Idyl*
xiv. 48. The Megarians, being filled with pride, asked
the god who were better than they. The first lines of the
reply they received are:

Γαίης μὲν πάσης τὸ Πελασγικὸν Ἄργος ἄμεινον,
ἵπποι Θρηΐκιαι, Λακεδαιμόνιαι δὲ γυναῖκες.

say. " But is not a beautiful mare beautiful, which even the god praised in his oracle ? "[1] What shall we say, Hippias ? Shall we not say that the mare is beautiful, I mean the beautiful mare ? For how could we dare to deny that the beautiful thing is beautiful ?

HIPP. Quite true, Socrates ; for what the god said is quite correct, too ; for very beautiful mares are bred in our country.

SOC. " Very well," he will say, " and how about a beautiful lyre ? Is it not beautiful ? " Shall we agree, Hippias ?

HIPP. Yes.

SOC. After this, then, the man will ask, I am sure, judging by his character : " You most excellent man, how about a beautiful pot ? Is it, then, not beautiful ? "

HIPP. Socrates, who is the fellow ? What an uncultivated person, who has the face to mention such worthless things in a dignified discussion !

SOC. That's the kind of person he is, Hippias, not elegant, but vulgar, thinking of nothing but the truth. But nevertheless the man must be answered, and I will declare my opinion beforehand : if the pot were made by a good potter, were smooth and round and well fired, as are some of the two-handled pots, those that hold six choes,[2] very beautiful ones—

" Better than all other land is the land of Pelasgian Argos,
    Thracian mares are the best, and the Lacedaemonian
        women."

To be sure, nothing is said about the beauty of the mares, and the reference to Elis contained in παρ' ἡμῖν just below is hard to reconcile with the Thracian mares of the oracle.

[2] The χοῦς was 5·76 pints.

PLATO

E τοιαύτην ἐρωτῴη χύτραν, καλὴν ὁμολογητέον εἶναι. πῶς γὰρ ἂν φαῖμεν καλὸν ὂν μὴ καλὸν εἶναι;

ιπ. Οὐδαμῶς, ὦ Σώκρατες.

ΣΩ. " Οὐκοῦν καὶ χύτρα," φήσει, " κωλὴ καλόν; ἀποκρίνου."

ιπ. Ἀλλ' οὕτως, ὦ Σώκρατες, ἔχει, οἶμαι· καλὸν μὲν καὶ τοῦτο τὸ¹ σκεῦός ἐστι καλῶς εἰργασμένον, ἀλλὰ τὸ ὅλον τοῦτο οὐκ ἔστιν ἄξιον κρίνειν ὡς ὂν καλὸν πρὸς ἵππον τε καὶ παρθένον καὶ τἆλλα πάντα τὰ καλά.

289 ΣΩ. Εἶεν· μανθάνω, ὦ Ἱππία, ὡς ἄρα χρὴ ἀντιλέγειν πρὸς τὸν ταῦτα ἐρωτῶντα τάδε· ὦ ἄνθρωπε, ἀγνοεῖς ὅτι τὸ τοῦ Ἡρακλείτου εὖ ἔχει, ὡς ἄρα " πιθήκων ὁ κάλλιστος αἰσχρὸς ἀνθρώπων² γένει συμβάλλειν," καὶ χυτρῶν ἡ καλλίστη αἰσχρὰ παρθένων γένει συμβάλλειν, ὥς φησιν Ἱππίας ὁ σοφός. οὐχ οὕτως, ὦ Ἱππία;

ιπ. Πάνυ μὲν οὖν, ὦ Σώκρατες, ὀρθῶς ἀπεκρίνω.

11. ΣΩ. Ἄκουε δή. μετὰ τοῦτο γὰρ εὖ οἶδ' ὅτι φήσει· " τί δέ, ὦ Σώκρατες; τὸ τῶν παρθένων

B γένος θεῶν γένει ἄν τις συμβάλλῃ, οὐ ταὐτὸν πείσεται ὅπερ τὸ τῶν χυτρῶν τῷ τῶν παρθένων συμβαλλόμενον; οὐχ ἡ καλλίστη παρθένος αἰσχρὰ φανεῖται; ἢ οὐ καὶ Ἡράκλειτος αὐτὸ³ τοῦτο λέγει, ὃν σὺ ἐπάγεις, ὅτι ἀνθρώπων ὁ σοφώτατος πρὸς θεὸν πίθηκος φανεῖται καὶ σοφίᾳ καὶ κάλλει καὶ τοῖς ἄλλοις πᾶσιν;" ὁμολογήσωμεν,⁴ ὦ⁵ Ἱππία, τὴν καλλίστην παρθένον πρὸς θεῶν γένος αἰσχρὰν εἶναι;

ιπ. Τίς γὰρ ἂν ἀντείποι τούτῳ γε, ὦ Σώκρατες;

¹ τοῦτο τὸ F : τοῦτο TW.
² ἀνθρώπων Bekker : ἄλλῳ TWF.

364

GREATER HIPPIAS

if that were the kind of pot he asked about, we must agree that it is beautiful ; for how could we say that being beautiful it is not beautiful ?

HIPP. We could not at all, Socrates.

SOC. " Then," he will say, " a beautiful pot also is beautiful, is it not ? Answer."

HIPP. Well, Socrates, it is like this, I think. This utensil, when well wrought, is beautiful, but absolutely considered it does not deserve to be regarded as beautiful in comparison with a mare and a maiden and all the beautiful things.

SOC. Very well ; I understand, Hippias, that the proper reply to him who asks these questions is this : " Sir, you are not aware that the saying of Heracleitus is good, that ' the most beautiful of monkeys is ugly compared with the race of man,' and the most beautiful of pots is ugly compared with the race of maidens, as Hippias the wise man says." Is it not so, Hippias ?

HIPP. Certainly, Socrates ; you replied rightly.

SOC. Listen then. For I am sure that after this he will say : " Yes, but, Socrates, if we compare maidens with gods, will not the same thing happen to them that happened to pots when compared with maidens ? Will not the most beautiful maiden appear ugly ? Or does not Heracleitus, whom you cite, mean just this, that the wisest of men, if compared with a god, will appear a monkey, both in wisdom and in beauty and in everything else ? Shall we agree, Hippias, that the most beautiful maiden is ugly if compared with the gods ?

HIPP. Yes, for who would deny that, Socrates ?

---

³ αὐτὸ F : ταὐτὸ TW.
⁴ ὁμολογήσωμεν W : ὁμολογήσομεν TF.
⁵ ὦ add. Coisl. : om. TWF.

365

PLATO

C ΣΩ. Ἂν τοίνυν ταῦτα ὁμολογήσωμεν, γελάσεταί
τε καὶ ἐρεῖ· " Ὦ Σώκρατες, μέμνησαι οὖν ὅ τι
ἠρωτήθης;" " Ἔγωγε," φήσω, " ὅτι αὐτὸ τὸ καλὸν
ὅ τί ποτ' ἔστιν." " Ἔπειτα," φήσει, " ἐρωτηθεὶς
τὸ καλὸν ἀποκρίνει ὃ τυγχάνει ὄν, ὡς αὐτὸς φῄς,
οὐδὲν μᾶλλον καλὸν ἢ αἰσχρόν;" Ἔοικε, φήσω·
ἢ τί μοι συμβουλεύεις, ὦ φίλε, φάναι;

III. ΙΠ. Τοῦτ' ἔγωγε· καὶ γὰρ¹ δὴ πρός γε θεοὺς ὅτι
οὐ καλὸν τὸ ἀνθρώπειον γένος, ἀληθῆ ἐρεῖ.

ΣΩ. " Εἰ δέ σε ἠρόμην," φήσει, " ἐξ ἀρχῆς τι
D ἐστι καλόν τε καὶ αἰσχρόν, εἴ μοι ἅπερ νῦν ἀπεκρίνω,
ἆρ' οὐκ ἂν ὀρθῶς ἀπεκέκρισο; ἔτι δὲ καὶ δοκεῖ σοι
αὐτὸ τὸ καλόν, ᾧ καὶ τἆλλα πάντα κοσμεῖται καὶ
καλὰ φαίνεται, ἐπειδάν τῳ προσγένηται ἐκεῖνο τὸ
εἶδος, τοῦτ' εἶναι παρθένος ἢ ἵππος ἢ λύρα;"

ΙΠ. Ἀλλὰ μέντοι, ὦ Σώκρατες, εἰ τοῦτό γε
ζητεῖ, πάντων ῥᾷστον ἀποκρίνασθαι αὐτῷ τί ἐστι
τὸ καλόν ᾧ καὶ τἆλλα πάντα κοσμεῖται καὶ προσ-
E γενομένου αὐτοῦ καλὰ φαίνεται. εὐηθέστατος οὖν
ἐστιν ὁ ἄνθρωπος καὶ οὐδὲν ἐπαΐει περὶ καλῶν
κτημάτων. ἐὰν γὰρ αὐτῷ ἀποκρίνῃ ὅτι τοῦτ'
ἐστιν ὃ ἐρωτᾷς τὸ καλὸν οὐδὲν ἄλλο ἢ χρυσός,
ἀπορήσει καὶ οὐκ ἐπιχειρήσει σε ἐλέγχειν. ἴσμεν
γάρ που πάντες ὅτι ὅπου ἂν τοῦτο προσγένηται,
κἂν² πρότερον αἰσχρὸν φαίνηται, καλὸν φανεῖται
χρυσῷ γε κοσμηθέν.

ΣΩ. Ἄπειρος εἶ τοῦ ἀνδρός, ὦ Ἱππία, ὡς
σχέτλιός ἐστι καὶ οὐδὲν ῥᾳδίως ἀποδεχόμενος.

¹ γὰρ F: om. TW.   ² κἂν F: καὶ TW.
366

soc. If, then, we agree to that, he will laugh and say : " Socrates, do you remember the question you were asked ? "   " I do," I shall say, " the question was what the absolute beautiful is."   " Then," he will say, " when you were asked for the beautiful, do you give as your reply what is, as you yourself say, no more beautiful than ugly ? "   " So it seems," I shall say ; or what do you, my friend, advise me to say ?

hipp. That is what I advise ; for, of course, in saying that the human race is not beautiful in comparison with gods, you will be speaking the truth.

soc. " But if I had asked you," he will say, " in the beginning what is beautiful and ugly, if you had replied as you now do, would you not have replied correctly ?   But do you still think that the absolute beautiful, by the addition of which all other things are adorned and made to appear beautiful, when its form is added to any of them—do you think that is a maiden or a mare or a lyre ? "

hipp. Well, certainly, Socrates, if that is what he is looking for, nothing is easier than to answer and tell him what the beautiful is, by which all other things are adorned and by the addition of which they are made to appear beautiful.   So the fellow is very simple-minded and knows nothing about beautiful possessions.   For if you reply to him : " This that you ask about, the beautiful, is nothing else but gold," he will be thrown into confusion and will not attempt to confute you.   For we all know, I fancy, that wherever this is added, even what before appears ugly will appear beautiful when adorned with gold.

soc. You don't know the man, Hippias, what a wretch he is, and how certain not to accept anything easily.

ιπ. Τί οὖν τοῦτο, ὦ Σώκρατες; τὸ γὰρ ὀρθῶς
290 λεγόμενον ἀνάγκη αὐτῷ ἀποδέχεσθαι, ἢ μὴ ἀπο-
δεχομένῳ καταγελάστῳ εἶναι.

12. ΣΩ. Καὶ μὲν δὴ ταύτην γε τὴν ἀπόκρισιν, ὦ
ἄριστε, οὐ μόνον οὐκ ἀποδέξεται, ἀλλὰ καὶ πάνυ με
τωθάσεται, καὶ ἐρεῖ· " ὦ τετυφωμένε σύ, Φειδίαν
οἴει κακὸν εἶναι δημιουργόν;" καὶ ἐγώ, οἶμαι,
ἐρῶ ὅτι Οὐδ᾽ ὁπωστιοῦν.

ιπ. Καὶ ὀρθῶς γ᾽ ἐρεῖς, ὦ Σώκρατες.

ΣΩ. Ὀρθῶς μέντοι. τοιγάρτοι ἐκεῖνος, ἐπειδὰν
ἐγὼ ὁμολογῶ ἀγαθὸν εἶναι δημιουργὸν τὸν Φειδίαν,
B " Εἶτα," φήσει, " οἴει, τοῦτο τὸ καλὸν ὃ σὺ λέγεις
ἠγνόει Φειδίας;" καὶ ἐγώ· Τί μάλιστα; φήσω.
" "Ὅτι, ἐρεῖ, τῆς Ἀθηνᾶς τοὺς ὀφθαλμοὺς οὐ
χρυσοῦς ἐποίησεν, οὐδὲ τὸ ἄλλο πρόσωπον οὐδὲ
τοὺς πόδας οὐδὲ τὰς χεῖρας, εἴπερ χρυσοῦν γε δὴ
ὂν κάλλιστον ἔμελλε φαίνεσθαι, ἀλλ᾽ ἐλεφάντινον·
δῆλον ὅτι τοῦτο ὑπὸ ἀμαθίας ἐξήμαρτεν, ἀγνοῶν
ὅτι χρυσὸς ἄρ᾽ ἐστὶν ὁ πάντα καλὰ ποιῶν, ὅπου ἂν
προσγένηται." ταῦτα οὖν λέγοντι τί ἀποκρινώμεθα,
ὦ Ἱππία;

C ιπ. Οὐδὲν χαλεπόν· ἐροῦμεν γὰρ ὅτι ὀρθῶς
ἐποίησε. καὶ γὰρ τὸ ἐλεφάντινον, οἶμαι, καλόν
ἐστιν.

ΣΩ. " Τοῦ οὖν ἕνεκα," φήσει, " οὐ καὶ τὰ μέσα
τῶν ὀφθαλμῶν ἐλεφάντινα εἰργάσατο, ἀλλὰ λίθινα,
ὡς οἷόν τ᾽ ἦν ὁμοιότητα τοῦ λίθου τῷ ἐλέφαντι
ἐξευρών; ἢ καὶ ὁ λίθος ὁ καλὸς καλόν ἐστι;"
φήσομεν, ὦ[1] Ἱππία;

ιπ. Φήσομέν τοι, ὅταν γε πρέπων ᾖ.

ΣΩ. " "Ὅταν δὲ μὴ πρέπων, αἰσχρόν;" ὁμολογῶ
ἢ μή;

368

HIPP. What of that, then, Socrates ? For he must perforce accept what is correct, or if he does not accept it, be ridiculous.

soc. This reply, my most excellent friend, he not only will certainly not accept, but he will even jeer at me grossly and will say : " You lunatic, do you think Pheidias is a bad craftsman ? " And I shall say, " Not in the least."

HIPP. And you will be right, Socrates.

soc. Yes, to be sure. Consequently when I agree that Pheidias is a good craftsman, " Well, then," he will say, " do you imagine that Pheidias did not know this beautiful that you speak of ? " " Why do you ask that ? " I shall say. " Because," he will say, " he did not make the eyes of his Athena of gold, nor the rest of her face, nor her hands and feet, if, that is, they were sure to appear most beautiful provided only they were made of gold, but he made them of ivory ; evidently he made this mistake through ignorance, not knowing that it is gold which makes everything beautiful to which it is added." When he says that, what reply shall we make to him, Hippias ?

HIPP. That is easy ; for we shall say that Pheidias did right ; for ivory, I think, is beautiful.

soc. " Why, then," he will say, " did he not make the middle parts of the eyes also of ivory, but of stone, procuring stone as similar as possible to the ivory ? Or is beautiful stone also beautiful ? " Shall we say that it is, Hippias ?

HIPP. Surely we shall say so, that is, where it is appropriate.

soc. " But ugly when not appropriate ? " Shall I agree, or not ?

---

[1] ὦ WF : om. T.

PLATO

ιπ. Ὁμολόγει, ὅταν γε μὴ πρέπῃ.

D ΣΩ. "Τί δὲ δή; ὁ ἐλέφας καὶ ὁ χρυσός," φήσει, "ὦ σοφὲ σύ, οὐχ ὅταν μὲν πρέπῃ, καλὰ ποιεῖ φαίνεσθαι, ὅταν δὲ μή, αἰσχρά;" ἔξαρνοι ἐσόμεθα ἢ ὁμολογήσομεν αὐτῷ ὀρθῶς λέγειν αὐτόν;

ιπ. Ὁμολογήσομεν τοῦτό γε, ὅτι ὃ ἂν πρέπῃ ἑκάστῳ, τοῦτο¹ καλὸν ποιεῖ ἕκαστον.

ΣΩ. "Πότερον οὖν² πρέπει," φήσει, "ὅταν τις τὴν χύτραν ἣν ἄρτι ἐλέγομεν, τὴν καλήν, ἕψῃ ἔτνους καλοῦ μεστήν, χρυσῆ τορύνη αὐτῇ ἢ συκίνη;"

13. ιπ. Ἡράκλεις, οἷον λέγεις ἄνθρωπον, ὦ
E Σώκρατες. οὐ βούλει μοι εἰπεῖν τίς ἐστιν;

ΣΩ. Οὐ γὰρ ἂν γνοίης, εἴ σοι εἴποιμι τοὔνομα.

ιπ. Ἀλλὰ καὶ νῦν ἔγωγε γιγνώσκω ὅτι ἀμαθής τίς ἐστιν.

ΣΩ. Μέρμερος πάνυ ἐστίν, ὦ Ἱππία· ἀλλ' ὅμως τί φήσομεν; ποτέραν πρέπειν τοῖν τορύναιν τῷ ἔτνει καὶ τῇ χύτρᾳ; ἢ δῆλον ὅτι τὴν συκίνην; εὐωδέστερον γάρ που τὸ ἔτνος ποιεῖ, καὶ ἅμα, ὦ ἑταῖρε, οὐκ ἂν συντρίψασα ἡμῖν τὴν χύτραν ἐκχέαι τὸ ἔτνος καὶ τὸ πῦρ ἀποσβέσειεν καὶ τοὺς μέλλοντας ἑστιᾶσθαι ἄνευ ὄψου ἂν³ πάνυ γενναίου ποιήσειεν· ἡ δὲ χρυσῆ ἐκείνη πάντ' ἂν ταῦτα ποιήσειεν, ὥστ'
291 ἐμοί γε δοκεῖν⁴ τὴν συκίνην ἡμᾶς μᾶλλον φάναι πρέπειν ἢ τὴν χρυσῆν, εἰ μή τι σὺ ἄλλο λέγεις.

ιπ. Πρέπει μὲν γάρ, ὦ Σώκρατες, μᾶλλον· οὐ μέντ' ἂν ἔγωγε τῷ ἀνθρώπῳ τοιαῦτ' ἐρωτῶντι διαλεγοίμην.

---

¹ τοῦτο F : τοῦτον TW.
² οὖν F : om. TW.
³ ὄψου ἂν W : ὄψου TF.
⁴ ὥστ' ἔμοιγε δοκεῖν F : ὥς γε μοι δοκεῖ TW.

370

HIPP. Agree, that is, when it is not appropriate.

soc. " What then ? Do not gold and ivory," he will say, " when they are appropriate, make things beautiful, and when they are not appropriate, ugly ? " Shall we deny that, or agree that what he says is correct ?

HIPP. We shall agree to this, at any rate, that whatever is appropriate to any particular thing makes that thing beautiful.

soc. " Well, then," he will say, " when some one has boiled the pot of which we were speaking just now, the beautiful one, full of beautiful soup, is a golden ladle appropriate to it, or one made of fig wood ? "

HIPP. Heracles ! What a fellow this is that you speak of ! Won't you tell me who he is ?

soc. You would not know him if I should tell you his name.

HIPP. But even now I know that he is an ignoramus.

soc. He is a great nuisance, Hippias ; but yet, what shall we say ? Which of the two ladles shall we say is appropriate to the soup and the pot ? Is it not evidently the one of fig wood ? For it is likely to make the soup smell better, and besides, my friend, it would not break the pot, thereby spilling the soup, putting out the fire, and making those who are to be entertained go without their splendid soup ; whereas the golden ladle would do all those things, so that it seems to me that we must say that the wooden ladle is more appropriate than the golden one, unless you disagree.

HIPP. No, for it is more appropriate, Socrates ; however, I, for my part, would not talk with the fellow when he asks such questions.

PLATO

ΣΩ. Ὀρθῶς γε, ὦ φίλε· σοὶ μὲν γὰρ οὐκ ἂν πρέποι τοιούτων ὀνομάτων ἀναπίμπλασθαι, καλῶς μὲν οὑτωσὶ ἀμπεχομένῳ, καλῶς δὲ ὑποδεδεμένῳ, εὐδοκιμοῦντι δὲ ἐπὶ σοφίᾳ ἐν πᾶσι τοῖς Ἕλλησιν· ἀλλ᾽ ἐμοὶ οὐδὲν πρᾶγμα φύρεσθαι πρὸς τὸν ἄνθρω-
B πον· ἐμὲ οὖν προδίδασκε καὶ ἐμὴν χάριν ἀποκρί-νου. " Εἰ γὰρ δὴ πρέπει γε μᾶλλον ἢ συκίνη τῆς χρυσῆς," φήσει ὁ ἄνθρωπος, " ἄλλο τι ἢ καὶ καλ-λίων ἂν εἴη, ἐπειδήπερ τὸ πρέπον, ὦ Σώκρατες, κάλλιον ὡμολόγησας εἶναι τοῦ μὴ πρέποντος;" ἄλλο τι ὁμολογῶμεν, ὦ Ἱππία, τὴν συκίνην καλλίω τῆς χρυσῆς εἶναι;

ΙΠ. Βούλει σοι εἴπω, ὦ Σώκρατες, ὃ εἰπὼν εἶναι τὸ καλὸν ἀπαλλάξεις σαυτὸν[1] τῶν πολλῶν λόγων;

C ΣΩ. Πάνυ μὲν οὖν· μὴ μέντοι πρότερόν γε πρὶν ἄν μοι εἴπῃς ποτέραν ἀποκρίνωμαι οἷν ἄρτι ἔλεγον τοῖν τορύναιν πρέπουσάν τε καὶ καλλίω εἶναι.

ΙΠ. Ἀλλ᾽, εἰ βούλει, αὐτῷ ἀπόκριναι, ὅτι ἡ ἐκ τῆς συκῆς εἰργασμένη.

ΣΩ. Λέγε δὴ νυνὶ ὃ ἄρτι ἔμελλες λέγειν. ταύτῃ μὲν γὰρ τῇ ἀποκρίσει, ἂν[2] φῶ τὸ καλὸν χρυσὸν εἶναι, οὐδὲν ὡς ἔοικέ μοι ἀναφανήσεται κάλλιον ὂν χρυσὸς ἢ ξύλον σύκινον· τὸ δὲ νῦν τί αὖ λέγεις τὸ καλὸν εἶναι;

D ΙΠ. Ἐγώ σοι ἐρῶ. ζητεῖν γάρ μοι δοκεῖς τοιοῦτόν τι τὸ καλὸν ἀποκρίνασθαι, ὃ μηδέποτε αἰσχρὸν μηδαμοῦ μηδενὶ φανεῖται.

ΣΩ. Πάνυ μὲν οὖν, ὦ Ἱππία· καὶ καλῶς γε νῦν ὑπολαμβάνεις.

---

[1] σαυτὸν corr. Coisl.: αὑτὸν W : αὐτὸν TF.
[2] ἂν Hermann : ἢ ἂν TW : ἢ ἂν F.

soc. Quite right, my friend; for it would not
be appropriate for you to be filled up with such
words, you who are so beautifully clad, so beautifully shod, and so famous for your wisdom among
all the Greeks; but for me it doesn't matter if I
do associate with the fellow; so instruct me and
for my sake answer him. " For if the wooden one
is more appropriate than the golden one," the fellow
will say, " would it not be more beautiful, since
you agreed, Socrates, that the appropriate is more
beautiful than that which is not appropriate ? "
Shall we not agree, Hippias, that the wooden one
is more beautiful than the golden ?

hipp. Do you wish me to tell you, Socrates,
what definition of the beautiful will enable you to
free yourself from long discussion ?

soc. Certainly; but not until after you have
told me which of the two ladles I just spoke of I
shall reply is appropriate and more beautiful.

hipp. Well, if you like, reply to him that it is
the one made of fig wood.

soc. Now, then, say what you were just now going
to say. For by this reply, if I say that the beautiful is gold, it seems to me that gold will be shown
to be no more beautiful than fig wood; but what
do you now, once more, say that the beautiful is ?

hipp. I will tell you; for you seem to me to be
seeking to reply that the beautiful is something of
such sort that it will never appear ugly anywhere
to anybody.

soc. Certainly, Hippias; now you understand
beautifully.

PLATO

ιπ. Ἄκουε δή· πρὸς γὰρ τοῦτ᾽ ἴσθι, ἐάν τις ἔχῃ ὅ τι ἀντείπῃ, φάναι ἐμὲ μηδ᾽ ὁτιοῦν ἐπαΐειν.[1]

ΣΩ. Λέγε δὴ ὡς τάχιστα πρὸς θεῶν.

ιπ. Λέγω τοίνυν ἀεὶ καὶ παντὶ καὶ πανταχοῦ κάλλιστον εἶναι ἀνδρί, πλουτοῦντι, ὑγιαίνοντι, τιμωμένῳ ὑπὸ τῶν Ἑλλήνων, ἀφικομένῳ εἰς γῆρας, τοὺς αὑτοῦ γονέας τελευτήσαντας καλῶς περιστεί-
E λαντι, ὑπὸ τῶν αὑτοῦ ἐκγόνων καλῶς καὶ μεγαλο-πρεπῶς ταφῆναι.

14. ΣΩ. Ἰοὺ ἰού, ὦ Ἱππία, ἢ θαυμασίως τε καὶ μεγάλως καὶ ἀξίως σαυτοῦ εἴρηκας· καὶ νὴ τὴν Ἥραν ἄγαμαί σου ὅτι μοι δοκεῖς εὐνοϊκῶς, καθ᾽ ὅσον οἷός τ᾽ εἶ, βοηθεῖν· ἀλλὰ γὰρ τοῦ ἀνδρὸς οὐ τυγχάνομεν, ἀλλ᾽ ἡμῶν δὴ νῦν καὶ πλεῖστον καταγελάσεται, εὖ ἴσθι.

ιπ. Πονηρόν γ᾽, ὦ Σώκρατες, γέλωτα· ὅταν γὰρ πρὸς ταῦτα ἔχῃ μὲν μηδὲν ὅ τι λέγῃ, γελᾷ δέ, αὑτοῦ
292 καταγελάσεται καὶ ὑπὸ τῶν παρόντων αὐτὸς ἔσται καταγέλαστος.

ΣΩ. Ἴσως οὕτως ἔχει· ἴσως μέντοι ἐπί γε ταύτῃ τῇ ἀποκρίσει, ὡς ἐγὼ μαντεύομαι, κινδυνεύσει οὐ μόνον μου καταγελᾶν.

ιπ. Ἀλλὰ τί μήν;

ΣΩ. Ὅτι, ἂν τύχῃ βακτηρίαν ἔχων, ἂν μὴ ἐκφύγω φεύγων αὐτόν, εὖ μάλα μου ἐφικέσθαι πειράσεται.

ιπ. Πῶς λέγεις; δεσπότης τίς σου ὁ ἄνθρωπός ἐστιν, καὶ τοῦτο ποιήσας οὐκ ἀχθήσεται[2] καὶ δίκας ὀφλήσει; ἢ οὐκ ἔνδικος ὑμῖν ἡ πόλις ἐστίν, ἀλλ᾽
B ἐᾷ ἀδίκως τύπτειν ἀλλήλους τοὺς πολίτας;

---

[1] ἐπαΐειν F : ἐπαινεῖν TW.
[2] ἀχθήσεται F : ἀχθέσεται TW : ἀπαχθήσεται Naber.

374

HIPP. Listen, then; for, mind you, if anyone has anything to say against this, you may say I know nothing at all.

soc. Then for Heaven's sake, speak as quickly as you can.

HIPP. I say, then, that for every man and everywhere it is most beautiful to be rich and healthy, and honoured by the Greeks, to reach old age, and, after providing a beautiful funeral for his deceased parents, to be beautifully and splendidly buried by his own offspring.

soc. Bravo, bravo, Hippias! You have spoken in a way that is wonderful and great and worthy of you; and now, by Hera, I thank you, because you are kindly coming to my assistance to the best of your ability. But our shots are not hitting the man; no, he will laugh at us now more than ever, be sure of that.

HIPP. A wretched laugh, Socrates; for when he has nothing to say to this, but laughs, he will be laughing at himself and will himself be laughed at by those present.

soc. Perhaps that is so; perhaps, however, after this reply, he will, I foresee, be likely to do more than laugh at me.

HIPP. Why do you say that, pray?

soc. Because, if he happens to have a stick, unless I get away in a hurry, he will try to fetch me a good one.

HIPP. What? Is the fellow some sort of master of yours, and if he does that, will he not be arrested and have to pay for it? Or does your city disregard justice and allow the citizens to beat one another unjustly?

ΣΩ. Οὐδ' ὁπωστιοῦν ἐᾷ.

ΙΠ. Οὐκοῦν δώσει δίκην ἀδίκως γέ σε τύπτων.

ΣΩ. Οὔ μοι δοκεῖ, ὦ Ἱππία, οὔκ, εἰ ταῦτά γε ἀποκριναίμην, ἀλλὰ δικαίως, ἔμοιγε δοκεῖ.

ΙΠ. Καὶ ἐμοὶ τοίνυν δοκεῖ, ὦ Σώκρατες, ἐπειδήπερ γε αὐτὸς ταῦτα οἴει.

ΣΩ. Οὐκοῦν εἴπω σοι καὶ ᾗ αὐτὸς οἴομαι δικαίως ἂν τύπτεσθαι ταῦτα ἀποκρινόμενος; ἢ καὶ σύ με ἄκριτον τυπτήσεις; ἢ δέξει λόγον;

C ΙΠ. Δεινὸν γὰρ ἂν εἴη, ὦ Σώκρατες, εἰ μὴ δεχοίμην· ἀλλὰ πῶς λέγεις;

15. ΣΩ. Ἐγώ σοι ἐρῶ, τὸν αὐτὸν τρόπον ὅνπερ νῦν δὴ μιμούμενος ἐκεῖνον, ἵνα μὴ πρὸς σὲ λέγω ῥήματα, οἷα ἐκεῖνος εἰς ἐμὲ ἐρεῖ, χαλεπά τε καὶ ἀλλόκοτα. εὖ γὰρ ἴσθι, " Εἰπέ μοι," φήσει, " ὦ Σώκρατες, οἴει ἂν ἀδίκως πληγὰς λαβεῖν, ὅστις διθύραμβον τοσουτονὶ ᾄσας οὕτως ἀμούσως πολὺ ἀπῇσας ἀπὸ τοῦ ἐρωτήματος;" Πῶς δή; φήσω ἐγώ. "Ὅπως;" φήσει· "οὐχ οἷός τ' εἶ μεμνῆ-
D σθαι ὅτι τὸ καλὸν αὐτὸ ἠρώτων, ὃ παντὶ ᾧ ἂν προσγένηται, ὑπάρχει ἐκείνῳ καλῷ εἶναι, καὶ λίθῳ καὶ ξύλῳ καὶ ἀνθρώπῳ καὶ θεῷ καὶ πάσῃ[1] πράξει καὶ παντὶ μαθήματι; αὐτὸ γὰρ ἔγωγε, ὦ ἄνθρωπε, κάλλος ἐρωτῶ ὅ τι ἐστίν, καὶ οὐδέν σοι μᾶλλον γεγωνεῖν δύναμαι ἢ εἴ μοι παρεκάθησο λίθος, καὶ οὗτος μυλίας, μήτε ὦτα μήτ' ἐγκέφαλον ἔχων." εἰ οὖν φοβηθεὶς εἴποιμι ἐγὼ ἐπὶ τούτοις τάδε, ἆρα οὐκ ἂν ἄχθοιο, ὦ Ἱππία; "Ἀλλὰ μέντοι τόδε τὸ
E καλὸν εἶναι Ἱππίας ἔφη· καίτοι ἐγὼ αὐτὸν ἠρώτων

[1] πάσῃ F : ἀπάσῃ TW.

soc. Oh no ; that is not allowed at all.

hipp. Then he will have to pay a penalty for beating you unjustly.

soc. I do not think so, Hippias. No, if I were to make that reply, the beating would be just, I think.

hipp. Then I think so, too, Socrates, since that is your own belief.

soc. Shall I, then, not tell you why it is my own belief that the beating would be just, if I made that reply ? Or will you also beat me without trial ? Or will you listen to what I have to say ?

hipp. It would be shocking if I would not listen ; but what have you to say ?

soc. I will tell you, imitating him in the same way as a while ago, that I may not use to you such harsh and uncouth words as he uses to me. For you may be sure, " Tell me, Socrates," he will say, " do you think it would be unjust if you got a beating for singing such a long dithyramb so unmusically and so far from the question ? " " How so ? " I shall say. " How so ? " he will say ; " are you not able to remember that I asked for the absolute beautiful, by which everything to which it is added has the property of being beautiful, both stone and stick and man and god and every act and every acquisition of knowledge ? For what I am asking is this, man : what is absolute beauty ? and I cannot make you hear what I say any more than if you were a stone sitting beside me, and a millstone at that, having neither ears nor brain." Would you, then, not be angry, Hippias, if I should be frightened and should reply in this way ? " Well, but Hippias said that this was the beautiful ; and

PLATO

οὕτως ὥσπερ σὺ ἐμέ, ὃ πᾶσι καλὸν καὶ ἀεί ἐστι."
πῶς οὖν φῄς; οὐκ ἀχθέσει, ἂν εἴπω ταῦτα;

ΙΠ. Εὖ γ᾽ οὖν οἶδα, ὦ Σώκρατες, ὅτι πᾶσι καλὸν
τοῦτ᾽ ἐστίν ὃ ἐγὼ εἶπον καὶ δόξει.

ΣΩ. "Ἦ καὶ ἔσται;" φήσει· "ἀεὶ γάρ που
καλὸν τό γε καλόν."[1]

ΙΠ. Πάνυ γε.

ΣΩ. "Οὐκοῦν καὶ ἦν;" φήσει.

ΙΠ. Καὶ ἦν.

ΣΩ. "Ἦ καὶ τῷ Ἀχιλλεῖ," φήσει, "ὁ ξένος ὁ
Ἠλεῖος ἔφη καλὸν εἶναι ὑστέρῳ τῶν προγόνων
ταφῆναι, καὶ τῷ πάππῳ αὐτοῦ Αἰακῷ, καὶ τοῖς
293 ἄλλοις ὅσοι ἐκ θεῶν γεγόνασι, καὶ αὐτοῖς τοῖς
θεοῖς;"

16. ΙΠ. Τί τοῦτο; βάλλ᾽ ἐς μακαρίαν! τοῦ ἀνθρώπου οὐδ᾽ εὔφημα, ὦ Σώκρατες, ταῦτά γε τὰ
ἐρωτήματα.

ΣΩ. Τί δέ; τὸ ἐρομένου[2] ἑτέρου φάναι ταῦθ᾽
οὕτως ἔχειν οὐ πάνυ δύσφημον;

ΙΠ. Ἴσως.

ΣΩ. "Ἴσως τοίνυν σὺ εἶ οὗτος," φήσει, "ὃς
παντὶ φῂς καὶ ἀεὶ καλὸν εἶναι ὑπὸ μὲν τῶν ἐκγόνων
ταφῆναι, τοὺς δὲ γονέας θάψαι· ἢ οὐχ εἷς τῶν
ἁπάντων καὶ Ἡρακλῆς ἦν καὶ οὓς νῦν δὴ ἐλέγομεν
πάντες;"

ΙΠ. Ἀλλ᾽ οὐ τοῖς θεοῖς ἔγωγε ἔλεγον.

B   ΣΩ. "Οὐδὲ τοῖς ἥρωσιν, ὡς ἔοικας."

ΙΠ. Οὐχ ὅσοι γε θεῶν παῖδες ἦσαν.

ΣΩ. "Ἀλλ᾽ ὅσοι μή;"

ΙΠ. Πάνυ γε.

---

[1] καλὸν τό γε καλόν W : τό γε καλὸν καλόν F : τό γε καλὸν TP.
[2] ἐρομένου Bipontina : ἐρωμένου F : ἐρωτωμένου TW.

378

yet I asked him, just as you asked me, what is beautiful to all and always." What do you say? Will you not be angry if I say that?

HIPP. I know very well, Socrates, that this which I said was beautiful is beautiful to all and will seem so.

SOC. " And will it be so, too ? " he will say ; " for the beautiful is always beautiful, is it not ? "

HIPP. Certainly.

SOC. " Then was it so, too ? " he will say.

HIPP. It was so, too.

SOC. " And," he will say, " did the stranger from Elis say also that for Achilles it was beautiful to be buried later than his parents, and for his grandfather Aeacus, and all the others who were born of gods, and for the gods themselves ? "

HIPP. What's that ? Confound it ! These questions of the fellow's are not even respectful to religion.

SOC. Well, then, when another asks the question, perhaps it is not quite disrespectful to religion to say that these things are so ?

HIPP. Perhaps.

SOC. " Perhaps, then, you are the man," he will say, " who says that it is beautiful for every one and always to be buried by one's offspring, and to bury one's parents ; or was not Heracles included in ' every one,' he and all those whom we just now mentioned ? "

HIPP. But I did not say it was so for the gods.

SOC. " Nor for the heroes either, apparently."

HIPP. Not those who were children of gods.

SOC. " But those who were not ? "

HIPP. Certainly.

PLATO

ΣΩ. " Οὐκοῦν κατὰ τὸν σὸν αὖ λόγον, ὡς φαίνεται, τῶν ἡρώων τῷ μὲν Ταντάλῳ καὶ τῷ Δαρδάνῳ καὶ τῷ Ζήθῳ δεινόν τε καὶ ἀνόσιον καὶ αἰσχρόν ἐστι, Πέλοπι δὲ καὶ τοῖς ἄλλοις τοῖς οὕτω γεγονόσι καλόν."

ΙΠ. Ἔμοιγε δοκεῖ.

ΣΩ. " Σοὶ τοίνυν δοκεῖ," φήσει, " ὃ ἄρτι οὐκ ἔφησθα, τὸ θάψαντι τοὺς προγόνους ταφῆναι ὑπὸ
C τῶν ἐκγόνων ἐνίοτε καὶ ἐνίοις αἰσχρὸν εἶναι· ἔτι δὲ μᾶλλον, ὡς ἔοικεν, ἀδύνατον πᾶσι τοῦτο γενέσθαι καὶ εἶναι καλόν, ὥστε τοῦτό γε ὥσπερ καὶ τὰ ἔμπροσθεν ἐκεῖνα,[1] ἥ τε παρθένος καὶ ἡ χύτρα, ταὐτὸν πέπονθε, καὶ ἔτι γελοιοτέρως τοῖς μέν ἐστι καλόν, τοῖς δ' οὐ καλόν. καὶ οὐδέπω καὶ τήμερον," φήσει, " οἷός τ' εἶ, ὦ Σώκρατες, περὶ τοῦ καλοῦ ὅ τι ἐστὶ τὸ ἐρωτώμενον ἀποκρίνασθαι." ταῦτά μοι καὶ τοιαῦτα ὀνειδιεῖ δικαίως, ἐὰν αὐτῷ οὕτως ἀποκρίνωμαι.

D 17. Τὰ μὲν οὖν πολλά, ὦ Ἱππία, σχεδόν τί μοι οὕτω διαλέγεται· ἐνίοτε δ' ὥσπερ ἐλεήσας μου τὴν ἀπειρίαν καὶ ἀπαιδευσίαν αὐτός μοι προβάλλει ἐρωτῶν εἰ τοιόνδε μοι δοκεῖ εἶναι τὸ καλόν, ἢ καὶ περὶ ἄλλου ὅτου ἂν τύχῃ πυνθανόμενος καὶ περὶ οὗ ἂν λόγος ᾖ.

ΙΠ. Πῶς τοῦτο λέγεις, ὦ Σώκρατες;

ΣΩ. Ἐγώ σοι φράσω. " Ὦ δαιμόνιε," φησί, " Σώκρατες, τὰ μὲν τοιαῦτα ἀποκρινόμενος καὶ οὕτω παῦσαι—λίαν γὰρ εὐήθη τε καὶ εὐεξέλεγκτά ἐστιν—ἀλλὰ τὸ τοιόνδε σκόπει εἴ σοι δοκεῖ καλὸν
E εἶναι, οὗ καὶ νῦν δὴ ἐπελαβόμεθα ἐν τῇ ἀποκρίσει,

[1] ἐκεῖνα F : κεῖνα TW.

380

GREATER HIPPIAS

soc. "Then again, according to your statement, among the heroes it is terrible and impious and disgraceful for Tantalus and Dardanus and Zethus, but beautiful for Pelops [1] and the others who were born as he was?"

hipp. I think so.

soc. "You think, then, what you did not say just now, that to bury one's parents and be buried by one's offspring is sometimes and for some persons disgraceful; and it is still more impossible, as it seems, for this to become and to be beautiful for all, so that the same thing has happened to this as to the things we mentioned before, the maiden and the pot, in a still more ridiculous way than to them; it is beautiful for some and not beautiful for others. And you are not able yet, even to-day, Socrates," he will say, "to answer what is asked about the beautiful, namely what it is." With these words and the like he will rebuke me, if I reply to him in this way. For the most part, Hippias, he talks with me in some such way as that; but sometimes, as if in pity for my inexperience and lack of training, he himself volunteers a question, and asks whether I think the beautiful is so and so—or whatever else it is which happens to be the subject of our questions and our discussion.

hipp. What do you mean by that, Socrates?

soc. I will tell you. "Oh, my dear Socrates," he says, "stop making replies of this sort and in this way—for they are too silly and easy to refute; but see if something like this does not seem to you to be beautiful, which we got hold of just now in

[1] Pelops as the son of a mortal (Tantalus); the others mentioned were sons of gods.

ἡνίκ᾽ ἔφαμεν τὸν χρυσὸν οἷς μὲν πρέπει καλὸν
εἶναι, οἷς δὲ μή, οὔ, καὶ τἆλλα πάντα οἷς ἂν τοῦτο
προσῇ· αὐτὸ δὴ τοῦτο τὸ πρέπον καὶ τὴν φύσιν
αὐτοῦ τοῦ πρέποντος σκόπει εἰ τοῦτο τυγχάνει ὂν
τὸ καλόν.'' ἐγὼ μὲν οὖν εἴωθα συμφάναι τὰ
τοιαῦθ᾽ ἑκάστοτε· οὐ γὰρ ἔχω ὅ τι λέγω· σοὶ δ᾽
οὖν δοκεῖ τὸ πρέπον καλὸν εἶναι;

ιπ. Πάντως δήπου, ὦ Σώκρατες.

σω. Σκοπώμεθα, μή πῃ ἄρ᾽ ἐξαπατώμεθα.

ιπ. Ἀλλὰ χρὴ σκοπεῖν.

σω. Ὅρα τοίνυν· τὸ πρέπον ἆρα τοῦτο λέγομεν
294 ὃ παραγενόμενον ποιεῖ ἕκαστα φαίνεσθαι καλὰ
τούτων οἷς ἂν παρῇ, ἢ ὃ εἶναι ποιεῖ, ἢ οὐδέτερα
τούτων;

ιπ. Ἔμοιγε δοκεῖ.

σω. Πότερα;

ιπ. Ὃ ποιεῖ φαίνεσθαι καλά· ὥσπερ γε ἐπειδὰν
ἱμάτιά τις λάβῃ ἢ ὑποδήματα ἁρμόττοντα, κἂν ᾖ
γελοῖος, καλλίων φαίνεται.[1]

σω. Οὐκοῦν εἴπερ καλλίω ποιεῖ φαίνεσθαι ἢ ἔστι
τὸ πρέπον, ἀπάτη τις ἂν εἴη περὶ τὸ καλὸν τὸ
πρέπον, καὶ οὐκ ἂν εἴη τοῦτο ὃ ἡμεῖς ζητοῦμεν, ὦ
B Ἱππία; ἡμεῖς γάρ που ἐκεῖνο ἐζητοῦμεν, ᾧ πάντα
τὰ καλὰ πράγματα καλά ἐστιν· ὥσπερ ᾧ πάντα τὰ
μεγάλα ἐστὶ μεγάλα, τῷ ὑπερέχοντι· τούτῳ γὰρ
πάντα μεγάλα ἐστί. καὶ ἐὰν[2] μὴ φαίνηται, ὑπερέχῃ
δέ, ἀνάγκη αὐτοῖς μεγάλοις εἶναι· οὕτω δή, φαμέν,
καὶ τὸ καλόν, ᾧ καλὰ πάντα ἐστίν, ἄν τ᾽ οὖν

---

[1] Πότερα . . . ζητοῦμεν (294 c) all given to Socrates in the
mss. : πότερα om. Baumann ; the arrangement given above is
due to Apelt.

[2] καὶ ἐὰν W : καὶ ἂν T : κἂν F.

our reply, when we said that gold was beautiful
for those things for which it was appropriate, but
not for those for which it was not, and that all the
other things were beautiful to which this quality
pertains ; so examine this very thing, the appropriate, and see if it is perchance the beautiful."
Now I am accustomed to agree to such things every
time ; for I don't know what to say ; but now does
it seem to you that the appropriate is the beautiful ?

HIPP. Yes, certainly, Socrates.

SOC. Let us consider, lest we make a mistake
somehow.

HIPP. Yes, we must consider.

SOC. See, then ; do we say that the appropriate
is that which, when it is added, makes each of those
things to which it is added appear beautiful, or which
makes them be beautiful, or neither of these ?

HIPP. I think so.

SOC. Which ?

HIPP. That which makes them appear beautiful ;
as when a man takes clothes or shoes that fit, even
if he be ridiculous, he appears more beautiful.

SOC. Then if the appropriate makes him appear
more beautiful than he is, the appropriate would
be a sort of deceit in respect to the beautiful, and
would not be that which we are looking for, would
it, Hippias ? For we were rather looking for that
by which all beautiful things are beautiful—like
that by which all great things are great, that is,
excess ; for it is by this that all great things are
great ; for even if they do not appear great, but
exceed, they are of necessity great ; so, then, we
say, what would the beautiful be, by which all
things are beautiful, whether they appear so or

383

φαίνηται ἄν τε μή, τί ἂν εἴη; τὸ μὲν γὰρ πρέπον
οὐκ ἂν εἴη· καλλίω γὰρ ποιεῖ φαίνεσθαι ἢ¹ ἔστιν,
ὡς ὁ σὸς λόγος, οἷα δ᾽ ἔστιν οὐκ ἐᾷ φαίνεσθαι. τὸ
C δὲ ποιοῦν εἶναι καλά, ὅπερ νῦν δὴ εἶπον, ἐάν τε
φαίνηται ἐάν τε μή, πειρατέον λέγειν τί ἐστι·
τοῦτο γὰρ ζητοῦμεν, εἴπερ τὸ καλὸν ζητοῦμεν.

ιπ. Ἀλλὰ τὸ πρέπον, ὦ Σώκρατες, καὶ εἶναι καὶ
φαίνεσθαι ποιεῖ καλὰ παρόν.

σω. Ἀδύνατον ἄρα τῷ ὄντι καλὰ ὄντα μὴ
φαίνεσθαι καλὰ εἶναι, παρόντος γε τοῦ ποιοῦντος
φαίνεσθαι;

ιπ. Ἀδύνατον.

18. σω. Ὁμολογήσομεν οὖν τοῦτο, ὦ Ἱππία,
πάντα τὰ τῷ ὄντι καλὰ καὶ νόμιμα καὶ ἐπιτηδεύματα καὶ δοξάζεσθαι καλὰ εἶναι καὶ φαίνεσθαι
D ἀεὶ πᾶσιν, ἢ πᾶν τοὐναντίον ἀγνοεῖσθαι καὶ πάντων
μάλιστα ἔριν καὶ μάχην περὶ αὐτῶν εἶναι καὶ ἰδίᾳ
ἑκάστοις καὶ δημοσίᾳ ταῖς πόλεσιν;

ιπ. Οὕτω μᾶλλον, ὦ Σώκρατες· ἀγνοεῖσθαι.

σω. Οὐκ ἄν, εἴ γέ που τὸ φαίνεσθαι αὐτοῖς
προσῆν· προσῆν δ᾽ ἄν, εἴπερ τὸ πρέπον καλὸν ἦν
καὶ μὴ μόνον καλὰ ἐποίει εἶναι ἀλλὰ καὶ φαίνεσθαι.
ὥστε τὸ πρέπον, εἰ μὲν τὸ καλὰ ποιοῦν ἐστιν εἶναι,
τὸ μὲν καλὸν ἂν εἴη ὃ ἡμεῖς ζητοῦμεν, οὐ μέντοι
τό γε ποιοῦν φαίνεσθαι· εἰ δ᾽ αὖ τὸ φαίνεσθαι

¹ ἢ F : ᾖ TW.

not? For it could not be the appropriate, since that, by your statement, makes things appear more beautiful than they are, but does not let them appear such as they are. But we must try to say what that is which makes things be beautiful, as I said just now, whether they appear so or not; for that is what we are looking for, since we are looking for the beautiful.

HIPP. But the appropriate, Socrates, makes things both be and appear beautiful by its presence.

SOC. Is it impossible, then, for things which are really beautiful not to appear to be beautiful, at any rate when that is present which makes them appear so?

HIPP. It is impossible.

SOC. Shall we, then, agree to this, Hippias, that all things which are really beautiful, both uses and pursuits, are always believed to be beautiful by all, and appear so to them, or, quite the contrary, that people are ignorant about them, and that there is more strife and contention about them than about anything else, both in private between individuals and in public between states?

HIPP. The latter rather, Socrates; that people are ignorant about them.

SOC. They would not be so, if the appearance of beauty were added to them; and it would be added, if the appropriate were beautiful and made things not only to be beautiful, but also to appear so. So that the appropriate, if it is that which makes things be beautiful, would be the beautiful which we are looking for, but would not be that which makes things appear beautiful; but if, on the other hand, the appropriate is that which makes

Ε ποιοῦν ἐστὶ τὸ πρέπον, οὐκ ἂν εἴη τὸ καλὸν ὃ ἡμεῖς
ζητοῦμεν. εἶναι γὰρ ἐκεῖνό γε ποιεῖ, φαίνεσθαι δὲ
καὶ εἶναι ποιεῖν¹ οὐ μόνον καλὰ οὐκ ἄν ποτε δύναιτο
τὸ αὐτό, ἀλλ' οὐδὲ ἄλλο ὁτιοῦν. ἑλώμεθα δὴ
πότερα δοκεῖ τὸ πρέπον εἶναι τὸ φαίνεσθαι καλὰ
ποιοῦν, ἢ τὸ εἶναι.

ιπ. Τὸ φαίνεσθαι, ἔμοιγε δοκεῖ, ὦ Σώκρατες.

σω. Βαβαί, οἴχεται ἄρ' ἡμᾶς διαπεφευγός, ὦ
Ἱππία, τὸ καλὸν γνῶναι ὅ τί ποτ'² ἐστίν, ἐπειδή γε
τὸ πρέπον ἄλλο τι ἐφάνη ὂν ἢ καλόν.

ιπ. Ναὶ μὰ Δία, ὦ Σώκρατες, καὶ μάλα ἔμοιγε
ἀτόπως.

295 σω. Ἀλλὰ μέντοι, ὦ ἑταῖρε, μήπω γε ἀνῶμεν
αὐτό· ἔτι γάρ τινα ἐλπίδα ἔχω ἐκφανήσεσθαι, τί
ποτ' ἐστὶν τὸ καλόν.

ιπ. Πάντως δήπου, ὦ Σώκρατες· οὐδὲ γὰρ χαλεπόν ἐστιν εὑρεῖν. ἐγὼ μὲν οὖν οἶδ' ὅτι, εἰ ὀλίγον
χρόνον εἰς ἐρημίαν ἐλθὼν σκεψαίμην πρὸς ἐμαυτόν,
ἀκριβέστερον ἂν³ αὐτό σοι εἴποιμι τῆς ἀπάσης
ἀκριβείας.

19. σω. Ἃ μὴ μέγα, ὦ Ἱππία, λέγε, ὁρᾷς ὅσα
πράγματα ἡμῖν ἤδη παρέσχηκε· μὴ καὶ ὀργισθὲν
Β ἡμῖν ἔτι μᾶλλον ἀποδρᾷ. καίτοι οὐδὲν λέγω· σὺ
μὲν γάρ, οἶμαι, ῥᾳδίως αὐτὸ εὑρήσεις, ἐπειδὰν
μόνος γένῃ. ἀλλὰ πρὸς θεῶν ἐμοῦ ἐναντίον αὐτὸ
ἔξευρε, εἰ δὲ βούλει, ὥσπερ νῦν ἐμοὶ συζήτει· καὶ
ἐὰν μὲν εὕρωμεν, κάλλιστα ἕξει· εἰ δὲ μή, στέρξω,
οἶμαι, ἐγὼ τῇ ἐμῇ τύχῃ, σὺ δ' ἀπελθὼν ῥᾳδίως
εὑρήσεις. καὶ ἐὰν νῦν εὕρωμεν, ἀμέλει οὐκ ὀχληρὸς

¹ καὶ εἶναι ποιεῖν Heindorf: ποιεῖν καὶ εἶναι Hirschig: καὶ
ποιεῖν εἶναι TWF: Burnet brackets ποιεῖν.
² ὅ τί ποτ' F: ὅ τί ποτὲ T.   ³ ἂν F: om. TW.

things appear beautiful, it would not be the beautiful
for which we are looking. For that makes things
be beautiful, but the same element could not make
things both appear and be beautiful, nor could it
make them both appear and be anything else whatsoever. Let us choose, then, whether we think
that the appropriate is that which makes things
appear or be beautiful.

HIPP That which makes them appear so, in my
opinion, Socrates.

soc. Whew! Our perception of what the beautiful is has fled away and gone, Hippias, since the
appropriate has been found to be something other
than the beautiful.

HIPP. Yes, by Zeus, Socrates, and to me that is
very queer

soc. However, my friend, let us not yet give it up,
for I still have hopes that what the beautiful is will
be made clear.

HIPP. Certainly, to be sure, Socrates, for it is
not hard to find. Now I know that if I should go
away into solitude and meditate alone by myself,
I could tell it to you with the most perfect accuracy.

soc. Ah, don't boast, Hippias. You see how
much trouble it has caused us already; I'm afraid
it may get angry and run away more than ever.
And yet that is nonsense; for you, I think, will
easily find it when you go away by yourself. But
for Heaven's sake, find it in my presence, or, if
you please, join me, as you are now doing, in looking
for it. And if we find it, that will be splendid, but
if we do not, I shall, I suppose, accept my lot, and
you will go away and find it easily. And if we
find it now, I shall certainly not be a nuisance to

387

PLATO

ἔσομαί σοι πυνθανόμενος, ὅ τι ἦν ἐκεῖνο ὃ κατὰ
C σαυτὸν ἐξεῦρες· νῦν δὲ θέασαι αὖ τόδ᾽ εἴ¹ σοι δοκεῖ
εἶναι τὸ καλόν· λέγω δὴ αὐτὸ εἶναι—ἀλλὰ γὰρ
ἐπισκόπει μοι πάνυ προσέχων τὸν νοῦν, μὴ παραληρήσω—τοῦτο γὰρ δὴ ἔστω ἡμῖν καλόν, ὃ ἂν
χρήσιμον ᾖ. εἶπον δὲ ἐκ τῶνδε ἐννοούμενος· καλοί,
φαμέν, οἱ ὀφθαλμοί εἰσιν, οὐχ οἳ ἂν δοκῶσι τοιοῦτοι
εἶναι οἷοι μὴ δυνατοὶ ὁρᾶν, ἀλλ᾽ οἳ ἂν δυνατοί τε
καὶ χρήσιμοι πρὸς τὸ ἰδεῖν. ἦ γάρ,

ιπ. Ναί.

σω. Οὐκοῦν καὶ τὸ ὅλον σῶμα οὕτω λέγομεν
καλὸν εἶναι, τὸ μὲν πρὸς δρόμον, τὸ δὲ πρὸς πάλην,
D καὶ αὖ τὰ ζῷα πάντα, ἵππον καλὸν καὶ ἀλεκτρυόνα
καὶ ὄρτυγα, καὶ τὰ σκεύη πάντα καὶ τὰ ὀχήματα
τά τε πεζὰ καὶ τὰ ἐν τῇ θαλάττῃ πλοῖά τε καὶ
τριήρεις, καὶ τά γε ὄργανα πάντα τά τε ὑπὸ τῇ
μουσικῇ καὶ τὰ ὑπὸ ταῖς ἄλλαις τέχναις, εἰ δὲ
βούλει, τὰ ἐπιτηδεύματα καὶ τοὺς νόμους, σχεδόν
τι πάντα ταῦτα καλὰ προσαγορεύομεν τῷ αὐτῷ
τρόπῳ· ἀποβλέποντες πρὸς ἕκαστον αὐτῶν, ᾗ
πέφυκεν, ᾗ εἴργασται, ᾗ κεῖται, τὸ μὲν χρήσιμον
καὶ ᾗ χρήσιμον καὶ πρὸς ὃ χρήσιμον καὶ ὁπότε
E χρήσιμον καλὸν φαμεν εἶναι, τὸ δὲ ταύτῃ πάντῃ
ἄχρηστον αἰσχρόν· ἆρ᾽ οὖν οὐ καὶ σοὶ δοκεῖ οὕτως,
ὦ Ἱππία;

ιπ. Ἔμοιγε.

20. σω. Ὀρθῶς ἄρα νῦν λέγομεν, ὅτι τυγχάνει
παντὸς ὂν μᾶλλον καλὸν τὸ χρήσιμον;

ιπ. Ὀρθῶς μέντοι, ὦ Σώκρατες.

σω. Οὐκοῦν τὸ δυνατὸν ἕκαστον ἀπεργάζεσθαι,

¹ αὖ τόδ᾽ εἰ Hermann : αὐτὸ εἰ TW : αὐτὸ ὃ F.

388

you by asking what that was which you found by
yourself; but now once more see if this is in your
opinion the beautiful: I say, then, that it is—but
consider, paying close attention to me, that I may
not talk nonsense—for I say, then, whatever is
useful shall be for us beautiful. But I said it with
this reason for my thought; beautiful eyes, we
say, are not such as seem to be so, which are unable
to see, but those which are able and useful for seeing.
Is that right?

HIPP. Yes.

SOC. Then, too, in the same way we say that
the whole body is beautiful, part of it for running,
part for wrestling; and again all the animals, a
beautiful horse or cock or quail; and all utensils
and land vehicles, and on the sea freight-ships and
ships of war; and all instruments in music and in
the other arts, and, if you like, customs and laws
also—pretty well all these we call beautiful in the
same way; looking at each of them—how it is formed
by nature, how it is wrought, how it has been enacted
—the useful we call beautiful, and beautiful in the
way in which it is useful, and for the purpose for
which it is useful, and at the time when it is useful;
and that which is in all these aspects useless we
say is ugly. Now is not this your opinion also,
Hippias?

HIPP. It is.

SOC. Then are we right in saying that the useful
rather than everything else is beautiful?

HIPP. We are right, surely, Socrates.

SOC. Now that which has power to accomplish

εἰς ὅπερ δυνατόν, εἰς τοῦτο καὶ χρήσιμον, τὸ δὲ
ἀδύνατον ἄχρηστον;

ιπ. Πάνυ γε.

σω. Δύναμις μὲν ἄρα καλόν, ἀδυναμία δὲ αἰσχρόν;

ιπ. Σφόδρα γε. τά τε οὖν¹ ἄλλα, ὦ Σώκρατες,
296 μαρτυρεῖ ἡμῖν ὅτι τοῦτο οὕτως ἔχει, ἀτὰρ οὖν καὶ
τὰ πολιτικά· ἐν γὰρ τοῖς πολιτικοῖς τε καὶ τῇ
αὑτοῦ πόλει τὸ μὲν δυνατὸν εἶναι πάντων κάλλιστον,
τὸ δὲ ἀδύνατον πάντων αἴσχιστον.

σω. Εὖ λέγεις. ἆρ' οὖν πρὸς θεῶν, ὦ Ἱππία,²
διὰ ταῦτα καὶ ἡ σοφία πάντων κάλλιστον, ἡ δὲ
ἀμαθία πάντων αἴσχιστον;

ιπ. Ἀλλὰ τί οἴει, ὦ Σώκρατες;

σω. Ἔχε δὴ ἠρέμα, ὦ φίλε ἑταῖρε· ὡς φοβοῦμαι,
τί ποτ' αὖ λέγομεν.

B ιπ. Τί δ' αὖ φοβεῖ, ὦ Σώκρατες, ἐπεὶ νῦν γέ σοι
ὁ λόγος παγκάλως προβέβηκεν;

σω. Βουλοίμην ἄν, ἀλλά μοι τόδε συνεπίσκεψαι·
ἆρ' ἄν τίς τι ποιήσειεν ὃ μήτ' ἐπίσταιτο μήτε τὸ
παράπαν δύναιτο;

ιπ. Οὐδαμῶς· πῶς γὰρ ἂν ὅ γε μὴ δύναιτο;

σω. Οἱ οὖν ἐξαμαρτάνοντες καὶ κακὰ ἐργαζό-
μενοί τε καὶ ποιοῦντες ἄκοντες, ἄλλο τι οὗτοι, εἰ
μὴ ἐδύναντο ταῦτα ποιεῖν, οὐκ ἄν ποτε ἐποίουν;

C ιπ. Δῆλον δή.

σω. Ἀλλὰ μέντοι δυνάμει γε δύνανται οἱ δυνάμε-
νοι· οὐ γάρ που ἀδυναμίᾳ γε.

¹ οὖν TW : γοῦν F.
² ὦ ἱππία W : ἱππία TF.

anything is useful for that for which it has power, but that which is powerless is useless, is it not ?

HIPP. Certainly.

soc. Power, then, is beautiful, and want of power is disgraceful or ugly.

HIPP. Decidedly. Now other things, Socrates, testify for us that this is so, but especially political affairs ; for in political affairs and in one's own state to be powerful is the most beautiful of all things, but to be powerless is the most disgraceful of all.

soc. Good ! Then, for Heaven's sake, Hippias, is wisdom also for this reason the most beautiful of all things and ignorance the most disgraceful of all things ?

HIPP. Well, what do you suppose, Socrates ?

soc. Just keep quiet, my dear friend ; I am so afraid and wondering what in the world we are saying again.

HIPP. What are you afraid of again, Socrates, since now your discussion has gone ahead most beautifully ?

soc. I wish that might be the case ; but consider this point with me : could a person do what he did not know how and was utterly powerless to do ?

HIPP. By no means ; for how could he do what he was powerless to do ?

soc. Then those who commit errors and accomplish and do bad things involuntarily, if they were powerless to do those things, would not do them ?

HIPP. Evidently not.

soc. But yet it is by power that those are powerful who are powerful ; for surely it is not by powerlessness.

391

PLATO

ιπ. Οὐ δῆτα.

σω. Δύνανται δέ γε πάντες ποιεῖν οἱ ποιοῦντες ἃ ποιοῦσιν;

ιπ. Ναί.

σω. Κακὰ δέ γε πολὺ πλείω ποιοῦσιν ἢ ἀγαθὰ πάντες ἄνθρωποι, ἀρξάμενοι ἐκ παίδων, καὶ ἐξαμαρτάνουσιν ἄκοντες.

ιπ. Ἔστι ταῦτα.

σω. Τί οὖν; ταύτην τὴν δύναμιν καὶ ταῦτα τὰ χρήσιμα, ἃ ἂν ᾖ ἐπὶ τὸ κακόν τι ἐργάζεσθαι χρήσιμα, ἆρα φήσομεν ταῦτα εἶναι καλά, ἢ πολλοῦ δεῖ;

D ιπ. Πολλοῦ, ἔμοιγε δοκεῖ, ὦ Σώκρατες.

σω. Οὐκ ἄρα, ὦ Ἱππία, τὸ δυνατόν τε καὶ τὸ χρήσιμον ἡμῖν, ὡς ἔοικεν, ἐστὶ τὸ καλόν.

ιπ. Ἐάν γε, ὦ Σώκρατες, ἀγαθὰ δύνηται καὶ ἐπὶ τοιαῦτα χρήσιμον ᾖ.

21. σω. Ἐκεῖνο μὲν τοίνυν οἴχεται, τὸ δυνατόν τε καὶ χρήσιμον ἁπλῶς εἶναι καλόν· ἀλλ' ἄρα τοῦτ' ἦν ἐκεῖνο, ὦ Ἱππία, ὃ ἐβούλετο ἡμῶν ἡ ψυχὴ εἰπεῖν, ὅτι τὸ χρήσιμόν τε καὶ τὸ δυνατὸν ἐπὶ τὸ ἀγαθόν τι ποιῆσαι, τοῦτ' ἐστὶ τὸ καλόν;

E ιπ. Ἔμοιγε δοκεῖ.

σω. Ἀλλὰ μὴν τοῦτό γε ὠφέλιμόν ἐστιν. ἢ οὔ;

ιπ. Πάνυ γε.

σω. Οὕτω δὴ καὶ τὰ καλὰ σώματα καὶ τὰ καλὰ νόμιμα καὶ ἡ σοφία καὶ ἃ νῦν δὴ ἐλέγομεν πάντα καλά ἐστιν ὅτι ὠφέλιμα.

ιπ. Δῆλον ὅτι.

σω. Τὸ ὠφέλιμον ἄρα ἔοικεν ἡμῖν εἶναι τὸ καλόν, ὦ Ἱππία.

ιπ. Πάντως δήπου, ὦ Σώκρατες.

HIPP. Certainly not.

SOC. And all who do, have power to do what they do ?

HIPP. Yes.

SOC. Men do many more bad things than good, from childhood up, and commit many errors involuntarily.

HIPP. That is true.

SOC. Well, then, this power and these useful things, which are useful for accomplishing something bad—shall we say that they are beautiful, or far from it ?

HIPP. Far from it, in my opinion, Socrates.

SOC. Then, Hippias, the powerful and the useful are not, as it seems, our beautiful.

HIPP. They are, Socrates, if they are powerful and useful for good.

SOC. Then that assertion, that the powerful and useful are beautiful without qualification, is gone ; but was this, Hippias, what our soul wished to say, that the useful and the powerful for doing something good is the beautiful ?

HIPP. Yes, in my opinion.

SOC. But surely this is beneficial ; or is it not ?

HIPP. Certainly.

SOC. So by this argument the beautiful persons and beautiful customs and all that we mentioned just now are beautiful because they are beneficial.

HIPP. Evidently.

SOC. Then the beneficial seems to us to be the beautiful, Hippias.

HIPP. Yes, certainly, Socrates.

ΣΩ. Ἀλλὰ μὴν τό γε ὠφέλιμον τὸ ποιοῦν ἀγαθόν ἐστιν.

ΙΠ. Ἔστι γάρ.

ΣΩ. Τὸ ποιοῦν δέ γ' ἐστὶν οὐκ ἄλλο τι ἢ τὸ αἴτιον· ἢ γάρ;

ΙΠ. Οὕτως.

ΣΩ. Τοῦ ἀγαθοῦ ἄρα αἴτιόν ἐστιν τὸ καλόν.

297 ΙΠ. Ἔστι γάρ.

ΣΩ. Ἀλλὰ μὴν τό γε αἴτιον, ὦ Ἱππία, καὶ οὗ ἂν αἴτιον ᾖ τὸ αἴτιον, ἄλλο ἐστίν· οὐ γάρ που τό γε αἴτιον αἰτίου αἴτιον ἂν εἴη. ὧδε δὲ σκόπει· οὐ τὸ αἴτιον ποιοῦν ἐφάνη;

ΙΠ. Πάνυ γε.

ΣΩ. Οὐκοῦν ὑπὸ τοῦ ποιοῦντος ποιεῖται οὐκ ἄλλο τι ἢ τὸ γιγνόμενον, ἀλλ' οὐ τὸ ποιοῦν;

ΙΠ. Ἔστι ταῦτα.

ΣΩ. Οὐκοῦν ἄλλο τι τὸ γιγνόμενον, ἄλλο δὲ τὸ ποιοῦν;

ΙΠ. Ναί.

ΣΩ. Οὐκ ἄρα τό γ' αἴτιον αἴτιον αἰτίου ἐστίν, ἀλλὰ τοῦ γιγνομένου ὑφ' ἑαυτοῦ.

B ΙΠ. Πάνυ γε.

ΣΩ. Εἰ ἄρα τὸ καλόν ἐστιν αἴτιον ἀγαθοῦ, γίγνοιτ' ἂν ὑπὸ τοῦ καλοῦ τὸ ἀγαθόν· καὶ διὰ ταῦτα, ὡς ἔοικε, σπουδάζομεν καὶ τὴν φρόνησιν καὶ τἆλλα πάντα τὰ καλά, ὅτι τὸ ἔργον αὐτῶν καὶ τὸ ἔκγονον σπουδαστόν ἐστι, τὸ ἀγαθόν, καὶ κινδυνεύει ἐξ ὧν εὑρίσκομεν ἐν[1] πατρός τινος ἰδέᾳ εἶναι τὸ καλὸν τοῦ ἀγαθοῦ.

ΙΠ. Πάνυ μὲν οὖν· καλῶς γὰρ λέγεις, ὦ Σώκρατες.

---

[1] ἐν F: om. TW.

soc. But the beneficial is that which creates good.

hipp. Yes, it is.

soc. But that which creates is nothing else than the cause ; am I right ?

hipp. It is so.

soc. Then the beautiful is the cause of the good.

hipp. Yes, it is.

soc. But surely, Hippias, the cause and that of which the cause is the cause are different ; for the cause could not well be the cause of the cause. But look at it in this way : was not the cause seen to be creating ?

hipp. Yes, certainly.

soc. By that which creates, then, only that is created which comes into being, but not that which creates.[1] Is not that true ?

hipp. That is true.

soc. The cause, then, is not the cause of the cause, but of that which comes into being through it.

hipp. Certainly.

soc. If, then, the beautiful is the cause of good, the good would come into being through the beautiful ; and this is why we are eager for wisdom and all the other beautiful things, because their offspring, the good, is worthy of eagerness, and, from what we are finding, it looks as if the beautiful were a sort of father of the good.

hipp. Certainly ; for what you say is well said, Socrates.

[1] *i.e.* the creative force creates the thing created, not the creative force.

PLATO

ΣΩ. Οὐκοῦν καὶ τόδε καλῶς λέγω, ὅτι οὔτε ὁ πατὴρ υἱός ἐστιν, οὔθ' ὁ υἱὸς πατήρ;

C ΙΠ. Καλῶς μέντοι.

ΣΩ. Οὐδέ γε τὸ αἴτιον γιγνόμενόν ἐστιν, οὐδὲ τὸ γιγνόμενον αὖ αἴτιον.

ΙΠ. Ἀληθῆ λέγεις.

ΣΩ. Μὰ Δί', ὦ ἄριστε, οὐδὲ ἄρα τὸ καλὸν ἀγαθόν ἐστιν, οὐδὲ τὸ ἀγαθὸν καλόν· ἢ¹ δοκεῖ σοι οἷόν τε εἶναι ἐκ τῶν προειρημένων;

ΙΠ. Οὐ μὰ τὸν Δία, οὔ μοι φαίνεται.

ΣΩ. Ἀρέσκει οὖν ἡμῖν καὶ ἐθέλοιμεν ἂν λέγειν, ὡς τὸ καλὸν οὐκ ἀγαθὸν οὐδὲ τὸ ἀγαθὸν καλόν;

ΙΠ. Οὐ μὰ τὸν Δία, οὐ πάνυ μοι ἀρέσκει.

ΣΩ. Ναὶ μὰ τὸν Δία, ὦ Ἱππία· ἐμοὶ δέ γε πάντων
D ἥκιστ' ἀρέσκει ὧν εἰρήκαμεν λόγων.

ΙΠ. Ἔοικε γὰρ οὕτως.

22. ΣΩ. Κινδυνεύει ἄρα ἡμῖν, οὐχ ὥσπερ ἄρτι ἐφαίνετο κάλλιστος εἶναι τῶν λόγων τὸ ὠφέλιμον καὶ τὸ χρήσιμόν τε καὶ τὸ δυνατὸν ἀγαθόν τι ποιεῖν καλὸν εἶναι, οὐχ οὕτως ἔχειν, ἀλλ', εἰ οἷόν τέ ἐστιν, ἐκείνων εἶναι γελοιότερος τῶν πρώτων, ἐν οἷς τήν τε παρθένον ᾠόμεθα εἶναι τὸ καλὸν καὶ ἓν ἕκαστον τῶν ἔμπροσθεν λεχθέντων.

ΙΠ. Ἔοικεν.

ΣΩ. Καὶ ἐγὼ μέν γε οὐκ ἔτι ἔχω, ὦ Ἱππία, ὅποι τράπωμαι, ἀλλ' ἀπορῶ· σὺ δὲ ἔχεις τι λέγειν;

E ΙΠ. Οὐκ ἔν γε τῷ παρόντι, ἀλλ', ὥσπερ ἄρτι ἔλεγον, σκεψάμενος εὖ οἶδ' ὅτι εὑρήσω.

ΣΩ. Ἀλλ' ἐγώ μοι δοκῶ ὑπὸ ἐπιθυμίας τοῦ εἰδέναι οὐχ οἷός τε σὲ εἶναι περιμένειν μέλλοντα· καὶ γὰρ οὖν δή τι καὶ οἶμαι ἄρτι ηὐπορηκέναι.

¹ καλόν· ἢ corr. Coisl.: ἢ καλόν· ἢ T: ἢ καλὸν W: καλόν F.

396

soc. Then is this well said, too, that the father is not the son, and the son not father?

HIPP. To be sure it is well said.

soc. And neither is the cause that which comes into being, nor is that which comes into being the cause.

HIPP. True.

soc. By Zeus, my good friend, then neither is the beautiful good, nor the good beautiful; or does it seem to you possible, after what has been said?

HIPP. No, by Zeus, it does not appear so to me.

soc. Does it please us, and should we be willing to say that the beautiful is not good, and the good not beautiful?

HIPP. No, by Zeus, it does not please me at all.

soc. Right, by Zeus, Hippias! And it pleases me least of all the things we have said.

HIPP. Yes, that is likely.

soc. Then there is a good chance that the statement that the beneficial and the useful and the powerful to create something good are beautiful, is not, as it appeared to be, the most beautiful of our statements, but, if that be possible, is even more ridiculous than those first ones in which we thought the maiden was the beautiful, and each of the various other things we spoke of before.

HIPP. That is likely.

soc. And Hippias, I no longer know where to turn; I am at a loss; but have you anything to say?

HIPP. Not at the moment, but, as I said just now, I am sure I shall find it after meditation.

soc. But it seems to me that I am so eager to know that I cannot wait for you while you delay; for I believe I have just now found a way out. Just see;

397

ὅρα γάρ· εἰ ὃ ἂν χαίρειν ἡμᾶς ποιῇ, μήτι πάσας τὰς
ἡδονάς, ἀλλ' ὃ ἂν διὰ τῆς ἀκοῆς καὶ τῆς ὄψεως,
τοῦτο φαῖμεν εἶναι καλόν, πῶς τι ἄρ' ἂν ἀγωνιζοί-
298 μεθα; οἵ τέ γέ που καλοὶ ἄνθρωποι, ὦ Ἱππία, καὶ
τὰ ποικίλματα πάντα καὶ τὰ ζωγραφήματα καὶ τὰ
πλάσματα τέρπει ἡμᾶς ὁρῶντας, ἃ ἂν καλὰ ᾖ· καὶ
οἱ φθόγγοι οἱ καλοὶ καὶ ἡ μουσικὴ ξύμπασα καὶ οἱ
λόγοι καὶ αἱ μυθολογίαι ταὐτὸν τοῦτο ἐργάζονται,
ὥστ' εἰ ἀποκριναίμεθα τῷ θρασεῖ ἐκείνῳ ἀνθρώπῳ
ὅτι "Ὦ γενναῖε, τὸ καλόν ἐστι τὸ δι' ἀκοῆς τε καὶ
ὄψεως ἡδύ," οὐκ ἄν, οἴει, αὐτὸν τοῦ θράσους
ἐπίσχοιμεν;

ιπ. Ἐμοὶ γοῦν[1] δοκεῖ νῦν, ὦ Σώκρατες, εὖ λέγε-
B σθαι τὸ καλὸν ὃ ἔστιν.

σω. Τί δ' ἄρα; τὰ ἐπιτηδεύματα τὰ καλὰ καὶ
τοὺς νόμους, ὦ Ἱππία, δι' ἀκοῆς ἢ δι' ὄψεως φήσομεν
ἡδέα ὄντα καλὰ εἶναι, ἢ ἄλλο τι εἶδος ἔχειν;

ιπ. Ταῦτα δ' ἴσως, ὦ Σώκρατες, κἂν παραλάθοι
τὸν ἄνθρωπον.

σω. Μὰ τὸν κύνα, ὦ Ἱππία, οὐχ ὅν γ' ἂν ἐγὼ
C μάλιστα αἰσχυνοίμην ληρῶν καὶ προσποιούμενός τι
λέγειν μηδὲν λέγων.

ιπ. Τίνα τοῦτον;

σω. Σωκράτη τὸν Σωφρονίσκου, ὃς ἐμοὶ οὐδὲν ἂν
μᾶλλον ταῦτα ἐπιτρέποι ἀνερεύνητα ὄντα ῥᾳδίως
λέγειν ἢ ὡς εἰδότα ἃ μὴ οἶδα.

ιπ. Ἀλλὰ μὴν ἔμοιγε καὶ αὐτῷ, ἐπειδὴ σὺ εἶπες,
δοκεῖ τι ἄλλο εἶναι τοῦτο τὸ περὶ τοὺς νόμους.

23. σω. Ἔχ' ἡσυχῇ, ὦ Ἱππία· κινδυνεύομεν γάρ

----
[1] ἐμοιγοῦν Γ : ἔμοιγε οὖν TW.

how would it help us towards our goal if we were to say that that is beautiful which makes us feel joy ; I do not mean all pleasures, but that which makes us feel joy through hearing and sight ? For surely beautiful human beings, Hippias, and all decorations and paintings and works of sculpture which are beautiful, delight us when we see them ; and beautiful sounds and music in general and speeches and stories do the same thing, so that if we were to reply to that impudent fellow, " My excellent man, the beautiful is that which is pleasing through hearing and sight," don't you think that we should put a stop to his impudence ?

HIPP. To me, at any rate, Socrates, it seems that the nature of the beautiful is now well stated.

SOC. But what then ? Shall we say, Hippias, that beautiful customs and laws are beautiful because they are pleasing through hearing and sight, or that they have some other form of beauty ?

HIPP. Perhaps, Socrates, these things might slip past the man unnoticed.

SOC. No, by the dog, Hippias—not past the man before whom I should be most ashamed of talking nonsense and pretending that I was talking sense when I was not.

HIPP. What man is that ?

SOC. Socrates, the son of Sophroniscus, who would no more permit me to say these things carelessly without investigation than to say that I know what I do not know.

HIPP. But certainly I also, now that you have mentioned it, think that this about the laws is something different.

SOC. Not too fast, Hippias ; for very likely we have

399

τοι ἐν τῇ αὐτῇ ἐμπεπτωκότες ἀπορίᾳ περὶ τοῦ καλοῦ ἐν ᾗπερ νῦν δή,[1] οἴεσθαι ἐν ἄλλῃ τινὶ εὐπορίᾳ εἶναι.

ιπ. Πῶς τοῦτο λέγεις, ὦ Σώκρατες;

σω. Ἐγώ σοι φράσω ὅ γ' ἐμοὶ[2] καταφαίνεται, εἰ D ἄρα τὶ λέγω. ταῦτα μὲν γὰρ τὰ περὶ τοὺς νόμους τε καὶ τὰ ἐπιτηδεύματα τάχ' ἂν φανείη οὐκ ἐκτὸς ὄντα τῆς αἰσθήσεως ἢ διὰ τῆς ἀκοῆς τε καὶ ὄψεως ἡμῖν οὖσα τυγχάνει· ἀλλ' ὑπομείνωμεν τοῦτον τὸν λόγον, τὸ διὰ τούτων ἡδὺ καλὸν εἶναι, μηδὲν τὸ τῶν νόμων εἰς μέσον παράγοντες. ἀλλ' εἰ ἡμᾶς ἔροιτο εἴτε οὗτος ὃν λέγω, εἴτε ἄλλος ὁστισοῦν· " Τί δή, ὦ Ἱππία τε καὶ Σώκρατες, ἀφωρίσατε τοῦ ἡδέος τὸ ταύτῃ ἡδὺ ᾗ λέγετε[3] καλὸν εἶναι, τὸ δὲ E κατὰ τὰς ἄλλας αἰσθήσεις σίτων τε καὶ ποτῶν καὶ τῶν περὶ τἀφροδίσια καὶ τἆλλα πάντα τὰ τοιαῦτα οὔ φατε καλὰ εἶναι; ἢ οὐδὲ ἡδέα, οὐδὲ ἡδονὰς τὸ παράπαν ἐν τοῖς τοιούτοις φατὲ εἶναι, οὐδ' ἐν ἄλλῳ ἢ τῷ ἰδεῖν τε καὶ ἀκοῦσαι;" τί φήσομεν, ὦ Ἱππία;

ιπ. Πάντως δήπου φήσομεν, ὦ Σώκρατες, καὶ ἐν τοῖς ἄλλοις μεγάλας πάνυ ἡδονὰς εἶναι.

σω. " Τί οὖν," φήσει, " ἡδονὰς οὔσας οὐδὲν 299 ἧττον ἢ καὶ ἐκείνας ἀφαιρεῖσθε τοῦτο τοὔνομα καὶ ἀποστερεῖτε τοῦ καλὰς εἶναι;" " Ὅτι, φήσομεν, καταγελῴη[4] ἂν ἡμῶν οὐδεὶς ὅστις οὔ, εἰ φαῖμεν μὴ ἡδὺ εἶναι φαγεῖν, ἀλλὰ καλόν, καὶ ὄζειν ἡδὺ μὴ ἡδὺ ἀλλὰ καλόν· τὰ δέ που περὶ τὰ ἀφροδίσια πάντες ἂν ἡμῖν μάχοιντο ὡς ἥδιστον ὄν, δεῖν[5] δὲ

---

[1] νῦν δή later hands: δὴ νῦν TWF.
[2] γ' ἐμοί F: γέ μοι TW.
[3] λέγετε scr. Laurent. vii. 85: λέγεται TWF.
[4] καταγελῴη F: καταγελῶ TW.
[5] δεῖν Heindorf: δεῖ TWF.

fallen into the same perplexity about the beautiful in which we were a while ago, although we think we have found another way out.

HIPP. What do you mean by that, Socrates?

SOC. I will tell you what presents itself to me, if perhaps there may be some sense in it. For perhaps these matters of laws and customs might be shown to be not outside of the perception which we have through hearing and sight; but let us stick to the statement that that which is pleasing through the senses is beautiful, without interjecting the matter of the laws. But if this man of whom I speak, or anyone else whosoever, should ask us: "Hippias and Socrates, did you make the distinction that in the category of 'the pleasing' that which is pleasing in the way you mention is beautiful, whereas you say that that which is pleasing according to the other senses—those concerned with food and drink and sexual love and all such things—is not beautiful? Or do you say that such things are not even pleasing and that there is no pleasure at all in them, nor in anything else except sight and hearing?" What shall we say, Hippias?

HIPP. Certainly, by all means, Socrates, we shall say that there are very great pleasures in the other things also.

SOC. "Why, then," he will say, "if they are pleasures no less than the others, do you take from them this designation and deprive them of being beautiful?" "Because," we shall say, "everybody would laugh at us if we should say that eating is not pleasant but is beautiful, and that a pleasant odour is not pleasant but is beautiful; and as to the act of sexual love, we should all, no doubt, contend

401

αὐτό, ἐάν τις καὶ πράττῃ, οὕτω πράττειν, ὥστε
μηδένα ὁρᾶν, ὡς αἴσχιστον ὂν ὁρᾶσθαι." ταῦτα
ἡμῶν λεγόντων, ὦ Ἱππία, " Μανθάνω," ἂν ἴσως
φαίη, " καὶ ἐγὼ ὅτι πάλαι αἰσχύνεσθε ταύτας τὰς
B ἡδονὰς φάναι καλὰς εἶναι, ὅτι οὐ δοκεῖ τοῖς ἀνθρώ-
ποις· ἀλλ' ἐγὼ οὐ τοῦτο ἠρώτων, ὃ δοκεῖ τοῖς
πολλοῖς καλὸν εἶναι, ἀλλ' ὅ τι ἔστιν." ἐροῦμεν δή,
οἶμαι, ὅπερ ὑπεθέμεθα, ὅτι " Τοῦθ' ἡμεῖς γέ φαμεν
τὸ μέρος τοῦ ἡδέος, τὸ ἐπὶ τῇ ὄψει τε καὶ ἀκοῇ
γιγνόμενον, καλὸν εἶναι." ἀλλὰ ἔχεις τι χρῆσθαι
τῷ λόγῳ, ἤ τι καὶ ἄλλο ἐροῦμεν, ὦ Ἱππία;

ιπ. Ἀνάγκη πρός γε τὰ εἰρημένα, ὦ Σώκρατες,
μὴ ἄλλ' ἄττα ἢ ταῦτα λέγειν.

24. ΣΩ. " Καλῶς δὴ λέγετε," φήσει. " οὐκοῦν
C εἴπερ τὸ δι' ὄψεως καὶ ἀκοῆς ἡδὺ καλόν ἐστιν, ὃ μὴ
τοῦτο τυγχάνει ὂν τῶν ἡδέων, δῆλον ὅτι οὐκ ἂν
καλὸν εἴη;" ὁμολογήσομεν;

ιπ. Ναί.

ΣΩ. " Ἦ οὖν τὸ δι' ὄψεως ἡδύ," φήσει, " δι'
ὄψεως καὶ ἀκοῆς ἐστιν ἡδύ, ἢ τὸ δι' ἀκοῆς ἡδὺ δι'
ἀκοῆς καὶ ὄψεώς ἐστιν ἡδύ;" " Οὐδαμῶς," φήσομεν,
" τὸ διὰ τοῦ ἑτέρου ὂν τοῦτο δι' ἀμφοτέρων εἴη
ἄν—τοῦτο γὰρ δοκεῖς ἡμῖν λέγειν—ἀλλ' ἡμεῖς
D ἐλέγομεν, ὅτι καὶ ἑκάτερον τούτων αὐτὸ καθ' αὑτὸ
τῶν ἡδέων καλὸν εἴη, καὶ ἀμφότερα." οὐχ οὕτως
ἀποκρινούμεθα;

ιπ. Πάνυ μὲν οὖν.

ΣΩ. " Ἆρ' οὖν," φήσει, " ἡδὺ ἡδέος ὁτιοῦν

that it is most pleasant, but that one must, if he perform it, do it so that no one else shall see, because it is most repulsive to see." If we say this, Hippias, "I too understand," he will perhaps say, "that you have all along been ashamed to say that these pleasures are beautiful, because they do not seem so to people ; but that is not what I asked, what seems to most people to be beautiful, but what is so." We shall, then, I fancy, say, as we suggested, "We say that that part of the pleasant which comes by sight and hearing is beautiful." Do you think the statement is of any use, Hippias, or shall we say something else ?

HIPP. Inevitably, in view of what has been said, Socrates, we must say just that.

SOC. "Excellent !" he will say. "Then if that which is pleasant through sight and hearing is beautiful, that among pleasant things which does not happen to be of that sort would evidently not be beautiful ? " Shall we agree ?

HIPP. Yes.

SOC. "Is, then, that which is pleasant through sight," he will say, "pleasant through sight and hearing, or is that which is pleasant through hearing pleasant through hearing and sight ? " "No," we shall say, "that which is pleasant through each of these would not in the least be pleasant through both—for that is what you appear to us to mean— but we said that either of these pleasant things was beautiful alone by itself, and both together." Is not that the reply we shall make ?

HIPP. Certainly.

SOC. "Does, then," he will say, "any pleasant thing whatsoever differ from any pleasant thing

ὁτουοῦν διαφέρει τούτῳ, τῷ ἡδὺ εἶναι; μὴ γὰρ εἰ μείζων τις ἡδονὴ ἢ ἐλάττων ἢ μᾶλλον ἢ ἧττόν ἐστιν, ἀλλ' εἴ τις αὐτῷ τούτῳ διαφέρει, τῷ ἡ μὲν ἡδονὴ εἶναι, ἡ δὲ μὴ ἡδονή, τῶν ἡδονῶν;" "Οὐχ ἡμῖν γε δοκεῖ·" οὐ γάρ;

ιπ. Οὐ γὰρ οὖν δοκεῖ.

σω. "Οὐκοῦν," φήσει, "δι' ἄλλο τι ἢ ὅτι ἡδοναί εἰσι προείλεσθε ταύτας τὰς ἡδονὰς ἐκ τῶν Ε ἄλλων ἡδονῶν, τοιοῦτόν τι ὁρῶντες ἐπ' ἀμφοῖν, ὅτι ἔχουσί τι διάφορον τῶν ἄλλων, εἰς ὃ ἀποβλέποντες καλάς φατε αὐτὰς εἶναι; οὐ γάρ που[1] διὰ τοῦτο καλή ἐστιν ἡδονὴ ἡ διὰ τῆς ὄψεως, ὅτι δι' ὄψεώς ἐστιν· εἰ γὰρ τοῦτο αὐτῇ ἦν τὸ αἴτιον καλῇ εἶναι, οὐκ ἄν ποτε ἦν ἡ ἑτέρα, ἡ διὰ τῆς ἀκοῆς, καλή· οὔκουν ἔστι γε δι' ὄψεως ἡδονή." "'Αληθῆ λέγεις," φήσομεν;

ιπ. Φήσομεν γάρ.

300 σω. "Οὐδέ γ' αὖ ἡ δι' ἀκοῆς ἡδονή, ὅτι δι' ἀκοῆς ἐστί, διὰ ταῦτα τυγχάνει καλή· οὐ γὰρ ἄν ποτε αὖ ἡ διὰ τῆς ὄψεως καλὴ ἦν· οὔκουν ἔστι γε δι' ἀκοῆς ἡδονή." ἀληθῆ φήσομεν, ὦ Ἱππία, λέγειν τὸν ἄνδρα ταῦτα λέγοντα;

ιπ. 'Αληθῆ.

σω. "'Αλλὰ μέντοι ἀμφότεραί γ' εἰσὶ καλαί, ὡς φατέ." φαμὲν γάρ;

ιπ. Φαμέν.

σω. "Ἔχουσιν ἄρα τι τὸ αὐτὸ ὃ ποιεῖ αὐτὰς καλὰς εἶναι, τὸ κοινὸν τοῦτο, ὃ καὶ ἀμφοτέραις

---

[1] που F : πω TW.

404

whatsoever by this, by being pleasant ? I ask not whether any pleasure is greater or smaller or more or less, but whether it differs by just this very thing, by the fact that one of the pleasures is a pleasure and the other is not a pleasure." " We do not think so." Do we ?

HIPP. No, we do not.

SOC. " Is it not, then," he will say, " for some other reason than because they are pleasures that you chose these pleasures out from the other pleasures— it was because you saw some quality in both, since they have something different from the others, in view of which you say that they are beautiful ? For the reason why that which is pleasant through sight is beautiful, is not, I imagine, because it is through sight ; for if that were the cause of its being beautiful, the other pleasure, that through hearing, would not be beautiful ; it certainly is not pleasure through sight." Shall we say " What you say is true ? "

HIPP. Yes, we shall.

SOC. " Nor, again, is the pleasure through hearing beautiful for the reason that it is through hearing ; for in that case, again, the pleasure through sight would not be beautiful ; it certainly is not pleasure through hearing." Shall we say, Hippias, that the man who says that speaks the truth ?

HIPP. Yes, he speaks the truth.

SOC. " But yet both are beautiful, as you say." We do say that, do we not ?

HIPP. We do.

SOC. " They have, then, something identical which makes them to be beautiful, this common quality which pertains to both of them in common and to

405

PLATO

B αὑταῖς ἔπεστι κοινῇ καὶ ἑκατέρᾳ ἰδίᾳ· οὐ γὰρ ἂν
που ἄλλως ἀμφότεραί τε καλαὶ ἦσαν καὶ ἑκατέρα.''
ἀποκρίνου ἐμοὶ ὡς ἐκείνῳ.

ιπ. Ἀποκρίνομαι, καὶ ἐμοὶ δοκεῖ ἔχειν ὡς
λέγεις.

σω. Εἰ ἄρα τι αὗται αἱ ἡδοναὶ ἀμφότεραι πεπόν-
θασιν, ἑκατέρα δὲ μή, οὐκ ἂν τούτῳ γε τῷ παθή-
ματι εἶεν καλαί.

ιπ. Καὶ πῶς ἂν εἴη τοῦτο, ὦ Σώκρατες, μηδε-
τέρας πεπονθυίας τι τῶν ὄντων ὁτιοῦν, ἔπειτα
τοῦτο τὸ πάθος, ὃ μηδετέρα πέπονθεν, ἀμφοτέρας
πεπονθέναι;

C σω. Οὐ δοκεῖ σοι;

ιπ. Πολλὴ γὰρ ἄν μ' ἔχοι ἀπειρία καὶ τῆς τούτων φύσεως καὶ τῆς τῶν παρόντων λέξεως λόγων.

25. σω. Ἡδέως γε, ὦ Ἱππία. ἀλλὰ γὰρ ἐγὼ
ἴσως κινδυνεύω δοκεῖν μέν τι ὁρᾶν οὕτως ἔχον ὡς
σὺ φῂς ἀδύνατον εἶναι, ὁρῶ δ' οὐδέν.

ιπ. Οὐ κινδυνεύεις, ὦ Σώκρατες, ἀλλὰ πάνυ
ἑτοίμως παρορᾷς.

σω. Καὶ μὴν πολλά γέ μοι προφαίνεται τοιαῦτα
πρὸ τῆς ψυχῆς, ἀλλὰ ἀπιστῶ αὐτοῖς, ὅτι σοὶ μὲν
D οὐ φαντάζεται, ἀνδρὶ πλεῖστον ἀργύριον εἰργα-
σμένῳ τῶν νῦν ἐπὶ σοφίᾳ, ἐμοὶ δέ, ὃς οὐδὲν πώποτε
ἠργασάμην· καὶ ἐνθυμοῦμαι, ὦ ἑταῖρε, μὴ παίζῃς
πρός με καὶ ἑκὼν ἐξαπατᾷς· οὕτω μοι σφόδρα καὶ
πολλὰ καταφαίνεται.

ιπ. Οὐδεὶς σοῦ, ὦ Σώκρατες, κάλλιον εἴσεται
εἴτε παίζω εἴτε μή, ἐὰν ἐπιχειρήσῃς λέγειν τὰ προ-
φαινόμενά σοι ταῦτα· φανήσει γὰρ οὐδὲν λέγων.

each individually ; for otherwise they would not both collectively and each individually be beautiful." Answer me, as if you were answering him.

HIPP. I answer, and I think it is as you say.

SOC. If, then, these pleasures are both affected in any way collectively, but each individually is not so affected, it is not by this affection that they would be beautiful.

HIPP. And how could that be, Socrates, when neither of them individually is affected by some affection or other, that then both are affected by that affection by which neither is affected ?

SOC. You think it cannot be ?

HIPP. I should have to be very inexperienced both in the nature of these things and in the language of our present discussion.

SOC. Very pretty, Hippias. But there is a chance that I think I see a case of that kind which you say is impossible, but do not really see it.

HIPP. There's no chance about it, Socrates, but you quite purposely see wrongly.

SOC. And certainly many such cases appear before my mind, but I mistrust them because they do not appear to you, a man who has made more money by wisdom than anyone now living, but to me who never made any money at all ; and the thought disturbs me, my friend, that you are playing with me and purposely deceiving me, they appear to me in such numbers and with such force.

HIPP. Nobody, Socrates, will know better than you whether I am playing with you or not, if you proceed to tell these things that appear to you ; for it will be apparent to you that you are talking

PLATO

οὐ γὰρ μήποτε εὕρῃς, ὃ μήτ᾽[1] ἐγὼ πέπονθα μήτε
σύ, τοῦτ᾽ ἀμφοτέρους ἡμᾶς πεπονθότας.

E   ΣΩ. Πῶς λέγεις, ὦ Ἱππία; ἴσως μὲν τὶ[2] λέγεις,
ἐγὼ δ᾽ οὐ μανθάνω· ἀλλά μου σαφέστερον ἄκουσον
ὃ βούλομαι λέγειν. ἐμοὶ γὰρ φαίνεται, ὃ μήτ᾽ ἐγὼ
πέπονθα εἶναι μήτ᾽ εἰμὶ μηδ᾽ αὖ σὺ εἶ, τοῦτ᾽
ἀμφοτέρους πεπονθέναι ἡμᾶς οἷόν τ᾽ εἶναι· ἕτερα
δ᾽ αὖ, ἃ ἀμφότεροι πεπόνθαμεν εἶναι, ταῦτα
οὐδέτερον εἶναι ἡμῶν.

ιπ. Τέρατα αὖ ἀποκρινομένῳ ἔοικας, ὦ Σώκρατες, ἔτι μείζω ἢ ὀλίγον πρότερον ἀπεκρίνω.
σκόπει γάρ· πότερον εἰ ἀμφότεροι δίκαιοί ἐσμεν,
301 οὐ καὶ ἑκάτερος ἡμῶν εἴη ἄν, ἢ εἰ ἄδικος ἑκάτερος,
οὐ καὶ ἀμφότεροι αὖ, ἢ εἰ ὑγιαίνοντες, οὐ καὶ
ἑκάτερος; ἢ εἰ κεκμηκώς τι ἢ τετρωμένος ἢ
πεπληγμένος ἢ ἄλλ᾽ ὁτιοῦν πεπονθὼς ἑκάτερος
ἡμῶν εἴη, οὐ καὶ ἀμφότεροι ἂν τοῦτο πεπόνθοιμεν;
ἔτι τοίνυν εἰ χρυσοῖ ἢ ἀργυροῖ ἢ ἐλεφάντινοι, εἰ δὲ
βούλει, γενναῖοι ἢ σοφοὶ ἢ τίμιοι ἢ γέροντές γε ἢ
νέοι ἢ ἄλλο ὅ τι βούλει τῶν ἐν ἀνθρώποις ἀμφότεροι
τύχοιμεν ὄντες, ἆρ᾽ οὐ μεγάλη ἀνάγκη καὶ ἑκάτερον ἡμῶν τοῦτ᾽ εἶναι;

B   ΣΩ. Πάντως γε δήπου.

ιπ. Ἀλλὰ γὰρ δὴ σύ, ὦ Σώκρατες, τὰ μὲν ὅλα
τῶν πραγμάτων οὐ σκοπεῖς, οὐδ᾽ ἐκεῖνοι οἷς σὺ
εἴωθας διαλέγεσθαι, κρούετε δὲ ἀπολαμβάνοντες τὸ
καλὸν καὶ ἕκαστον τῶν ὄντων ἐν τοῖς λόγοις κατα-
τέμνοντες. διὰ ταῦτα οὕτω μεγάλα ὑμᾶς λανθάνει
καὶ διανεκῆ σώματα τῆς οὐσίας πεφυκότα. καὶ
νῦν τοσοῦτόν σε λέληθεν, ὥστε οἴει εἶναί τι ἢ

---

[1] μήτ᾽ F : μήποτ᾽ TW.
[2] μεν τι F : μέντοι τί TW.

nonsense. For you will never find that you and I
are both affected by an affection by which neither
of us is affected.

soc. What are you saying, Hippias? Perhaps
you are talking sense, and I fail to understand;
but let me tell more clearly what I wish to say.
For it appears to me that it is possible for us both
to be so affected as to be something which I am not
so affected as to be, and which I am not and you
are not either; and again for neither of us to be
so affected as to be other things which we both are.

HIPP. Your reply, Socrates, seems to involve
miracles again even greater than those of your
previous reply. For consider: if we are both just,
would not each of us be just also, and if each is
unjust, would not both again also be unjust, or if
both are healthy, each of us also? Or if each of
us were to be tired or wounded or struck or affected
in any other way whatsoever, should we not both of
us be affected in the same way? Then, too, if we
were to be golden or of silver or of ivory, or, if you
please, noble or wise or honoured or old or young or
whatever else you like of all that flesh is heir to, is
it not quite inevitable that each of us be that also?

soc. Absolutely.

HIPP. But you see, Socrates, you do not consider
the entirety of things, nor do they with whom you
are in the habit of conversing, but you all test the
beautiful and each individual entity by taking them
separately and cutting them to pieces. For this
reason you fail to observe that embodiments of
reality are by nature so great and undivided. And
now you have failed to observe to such a degree
that you think there is some affection or reality

PLATO

πάθος ἢ οὐσίαν, ἢ περὶ μὲν ἀμφότερα ταῦτα ἔστιν
C ἅμα, περὶ δὲ ἑκάτερον οὔ, ἢ αὖ περὶ μὲν ἑκάτερον,
περὶ δὲ ἀμφότερα οὔ· οὕτως ἀλογίστως καὶ ἀ-
σκέπτως καὶ εὐήθως καὶ ἀδιανοήτως διάκεισθε.

26. ΣΩ. Τοιαῦτα, ὦ Ἱππία, τὰ ἡμέτερά ἐστιν,
οὐχ οἷα βούλεταί τις, φασὶν ἄνθρωποι ἑκάστοτε
παροιμιαζόμενοι, ἀλλ' οἷα δύναται· ἀλλὰ σὺ ἡμᾶς
ὀνίνης ἀεὶ νουθετῶν. ἐπεὶ καὶ νῦν, πρὶν ὑπὸ σοῦ
ταῦτα νουθετηθῆναι, ὡς εὐήθως διεκείμεθα—ἔτι
σοι μᾶλλον ἐγὼ ἐπιδείξω εἰπὼν ἃ διενοούμεθα[1]
περὶ αὐτῶν, ἢ μὴ εἴπω;

D ΙΠ. Εἰδότι μὲν ἐρεῖς, ὦ Σώκρατες· οἶδα γὰρ
ἑκάστους τῶν περὶ τοὺς λόγους ὡς διάκεινται·
ὅμως δ' εἴ τι σοὶ ἥδιον, λέγε.

ΣΩ. Ἀλλὰ μὴν ἥδιόν γε. ἡμεῖς γάρ, ὦ βέλτιστε,
οὕτως ἀβέλτεροι ἦμεν, πρίν σε ταῦτ' εἰπεῖν, ὥστε
δόξαν εἴχομεν περὶ ἐμοῦ τε καὶ σοῦ ὡς ἑκάτερος
ἡμῶν εἷς ἐστί, τοῦτο δὲ ὃ ἑκάτερος ἡμῶν εἴη οὐκ
ἄρα εἴημεν ἀμφότεροι—οὐ γὰρ εἷς ἐσμέν, ἀλλὰ
E δύο—οὕτως εὐηθικῶς εἴχομεν· νῦν δὲ παρὰ σοῦ
ἤδη ἀνεδιδάχθημεν ὅτι εἰ μὲν δύο ἀμφότεροί ἐσμεν,
δύο καὶ ἑκάτερον ἡμῶν ἀνάγκη εἶναι, εἰ δὲ εἷς
ἑκάτερος, ἕνα καὶ ἀμφοτέρους ἀνάγκη· οὐ γὰρ
οἷόν τε διανεκεῖ λόγῳ τῆς οὐσίας κατὰ Ἱππίαν
ἄλλως ἔχειν, ἀλλ' ὃ ἂν ἀμφότερα ᾖ,[2] τοῦτο καὶ
ἑκάτερον, καὶ ὃ ἑκάτερον, ἀμφότερα εἶναι. πε-
πεισμένος δὴ νῦν ἐγὼ ὑπὸ σοῦ ἐνθάδε κάθημαι·
πρότερον μέντοι, ὦ Ἱππία, ὑπόμνησόν με· πότερον
εἷς ἐσμὲν ἐγώ τε καὶ σύ, ἢ σύ τε δύο εἶ κἀγὼ δύο;

---

[1] διενοούμεθα F : διανοούμεθα TW.
[2] ᾖ W : ἢ F : ἦν Tf.

which pertains to both of these together, but not to each individually, or again to each, but not to both ; so unreasoning and undiscerning and foolish and unreflecting is your state of mind.

soc. Human affairs, Hippias, are not what a man wishes, but what he can,[1] as the proverb goes which people are constantly citing ; but you are always aiding us with admonitions. For now too, until we were admonished by you of our foolish state of mind—shall I continue to speak and make you a still further exhibition of our thoughts on the subject, or shall I not speak ?

hipp. You will speak to one who knows, Socrates, for I know the state of mind of all who are concerned with discussions ; but nevertheless, if you prefer, speak.

soc. Well, I do prefer. For we, my friend, were so stupid, before you spoke, as to have an opinion concerning you and me, that each of us was one, but that we were not both that which each of us was—for we are not one, but two—so foolish were we. But now we have been taught by you that if we are both two, then each of us is inevitably two, and if each is one, then both are inevitably one ; for it is impossible, by the continuous doctrine of reality according to Hippias, that it be otherwise, but what we both are, that each is, and what each is, both are. So now I have been convinced by you, and I hold this position. But first, Hippias, refresh my memory : Are you and I one, or are you two and I two ?

---

[1] Suidas gives the proverb in the form : ζῶμεν γὰρ οὐχ ὡς θέλομεν, ἀλλ' ὡς δυνάμεθα. " Man proposes, but God disposes " would be an English equivalent.

PLATO

ιπ. Τί λέγεις, ὦ Σώκρατες;

Σω. Ταῦτα ἅπερ λέγω· φοβοῦμαι γάρ σε σαφῶς λέγειν, ὅτι μοι χαλεπαίνεις, ἐπειδὰν τὶ δόξῃς
302 σαυτῷ λέγειν· ὅμως δ' ἔτι μοι εἰπέ· οὐχ εἷς ἡμῶν ἑκάτερός ἐστι καὶ πέπονθε τοῦτο, εἷς εἶναι;

ιπ. Πάνυ γε.

Σω. Οὐκοῦν εἴπερ εἷς, καὶ περιττὸς ἂν εἴη ἑκάτερος ἡμῶν· ἢ οὐ τὸ ἓν περιττὸν ἡγεῖ;

ιπ. Ἔγωγε.

Σω. Ἦ καὶ ἀμφότεροι οὖν περιττοί ἐσμεν δύο ὄντες;

ιπ. Οὐκ ἂν εἴη, ὦ Σώκρατες.

Σω. Ἀλλ' ἄρτιοί γε ἀμφότεροι· ἢ γάρ;

ιπ. Πάνυ γε.

Σω. Μῶν οὖν, ὅτι ἀμφότεροι ἄρτιοι, τούτου ἕνεκα καὶ ἑκάτερος ἄρτιος ἡμῶν ἐστίν;

ιπ. Οὐ δῆτα.

Β Σω. Οὐκ ἄρα πᾶσα ἀνάγκη, ὡς νῦν δὴ ἔλεγες, ἃ ἂν ἀμφότεροι, καὶ ἑκάτερον, καὶ ἃ ἂν ἑκάτερος, καὶ ἀμφοτέρους εἶναι.

ιπ. Οὐ τά γε τοιαῦτα, ἀλλ' οἷα ἐγὼ πρότερον ἔλεγον.

27. Σω. Ἐξαρκεῖ, ὦ Ἱππία· ἀγαπητὰ γὰρ καὶ ταῦτα, ἐπειδὴ τὰ μὲν οὕτω φαίνεται, τὰ δ' οὐχ οὕτως ἔχοντα. καὶ γὰρ ἐγὼ ἔλεγον, εἰ μέμνησαι ὅθεν οὗτος ὁ λόγος ἐλέχθη,[1] ὅτι ἡ διὰ τῆς ὄψεως
C καὶ δι'[2] ἀκοῆς ἡδονὴ οὐ τούτῳ εἶεν καλαί, ὅ τι τυγχάνοιεν ἑκάτερα μὲν αὐτῶν εἶναι πεπονθυῖα, ἀμφότεραι δὲ μή, ἢ ἀμφότεραι μέν, ἑκάτερα δὲ μή, ἀλλ' ἐκείνῳ, ᾧ ἀμφότεραί τε καὶ ἑκάτερα, διότι συνεχώρεις ἀμφοτέρας τε αὐτὰς εἶναι καλὰς καὶ ἑκατέραν. τούτου δὴ ἕνεκα τῇ οὐσίᾳ τῇ ἐπ'
412

HIPP. What do you mean, Socrates ?

soc. Just what I say ; for I am afraid to speak plainly to you, because you are vexed with me, when you think you are talking sensibly ; however, tell me further : Is not each of us one and affected in such a way as to be one ?

HIPP. Certainly.

soc. Then each of us, if one, would be an odd number ; or do you not consider one an odd number ?

HIPP. I do.

soc. Then are we both an odd number, being two ?

HIPP. That could not be, Socrates.

soc. But we are both an even number, are we not ?

HIPP. Certainly.

soc. Then because we are both even, is each of us on that account even ?

HIPP. No, surely not.

soc. Then it is not absolutely inevitable, as you said just now, that what both are, each is, and what each is, both are.

HIPP. Not things of this sort, but such as I mentioned before.

soc. That suffices, Hippias ; for even this is welcome, since it appears that some things are so and some are not so. For I said, if you remember the beginning of this discussion, that pleasures through sight and through hearing were beautiful, not by that by which each of them was so affected as to be beautiful, but not both, nor both but not each, but by that by which both and each were so affected, because you conceded that both and each were beautiful. For this reason I thought that if both

---

[1] ἐλέχθη f : ἐδέχθη F : ἐλέγχθη T : ἠλέγχθη W (?).
[2] καὶ δι᾽ TW : καὶ F.

PLATO

ἀμφότερα ἑπομένη ᾤμην, εἴπερ ἀμφότερά ἐστι
καλά, ταύτῃ δεῖν αὐτὰ καλὰ εἶναι, τῇ δὲ κατὰ τὰ
ἕτερα ἀπολειπομένῃ μή· καὶ ἔτι νῦν οἴομαι. ἀλλά
μοι λέγε, ὥσπερ ἐξ ἀρχῆς· ἡ δι᾽ ὄψεως ἡδονὴ καὶ
ἡ δι᾽ ἀκοῆς, εἴπερ ἀμφότεραί τ᾽ εἰσὶ καλαὶ καὶ
D ἑκατέρα, ἆρα ὃ ποιεῖ αὐτὰς καλὰς οὐχὶ καὶ ἀμφοτέραις γε αὐταῖς ἕπεται καὶ ἑκατέρᾳ;

ιπ. Πάνυ γε.

σω. Ἆρ᾽ οὖν ὅτι ἡδονὴ ἑκατέρα τ᾽ ἐστὶ καὶ
ἀμφότεραι, διὰ τοῦτο ἂν εἶεν καλαί; ἢ διὰ τοῦτο
μὲν καὶ αἱ ἄλλαι πᾶσαι ἂν οὐδὲν τούτων ἧττον εἶεν
καλαί; οὐδὲν γὰρ ἧττον ἡδοναὶ ἐφάνησαν οὖσαι,
εἰ μέμνησαι.

ιπ. Μέμνημαι.

σω. Ἀλλ᾽ ὅτι γε δι᾽ ὄψεως καὶ ἀκοῆς αὗταί εἰσι,
διὰ τοῦτο ἐλέγετο καλὰς αὐτὰς εἶναι.

E ιπ. Καὶ ἐρρήθη οὕτως.

σω. Σκόπει δέ, εἰ ἀληθῆ λέγω. ἐλέγετο γάρ, ὡς
ἐγὼ μνήμης ἔχω, τοῦτ᾽ εἶναι καλὸν τὸ ἡδύ, οὐ πᾶν,
ἀλλ᾽ ὃ ἂν δι᾽ ὄψεως καὶ ἀκοῆς ᾖ.

ιπ. Ἀληθῆ.

σω. Οὐκοῦν τοῦτό γε τὸ πάθος ἀμφοτέραις μὲν
ἕπεται, ἑκατέρᾳ δ᾽ οὔ; οὐ γάρ που ἑκάτερόν γε
αὐτῶν, ὅπερ ἐν τοῖς πρόσθεν ἐλέγετο, δι᾽ ἀμφοτέρων
ἐστίν, ἀλλ᾽ ἀμφότερα μὲν δι᾽ ἀμφοῖν, ἑκάτερον δ᾽
οὔ· ἔστι ταῦτα;

ιπ. Ἔστιν.

σω. Οὐκ ἄρα τούτῳ γε ἑκάτερον αὐτῶν ἐστι
καλόν, ὃ μὴ ἕπεται ἑκατέρῳ· τὸ γὰρ ἀμφότερον
ἑκατέρῳ οὐχ ἕπεται· ὥστε ἀμφότερα μὲν αὐτὰ

414

are beautiful they must be beautiful by that essence which belongs to both, but not by that which is lacking in each ; and I still think so. But tell me, as in the beginning : If pleasure through sight and pleasure through hearing are both and each beautiful, does not that which makes them beautiful belong to both and to each ?

HIPP. Certainly.

SOC. Is it, then, for this reason, because each is a pleasure and both are pleasures, that they would be beautiful ? Or would all other pleasures be for this reason no less beautiful than they ? For we saw, if you remember, that they were no less pleasures.

HIPP. Yes, I remember.

SOC. But for this reason, because these pleasures were through sight and hearing, it was said that they are beautiful.

HIPP. Yes, that is what was said.

SOC. See if what I say is true. For it was said, if my memory serves me, that *this* " pleasant " was beautiful, not *all* " pleasant," but that which is through sight and hearing.

HIPP. True.

SOC. Now this quality belongs to both, but not to each, does it not ? For surely each of them, as was said before, is not through both senses, but both are through both, and each is not. Is that true ?

HIPP. It is.

SOC. Then it is not by that which does not belong to each that each of them is beautiful ; for " both " does not belong to each ; so that it is possible,

PLATO

φάναι καλὰ κατὰ τὴν ὑπόθεσιν ἔξεστιν, ἑκάτερον
303 δὲ οὐκ ἔξεστιν· ἢ πῶς λέγομεν[1]; οὐκ ἀνάγκη;

ΙΠ. Φαίνεται.

28. ΣΩ. Φῶμεν οὖν ἀμφότερα μὲν καλὰ εἶναι,
ἑκάτερον δὲ μὴ φῶμεν;

ΙΠ. Τί γὰρ κωλύει;

ΣΩ. Τόδε ἔμοιγε δοκεῖ, ὦ φίλε, κωλύειν, ὅτι ἦν
που ἡμῖν τὰ μὲν οὕτως ἐπιγιγνόμενα ἑκάστοις,
εἴπερ ἀμφοτέροις ἐπιγίγνοιτο, καὶ ἑκατέρῳ, καὶ
εἴπερ ἑκατέρῳ, καὶ ἀμφοτέροις, ἅπαντα ὅσα σὺ
διῆλθες· ἦ γάρ;

ΙΠ. Ναί.

ΣΩ. Ἃ δέ γε αὖ ἐγὼ διῆλθον, οὔ· ὧν δὴ ἦν καὶ
αὐτὸ τὸ ἑκάτερον καὶ τὸ ἀμφότερον. ἔστιν οὕτως;

ΙΠ. Ἔστιν.

Β   ΣΩ. Ποτέρων οὖν, ὦ Ἱππία, δοκεῖ σοι τὸ καλὸν
εἶναι; πότερον ὧν σὺ ἔλεγες; εἴπερ ἐγὼ ἰσχυρὸς
καὶ σύ, καὶ ἀμφότεροι, καὶ εἴπερ ἐγὼ δίκαιος καὶ
σύ, καὶ ἀμφότεροι, καὶ εἴπερ ἀμφότεροι, καὶ
ἑκάτερος· οὕτω δὴ καὶ εἴπερ ἐγὼ καλὸς καὶ σύ, καὶ
ἀμφότεροι, καὶ εἴπερ ἀμφότεροι, καὶ ἑκάτερος; ἢ
οὐδὲν κωλύει, ὥσπερ ἀρτίων ὄντων τινῶν ἀμφοτέρων τάχα μὲν ἑκάτερα περιττὰ εἶναι, τάχα δ'
ἄρτια, καὶ αὖ ἀρρήτων ἑκατέρων ὄντων τάχα μὲν
ῥητὰ τὰ συναμφότερα εἶναι, τάχα δ' ἄρρητα, καὶ
C   ἄλλα μυρία τοιαῦτα, ἃ δὴ καὶ ἐγὼ ἔφην ἐμοὶ
προφαίνεσθαι; ποτέρων δὴ τιθεῖς[2] τὸ καλόν; ἢ

[1] λέγομεν WF : λέγωμεν T.
[2] τιθεῖς F : τίθης T : τιθῆς W.

---

[1] See 300 E, 301 A.
[2] See 301 E, 302 A.   [3] See 300 C.

416

according to our hypothesis, to say that they both are beautiful, but not to say that each is so; or what shall we say? Is that not inevitable?

HIPP. It appears so.

SOC. Shall we say, then, that both are beautiful, but that each is not?

HIPP. What is to prevent?

SOC. This seems to me, my friend, to prevent, that there were some attributes thus belonging to individual things, which belonged, we thought, to each, if they belonged to both, and to both, if they belonged to each—I mean all those attributes which you specified.[1] Am I right?

HIPP. Yes.

SOC. But those again which I specified[2] did not; and among those were precisely "each" and "both." Is that so?

HIPP. It is.

SOC. To which group, then, Hippias, does the beautiful seem to you to belong? To the group of those that you mentioned? If I am strong and you also, are we both collectively strong, and if I am just and you also, are we both collectively just, and if both collectively, then each individually; so, too, if I am beautiful and you also, are we both collectively beautiful, and if both collectively, then each individually? Or is there nothing to prevent this, as in the case that when given things are both collectively even, they may perhaps individually be odd, or perhaps even, and again, when things are individually irrational quantities they may perhaps both collectively be rational, or perhaps irrational, and countless other cases which, you know, I said appeared before my mind?[3] To which group do

417

ὥσπερ ἐμοὶ περὶ αὐτοῦ καταφαίνεται, καὶ σοί;
πολλὴ γὰρ ἀλογία ἔμοιγε δοκεῖ εἶναι ἀμφοτέρους
μὲν ἡμᾶς εἶναι καλούς, ἑκάτερον δὲ μή, ἢ ἑκάτερον
μέν, ἀμφοτέρους δὲ μή, ἢ ἄλλο ὁτιοῦν τῶν τοιούτων.
οὕτως αἱρεῖ, ὥσπερ ἐγώ, ἢ κείνως[1];

ιπ. Οὕτως ἔγωγε, ὦ Σώκρατες.

σω. Εὖ γε σὺ ποιῶν, ὦ Ἱππία, ἵνα καὶ ἀπαλ-
D λαγῶμεν πλείονος ζητήσεως· εἰ γὰρ τούτων γ᾽ ἐστὶ
τὸ καλόν, οὐκ ἂν ἔτι εἴη τὸ δι᾽ ὄψεως καὶ ἀκοῆς
ἡδὺ καλόν. ἀμφότερα μὲν γὰρ ποιεῖ καλὰ τὸ δι᾽
ὄψεως καὶ ἀκοῆς, ἑκάτερον δ᾽ οὔ· τοῦτο δ᾽ ἦν
ἀδύνατον, ὡς ἐγώ τε καὶ σὺ δὴ ὁμολογοῦμεν, ὦ
Ἱππία.

ιπ. Ὁμολογοῦμεν γάρ.

σω. Ἀδύνατον ἄρα τὸ δι᾽ ὄψεως καὶ ἀκοῆς ἡδὺ
καλὸν εἶναι, ἐπειδή γε καλὸν γιγνόμενον τῶν ἀδυνά-
των τι παρέχεται.

ιπ. Ἔστι ταῦτα.

29. σω. '' Λέγετε δὴ πάλιν,'' φήσει, '' ἐξ ἀρχῆς,
E ἐπειδὴ τούτου διημάρτετε· τί φατε εἶναι τοῦτο τὸ
καλὸν τὸ ἐπ᾽ ἀμφοτέραις ταῖς ἡδοναῖς, δι᾽ ὅ τι
ταύτας πρὸ τῶν ἄλλων τιμήσαντες καλὰς ὠνομά-
σατε;'' ἀνάγκη δή μοι δοκεῖ εἶναι,[2] ὦ Ἱππία,
λέγειν ὅτι ἀσινέσταται αὗται τῶν ἡδονῶν εἰσὶ καὶ
βέλτισται, καὶ ἀμφότεραι καὶ ἑκατέρα· ἢ σύ τι
ἔχεις λέγειν ἄλλο, ᾧ διαφέρουσι τῶν ἄλλων;

ιπ. Οὐδαμῶς· τῷ ὄντι γὰρ βέλτισταί εἰσιν.

σω. '' Τοῦτ᾽ ἄρα,'' φήσει, '' λέγετε δὴ τὸ καλὸν
εἶναι, ἡδονὴν ὠφέλιμον;'' Ἐοίκαμεν, φήσω ἔγωγε·
σὺ δέ;

ιπ. Καὶ ἐγώ.

---

[1] κείνως T : ἐκείνως WF. [2] εἶναι TF : om. W.

GREATER HIPPIAS

you assign the beautiful? Or have you the same
view about it as I? For to me it seems great foolish-
ness that we collectively are beautiful, but each
of us is not so, or that each of us is so, but both are
not, or anything else of that sort. Do you choose
in this way, as I do, or in some other way?

HIPP. In this way, Socrates.

SOC. You choose well, Hippias, that we may be free
from the need of further search; for if the beautiful is in this group, that which is pleasing through
sight and hearing would no longer be the beautiful.
For the expression "through sight and hearing"
makes both collectively beautiful, but not each individually; and this was impossible, as you and I agree.

HIPP. Yes, we agree.

SOC. It is, then, impossible that the pleasant
through sight and hearing be the beautiful, since
in becoming beautiful it offers an impossibility.

HIPP. That is true.

SOC. "Then tell us again," he will say, "from
the beginning, since you failed this time; what
do you say that this 'beautiful,' belonging to both
the pleasures, is, on account of which you honoured
them before the rest and called them beautiful?"
It seems to me, Hippias, inevitable that we say
that these are the most harmless and the best of
pleasures, both of them collectively and each of
them individually; or have you anything else to
suggest, by which they excel the rest?

HIPP. Not at all; for really they are the best.

SOC. "This, then," he will say, "you say is the
beautiful, beneficial pleasure?" "It seems that
we do," I shall say; and you?

HIPP. I also.

419

PLATO

ΣΩ. "Οὐκοῦν ὠφέλιμον," φήσει, "τὸ ποιοῦν
τἀγαθόν,[1] τὸ δὲ ποιοῦν καὶ τὸ ποιούμενον ἕτερον
νῦν δὴ ἐφάνη, καὶ εἰς τὸν πρότερον λόγον ἥκει
ὑμῖν ὁ λόγος; οὔτε γὰρ τὸ ἀγαθὸν ἂν εἴη καλὸν
304 οὔτε τὸ καλὸν ἀγαθόν, εἴπερ ἄλλο αὐτῶν ἑκάτερόν
ἐστι." Παντός γε μᾶλλον, φήσομεν, ὦ Ἱππία,
ἂν σωφρονῶμεν· οὐ γάρ που θέμις τῷ ὀρθῶς
λέγοντι μὴ συγχωρεῖν.

ιπ. Ἀλλὰ δή γ᾽, ὦ Σώκρατες, τί οἴει ταῦτ᾽ εἶναι
ξυνάπαντα; κνήσματά[2] τοί ἐστι καὶ περιτμήματα
τῶν λόγων, ὅπερ ἄρτι ἔλεγον, κατὰ βραχὺ διηρη-
μένα· ἀλλ᾽ ἐκεῖνο καὶ καλὸν καὶ πολλοῦ ἄξιον, οἷόν
τ᾽ εἶναι εὖ καὶ καλῶς λόγον καταστησάμενον ἐν
δικαστηρίῳ ἢ ἐν βουλευτηρίῳ ἢ ἐπ᾽ ἄλλῃ τινὶ ἀρχῇ,
B πρὸς ἣν ἂν ὁ λόγος ᾖ, πείσαντα οἴχεσθαι φέροντα
οὐ τὰ σμικρότατα ἀλλὰ τὰ μέγιστα τῶν ἄθλων,
σωτηρίαν αὑτοῦ τε καὶ τῶν αὑτοῦ χρημάτων καὶ
φίλων. τούτων οὖν χρὴ ἀντέχεσθαι, χαίρειν ἐά-
σαντα τὰς σμικρολογίας ταύτας, ἵνα μὴ δοκῇ λίαν
ἀνόητος εἶναι λήρους καὶ φλυαρίας ὥσπερ νῦν
μεταχειριζόμενος.

30. ΣΩ. Ὦ Ἱππία φίλε, σὺ μὲν μακάριος εἶ, ὅτι
τε οἶσθα ἃ χρὴ ἐπιτηδεύειν ἄνθρωπον, καὶ ἐπιτετή-
δευκας ἱκανῶς, ὡς φῄς· ἐμὲ δὲ δαιμονία τις τύχη,
C ὡς ἔοικε, κατέχει, ὅστις πλανῶμαι μὲν καὶ ἀπορῶ
ἀεί, ἐπιδεικνὺς δὲ τὴν ἐμαυτοῦ ἀπορίαν ὑμῖν τοῖς
σοφοῖς λόγῳ αὖ ὑπὸ ὑμῶν προπηλακίζομαι, ἐπειδὰν
ἐπιδείξω. λέγετε γάρ με, ἅπερ καὶ σὺ νῦν λέγεις,
ὡς ἠλίθιά τε καὶ σμικρὰ καὶ οὐδενὸς ἄξια πράγμα-

---

[1] ποιοῦν τἀγαθόν F : ποιοῦντ᾽ ἀγαθόν TW.
[2] κνήσματά F (and Cobet) : κνίσματα TW.

soc. " Well, then," he will say, " beneficial is
that which creates the good, but that which creates
and that which is created were just now seen to be
different, and our argument has come round to the
earlier argument, has it not ? For neither could
the good be beautiful nor the beautiful good, if
each of them is different from the other." " Absolutely true," we shall say, if we are reasonable ;
for it is inadmissible to disagree with him who says
what is right.

HIPP. But now, Socrates, what do you think all
this amounts to ? It is mere scrapings and shavings
of discourse, as I said a while ago,[1] divided into bits ;
but that other ability is beautiful and of great
worth, the ability to produce a discourse well and
beautifully in a court of law or a council-house or
before any other public body before which the discourse may be delivered, to convince the audience
and to carry off, not the smallest, but the greatest
of prizes, the salvation of oneself, one's property,
and one's friends. For these things, therefore, one
must strive, renouncing these petty arguments,
that one may not, by busying oneself, as at present,
with mere talk and nonsense, appear to be a fool.

soc. My dear Hippias, you are blessed because
you know the things a man ought to practise, and
have, as you say, practised them satisfactorily. But
I, as it seems, am possessed by some accursed
fortune, so that I am always wandering and perplexed, and, exhibiting my perplexity to you wise
men, am in turn reviled by you in speech whenever
I exhibit it. For you say of me, what you are now
saying, that I busy myself with silly little matters

[1] See 301 B.

τεύομαι· ἐπειδὰν δὲ αὖ ἀναπεισθεὶς ὑφ' ὑμῶν λέγω
ἅπερ ὑμεῖς, ὡς πολὺ κράτιστόν ἐστιν οἷόν τ' εἶναι
λόγον εὖ καὶ καλῶς καταστησάμενον περαίνειν ἐν
D δικαστηρίῳ ἢ ἐν ἄλλῳ τινὶ συλλόγῳ, ὑπό τε ἄλλων
τινῶν τῶν ἐνθάδε καὶ ὑπὸ τούτου τοῦ ἀνθρώπου
τοῦ ἀεί με ἐλέγχοντος πάντα κακὰ ἀκούω. καὶ
γάρ μοι τυγχάνει ἐγγύτατα γένους ὢν καὶ ἐν τῷ
αὐτῷ οἰκῶν· ἐπειδὰν οὖν εἰσέλθω οἴκαδε εἰς ἐμαυτοῦ καί μου ἀκούσῃ ταῦτα λέγοντος, ἐρωτᾷ, εἰ
οὐκ αἰσχύνομαι τολμῶν περὶ καλῶν ἐπιτηδευμάτων
διαλέγεσθαι, οὕτω φανερῶς ἐξελεγχόμενος περὶ τοῦ
καλοῦ, ὅτι οὐδ' αὐτὸ τοῦτο ὅ τί ποτ' ἔστιν οἶδα.
" Καίτοι πῶς σὺ εἴσει," φησίν, "ἢ λόγον ὅστις
E καλῶς κατεστήσατο ἢ μή, ἢ ἄλλην πρᾶξιν ἡντινοῦν,
τὸ καλὸν ἀγνοῶν; καὶ ὁπότε οὕτω διάκεισαι, οἴει
σοι[1] κρεῖττον εἶναι ζῆν μᾶλλον ἢ τεθνάναι;" συμ-
βέβηκε δή μοι, ὅπερ λέγω, κακῶς μὲν ὑπὸ ὑμῶν
ἀκούειν καὶ ὀνειδίζεσθαι, κακῶς δὲ ὑπ' ἐκείνου·
ἀλλὰ γὰρ ἴσως ἀναγκαῖον ὑπομένειν ταῦτα πάντα·
οὐδὲν γὰρ ἄτοπον, εἰ ὠφελοίμην.[2] ἐγὼ οὖν μοι
δοκῶ, ὦ Ἱππία, ὠφελῆσθαι[3] ἀπὸ τῆς ἀμφοτέρων
ὑμῶν ὁμιλίας· τὴν γὰρ παροιμίαν ὅ τί ποτε λέγει,
τὸ " χαλεπὰ τὰ καλά," δοκῶ μοι εἰδέναι.

---

[1] οἴει σοι f: οἴσεῖ σοι W(T ?): ὃς εἶ σοι F.
[2] ὠφελοίμην later copyists: ὠφελούμην TW: ὠφελοῦμεν F.
[3] ὠφελῆσθαι W : ὠφελεῖσθαι TF.

of no account; but when in turn I am convinced by you and say what you say, that it is by far the best thing to be able to produce a discourse well and beautifully and gain one's end in a court of law or in any other assemblage, I am called everything that is bad by some other men here and especially by that man who is continually refuting me; for he is a very near relative of mine and lives in the same house. So whenever I go home to my own house, and he hears me saying these things, he asks me if I am not ashamed that I have the face to talk about beautiful practices, when it is so plainly shown, to my confusion, that I do not even know what the beautiful itself is. "And yet how are you to know," he will say, "either who produced a discourse, or anything else whatsoever, beautifully, or not, when you are ignorant of the beautiful? And when you are in such a condition, do you think it is better for you to be alive than dead?" So it has come about, as I say, that I am abused and reviled by you and by him. But perhaps it is necessary to endure all this, for it is quite reasonable that I might be benefited by it. So I think, Hippias, that I have been benefited by conversation with both of you; for I think I know the meaning of the proverb: "beautiful things are difficult."

LESSER HIPPIAS

INTRODUCTION TO THE *LESSER HIPPIAS*

In the *Lesser Hippias* the eminent sophist from Elis appears in much the same light as in the *Greater Hippias*. He has, as we are informed by the opening words of Eudicus, just finished a discourse conceived as an exhibition of his proficiency. Eudicus—who is mentioned in the *Greater Hippias*, but of whom nothing further is known than that his father's name was Apemantus—calls upon Socrates to ask the sophist some questions, and Socrates proceeds to ask what Hippias thinks of the relative merits of Achilles and Odysseus. This leads to a discussion of the true and the wily, or false, man, the conclusion of which is that he who best knows the truth is most able to tell falsehoods, and that therefore the true man is most false. Similar paradoxical conclusions are reached concerning various forms of physical excellence and of virtue, even of justice and of goodness itself. The success of Socrates in defeating the sophist is complete, but the final result of the dialogue is negative and unsatisfactory. The whole seems almost a *reductio ad absurdum* of the Socratic method.

Whether the dialogue is a genuine work of Plato, or not, is an open question. If it is Plato's, it must belong to the earlier years of his literary activity. There is, perhaps, nothing in it which Plato might not have written, but it may equally well be the work of

an imitator. The discourse which Hippias is supposed to have just finished may be the discourse on the beautiful pursuits proper for a young man, which the sophist says (*Gr. Hipp.* 286 B) he intends to deliver on the next day but one at the request of Eudicus. If there really is a reference here to the *Greater Hippias*, the *Lesser Hippias* cannot be genuine unless the other dialogue is also a work of Plato. But it is quite possible that the passage in the *Greater Hippias* was invented for the express purpose of making that dialogue appear to be the work of the author of the *Lesser Hippias*. It is, then, possible that the two dialogues may be by different authors, whether one or the other is by Plato, or not.

ΙΠΠΙΑΣ ΕΛΑΤΤΩΝ

[Η ΠΕΡΙ ΤΟΥ ΨΕΥΔΟΥΣ · ΑΝΑΤΡΕΠΤΙΚΟΣ]

ΤΑ ΤΟΥ ΔΙΑΛΟΓΟΥ ΠΡΟΣΩΠΑ

ΕΥΔΙΚΟΣ, ΣΩΚΡΑΤΗΣ, ΙΠΠΙΑΣ

St. I
p. 363 1. ΕΥ. Σὺ δὲ δὴ τί σιγᾷς, ὦ Σώκρατες, Ἱππίου
τοσαῦτα ἐπιδειξαμένου, καὶ οὐχὶ ἢ συνεπαινεῖς τι
τῶν εἰρημένων ἢ καὶ ἐλέγχεις, εἴ τί σοι μὴ καλῶς δοκεῖ εἰρηκέναι; ἄλλως τε ἐπειδὴ καὶ αὐτοὶ
λελείμμεθα, οἳ μάλιστ᾽ ἂν ἀντιποιησαίμεθα μετεῖναι ἡμῖν τῆς ἐν φιλοσοφίᾳ διατριβῆς.

ΣΩ. Καὶ μήν, ὦ Εὔδικε, ἔστι γε ἃ ἡδέως ἂν
B πυθοίμην Ἱππίου ὧν νῦν δὴ ἔλεγεν περὶ Ὁμήρου.
καὶ γὰρ τοῦ σοῦ πατρὸς Ἀπημάντου ἤκουον ὅτι ἡ
Ἰλιὰς κάλλιον εἴη ποίημα τῷ Ὁμήρῳ ἢ ἡ Ὀδύσσεια,
τοσούτῳ δὲ κάλλιον, ὅσῳ[1] ἀμείνων Ἀχιλλεὺς
Ὀδυσσέως εἴη· ἑκάτερον γὰρ τούτων[2] τὸ μὲν εἰς
Ὀδυσσέα ἔφη πεποιῆσθαι, τὸ δ᾽ εἰς Ἀχιλλέα.
περὶ ἐκείνου οὖν ἡδέως ἄν, εἰ βουλομένῳ ἐστὶν
Ἱππίᾳ, ἀναπυθοίμην ὅπως αὐτῷ δοκεῖ περὶ τοῖν
ἀνδροῖν τούτοιν, πότερον ἀμείνω φησὶν εἶναι,

[1] ὅσῳ W : ὅσον TF.
[2] τούτων F : τῶν ποιημάτων TW.

LESSER HIPPIAS

[OR ON FALSEHOOD : REFUTATIVE]

CHARACTERS

EUDICUS, SOCRATES, HIPPIAS

EUD. Why, then, are you silent, Socrates, when
Hippias has been delivering such a fine display ?
Why do you not join us in praising some part of his
speech, or else, if he seems to you to have been
wrong in any point, refute him—especially now that
we who might best claim to have a share in philosophical discussion have been left to ourselves ?

SOC. Indeed, Eudicus, there are some points in
what Hippias was just now saying of Homer, about
which I should like to question him. For I used to
hear your father Apemantus say that Homer's
Iliad was a finer poem than the *Odyssey*, and just as
much finer as Achilles was finer than Odysseus ; for
he said that one of these poems was made with
Odysseus, the other with Achilles as its subject.
So that is a point about which, if it is agreeable to
Hippias, I should like to ask—what he thinks about
these two men, which of them he says is the better ;

PLATO

C ἐπειδὴ καὶ ἄλλα πολλὰ καὶ παντοδαπὰ ἡμῖν ἐπι-
δέδεικται καὶ περὶ ποιητῶν τε ἄλλων καὶ περὶ
Ὁμήρου.

2. ΕΥ. Ἀλλὰ δῆλον ὅτι οὐ φθονήσει Ἱππίας, ἐάν
τι αὐτὸν ἐρωτᾷς, ἀποκρίνεσθαι. ἢ γάρ, ὦ Ἱππία,
ἐάν τι ἐρωτᾷ σε Σωκράτης, ἀποκρινεῖ; ἢ πῶς
ποιήσεις;

ΙΠ. Καὶ γὰρ ἂν δεινὰ ποιοίην, ὦ Εὔδικε, εἰ
Ὀλυμπίαζε μὲν εἰς τὴν τῶν Ἑλλήνων πανήγυριν,
ὅταν τὰ Ὀλύμπια ᾖ, ἀεὶ ἐπανιὼν οἴκοθεν ἐξ Ἤλιδος
εἰς τὸ ἱερὸν παρέχω ἐμαυτὸν καὶ λέγοντα ὅ τι ἂν
D τις βούληται ὧν ἄν μοι[1] εἰς ἐπίδειξιν παρεσκευα-
σμένον ᾖ, καὶ ἀποκρινόμενον τῷ βουλομένῳ ὅ τι ἂν
τις ἐρωτᾷ, νῦν δὲ τὴν Σωκράτους ἐρώτησιν φύγοιμι.

364 ΣΩ. Μακάριόν γε, ὦ Ἱππία, πάθος πέπονθας, εἰ
ἑκάστης Ὀλυμπιάδος οὕτως εὔελπις ὢν περὶ τῆς
ψυχῆς εἰς σοφίαν ἀφικνεῖ εἰς τὸ ἱερόν· καὶ θαυμά-
σαιμ' ἂν εἴ τις τῶν περὶ τὸ σῶμα ἀθλητῶν οὕτως
ἀφόβως τε καὶ πιστευτικῶς ἔχων τῷ σώματι
ἔρχεται αὐτόσε ἀγωνιούμενος, ὥσπερ σὺ φῂς τῇ
διανοίᾳ.

ΙΠ. Εἰκότως, ὦ Σώκρατες, ἐγὼ τοῦτο πέπονθα·
ἐξ οὗ γὰρ ἦργμαι Ὀλυμπίασιν ἀγωνίζεσθαι, οὐδενὶ πώποτε κρείττονι εἰς οὐδὲν ἐμαυτοῦ ἐνέτυχον.

3. ΣΩ. Καλόν γε λέγεις, ὦ Ἱππία, καὶ τῇ
Ἠλείων πόλει τῆς σοφίας ἀνάθημα τὴν δόξαν
B εἶναι τὴν σὴν καὶ τοῖς γονεῦσι τοῖς σοῖς. ἀτὰρ τί
δὴ λέγεις ἡμῖν περὶ τοῦ Ἀχιλλέως τε καὶ τοῦ
Ὀδυσσέως; πότερον ἀμείνω καὶ κατὰ τί φῂς
εἶναι; ἡνίκα μὲν γὰρ πολλοὶ ἔνδον ἦμεν καὶ σὺ
τὴν ἐπίδειξιν ἐποιοῦ, ἀπελείφθην σου τῶν λεγο-

[1] μοι TW : ἐμοί F.

430

for he has told us in his exhibition many other things of all sorts about Homer and other poets.

EUD. It is plain enough that Hippias will not object to answering if you ask him a question. Oh, Hippias, if Socrates asks you a question, will you answer ? or what will you do ?

HIPP. Why, Eudicus, it would be strange conduct on my part, if I, who always go up to Olympia to the festival of the Greeks from my home at Elis, and entering the sacred precinct, offer to speak on anything that anyone chooses of those subjects which I have prepared for exhibition, and to answer any questions that anyone asks—should now avoid being questioned by Socrates.

SOC. You are in a state of blessedness, Hippias, if at every Olympiad you come to the sanctuary with such fair hopes concerning your soul and its wisdom ; and I should be surprised if any of the physical athletes when he goes to that same place to take part in the contests, has such fearless confidence in his body as you have in your intellect.

HIPP. Naturally, Socrates, I am in this state : for since I began to contend at the Olympic games, I have never yet met anyone better than myself in anything.

SOC. That is splendid, Hippias ! Your reputation will be a monument of wisdom for the city of Elis and for your parents. But now what do you say about Achilles and Odysseus ? Which do you say is the better and in what respect ? For when there were many of us in the room, and you were making your exhibition, I could not keep up with what you were

PLATO

μένων· ὤκνουν γὰρ ἐπανερέσθαι, διότι ὄχλος τε
πολὺς ἔνδον ἦν, καὶ μή σοι ἐμποδὼν εἴην ἐρωτῶν
τῇ ἐπιδείξει· νυνὶ δὲ ἐπειδὴ ἐλάττους τέ ἐσμεν καὶ
Εὔδικος ὅδε κελεύει ἐρέσθαι, εἰπέ τε καὶ δίδαξον
C ἡμᾶς σαφῶς, τί ἔλεγες περὶ τούτοιν τοῖν ἀνδροῖν;
πῶς διέκρινες αὐτούς;

ιπ. Ἀλλ᾿ ἐγώ σοι, ὦ Σώκρατες, ἐθέλω ἔτι
σαφέστερον ἢ τότε διελθεῖν ἃ λέγω καὶ περὶ τούτων
καὶ ἄλλων.[1] φημὶ γὰρ Ὅμηρον πεποιηκέναι ἄριστον μὲν ἄνδρα Ἀχιλλέα τῶν εἰς Τροίαν ἀφικομένων,
σοφώτατον δὲ Νέστορα, πολυτροπώτατον δὲ
Ὀδυσσέα.

σω. Βαβαί, ὦ Ἱππία· ἆρ᾿ ἄν τί μοι χαρίσαιο
τοιόνδε, μή μου καταγελᾶν, ἐὰν μόγις[2] μανθάνω τὰ
D λεγόμενα καὶ πολλάκις ἀνερωτῶ; ἀλλά μοι πειρῶ
πράως τε καὶ εὐκόλως ἀποκρίνεσθαι.

ιπ. Αἰσχρὸν γὰρ ἂν εἴη, ὦ Σώκρατες, εἰ ἄλλους
μὲν αὐτὰ ταῦτα παιδεύω καὶ ἀξιῶ διὰ ταῦτα χρήματα λαμβάνειν, αὐτὸς δὲ ὑπὸ σοῦ ἐρωτώμενος μὴ
συγγνώμην τ᾿ ἔχοιμι καὶ πράως ἀποκρινοίμην.

4. σω. Πάνυ καλῶς λέγεις. ἐγὼ γάρ τοι, ἡνίκα
μὲν ἄριστον τὸν Ἀχιλλέα ἔφησθα πεποιῆσθαι,
ἐδόκουν σου μανθάνειν ὅ τι ἔλεγες, καὶ ἡνίκα τὸν
E Νέστορα σοφώτατον· ἐπειδὴ δὲ τὸν Ὀδυσσέα
εἶπες ὅτι πεποιηκὼς εἴη ὁ ποιητὴς πολυτροπώτατον,
τοῦτο δ᾿, ὥς γε πρὸς σὲ τἀληθῆ εἰρῆσθαι, παντάπασιν οὐκ οἶδ᾿ ὅ τι λέγεις. καί μοι εἰπέ, ἄν τι
ἐνθένδε μᾶλλον μάθω· ὁ Ἀχιλλεὺς οὐ πολύτροπος
τῷ Ὁμήρῳ πεποίηται;

ιπ. Ἥκιστά γε, ὦ Σώκρατες, ἀλλ᾿ ἁπλούστατος,[3]
ἐπεὶ καὶ ἐν Λιταῖς, ἡνίκα πρὸς ἀλλήλους ποιεῖ

[1] ἄλλων TW : περὶ ἄλλον F.

432

saying : for I hesitated to ask questions, because there was a great crowd in the room, also for fear of hindering your exhibition by doing so ; but now, since we are fewer and Eudicus here urges me to question you, speak and tell us clearly what you said about these two men ; how did you distinguish them ?

HIPP. Why I am glad, Socrates, to explain to you still more clearly what I say about these and others also. For I say that Homer made Achilles the bravest man of those who went to Troy, and Nestor the wisest, and Odysseus the wiliest.

SOC. Oh dear, Hippias ! Would you do me the favour not to laugh at me if I find it hard to understand what you say, and keep asking questions over and over ? Please try to answer me gently and courteously.

HIPP. Of course ; for it would be a disgrace, Socrates, if I, who teach others good manners and charge them money for it, should not myself, when questioned by you, be considerate and reply gently.

SOC. That is excellent. For when you said that the poet made Achilles the bravest of men, and Nestor the wisest, I thought I understood what you meant ; but when you said that he made Odysseus the wiliest, to tell you the truth, I do not in the least know what you mean by that. Now tell me, and perhaps it may result in my understanding better. Has not Homer made Achilles wily ?

HIPP. Not at all, Socrates ; he made him most simple ; for in " The Prayers," when he depicts them

---

² μόγις F : μόλις TW.
³ ἁπλούστατω TW : ἁπλούστατος καὶ ἀληθέστατος F.

PLATO

αὐτοὺς διαλεγομένους, λέγει αὐτῷ ὁ Ἀχιλλεὺς
πρὸς τὸν Ὀδυσσέα,

365 Διογενὲς Λαερτιάδη, πολυμήχαν᾽ Ὀδυσσεῦ,
χρὴ μὲν δὴ τὸν μῦθον ἀπηλεγέως ἀποειπεῖν,
ὥσπερ¹ δὴ κρανέω τε καὶ ὡς τελέεσθαι² ὀΐω,
[ὡς μή μοι τρύζητε παρήμενοι ἄλλοθεν ἄλλος.]
ἐχθρὸς γάρ μοι κεῖνος ὁμῶς Ἀΐδαο πύλῃσιν,
B ὅς χ᾽ ἕτερον μὲν κεύθῃ ἐνὶ φρεσίν, ἄλλο δὲ εἴπῃ.
αὐτὰρ ἐγὼν ἐρέω, ὡς καὶ τετελεσμένον ἔσται.

ἐν τούτοις δηλοῖ τοῖς ἔπεσι τὸν τρόπον ἑκατέρου τοῦ
ἀνδρός, ὡς ὁ μὲν Ἀχιλλεὺς εἴη ἀληθής τε καὶ
ἁπλοῦς, ὁ δὲ Ὀδυσσεὺς πολύτροπός τε καὶ ψευδής·
ποιεῖ γὰρ τὸν Ἀχιλλέα εἰς τὸν Ὀδυσσέα λέγοντα
ταῦτα τὰ ἔπη.

ΣΩ. Νῦν ἤδη, ὦ Ἱππία, κινδυνεύω μανθάνειν
ὃ λέγεις· τὸν πολύτροπον ψευδῆ λέγεις, ὥς γε
φαίνεται.
C ιπ. Μάλιστα, ὦ Σώκρατες· τοιοῦτον γὰρ πε-
ποίηκε τὸν Ὀδυσσέα Ὅμηρος πολλαχοῦ καὶ ἐν
Ἰλιάδι καὶ ἐν Ὀδυσσείᾳ.

ΣΩ. Ἐδόκει ἄρα, ὡς ἔοικεν, Ὁμήρῳ ἕτερος μὲν
εἶναι ἀνὴρ ἀληθής, ἕτερος δὲ ψευδής, ἀλλ᾽ οὐχ ὁ
αὐτός.

ιπ. Πῶς γὰρ οὐ μέλλει, ὦ Σώκρατες;
ΣΩ. Ἦ καὶ σοὶ δοκεῖ αὐτῷ, ὦ Ἱππία;
ιπ. Πάντων μάλιστα· καὶ γὰρ ἂν δεινὸν εἴη, εἰ
μή.
5. ΣΩ. Τὸν μὲν Ὅμηρον τοίνυν ἐάσωμεν, ἐπειδὴ
D καὶ ἀδύνατον ἐπανερέσθαι τί ποτε νοῶν ταῦτα

¹ ὥσπερ TWF: ἧπερ S and mss. of Homer.
² τελέεσθαι T: τετελέεσθαι W: τετελέσθαι F (for τελέεσθαι ὀΐω
434

talking with one another, he makes Achilles say
to Odysseus.[1]

Zeus-born son of Laertes, wily Odysseus, I must speak
out the word without refraining, as I shall act and think
will be accomplished [and pray do not mutter in discord
sitting here beside me]. For hateful to me as the gates
of Hades is he who hides one thing in his heart and says
another. But I shall speak that which shall be accomplished.

In these lines he makes plain the character of
each of the men, that Achilles is true and simple, and
Odysseus wily and false ; for he represents Achilles
as saying these lines to Odysseus.

soc. Now at last, Hippias, I think I understand
what you mean ; you mean that the wily man is
false, apparently.

hipp. Certainly, Socrates ; for Homer represents
Odysseus as that sort of a man in many passages of
both *Iliad* and *Odyssey*.

soc. Homer, then, as it seems, thought that a true
man was one man and a false man another, but not
the same.

hipp. Of course he did, Socrates.

soc. And do you think so yourself, Hippias ?

hipp. Most assuredly ; for it would be strange
if I did not.

soc. Then let us drop Homer, since it is impossible
to ask him what he meant when he made those

---

[1] *Iliad*, ix. 308 ff. The division into twenty-four books
was made in Alexandrian times. Before that division was
made (and even after) references were made to parts of the
Iliad and *Odyssey* by descriptive titles, " The Prayers," " The
Catalogue of Ships," and the like.

S and the mss. of Homer read τετελεσμένον ἔσται, after which
follows *Il.* ix. 311, ὡς μή μοι τρύξητε παρήμενοι ἄλλοθεν ἄλλος,
which the other mss. of Plato omit).

PLATO

ἐποίησε τὰ ἔπη· σὺ δ' ἐπειδὴ φαίνει ἀναδεχόμενος
τὴν αἰτίαν, καὶ σοὶ συνδοκεῖ ταῦτα ἅπερ φῂς
Ὅμηρον λέγειν, ἀπόκριναι κοινῇ ὑπὲρ Ὁμήρου τε
καὶ σαυτοῦ.

ιπ. Ἔσται ταῦτα· ἀλλ' ἐρώτα ἔμβραχυ ὅ τι
βούλει.

σω. Τοὺς ψευδεῖς λέγεις οἷον ἀδυνάτους τι
ποιεῖν, ὥσπερ τοὺς κάμνοντας, ἢ δυνατούς τι ποιεῖν;

ιπ. Δυνατοὺς ἔγωγε καὶ μάλα σφόδρα ἄλλα τε
πολλὰ καὶ ἐξαπατᾶν ἀνθρώπους.

E σω. Δυνατοὶ μὲν δή, ὡς ἔοικεν, εἰσὶ κατὰ τὸν σὸν
λόγον καὶ πολύτροποι· ἢ γάρ;

ιπ. Ναί.

σω. Πολύτροποι δ' εἰσὶ καὶ ἀπατεῶνες ὑπὸ
ἠλιθιότητος καὶ ἀφροσύνης, ἢ ὑπὸ πανουργίας καὶ
φρονήσεώς τινος;

ιπ. Ὑπὸ πανουργίας πάντων μάλιστα καὶ φρονήσεως.

σω. Φρόνιμοι μὲν ἄρα εἰσίν, ὡς ἔοικεν.

ιπ. Ναὶ μὰ Δία, λίαν γε.

σω. Φρόνιμοι δὲ ὄντες οὐκ ἐπίστανται ὅ τι ποιοῦσιν, ἢ ἐπίστανται[1];

ιπ. Καὶ μάλα σφόδρα ἐπίστανται· διὰ ταῦτα καὶ
κακουργοῦσιν.

σω. Ἐπιστάμενοι δὲ ταῦτα ἃ ἐπίστανται πότερον
ἀμαθεῖς εἰσὶν ἢ σοφοί;

366 ιπ. Σοφοὶ μὲν οὖν αὐτά γε ταῦτα, ἐξαπατᾶν.

6. σω. Ἔχε δή· ἀναμνησθῶμεν τί ἐστιν ὃ λέγεις.
τοὺς ψευδεῖς φῂς εἶναι δυνατοὺς καὶ φρονίμους καὶ
ἐπιστήμονας καὶ σοφοὺς εἰς ἅπερ ψευδεῖς;

ιπ. Φημὶ γὰρ οὖν.

---

[1] ὅ τι ποιοῦσιν ἢ ἐπίστανται F : om. TW.

436

verses ; but since you come forward to take up his cause, and agree in this which you say is his meaning, do you answer for Homer and yourself in common.

HIPP. Very well ; ask briefly whatever you like.

SOC. Do you say that the false are, like the sick, without power to do anything, or that they have power to do something ?

HIPP. I say that they have great power to do many things, and especially to deceive people.

SOC. They are, then, powerful, according to you, and wily, are they not ?

HIPP. Yes.

SOC. But are they wily and deceivers by reason of simplicity and folly, or by reason of shrewdness and a sort of intelligence ?

HIPP. By shrewdness, most assuredly, and intelligence.

SOC. They are intelligent, then, as it seems.

HIPP. Yes, by Zeus, too much so.

SOC. And being intelligent, do they know what they are doing, or do they not know ?

HIPP. Yes, they know very well ; that is why they do harm.

SOC. And knowing these things which they know, are they ignorant, or wise ?

HIPP. Wise, surely, in just this, deception.

SOC. Stop. Let us recall what you say. You say that the false are powerful and intelligent, and knowing and wise in those things in which they are false ?

HIPP. Yes, I do.

PLATO

ΣΩ. Ἄλλους δὲ τοὺς ἀληθεῖς τε καὶ ψευδεῖς, καὶ ἐναντιωτάτους ἀλλήλοις;

ΙΠ. Λέγω ταῦτα.

ΣΩ. Φέρε δή· τῶν μὲν δυνατῶν τινὲς καὶ σοφῶν, ὡς ἔοικεν, εἰσὶν οἱ ψευδεῖς κατὰ τὸν σὸν λόγον.

ΙΠ. Μάλιστά γε.

B ΣΩ. Ὅταν δὲ λέγῃς δυνατοὺς καὶ σοφοὺς εἶναι τοὺς ψευδεῖς εἰς αὐτὰ ταῦτα, πότερον λέγεις δυνατοὺς εἶναι ψεύδεσθαι ἐὰν βούλωνται, ἢ ἀδυνάτους εἰς ταῦτα ἅπερ ψεύδονται;

ΙΠ. Δυνατοὺς ἔγωγε.

ΣΩ. Ὡς ἐν κεφαλαίῳ ἄρα εἰρῆσθαι, οἱ ψευδεῖς εἰσιν οἱ¹ σοφοί τε καὶ δυνατοὶ ψεύδεσθαι.

ΙΠ. Ναί.

ΣΩ. Ἀδύνατος ἄρα ψεύδεσθαι ἀνὴρ καὶ ἀμαθὴς οὐκ ἂν εἴη ψευδής.

ΙΠ. Ἔχει οὕτως.

ΣΩ. Δυνατὸς δέ γ' ἐστὶν ἕκαστος ἄρα, ὃς ἂν ποιῇ C τότε ὃ ἂν βούληται, ὅταν βούληται· οὐχ ὑπὸ νόσου λέγω ἐξειργόμενον οὐδὲ τῶν τοιούτων, ἀλλὰ ὥσπερ σὺ δυνατὸς εἶ γράψαι τοὐμὸν ὄνομα ὅταν βούλῃ, οὕτω λέγω. ἢ² οὐχ, ὃς ἂν οὕτως ἔχῃ, καλεῖς σὺ δυνατόν;

ΙΠ. Ναί.

7. ΣΩ. Λέγε δή μοι, ὦ Ἱππία, οὐ σὺ μέντοι ἔμπειρος εἶ λογισμῶν καὶ λογιστικῆς;

ΙΠ. Πάντων μάλιστα, ὦ Σώκρατες.

ΣΩ. Οὐκοῦν εἰ καί τίς σε ἔροιτο, τὰ τρὶς ἑπτακόσια ὁπόσος ἐστὶν ἀριθμός, εἰ βούλοιο, πάντων D τάχιστα καὶ μάλιστ' ἂν εἴποις τἀληθῆ περὶ τούτου;

ΙΠ. Πάνυ γε.

¹ οἱ F: om. TW.   ² ἢ TW: ἀρ' F.
438

soc. And that the true and the false are different and complete opposites of one another ?

hipp. I do.

soc. Well, then, the false are among the powerful and the wise, according to your statement.

hipp. Certainly.

soc. And when you say that the false are powerful and wise for falsehood, do you mean that they have power to utter falsehoods if they like, or that they are powerless in respect to the falsehoods which they utter ?

hipp. That they have power.

soc. In short, then, the false are those who are wise and powerful in uttering falsehoods.

hipp. Yes.

soc. A man, then, who has not the power to utter falsehoods and is ignorant would not be false.

hipp. That is true.

soc. Well, but every man has power who does what he wishes at the time when he wishes ; I am not speaking of one who is prevented by disease or that sort of thing, but as I might say of you that you have power to write my name when you wish ; or do you not say that a man has power who is in such a condition ?

hipp. Yes, I do.

soc. Tell me, then, Hippias, are you not skilful in arithmetical calculations ?

hipp. Most assuredly, Socrates.

soc. Then if some one were to ask you what the product of three times seven hundred is, you could, if you wished, tell him the truth about that more quickly and better than anyone else ?

hipp. Certainly.

ΣΩ. Ἆρα ὅτι δυνατώτατός τε εἶ καὶ σοφώτατος κατὰ ταῦτα;

ΙΠ. Ναί.

ΣΩ. Πότερον οὖν σοφώτατός τε εἶ καὶ δυνατώτατος μόνον, ἢ καὶ ἄριστος ταῦτα ἅπερ δυνατώτατός τε καὶ σοφώτατος, τὰ λογιστικά;

ΙΠ. Καὶ ἄριστος δήπου, ὦ Σώκρατες.

ΣΩ. Τὰ μὲν δὴ ἀληθῆ σὺ ἂν δυνατώτατα εἴποις περὶ τούτων· ἦ γάρ;

ΙΠ. Οἶμαι ἔγωγε.

E   ΣΩ. Τί δὲ τὰ ψευδῆ περὶ τῶν αὐτῶν τούτων; καί μοι, ὥσπερ τὰ πρότερα, γενναίως καὶ μεγαλοπρεπῶς ἀπόκριναι, ὦ Ἱππία· εἴ τίς σε ἔροιτο τὰ τρὶς ἑπτακόσια πόσα ἐστί, πότερον σὺ ἂν μάλιστα ψεύδοιο καὶ ἀεὶ κατὰ ταὐτὰ ψευδῆ λέγοις περὶ τούτων, βουλόμενος ψεύδεσθαι καὶ μηδέποτε ἀληθῆ
367 ἀποκρίνεσθαι, ἢ ὁ ἀμαθὴς εἰς λογισμοὺς δύναιτ' ἂν σοῦ μᾶλλον ψεύδεσθαι βουλομένου; ἢ ὁ μὲν ἀμαθὴς πολλάκις ἂν βουλόμενος ψευδῆ λέγειν τἀληθῆ ἂν εἴποι ἄκων, εἰ τύχοι, διὰ τὸ μὴ εἰδέναι, σὺ δὲ ὁ σοφός, εἴπερ βούλοιο ψεύδεσθαι, ἀεὶ ἂν κατὰ τὰ αὐτὰ ψεύδοιο;

ΙΠ. Ναί, οὕτως ἔχει ὡς σὺ λέγεις.

ΣΩ. Ὁ ψευδὴς οὖν πότερον περὶ μὲν τἆλλα ψευδής ἐστιν, οὐ μέντοι περὶ ἀριθμόν,[1] οὐδὲ ἀριθμῶν[2] ἂν ψεύσαιτο;

ΙΠ. Καὶ ναὶ μὰ Δία περὶ ἀριθμόν.

8. ΣΩ. Θῶμεν ἄρα καὶ τοῦτο, ὦ Ἱππία, περὶ
B λογισμόν τε καὶ ἀριθμὸν εἶναί τινα ἄνθρωπον ψευδῆ;

[1] ἀριθμὸν corr. Ven. 185: ἀριθμῶν TWF.
[2] ἀριθμῶν scr. Ven. 185: ἀριθμὸν TWF.

soc. Because you are the most powerful and wisest of men in these matters ?

hipp. Yes.

soc. Are you, then, merely wisest and most powerful, or are you also best in those matters in which you are most powerful and wisest, namely calculations ?

hipp. Best also, to be sure, Socrates.

soc. Then you would have the greatest power to tell the truth about these things, would you not ?

hipp. I think so.

soc. But what of falsehoods about these same things ? And please answer this with the same splendid frankness as my previous questions, Hippias. If some one were to ask you how much three times seven hundred is, would you have the most power to tell falsehoods and always uniformly to say false things about these matters, if you wished to tell falsehoods and never to reply truly ; or would he who is ignorant of calculations have more power to tell falsehoods than you, if you wished to do so ? Or would the ignorant man often, when he wished to tell falsehoods, involuntarily tell the truth, if it so happened, because he did not know, whereas you, the wise man, if you wished to tell falsehoods, would tell them always and uniformly ?

hipp. Yes, it is as you say.

soc. Is the false man, then, false about other things, but not about number, and would he not tell falsehoods when dealing with number ?

hipp. He is false about number also, by Zeus.

soc. Shall we, then, assume this also, that there is such a person as a man who is false about calculation and number ?

ΙΠ. Ναί.

ΣΩ. Τίς οὖν ἂν εἴη οὗτος; οὐχὶ δεῖ ὑπάρχειν αὐτῷ,[1] εἴπερ μέλλει ψευδὴς ἔσεσθαι, ὡς σὺ ἄρτι ὡμολόγεις, δυνατὸν εἶναι ψεύδεσθαι; ὁ γὰρ ἀδύνατος ψεύδεσθαι, εἰ μέμνησαι, ὑπὸ σοῦ ἐλέγετο ὅτι οὐκ ἄν ποτε ψευδὴς γένοιτο.

ΙΠ. Ἀλλὰ μέμνημαι, καὶ ἐλέχθη οὕτως.

ΣΩ. Οὐκοῦν ἄρτι ἐφάνης σὺ δυνατώτατος ὢν ψεύδεσθαι περὶ λογισμῶν[2];

ΙΠ. Ναί, ἐλέχθη γέ τοι καὶ τοῦτο.

C   ΣΩ. Ἆρ᾽ οὖν καὶ δυνατώτατος εἶ ἀληθῆ λέγειν περὶ λογισμῶν;

ΙΠ. Πάνυ γε.

ΣΩ. Οὐκοῦν ὁ αὐτὸς ψευδῆ καὶ ἀληθῆ λέγειν περὶ λογισμῶν δυνατώτατος.[3] οὗτος δ᾽ ἐστὶν ὁ ἀγαθὸς περὶ τούτων, ὁ λογιστικός.

ΙΠ. Ναί.

ΣΩ. Τίς οὖν ψευδὴς περὶ λογισμὸν[4] γίγνεται, ὦ Ἱππία, ἄλλος ἢ ὁ ἀγαθός; ὁ αὐτὸς[5] γὰρ καὶ δυνατός· οὗτος δὲ καὶ ἀληθής.

ΙΠ. Φαίνεται.

ΣΩ. Ὁρᾷς οὖν, ὅτι ὁ αὐτὸς ψευδής τε καὶ ἀληθὴς περὶ τούτων, καὶ οὐδὲν ἀμείνων ὁ ἀληθὴς τοῦ ψεύδους; ὁ αὐτὸς γὰρ δήπου ἐστὶ καὶ οὐκ ἐναντιώ-
D ται α ἔχει, ὥσπερ σὺ ᾤου ἄρτι.

ΙΠ. Οὐ φαίνεται ἐνταῦθά γε.

ΣΩ. Βούλει οὖν σκεψώμεθα καὶ ἄλλοθι;

ΙΠ. Εἴ[6] γε σὺ βούλει.

---

[1] αὐτῷ F : αὐτὸν TWf.
[2] λογισμῶν corr. Coisl. : λογισμὸν TWF.
[3] δυνατώτατος F : δυνατὸς TWf.
[4] λογισμὸν F : λογισμῶν TW.

LESSER HIPPIAS

HIPP. Yes.

soc. Now who would that man be? Must he not, as you just now agreed, have power to tell falsehoods, if he is to be false? For it was said by you, if you recollect, that he who has not the power to tell falsehoods would never be false.

HIPP. Yes, I recollect, that was said.

soc. And just now you were found to have most power to tell falsehoods about calculations, were you not?

HIPP. Yes, that also was said.

soc. Have you, then, also most power to tell the truth about calculations?

HIPP. Certainly.

soc. Then the same man has most power to speak both falsehood and truth about calculations; and this man is the one who is good in respect to them, namely the calculator.

HIPP. Yes.

soc. Who, then, becomes false in respect to calculation, Hippias, other than the good man? For the same man is also powerful; and he is also true.

HIPP. So it appears.

soc. You see, then, that the same man is both false and true in respect to these matters, and the true is in no wise better than the false? For he is indeed the same man, and the two are not utter opposites, as you thought just now.

HIPP. Apparently not, at least in this field.

soc. Shall we, then, investigate elsewhere?

HIPP. If you like

5 ὁ αὐτὸς F: οὗτος TW.
6 εἰ Bekker: εἰ ἄλλως TWF.

443

9. ΣΩ. Οὐκοῦν καὶ γεωμετρίας ἔμπειρος εἶ;

ΙΠ. Ἔγωγε.

ΣΩ. Τί οὖν; οὐ καὶ ἐν γεωμετρίᾳ οὕτως ἔχει· ὁ αὐτὸς δυνατώτατος ψεύδεσθαι καὶ ἀληθῆ λέγειν περὶ τῶν διαγραμμάτων, ὁ γεωμετρικός;

ΙΠ. Ναί.

ΣΩ. Περὶ ταῦτα οὖν ἀγαθὸς ἄλλος τις ἢ οὗτος;

Ε   ΙΠ. Οὐκ ἄλλος.

ΣΩ. Οὐκοῦν ὁ ἀγαθὸς καὶ σοφὸς γεωμέτρης δυνατώτατός γε ἀμφότερα; καὶ εἴπερ τις ἄλλος ψευδὴς περὶ διαγράμματα, οὗτος ἂν εἴη, ὁ ἀγαθός; οὗτος γὰρ δυνατός, ὁ δὲ κακὸς ἀδύνατος ἦν ψεύδεσθαι· ὥστε οὐκ ἂν γένοιτο ψευδὴς ὁ μὴ δυνάμενος ψεύδεσθαι, ὡς ὡμολόγηται.

ΙΠ. Ἔστι ταῦτα.

ΣΩ. Ἔτι τοίνυν καὶ τὸν τρίτον ἐπισκεψώμεθα, τὸν ἀστρονόμον· ἧς αὖ σὺ τέχνης ἔτι μᾶλλον ἐπιστή-
368 μων οἴει εἶναι ἢ τῶν ἔμπροσθεν· ἦ γάρ, ὦ Ἱππία;

ΙΠ. Ναί.

ΣΩ. Οὐκοῦν καὶ ἐν ἀστρονομίᾳ ταὐτὰ ταῦτα[1] ἐστιν;

ΙΠ. Εἰκός γε, ὦ Σώκρατες.

ΣΩ. Καὶ ἐν ἀστρονομίᾳ ἄρα εἴπερ τις καὶ ἄλλος ψευδής, ὁ ἀγαθὸς ἀστρονόμος ψευδὴς ἔσται, ὁ δυνατὸς ψεύδεσθαι. οὐ γὰρ ὅ γε ἀδύνατος· ἀμαθὴς γάρ.

ΙΠ. Φαίνεται οὕτως.

ΣΩ. Ὁ αὐτὸς ἄρα καὶ ἐν ἀστρονομίᾳ ἀληθής τε καὶ ψευδὴς ἔσται.

ΙΠ. Ἔοικεν.

10. ΣΩ. Ἴθι δή, ὦ Ἱππία, ἀνέδην οὑτωσὶ ἐπί-

____
[1] ταὐτὰ ταῦτα Tf: ταυτα WF.

444

soc. Well, then, are you expert in geometry also ?

hipp. I am.

soc. Well, has not the same man most power to speak falsehood and truth about geometry, namely the geometrician ?

hipp. Yes.

soc. In respect to that, then, is any other good than he ?

hipp. No, no other.

soc. The good and wise geometrician, then, has the most power in both respects, has he not ? And if anyone is false in respect to diagrams, it would be this man, the good geometrician ? For he has the power, and the bad one was powerless, to speak falsehood ; so that he who has no power to speak falsehood would not become false, as has been agreed.

hipp. That is true.

soc. Let us, then, investigate also the third man, the astronomer, whose art you think you know even better than those of the previous ones ; do you not, Hippias ?

hipp. Yes.

soc. Are not the same things true in astronomy also ?

hipp. Probably, Socrates.

soc. Then in astronomy also, if anyone is false, the good astronomer will be false, he who has power to speak falsehood. For he who has not power will not ; for he is ignorant.

hipp. So it appears.

soc. The same man, then, in astronomy will be true and false.

hipp. So it seems.

soc. Come now, Hippias, consider generally in

B σκέψαι κατὰ πασῶν τῶν ἐπιστημῶν, εἴ πού ἐστιν
ἄλλως ἔχον ἢ οὕτως. πάντως δὲ πλείστας τέχνας
πάντων σοφώτατος εἶ ἀνθρώπων, ὡς ἐγώ ποτέ σου
ἤκουον μεγαλαυχουμένου, πολλὴν σοφίαν καὶ ζη-
λωτὴν σαυτοῦ διεξιόντος ἐν ἀγορᾷ ἐπὶ ταῖς τραπέ-
ζαις. ἔφησθα δὲ ἀφικέσθαι ποτὲ εἰς Ὀλυμπίαν ἃ
εἶχες περὶ τὸ σῶμα ἅπαντα σαυτοῦ ἔργα ἔχων·
πρῶτον μὲν δακτύλιον—ἐντεῦθεν γὰρ ἤρχου—ὃν
C εἶχες σαυτοῦ ἔχειν ἔργον, ὡς ἐπιστάμενος δακτυ-
λίους γλύφειν, καὶ ἄλλην σφραγῖδα σὸν ἔργον· καὶ
στλεγγίδα[1] καὶ λήκυθον, ἃ αὐτὸς ἠργάσω· ἔπειτα
ὑποδήματα ἃ εἶχες ἔφησθα αὐτὸς σκυτοτομῆσαι,
καὶ τὸ ἱμάτιον ὑφῆναι καὶ τὸν χιτωνίσκον· καὶ ὅ γε
πᾶσιν ἔδοξεν ἀτοπώτατον καὶ σοφίας πλείστης
ἐπίδειγμα, ἐπειδὴ τὴν ζώνην ἔφησθα τοῦ χιτω-
νίσκου, ἣν εἶχες, εἶναι μὲν οἷαι αἱ Περσικαὶ τῶν
πολυτελῶν, ταύτην δὲ αὐτὸς πλέξαι· πρὸς δὲ τούτοις ποιήματα ἔχων ἐλθεῖν, καὶ ἔπη καὶ τραγῳδίας
καὶ διθυράμβους, καὶ καταλογάδην πολλοὺς λόγους
D καὶ παντοδαποὺς συγκειμένους· καὶ περὶ τῶν τεχ-
νῶν δὴ ὧν ἄρτι ἐγὼ ἔλεγον ἐπιστήμων[2] ἀφικέσθαι διαφερόντως τῶν ἄλλων, καὶ περὶ ῥυθμῶν καὶ
ἁρμονιῶν καὶ γραμμάτων ὀρθότητος, καὶ ἄλλα ἔτι
πρὸς τούτοις πάνυ πολλά, ὡς ἐγὼ δοκῶ μνημο-
νεύειν· καίτοι τό γε μνημονικὸν ἐπελαθόμην σου, ὡς
ἔοικε, τέχνημα, ἐν ᾧ σὺ οἴει λαμπρότατος εἶναι·
E οἶμαι δὲ καὶ ἄλλα πάμπολλα ἐπιλελῆσθαι. ἀλλ'
ὅπερ ἐγὼ λέγω, καὶ εἰς τὰς σαυτοῦ τέχνας βλέψας
—ἱκαναὶ δέ—καὶ εἰς τὰς τῶν ἄλλων εἰπέ μοι, ἐάν
που εὕρῃς ἐκ τῶν ὡμολογημένων ἐμοί τε καὶ σοί,

---

[1] στλεγγίδα Wt: σλεγγίδα T: στεγγίδα F.
[2] ἐπιστήμων f: ἐπιστήμην F: ἐπιστημῶν TW.

this way concerning all the sciences, whether this is the case, or not. Certainly you are the wisest of men in the greatest number of arts, as I once heard you boast, recounting your great and enviable wisdom in the market-place at the tables of the money-changers. You said that once, when you went to Olympia, everything you had on your person was your own work; first the ring—for you began with that—which you had was your own work, showing that you knew how to engrave rings, and another seal was your work, and a strigil and an oil-flask were your works; then you said that you yourself had made the sandals you had on, and had woven your cloak and tunic; and, what seemed to every one most unusual and proof of the most wisdom, was when you said that the girdle you wore about your tunic was like the Persian girdles of the costliest kind, and that you had made it yourself. And in addition you said that you brought with you poems, both epics and tragedies and dithyrambs, and many writings of all sorts composed in prose; and that you were there excelling all others in knowledge of the arts of which I was speaking just now, and of the correctness of rhythms and harmonies and letters, and many other things besides, as I seem to remember; and yet I forgot your art of memory, as it seems, in which you think you are most brilliant; and I fancy I have forgotten a great many other things. But, as I say, look both at your own arts—and there are plenty of them—and at those of others, and tell me if you find, in accordance with the agreements you and I have reached, any point where

447

PLATO

ὅπου ἐστὶν ὁ μὲν ἀληθής, ὁ δὲ ψευδής, χωρὶς καὶ οὐχ ὁ αὐτός; ἐν ᾗτινι βούλει σοφίᾳ τοῦτο σκέψαι 369 ἢ πανουργίᾳ ἢ ὁτιοῦν χαίρεις ὀνομάζων· ἀλλ' οὐχ εὑρήσεις, ὦ ἑταῖρε· οὐ γὰρ ἔστιν· ἐπεὶ σὺ εἰπέ.

11. ιπ. Ἀλλ' οὐκ ἔχω, ὦ Σώκρατες, νῦν γε οὕτως.

σω. Οὐδέ γε ἕξεις, ὡς ἐγὼ οἶμαι· εἰ δ' ἐγὼ ἀληθῆ λέγω, μέμνησαι ὃ ἡμῖν συμβαίνει ἐκ τοῦ λόγου, ὦ Ἱππία.

ιπ. Οὐ πάνυ τι ἐννοῶ, ὦ Σώκρατες, ὃ λέγεις.

σω. Νυνὶ γὰρ ἴσως οὐ χρῇ[1] τῷ μνημονικῷ τεχνή-ματι· δῆλον γὰρ ὅτι οὐκ οἴει δεῖν· ἀλλ' ἐγώ σε ὑπομνήσω. οἶσθα ὅτι τὸν μὲν Ἀχιλλέα ἔφησθα B ἀληθῆ εἶναι, τὸν δὲ Ὀδυσσέα ψευδῆ καὶ πολύτροπον;

ιπ. Ναί.

σω. Νῦν οὖν αἰσθάνει ὅτι ἀναπέφανται ὁ αὐτὸς ὢν ψευδής τε καὶ ἀληθής, ὥστε εἰ ψευδὴς ὁ Ὀδυσ-σεὺς ἦν, καὶ ἀληθὴς γίγνεται, καὶ εἰ ἀληθὴς ὁ Ἀχιλλεύς, καὶ ψευδής, καὶ οὐ διάφοροι ἀλλήλων οἱ ἄνδρες οὐδ' ἐναντίοι, ἀλλ' ὅμοιοι;

ιπ. Ὦ Σώκρατες, ἀεὶ σύ τινας τοιούτους πλέκεις λόγους, καὶ ἀπολαμβάνων ὃ ἂν ᾖ δυσχερέστατον τοῦ λόγου, τούτου ἔχει κατὰ σμικρὸν ἐφαπτόμενος, C καὶ οὐχ ὅλῳ ἀγωνίζει τῷ πράγματι περὶ ὅτου ἂν ὁ λόγος ᾖ· ἐπεὶ καὶ νῦν, ἐὰν βούλῃ, ἐπὶ πολλῶν τεκμηρίων ἀποδείξω σοι ἱκανῷ λόγῳ Ὅμηρον Ἀχιλλέα πεποιηκέναι ἀμείνω Ὀδυσσέως καὶ ἀ-ψευδῆ, τὸν δὲ δολερόν τε καὶ πολλὰ ψευδόμενον καὶ χείρω Ἀχιλλέως. εἰ δὲ βούλει, σὺ αὖ ἀντιπαρά-

---

[1] χρῇ t: χρὴ TF: χρῇ W.

448

one man is true and another false, where they are separate and not the same. Look for this in any branch whatsoever of wisdom or shrewdness or whatever you choose to call it; but you will not find it, my friend, for it does not exist; just tell me.

HIPP. But I cannot, Socrates, at least, not now offhand.

SOC. And you never will be able to tell me, I fancy; but if what I say is true, Hippias, you remember what results from our argument.

HIPP. I do not at all understand what you mean, Socrates.

SOC. No, for perhaps you are not using your art of memory; for you evidently think it is not necessary; but I will remind you. Do you remember that you said that Achilles was true and Odysseus was false and wily?

HIPP. Yes.

SOC. Do you now, then, perceive that the same man has been found to be false and true, so that if Odysseus was false, he becomes also true, and if Achilles was true, he becomes also false, and the two men are not different from one another, nor opposites, but alike?

HIPP. Socrates, you are always making intricate arguments of this sort, and, picking out the most difficult part of the argument, you stick to it in detail, and you do not discuss the whole subject with which the argument deals; for now, if you like, I will prove to you by satisfactory argument based on many pieces of evidence, that Homer made Achilles better than Odysseus and free from falsehood, and Odysseus crafty and a teller of many falsehoods and inferior to Achilles. And, if you

449

βάλλε λόγον παρὰ λόγον, ὡς ὁ ἕτερος ἀμείνων ἐστί·
καὶ μᾶλλον εἴσονται οὗτοι, ὁπότερος ἄμεινον λέγει.

D 12. ΣΩ. Ὦ Ἱππία, ἐγώ τοι οὐκ ἀμφισβητῶ μὴ
οὐχὶ σὲ εἶναι σοφώτερον ἢ ἐμέ· ἀλλ' ἀεὶ εἴωθα,
ἐπειδάν τις λέγῃ τι, προσέχειν τὸν νοῦν, ἄλλως τε
καὶ ἐπειδάν μοι δοκῇ σοφὸς εἶναι ὁ λέγων, καὶ
ἐπιθυμῶν μαθεῖν ὅ τι λέγει διαπυνθάνομαι καὶ
ἐπανασκοπῶ καὶ συμβιβάζω τὰ λεγόμενα, ἵνα
μάθω· ἐὰν δὲ φαῦλος δοκῇ μοι εἶναι ὁ λέγων, οὔτε
ἐπανερωτῶ οὔτε μοι μέλει ὧν λέγει. καὶ γνώ-
σει τούτῳ οὓς ἂν ἐγὼ ἡγῶμαι σοφοὺς εἶναι·
εὑρήσεις γάρ με λιπαρῆ ὄντα περὶ τὰ λεγόμενα ὑπὸ
E τούτου καὶ πυνθανόμενον παρ' αὐτοῦ, ἵνα μαθών τι
ὠφεληθῶ. ἐπεὶ καὶ νῦν ἐννενόηκα σοῦ λέγοντος,
ὅτι ἐν τοῖς ἔπεσιν οἷς σὺ ἄρτι ἔλεγες, ἐνδεικνύμενος
τὸν Ἀχιλλέα εἰς τὸν Ὀδυσσέα λέγειν ὡς ἀλαζόνα
ὄντα, ἄτοπόν μοι δοκεῖ εἶναι, εἰ σὺ ἀληθῆ λέγεις,
370 ὅτι ὁ μὲν Ὀδυσσεὺς οὐδαμοῦ φαίνεται ψευσάμενος,
ὁ πολύτροπος, ὁ δὲ Ἀχιλλεὺς πολύτροπός τις
φαίνεται κατὰ τὸν σὸν λόγον· ψεύδεται γοῦν.
προειπὼν γὰρ ταῦτα τὰ ἔπη, ἅπερ καὶ σὺ εἶπες
ἄρτι,

ἐχθρὸς γάρ μοι κεῖνος ὁμῶς Ἀΐδαο πύλῃσιν,
ὅς χ' ἕτερον μὲν κεύθῃ ἐνὶ φρεσίν, ἄλλο δὲ εἴπῃ,

B ὀλίγον ὕστερον λέγει ὡς οὔτ' ἂν ἀναπεισθείη ὑπὸ
τοῦ Ὀδυσσέως τε καὶ τοῦ Ἀγαμέμνονος οὔτε
μένοι τὸ παράπαν ἐν τῇ Τροίᾳ, ἀλλ'

αὔριον ἱρὰ Διὶ ῥέξας, φησί, καὶ πᾶσι θεοῖσιν,
νηήσας εὖ νῆας, ἐπὴν ἅλαδε προερύσσω,
ὄψεαι, αἴ κ' ἐθέλησθα καὶ αἴ κέν τοι τὰ μεμήλῃ,
ἦρι μάλ' Ἑλλήσποντον ἐπ' ἰχθυόεντα πλεούσας

like, do you oppose argument to argument, maintaining that the other is better; and these gentlemen here will determine which of us speaks better.

soc. Hippias, I do not doubt that you are wiser than I; but it is always my custom to pay attention when anyone is speaking, especially when the speaker seems to me to be wise; and because I desire to learn what he means, I question him thoroughly and examine and compare the things he says, in order that I may learn. But if the speaker seems to me to be worthless, I neither ask questions nor care what he says. And by this you will recognize whom I regard as wise; for you will find me persistently asking such a man questions about what he says, in order that I may profit by learning something. And so now I noticed when you were speaking, that in the lines which you repeated just now to show that Achilles speaks to Odysseus as to a deceiver, it seems to me very strange, if what you say is true, that Odysseus the wily is nowhere found to have spoken falsely, but Achilles is found to be a wily sort of person, according to your argument; at any rate, he speaks falsely. For he begins by speaking these lines which you just quoted: "For hateful to me as the gates of Hades is he who hides one thing in his heart and says another," and a little later says that he would not be persuaded by Odysseus and Agamemnon and would not stay at Troy at all, but, he says—

To-morrow, after sacrificing to Zeus and all the gods, I will load my ships well and drag them into the sea; then you shall see, if you like and if it interests you, early in the morning my ships sailing the fishy Hellespont and

C νῆας ἐμάς, ἐν δ' ἄνδρας ἐρεσσέμεναι μεμαῶτας·
εἰ δέ κεν εὐπλοΐην δώῃ κλυτὸς Ἐννοσίγαιος,
ἤματί κεν τριτάτῳ Φθίην ἐρίβωλον ἱκοίμην.

ἔτι δὲ πρότερον τούτων πρὸς τὸν Ἀγαμέμνονα
λοιδορούμενος εἶπε·

νῦν δ' εἶμι Φθίηνδ', ἐπειὴ πολὺ λώϊόν[1] ἐστιν
οἴκαδ' ἴμεν σὺν νηυσὶ κορωνίσιν, οὐδέ σ' ὀΐω
D ἐνθάδ' ἄτιμος ἐὼν ἄφενος καὶ πλοῦτον ἀφύξειν.

ταῦτα εἰπὼν τοτὲ μὲν ἐναντίον τῆς στρατιᾶς
ἁπάσης,[2] τοτὲ δὲ πρὸς τοὺς ἑαυτοῦ ἑταίρους
οὐδαμοῦ φαίνεται οὔτε παρασκευασάμενος οὔτ'
ἐπιχειρήσας καθέλκειν τὰς ναῦς ὡς ἀποπλευσού-
μενος οἴκαδε, ἀλλὰ πάνυ γενναίως ὀλιγωρῶν τοῦ
τἀληθῆ λέγειν. ἐγὼ μὲν οὖν, ὦ Ἱππία, καὶ ἐξ
ἀρχῆς σε ἠρόμην ἀπορῶν ὁπότερος τούτων τοῖν
E ἀνδροῖν ἀμείνων πεποίηται τῷ ποιητῇ, καὶ ἡγού-
μενος ἀμφοτέρω ἀρίστω εἶναι καὶ δύσκριτον ὁπότερος ἀμείνων εἴη καὶ περὶ ψεύδους καὶ ἀληθείας
καὶ τῆς ἄλλης ἀρετῆς· ἀμφοτέρω γὰρ καὶ κατὰ
τοῦτο παραπλησίω ἐστόν.

13. ιπ. Οὐ γὰρ καλῶς σκοπεῖς, ὦ Σώκρατες.
ἃ μὲν γὰρ ὁ Ἀχιλλεὺς ψεύδεται, οὐκ ἐξ ἐπιβουλῆς
φαίνεται ψευδόμενος ἀλλ' ἄκων, διὰ τὴν συμφορὰν
τὴν τοῦ στρατοπέδου ἀναγκασθεὶς καταμεῖναι καὶ
βοηθῆσαι· ἃ δὲ ὁ Ὀδυσσεύς, ἑκών τε καὶ ἐξ
ἐπιβουλῆς.

σω. Ἐξαπατᾷς με, ὦ φίλτατε Ἱππία, καὶ αὐτὸς
τὸν Ὀδυσσέα μιμεῖ.

---

[1] λώϊόν TW : λῶόν F : φέρτερον mss. of Homer.
[2] ἁπάσης F : πάσης TW.

my men eagerly rowing in them ; and if the glorious Earth-shaker should grant me a fair voyage, on the third day I should come to fertile Phthia.[1]

And even before that, when he was reviling Agamemnon, he said :

And now I shall go to Phthia, since it is far better to go home with my beaked ships, and I do not intend to stay here without honour, and heap up wealth and riches for you.[2]

After he has said these things, at one time in the presence of the whole army and at another before his own comrades, he is nowhere found to have either prepared or attempted to drag down his ships to sail home, but he shows quite superb disregard of truth-speaking. Now I, Hippias, asked my question in the first place because I was perplexed as to which of the two men is represented as better by the poet, and because I thought both were very good, and it was hard to decide which was better, both in regard to falsehood and truth and to virtue in general ; for both are similar in this matter.

HIPP. That is because you do not look at it aright, Socrates. For the falsehoods that Achilles utters, he utters evidently not by design, but against his will, since he is forced by the misfortune of the army to remain and give assistance ; but Odysseus utters his falsehoods voluntarily and by design.

SOC. You are deceiving me, beloved Hippias, and are yourself imitating Odysseus.

[1] *Iliad* ix. 357 ff.   [2] *Ibid.* i. 169 ff.

371   ιπ. Οὐδαμῶς, ὦ Σώκρατες· λέγεις δὴ τί καὶ πρὸς τί;

ΣΩ. "Ὅτι οὐκ ἐξ ἐπιβουλῆς φῂς τὸν Ἀχιλλέα ψεύδεσθαι, ὃς ἦν οὕτω γόης καὶ ἐπίβουλος πρὸς τῇ ἀλαζονείᾳ,[1] ὡς πεποίηκεν Ὅμηρος, ὥστε καὶ τοῦ Ὀδυσσέως τοσοῦτον φαίνεται φρονεῖν πλέον πρὸς τὸ ῥᾳδίως λανθάνειν αὐτὸν ἀλαζονευόμενος, ὥστε ἐναντίον αὐτοῦ αὐτὸς ἑαυτῷ ἐτόλμα ἐναντία λέγειν καὶ ἐλάνθανεν τὸν Ὀδυσσέα· οὐδὲν γοῦν φαίνεται

B εἰπὼν πρὸς αὐτὸν ὡς αἰσθανόμενος αὐτοῦ ψευδομένου ὁ Ὀδυσσεύς.

ιπ. Ποῖα δὴ ταῦτα λέγεις, ὦ Σώκρατες;

ΣΩ. Οὐκ οἶσθα ὅτι λέγων ὕστερον ἢ ὡς[2] πρὸς τὸν Ὀδυσσέα ἔφη ἅμα τῇ ἠοῖ ἀποπλευσεῖσθαι, πρὸς τὸν Αἴαντα οὐκ αὖ φησὶν ἀποπλευσεῖσθαι, ἀλλὰ ἄλλα λέγει;

ιπ. Ποῦ δή;

ΣΩ. Ἐν οἷς λέγει

οὐ γὰρ πρὶν πολέμοιο μεδήσομαι αἱματόεντος,
C   πρίν γ' υἱὸν Πριάμοιο δαΐφρονος, Ἕκτορα δῖον,
Μυρμιδόνων ἐπί τε κλισίας καὶ νῆας ἱκέσθαι
κτείνοντ' Ἀργείους, κατά τε φλέξαι[3] πυρὶ νῆας·
ἀμφὶ δέ μιν[4] τῇ 'μῇ κλισίῃ καὶ νηῒ μελαίνῃ
Ἕκτορα καὶ μεμαῶτα μάχης σχήσεσθαι ὀίω.

σὺ δὴ οὖν, ὦ Ἱππία, πότερον οὕτως ἐπιλήσμονα
D οἴει εἶναι τὸν τῆς Θέτιδός τε καὶ ὑπὸ τοῦ σοφωτάτου Χείρωνος πεπαιδευμένον, ὥστε ὀλίγον πρότερον λοιδοροῦντα τοὺς ἀλαζόνας τῇ ἐσχάτῃ λοιδορίᾳ

---

[1] τῇ ἀλαζονείᾳ Bekker: τὴν ἀλαζονείαν TWF.
[2] ἢ ὡς WF: πως Τ.

454

LESSER HIPPIAS

HIPP. Not at all, Socrates. What do you mean and to what do you refer?

SOC. That you say Achilles did not speak falsely by design, he who was not only a deceiver, but was also such a cheat and plotter, as Homer has represented him, that he is seen to be so much more clever than Odysseus in deceiving him unnoticed without difficulty, that he dared to contradict himself in his presence, and Odysseus did not notice it; at any rate Odysseus does not appear to have said anything to him which indicates that he noticed his falsehood.

HIPP. What is this that you say, Socrates?

SOC. Don't you know that after he said to Odysseus that he was going to sail away at daybreak, in speaking to Ajax he does not repeat that he is going to sail away, but says something different?

HIPP. Where, pray?

SOC. Where he says:

For I shall not be mindful of bloody war until warlike Priam's son, the glorious Hector, shall reach the tents and ships of the Myrmidons through slaughter of Argives and shall burn the ships with fire. But at my tent and my black ship I think Hector, though eager for battle, will come to a halt.[1]

Now, Hippias, do you think the son of Thetis and pupil of the most wise Cheiron was so forgetful, that, although a little earlier he had reviled deceivers in the most extreme terms, he himself immediately

[1] *Iliad*, ix. 360 ff.

---

[3] κατά τε φλέξαι TWf (but σμυ above, W): κατέφλεξε F: κατά τε σμῦξαι S and vulg. of Homer.
[4] μιν TW: μὴν F: τοι MSS. of Homer.

455

PLATO

αὐτὸν παραχρῆμα πρὸς μὲν τὸν Ὀδυσσέα φάναι
ἀποπλευσεῖσθαι, πρὸς δὲ τὸν Αἴαντα μενεῖν,[1] ἀλλ'
οὐκ ἐπιβουλεύοντά τε καὶ ἡγούμενον ἀρχαῖον εἶναι
τὸν Ὀδυσσέα καὶ αὐτοῦ αὐτῷ τούτῳ τῷ τεχνάζειν
τε καὶ ψεύδεσθαι περιέσεσθαι;

14. ιπ. Οὔκουν ἔμοιγε δοκεῖ, ὦ Σώκρατες· ἀλλὰ
E καὶ αὐτὰ ταῦτα ὑπὸ εὐνοίας[2] ἀναπεισθεὶς πρὸς τὸν
Αἴαντα ἄλλα εἶπεν ἢ πρὸς τὸν Ὀδυσσέα· ὁ δὲ
Ὀδυσσεὺς ἅ τε ἀληθῆ λέγει, ἐπιβουλεύσας ἀεὶ
λέγει, καὶ ὅσα ψεύδεται, ὡσαύτως.

ΣΩ. Ἀμείνων ἄρ' ἐστίν, ὡς ἔοικεν, ὁ Ὀδυσσεὺς
Ἀχιλλέως.

ιπ. Ἥκιστά γε δήπου, ὦ Σώκρατες.

ΣΩ. Τί δέ; οὐκ ἄρτι ἐφάνησαν οἱ ἑκόντες
ψευδόμενοι βελτίους ἢ οἱ ἄκοντες;

ιπ. Καὶ πῶς ἄν, ὦ Σώκρατες, οἱ ἑκόντες ἀδικοῦν-
372 τες καὶ ἑκόντες ἐπιβουλεύσαντες καὶ κακὰ ἐργασά-
μενοι βελτίους ἂν εἶεν τῶν ἀκόντων, οἷς πολλὴ
δοκεῖ συγγνώμη εἶναι, ἐὰν μὴ εἰδώς τις ἀδικήσῃ ἢ
ψεύσηται ἢ ἄλλο τι[3] κακὸν ποιήσῃ; καὶ οἱ νόμοι
δήπου πολὺ χαλεπώτεροί εἰσι τοῖς ἑκοῦσι κακὰ
ἐργαζομένοις καὶ ψευδομένοις ἢ τοῖς ἄκουσιν.

15. ΣΩ. Ὁρᾷς, ὦ Ἱππία, ὅτι ἐγὼ ἀληθῆ λέγω,
B λέγων ὡς λιπαρής εἰμι πρὸς τὰς ἐρωτήσεις τῶν
σοφῶν; καὶ κινδυνεύω ἓν μόνον ἔχειν τοῦτο ἀγαθόν,
τἆλλα ἔχων πάνυ γε φαῦλα· τῶν μὲν γὰρ πραγμάτων ᾗ ἔχει ἔσφαλμαι, καὶ οὐκ οἶδ' ὅπη ἐστί.
τεκμήριον δέ μοι τούτου ἱκανόν, ὅτι ἐπειδὰν συγ-

---

[1] μενεῖν] μένειν TWF.
[2] εὐνοίας F: εὐηθείας TWf.   [3] τι WF: om. T.

456

LESSER HIPPIAS

said to Odysseus that he was going to sail away and
to Ajax that he was going to stay, and was not
acting by design and in the belief that Odysseus
was behind the times and that he himself would get
the better of him in just this matter of contrivance
and falsehood?

HIPP. No, I do not agree, Socrates; but in this
case also Achilles was induced by the goodness of
his heart to say to Ajax something different from
what he had said to Odysseus; whereas Odysseus,
when he speaks the truth always speaks with design,
and when he speaks falsehood likewise.

SOC. Then Odysseus, as it seems, is better than
Achilles.

HIPP. Not in the least, Socrates.

SOC. How is that? Were not those who utter
falsehoods voluntarily found to be better than
those who do so involuntarily?

HIPP. And how, Socrates, could those who
voluntarily do wrong and voluntarily and designedly
do harm be better than those who do so involuntarily?
And there seems to be good reason to forgive a man
who unwittingly does wrong or speaks falsehood
or does any other evil. And the laws surely are
much more severe towards those who do evil and
tell falsehoods voluntarily, than towards those who
do so involuntarily.

SOC. Do you see, Hippias, that I speak the truth
when I say that I am persistent in questioning wise
men? And this is probably the only good thing
about me, as I am otherwise quite worthless; for
I am all wrong about facts, and do not know the
truth about them. And it is to me sufficient proof
of the truth of this, that when I come into contact

457

PLATO

γένωμαί τῳ ὑμῶν τῶν εὐδοκιμούντων ἐπὶ σοφίᾳ καὶ
οἷς οἱ Ἕλληνες πάντες μάρτυρές εἰσι τῆς σοφίας,
φαίνομαι οὐδὲν εἰδώς· οὐδὲν γάρ μοι δοκεῖ τῶν
C αὐτῶν καὶ ὑμῖν, ὡς ἔπος εἰπεῖν· καίτοι τί μεῖζον
ἀμαθίας τεκμήριον ἢ ἐπειδάν τις σοφοῖς ἀνδράσι
διαφέρηται; ἐν δὲ τοῦτο θαυμάσιον ἔχω ἀγαθόν,
ὅ με σώζει· οὐ γὰρ αἰσχύνομαι μανθάνων, ἀλλὰ
πυνθάνομαι καὶ ἐρωτῶ καὶ χάριν πολλὴν ἔχω τῷ
ἀποκρινομένῳ, καὶ οὐδένα πώποτε ἀπεστέρησα
χάριτος. οὐ γὰρ πώποτε ἔξαρνος ἐγενόμην μαθών
τι, ἐμαυτοῦ ποιούμενος τὸ μάθημα εἶναι ὡς εὕρημα·
ἀλλ᾽ ἐγκωμιάζω τὸν διδάξαντά με ὡς σοφὸν ὄντα,
ἀποφαίνων ἃ ἔμαθον παρ᾽ αὐτοῦ. καὶ δὴ καὶ νῦν
D ἃ σὺ λέγεις οὐχ ὁμολογῶ σοι, ἀλλὰ διαφέρομαι
πάνυ σφόδρα· καὶ τοῦτ᾽ εὖ οἶδα ὅτι δι᾽ ἐμὲ γίγνεται,
ὅτι τοιοῦτός εἰμι οἷόσπερ εἰμί, ἵνα μηδὲν ἐμαυτὸν
μεῖζον εἴπω. ἐμοὶ γὰρ φαίνεται, ὦ Ἱππία, πᾶν
τοὐναντίον ἢ ὃ σὺ λέγεις· οἱ βλάπτοντες τοὺς
ἀνθρώπους καὶ ἀδικοῦντες καὶ ψευδόμενοι καὶ
ἐξαπατῶντες καὶ ἁμαρτάνοντες ἑκόντες, ἀλλὰ μὴ
ἄκοντες, βελτίους εἶναι ἢ οἱ ἄκοντες. ἐνίοτε μέντοι
καὶ τοὐναντίον δοκεῖ μοι τούτων καὶ πλανῶμαι περὶ
E ταῦτα, δῆλον ὅτι διὰ τὸ μὴ εἰδέναι· νυνὶ δὲ ἐν τῷ
παρόντι μοι ὥσπερ καταβολὴ περιελήλυθε, καὶ
δοκοῦσί μοι οἱ ἑκόντες ἐξαμαρτάνοντες περί τι
βελτίους εἶναι τῶν ἀκόντων. αἰτιῶμαι δὲ τοῦ νῦν
παρόντος παθήματος τοὺς ἔμπροσθεν λόγους αἰτίους
εἶναι, ὥστε φαίνεσθαι νῦν ἐν τῷ παρόντι τοὺς
ἄκοντας τούτων ἕκαστα ποιοῦντας πονηροτέρους ἢ

with one of you who are famous for wisdom, and to whose wisdom all the Greeks bear witness, I am found to know nothing; for there is hardly a single thing about which you and I have the same opinion; and yet what greater proof of ignorance is there than when one disagrees with a wise man? But I have this one remarkable good quality, which is my salvation; for I am not afraid to learn, but I inquire and ask questions and am very grateful to him who answers, and I never failed in gratitude to anyone; for when I have learned anything I have never denied it, pretending that the information was a discovery of my own; but I praise the wisdom of him who instructed me and proclaim what I learned from him. And so now I do not agree with what you say, but disagree very strongly; and I know very well that this is my own fault, because I am the sort of man I am—not to give myself any greater title. For my opinion, Hippias, is the exact opposite of what you say; I think that those who injure people and do wrong and speak falsehood and cheat and err voluntarily, not involuntarily, are better than those who do so involuntarily. Sometimes, however, the opposite of this seems to me to be the case, and I am all astray about these matters, evidently because I am ignorant; but now at the present moment a sort of paroxysm of my disease has come upon me, and those who err in respect to anything voluntarily appear to me better than those who err involuntarily. And I lay the blame for my present condition upon our previous argument, which causes those who do any of these things involuntarily to appear to me at this moment worse than those who do them volun-

τοὺς ἑκόντας. σὺ οὖν χάρισαι καὶ μὴ φθονήσῃς
ἰάσασθαι τὴν ψυχήν μου· πολὺ γάρ τοι μεῖζόν με
ἀγαθὸν ἐργάσει ἀμαθίας παύσας τὴν ψυχὴν ἢ νόσου
373 τὸ σῶμα. μακρὸν μὲν οὖν λόγον εἰ θέλεις λέγειν,
προλέγω σοι ὅτι οὐκ ἄν με ἰάσαιο—οὐ γὰρ ἂν
ἀκολουθήσαιμι—ὥσπερ δὲ ἄρτι εἰ θέλεις μοι ἀποκρίνεσθαι, πάνυ ὀνήσεις, οἶμαι δὲ οὐδ' αὐτὸν σὲ
βλαβήσεσθαι. δικαίως δ' ἂν καὶ σὲ παρακαλοίην,
ὦ παῖ Ἀπημάντου· σὺ γάρ με ἐπῆρας¹ Ἱππίᾳ δια-
λέγεσθαι· καὶ νῦν, ἐὰν μή μοι ἐθέλῃ Ἱππίας ἀποκρίνεσθαι δέου αὐτοῦ ὑπὲρ² ἐμοῦ.

ΕΤ. Ἀλλ', ὦ Σώκρατες, οἶμαι οὐδὲν δεήσεσθαι
Β Ἱππίαν τῆς ἡμετέρας δεήσεως· οὐ γὰρ τοιαῦτα
αὐτῷ ἐστι τὰ προειρημένα, ἀλλ' ὅτι οὐδενὸς ἂν
φύγοι ἀνδρὸς ἐρώτησιν. ἦ γάρ, ὦ Ἱππία; οὐ
ταῦτα ἦν ἃ ἔλεγες;

ΙΠ. Ἔγωγε· ἀλλὰ Σωκράτης, ὦ Εὔδικε, ἀεὶ
ταράττει ἐν τοῖς λόγοις καὶ ἔοικεν ὥσπερ κακουρ-
γοῦντι.

ΣΩ. Ὦ βέλτιστε Ἱππία, οὔτι ἑκών γε ταῦτα
ἐγὼ ποιῶ—σοφὸς γὰρ ἂν ἦ³ καὶ δεινὸς κατὰ τὸν σὸν
λόγον—ἀλλὰ ἄκων, ὥστε μοι συγγνώμην ἔχε· φῂς
γὰρ αὖ δεῖν, ὃς ἂν κακουργῇ ἄκων, συγγνώμην
ἔχειν.

C ΕΤ. Καὶ μηδαμῶς γε, ὦ Ἱππία, ἄλλως ποίει,
ἀλλὰ καὶ ἡμῶν ἕνεκα καὶ τῶν προειρημένων σοι
λόγων ἀποκρίνου ἃ ἄν σε ἐρωτᾷ Σωκράτης.

ΙΠ. Ἀλλ' ἀποκρινοῦμαι, σοῦ γε δεομένου. ἀλλ'
ἐρώτα ὅ τι βούλει.

16. ΣΩ. Καὶ μὴν σφόδρα γε ἐπιθυμῶ, ὦ Ἱππία,

---

¹ ἐπῆρας F : ἐπῆρας T : ἀπῆρας W.
² ὑπὲρ F : περὶ TW.   ³ ἦ F : ἦν TW.

tarily. So please do me a favour and do not refuse
to cure my soul; for you will be doing me much
more good if you cure my soul of ignorance, than
if you were to cure my body of disease. Now if
you choose to deliver a long speech, I tell you beforehand that you would not cure me—for I could not
follow you—but if you are willing to answer me,
as you did just now, you will do me a great deal
of good, and I think you yourself will not be injured,
either. And I might fairly call upon you also,
son of Apemantus, for help; for you stirred me up
to converse with Hippias; so now, if Hippias is
unwilling to answer me, ask him in my behalf to
do so.

EUD. Well, Socrates, I imagine Hippias will need
no asking from us; for that is not what he announced;
he announced that he would not avoid the questioning of any man. How is that, Hippias? Is not
that what you said?

HIPP. Yes, I did; but Socrates, Eudicus, always
makes confusion in arguments, and seems to want
to make trouble.

soc. Most excellent Hippias, I do not do these
voluntarily at all—for then I should be wise and
clever, according to you—but involuntarily, so
forgive me; for you say,[1] too, that he who does evil
involuntarily ought to be forgiven.

EUD. And do not refuse, Hippias; but for our sake,
and also because of your previous announcements,
answer any questions Socrates asks you.

HIPP. Well, I will answer since you request it.
Ask whatever questions you like.

soc. I certainly have a great desire, Hippias, to

[1] See 372.

PLATO

διασκέψασθαι τὸ νῦν δὴ λεγόμενον, πότεροί ποτε
ἀμείνους, οἱ ἑκόντες ἢ οἱ ἄκοντες ἁμαρτάνοντες.
οἶμαι οὖν ἐπὶ τὴν σκέψιν ὀρθότατ᾽ ἂν ὧδε ἐλθεῖν.
ἀλλ᾽ ἀπόκριναι· καλεῖς τινα δρομέα ἀγαθόν;

D ιπ. Ἔγωγε.

ϲω. Καὶ κακόν;

ιπ. Ναί.

ϲω. Οὐκοῦν ἀγαθὸς μὲν ὁ εὖ θέων, κακὸς δὲ ὁ
κακῶς;

ιπ. Ναί.

ϲω. Οὐκοῦν ὁ βραδέως θέων κακῶς θεῖ, ὁ δὲ
ταχέως εὖ;

ιπ. Ναί.

ϲω. Ἐν δρόμῳ μὲν ἄρα καὶ τῷ θεῖν τάχος μὲν
ἀγαθόν, βραδυτὴς δὲ κακόν;

ιπ. Ἀλλὰ τί μέλλει;

ϲω. Πότερος οὖν ἀμείνων δρομεύς, ὁ ἑκὼν βραδέως θέων ἢ ὁ ἄκων;

ιπ. Ὁ ἑκών.

ϲω. Ἆρ᾽ οὖν οὐ ποιεῖν τί ἐστι τὸ θεῖν;

ιπ. Ποιεῖν μὲν οὖν.

E ϲω. Εἰ δὲ ποιεῖν, οὐ καὶ ἐργάζεσθαί τι;

ιπ. Ναί.

ϲω. Ὁ κακῶς ἄρα θέων κακὸν καὶ αἰσχρὸν ἐν
δρόμῳ τοῦτο ἐργάζεται;

ιπ. Κακόν· πῶς γὰρ οὔ;

ϲω. Κακῶς δὲ θεῖ ὁ βραδέως θέων;

ιπ. Ναί.

ϲω. Οὐκοῦν ὁ μὲν ἀγαθὸς δρομεὺς ἑκὼν τὸ
κακὸν τοῦτο ἐργάζεται καὶ τὸ αἰσχρόν, ὁ δὲ κακὸς
ἄκων;

ιπ. Ἔοικέν γε.

investigate what we are just at present talking about,
namely which are better, those who err voluntarily
or those who err involuntarily. Now I think the
best way to go at the investigation is this. Just
answer. Do you call some one a good runner?

HIPP. I do.

SOC. And a bad one?

HIPP. Yes.

SOC. Now, he who runs well is a good runner, and
he who runs badly a bad one; is it not so?

HIPP. Yes.

SOC. Then does not he who runs slowly run badly,
and he who runs fast run well?

HIPP. Yes.

SOC. In a race, then, and in running, rapidity is a
good thing, and slowness an evil.

HIPP. Why, of course.

SOC. Which, then, is the better runner, he who runs
slowly voluntarily or he who does so involuntarily?

HIPP. He who does it voluntarily.

SOC. Well, then, is not running doing something?

HIPP. Yes, it is doing.

SOC. And if doing, is it not also performing some
act?

HIPP. Yes.

SOC. Then he who runs badly performs a bad and
disgraceful act in a race?

HIPP. Yes, a bad act of course.

SOC. But he runs badly who runs slowly?

HIPP. Yes.

SOC. Then the good runner performs this bad and
disgraceful act voluntarily, and the bad runner
involuntarily?

HIPP. So it seems.

PLATO

ΣΩ. Ἐν δρόμῳ μὲν ἄρα πονηρότερος ὁ ἄκων κακὰ ἐργαζόμενος ἢ ὁ ἑκών;

ΙΠ. Ἐν δρόμῳ γε.

374 ΣΩ. Τί δ᾽ ἐν πάλῃ; πότερος παλαιστὴς ἀμείνων, ὁ ἑκὼν πίπτων ἢ ὁ ἄκων;

ΙΠ. Ὁ ἑκών, ὡς ἔοικεν.[1]

ΣΩ. Πονηρότερον δὲ καὶ αἴσχιον ἐν πάλῃ τὸ πίπτειν ἢ τὸ καταβάλλειν;

ΙΠ. Τὸ πίπτειν.

ΣΩ. Καὶ ἐν πάλῃ ἄρα ὁ ἑκὼν τὰ πονηρὰ καὶ αἰσχρὰ ἐργαζόμενος βελτίων παλαιστὴς ἢ ὁ ἄκων.

ΙΠ. Ἔοικεν.

ΣΩ. Τί δὲ ἐν τῇ ἄλλῃ πάσῃ τῇ τοῦ σώματος χρείᾳ; οὐχ ὁ βελτίων τὸ σῶμα δύναται ἀμφότερα ἐργάζεσθαι, καὶ τὰ ἰσχυρὰ καὶ τὰ ἀσθενῆ, καὶ τὰ B αἰσχρὰ καὶ τὰ καλά· ὥστε ὅταν κατὰ τὸ σῶμα πονηρὰ ἐργάζηται, ἑκὼν ἐργάζεται ὁ βελτίων τὸ σῶμα, ὁ δὲ πονηρότερος ἄκων;

ΙΠ. Ἔοικεν καὶ τὰ[2] κατὰ τὴν ἰσχὺν οὕτως ἔχειν.

ΣΩ. Τί δὲ κατ᾽ εὐσχημοσύνην, ὦ Ἱππία; οὐ τοῦ βελτίονος σώματός ἐστιν ἑκόντος τὰ αἰσχρὰ καὶ πονηρὰ σχήματα σχηματίζειν, τοῦ δὲ πονηροτέρου ἄκοντος; ἢ πῶς σοι δοκεῖ;

ΙΠ. Οὕτως.

ΣΩ. Καὶ ἀσχημοσύνη ἄρα ἡ μὲν ἑκούσιος πρὸς C ἀρετῆς ἐστιν, ἡ δὲ ἀκούσιος πρὸς πονηρίας σώματος.

[1] ὡς ἔοικε F: ἔοικεν TW.
[2] καὶ τὰ TWF: om. edd.

464

LESSER HIPPIAS

soc. In running, then, he who does bad acts involuntarily is worse than he who does them voluntarily?

HIPP. Yes, in running.

soc. And how is it in wrestling? Which is the better wrestler, he who is thrown voluntarily, or involuntarily?

HIPP. He who is thrown voluntarily, as it seems.

soc. But is it worse and more disgraceful in a wrestling match to be thrown or to throw one's opponent?

HIPP. To be thrown.

soc. In wrestling also, then, he who performs bad and disgraceful acts voluntarily is a better wrestler than he who performs them involuntarily.

HIPP. So it seems.

soc. And how is it in every other bodily exercise? Is not he who is the better man in respect to his body able to perform both kinds of acts, the strong and the weak, the disgraceful and the fine, so that whenever he performs bad acts of a bodily kind, he who is the better man in respect to his body does them voluntarily, but he who is worse does them involuntarily?

HIPP. That seems to be the case in matters of strength also.

soc. And how about grace, Hippias? Does not the better body take ugly and bad postures voluntarily, and the worse body involuntarily? Or what is your opinion?

HIPP. That is my opinion.

soc. Then ungracefulness when voluntary is associated with excellence of the body, but when involuntary with faultiness.

465

PLATO

ιπ. Φαίνεται.

Σω. Τί δὲ φωνῆς πέρι λέγεις; ποτέραν φῂς εἶναι βελτίω, τὴν ἑκουσίως ἀπᾴδουσαν ἢ τὴν ἀκουσίως;

ιπ. Τὴν ἑκουσίως.

Σω. Μοχθηροτέραν δὲ τὴν ἀκουσίως;

ιπ. Ναί.

Σω. Δέξαιο δ' ἂν πότερον τἀγαθὰ κεκτῆσθαι ἢ τὰ κακά;

ιπ. Τἀγαθά.

Σω. Πότερον οὖν ἂν δέξαιο πόδας κεκτῆσθαι ἑκουσίως χωλαίνοντας ἢ ἀκουσίως;

ιπ. Ἑκουσίως.

D Σω. Χωλεία δὲ ποδῶν οὐχὶ πονηρία καὶ ἀσχημοσύνη ἐστίν;

ιπ. Ναί.

Σω. Τί δέ; ἀμβλυωπία οὐ πονηρία ὀφθαλμῶν;

ιπ. Ναί.

Σω. Ποτέρους οὖν ἂν βούλοιο ὀφθαλμοὺς κεκτῆσθαι καὶ ποτέροις συνεῖναι; οἷς ἑκὼν ἄν τις ἀμβλυώττοι καὶ παρορῴη ἢ οἷς ἄκων;

ιπ. Οἷς ἑκών.

Σω. Βελτίω ἄρα ἥγησαι τῶν σαυτοῦ τὰ ἑκουσίως πονηρὰ ἐργαζόμενα ἢ τὰ ἀκουσίως;

ιπ. Τὰ γοῦν τοιαῦτα.

Σω. Οὐκοῦν πάντα, οἷον καὶ ὦτα καὶ ῥῖνας καὶ στόμα καὶ πάσας τὰς αἰσθήσεις, εἷς λόγος συνέχει,
E τὰς μὲν ἀκόντως κακὰ ἐργαζομένας ἀκτήτους εἶναι

466

HIPP. Apparently.

SOC. And what do you say about the voice? Which do you say is the better? That which sings out of tune voluntarily, or involuntarily?

HIPP. That which does it voluntarily.

SOC. And that which does it involuntarily is the worse?

HIPP. Yes.

SOC. Would you choose to possess good or bad things?

HIPP. Good ones.

SOC. Would you, then, choose to possess feet that limp voluntarily, or involuntarily?

HIPP. Voluntarily.

SOC. But is not a limp faultiness and ungracefulness of the feet?

HIPP. Yes.

SOC. Well, is not dimness of sight faultiness of the eyes?

HIPP. Yes.

SOC. Which eyes, then, would you choose to possess and live with? Those with which one would see dimly and incorrectly voluntarily, or involuntarily?

HIPP. Those with which one would do so voluntarily.

SOC. Those parts, then, of yourself which voluntarily act badly you consider better than those which do so involuntarily?

HIPP. Yes; that is, in matters of that sort.

SOC. Well, then, one statement embraces all alike, such as ears and nose and mouth and all the senses —that those which act badly involuntarily are undesirable because they are bad, and those

ὡς πονηρὰς οὔσας, τὰς δὲ ἑκουσίως κτητὰς ὡς
ἀγαθὰς οὔσας.

ιπ. Ἔμοιγε δοκεῖ.

17. ΣΩ. Τί δέ; ὀργάνων ποτέρων βελτίων ἡ
κοινωνία, οἷς ἑκών τις κακὰ ἐργάζεται ἢ οἷς ἄκων;
οἷον πηδάλιον, ᾧ ἄκων κακῶς τις κυβερνήσει,
βέλτιον, ἢ ᾧ ἑκών;

ιπ. Ὧι ἑκών.

ΣΩ. Οὐ καὶ τόξον ὡσαύτως καὶ λύρα καὶ αὐλοὶ
καὶ τἆλλα ξύμπαντα;

ιπ. Ἀληθῆ λέγεις.

375 ΣΩ. Τί δέ; ψυχὴν κεκτῆσθαι ἵππου, ᾗ ἑκών τις
κακῶς ἱππεύσει, ἄμεινον[1] ἢ ᾗ[2] ἄκων;

ιπ. Ἧι ἑκών.

ΣΩ. Ἀμείνων ἄρα ἐστίν.

ιπ. Ναί.

ΣΩ. Τῇ ἀμείνονι ἄρα ψυχῇ ἵππου τὰ τῆς ψυχῆς
ἔργα ταύτης τὰ πονηρὰ ἑκουσίως ἂν ποιοῖ, τῇ δὲ
τῆς πονηρᾶς[3] ἀκουσίως;

ιπ. Πάνυ γε.

ΣΩ. Οὐκοῦν καὶ κυνὸς καὶ τῶν ἄλλων ζῴων
πάντων;

ιπ. Ναί.

ΣΩ. Τί δὲ δή; ἀνθρώπου ψυχὴν ἐκτῆσθαι τοξό-
του ἄμεινόν[4] ἐστιν, ἥτις ἑκουσίως ἁμαρτάνει τοῦ
B σκοποῦ, ἢ ἥτις ἀκουσίως;

ιπ. Ἥτις ἑκουσίως.

ΣΩ. Οὐκοῦν καὶ[5] αὕτη ἀμείνων εἰς τοξικήν ἐστιν;

ιπ. Ναί.

---

[1] ἄμεινον f : ἄμινον F : ἀμείνων TW.   [2] ᾗ add. corr. Coisl.
[3] τῇ δὲ τῆς πονηρᾶς W : τῇ δὲ τῆς πονηρίας Tf : τῃ δὲ τῇ
πονηρᾳ F.

468

which do so voluntarily are desirable because they are good.

HIPP. I think so.

SOC. Well now, which instruments are better to have to do with, those with which a man does bad work voluntarily, or involuntarily? For instance, is a rudder better with which a man will involuntarily steer badly, or one with which he will do so voluntarily?

HIPP. One with which he will do so voluntarily.

SOC. And is not the same true of a bow and a lyre and flutes and all the rest?

HIPP. Quite true.

SOC. Well now, would you choose to possess a horse of such spirit that you would ride him badly voluntarily, or involuntarily?

HIPP. Voluntarily.

SOC. Then that spirit is better.

HIPP. Yes.

SOC. Then with the horse of better spirit one would do voluntarily the bad acts of that spirit, but with the one of worse spirit involuntarily?

HIPP. Certainly.

SOC. And is not that true of a dog, and all other animals?

HIPP. Yes.

SOC. Well now, then, in the case of an archer is it better to possess the mind which voluntarily misses the mark, or that which does so involuntarily?

HIPP. That which does so voluntarily.

SOC. Then that is the better mind for the purpose of archery?

HIPP. Yes.

---

⁴ ἄμεινον F: ἀμείνονος TW.   ⁵ καὶ F: om. TW.

ΣΩ. Καὶ ψυχὴ ἄρα ἀκουσίως ἁμαρτάνουσα πονηροτέρα ἢ ἑκουσίως;

ΙΠ. Ἐν τοξικῇ γε.

ΣΩ. Τί δ' ἐν ἰατρικῇ; οὐχὶ ἡ ἑκοῦσα κακὰ ἐργαζομένη περὶ τὰ σώματα ἰατρικωτέρα;

ΙΠ. Ναί.

ΣΩ. Ἀμείνων ἄρα αὕτη ἐν ταύτῃ τῇ τέχνῃ τῆς μή.[1]

ΙΠ. Ἀμείνων.

ΣΩ. Τί δέ; ἡ κιθαριστικωτέρα καὶ αὐλητικω-
C τέρα καὶ τἆλλα πάντα τὰ κατὰ τὰς τέχνας τε καὶ τὰς ἐπιστήμας, οὐχὶ ἡ ἀμείνων ἑκοῦσα τὰ κακὰ ἐργάζεται καὶ τὰ αἰσχρὰ καὶ ἐξαμαρτάνει, ἡ δὲ πονηροτέρα ἄκουσα;

ΙΠ. Φαίνεται.

ΣΩ. Ἀλλὰ μήν που τάς γε τῶν δούλων ψυχὰς κεκτῆσθαι δεξαίμεθ' ἂν μᾶλλον τὰς ἑκουσίως ἢ τὰς ἀκουσίως ἁμαρτανούσας τε καὶ κακουργούσας, ὡς ἀμείνους οὔσας εἰς ταῦτα.

ΙΠ. Ναί.

ΣΩ. Τί δέ; τὴν ἡμετέραν αὐτῶν οὐ βουλοίμεθ' ἂν ὡς βελτίστην ἐκτῆσθαι;

ΙΠ. Ναί.

D ΣΩ. Οὐκοῦν βελτίων ἔσται, ἐὰν ἑκοῦσα κακουργῇ τε καὶ ἐξαμαρτάνῃ, ἢ ἐὰν ἄκουσα;

ΙΠ. Δεινὸν μέντ' ἂν εἴη, ὦ Σώκρατες, εἰ οἱ ἑκόντες ἀδικοῦντες βελτίους ἔσονται ἢ οἱ ἄκοντες.

ΣΩ. Ἀλλὰ μὴν φαίνονταί[2] γε ἐκ τῶν εἰρημένων.

ΙΠ. Οὔκουν ἔμοιγε.

---

[1] μή Schleiermacher: μὴ ἰατρικῆς TWF.
[2] φαίνονται F: φαίνεται TW.

soc. Is, then, the mind also which errs involuntarily worse than that which errs voluntarily?

hipp. Yes, in the case of archery.

soc. And how is it in the art of medicine? Is not the mind which does harm to the patients' bodies voluntarily the more scientific?

hipp. Yes.

soc. In this art, then, this mind is better than the other.

hipp. It is better.

soc. Well now, the more musical, whether with lyre or with flute, and in everything else that concerns all the other arts and sciences—is not that mind better which voluntarily does bad and disgraceful things and commits errors, whereas that which does so involuntarily is worse?

hipp. Apparently.

soc. And surely we should prefer to possess slaves of such minds that they voluntarily commit errors and do mischief, rather than such as do so involuntarily; we should think them better fitted for their duties.

hipp. Yes.

soc. Well now, should we not wish to possess our own mind in the best possible condition?

hipp. Yes.

soc. Will it, then, be better if it does evil and errs voluntarily, or involuntarily?

hipp. But it would be a terrible thing, Socrates, if those who do wrong voluntarily are to be better than those who do so involuntarily.

soc. But surely they appear, at least, to be so, from what has been said.

hipp. Not to me.

18. ΣΩ. Ἐγὼ δ' ᾤμην, ὦ Ἱππία, καὶ σοὶ φανῆναι. πάλιν δ' ἀπόκριναι· ἡ δικαιοσύνη οὐχὶ ἢ
δύναμίς τίς ἐστιν ἢ ἐπιστήμη ἢ ἀμφότερα; ἢ οὐκ
ἀνάγκη ἕν γέ τι τούτων εἶναι τὴν δικαιοσύνην;

E ΙΠ. Ναί.[1]

ΣΩ. Οὐκοῦν εἰ μὲν δύναμίς ἐστι τῆς ψυχῆς ἡ
δικαιοσύνη, ἡ δυνατωτέρα ψυχὴ δικαιοτέρα ἐστί;
βελτίων γάρ που ἡμῖν ἐφάνη, ὦ ἄριστε, ἡ τοιαύτη.

ΙΠ. Ἐφάνη γάρ.

ΣΩ. Τί δ' εἰ ἐπιστήμη; οὐχ ἡ σοφωτέρα ψυχὴ
δικαιοτέρα, ἡ δὲ ἀμαθεστέρα ἀδικωτέρα;

ΙΠ. Ναί.

ΣΩ. Τί δ' εἰ ἀμφότερα; οὐχ ἡ ἀμφοτέρας
ἔχουσα, ἐπιστήμην καὶ δύναμιν, δικαιοτέρα, ἡ δὲ
ἀμαθεστέρα ἀδικωτέρα; οὐχ οὕτως ἀνάγκη ἔχειν;

ΙΠ. Φαίνεται.

ΣΩ. Οὐκοῦν ἡ δυνατωτέρα καὶ σοφωτέρα αὕτη
ἀμείνων οὖσα ἐφάνη καὶ ἀμφότερα μᾶλλον δυναμένη
ποιεῖν, καὶ τὰ καλὰ καὶ τὰ αἰσχρά, περὶ πᾶσαν
ἐργασίαν;

376 ΙΠ. Ναί.

ΣΩ. Ὅταν ἄρα τὰ αἰσχρὰ ἐργάζηται, ἑκοῦσα
ἐργάζεται διὰ δύναμιν καὶ τέχνην· ταῦτα δὲ δικαιοσύνης φαίνεται, ἤτοι ἀμφότερα ἢ τὸ ἕτερον.

ΙΠ. Ἔοικεν.

ΣΩ. Καὶ τὸ μέν γε ἀδικεῖν κακὰ ποιεῖν ἐστί, τὸ
δὲ μὴ ἀδικεῖν καλά.

ΙΠ. Ναί.

ΣΩ. Οὐκοῦν ἡ δυνατωτέρα καὶ ἀμείνων ψυχή,

---

[1] ναί add. recc.: om. TWF.

LESSER HIPPIAS

soc. I thought, Hippias, they appeared to be so to you also. But now once more answer me : Is not justice either a sort of power or knowledge, or both ? Or must not justice inevitably be one or other of these ?

HIPP. Yes.

soc. Then if justice is a power of the soul, the more powerful soul is the more just, is it not ? For we found, my friend, that such a soul was better.

HIPP. Yes, we did.

soc. And what if it be knowledge ? Is not the wiser soul more just, and the more ignorant more unjust ?

HIPP. Yes.

soc. And what if it be both ? Is not the soul which has both, power and knowledge, more just, and the more ignorant more unjust ? Is that not inevitably the case ?

HIPP. It appears to be.

soc. This more powerful and wiser soul, then, was found to be better and to have more power to do both good and disgraceful acts in every kind of action was it not ?

HIPP. Yes.

soc. Whenever, then, it does disgraceful acts, it does them voluntarily, by reason of power and art ; and these, either one or both of them, are attributes of justice.

HIPP. So it seems.

soc. And doing injustice is doing evil acts, and not doing injustice is doing good acts.

HIPP. Yes.

soc. Will not, then, the more powerful and better

473

PLATO

ὅταν περ ἀδικῇ, ἑκοῦσα ἀδικήσει, ἡ δὲ πονηρὰ
ἄκουσα;

ιπ. Φαίνεται.

B ΣΩ. Οὐκοῦν ἀγαθὸς ἀνὴρ ὁ τὴν ἀγαθὴν ψυχὴν
ἔχων, κακὸς δὲ ὁ τὴν κακήν;

ιπ. Ναί.

ΣΩ. Ἀγαθοῦ μὲν ἄρα ἀνδρός ἐστιν ἑκόντα ἀδικεῖν, κακοῦ δὲ ἄκοντα, εἴπερ ὁ ἀγαθὸς ἀγαθὴν
ψυχὴν ἔχει.

ιπ. Ἀλλὰ μὴν ἔχει γε.

ΣΩ. Ὁ ἄρα ἑκὼν ἁμαρτάνων καὶ αἰσχρὰ καὶ
ἄδικα ποιῶν, ὦ Ἱππία, εἴπερ τίς ἐστιν οὗτος, οὐκ
ἂν ἄλλος εἴη ἢ ὁ ἀγαθός.

ιπ. Οὐκ ἔχω ὅπως σοι συγχωρήσω, ὦ Σώκρατες, ταῦτα.

ΣΩ. Οὐδὲ γὰρ ἐγὼ ἐμοί, ὦ Ἱππία· ἀλλ᾽ ἀναγ-
C καῖον οὕτω φαίνεσθαι νῦν γε ἡμῖν ἐκ τοῦ λόγου.
ὅπερ μέντοι πάλαι ἔλεγον, ἐγὼ περὶ ταῦτα ἄνω καὶ
κάτω πλανῶμαι καὶ οὐδέποτε ταὐτά μοι δοκεῖ· καὶ
ἐμὲ μὲν οὐδὲν θαυμαστὸν πλανᾶσθαι οὐδὲ ἄλλον
ἰδιώτην· εἰ δὲ καὶ ὑμεῖς πλανήσεσθε οἱ σοφοί,
τοῦτο ἤδη καὶ ἡμῖν δεινόν, εἰ μηδὲ παρ᾽ ὑμᾶς
ἀφικόμενοι παυσόμεθα τῆς πλάνης.

soul, when it does injustice, do it voluntarily, and the bad soul involuntarily ?

HIPP. Apparently.

SOC. Is not, then, a good man he who has a good soul, and a bad man he who has a bad one ?

HIPP. Yes.

SOC. It is, then, in the nature of the good man to do injustice voluntarily, and of the bad man to do it involuntarily, that is, if the good man has a good soul.

HIPP. But surely he has.

SOC. Then he who voluntarily errs and does disgraceful and unjust acts, Hippias, if there be such a man, would be no other than the good man.

HIPP. I cannot agree with you, Socrates, in that.

SOC. Nor I with myself, Hippias ; but that appears at the moment to be the inevitable result of our argument ; however, as I was saying all along, in respect to these matters I go astray, up and down, and never hold the same opinion ; and that I, or any other ordinary man, go astray is not surprising ; but if you wise men likewise go astray, that is a terrible thing for us also, if even when we have come to you we are not to cease from our straying.

INDEX

Absolute, 209, 215, 217, 225, 227, 229, 261, 267, 279, 291, 361, 367, 377
Acesimbrotus, 43
Achilles, 151, 379, 426, 429, 431, 433, 435, 449, 451, 453, 455
Adeimantus, 195, 199
Aeacus, 379
Agamemnon, 45, 451, 453
Agis, 43
Ajax, 151, 455, 457
All, 205
Anaxagoras, 61, 89, 91, 103, 339, 343
Antiphon, 195, 199, 201, 235
Antisthenes, 235
Apemantus, 355, 426, 429, 461
Aphrodite, 81
Aplun, 79
Apollo, 75, 77
Apoluon, 79
Appropriate, 369, 371, 373, 383, 385, 387
Archepolis, 43
Archer, 469
Ares, 75, 81, 85
Aristoteles, 195, 196, 203, 231, 237
Artemis, 81
Astronomer, 445
Astyanax, 35, 37, 39, 48
Athena, 75, 81, 83, 117
Athenaa, 85
Atreus, 45, 47

Batieia, 35
Beautiful, 113, 211, 334-423 *passim*; absolute, 361, 367, 377; body, 389; cause of good, 395; not good, 397; customs and laws, 399, 401; eyes, 389; funeral, 375; instruments, 389; gold, 367, 383; ivory, 369; lyre, 363; maiden, 361; mare, 363; monkey, 365; pleasures, 401-419; pot, 363, 365; power,

391; pursuits, 355, 359; stone, 369; useful, 389; wisdom, 391
Being, 255
Beneficial, 349, 351, 393, 395, 397, 419, 421
Bias, 339
Body, 61, 63, 71, 73, 389, 465
Borer, 21, 23, 27
Both, 255, 257, 411, 413, 415, 417
Bow, 469

Calculations, 439, 441, 443
Callias, 5, 33
Carpenter, 23, 25, 29, 31
Cause, 395
Cephalus, 195, 199
Change, 241, 319, 321, 323, 327
Cheiron, 455
Chrysippus, 45
Consonants, 139
Contacts, 275, 277
Convention, in giving names, 3-191 *passim*
Cratylus, 3, 4, 5, 7, 9, 31, 85, 87, 149-191 *passim*
Cronus, 49, 67, 69, 75

Daedalus, 339
Dardanus, 381
Demeter, 75
Dia, 49
Dialectician, 31
Didoinysus, 81
Diogenes Laertius, 5, 195
Dionysodorus, 17 n.
Dionysus, 81
Diphilus, 59
Dog, 469

Eiremes, 87
Elements, of names, 131, 171; 309, 311

477

INDEX

478

INDEX

INDEX